Giordano Bruno
AND THE
HERMETIC TRADITION

Giordano Bruno

AND THE

HERMETIC TRADITION

Frances A. Yates

Vintage Books
A Division of Random House
New York

CONTENTS

ILLUSTRATIONS

PREFACE

MANY years ago I planned to make an English translation of Giordano Bruno's *La cena de le ceneri* with an introduction emphasising the boldness with which this advanced philosopher of the Renaissance accepted the Copernican theory. But as I followed Bruno along the Strand to the house in Whitehall where he was to expound the Copernican theory to knights and doctors, doubts arose. Was that journey imaginary and was the Supper really held at the French embassy? And was the Copernican theory really the subject of the debate or was there something else implied in it? The Bruno problem remained with me thereafter as the real centre of all my studies; masses of notes and manuscript accumulated but full understanding eluded me. Some major clue was missing.

During the last twenty-five years certain scholars have been drawing attention to the significance of the influence of Hermetism in the Italian Renaissance. The fundamental bibliographical studies of P. O. Kristeller have shown the importance and diffusion of Ficino's translation of the *Corpus Hermeticum*. E. Garin has subtly indicated Hermetic strands in Renaissance thought, particularly in his *Medioevo e Rinascimento* and in essays now republished in the book *La cultura filosofica del Rinascimento italiano*. He also inspired a group of students to undertake detailed investigations of Hermetic influence on individual writers, published as *Testi umanistici su l'ermetismo*. Several French scholars are aware of Renaissance Hermetism. In England, D. P. Walker has examined the *prisca theologia* in an important article, and has analysed Ficino's use of the Hermetic *Asclepius* in his book *Spiritual and Demonic Magic from Ficino to Campanella*. This book brings out for the first time shades of difference in Renaissance attitudes to magic and indicates the bearing of the subject on religious issues.

No one had as yet spoken of Bruno in connection with Hermetism, nor, in spite of my interest in all these studies, did the possibility of such a connection occur to me for some time. I had long known that Bruno's works, particularly those on memory, are full of magic (a fact which did not escape Lynn Thorndike in his *History of Magic and Experimental Science*), but I did not realise that his magic belongs with his philosophy as part of a Hermetic philosophy. It was not until a few years ago that it dawned upon me, quite suddenly, that Renaissance Hermetism provides the long-sought-for major clue to Bruno. The right key was found at last; my former Bruno studies fell into place; and this book was written fairly quickly.

It is obvious that the book is not a monograph on Bruno; it sets out to do only what its title states, to place him in the Hermetic tradition. Before a final reassessment of Bruno is possible other studies are necessary, particularly an elucidation of his place in the history of the classical art of memory which he transformed into a magico-religious technique. Some of the references to Bruno's mnemonics in the present book may seem rather obscure, but I hope to treat further of this subject in another book. There is a great omission in this book, namely the influence on Bruno of Ramon Lull which I have hardly mentioned, nor have I used his many works on Lullism. Here again a study of Bruno and the Lullian tradition is needed which one day I hope that I may be able to produce. The three strands of the Hermetism, the mnemonics, the Lullism are all interwoven in Bruno's complex personality, mind, and mission. All three have a history running from the Middle Ages through the Renaissance up to the dividing line of Descartes and the seventeenth century.

I am indebted throughout the present book to the Nock-Festugière edition and French translation of the *Corpus Hermeticum* and to A.-J. Festugière's book *La Révélation d'Hermès Trismégiste*. Though Renaissance Hermetism has not been set out before in the way in which I attempt to do it in the first ten chapters, these chapters owe much to others, particularly in parts of IV, VII, IX, and X to Walker; the theme of VIII has been hinted at by Garin. My knowledge of Cabala is derived almost entirely from the works of G. G. Scholem; my persistence in spelling the word in this way is part of the general plan of approaching the ancient wisdoms from the point of view of the Renaissance; this is how Pico and Bruno spell it. The nine chapters on Bruno present him as a variation on the Hermetic-Cabalist tradition. This is so revolutionary that I have not been able to use much of the vast literature on Bruno, save for biographical and documentary material and some other works which are acknowledged in the notes. I have used G. Aquilecchia's revised edition of the Gentile edition of Bruno's Italian dialogues, and Aquilecchia's edition of the two newly discovered Latin works. The treatment of Campanella as a sequel to Bruno is new, though indebted to Walker's analysis of Campanella's magic and to the labours of L. Firpo. The last two chapters emphasise the weakening of Hermetic influence through the dating of the *Hermetica* and its survival in esoteric writers and societies (both these points have been briefly indicated by Garin). The emergence of seventeenth-century thought in Mersenne, Kepler, and Descartes is seen against the background of the Hermetic tradition.

There has inevitably been over-simplification in this account of an immensely complex theme, and my purpose of leading up to, and away from, Giordano Bruno may have influenced my choice of material. The full history of Hermetism has yet to be written; it should include the Middle Ages and continue far later than the date to which I have taken it. I am aware that I take risks as I strike a course through ways of thinking so unfamiliar and obscure as those of the Renaissance Hermetists, and I cannot hope to have made no mistakes. If this book draws more attention to a most important subject and stimulates others to labour in this field it will have done its work.

Since the book has been so long in the making, perhaps I may thank those who have helped me in chronological order. Through our common interest in Bruno I came to know Dorothea Waley Singer, whose kindness and encouragement marked a turning point in my life, for she introduced me to Edgar Wind, the late Fritz Saxl, and Gertrud Bing, and I began to frequent the Warburg Institute, then in its first London home on Millbank. Eventually, through the generosity and foresight of those in authority, the Warburg Institute and its library became a part of the University of London. Towards the end of the war, Saxl invited me to join the staff, and so for many years I have had the advantage of using the library founded by Aby Warburg and now maintained by London University. This unique library influences all those who use it through the distinctive arrangement of the books which reflects the mind of its founder. I have also had the inestimable advantage of the friendship of members of the staff of the Institute. G. Bing has known my Bruno studies over many years, constantly supporting me with understanding and encouragement. The present Director of the Institute, Ernst Gombrich, has stimulated, advised, and helped about the book with his great forbearance and kindness.

Many have been the conversations on subjects of mutual interest with Perkin Walker, now on the staff of the Institute. All these read the book in manuscript, making valuable criticisms; G. Bing also read it in proof. One hardly knows how much one owes to friendship and to talk with friends, nor how to thank for it. Other old friends now in the United States are Charles Mitchell (heated arguments, often in stations and trains) and Rudolf Wittkower, who gave valuable advice at an important juncture. G. Aquilecchia, long a fellow-Brunian, kindly allowed me to see some unpublished material. O. Kurz, J. Trapp, and all the librarians of the Institute have given of their knowledge: the staff of the photographic collection has been unfailingly helpful.

I have constantly used the London Library to the staff of which my thanks are due. The debt to the library of the British Museum and its staff is, needless to say, impossible to reckon.

My sister, R. W. Yates, has read the book in manuscript and in proof many times, with tireless care in helping with corrections and suggestions, also supporting my life in countless ways. Other members of my family were still alive when my Bruno studies began, and I think of them now in conclusion.

FRANCES A. YATES
Reader in the History of the Renaissance
University of London

Warburg Institute,
University of London

ABBREVIATIONS

Bibliografia   V. Salvestrini, *Bibliografia di Giordano Bruno* (1582–1950), seconda edizione postuma a cura di Luigi Firpo, Florence, 1958.

C.H.   *Corpus Hermeticum*, Paris, 1945 and 1954. Vol. I, *Corpus Hermeticum*, I–XII, texte établi par A. D. Nock et traduit par A.-J. Festugière. Vol. II, *Corpus Hermeticum*, XIII–XVIII, *Asclepius*, texte établi par A. D. Nock et traduit par A.-J. Festugière. Vol. III, Fragments extraits de Stobèe, I–XXII, texte établi et traduit par A.-J. Festugière, Vol. IV, Fragments extraits de Stobée, XXIII–XXIX, texte établi et traduit par A.-J. Festugière; Fragments divers, texte établi par A. D. Nock et traduit par A.-J. Festugière.

Dial. ital.   Giordano Bruno, *Dialoghi italiani*, con note da Giovanni Gentile, terza edizione a cura di Giovanni Aquilecchia, Florence, 1957 (one vol.).

Documenti   *Documenti della vita di Giordano Bruno*, a cura di Vincenzo Spampanato, Florence, 1933.

Festugière   A.-J. Festugière, *La Révélation d'Hermès Trismégiste*, Paris, 1950–4 (four vols.).

Ficino   Marsilio Ficino, *Opera omnia*, Bâle, 1576 (two vols., consecutively paged).

Garin, Cultura   Eugenio Garin, *La cultura filosofica del Rinascimento italiano*, Florence, 1961.

J.W.C.I.   *Journal of the Warburg and Courtauld Institutes.*

Kristeller, Studies   Paul Oskar Kristeller, *Studies in Renaissance Thought and Letters*, Rome, 1956.

Kristeller, Suppl. Fic.   Paul Oskar Kristeller, *Supplementum Ficinianum*, Florence, 1937 (two vols.).

Op. lat.   Giordano Bruno, *Opere latine*, ed. F. Fiorentino, V. Imbriani, C. M. Tallarigo, F. Tocco, H. Vitelli, Naples and Florence, 1879–91 (three vols. in eight parts). Facsimile reprint, 1962 (Friedrich Fromman Verlag Gunther Holzboog, Stuttgart-Bad Cannstatt).

Pico   Giovanni Pico della Mirandola, *Opera omnia*, Bâle, 1572 (one vol.).

Scott   *Hermetica*, ed. W. Scott, Oxford, 1924–36 (four vols.).

Sommario   Angelo Mercati, *Il sommario del processo di Giordano Bruno*, Città del Vaticano, 1942.

Test. uman.   *Testi umanistici sul' ermetismo*, testi di Ludovico Lazzarelli, F. Giorgio Veneto, Cornelio Agrippa di Nettesheim, a cura di E. Garin, M. Brini, C. Vasoli, P. Zambelli, Rome, 1955.

Thorndike   Lynn Thorndike, *A History of Magic and Experimental Science*, Columbia University Press, 1923–41 (six vols.).

Walker   D. P. Walker, *Spiritual and Demonic Magic from Ficino to Campanella*, The Warburg Institute, University of London, 1958.

Chapter I

❖❖❖❖❖❖❖❖❖❖❖❖❖❖❖❖❖❖❖❖❖❖❖❖❖❖❖❖❖❖❖❖❖❖❖❖

HERMES TRISMEGISTUS

❖❖❖❖❖❖❖❖❖❖❖❖❖❖❖❖❖❖❖❖❖❖❖❖❖❖❖❖❖❖❖❖❖❖❖❖

THE great forward movements of the Renaissance all derive their vigour, their emotional impulse, from looking backwards. The cyclic view of time as a perpetual movement from pristine golden ages of purity and truth through successive brazen and iron ages still held sway and the search for truth was thus of necessity a search for the early, the ancient, the original gold from which the baser metals of the present and the immediate past were corrupt degenerations. Man's history was not an evolution from primitive animal origins through ever growing complexity and progress; the past was always better than the present, and progress was revival, rebirth, renaissance of antiquity. The classical humanist recovered the literature and the monuments of classical antiquity with a sense of return to the pure gold of a civilisation better and higher than his own. The religious reformer returned to the study of the Scriptures and the early Fathers with a sense of recovery of the pure gold of the Gospel, buried under later degenerations.

These are truisms, and it is also obvious that both these great returning movements were not mistaken as to the date of the earlier, better period to which they turned. The humanist knew the date of Cicero, knew the correct date of his golden age of classical culture; the reformer, even if not clear as to the date of the Gospels, knew that he was trying to return to the earliest centuries of Christianity. But the returning movement of the Renaissance with which this book will be concerned, the return to a pure golden age of magic, was based on a radical error in dating.

I

The works which inspired the Renaissance Magus, and which he believed to be of profound antiquity, were really written in the second to the third centuries A.D. He was not returning to an Egyptian wisdom, not much later than the wisdom of the Hebrew patriarchs and prophets, and much earlier than Plato and the other philosophers of Greek antiquity, who had all—so the Renaissance Magus firmly believed—drunk from its sacred fountain. He is returning to the pagan background of early Christianity, to that religion of the world, strongly tinged with magic and oriental influences, which was the gnostic version of Greek philosophy, and the refuge of weary pagans seeking an answer to life's problems other than that offered by their contemporaries, the early Christians.

The Egyptian God, Thoth, the scribe of the gods and the divinity of wisdom, was identified by the Greeks with their Hermes and sometimes given the epithet of "Thrice Great".[1] The Latins took over this identification of Hermes or Mercurius with Thoth, and Cicero in his *De natura deorum* explains that there were really five Mercuries, the fifth being he who killed Argus and consequently fled in exile to Egypt where he "gave the Egyptians their laws and letters" and took the Egyptian name of Theuth or Thoth.[2] A large literature in Greek developed under the name of Hermes Trismegistus, concerned with astrology and the occult sciences, with the secret virtues of plants and stones and the sympathetic magic based on knowledge of such virtues, with the making of talismans for drawing down the powers of the stars, and so on. Besides these treatises or recipes for the practice of astral magic going under the name of Hermes, there also developed a philosophical literature to which the same revered name was attached. It is not known when the Hermetic framework was first used for philosophy, but the *Asclepius* and the *Corpus Hermeticum*, which are the most important of the philosophical *Hermetica* which have come down to us, are probably to be dated between A.D. 100 and 300.[3] Though cast in a pseudo-Egyptian framework, these works have been thought by many scholars to contain very few genuine Egyptian elements. Others would allow for some influence of native Egyptian beliefs upon them.[4] In any case,

[1] Festugière, I, pp. 67 ff.   [2] Cicero, *De nat. deor.*, III, 22.
[3] *C.H.*, I, p. v. (preface by Nock); Festugière, III, p. 1.
[4] As Bloomfield says, "Scholarship has veered from one extreme to the other on this question of the Egyptian elements in Hermeticism" (see

2

however, they were certainly not written in remotest antiquity by an all-wise Egyptian priest, as the Renaissance believed, but by various unknown authors, all probably Greeks,[1] and they contain popular Greek philosophy of the period, a mixture of Platonism and Stoicism, combined with some Jewish and probably some Persian influences. They are very diverse, but they all breathe an atmosphere of intense piety. The *Asclepius* purports to describe the religion of the Egyptians, and by what magic rites and processes the Egyptians drew down the powers of the cosmos into the statues of their gods. This treatise has come down to us through the Latin translation formerly attributed to Apuleius of Madaura.[2] The *Pimander* (the first of the treatises in the *Corpus Hermeticum*, the collection of fifteen Hermetic dialogues[3]) gives an account of the creation of the world which is in parts reminiscent of *Genesis*. Other treatises describe the ascent of the soul through the spheres of the planets to the divine realms above them, or give ecstatic descriptions of a process of regeneration by which the soul casts off the chains which bind it to the material world and becomes filled with divine powers and virtues.

In the first volume of his work, *La Révélation d'Hermès Trismégiste*,[4] Festugière has analysed the state of mind of the epoch, roughly the second century after the birth of Christ, in which the *Asclepius* and the Hermetic treatises which have reached us in the *Corpus Hermeticum* collection were written. Externally that world

[1] According to Nock and Festugière; see *C.H.*, *loc. cit.*; Festugière, I, pp. 85 ff.

[2] The attribution, which is incorrect, dates from the ninth century; see *C.H.*, II, p. 259: on the Coptic version, see below, p. 431, note 2.

[3] It is not known when the *Corpus Hermeticum* was first put together as a collection, but it was already known in this form to Psellus in the eleventh century; see *C.H.*, I, pp. xlvii–l (preface by Nock).

[4] Festugière, I, pp. 1 ff.

M. W. Bloomfield, *The Seven Deadly Sins*, Michigan, 1952, p. 342, and the references there given). Festugière allows hardly anything to it and concentrates almost entirely on the Greek influences in the *Hermetica*. A cautious summary by Bloomfield (*op. cit.*, p. 46) is as follows: "These writings are chiefly the product of Egyptian Neoplatonists who were greatly influenced by Stoicism, Judaism, Persian theology and possibly by native Egyptian beliefs, as well as, of course, by Plato, especially the *Timaeus*. They were perhaps the bible of an Egyptian mystery religion, which possibly in kernel went back to the second century B.C." The mystery cult theory is opposed by Festugière, I, pp. 81 ff.

3

was highly organised and at peace. The *pax Romana* was at the height of its efficiency and the mixed populations of the Empire were governed by an efficient bureaucracy. Communications along the great Roman roads were excellent. The educated classes had absorbed the Graeco-Roman type of culture, based on the seven liberal arts. The mental and spiritual condition of this world was curious. The mighty intellectual effort of Greek philosophy was exhausted, had come to a standstill, to a dead end, perhaps because Greek thinking never took the momentous step of experimental verification of its hypotheses—a step which was not to be taken until fifteen centuries later with the birth of modern scientific thinking in the seventeenth century. The world of the second century was weary of Greek dialectics which seemed to lead to no certain results. Platonists, Stoics, Epicureans could only repeat the theories of their various schools without making any further advances, and the tenets of the schools were boiled down in text-book form, in manuals which formed the basis of philosophical instruction within the Empire. In so far as it is Greek in origin, the philosophy of the Hermetic writings is of this standardised type, with its smattering of Platonism, Neoplatonism, Stoicism, and the other Greek schools of thought.

This world of the second century was, however, seeking intensively for knowledge of reality, for an answer to its problems which the normal education failed to give. It turned to other ways of seeking an answer, intuitive, mystical, magical. Since reason seemed to have failed, it sought to cultivate the *Nous*, the intuitive faculty in man. Philosophy was to be used, not as a dialectical exercise, but as a way of reaching intuitive knowledge of the divine and of the meaning of the world, as a gnosis, in short, to be prepared for by ascetic discipline and a religious way of life. The Hermetic treatises, which often take the form of dialogues between master and disciple, usually culminate in a kind of ecstasy in which the adept is satisfied that he has received an illumination and breaks out into hymns of praise. He seems to reach this illumination through contemplation of the world or the cosmos, or rather through contemplation of the cosmos as reflected in his own *Nous* or *mens* which separates out for him its divine meaning and gives him a spiritual mastery over it, as in the familiar gnostic revelation or experience of the ascent of the soul through the spheres of the planets to become immersed in the divine. Thus that religion of

4

the world which runs as an undercurrent in much of Greek thought, particularly in Platonism and Stoicism, becomes in Hermetism actually a religion, a cult without temples or liturgy, followed in the mind alone, a religious philosophy or philosophical religion containing a gnosis.

The men of the second century were thoroughly imbued with the idea (which the Renaissance imbibed from them) that what is old is pure and holy, that the earliest thinkers walked more closely with the gods than the busy rationalists, their successors. Hence the strong revival of Pythagoreanism in this age. They also had the impression that what is remote and far distant is more holy[1]; hence their cult of the "barbarians", of Indian gymnosophists, Persian Magi, Chaldean astrologers, whose approach to knowledge was felt to be more religious than that of the Greeks.[2] In the melting-pot of the Empire, in which all religions were tolerated, there was ample opportunity for making acquaintance with oriental cults. Above all, it was the Egyptians who were revered in this age. Egyptian temples were still functioning, and devout seekers after religious truth and revelation in the Graeco-Roman world would make pilgrimages to some remotely situated Egyptian temple and pass the night in its vicinity in the hope of receiving some vision of divine mysteries in dreams.[3] The belief that Egypt was the original home of all knowledge, that the great Greek philosophers had visited it and conversed with Egyptian priests, had long been current, and, in the mood of the second century, the ancient and mysterious religion of Egypt, the supposed profound knowledge of its priests, their ascetic way of life, the religious magic which they were thought to perform in the subterranean chambers of their temples, offered immense attractions. It is this pro-Egyptian mood of the Graeco-Roman world which is reflected in the Hermetic *Asclepius* with its strange description of the magic by which the Egyptian priests animated the statues of their gods, and its moving prophecy that the most ancient Egyptian religion is destined to come to an end. "In that hour", so the supposed Egyptian priest, Hermes Trismegistus, tells his disciple, Asclepius, "In that hour, weary of life, men will no longer regard the world as the worthy object of their admiration and reverence. This All, which is a good thing, the best that can be seen in the past, the present,

---

[1] *Ibid.*, I, pp. 14 ff.   [2] *Ibid.*, I, pp. 19 ff.   [3] *Ibid.*, I, pp. 46 ff.

and the future, will be in danger of perishing; men will esteem it a burden; and thenceforward this whole of the universe will be despised and no longer cherished, this incomparable work of God, glorious construction, all-good creation made up of an infinite diversity of forms, instrument of the will of God who, without envy, lavishes his favour upon his work, in which is assembled in one all, in a harmonious diversity, all that can be seen which is worthy of reverence, praise and love."[1] Thus Egypt, and its magical religion, becomes identified with the Hermetic religion of the world.

So we can understand how the content of the Hermetic writings fostered the illusion of the Renaissance Magus that he had in them a mysterious and precious account of most ancient Egyptian wisdom, philosophy, and magic. Hermes Trismegistus, a mythical name associated with a certain class of gnostic philosophical revelations or with magical treatises and recipes, was, for the Renaissance, a real person, an Egyptian priest who had lived in times of remote antiquity and who had himself written all these works. The scraps of Greek philosophy which he found in these writings, derived from the somewhat debased philosophical teaching current in the early centuries A.D., confirmed the Renaissance reader in his belief that he had here the fount of pristine wisdom whence Plato and the Greeks had derived the best that they knew.

This huge historical error was to have amazing results.

It was on excellent authority that the Renaissance accepted Hermes Trismegistus as a real person of great antiquity and as the author of the Hermetic writings, for this was implicitly believed by leading Fathers of the Church, particularly Lactantius and Augustine. Naturally, it would not have occurred to anyone to doubt that these overwhelmingly authoritative writers must be right, and it is indeed a remarkable testimony to the prominence and importance of the Hermetic writings and to the early and complete success of the Hermes Trismegistus legend as to their authorship and antiquity that Lactantius, writing in the third century, and Augustine in the fourth, both accept the legend unquestioningly.

After quoting Cicero on the fifth Mercury as he "who gave

[1] *C.H.*, II, p. 328.

letters and laws to the Egyptians", Lactantius, in his *Institutes*, goes on to say that this Egyptian Hermes "although he was a man, yet he was of great antiquity, and most fully imbued with every kind of learning, so that the knowledge of many subjects and arts acquired for him the name of Trismegistus. He wrote books and those in great number, relating to the knowledge of divine things, in which he asserts the majesty of the supreme and only God, and makes mention of Him by the same names which we use—God and Father."[1] By these "many books", Lactantius certainly means some of the Hermetic writings which have come down to us, for he makes several quotations from some of the treatises of the *Corpus Hermeticum* and also from the *Asclepius*.[2] The very early date at which Lactantius would place Hermes Trismegistus and his books may be inferred from a remark in his *De ira Dei* where he says that Trismegistus is much more ancient than Plato and Pythagoras.[3]

There are many other quotations from, and references to Hermes Trismegistus in Lactantius' *Institutes*. He evidently thought that Hermes was a valuable ally in his campaign of using pagan wisdom in support of the truth of Christianity. In the quotation just made, he has pointed out that Hermes, like the Christians, speaks of God as "Father"; and in fact the word Father is not infrequently used of the supreme being in the Hermetic writings. Still more telling, however, was Hermes' use of the expression "Son of God" for the demiurge. To demonstrate this remarkable confirmation of the truth of Christianity by this most ancient writer, Lactantius quotes, in Greek, a passage from the *Asclepius* (one of the quotations which has preserved for us fragments of the lost Greek original):

> Hermes, in the book which is entitled *The Perfect Word*, made use of these words: "The Lord and Creator of all things, whom we have thought right to call God, since He made the second God visible and sensible. . . . Since, therefore, He made Him first, and alone, and one only, He appeared to Him beautiful, and most full of all good things; and He hallowed Him, and altogether loved Him as His own Son."[4]

[1] Lactantius, *Div. Inst.*, I, vi; English translation by W. Fletcher, *The Works of Lactantius*, Edinburgh, 1871, I, p. 15.

[2] On quotations by Lactantius from the *Hermetica*, see *C.H.*, I, p. xxxviii; II, pp. 259, 276–7.

[3] Lactantius, *De ira Dei*, XI; Fletcher's translation, II, p. 23.

[4] Lactantius, *Div. Inst.*, IV, vi; Fletcher's translation, I, p. 220. Lactantius is quoting from *Asclepius*, 8 (*C.H.*, II, p. 304).

The Perfect Word, or *Sermo Perfectus*, is a correct translation of the original Greek title of the *Asclepius*,[1] and the passage which Lactantius quotes in Greek corresponds roughly to a passage in our Latin translation. Thus the *Asclepius*, the work which contains the weird description of how the Egyptians fabricated their idols and the Lament for the Egyptian religion, becomes sanctified because it contains a prophecy concerning the Son of God.

It was not only in the *Asclepius* that the Hermetic writers used the expression "Son of God". At the beginning of *Pimander*, which is the Hermetic account of creation, the act of creation is said to be through a luminous Word, who is the Son of God.[2] When discussing the Son of God as the creative Word, with quotations from the Scriptures, Lactantius brings in Gentile confirmation, pointing out that the Greeks speak of Him as the Logos, and also Trismegistus. He was doubtless thinking of the passage on the creative Word as the Son of God in the *Pimander*, and he adds that "Trismegistus, who by some means or other searched into almost all truth, often described the excellence and the majesty of the Word."[3]

Indeed, Lactantius regards Hermes Trismegistus as one of the most important of the Gentile seers and prophets who foresaw the coming of Christianity, because he spoke of the Son of God and of the Word. In three passages of the *Institutes* he cites Trismegistus with the Sibyls as testifying to the coming of Christ.[4] Lactantius nowhere says anything against Hermes Trismegistus. He is always the most ancient and all-wise writer, the tenor of whose works is agreeable to Christianity and whose mention of God the Son places him with the Sibyls as a Gentile prophet. In

[1] See *C.H.*, II, pp. 276–7.

[2] See below, p. 23.

[3] Lactantius, *Div. Inst.*, IV, xi; Fletcher's translation, I, p. 226.

[4] Lactantius, *Div. Inst.*, I, vi; IV, vi; VIII, xviii; Fletcher's translation, I, pp. 14–19; 220–2; 468–9.

The Sibylline Oracles themselves were no more genuinely antique than the *Hermetica*. Forged Sibylline prophecies of Jewish origin appeared at some uncertain date, and were later manipulated by the Christians. It seems difficult to distinguish what is of Jewish and what is of Christian origin in the *Oracula Sibyllina*. See M. J. Lagrange, *Le judaisme avant Jésus-Christ*, Paris, 1931, pp. 505–11; A. Puech, *Histoire de la littérature grecque chrétienne*, Paris, 1928, II, pp. 603–15; and the note by G. Bardy in *Oeuvres de Saint Augustin*, Desclée de Brouwer, Vol. 36, 1960, pp. 755–9.

general passages Lactantius condemns the worshipping of images, and he also thinks that the demons used by Magi are evil fallen angels.[1] These things are, however, never associated by him with Trismegistus, who always appears as a revered authority on divine truths. It is no wonder that Lactantius became a favourite Father for the Renaissance Magus who wished to remain a Christian.

Augustine was, however, a difficulty for the Renaissance Magus who wished to remain a Christian, for Augustine in the *De Civitate Dei* delivers a severe condemnation of what "Hermes the Egyptian, called Trismegistus" wrote concerning idols, that is to say of the passage in the *Asclepius*, which he quotes at length, on how the Egyptians in their magical religion animated the statues of their gods by magic means, by drawing spirits into them.[2] Augustine is using, not a Greek text of the *Asclepius*, as Lactantius had done, but the same Latin translation which we have, and which must therefore be at least as early as the fourth century.[3] As mentioned before, this translation used to be attributed to Apuleius of Madaura.

The context in which Augustine makes his attack on the idolatrous passage in the *Asclepius* is important. He has been attacking magic in general and in particular the views on spirits or *daemones* held by Apuleius of Madaura.[4]

Apuleius of Madaura is a striking example of one of those men, highly educated in the general culture of the Graeco-Roman world who, weary of the stale teachings of the schools, sought for salvation in the occult, and particularly in the Egyptian type of the occult. Born *circa* A.D. 123, Apuleius was educated at Carthage and at Athens and later travelled to Egypt where he became involved in a lawsuit in which he was accused of magic. He is famous for his wonderful novel, popularly known as *The Golden Ass*,[5] the hero of which is transformed by witches into an ass, and after many sufferings in his animal form, is transformed back into human shape after an ecstatic vision of the goddess Isis, which comes to him on a lonely seashore whither he has wandered in

[1] Lactantius, *Div. Inst.*, II, xv.

[2] Augustine, *De civ. Dei*, VIII, xxiii–xxvi. He is quoting from *Asclepius*, 23, 24, 37; see *C.H.*, II, pp. 325 ff.

[3] *C.H.*, II, p. 259.   [4] *De civ. Dei*, VIII, xiii–xxii.

[5] This is the title of the sixteenth-century English translation by William Adlington.

despair. Eventually he becomes a priest of Isis in an Egyptian temple. The whole mood of this novel, with its ethical theme (for the animal form is a punishment for transgression), its ecstatic initiation or illumination, its Egyptian colouring, is like the mood of the Hermetic writings. Though Apuleius was not really the translator of the *Asclepius*, that work would certainly have appealed to him.

Augustine calls Apuleius a Platonist, and he attacks him for the views on airy spirits or *daemones* which he held to be intermediaries between gods and men in his work on the "demon" of Socrates. Augustine regards this as impious, not because he disbelieves in airy spirits or demons but because he thinks they are wicked spirits or devils. He then goes on to attack Hermes Trismegistus for praising the Egyptians for the magic by which they drew such spirits or demons into the statues of their gods, thus animating the statues, or making them into gods. Here he quotes verbally the god-making passage in the *Asclepius*. He then discusses the prophecy that the Egyptian religion will come to an end, and the lament for its passing, which he interprets as a prophecy of the ending of idolatry by the coming of Christianity. Here too, therefore, Hermes Trismegistus is a prophet of the coming of Christianity, but all credit for this is taken away by Augustine's statement that he had this foreknowledge of the future from the demons whom he worshipped.

> Hermes presages these things as the devil's confederate, suppressing the evidence of the Christian name, and yet foretelling with a sorrowful intimation, that from it should proceed the wreck of all their idolatrous superstitions: for Hermes was one of those who (as the apostle says), "Knowing God, glorified Him not as God, nor were thankful, but became vain in their imaginations, and their foolish heart was full of darkness. . . ."[1]

Yet, continues Augustine, "this Hermes says much of God according to the truth", though in his admiration for the Egyptian idolatry he was blind, and his prophecy of its passing he had from the devil. In contrast, he quotes a true prophet, like Isaiah, who said, "The idols of Egypt shall be moved at His presence, and the heart of Egypt shall melt in the midst of her."[2]

Augustine says nothing whatever about Hermes' mention of the

---

[1] *De civ. Dei*, VIII, xxiii, quoted in the English translation by John Healey. The quotation is from Romans, I, xxi.

[2] Isaiah, XIX, i.

"Son of God", and his whole treatment of the subject is perhaps, in part, a reply to Lactantius' glorification of Hermes as a Gentile prophet.

Augustine's views on Hermes naturally presented a difficulty for the many devout admirers of the Hermetic writings in the Renaissance. Various courses were open to them. One was to affirm that the idolatrous passage in the *Asclepius* was an interpolation made in the Latin translation by the magician, Apuleius, and was not in the lost Greek original by Hermes. This course was adopted by several Hermetists of the sixteenth century, as will be seen later.[1] But to the Renaissance Magus, the magic in the *Asclepius* was the most attractive part of the Hermetic writings. How was a Christian Magus to get round Augustine? Marsilio Ficino did it by quoting Augustine's condemnation, and then ignoring it, though timidly, by practising magic. Giordano Bruno was to take the bolder course of maintaining that the magical Egyptian religion of the world was not only the most ancient but also the only true religion, which both Judaism and Christianity had obscured and corrupted.

There is another passage on Hermes Trismegistus in the *De Civitate Dei*, widely separated from the one on the Egyptian idolatry and in quite a different context. Augustine is affirming the extreme antiquity of the Hebrew tongue and that the Hebrew prophets and patriarchs are much earlier than any of the Gentile philosophers, and the wisdom of the patriarchs earlier than the Egyptian wisdom.

> And what was their [the Egyptian's] goodly wisdom, think you? Truly nothing but astronomy, and such other sciences as rather seemed to exercise the wit than to elevate the knowledge. For as for morality, it stirred not in Egypt until Trismegistus' time, who was indeed long before the sages and philosophers of Greece, but after Abraham, Isaac, Jacob, Joseph, yea and Moses also; for at the time when Moses was born, was Atlas, Prometheus' brother, a great astronomer, living, and he was grandfather by the mother's side to the elder Mercury, who begat the father of this Trismegistus.[2]

Augustine thus confirmed with the great weight of his authority the extreme antiquity of Hermes Trismegistus, who was "long before the sages and philosophers of Greece". And by giving him

---

[1] See below, pp. 169, 172–3.

[2] *De civ. Dei*, XVIII, xxix; quoted in John Healey's translation.

this curious genealogy, whereby he is dated three generations later than a contemporary of Moses, Augustine raised a question which was to be much debated concerning the relative dates of Moses and Hermes. Was Hermes slightly later than Moses, though much earlier than the Greeks, as Augustine said ? Was he contemporary with Moses, or earlier than Moses ? All these views were to be held by later Hermetists and Magi. The need to date him in relation to Moses was stimulated by the affinities with *Genesis* which must strike every reader of the Hermetic *Pimander*.

From other early Christian writers, more about Hermes Trismegistus could be learned,[1] particularly from Clement of Alexandria, who, in his striking description of the procession of the Egyptian priests, says that the singer at the head of the procession carried two books of music and hymns by Hermes; the horoscopus carried four books by Hermes on the stars. In the course of this description, Clement states that there are forty-two books by Hermes Trismegistus, thirty-six of which contain the whole of the philosophy of the Egyptians, the other six being on medicine.[2] It is very improbable that Clement knew any of the *Hermetica* which have come down to us,[3] but the Renaissance reader believed that he had in the *Corpus Hermeticum* and the *Asclepius* precious survivors of that great sacred library of which Clement speaks.

About 1460, a Greek manuscript was brought to Florence from Macedonia by a monk, one of those many agents employed by Cosimo de' Medici to collect manuscripts for him. It contained a copy of the *Corpus Hermeticum*, not quite a complete copy, for it included fourteen only of the fifteen treatises of the collection, the last one being missing.[4] Though the Plato manuscripts were

---

[1] See the collection of *Testimonia* in Scott, Vol. I.

[2] Clement of Alexandria, *Stromata*, VI, iv, xxxv–xxxviii. Cf. Festugière, I, pp. 75 ff.

[3] Clement does not mention the Hermetic writings, from which Scott concludes (I, pp. 87–90) that either he did not know them, or knew that they were not of very ancient date.

[4] The manuscript from which Ficino made his translation is in the Biblioteca Laurenziana (Laurentianus, LXXI 33 (A)). See Kristeller, *Studies*, p. 223; the eleventh chapter in this book is a republication in revised form of an article which Kristeller first published in 1938 and which was the pioneer study of Ficino's translation of the *Corpus Hermeticum*. All students of Hermetism in the Renaissance are deeply indebted to Kristeller's work.

already assembled, awaiting translation, Cosimo ordered Ficino to put these aside and to translate the work of Hermes Trismegistus at once, before embarking on the Greek philosophers. It is Ficino himself who tells us this, in that dedication to Lorenzo de' Medici of the Plotinus commentaries in which he describes the impetus given to Greek studies by the coming of Gemistus Pletho and other Byzantine scholars to the Council of Florence, and how he himself was commissioned by Cosimo to translate the treasures of Greek philosophy now coming into the West from Byzantium. Cosimo, he says, had handed over to him the works of Plato for translation. But in the year 1463 word came to Ficino from Cosimo that he must translate Hermes first, at once, and go on afterwards to Plato; "mihi Mercurium primo Termaximum, mox Platonem mandavit interpretandum".[1] Ficino made the translation in a few months, whilst the old Cosimo, who died in 1464, was still alive. Then he began on Plato.[2]

It is an extraordinary situation. There are the complete works of Plato, waiting, and they must wait whilst Ficino quickly translates Hermes, probably because Cosimo wants to read him before he dies. What a testimony this is to the mysterious reputation of the Thrice Great One! Cosimo and Ficino knew from the Fathers that Hermes Trismegistus was much earlier than Plato. They also knew the Latin *Asclepius* which whetted the appetite for more ancient Egyptian wisdom from the same pristine source.[3] Egypt was before Greece; Hermes was earlier than Plato. Renaissance

[1] Dedication by Ficino to Lorenzo de' Medici of his epitome and commentaries on Plotinus; Ficino, p. 1537.

[2] "Mercurium paucis mensibus eo uiuente (referring to Cosimo) peregi. Platonem tunc etiam sum aggressus"; Ficino, *loc. cit.* Cf. Kristeller, *Studies*, p. 223; A. Marcel, *Marsile Ficin*, Paris, 1958, pp. 255 ff.

[3] In order to understand this enthusiasm, a history of Hermetism in the Middle Ages and in the Renaissance before Ficino is needed. For some indications of the influence of the *Asclepius* in the Middle Ages, see *C.H.* II, pp. 267–75. Interest in Hermetism (based chiefly on *Asclepius* and on the pseudo-Hermetic *Liber Hermetis Mercurii Triplicis de VI rerum principiis* is one of the marks of the twelfth-century Renaissance. For the influence of these works on Hugh of St. Victor, see the *Didascalicon*, translated Jerome Taylor, Columbia, 1961, introduction pp. 19 ff. and notes.

Many of the magical, alchemical, and astrological writings going under the name of Hermes were of course known in the Middle Ages, see below, pp. 48–9.

respect for the old, the primary, the far-away, as nearest to divine truth, demanded that the *Corpus Hermeticum* should be translated before Plato's *Republic* or *Symposium*, and so this was in fact the first translation that Ficino made.

Ficino gave his translation the title of *Pimander*, which is really the title of only the first treatise in the *Corpus Hermeticum*, but which he extended to cover the whole *Corpus*, or rather the first fourteen of its items which were all that his manuscript contained. He dedicated the translation to Cosimo, and this dedication, or *argumentum* as he calls it, reveals the state of mind, the attitude of profound awe and wonder, in which he had approached this marvellous revelation of ancient Egyptian wisdom.

> In that time in which Moses was born flourished Atlas the astrologer, brother of Prometheus the physicist and maternal uncle of the elder Mercury whose nephew was Mercurius Trismegistus.[1]

So the *argumentum* begins, with a slightly garbled version of the Augustinian genealogy of Hermes, which at once places him in extreme antiquity, and almost in a Mosaic context.

Augustine has written of Mercurius, continues Ficino, also Cicero and Lactantius. He repeats the information from Cicero that Mercurius "gave laws and letters" to the Egyptians, adding that he founded the city called Hermopolis. He was an Egyptian priest, the wisest of them all, supreme as philosopher for his vast knowledge, as priest for his holiness of life and practice of the divine cults, and worthy of kingly dignity as administrator of the laws, whence he is rightly called Termaximus, the Three Times Great.[2]

> He is called the first author of theology: he was succeeded by Orpheus, who came second amongst ancient theologians: Aglaophemus, who had been initiated into the sacred teaching of Orpheus, was succeeded in theology by Pythagoras, whose disciple was Philolaus, the teacher of our Divine Plato. Hence there is one ancient theology (*prisca theologia*) . . . taking its origin in Mercurius and culminating in the Divine Plato.[3]

It is in this preface to the *Pimander* that Ficino gives for the first time his genealogy of wisdom which he worked out, not

---

[1] *Argumentum* before Ficino's *Pimander* (Ficino, p. 1836).

[2] This explanation of the meaning of "Thrice Great" is found in the Middle Ages; see below, pp. 48–9.

[3] Ficino, *loc. cit.*

mainly from Gemistus Pletho, who does not mention Trismegistus, but from the Fathers, particularly Augustine, Lactantius, and Clement. He was to repeat the genealogy of wisdom many times later: Hermes Trismegistus always has either the first place in it, or is second only to Zoroaster (who was Pletho's favourite as the first *priscus theologus*), or is bracketed first with Zoroaster.[1] The genealogy of the *prisca theologia* forcibly demonstrates the extreme importance which Ficino assigned to Hermes as the *fons et origo* of a wisdom tradition which led in an unbroken chain to Plato. Much other evidence could be quoted from his works of Ficino's unquestioning belief in the primacy and importance of Hermes, and this attitude impressed an early biographer of the Florentine philosopher who says that "he (Ficino) held it as a secure and firm opinion that the philosophy of Plato took its origin from that of Mercurius, whose teachings seemed to him closer to the doctrine of Orpheus and in certain ways to our own Theology (that is, to Christianity) than those of Pythagoras."[2]

Mercurius wrote many books pertaining to the knowledge of divine things, continues Ficino in his preface to the *Pimander*, in which he reveals arcane mysteries. Nor is it only as a philosopher that he speaks but sometimes as a prophet he sings of the future. He foresaw the ruin of the early religion and the birth of a new faith, and the coming of Christ. Augustine doubts whether he did

[1] In the *Theologia Platonica*, Ficino gives the genealogy as (1) Zoro-aster, (2) Mercurius Trismegistus, (3) Orpheus, (4) Aglaophemus, (5) Pythagoras, (6) Plato (Ficino, p. 386). In the preface to the Plotinus commentaries, Ficino says that divine theology began simultaneously with Zoroaster among the Persians and with Mercurius among the Egyptians; then goes on to Orpheus, Aglaophemus, Pythagoras, Plato (*ibid.*, p. 1537).

This equating of Zoroaster with Hermes brings Ficino's genealogy into some conformity with that of Gemistus Pletho, for whom the most ancient source of wisdom is Zoroaster, after whom he puts a different string of intermediaries to those given by Ficino, but arrives eventually, like Ficino, at Pythagoras and Plato. See the passages quoted from Pletho's commentary on the *Laws* and from his reply to Scholarios in F. Masai, *Pléthon et le Platonisme de Mistra*, Paris, 1956, pp. 136, 138.

For a valuable study of Ficino's genealogies of wisdom, see D. P. Walker, "The *Prisca Theologia* in France", *J.W.C.I.*, 1954 (XVII), pp. 204–59.

[2] *Vita di Ficino*, published from a manuscript of *circa* 1591 in Marcel, *op. cit.*, p. 716.

not know this through the stars or the revelation of demons, but Lactantius does not hesitate to place him among the Sibyls and the prophets.[1]

These remarks (which we have paraphrased, not fully translated, from the *argumentum*) show Ficino's effort to avoid Augustine's condemnation of his hero for the Egyptian idolatry in the *Asclepius*, which he does by emphasising the favourable view of Lactantius. He next goes on to say that of the many works which Mercurius wrote, two principally are divine, the one called *Asclepius*, which Apuleius the Platonist translated into Latin, and the one called *Pimander* (that is the *Corpus Hermeticum*), which has been brought out of Macedonia into Italy and which he himself, by command of Cosimo, has now translated into Latin. He believes that it was first written in Egyptian and was translated into Greek to reveal to the Greeks the Egyptian mysteries.

The *argumentum* ends on a note of ecstasy which reflects those gnostic initiations with which the *Hermetica* are concerned. In this work, so Ficino believes, there shines a light of divine illumination. It teaches us how, rising above the deceptions of sense and the clouds of fantasy, we are to turn our mind to the Divine Mind, as the moon turns to the sun, so that Pimander, that is the Divine Mind, may flow into our mind and we may contemplate the order of all things as they exist in God.

In the introduction to his edition of the *Hermetica*, Scott outlined Ficino's attitude to these works as follows:

> Ficino's theory of the relation between Hermes Trismegistus and the Greek philosophers was based partly on data supplied by early Christian writers, especially Lactantius and Augustine, and partly on the internal evidence of the *Corpus Hermeticum* and the Latin *Asclepius* of Pseudo-Apuleius. He saw . . . that the resemblance between the Hermetic doctrines and those of Plato was such as to imply some historical connection; but accepting it as a known fact that the author of the *Hermetica* was a man who lived about the time of Moses, he inverted the true relation and thought that Plato had derived his theology, through Pythagoras, from Trismegistus. And his view was adopted, at least in its main outlines, by all who dealt with the subject down to the end of the sixteenth century.[2]

[1] In his work on the Christian religion (*De Christ. relig.*, XXV), Ficino puts Hermes with the Sibyls as testifying with them to the coming of Christ (Ficino, p. 29).

[2] Scott, I, p. 31. The end of the sixteenth century is too early a date at which to put the ending of this illusion; see below, chapter XXI.

This is undoubtedly a fact, and one which all students of the Renaissance Neoplatonism which Ficino's translations and works inaugurated would do well to bear in mind. It has not been sufficiently investigated what was the effect on Ficino of his awe-struck approach to the *Hermetica* as the *prisca theologia*, the pristine fount of illumination flowing from the Divine *Mens*, which would lead him to the original core of Platonism as a gnosis derived from Egyptian wisdom.

Contemporaries shared with Ficino his estimate of the extreme importance of the Hermetic writings for, as P. O. Kristeller has pointed out, his *Pimander* had an immense diffusion.[1] A very large number of manuscripts of it exist, more than of any other work by Ficino. It was printed for the first time in 1471 and went through sixteen editions to the end of the sixteenth century, not counting those in which it appears with the other works. An Italian translation of it by Tommaso Benci was printed at Florence in 1548. In 1505, Lefèvre d'Etaples brought together into one volume Ficino's *Pimander* and the translation of the *Asclepius* by Pseudo-Apuleius. The bibliography of the editions, translations, collections, commentaries on the Hermetic writings in the sixteenth century is long and complicated,[2] testifying to the profound and enthusiastic interest aroused by Hermes Trismegistus throughout the Renaissance.

The ban of the mediaeval Church on magic had forced it into dark holes and corners, where the magician plied his abominated art in secrecy. Respectable people might sometimes employ him surreptitiously and he was much feared. But he was certainly not publicly admired as a religious philosopher. Renaissance magic, which was a reformed and learned magic and always disclaimed any connection with the old ignorant, evil, or black magic, was often an adjunct of an esteemed Renaissance philosopher. This new status of magic was undoubtedly mainly due to that great flood of literature which came in from Byzantium, so much of which dated from those early centuries after Christ in which the reigning philosophies were tinged with occultism. The learned and assiduous reader of such authors as Iamblichus, Porphyry, or even

[1] Kristeller, *Studies*, pp. 223 ff.; *Suppl. Fic.*, I, pp. lvii–lviii, cxxix–cxxxi.

[2] Scott, I, pp. 31 ff., and see further below, pp. 170–0, 179, 181–2.

of Plotinus, could no longer regard magic as the trade of ignorant and inferior persons. And the genealogy of ancient wisdom, which Ficino did so much to propagate, was also favourable to a revival of magic, for so many of the *prisci theologi* were *prisci magi*, and the literature which supported their claims also really dated from the occultist early centuries A.D. To the most ancient Zoroaster, who sometimes changes place with Hermes as the earliest in the chain of wisdom, were attributed the *Chaldean Oracles*, which were not, as supposed, documents of extreme antiquity but dated from the second century A.D.[1] The incantatory magic supposed to have been taught by Orpheus, who comes second in the chain of *prisci theologi*, was based on the Orphic hymns, most of which date from the second or third century A.D.[2] Thus Hermes Trismegistus was not the only most ancient theologian or Magus whose sacred literature was badly misdated.

Nevertheless it is probable that Hermes Trismegistus is the most important figure in the Renaissance revival of magic. Egypt was traditionally associated with the darkest and strongest magic, and now there were brought to light the writings of an Egyptian priest which revealed an extraordinary piety, confirming the high opinion of him which the Christian Father, Lactantius, had expressed, and whom the highest authorities regarded as the source of Plato. It was, almost certainly, the discovery of the *Corpus Hermeticum*, which demonstrated the piety of Hermes and associated him so intimately with the reigning Platonic philosophy, which rehabilitated his *Asclepius*, condemned by Augustine as containing bad demonic magic. The extraordinarily lofty position

---

[1] Pletho firmly believed in the extreme antiquity of these Oracles (see Masai, *op. cit.*, pp. 136, 137, 375, etc.) which are for him the early fount of Zoroastrian wisdom the streams from which eventually reached Plato. This exactly corresponds to Ficino's attitude to the *Hermetica*. It was not difficult for Ficino to mingle the waters of these two pristine founts, since they were roughly contemporaneous and similar in their atmosphere. Speaking of the *Hermetica*, Nock says, "Comme les *Oracles Chaldaïques*, ouvrage du temps de Marc-Aurèle, ils nous révèlent une manière de penser, ou plutôt une manière d'user de la pensée, analogue à une sorte de procédé magique . . ." (*C.H.*, I, p. vii).

The *Chaldean Oracles* were edited by W. Kroll, *De oraculis chaldaicis* in *Breslauer Philolog. Abhandl.*, VII (1894), pp. 1–76.

[2] On the *Orphica* in the Renaissance, see D. P. Walker, "Orpheus the Theologian and the Renaissance Platonists", *J.W.C.I.*, 1953 (XVI), pp. 100–20.

assigned to Hermes Trismegistus in this new age rehabilitated Egypt and its wisdom, and therefore the magic with which that wisdom was associated.

Chapter II

FICINO'S *PIMANDER* AND THE *ASCLEPIUS*

IN this chapter I shall give compressed accounts of the contents of four selected treatises of the *Corpus Hermeticum*, chosen only from amongst those fourteen which Ficino translated and to which he gave the general title *Pimander*. I shall indicate the more important points from Ficino's commentaries on these works, trying to bring out his awe-struck wonder at the intuitions into Mosaic and even Christian truths which this most ancient Egyptian author seemed to him to have had mysteriously revealed to him. Finally, a compressed account of the contents of the *Asclepius* will be given. In this way it is hoped to bring before the reader some impression of the two works which Ficino in his *argumentum* before the *Pimander* associates together as the two "divine books" of Hermes Trismegistus, namely the book "On the Power and Wisdom of God" (the fourteen treatises of his *Pimander*) and the book "On the Divine Will" (the *Asclepius*). It is, I believe, necessary for the understanding of the Renaissance attitude to the magic in the *Asclepius* to read that work in the context of the extraordinary piety and knowledge of divine things which the *Pimander* seemed to reveal.

The reader whose interest may be aroused in the true nature of these works as documents for pagan gnosticism in the early centuries A.D. may be referred to Festugière's massive volumes on *La Révélation d'Hermès Trismégiste* in which he treats exhaustively of their philosophical sources and brilliantly reconstructs the social and religious atmosphere of their period.[1] The writers could have used some Hebrew sources,[2] as well as the current Graeco-Roman philosophy, and, in view of their real date after Christ, they could have heard something of Christianity and of the Christian's "Son of God".[3] But for our purposes here, the critical and historical problems of the Hermetic literature are irrelevant, for they would have been entirely unknown to Ficino and his readers, and we are going to try to approach these documents imaginatively as Ficino and the whole Renaissance after him approached them, as revelations of most ancient Egyptian wisdom by a writer who lived long before Plato and even longer before Christ. To keep up this illusion I shall give the five treatises here analysed "Egyptian" titles, and I shall refer throughout to their author as "Hermes Trismegistus". For it seems to me that it is only by entering with some degree of sympathy into the huge illusion of their vast antiquity and Egyptian character that one can hope to realise the tremendous impact which these works made on the Renaissance reader.

Before, however, we plunge into the great Egyptian illusion, some critical remarks are necessary.

These writings are really by different unknown authors and no doubt of considerably varying dates. Even the individual treatises are often composites, made up of different tracts grouped together into a whole. Their contents are therefore very various, and often contradictory. No really coherent system can be drawn from them as a whole. Nor are they intended to be a system of rationally

[1] Needless to say, the works of Reitzenstein, particularly his *Poimandres* (Leipzig, 1904) are still fundamental for this subject. W. Scott's prefaces and critical apparatus in his edition of the *Hermetica* have been consulted as well as the prefaces and notes in the Nock-Festugière edition. Other useful works are A. D. Nock, *Conversion*, Oxford, 1933; C. H. Dodd, *The Bible and the Greeks*, London, 1935; R. Mc. L. Wilson, *The Gnostic Problem*, London, 1958.

[2] There is general agreement that the first treatise of the *Corpus Hermeticum*, the *Pimander*, contains some Jewish elements but opinions differ as to the amount of the writers' indebtedness to Hellenised Judaism.

[3] Most scholars are of the opinion that there is very little, if any, Christian influence in the *Hermetica*. Dodd, who stresses the Jewish influence, thinks that "features of the *Hermetica* in which Christian influence might be suspected, can be accounted for by Hellenistic-Jewish ideas which lie behind both the *Hermetica* and the New Testament" (*op. cit.*, p. xv, note).

thought out philosophy. They are records of individual souls seeking revelation, intuition into the divine, personal salvation, gnosis, without the aid of a personal God or Saviour, but through a religious approach to the universe. It is this religious approach, their character as documents of religious experiences, which give the *Hermetica* a unity which they entirely lack as a thought system.

The cosmological framework which they take for granted is always astrological, even where this is not expressly stated. The material world is under the rule of the stars, and of the seven planets, the "Seven Governors". The laws of the nature within which the religious gnostic lives are the astrological laws, and they are the setting of his religious experience.

There is, however, a fundamental difference in the attitude to the star-ruled world among the various authors of the *Hermetica*. Festugière has classified these writings as belonging to two types of gnosis, namely pessimist gnosis, or optimist gnosis.[1] For the pessimist (or dualist) gnostic, the material world heavily impregnated with the fatal influence of the stars is in itself evil; it must be escaped from by an ascetic way of life which avoids as much as possible all contact with matter, until the lightened soul rises up through the spheres of the planets, casting off their evil influences as it ascends, to its true home in the immaterial divine world. For the optimist gnostic, matter is impregnated with the divine, the earth lives, moves, with a divine life, the stars are living divine animals, the sun burns with a divine power, there is no part of Nature which is not good for all are parts of God.

The following accounts of the contents of the five Hermetic writings chosen are partly analysis, partly direct quotation.[2] I have made many omissions and have sometimes slightly rearranged the order. There is a good deal of diffuseness and repetition in these works, and I have tried to give their main gist as briefly as possible. (1) The Egyptian Genesis. *Pimander*. (*Corpus Hermeticum* I[3]; partly optimist and partly dualist gnosis.)

[1] Festugière, I, p. 84; II, pp. x–xi (classification of the individual *Hermetica* as optimist or pessimist in note to p. xi).

[2] They are in the nature of *précis*, with some direct quotation, and the reader must be warned not to use them as complete translations. In making them, I have had before me Festugière's French translation and Ficino's Latin translation. Unfortunately it is not possible to use Scott's English translation owing to the liberties which he took with the text.

[3] *C.H.*, I, pp. 7–19; Ficino, pp. 1837–9.

Pimander, who is the *Nous*, or divine *mens*, appears to Trismegistus when his corporeal senses are bound as in a heavy sleep. Trismegistus expresses his longing to know the nature of beings and to know God.

Pimander's aspect changes, and Trismegistus sees a limitless vision which is all light. Then a kind of obscurity or darkness appears, out of which comes a kind of fire in which is heard an indescribable sound, like a fiery groan, while from the light issues a holy Word, and a fire without mixture leaps from the moist region up to the sublime, and the air, being light, follows the fiery breath. "That light", says Pimander, "is I myself, *Nous*, thy God . . . and the luminous Word issuing from the *Nous* is the Son of God."

Trismegistus then sees within himself, in his own *Nous* or *mens*, the light and an innumerable number of Powers, a limitless world and the fire enveloped in an all powerful force. He asks Pimander, "Whence then arise the elements of nature?" and Pimander replies, "From the Will of God, which received into itself the Word. . . . And the *Nous*-God, existing as life and light, brought forth a second *Nous*-Demiurge, who being the god of fire and breath, fashioned the Governors, seven in number, who envelop with their circles the sensible world." The Word united itself with the *Nous*-Demiurge, being of the same substance, and the *Nous*-Demiurge conjointly with the Word moves the Seven Governors on which all the lower elemental world depends.

After the *Nous*-Demiurge-Word of fire and breath had fashioned the Seven Governors and set them in motion, there comes in Trismegistus' account the creation of Man, which is the direct action of the *Nous*-Father.

"Now the *Nous*, Father of all beings, being life and light, brought forth a Man similar to himself, whom he loved as his own child. For the Man was beautiful, reproducing the image of his Father: for it was indeed with his own form that God fell in love and gave over to him all his works. Now, when he saw the creation which the Demiurge had fashioned in the fire, the Man wished also to produce a work, and permission to do this was given him by the Father. Having thus entered into the demiurgic sphere, in which he had full power, the Man saw the works of his brother, and the Governors fell in love with him, and each gave to him a part in their own rule. Then, having learned their essence and

23

having received participation in their nature, he wished to break through the periphery of the circles and to know the power of Him who reigns above the fire.

Then Man, who had full power over the world of mortal beings and of animals, leant across the armature of the spheres, having broken through their envelopes, and showed to the Nature below the beautiful form of God. When she saw that he had in him the inexhaustible beauty and all the energy of the Governors, joined to the form of God, Nature smiled with love, for she had seen the features of that marvellously beautiful form of Man reflected in the water and his shadow on the earth. And he, having seen this form like to himself in Nature, reflected in the water, he loved her and wished to dwell with her. The moment he wished this he accomplished it and came to inhabit the irrational form. Then Nature having received her loved one, embraced him, and they were united, for they burned with love."

Man having taken on a mortal body, in order to live with Nature, is alone of all terrestrial beings of a double nature, mortal through his body, immortal through the essential Man. Although in fact immortal and having power over all things, he has also through his body the condition of mortality, being under Destiny and the slave of the armature of the spheres. "Now", says Pimander, "I will reveal to you a mystery which has been hidden until now. Nature being united to Man in love produced an amazing prodigy. Man, as I said, had in him the nature of the assembly of the Seven, composed of fire and breath. Nature from her union with Man brought forth seven men corresponding to the natures of the Seven Governors, being both male and female and rising up towards the sky." The generation of the seven first men was made in the following fashion. Female was the earth, water the generative element; the fire brought things to maturity, and from ether Nature received the vital breath, and she produced the bodies with the form of Man. As for Man, from life and light which he had been, he changed to soul and intellect, the life changing to soul and the light to intellect. And all the beings of the sensible world remained in this state until the end of a period.

At the end of this period, continues Pimander, the link which bound all things was broken by the will of God. Man and all animals, which till then had been both male and female, separated into two sexes and God spoke the word, increase and multiply.

24

Then Providence, through destiny and the armature of the spheres, established the generations, and all living things multiplied, each according to their species.

Pimander gives Trismegistus advice as to how he is to comport himself in life in view of the mystery which has been imparted to him. He is to know himself, because "he who knows himself goes towards himself", that is towards his true nature. "You are light and life, like God the Father of whom Man was born. If therefore you learn to know yourself as made of light and life . . . you will return to life." Only the man who has intellect (not all men have it) can thus know himself. And Trismegistus must live a pure and holy life, rendering the Father propitious to him through filial love and uttering benedictions and hymns.

Trismegistus gives thanks to Pimander for having revealed all things to him, but wishes also to know about the "ascension". Pimander explains that at death the mortal body dissolves into its corporeal elements but the spiritual man goes up through the armature of the spheres leaving at each sphere a part of his mortal nature and the evil it contains. Then, when entirely denuded of all that the spheres had imprinted on him, he enters into the "ogdoadic" nature, hears the Powers singing hymns to God and becomes mingled with the Powers.

Trismegistus is now dismissed by Pimander, "after having been invested with powers and instructed in the nature of the All and the supreme vision." He begins to preach to the people urging them to leave their errors and to take part in immortality.

And Trismegistus "engraved within himself the benefit of Pimander".[1]

Ficino, in his commentary on this treatise, is immensely struck by remarkable resemblances to the book of *Genesis*. "Here Mercurius is seen to be treating of the Mosaic mysteries", he begins, and then goes on to make obvious comparisons. Moses saw a darkness over the face of the abyss and the Spirit of God brooding over the waters: Mercurius sees a darkness and the Word of God warming the humid nature. Moses announced the creation by the powerful Word of God. Mercurius actually states that that shining Word, which illuminates all things, is the Son of God. And if it is

[1] "Ego autem Pimandri beneficium inscripsi penetralibus animi . . ." (Ficino's translation, Ficino, p. 1839).

possible to ascribe to a man born before the Incarnation such knowledge, he saw the Son being born of the Father and the Spirit proceeding from the Father and the Son. He saw the creation being made by the Divine Word, and man being made in the image of God, then his fall from the intelligible sphere into the body. He actually uses almost the same words as Moses when describing God's command to the species to increase and multiply. Then he instructs us how we may rise again to that intelligible and immortal nature from which we have degenerated. Moses was the law-giver of the Hebrews, Mercurius of the Egyptians, and he gives holy advice to his flock on how to live, praising the Father of all with hymns and thanksgivings and contemplating the life and the light.[1]

As the above abstract of the commentary on the *Pimander* shows it was above all what he took to be the resemblances to Moses (not so much to Plato) in this work which profoundly impressed Ficino. This was why, so he must have thought, the Fathers made such a point of dating Trismegistus in relation to Moses, because he seemed like an Egyptian Moses. Ficino continued to ponder over these marvels in later years; in the *Theologia Platonica* he actually allowed himself to wonder whether, after all, Hermes Trismegistus *was* Moses. After speaking in that work of the account of creation in the *Timaeus* he adds: "Trismegistus Mercurius teaches more clearly such an origin of the generation of the world. Nor need we wonder that this man knew so much, if this Mercurius was the same man as Moses, as Artapanus the historian shows with many conjectures.[2]"

And Trismegistus is even better than Moses because he saw, long before the Incarnation, that the creative Word was the Son of God. "Ille (Moses) potenti verbo domini cuncta creata nunciat, hic (Mercurius) verbum illud lucens, quod omnia illuminet . . . filium Dei esse asseverat. . . ." Probably Ficino is here thinking of a comparison with the beginning of St. John's Gospel. As Ficino hurriedly translated the *Pimander* for Cosimo he would have realised how right Lactantius had been when he said that Tris-

[1] Ficino, *loc. cit.*

[2] *Theologia Platonica*, VIII, I (Ficino, p. 400).

Ficino probably got his information about Artapanus from Eusebius, *De praeparatione evangelicae*, IX, 27, 6. Artapanus was a Hellenised Jew; see Festugière, I, pp. 70, 384.

megistus "by some means or other searched into almost all truth" and "often described the excellence and the Majesty of the Word", calling him "Son of God", not only in the *Pimander*, but also in the *Asclepius*.

Thus an odour of sanctity surrounds the author of the Egyptian Genesis, who is so like Moses, who prophesies Christianity, and who teaches a devout way of life in loving devotion to God the Father.

Nevertheless it is most obvious that there are, as Ficino significantly fails to point out, radical differences of many kinds between the Mosaic Genesis and the Egyptian Genesis. Particularly do they differ most profoundly in their account of the nature of Man and the character of his Fall.

It is true that the Mosaic Genesis, like the Egyptian Genesis, says that Man was made in the image of God and was given dominion over all creatures, but it is never said in the Mosaic Genesis that this meant that Adam was created as a divine being, having the divine creative power. Not even when Adam walked with God in the Garden of Eden before the Fall is this said of him. When Adam, tempted by Eve and the serpent, wished to eat of the Tree of Knowledge and become like God, this was the sin of disobedience, punished by the exile from the Garden of Eden. But in the Egyptian Genesis the newly created Man, seeing the newly created Seven Governors (the planets) on whom all things depend, wishes to create, to make something like that. Nor is this treated as a sin of disobedience.[1] He is allowed into the society of the Seven Governors who love him and impart to him their powers. This Egyptian Adam is more than human; he is divine and belongs to the race of the star demons, the divinely created governors of the lower world. He is even stated to be "brother" to the creative Word-Demiurge—Son of God, the "second god" who moves the stars.

It is true that he falls, but this fall is in itself an act of his power. He can lean down through the armature of the spheres, tear open

[1] Festugière thinks that though man's desire to create was not a fault, since permission to do so was given to him by the Father, yet his entry immediately afterwards into the demiurgic sphere of the Seven Governors was already a punishment, a beginning of his fall into matter (*Révélation*, III, pp. 87 ff.). Dodd's interpretation (*op. cit.*, p. 153) is similar. Both writers stress the difference between Hermetic man and Mosaic man, the one created divine, the other created out of the dust of the earth. The fall of Hermetic man is more like the fall of Lucifer than the fall of Adam.

their envelopes and come down to show himself to Nature. He does this of his own free will moved by love of the beautiful Nature which he himself helped to create and maintain, through his participation in the nature of the Seven Governors. He was moved to do this by love of his own image, reflected in the face of Nature (just as God loved Man, seeing in him his own beautiful image). And Nature recognises his power, the powers of the Seven Governors in him, and is united to him in love.

It is true that this is a Fall which involves loss, that Man in coming down to Nature and taking on a mortal body puts this mortal body, puts his mortal part, under the dominion of the stars, and it is perhaps punished by the separation into two sexes (after the curious period of the Seven sexless men engendered by Man and Nature). But man's immortal part remains divine and creative. He consists, not of a human soul and a body, but of a divine, creative, immortal essence and a body. And this divinity, this power, he recovers in the vision of the divine *mens*, which is like his own divine *mens*, shown him by Pimander. Pimander leaves Trismegistus after he has been *"invested with powers* and instructed in the nature of the All and the supreme vision."

In short, the Egyptian Genesis tells the story of the creation and fall of a divine man, a man intimately related to the star-demons in his very origin, Man as Magus. The Egyptian Genesis tallies well with that famous outbreak in the *Asclepius* on man as the *magnum miraculum* (with which Pico della Mirandola was to open his Oration on the Dignity of Man):

> What a great miracle is Man, O Asclepius, a being worthy of reverence and honour. For he passes into the nature of a god as though he were himself a god; he has familiarity with the race of demons, knowing that he is issued from the same origin; he despises that part of his nature which is only human, for he has put his hope in the divinity of the other part.[1]

(2) Egyptian Regeneration. *The Secret Discourse on the Mountain of Hermes Trismegistus to his Son Tat. (Corpus Hermeticum,* XIII[2]; dualist gnosis.)

Tat asks his father, Trismegistus, to teach him about the doctrine of regeneration, for he has fortified his spirit against the illusion of the world and is ready for the final initiation. Trismegistus tells

---

[1] See below, p. 35.

[2] *C.H.*, II, pp. 200–09; Ficino, pp. 1854–6.

him that regenerated man is born of intelligent wisdom in silence
and the seed is the True Good, sown in him by the Will of God.
The man thus born again "will be god, the son of God, all in all,
composed of all the Powers." Trismegistus has had the regenerative experience. With growing excitement, Tat implores him to
pass it on to him. "Who is the operator in the work of regeneration?" he asks, and the reply is, "The Son of God, a man like
other men, by the will of God." Tat asks what truth is, and he is
told that it is "that which is not polluted, which has no limit, no
colour, no form, is motionless, naked, shining, which can only be
apprehended by itself, the unalterable Good, the Incorporeal." It
cannot be perceived by the senses and can only be known by the
effects of its power and energy, which demands that a person must
be capable of understanding birth in God. "Am I not capable of
this, O Father?" cries Tat, and the answer is that he must draw
it to himself and it will come; wish it and it will be produced;
arrest the activity of the bodily senses and the divinity will be
born in him; purify himself from the "irrational punishments of
matter". Terrible and numerous are these "punishments", and the
chief of them are twelve in number, namely Ignorance, Sadness,
Incontinence, Concupiscence, Injustice, Cupidity, Deceit, Envy,
Fraud, Anger, Precipitation, Malice. These are the punishments
which, through his imprisonment in the body, force the interior
man to suffer through the senses.

Now, in a religious silence, Tat experiences the work of regeneration and the Powers of God come into him and drive out
the Punishments. Knowledge replaces Ignorance; Joy repulses
Sadness; Continence, Incontinence; Endurance, Concupiscence;
Justice, Injustice; Generosity, Cupidity; Truth, Deceit. With the
arrival of Truth comes the Good, accompanied by Life and Light,
and all the remaining Punishments are driven out. The Decade
of the Powers has cancelled the Dodecade of the Punishments.

When his regenerative experience is completed, Trismegistus
leads Tat out of the "tent" (translated *tabernaculum* by Ficino)
under which he had been and which was constituted by the circle
of the zodiac. As Festugière explains, the twelve vices or "punishments" come from the twelve signs of the zodiac which oppressed
Tat when he was still material and under the influence of matter.
Festugière compares this with the ascent through the spheres in
the *Pimander*, where there are seven vices with the planets which

the initiate abandons on his upward path.[1] The punishments of matter are thus really the influences of the stars, for which are substituted, in the regenerative experience, Virtues which are Divine Powers which free the soul from the material weight of the heaven and its influences. The Powers are One in the Word, and the soul thus regenerated becomes itself the Word and a Son of God.[2]

Trismegistus has passed on to Tat the experience which he himself has had, and the Powers sing in Tat the Hymn of Regeneration. "Let all nature listen to the hymn. . . . I will sing the Lord of Creation, the All, the One. Open, oh heavens, winds retain your breath, let the immortal circle of God listen to my word. . . . Powers which are in me sing to the One, the All. . . . I give thee thanks, Father, energy of the Powers; I give thee thanks, God, power of my energies. . . . This is what the Powers cry which are in me. . . . This is what the man who belongs to thee cries through the fire, through the air, through the earth, through the water, through the breath, through all thy creatures. . . ."

In his commentary on this treatise,[3] Ficino compares the driving out of the *ultores* and their replacement by the *Potestates Dei* with the Christian experience of regeneration in Christ, the Word and the Son of God. In fact, as Festugière points out,[4] this gnostic experience does seem to be something like a gift of grace which cancels the predestination of the stars.

I append a table of the Punishments and Powers as translated into Latin by Ficino. He translated Incontinence as Inconstancy and, in the text of the translation, forgot Concupiscence which, however, he gives as Luxuria in the list of Punishments in his commentary. Since he does not list the Powers in the commentary, we have no opposite for his Luxuria, which should, of course, be Castitas (or, if the Endurance of the text had been translated, Fortitudo).

---

[1] Festugière, III, pp. 90, 154, 156, etc. See also the valuable discussion of this treatise, and of the association of the vices with the zodiac and the planets, in M. W. Bloomfield, *The Seven Deadly Sins*, Michigan, 1952, pp. 48 ff.

[2] On the Powers, see Festugière, III, pp. 153 ff.

[3] Ficino, p. 1856.

[4] Festugière, IV, p. 253.

Punishments	Powers
Ignorantia	Cognitio Dei
Tristitia	Gaudium
Inconstantia	Constantia
Cupiditas	Continentia
Luxuria	Castitas ? Fortitudo ?
Injustitia	Justitia
Deceptio	Veritas
Invidia	Bonum
Fraus	Lumen
Ira	Vita
Temeritas	
Malitia	

It is probable that this Gospel according to Hermes Trismegistus meant a great deal to Ficino, who desperately feared the stars. Like the creation by the Word in *Pimander*, it may well have seemed to him to accord with St. John. "In Him was life; and the life was the light of men", and to as many as received Him "to them gave He power to become the sons of God."[1]

(3) Egyptian Reflection of the Universe in the Mind. *The Mind to Hermes*. (*Corpus Hermeticum* XI[2]; optimist gnosis.)

(The *mens* is supposed throughout to be addressing Hermes.)

Eternity is the Power of God, and the work of Eternity is the world, which has no beginning, but is continually becoming by the action of Eternity. Therefore nothing that is in the world will ever perish or be destroyed, for Eternity is imperishable.

And all this great body of the world is a soul, full of intellect and of God, who fills it within and without and vivifies the All.

Contemplate through me (that is through the *mens*) the world, and consider its beauty. See the hierarchy of the seven heavens and their order. See that all things are full of light. See the earth, settled in the midst of the All, the great nurse who nourishes all terrestrial creatures. All is full of soul, and all beings are in movement. Who has created these things ? The One God, for God is One. You see that the world is always one, the sun, one, the moon, one, the divine activity, one; God too, is One. And since all is living, and life is also one, God is certainly One. It is by the

[1] St. John, I, iv, xii.
[2] *C.H.*, I, pp. 147–57; Ficino, pp. 1850–52.

action of God that all things come into being. Death is not the destruction of the assembled elements in a body, but the breaking of their union. The change is called death because the body dissolves, but I declare to you, my dear Hermes, that the beings who are thus dissolved are but transformed.

All beings are in God but not as though placed in a place, for it is not thus that they are placed in the incorporeal faculty of representation. Judge of this from your own experience. Command your soul to be in India, to cross the ocean; in a moment it will be done. Command it to fly up to heaven. It will not need wings; nothing can prevent it. And if you wish to break through the vault of the universe and to contemplate what is beyond—if there is anything beyond the world—you may do it.

See what power, what swiftness you possess. It is so that you must conceive of God; all that is, he contains within himself like thoughts, the world, himself, the All. Therefore unless you make yourself equal to God, you cannot understand God: for the like is not intelligible save to the like. Make yourself grow to a greatness beyond measure, by a bound free yourself from the body; raise yourself above all time, become Eternity; then you will understand God. Believe that nothing is impossible for you, think yourself immortal and capable of understanding all, all arts, all sciences, the nature of every living being. Mount higher than the highest height; descend lower than the lowest depth. Draw into yourself all sensations of everything created, fire and water, dry and moist, imagining that you are everywhere, on earth, in the sea, in the sky, that you are not yet born, in the maternal womb, adolescent, old, dead, beyond death. If you embrace in your thought all things at once, times, places, substances, qualities, quantities, you may understand God.

Say no longer that God is invisible. Do not speak thus, for what is more manifest than God. He has created all only that you may see it through the beings. For that is the miraculous power of God, to show himself through all beings. For nothing is invisible, even of the incorporeals. The intellect makes itself visible in the act of thinking, God in the act of creating.

Ficino's commentary on this treatise is merely a short résumé. The reader will notice that the view of the world on which this Egyptian revelation (really optimist type of gnosis) is based differs fundamentally from the preceding revelation (based on a pessimist type of gnosis). In the revelation of Hermes to Tat, matter was evil and the work of regeneration consisted in escaping from its power through the infusion into the soul of divine Powers or Virtues. Here the world is good, for it is full of God. The gnosis consists in reflecting the world within the mind, for so we shall know the God who made it.

Yet also in the pessimist gnosis, described in the regeneration of Tat, the world was reflected in his mind. After his regeneration, he cried to God through the creatures, and became Eternity, the Aion, as here. The principle of world-reflection in the mind thus belongs to both types of gnosis, but with a different emphasis. In the one the adept is released by his vision from evil powers in matter and there is a strong ethical element. In the other, the vision is of God in nature, a kind of pantheism; the material world is full of the divine, and the gnosis consists in fully grasping it, as it is, and holding it within the mind.

For the Renaissance enthusiast, believing all to be the work of one man, the most ancient Egyptian, Hermes Trismegistus, these distinctions would be blurred.

(4) Egyptian Philosophy of Man and of Nature: Earth Movement. *Hermes Trismegistus to Tat on the Common Intellect.* (*Corpus Hermeticum* XII[1]; optimist gnosis.)

The intellect, O Tat, is drawn from the very substance of God. In men, this intellect is God; and so some men are gods and their humanity is near to the divinity. When man is not guided by intellect, he falls below himself into an animal state. All men are subject to destiny but those in possession of the word, in whom intellect commands, are not under it in the same manner as others. God's two gifts to man of intellect and the word have the same value as immortality. If man makes right use of these, he differs in no way from the immortals.

The world, too, is a god, image of a greater god. United to him and conserving the order and will of the Father, it is the totality of life. There is nothing in it, through all the duration of the cyclic return willed by the Father, which is not alive. The Father has willed that the world should be living so long as it keeps its cohesion; hence the world is necessarily god. How then could it

---

[1] *C.H.*, I, pp. 174–83; Ficino, pp. 1852–4.

be that in that which is god, which is the image of the All, there should be dead things? For death is corruption and corruption is destruction, and it is impossible that anything of God could be destroyed.

Do not the living beings in the world die, O Father, although they are parts of the world?

Hush, my child, for you are led into error by the denomination of the phenomenon. Living beings do not die, but, being composite bodies they are dissolved; this is not death but the dissolution of a mixture. If they are dissolved, it is not to be destroyed but to be renewed. What in fact is the energy of life? Is it not movement? What is there in the world which is immobile? Nothing.

But the earth at least, does it not seem to be immobile?

No. On the contrary, alone of all beings it is both subject to a multitude of movements and stable. It would be absurd to suppose that this nurse of all beings should be immobile, she who gives birth to all things, for without movement it is impossible to give birth. All that is in the world, without exception, is in movement, and that which is in movement is also in life. Contemplate then the beautiful arrangement of the world and see that it is alive, and that all matter is full of life.

Is God then in matter, O Father?

Where could matter be placed if it existed apart from God? Would it not be a confused mass, unless it were put to work? And if it is put to work by whom is that done? The energies which operate in it are parts of God. Whether you speak of matter or bodies or substance, know that these things are energies of God, of God who is the All. In the All there is nothing which is not God. Adore this Word, my child, and render it a cult.

Again, Ficino's commentary on this is little more than a résumé.

The piece again gives "Egyptian" philosophy of the optimist gnosis, repeating much that is in other treatises. The fundamental tenet that man through his intellect is divine, and that gnosis consists in becoming, or rebecoming a god in order to see God, comes out clearly.

The emphasis of "Egyptian" natural philosophy (optimist gnosis) on the divinity, eternity, and life of the world and of matter is also strongly restated. In this divine and living world, nothing can die and everything moves, including the earth.

This philosophy, in which divine man through his divine intellect participates in the intellect infused throughout the living world of divine nature, is the ideal philosophy for Man as Magus, as the *Asclepius* will show.

(5) Egyptian Religion. The *Asclepius*[1] or *The Perfect Word* (that the latter is the correct title would have been known from Lactantius who calls it *Sermo Perfectus*; optimist gnosis).

Hermes Trismegistus, Asclepius, Tat, and Hammon meet together in an Egyptian temple. No others were admitted, for it would be impious to divulge to the masses a teaching entirely filled with the divine majesty. When the fervour of the four men and the presence of God had filled the holy place, the divine love (*divinus Cupido*)[2] began to speak through the lips of Hermes.

All descends from heaven, from the One who is the All, by the intermediary of the heaven. Attend carefully to this, with full application of your divine intellect, for the doctrine of the divinity is like a torrential flood coming down from the heights with violent impetuosity. From the celestial bodies there are spread throughout the world continual effluvia, through the souls of all species and of all individuals from one end to the other of nature. Matter has been prepared by God to be the receptacle of all forms; and nature, imprinting the forms by means of the four elements, prolongs up to heaven the series of beings.

All species reproduce their individuals, whether demons, men, birds, animals, and so on. The individuals of the human race are diverse; having come down from on high where they had commerce with the race of demons they contract links with all other species. That man is near to the gods who, thanks to the spirit which relates him to the gods, has united himself to them with a religion inspired by heaven.

And so, O Asclepius, man is a *magnum miraculum*, a being worthy of reverence and honour. For he goes into the nature of a god as though he were himself a god; he has familiarity with the race of demons, knowing that he is of the same origin; he despises that part of his nature which is only human for he has put his hope in the divinity of the other part.[3]

Man is united to the gods by what he has of the divine, his intellect; all other creatures are bound to him by the celestial plan

[1] *C.H.*, II, pp. 296–355. [2] *Ibid.*, p. 297. [3] *Ibid.*, pp. 301–2.

and he attaches them to himself by knots of love. This union of gods with men is not for all men but only for those who have the faculty of intellection. Thus alone among creatures, man is double, one part like God, the other formed of the elements. The reason why man was condemned to this double nature is as follows.

When God had created the second god, he seemed to him beautiful and he loved him as the offspring of his divinity[1] ("as his Son" according to Lactantius, who regards this as one of the passages in which Hermes prophesies Christianity).[2] But there had to be another being who could contemplate what God had made and so he created man. Seeing that man could not regulate all things unless he gave him a material envelope he gave him a body. Thus man was formed from a double origin, so that he could both admire and adore celestial things and take care of terrestrial things and govern them.

The soul of the gods is said to be all intellect, but this is true only of the superior gods, for there are many gods, some intelligible, some sensible.

The chief or principal gods are as follows (I here combine two passages on the principal gods).

The Ruler of Heaven is Jupiter; and through the intermediary of heaven he dispenses life to all beings. (Possibly an earlier statement that it is breath or *spiritus* which keeps life in all the beings of the world relates to this supremacy of Jupiter, the god of Air.) Jupiter occupies a place intermediary between heaven and earth.

The Sun, or Light, for it is through the intermediary of the solar circle that light is spread to all. The Sun illuminates the other stars not so much by the power of his light as by his divinity and sanctity. He must be held as the second god. The world is living and all things in it are alive and it is the sun which governs all living things.

Next in the order of gods are the Thirty-Six, which are called Horoscopes,[3] that is stars fixed in the same place who have for their chief a god called Pantomorph or Omniform who imposes their particular forms on the individual of each species. No individual form can be born exactly the same as another; these forms change as many times an hour as there are moments within the circle in the interior of which resides the great god Omniform. (These thirty-six gods are the decans, or divisions of ten degrees into

[1] *Ibid.*, pp. 304–5.   [2] See above, p. 7.   [3] *C.H.*, II, p. 319.

which the 360 degrees of the circle of the zodiac are divided.[1] Note in the Egyptian theological system here presented the great importance of the sun and the zodiac with its decans.)

Finally, in the list of gods come the seven spheres who have as their ruler Fortune or Destiny. Air is the instrument or organ of all these gods.

Having spoken of the society which unites gods and men, you must know, O Asclepius, the power and force of man. Just as the Lord and Father is the creator of the gods of heaven, so man is the author of the gods who reside in the temples. Not only does he receive life, but he gives it in his turn. Not only does he progress towards God, but he *makes gods*.

Do you mean the statues, O Trismegistus?

Yes, the statues, Asclepius. They are animated statues full of *sensus* and *spiritus* who can accomplish many things, foretelling the future, giving ills to men and curing them.[2]

(I attach here a later passage on the man-made gods.)

What we have said about man is already marvellous, but most marvellous of all is that he has been able to discover the nature of the gods and to reproduce it. Our first ancestors invented the art of making gods. They mingled a virtue, drawn from material nature, to the substance of the statues, and "since they could not actually create souls, after having evoked the souls of demons or angels, they introduced these into their idols by holy and divine rites, so that the idols had the power of doing good and evil." These terrestrial or man-made gods result from a composition of herbs, stones, and aromatics which contain in themselves an occult virtue of divine efficacy. And if one tries to please them with numerous sacrifices, hymns, songs of praise, sweet concerts which recall the harmony of heaven, this is in order that the celestial element which has been introduced into the idol by the repeated practice of the celestial rites may joyously support its long dwelling amongst men. That is how man makes gods.[3] Hermes adds as examples of such gods, the worship of Asclepius, of his own ancestor, Hermes, and of Isis (implying the cult of the statues of these divinities); and he mentions here, too, the Egyptian worship of animals.

(I revert now to an earlier part of the *Asclepius*.)

[1] On the decans, see below, pp. 45–7.
[2] *C.H.*, II, pp. 325–6.   [3] *Ibid.*, pp. 347–9.

Yet the religion of Egypt, and its wise and true cult of the divine
All in One, is destined to pass away.

THE LAMENT[1] (OR THE APOCALYPSE)

There will come a time when it will be seen that in vain have
the Egyptians honoured the divinity with a pious mind and with
assiduous service. All their holy worship will become inefficacious.
The gods, leaving the earth, will go back to heaven; they will
abandon Egypt; this land, once the home of religion, will be
widowed of its gods and left destitute. Strangers will fill this
country, and not only will there no longer be care for religious
observances, but, a yet more painful thing, it will be laid down
under so-called laws, under pain of punishments, that all must
abstain from acts of piety or cult towards the gods. Then this most
holy land, the home of sanctuaries and temples, will be covered
with tombs and the dead. O Egypt, Egypt, there will remain of
thy religion only fables, and thy children in later times will not
believe them; nothing will survive save words engraved on stones
to tell of thy pious deeds. The Scythian or the Indian, or some
other such barbarous neighbour will establish himself in Egypt.
For behold the divinity goes back up to heaven; and men, abandoned, all die, and then, without either god or man, Egypt will be
nothing but a desert. . . .

Why weep, O Asclepius? Egypt will be carried away to worse
things than this; she will be polluted with yet graver crimes. She,
hitherto most holy, who so much loved the gods, only country of
the earth where the gods made their home in return for her
devotion, she who taught men holiness and piety, will give example
of the most atrocious cruelty. In that hour, weary of life, men will
no longer regard the world as worthy object of their admiration
and reverence. This All, which is a good thing, the best that can
be seen in the past, the present and the future, will be in danger of
perishing; men will esteem it a burden; and thenceforward they
will despise and no longer cherish this whole of the universe,
incomparable work of God, glorious construction, good creation
made up of an infinite diversity of forms, instrument of the will of
God who, without envy, pours forth his favour on all his work, in

[1] *Ibid.*, pp. 326 ff.

which is assembled in one whole, in a harmonious diversity, all that can be seen that is worthy of reverence, praise and love. For darkness will be preferred to light; it will be thought better to die than to live; none will raise his eyes towards heaven; the pious man will be thought mad, the impious, wise; the frenzied will be thought brave, the worst criminal a good man. The soul and all the beliefs attached to it, according to which the soul is immortal by nature or foresees that it can obtain immortality as I have taught you—this will be laughed at and thought nonsense. And believe me, it will be considered a capital crime under the law to give oneself to the religion of the mind. A new justice will be created and new laws. Nothing holy, nothing pious, nothing worthy of heaven and of the gods who dwell there, will be any more spoken of nor will find credence in the soul.

The gods will separate themselves from men, deplorable divorce. Only the evil angels will remain who will mingle with men, and constrain them by violence—miserable creatures—to all the excesses of criminal audacity, engaging them in wars, brigandage, frauds, and in everything which is contrary to the nature of the soul. Then the earth will lose its equilibrium, the sea will no longer be navigable, the heaven will no longer be full of stars, the stars will stop their courses in the heaven. Every divine voice will be silenced, and will be silent. The fruits of the earth will moulder, the soil will be no longer fertile, the air itself will grow thick with a lugubrious torpor.

Such will be the old age of the world, irreligion, disorder, confusion of all goods. When all these things have come to pass, O Asclepius, then the Lord and Father, the god first in power and the demiurge of the One God, having considered these customs and voluntary crimes, endeavouring by his will, which is the divine will, to bar the way to vices and universal corruption and to correct errors, he will annihilate all malice, either by effacing it in a deluge or by consuming it by fire, or destroying it by pestilential maladies diffused in many places. Then he will bring back the world to its first beauty, so that this world may again be worthy of reverence and admiration, and that God also, creator and restorer of so great a work, may be glorified by the men who shall live then in continual hymns of praise and benedictions. That is what the rebirth of the world will be; a renewal of all good things, a holy and most solemn restoration of Nature herself, imposed by force in the course of time . . . by the will of God.

We have no commentary by Ficino on the *Asclepius*, for the commentary supposedly by him which is printed with the *Asclepius* in his collected works is now known to have been not by Ficino, but by Lefèvre d'Etaples.¹ In that commentary Lefèvre d'Etaples expresses strong disapproval of the "god-making" passage.² This disapproval can now be totally dissociated from Ficino, since it was not he who wrote the commentary.

The best guide to what Ficino thought of the *Asclepius* is thus the *argumentum* before his translation of the *Corpus Hermeticum*, called by him *Pimander*, where he says that of the many works of Hermes Trismegistus, two are "divine", the one the work on the Divine Will, the other on the Power and Wisdom of God. The first of these is called the *Asclepius*, the second *Pimander*.³

Thus the *Asclepius* is for Ficino, a "divine" work on the Will of God, intimately associated with the other "divine" work by this most holy and ancient Egyptian, the *Pimander*, on the Power and Wisdom of God.

My purpose in bringing together in this chapter accounts of four works in the *Corpus Hermeticum* together with an account of the *Asclepius* has been to suggest how, for Ficino and his readers, what they thought to be the Mosaic piety of the Egyptian Genesis,

---

¹ In 1505, Lefèvre d'Etaples published at Paris Ficino's *Pimander* together with the *Asclepius* with commentaries by himself. The two works were thereafter often published together, and eventually passed together into the collected editions of Ficino's works, in which it is not mentioned that the commentaries on the *Asclepius* are not by Ficino but by Lefèvre d'Etaples. For instance, in the edition of Ficino's *Opera* from which all the quotations in this book are made, Ficino's *Pimander*, with his commentaries (Ficino, pp. 1836–57) is immediately followed (pp. 1858–72) by the *Asclepius* with commentaries which the unwary reader naturally supposes are also by Ficino. P. O. Kristeller first cleared up this error in *Suppl. Fic.*, I, pp. cxxx ff.; see also Kristeller, *Studies*, pp. 223 ff.

² See Ficino, pp. 1866–7, 1870, for the commentaries on the *Asclepius* (really by Lefèvre d'Etaples) in which the Egyptian idolatry and magical practices described in that work are condemned. Cf. D. P. Walker, "The *Prisca Theologia* in France", *J.W.C.I.*, 1954 (XVII), p. 238.

³ "E multis denique Mercurii libris, duo sunt diuine praecipue, unus de Voluntate diuina, alter de Potestate, & sapientia Dei. Ille Asclepius, hic Pimander inscribitur." Ficino's *argumentum* before his *Pimander* (Ficino, p. 1836).

and the Christian piety of Egyptian regeneration, would have rehabilitated in their eyes the Egyptian religion of the *Asclepius*. They would observe that much of the same philosophy and general outlook of works in the *Corpus Hermeticum* is repeated in the *Asclepius*. Thus the latter work would seem the revelation of the religious cult which went with the "religion of the mind", or religion of the mind in relation to the world, which this holy Egyptian, both in various passages in the *Corpus Hermeticum*, and in the *Asclepius*, associated prophetically with the "Son of God". In the light of the newly discovered *Corpus*, and its translation in Ficino's eagerly read *Pimander*, it would have seemed that Augustine must have been mistaken in interpreting the Lament as a true prophecy, though inspired by devils, of the coming of Christianity to abolish Egyptian idolatry. Surely, on the contrary, the work which Lactantius had called the *Sermo Perfectus* contained the final initiation into the religious cult practised by the holy Hermes.

And that cult involved the practice of astral magic. The statues in the temples, the "terrestrial gods", were animated by knowing the occult properties of substances, by arranging them in accordance with the principles of sympathetic magic, and by drawing down into them the life of the celestial gods by invocations. So it would become a legitimate practice for a philosopher, even a devout practice associated with his religion, to "draw down the life of the heaven" by sympathetic astral magic, as Ficino advised in his work on magic, the *De vita coelitus comparanda*.

The rehabilitation of the *Asclepius*, through the discovery of the *Corpus Hermeticum*, is, I believe, one of the chief factors in the Renaissance revival of magic. And this can only be understood by reading the *Asclepius* in the context of Ficino's *Pimander*, and the pious interpretations of it in his commentary.

The attitude to the famous Lament of the *Asclepius* would also change. This moving and beautiful piece of pro-Egyptian rhetoric is suffused with a moral indignation reminiscent of Hebrew prophecy, by which the author may indeed have been influenced. The passing of the holy Egyptian religion is identified with a breaking up of the moral law, and its eventual restoration with the restoration of morality. The decay of the "religion of the world" brought with it the decay of ethics and utter moral confusion. Hence the pious and good man should hope for its promised return, and the Lament could begin to look quite differently from the way

Augustine saw it, could begin to seem like an injunction to infuse into a decayed Christianity something of the Egyptian spirit of piety and morality.

The first thing which meets the eye of the worshipper, or the tourist, who enters the cathedral of Siena is the portrait of Hermes Trismegistus on the famous mosaic pavement (frontispiece). On either side of Hermes stand two Sibyls, holding their prophecies of the coming of Christianity, and behind these two are ranged the rest of the ten, all with their prophecies. Obviously here we have Hermes Trismegistus with the Sibyls, as in Lactantius, as the great Gentile prophet of Christianity. The inscription under his feet dates the revered figure even earlier than Augustine or Lactantius had done, for it describes him as "Hermes Mercurius Contemporaneous Moyse". An oriental-looking figure wearing a turban and perhaps intended to be Moses his "contemporary" stands in a deferential attitude, almost bowing, on Hermes' right; and behind this figure is a grave personage perhaps intended to represent some pious Egyptian participator in the Hermetic dialogues, Asclepius, for example, or Tat.

The left hand of Hermes rests on a tablet, supported by sphinxes, on which is this inscription:

> DEUS OMNIUM CREATOR
> SECUM DEUM FECIT
> VISIBILEM ET HUNC
> FECIT PRIMUM ET SOLUM
> QUO OBLECTATUS EST
> VALDE AMAVIT PROPRIUM
> FILIUM QUI APPELLATUR
> SANCTUM VERBUM.

As Scott has pointed out,[1] this inscription is an abbreviated Latin translation of the passage in the *Asclepius* as quoted from the Greek by Lactantius and which that Father emphasised so strongly for its mention of the "Son of God". "The Lord and Creator of all things, whom we have the right to call God, since he made the second God visible and sensible. . . . Since, therefore, he made him first, and alone, and one only, he appeared to him beautiful, and most full of all good things; and he hallowed him

[1] Scott, I, p. 32.

and altogether loved him as his own Son."[1] All the points in the inscription are found here, except the last one "qui appellatur Sanctum Verbum", which brings in Hermes' other prophecy about the Word as the Son of God—also pointed out by Lactantius—at the beginning of *Pimander*.[2]

The suppliant Moses (if this figure is indeed intended to be Moses) holds a book which is also held by Hermes. On this book is written:

SUSCIPITE O LICTERAS ET LEGES EGIPTII

"Take up letters and laws, O Egyptians". The phrase is obviously derived from Cicero's description, which Lactantius quotes, of Hermes Trismegistus as he who gave to the Egyptians their letters and laws (*Aegyptiis leges et litteras tradidisse*).[3] But the phrase is most significantly changed in the inscription.

TAKE UP THY LETTERS AND LAWS O EGYPTIANS

would seem to mean a supplication from the lawgiver of the Hebrews (if the suppliant figure is Moses) to the lawgiver of the Egyptians to revive Egyptian piety and morality.

The mosaics of Hermes Trismegistus and the Sibyls were laid down in the duomo of Siena during the fourteen-eighties.[4] The representation of Hermes Trismegistus in this Christian edifice, so prominently displayed near its entrance and giving him so lofty a spiritual position, is not an isolated local phenomenon but a symbol of how the Italian Renaissance regarded him and a prophecy of what was to be his extraordinary career throughout Europe in the sixteenth century and well on into the seventeenth century.

[1] Lactantius, *Div. Inst.*, IV, vi; Fletcher's English translation, I, p. 221; *C.H.*, II, pp. 304–5; see above, p. 7.

[2] *C.H.*, I, p. 8; Ficino p. 1837. Lactantius, *Div. Inst.*, IV, viii, ix; Fletcher's translation, I, pp. 224, 226.

[3] Cicero, *De nat. deor.*, III, 22; quoted by Lactantius, *Div. Inst.*, I, vi (Fletcher's translation, I, p. 15). The quotation from Cicero is made in a passage in which Lactantius is putting Hermes with the Sibyls, so it could have been suggested to the designer of the mosaic by Lactantius, not directly by Cicero.

[4] See R. H. Cust, *The Pavement Masters of Siena*, London, 1901, pp. 23, 31. Hermes was known as a Gentile prophet in the Middle Ages and this is not the earliest representation of him with the Sibyls; but it is the first which shows him in his full Renaissance glory.

❖❖

Chapter III

HERMES TRISMEGISTUS AND MAGIC

❖❖

THE Hermetic literature divides into two branches. On the one hand there are the philosophical treatises, such as those in the *Corpus Hermeticum*, and the *Asclepius*, to which can be added some other specimens of this literature, particularly the fragments preserved in the anthology of excerpts compiled by Stobaeus.[1] On the other hand there is the astrological, alchemical, and magical literature, much of which also went under the name of Hermes Trismegistus. These two branches cannot be kept entirely separate from one another.[2] Not only do we have in the *Asclepius* an actual description of magical practices in the admiring reference to the methods by which the Egyptians "made gods", but also even the loftiest and most mystical of the philosophical Hermetic treatises presuppose, as we have seen, an astrological pattern in the cosmos. Gnosticism and magic go together. The pessimist gnostic needs to know the magical passwords and signs by which he may rid himself of the evil material

---

[1] Text of the Stobaeus fragments, with French translation, in *C.H.*, vols. III and IV.

[2] Scott tried to make such a separation, treating the philosophical *Hermetica* as quite distinct from, and infinitely superior to, the "masses of rubbish" going under the name of Hermes (Scott, I, p. 1). Festugière, on the other hand, devotes the first volume of his *Révélation* to "L'Astrologie et les Sciences Occultes" in which he treats of the magical and astrological texts as the necessary preliminary to the study of the philosophical *Hermetica*. Cf. also Thorndike, I, pp. 287 ff.

power of the stars in his upward ascent through the spheres. The optimist gnostic has no fear to draw down by sympathetic magic, invocations, talismans, those same powers of the universe which he believes to be good.

The methods of sympathetic magic[1] presuppose that continual effluvia of influences pouring down onto the earth from the stars of which the author of the *Asclepius* speaks. It was believed that these effluvia and influences could be canalised and used by an operator with the requisite knowledge. Every object in the material world was full of occult sympathies poured down upon it from the star on which it depended. The operator who wished to capture, let us say, the power of the planet Venus, must know what plants belonged to Venus, what stones and metals, what animals, and use only these when addressing Venus. He must know the images of Venus and know how to inscribe these on talismans made of the right Venus materials and at the right astrological moment. Such images were held to capture the spirit or power of the star and to hold or store it for use. Not only the planets had attached to each of them a complicated pseudo-science of occult sympathies and image-making, but the twelve signs of the zodiac each had their plants, animals, images, and so on, and indeed so had all the constellations and stars of the heavens. For the All was One, united by an infinitely complex system of relationships. The magician was one who knew how to enter into this system, and use it, by knowing the links of the chains of influences descending vertically from above, and establishing for himself a chain of ascending links by correct use of the occult sympathies in terrestrial things, of celestial images, of invocations and names, and the like. The methods and the cosmological background presupposed are the same whether the magician is using these forces to try to obtain concrete material benefits for himself, or whether he is using them religiously, as in the hieratic magic described in the *Asclepius*, for insight into the divine forces in nature and to assist his worship of them.

Into the Hellenistic astrology which is the background of the philosophical *Hermetica* an Egyptian element had been absorbed, namely the thirty-six decans, or thirty-six gods who ruled over the divisions into ten of the 360 degrees of the circle of the

---

[1] For a good summary of the subject, see Festugière, I, pp. 89 ff.

45

zodiac.[1] That strange people, the Egyptians, had divinised time, not merely in the abstract sense but in the concrete sense that each moment of the day and night had its god who must be placated as the moments passed. The decans, as they came to be called in Hellenistic times, were really Egyptian sidereal gods of time who had become absorbed in the Chaldean astrology and affiliated to the zodiac. They all had images, which vary in different lists of them, and these lists of the powerful images of the decans had come out of the archives of the Egyptian temples. The decans had various aspects. They had definite astrological significance, as "Horoscopes" presiding over the forms of life born within the time periods over which they presided, and they were assimilated to the planets domiciled in their domain, and to the signs of the zodiac, three decans going with each sign as its three "faces". But they were also gods, and powerful Egyptian gods, and this side of them was never forgotten, giving them a mysterious importance. The high place which the author of the *Asclepius* assigns to the "Thirty-Six Horoscopes" in his list of gods is a genuinely Egyptian feature of that work, and in one of the Stobaeus fragments we hear, within the familiar framework of a conversation between Hermes and his son Tat, of the great importance of the Thirty-Six.

We have said, my child, that there is a body which envelops the whole ensemble of the world: you should represent it to yourself as a circular figure, for thus is the All.

I represent to myself such a figure, as you say, O father.

Represent now to yourself that, below the circle of this body, are ranged the thirty-six decans, in the middle between the universal circle and the circle of the zodiac, separating these two circles, and, as it were sustaining the circle of the All and circumscribing the zodiac, moving along the zodiac with the planets, and having the same force as the movement of the All, alternatively with the Seven. . . . Pay attention to this: since the decans command over the planets and we are under the domination of the seven, do you not see how there

[1] On the decans, see Festugière, I, pp. 115 ff.; Bouché-Leclercq, *L'Astrologie grecque*, Paris, 1899, pp. 215 ff.; F. Boll, *Sphaera*, Leipzig, 1903, pp. 15 ff., 176 ff.; O. Neugebauer, *The Exact Sciences in Antiquity* (Princeton, 1952), Harper Torchbook Reprint, 1962, pp. 81 ff. The specialised study of the decan images is that by W. Gundel, *Dekane und Dekansternbilder*, Studien der Bibliothek Warburg, XIX, 1936.

comes to us a certain influence of the decans, whether through the children of the decans, or through the intermediary of the planets ?[1]

The decans appear here as powerful divine or demonic forces, close to the circle of the All, and above the circles of the zodiac and the planets and operating on things below either directly through their children or sons, the demons, or through the intermediary of the planets.

Thus the philosophical *Hermetica* belong into the same framework of thought as the practical *Hermetica*, the treatises on astrology or alchemy, the lists of plants, animals, stones and the like grouped according to their occult sympathies with the stars, the lists of images of planets, signs, decans, with instructions as to how to make magical talismans from them. The following are only a few examples from this vast and complex literature ascribed to Hermes Trismegistus. There is a treatise supposedly by Hermes on the names and powers of the twelve signs of the zodiac[2]; others on which plants go with the signs and the planets[3]; a book of Hermes Trismegistus to Asclepius on the occult virtues of animals[4]; a treatise on astrological medicine dedicated by Hermes to Ammon the Egyptian which describes how to treat illnesses caused by bad stellar influences by building up links with the methods of sympathetic magic and talismans to draw down, either an increase of good virtue from the star which has been causing the trouble or bringing in influences from another star.[5]

The name of Hermes Trismegistus seems to have been particularly strongly connected with the lists of images of the decans. The

[1] *C.H.*, III, pp. 34,36 (Stobaeus Excerpt, VI). In the notes to this passage (*ibid.*, p. L), Festugière explains the children or sons of the decans as demons. Cf. also *Révélation*, I, pp. 118–20; Scott, III, p. 374 (where a diagram is given to illustrate the fact that, according to this passage, the decans are outside and above the circle of the zodiac).

[2] See Thorndike, I, p. 291; Festugière, I, pp. 111–12.

[3] Thorndike, *loc. cit.*; Festugière, *ibid.*, pp. 143 ff.

[4] Festugière, *ibid.*, pp. 207 ff., discussing the "Livre court médical d'Hermès Trismégiste selon la science astrologique et l'influx naturel des animaux, publié à l'adresse de son disciple Asklépios." As can be seen from this French translation of the title, this type of treatise often brings in the same characters as those whom we meet in the philosophical *Hermetica*. This treatise on animals is addressed by Hermes to Asclepius, like the *Asclepius*.

[5] See Thorndike, I, p. 291; Festugière, I, pp. 130–1.

Liber Hermetis Trismegisti,[1] a treatise on astrology and astrological magic which has been brought to light in recent years begins with the decans, and the *Liber Sacer*,[2] or sacred book, of Hermes, is a list of decan images, and of the stones and plants in sympathy with each decan, with instructions as to how to engrave the images on the correct stone, which is to be fixed into a ring together with the relativ: plant; the wearer of the ring must abstain from all foods antipathetic to the decan.

In short, Hermes Trismegistus is indeed a name to conjure with in all this type of literature concerned with occult sympathies and talismans. Again in his capacity as Hermes-Thoth, inventor of language, of words which bind and unbind, he plays a rôle in magic,[3] and some of the magical prayers and invocations assigned to him are like those in the *Corpus Hermeticum*.

The name of Hermes Trismegistus was well known in the Middle Ages and was connected with alchemy, and magic, particularly with magic images or talismans.[4] The Middle Ages feared whatever they knew of the decans as dangerous demons, and some of the books supposedly by Hermes were strongly censured by Albertus Magnus as containing diabolical magic.[5] The Augustinian censure of the demon-worship in the *Asclepius* (by which he may have meant in particular, decan-worship) weighed heavily upon that work. However, mediaeval writers interested in natural philosophy speak of him with respect; for Roger Bacon he was the "Father of Philosophers",[6] and he is sometimes given a genealogy which makes him even more ancient than Ficino or the designer of the Siena mosaic thought. In the preface to a twelfth-century translation of an alchemical work, it is stated that there were three Hermeses, namely Enoch, Noah, and the king, philosopher, and prophet who reigned in Egypt after the Flood and was called Hermes Triplex. The same genealogy of

[1] Festugière, I, pp. 112 ff. The *Liber Hermetis* was discovered by Gundel and published by him in 1936.

[2] Festugière, I, pp. 139 ff.

[3] *Ibid.*, pp. 283 ff.

[4] Thorndike, II, pp. 214 ff.; Festugière, I, pp. 105 ff.

[5] In his *Speculum astronomiae*; see Albertus Magnus, *Opera*, ed. Borgnet, X, p. 641; and cf. Thorndike, II, p. 220. Albertus Magnus is one of the mediaeval writers who perhaps knew the Latin *Asclepius* (see *C.H.*, II, pp. 268–9).

[6] Thorndike, II, p. 219.

"Hermes Mercurius Triplex" is also given in a thirteenth-century treatise on astrology, and the same explanation of why he is "three-fold".[1] It will be remembered that Ficino in his *argumentum* before the *Pimander* gives a similar explanation of "Trismegistus" as referring to Hermes in his triple capacity of priest, philosopher, and king or law-giver. The mediaeval genealogy, however, takes Hermes Triplex back before Moses to the time of Noah.

There is an extremely comprehensive treatise on sympathetic and astral magic, with particular reference to talismans, which goes under the name of *Picatrix*. Though the authorship of *Picatrix* is not assigned to Hermes Trismegistus, the work frequently mentions him with great respect and it is important because it may have been one of Ficino's authorities on talismans and sympathetic magic.

Like many of the magical works attributed to Hermes which reached the Western Middle Ages and the Renaissance, the *Picatrix* was originally written in Arabic,[2] probably in the twelfth century. There was a big influence of Hermetic and gnostic literature and ideas on the Arabic world and particularly among the Arabs of Harran. Talismanic magic was practised by these Arabs, and the influence came through the Sabeans who were immersed in Hermetism, in both its philosophical and religious, and its magical aspects. *Picatrix* is by an Arabic writer under strong Sabean, that is to say, Hermetic, influence, and he gives

[1] *Ibid.*, pp. 215, 222. These are perhaps echoes of the twelfth-century pseudo-Hermetic *Liber Hermetis Mercurii Triplicis de VI rerum principiis*, which has been published by Th. Silverstein in *Archives d'histoire doctrinale et littéraire du Moyen Age*, 1955 (22), pp. 217–302. On the influence of this work, see above, p. 13, note 3.

[2] The Arabic text of *Picatrix*, ed. H. Ritter, is published in *Studien der Bibliothek Warburg*, Vol. XII, 1933, A German translation by H. Ritter and M. Plessner of the Arabic text is published in *Studies of the Warburg Institute*, University of London, Vol. 27, 1962; an outline in English of the contents of the Arabic text is given in this volume.

Besides these editions, see on the *Picatrix*, H. Ritter, Picatrix, ein arabisches Handbuch hellenistischer Magie, in *Vorträge der Bibliothek Warburg*, 1922; Thorndike, II, pp. 813 ff.; Festugière, I, pp. 389, 397 (in the appendix on Arabic Hermetic literature by Louis Massignon); Garin, *Cultura*, pp. 159 ff.

his lists of magic images, his practical advice on magical procedures, in an elaborate philosophical setting, the philosophy expounded being in many respects similar to that which we find in some treatises of the *Corpus Hermeticum* and in the *Asclepius*. Ficino and his friends would be able to recognise in the *Picatrix* many of the ideas and philosophico-religious sentiments expressed by the wonderful author of *Pimander*, the Egyptian Moses and the prophet of Christianity, and yet here this philosophy is in a context of practical magic, how to make talismans, how to draw down the influences of the stars by establishing the chains of links and correspondencies with the upper world.

The Latin translation of *Picatrix*[1] is shorter than the Arabic text; in the proem it is stated that the work has been translated from Arabic into Spanish by order of Alfonso the Wise, but this Spanish translation has not survived. The Latin *Picatrix* was certainly circulating a good deal in the Italian Renaissance.[2] There was a copy of *Picatrix* in Pico della Mirandola's library.[3] It was known to Ludovico Lazzarelli,[4] a most ardent Hermetist contemporary with Pico. Giovanni Francesco Pico, nephew of the great Pico, shows some knowledge of it in a work written after his uncle's death.[5] Symphorien Champier, who edited a new edition of the *Hermetica* but was anxious to dissociate Christian Hermetism from the magic of the *Asclepius*, speaks of *Picatrix* (in 1514) with disapproval and accuses Peter of Abano of having borrowed from it.[6] The popularity of this text-book of magic is

[1] Of this Latin translation there is as yet no edition. But it is the Latin translation which was used in the Renaissance, not the Arabic original, and, since it differs somewhat from the Arabic original, it must be used by students of Renaissance writers.

The manuscript of the Latin *Picatrix* which I have used is Sloane, 1305. Though a seventeenth-century manuscript, it corresponds closely to earlier manuscripts (see Thorndike, II, p. 822) and it has the advantage of being written in a clear and legible hand.

[2] E. Garin, *Medioevo e Rinascimento*, Florence, 1954, pp. 175 ff.; *Cultura*, pp. 159 ff.

[3] P. Kibre, *The Library of Pico della Mirandola*, New York, 1936, p. 263; cf. Garin, *Cultura*, p. 159.

[4] See Ludovico Lazzarelli, "Testi scelti", ed. M. Brini, in *Test. uman.*, p. 75.

[5] G. F. Pico, *Opera*, Bâle, 1572–3, II, p. 482; cf. Thorndike, VI, p. 468.

[6] In his criticism of the errors of Abano; cf. Thorndike, II, p. 814; V, pp. 119, 122.

attested by the fact that Rabelais directed one of his shafts at it when he spoke of "le reuerend pere en Diable Picatris, recteur de la faculté diabologique".[1] The secretive way in which such a book circulated is described by Agrippa D'Aubigné in a letter written between 1572 and 1575 in which he says that King Henri III of France had imported some magical books from Spain which he was allowed to see, after much difficulty and not without solemnly swearing not to copy them; amongst them were "les commantaires de Dom Jouan Picatrix de Tollede".[2]

Thus there is a good deal of evidence that this *Picatrix*, though it was never printed, had a considerable circulation in manuscript during the fifteenth and sixteenth centuries. Since there is no manuscript of it earlier than the fifteenth century,[3] it is possible that it began to circulate in the same century as that which saw the apotheosis of Hermes Trismegistus.

The *Picatrix* opens with pious prayers and promises to reveal profound secrets. For knowledge is the best gift of God to man, to know what is the root and principle of all things. The primal truth is not a body, but it is One, One Truth, One Unity. All things come from it and through it receive truth and unity in the perpetual movement of generation and corruption. There is a hierarchy in things, and lower things are raised to higher things; and higher things descend to lower things. Man is a little world reflecting the great world of the cosmos, but through his intellect the wise man can raise himself above the seven heavens.

From this short sample of the philosophy of *Picatrix*, it can be seen that the magician bases himself upon a gnosis, an insight into the nature of the All.

The order of nature is further expounded in two passages.[4] God or the *prima materia* is without form. There derives from the formless incorporeal One the series of

Intellectus or *mens*
Spiritus
Materia, or material nature, the elements and the *elementata*.

---

[1] *Pantagruel*, III, 23; cited by Thorndike, II, p. 814.

[2] Agrippa d'Aubigné, *Œuvres completes*, ed. E. Réaume and F. de Caussade, Paris, 1873, I, p. 435.

[3] On the manuscripts, see Thorndike, II, pp. 822–4.

[4] *Picatrix*, Lib. I, cap. 7, and Lib. IV, cap. I (Sloane 1305, ff. 21 *verso* ff.; ff. 95 *recto* ff.).

Spiritus descends from the above to the below and resides in the place where it is caught (*ubi captus est*). Or, as it is put in another chapter[1] "the virtues of the superior bodies are the form and power of the inferiors, and the form of the inferiors is of a material related to the virtues of the superiors; and they are as it were joined together, because their corporeal material (of terrestrial things) and their spiritual material (of the stars) are one material." The whole art of magic thus consists in capturing and guiding the influx of *spiritus* into *materia*.

The most important of the means of doing this is through the making of talismans, images of the stars inscribed on the correct materials, at the right times, in the right frame of mind, and so on. The whole of the first two long and complicated books of *Picatrix* is devoted to this most difficult art which demands a deep knowledge of astronomy, mathematics, music, metaphysics, and indeed practically everything, for the introduction of *spiritus* into talismans is a most tricky business and no one can succeed in it unless he is a resolute philosopher.

Lists of the images suitable for use on talismans are given, of which the following are a few examples from the lists of planet images.[2]

Two images of Saturn.

"The form of a man with a crow's face and foot, sitting on a throne, having in his right hand a spear and in his left a lance or an arrow."

"The form of a man standing on a dragon, clothed in black and holding in his right hand a sickle and in his left a spear."

Two images of Jupiter.

"The form of a man sitting on an eagle, clothed in a garment, with eagles beneath his feet. . . ."

"The form of a man with a lion's face and bird's feet, below them a dragon with seven heads, holding an arrow in his right hand. . . ."

An image of Mars.

"The form of a man, crowned, holding a raised sword in his right hand."

An image of Sol.

"The form of a king sitting on a throne, with a crown on his head and beneath his feet the figure (magic character) of the sun."

[1] *Picatrix*, Lib. II, cap. 12 (Sloane 1305, ff. 52 *recto* ff.).
[2] The planet images are listed in Lib. II, cap. 10 (Sloane 1305, ff. 43 *recto* ff.).

An image of Venus.

"The form of a woman with her hair unbound riding on a stag, having in her right hand an apple, and in her left, flowers, and dressed in white garments."

An image of Mercury.

"The form of a man having a cock on his head, on a throne, having feet like those of an eagle, with fire in the palm of his left hand and having below his feet this sign (a magic character)."

An image of Luna.

"The form of a woman with a beautiful face on a dragon, with horns on her head, with two snakes wound around her. . . . A snake is wound around each of her arms, and above her head is a dragon, and another dragon beneath her feet, each of these dragons having seven heads."

As can be seen from these examples, the magic images of the planets are usually recognisably related to the classical forms of these gods and goddesses but with strange and barbaric additions and modifications.

There is a full list in *Picatrix* of the images of the thirty-six decans,[1] grouped with the signs of the zodiac to which they belong.

The images of the decans of Aries.

First decan. "A huge dark man with red eyes, holding a sword, and clad in a white garment."

Second decan. "A woman clad in green and lacking one leg."

Third decan. "A man holding a golden sphere and dressed in red."

And so the list goes on, for all the thirty-six decans belonging to the twelve signs, all with weird and barbaric images.

Having fully dealt with talismans and their manufacture in his first two books, the author of *Picatrix* discusses in his third book[2] what stones, plants, animals, and so on go with the different planets, signs, and so on, giving full lists, what parts of the body go with the signs, what are the colours of the planets, how to invoke the spirits of the planets by calling on their names and powers, and so on. The fourth book[3] deals with similar matters, and with fumigations and ends with orations to the planets.

The work is thus a most complete text-book for the magician,

---

[1] The lists of decan images are in Lib. II, cap. 11 (Sloane 1305, ff. 48 *verso* ff.).

[2] Sloane 1305, ff. 37 *recto* ff.

[3] Sloane 1305, ff. 95 *recto* ff.

giving the philosophy of nature on which talismanic and sympathetic magic is based together with full instructions for its practice. Its objects are strictly practical; the various talismans and procedures are used to gain specific ends, for the cure of diseases, for long life, for success in various enterprises, for escaping from prison, for overcoming one's enemies, for attracting the love of another person, and so on.

Hermes Trismegistus is often mentioned, as the source for some talismanic images and in other connections, but there is in particular one very striking passage in the fourth book of *Picatrix* in which Hermes is stated to have been the first to use magic images and is credited with having founded a marvellous city in Egypt.

> There are among the Chaldeans very perfect masters in this art and they affirm that Hermes was the first who constructed images by means of which he knew how to regulate the Nile against the motion of the moon. This man also built a temple to the Sun, and he knew how to hide himself from all so that no one could see him, although he was within it. It was he, too, who in the east of Egypt constructed a City twelve miles (*miliaria*) long within which he constructed a castle which had four gates in each of its four parts. On the eastern gate he placed the form of an Eagle; on the western gate, the form of a Bull; on the southern gate the form of a Lion, and on the northern gate he constructed the form of a Dog. Into these images he introduced spirits which spoke with voices, nor could anyone enter the gates of the City except by their permission. There he planted trees in the midst of which was a great tree which bore the fruit of all generation. On the summit of the castle he caused to be raised a tower thirty cubits high on the top of which he ordered to be placed a light-house (*rotunda*) the colour of which changed every day until the seventh day after which it returned to the first colour, and so the City was illuminated with these colours. Near the City there was abundance of waters in which dwelt many kinds of fish. Around the circumference of the City he placed engraved images and ordered them in such a manner that by their virtue the inhabitants were made virtuous and withdrawn from all wickedness and harm. The name of the City was Adocentyn.[1]

Passed through the vivid imagination of the Arab of Harran, we seem to have here something which reminds us of the hieratic

[1] *Picatrix*, Lib. IV, cap. 3 (Sloane 1305, f. III *recto*). In the Arabic original, the name of the City is "al-Ašmūnain"; see the German translation of the Arabic text (cited above, p. 49, note 2), p. 323.

religious magic described in the *Asclepius*. Here are the man-made gods, statues of the animal- and bird-shaped gods of Egypt, which Hermes Trismegistus has animated by introducing spirits into them so that they speak with voices and guard the gates of this magical Utopia. The colours of the planets flash from the central tower, and these images around the circumference of the City, are they perhaps images of the signs of the zodiac and the decans which Hermes has known how to arrange so that only good celestial influences are allowed into the City ? The law-giver of the Egyptians is giving laws which must perforce be obeyed, for he constrains the inhabitants of the City to be virtuous, and keeps them healthy and wise, by his powerful manipulation of astral magic. The tree of generation in the City may perhaps also mean that he controls the generative powers, so that only the good, the wise, the virtuous and the healthy are born.

In his striking passage about the City of Adocentyn, the author of *Picatrix* soars above the level of his utilitarian prescriptions of individual talismans as cures for tooth-ache, aids to business progress, means for downing rivals, and the like, to a wider view of the possibilities of magic. One might say that this City shows us Hermes Mercurius Triplex in his triple rôle of Egyptian priest and god-maker, of philosopher-magician, and of king and law-giver. Unfortunately no date is given for the founding of Adocentyn, so we have no means of knowing whether this took place in the time of Noah and soon after the Flood, or in the time of Moses, or not much later than Moses. But the pious admirer of those two "divine" books by the most ancient Hermes—the *Pimander* and the *Asclepius*—might surely have been much struck, by this vivid description of a City in which, as in Plato's ideal *Republic*, the wise philosopher is the ruler, and rules most forcibly by means of the priestly Egyptian magic such as is described in the *Asclepius*. The City of Adocentyn in which virtue is enforced on the inhabitants by magic helps also to explain why, when the magical Egyptian religion decayed, manners and morals went to rack and ruin, as is so movingly described in the Lament. And in the prophecy in the *Asclepius*, after the Lament, of the eventual restoration of the Egyptian religion, it is said:

The gods who exercise their dominion over the earth will be restored one day and installed in a City at the extreme limit of Egypt, a City which will be founded towards the setting sun, and into which will hasten, by land and by sea, the whole race of mortal men.[1]

In the context of the *Asclepius*, the City of Adocentyn might thus be seen, both as the ideal Egyptian society before its fall, and as the ideal pattern of its future and universal renovation.

The author of *Picatrix* also states, at the beginning of the passage quoted above, that Hermes Trismegistus built a Temple to the Sun, within which he presided invisibly, though this Sun Temple is not explicitly connected with his City. Hermes as a builder of a Temple to the Sun could also connect in the mind of the pious reader of *Pimander* (by which I mean, of course, the fourteen treatises of the *Corpus Hermeticum* which Ficino included under that title) and of the *Asclepius*, with the many passages on the sun in those works. For example, in the *Corpus Hermeticum V* it is stated that the sun is supreme among the gods of heaven[2]; in the *Corpus Hermeticum* X, the author, using Platonic terminology, compares the sun to the Good and its rays to the influx of the intelligible splendour.[3] And in the list of the gods of Egypt in the *Asclepius* the Sun ranks as far greater than one of the planets.[4] He is above the thirty-six horoscopes in the list of gods, and the thirty-six are above the spheres of the planets. To find Hermes Trismegistus in the *Picatrix* as the builder of a Temple of the Sun, would thus accord perfectly with the teaching of that holy *priscus theologus* in the *Pimander* and in the *Asclepius*.

When Marsilio Ficino began to dabble in his magic, which included a tentative use of talismans, there were plenty of mediaeval authorities which he might have used who give lists of talismanic images, amongst them Peter of Abano, who lists the decan images, and whom Ficino cites by name[5] in his treatise *De vita coelitus comparanda*, a possible translation of which might be "On capturing the life of the stars". He would also find much encouragement for the practice of magic in certain of the Neo-

---

[1] *Asclepius* (*C.H.*, II, p. 332).

[2] *C.H.*, I, p. 61; Ficino, p. 1843.

[3] *C.H.*, I, p. 114; Ficino, p. 1847.

[4] *Asclepius* (*C.H.*, II, pp. 318 ff.). Jupiter, as the heaven, and the Sun, rank as the highest gods in the list, followed by the thirty-six decans; last and below these are the planets, in which Jupiter and Sol figure again but now only in a lower capacity as planets. See above, pp. 36–7.

[5] See below, p. 73.

platonic authors whom he studied and translated, particularly Proclus, or Iamblichus "On the Egyptian Mysteries". Nevertheless, as D. P. Walker has shown, his chief incentive or exemplar was almost certainly the description of magic in the *Asclepius*.[1] Walker has suggested *Picatrix* as among the possible sources for Ficino's practical magic,[2] and as the above analysis of that work has shown, the pious admirer of the "divine" *Pimander* and the "divine" *Asclepius* would find much in this practical treatise on talismanic magic to remind him of the utterances of the most ancient Hermes Trismegistus in his two divine books. It could have been the *Picatrix*, read in the context of his Hermetic studies, which enabled the pious Christian Neoplatonic philosopher to make the transition to a practice of magic.

Magic had never died out during the Middle Ages, in spite of the efforts of the ecclesiastical authorities to exercise some check over it and to banish its more extreme forms. Nor was it by any means only in Florence and under cover of Ficino's Neoplatonism, that the interest in the magic images of the stars was reviving in Italy. On the other side of the Appenines, in Ferrara, the Duke Borso d'Este had covered a great room in his palace with a cycle of paintings representing the months of the year and showing, in its central band, the signs of the zodiac with the images of the thirty-six decans most strikingly painted. In this room, the decoration of which was finished before 1470,[3] we may see, in the lowest band of the frescoes the omniform life of the court of Ferrara and above it the images of the thirty-six strung out along the zodiac. The series begins with the three decans of Aries and their sign (Pl. 1a); though their forms are slightly variant from the images which we quoted from the list in *Picatrix* they are easily recognisable as in the main the same, the tall dark man in white (Pl. 1b), the woman who is hiding under her skirts the unfortunate fact that she has only one leg, the man holding a sphere or circle. Despite their charmingly modernised costumes, these are really the Egyptian gods of time, the demons banned by Augustine.

[1] See below, pp. 66-7.
[2] Walker, p. 36; Garin, *Cultura*, pp. 159 ff.
[3] P. D'Ancona, *Les Mois de Schifanoia à Ferrara*, Milan, 1954, p. 9. The identification of the strange images grouped with the signs of the zodiac as being the images of the decans was first made by A. Warburg, "Italienische Kunst und Internationale Astrologie im Palazzo Schifanoja zu Ferrara", *Gesammelte Schriften*, Leipzig, 1932, II, pp. 459 ff.

We are not, however, here concerned with revivals of star images in other centres and outside the main current of Florentine Neoplatonism. We are concerned with how it was that Marsilio Ficino, who took such extreme care to present the revival of Plato and Neoplatonism as a movement which could be accorded with Christianity, allowed a fringe of magic to penetrate into this movement, thus inaugurating those philosophies of the Renaissance in which magical undercurrents are never far absent. The theory of the *prisca theologia*, of the piety and antiquity of Hermes Trismegistus, *priscus theologus* and Magus, offered an excuse for Ficino's modern philosophical magic. The attraction of the *Asclepius* had probably already been exerting its pull in the earlier Renaissance,[1] and when Ficino—dropping Plato in order to translate the *Corpus Hermeticum* first—found here a new revelation of the sanctity of Hermes and a confirmation of Lactantius' high opinion of him as the prophet of the "Son of God", he felt authorised to adopt the Lactantian view and tried to evade the Augustinian warning. The presence of Hermes Trismegistus inside the Duomo of Siena in the character of a Gentile prophet which Lactantius had given him, is symptomatic of the success of this rehabilitation.

We must not forget that the other *prisci theologi*, such as Orpheus or Zoroaster, were also Magi, and also authorised by their antiquity revivals of forms of magic. Yet Hermes Trismegistus is the most important of the *prisci magi* from the point of view of the incorporation of magic with philosophy, for in his case there was a body of supposedly most ancient philosophical writings to be studied, and these writings, in addition to their echoes of Moses and their prophetic understandings of Christianity before Christ, also prophetically shadowed the teachings of the divine Plato.

Lactantius wrote his *Divine Institutes* in the context of the rather superficially Christianised Empire of Constantine, and his apologetics in that work are directed towards persuading pagans to become Christians by emphasising how much in paganism is close to Christianity, or prophetic of Christianity. Between Lactantius and Augustine there had taken place the pagan reaction under the

[1] E. Garin, *Medioevo e Rinascimento*, p. 155, mentions Salutati and Manetti as writers influenced by the *Asclepius* before Ficino's revival of Hermetism.

apostate Emperor Julian, with its attempt to drive out the new upstart religion by a return to the philosophical "religion of the world" and to the mystery cults. In his "Hymn to Helios", Julian worships the Sun as the supreme god, the image of the intelligible Good; and he says that there are also in the heavens a multitude of other gods.

> For as he (the Sun) divides the three spheres by four through the zodiac . . . so he divides the zodiac also into twelve divine powers; and again he divides every one of these twelve by three, so as to make thirty-six gods in all.[1]

Throughout Origen's reply to Celsus it is evident how large a part Egyptianism had played in the type of Neoplatonic religion which came back in the pagan reaction. Celsus argues about how much "one may learn from the Egyptians", and Origen quotes the following passage from his lost work:

> They (the Egyptians) say that the body of man has been put under the charge of thirty-six daemons, or ethereal gods of some sort. . . . Each daemon is in charge of a different part. And they know the names of the daemons in the local dialect, such as Chnoumen, Chnachoumen, Knat, Sikat, Biou, Erou, Erebiou, Rhamanoor, and Rheianoor, and all the other names which they use in their language. And by invoking these they heal the sufferings of the various parts. What is there to prevent anyone from paying honour both to these and to others if he wishes, so that we can be in good health rather than ill, and have good rather than bad luck, and be delivered from tortures and punishments?

To this Origen replies:

> By these remarks Celsus is trying to drag our souls down to the daemons, as though they had obtained charge over our bodies. He has such a low opinion of paying an undivided and indivisible honour to the God of the universe that he does not believe that the only God who is worshipped and splendidly honoured is sufficient to grant the man who honours Him, in consequence of the actual worship he offers to Him, a power which prevents the attacks of daemons against the righteous person. For he has never seen how, when the formula "in the name of Jesus" is pronounced by true believers, it has healed not a few people from diseases and demonic possession and other distresses. . . . According to Celsus we might practise magic and

---

[1] Julian, *Works*, Loeb edition, I, pp. 405, 407.

sorcery rather than Christianity, and believe in an unlimited number of daemons rather than in the self-evident, and manifest supreme God. . . .[1]

Writing after the pagan reaction, Augustine cannot accept Lactantius' hopeful view of Hermes Trismegistus as the holy prophet of Christianity, and utters his warning against the demon-worship of the *Asclepius*.

Yet even Augustine lent his support to the colossal misdating of that work, by which Hermes appears as prophesying the coming of Christianity, though he had this knowledge through the demons.

Believing in the immense antiquity of the *Corpus Hermeticum* and the *Asclepius*, and following Lactantius' estimate of their holy and divine character, the pious Christian, Ficino, returns in his study of them, not, as he thinks, to the antiquity of a *priscus theologus* who prophetically saw into Christian truth (and authorised the practice of magic), but to the type of pagan philosophical gnosis with Egyptianising and magical tendencies, which characterised the anti-Christian reaction under Julian the Apostate.

The type of magic with which we are to be concerned differs profoundly from astrology which is not necessarily magic at all but a mathematical science based on the belief that human destiny is irrevocably governed by the stars, and that therefore from the study of a person's horoscope, the position of the stars at the time of his birth, one can foretell his irrevocably foreordained future. This magic is astrological only in the sense that it too bases itself upon the stars, their images and influences, but it is a way of escaping from astrological determinism by gaining power over the stars, guiding their influences in the direction which the operator desires. Or, in the religious sense, it is a way of salvation, of escape from material fortune and destiny, or of obtaining insight into the divine. Hence "astrological magic" is not a correct description of it, and hereafter, for want of a better term, I shall call it "astral magic".

It is in a very timid hesitating and cautious manner that Ficino embarks on a mild form of astral magic, attempting to alter, to escape from, his Saturnian horoscope by capturing, guiding towards himself, more fortunate astral influences. Yet this compara-

[1] Origen, *Contra Celsum*, VIII, 58–9; translated H. Chadwick, Cambridge, 1953, pp. 496–7.

tively harmless attempt at astral medical therapy was to open a flood-gate through which an astonishing revival of magic poured all over Europe.

Chapter IV

<hr>

FICINO'S NATURAL MAGIC[1]

<hr>

FICINO, whose father was a physician, was himself a physician as well as a priest, and his *Libri de Vita*,[2] divided into three books and first published in 1489, is a treatise on medicine. It was absolutely inevitable that a medical treatise of the Middle Ages or the Renaissance should make use of astrological presuppositions universally taken for granted. Medical prescriptions were normally based on assumptions such as that the signs ruled different parts of the body, that different bodily temperaments were related to different planets. Much of Ficino's book could therefore be regarded, as he claimed, as normal medicine. Nevertheless he was also putting forward in it a subtle and imaginative kind of magic involving the use of talismans. He was nervously aware of possible dangers in this, and in his preliminary address he tells the reader that "if you do not approve of astronomical images" these may be omitted.[3]

The work is intended primarily for students who are liable

[1] Ficino's magic has been admirably discussed by D. P. Walker in his book on *Spiritual and Demonic Magic from Ficino to Campanella* to which I am greatly indebted in this chapter. I am also indebted to E. Garin's essay, "Le 'Elezioni' e il problema dell'astrologia" in *Umanesimo e esoterismo*, ed. E. Castelli, Archivio di Filosofia, Padua, 1960, pp. 7 ff.

[2] *Libri de vita* is the collective title of a work divided into three books, the third of which has the title *De vita coelitus comparanda*. On the many editions of the *Libri de vita*, which was evidently one of the most popular of Ficino's works, see Kristeller, *Suppl. Fic.*, I, pp. lxiv–lxvi. It is included in Ficino, *Opera*, pp. 530–73.

[3] Ficino, p. 530 (address to the reader before Lib. III, *De vita coelitus comparanda*).

through over-intense application to their studies to grow ill or melancholy.[1] This is because the nature of their occupations brings them under the influence of Saturn, for contemplation and hard abstract study belong to Saturn who is also the planet of the melancholy temperament, and the star which is inimical to the vital forces of life and youth. Melancholy students who have used up their vital powers in their studies, and the old in whom these forces are in any case declining, are therefore advised to avoid as far as possible plants, herbs, animals, stones, and the like belonging to Saturn, and to use and surround themselves with plants, herbs, animals, stones, people, belonging to the more fortunate, cheerful, and life-giving planets, of which the chief are Sol, Jupiter, and Venus. Ficino has many enthusiastic passages on the valuable "gifts" making for health and good spirits to be obtained from these planets, which he poetically describes more than once as "the Three Graces".[2] The equation of beneficent astral influences with the Three Graces may be derived from a passage in the Emperor Julian's Hymn to the Sun.[3] Gold is a metal full of Solar and Jovial spirit and therefore beneficial in combating melancholy. Green is a health-giving and life-giving colour, and the reader is urged to come to "Alma Venus"[4] and to walk in the green fields with her, plucking her flowers, such as roses, or the crocus, the golden flower of Jupiter. Ficino also gives advice on how to choose a non-Saturnian diet, and thinks that the use of pleasant odours and scents is beneficial. We might be in the consulting room of a rather expensive psychiatrist who knows that his patients can afford plenty of gold and holidays in the country, and flowers out of season.

Talismans are not mentioned until the third book, which is the one which has the title *De vita coelitus comparanda*. Its first chapter opens with some obscure philosophy.[5] It is clearly enough based on the well-known tripartite division of intellect, soul, and body,

[1] On Ficino and melancholy, see E. Panofsky and F. Saxl, *Dürer's Melencolia I, Studien der Bibliothek Warburg*, 2, 1923; L. Babb, *The Elizabethan Malady*, East Lansing, 1951.

[2] *Libri de vita*, II, III, 5, etc.; (Ficino, pp. 536–7).

[3] Julian, *Works*, Loeb edition, I, p. 407.

[4] *Libri de vita*, II, 14 (Ficino, pp. 520–1).

[5] *Libri de vita*, III (*De vita coelitus comparanda*), I (Ficino, pp. 532–3).

but apart from that it is somewhat confusing. There is an intellect of the world and a body of the world, and between them is the soul of the world. In the divine *mens* or intellect are the Ideas; in the soul of the world are "seminal reasons" as many in number as there are ideas in the *mens*, and corresponding to them or reflecting them; to these seminal reasons in the soul there correspond the species in matter, or in the body of the world, which correspond to the reasons or depend on them, or are formed by them. If these material forms degenerate they can be reformed in the "middle place", presumably by manipulating the next highest forms on which they depend. There are congruities between the "reasons" in the soul of the world and the lower forms, which Zoroaster called divine links and Synesius, magic spells. These links depend not so much on stars and demons as on the soul of the world, which is everywhere present. Wherefore the "more ancient Platonists" formed images in the heavens, images of the forty-eight constellations, twelve in the zodiac, and thirty-six outside it, images also of the thirty-six "faces" of the zodiac. From these ordered forms depend the forms of inferior things.

Ficino states in the sub-title to the *Liber de vita coelitus comparanda* that it is a commentary on a book on the same subject by Plotinus. He does not specify here of what passage in the *Enneads* he is thinking, but P. O. Kristeller has observed that in one manuscript the *De vita coelitus comparanda* appears among the commentaries on Plotinus at *Ennead*, IV, 3, xi.[1] Plotinus here says:

> I think . . . that those ancient sages, who sought to secure the presence of divine beings by the erection of shrines and statues, showed insight into the nature of the All; they perceived that, though this Soul (of the world) is everywhere tractable, its presence will be secured all the more readily when an appropriate receptacle is elaborated, a place especially capable of receiving some portion or phase of it, something reproducing it and serving like a mirror to catch an image of it.

> It belongs to the nature of the All to make its entire content reproduce, most felicitously, the Reason-Principles in which it participates; every particular thing is the image within matter of a Reason-Principle which itself images a pre-material Reason-Prin-

---

[1] Kristeller, *Suppl. Fic.*, I, p. lxxxiv; cf. Garin, *article cited*, pp. 18 ff. Walker (p. 3, note 2) points out that *Enn.* IV, 4, 30–42, may also be relevant.

ciple: thus every particular entity is linked to that Divine Being in whose likeness it is made. . . .[1]

We seem to have here the two main topics of which Ficino is speaking, but put in a different order, which makes the thought-sequences a little clearer. (1) How the ancient sages who understood the nature of the All drew down divine beings into their shrines by attracting or securing a part of the soul of the world. This corresponds to Ficino's mention of magic links or spells, described by Zoroaster or Synesius, which are congruities between reasons in the soul of the world and lower forms. Ficino follows this by the mention of star images, as though these were a part of the magical linking system, and indeed stating that from the ordering of these celestial images the forms of lower things depend. (2) The outline of Neoplatonic theory—which Ficino puts before the allusion to magic, and Plotinus after it—of the reflection of the Ideas in the divine intellect in their images or forms in the soul of the world, whence they are again reflected (through the intermediaries in the soul of the world) in material forms.

What would make sense of Ficino's introduction of the reference to celestial images in his commentary on the Plotinus passage would be if he thinks that such images are in some way organically related to those "seminal reasons" or "reason principles" in the soul of the world which are the reflection in that "middle place" of the Ideas in the divine mind. Hence such images would become forms of the Ideas, or ways of approaching the Ideas at a stage intermediary between their purely intellectual forms in the divine *mens* and their dimmer reflection in the world of sense, or body of the world. Hence it was by manipulating such images in this intermediary "middle place" that the ancient sages knew how to draw down a part of the soul of the world into their shrines.

There is, further, in Ficino's words, the notion that the material forms in the world of sense can be, as it were, re-formed, when they have degenerated, by manipulation of the higher images on which they depend. In his analysis of this passage, E. Garin has defined this process as the imitation or reconstruction of the higher images in such a way that the divine influences are recaptured and re-conducted into the deteriorated sensible forms.[2] Thus the priestly

[1] Plotinus, *Enn*, IV, 3, xi; English translation by S. MacKenna, London, 1956, p. 270.
[2] Garin, *article cited*, pp. 21 ff.

Magus plays a semi-divine rôle, maintaining by his understanding of the use of images the circuit which unites the highest divine world with the soul of the world and the world of sense.

In his article on "Icones Symbolicae", E. H. Gombrich has analysed the mode of thought, so difficult for a modern to understand, by which, for a Renaissance Neoplatonist, an "ancient" image, one which reached him from traditions going back, so he believed, into a remote past, did actually have within it the reflection of an Idea.[1] An ancient image of Justice was not just a picture but actually contained within it some echo, taste, substance, of the divine Idea of Justice. This helps us to understand the way in which Ficino thinks of those star images descending from "the more ancient Platonists", though, in the case of such images, the relation to the Idea is even closer, through the cosmology of *mens, anima mundi, corpus mundi* in which the images have a definite place.

Thus Ficino's commentary on the Plotinus passage becomes, by devious ways, a justification for the use of talismans, and of the magic of the *Asclepius*, on Neoplatonic grounds—on the grounds that the ancient sages and the modern users of talismans are not invoking devils but have a deep understanding of the nature of the All, and of the degrees by which the reflections of the Divine Ideas descend into the world here below.

As D. P. Walker has pointed out,[2] at the end of the *De vita coelitus comparanda* Ficino returns to the commentary on the Plotinus passage with which he had begun the book, and now he states that Plotinus in that passage was merely imitating, or repeating, what Hermes Trismegistus had said in his *Asclepius*. This means that the *De vita coelitus comparanda* is a commentary only secondarily on Plotinus and primarily on Trismegistus, or rather, on the passage in the *Asclepius* in which he described the magical Egyptian worship.

When any (piece of) matter is exposed to superior things . . . immediately it suffers a supernal influence through that most powerful agent, of marvellous force and life, which is everywhere present . . .

[1] E. H. Gombrich, "*Icones Symbolicae:* the Visual Image in Neoplatonic Thought", *J.W.C.I.*, 1948 (XI), pp. 163–92.
[2] Walker, pp. 40–1.

as a mirror reflects a face, or Echo the sound of a voice. Of this Plotinus gives an example when, imitating Mercurius, he says that the ancient priests, or Magi, used to introduce something divine and wonderful into their statues and sacrifices. He (Plotinus) holds, together with Trismegistus, that they did not introduce through these things spirits separated from matter (that is demons), but *mundana numina*, as I said at the beginning, and Synesius agrees. . . . Mercurius himself, whom Plotinus follows, says that he composed through aerial demons, not through celestial or higher demons, statues from herbs, trees, stones, aromatics having within them a natural divine power (as he says). . . . There were skilful Egyptian priests who, when they could not persuade men by reason that there are gods, that is some spirit above men, invented that illicit magic which by enticing demons into statues made these appear to be gods. . . . I at first thought, following the opinion of the Blessed Thomas Aquinas, that if they made statues which could speak, this could not have been only through stellar influence but through demons. . . . But now let us return to Mercurius and to Plotinus. Mercurius says that the priests drew suitable virtues from the nature of the world and mixed these together. Plotinus follows him, and thinks that all can be easily conciliated in the soul of the world for it generates and moves the forms of natural things through certain seminal reasons infused with its divinity. Which reasons he calls gods for they are not separated from the Ideas in the supreme mind.[1]

An interpretation of this passage is that Ficino used to agree with Thomas Aquinas, who explicitly condemns as demonic the magic in the *Asclepius*,[2] but since he has read Plotinus' commentary he understands that, though there may have been bad Egyptian priests who used demonic magic, Hermes Trismegistus was not one of them. His power came only from the world, from his insight into the nature of the All as a hierarchy in which the influence of the Ideas descends from the Intellect of the World, through the "seminal reasons" in the Soul of the World, to the material forms in the Body of the World.[3] Hence, celestial images would have their power from the "world" not from demons, being

[1] *De vita coelitus comparanda*, 26 (Ficino, pp. 571–2). Another important description of the hieratic magic which Ficino knew well was Proclus' *De Sacrificiis et Magia* which he translated (Ficino, pp. 1928–9), and on which see Festugière, I, pp. 134–6; cf. also Walker, pp. 36–7; Garin, *article cited*, pp. 19–20.
[2] *Contra Gentiles*, III, civ–cvi.
[3] cf. Walker, p. 43.

something in the nature of shadows of Ideas, intermediaries in the middle place between Intellect and Body, links in the chains by which the Neoplatonic Magus operates his magic and marries higher things to lower things.

Thus the magic of the *Asclepius*, reinterpreted through Plotinus, enters with Ficino's *De vita coelitus comparanda* into the Neoplatonic philosophy of the Renaissance, and, moreover, into Ficino's *Christian* Neoplatonism. The latter feat necessitated, as we have seen, much ingenious evasion of authoritative Christian pronouncements. When Ficino wrote the *De vita coelitus comparanda* he had perhaps recently been reading Origen against Celsus, which he cites in chapter XXI,[1] and where he might have noticed the quotation from Celsus where the pagan accuses the Christians of mocking the Egyptians "although they show many profound mysteries and teach that such worship (in the Egyptian magical religion) is respect to invisible ideas and not, as most people think, to ephemeral animals."[2] Eager to snatch at anything in favour of his hero, the holy Hermes Trismegistus, Ficino might have been encouraged by Origen's reply to this: "My good man, you commend the Egyptians with good reason for showing many mysteries which are not evil, and obscure explanations about their animals." Nevertheless, the context in which this remark is made is less encouraging, and Origen's whole effort was directed towards refuting Celsus' view of the history of religion, which was that an ancient good, religious tradition, of which the Egyptians were an example, had been corrupted, first by the Jews, and then still further destroyed by the Christians.

Ficino's magic is based on a theory of *spiritus* which has been admirably defined by D. P. Walker, to whose book the reader is referred for a full and scholarly discussion of this subject.[3] Ficino bases the theory of how we are to "draw down the life of heaven" upon the *spiritus* as the channel through which the influence of the stars is diffused. Between the soul of the world and its body there is a *spiritus mundi* which is infused throughout the

---

[1] Ficino, p. 562.

[2] Origen, *Contra Celsum*, trans. H. Chadwick, Cambridge, 1953, p. 139.

[3] Walker, pp. 1–24 and *passim*. Ficino's chief expositions of the *spiritus* theory in the *Libri de Vita* are in Lib. III (*De vita coelitus comparanda*), I, 3, 4, 11, 20, but the theory is assumed and referred to throughout.

universe and through which the stellar influences come down to man, who drinks them in through his own spirit, and to the whole *corpus mundi*. The *spiritus* is a very fine and subtle substance, and it was of this which Virgil spoke when he said:

> Spiritus intus alit, totamque infusa per artus
> mens agitat molem et magno se corpore miscet.[1]

It is to attract the *spiritus* of a particular planet that animals, plants, food, scents, colours, and so on associated with that planet are to be used. The *spiritus* is borne upon the air and upon the wind, and it is a kind of very fine air and also very fine heat. It is particularly through the rays of the Sun and of Jupiter that our spirit "drinks" the spirit of the world.

Now there is nothing about the *spiritus* theory in the passage in the *Enneads* which seems to be the chief basis of Ficino's commentary, and, though it may be obscurely referred to elsewhere by Plotinus, I have not been able to find in that philosopher any such clear-cut definition of the *spiritus mundi* as the vehicle of stellar influences and the basis of magical operations such as Ficino seems to be working from. Where he could have found such a clear-cut theory, and specifically in relation to practical magic and to talismans, was in the *Picatrix*. As we saw in the last chapter, the theory of magic in that work depends on the series *intellectus*, *spiritus*, *materia*; the material of lower things being intimately related to the *spiritus* material in the stars.[2] Magic consists in guiding or controlling the influx of *spiritus* into *materia*, and one of the most important ways of doing this is through talismans, for a talisman is a material object into which the *spiritus* of a star has been introduced and which stores the *spiritus*. This theory of pneumatic magic, Ficino could have studied in *Picatrix*, together with the lists of things which attract *spiritus*, full instructions for making talismans, and lists of images for using on talismans. The possibility that Ficino may have used *Picatrix* is increased by the similarity of some of the images which he describes to some of those in *Picatrix*.

Ficino's images are mostly in chapter XVIII of the *De vita coelitus comparanda*. After mentioning the images of the signs of

---

[1] Virgil, *Aeneid*, VI, 726–7. Quoted by Ficino in *De vita coelitus comparanda*, 3 (Ficino, p. 535).

[2] See above, pp. 51–2.

the zodiac, he says that there are also images of the faces of the signs, drawn from the Indians, Egyptians, and Chaldeans (lists of decan images do come from these sources), as for example:

> In the first face of Virgo a beautiful girl, seated, with ears of corn in her hand and nursing a child.[1]

This decan image in this actual form, with the child, is drawn not from *Picatrix*, but from Albumazar, whom Ficino mentions as the source. It is the only decan image which he describes—all his other images are planet images—and he is not sure whether it is right to use it. He then says that if you want to obtain gifts from Mercury, you should make his image on tin or silver, with the sign of Virgo and characters of Virgo and Mercury; and the decan image for the first face of Virgo may be added "if this is to be used". This talisman would thus consist of the image of Mercury, some signs and characters, and perhaps the Virgo image with the child. Note that the talisman is not a medical talisman, but to obtain intellectual "gifts" from Mercury.

To obtain long life, you may make the image of Saturn on a sapphire in this form: "An old man sitting on a high throne or on a dragon, with a hood of dark linen on his head, raising his hand above his head, holding a sickle or a fish, clothed in a dark robe." (*Homo senex in altiore cathedra sedens uel dracone, caput tectus panno quodam lineo fusco, manus supra caput erigens, falcem manutenens aut pisces, fusca indutus ueste.*[2]) This image is close to one in *Picatrix* and contains elements from two others. (Saturn images in *Picatrix*: *Forma hominis super altam cathedram elevatus & in eius capite pannum lineum lutosum, & in eius manu falcem tenentis: Forma hominis senex erecti, suas manus super caput ipsius erigentes, & in eis piscem tenentis . . .: Forma hominis super draconem erecti, in dextra manu falcem tenentis, in sinistra hastam habentis & nigris pannis induti.*[3]) For a long and happy life, says Ficino, you may make on a white, clear, stone an image of Jupiter as "A crowned man on an eagle or a dragon, clad in a yellow garment." (*Homo sedens super aquilam uel draconem coronatus . . . croceam induto uestem.*[4]) There is a very similar image of Jupiter in *Picatrix*.

---

[1] *De vita coelitus comparanda*, 18 (Ficino, p. 556).
[2] Ficino, pp. 556–7.
[3] *Picatrix*, Lib. II, cap. 10; Sloane, 1305, f. 43 *verso*.
[4] Ficino, p. 557.

(*Forma hominis super aquilam . . . omnia suis vestimenta sunt crocea.*[1])

For the curing of illnesses, Ficino advises the use of this image: "A king on a throne, in a yellow garment, and a crow and the form of the Sun" (*Rex in throno, crocea ueste, & coruum Solisque formam*).[2] The resemblance of this image to one in *Picatrix* is striking: *Forma regis supra cathedram sedentis, & in sui capite coronam habentis, et coruum ante se, et infra eius pedes istas figuras* (magic characters).[3] In *Picatrix* this is not a medical talisman, as in Ficino, but will enable a king to overcome all other kings.

For happiness and strength of body, Ficino advises an image of a young Venus, holding apples and flowers, and dressed in white and yellow. (*Veneris imaginem puellarem, poma floresque manu tenentem, croceis & albis indutam.*[4] The comparable Venus image in *Picatrix* is: *Forma mulieris capillis expansis & super ceruum equitantes in eius manu dextra malum habentis in sinistra vero flores et eius vestes ex coloribus albis.*[5])

An image of Mercury described by Ficino is "A helmeted man sitting on a throne, with eagle's feet, holding a cock or fire in his left hand. . . . (*Homo sedens in throno galeratus cristatusque, pedibus aquilinis, sinistra gallum tenens aut ignem . . . .*[6] A comparable Mercury image in *Picatrix* is: *Forma hominis in eius capite gallum habentis, & supra cathedram erecti & pedes similes pedibus aquilae & in palma sinistra manus ignem habentis.*[7]) Ficino says that this image of Mercury is good for wit and memory, or, if carved in marble, is good against fevers.

The resemblances between Ficino's talismans and those in *Picatrix* are not absolutely conclusive evidence that he used that work. He knew, and mentions, other source for images,[8] and the gods on his talismans are mainly composed of their normal forms,

---

[1] *Picatrix, loc. cit.* Sloane, 1305, *loc. cit.*

[2] Ficino, *loc. cit.*

[3] *Picatrix, loc. cit.*; Sloane, 1305, f. 45 *recto.*

[4] Ficino, *loc. cit.*

[5] *Picatrix, loc. cit.*; Sloane, 1305, f. 44 *verso.*

[6] Ficino, *loc. cit.*

[7] *Picatrix, loc. cit.*; Sloane, 1305, *loc. cit.*

[8] Particularly Peter of Abano. He never mentions *Picatrix* by name. Perhaps he thought that Abano was a safer source to mention. The later controversy accusing Abano of having borrowed from *Picatrix* (see above, p. 50) might have been indirectly aimed at Ficino.

such as Jupiter on an eagle, or Venus with flowers and apples. Nevertheless one does gain the impression that he had been looking through the chapter on planet images in *Picatrix*. What is interesting is that, on the whole, he seems to avoid decan images, concentrating almost entirely on planet images. This was noticed by W. Gundel, the great authority on decan images, who thinks that Ficino's partiality for planet images reflects a traditional rivalry between decan and planet images which Ficino decides in favour of the latter. "Bei Ficinus ist die alte Rivalität der grossen Systeme der dekan- und der planetengläubigen Astrologie zugunsten der Planeten entschieden."[1] One wonders if this choice was related to the avoidance of demonic magic. By avoiding the images of the decan demons and by using planet images—not to evoke the demons of the planets but only as images of "mundane gods", shadows of Ideas in the Soul of the world—the pious Neoplatonist could perhaps believe that he would be doing only a "world" magic, a natural magic with natural forces, not a demonic magic. Watching Ficino's anxieties and hesitations, one is amazed at the daring of those bold characters beyond the Appenines, in Ferrara or in Padua[2] who did not fear to decorate the walls of their apartments with the images of the terrible Thirty-Six.

It is very strange to follow the convolutions and involutions of Ficino's mind in this chapter XVIII. Before he introduces his lists of planetary talismans he has some curious remarks on the cross as a kind of talisman.[3] The force of the heavens is greatest when

---

[1] Gundel, *Dekane und Dekansternbilder*, p. 280.

[2] The images of the decans are shown in the astrological scheme on the walls of the Salone at Padua; this scheme was first fully interpreted by F. Saxl (*Sitzungsberichte der Heidelberger Akademie der Wissenschaft*, 1925-6, pp. 49-68) through study of the astrology of Guido Bonatti and of the *Astrolabium planum* of Peter of Abano, the figures of which are derived from Albumasar. Cf. J. Seznec, *The Survival of the Pagan Gods*, trans. B. F. Sessions, New York, 1953, pp. 73-4.

[3] "Tunc enim stellae magnopere sunt potentes, quando quatuor coeli tenent angulos imo cardines, orientis uidelicet occidentisque, & medii utrinque. Sic uero dispositae, radios ita conjiciunt in se inuicem, ut crucem inde constituant. Crucem ergo ueteres figuram esse dicebant, tum stellarum fortitudine factam, tum earundem fortitudinis susceptaculum, ideoque habere summam in imaginibus potestatem, ac uires & spiritus suscipere Planetarum. Haec autem opinio ab Aegyptijs uel inducta est, uel maxime confirmata. Inter quorum characteres crux una erat insignis uitam eorum more futuram significans, eamque figuram pectori Serapidis

the celestial rays come down perpendicularly and at right angles, that is to say in the form of a cross joining the four cardinal points. The Egyptians hence used the form of the cross, which to them also signified the future life, and they sculptured that figure on the breast of Serapis. Ficino, however, thinks that the use of the cross among the Egyptians was not so much on account of its power in attracting the gifts of the stars, but as a prophecy of the coming of Christ, made by them unknowingly. Thus the sanctity of the Egyptians as prophets of Christianity through their use of the cross as a talisman comes in as an appropriate introduction to the list of talismanic images.

After this list, Ficino makes great play with the recommendation by doctors, particularly Peter of Abano, of the use of talismans in medicine. Then, after some references to Porphyry and Plotinus, he comes to Albertus Magnus, described as Professor of Astrology and Theology, who in his *Speculum astronomiae* has distinguished between false and true use of talismans.[1] Next he again worries over what Thomas Aquinas has said in the *Contra Gentiles*, finally reaching a position which he imagines is near to that of Thomas, namely that the talismans have their power mainly from the materials of which they are made, not from the images.[2] Yet if they are made under the influence of a harmony, similar to the celestial harmony, this excites their virtue.

In short, by devious means, Ficino has extracted his use of talismans from blame. I believe that he is thinking primarily of planetary talismans, and of these used not in a "demonic" manner but, as Walker has said, with "spiritual" magic, a magic using the *spiritus mundi*, to be attracted mainly through groupings of plants, metals, and so on, but also through use of planetary talismans which address the stars as world forces, or natural forces, and not as demons.[3]

"Why, then, should we not permit ourselves a universal image, that is an image of the universe itself? From which it might be

[1] Ficino, p. 558.
[2] *Ibid.*, *loc. cit.*; cf. Walker, p. 43.
[3] But cf. Walker's discussion (pp. 44–53) of "Ficino and the demons".

insculpebant. Ego uero quod de crucis excellentia fuit apud Aegyptios ante Christum, non tam muneris stellarum testimonium fuisse arbitror, quam uirtutis praesagium, quam a Christo esset acceptura . . ." Ficino, p. 556.

hoped to obtain much benefit from the universe." This cry comes at the beginning of chapter XIX, after the long defence of planetary images, used in a "natural" way, in the preceding chapter. This universal image or "figure of the world" (*mundi figura*) may be made in brass, combined with gold and silver. (These are the metals of Jupiter, Sol, and Venus.) It should be begun in an auspicious time, when Sol enters the first degree of Aries. It should not be worked at on the Sabbath, the day of Saturn. It should be completed in Venus "to signify its absolute beauty". Colours as well as lines, or lineaments, should be inserted into the work. "There are three universal and singular colours of the world, green, gold, and blue, dedicated to the Three Graces of heaven", which are Venus, Sol, and Jupiter. "They judge therefore that in order to capture the gifts of the celestial graces, these three colours should be frequently used, and into the formula of the world which you are making should be inserted the blue colour of the sphere of the world. They think that gold should be added to the precious work made like the heaven itself, and stars, and Vesta, or Ceres, that is the earth, dressed in green."[1]

There is a good deal which I have not been able to understand in this description. The figure seems to refer to a New Year as a new birthday of the world, or even to the first birthday of the world, the creation (Pico della Mirandola's *Heptaplus* is mentioned). But in general it may be said that the making of this magical or talismanic object belongs into the context of the *Libri de vita* as a whole which have all been concerned with various techniques for drawing down, or drinking in, the influences of the Sun, of Venus, and of Jupiter, as health-giving, rejuvenating, anti-Saturnian powers. The object described, or hinted at (for the description is very vague) would seem to be a model of the heavens constructed so as to concentrate on drawing down the fortunate influences of Sol, Venus, Jupiter. Certainly the colours of these planets are to predominate in it, and it may probably be presumed that their images are depicted in it. The inclusion of Ceres in green as the earth is understandable, but Vesta is strange.

Such an object, Ficino seems to say, may be worn, or placed opposite to be looked at,[2] suggesting that it is perhaps a medal, perhaps an elaborate jewel.

[1] Ficino, p. 559.
[2] "uel gestabit, uel oppositam intuebitur" (*ibid., loc. cit.*).

He then says that the figure of the world may be constructed so as to reproduce the motion of the spheres, as was done by Archimedes, and has been done recently by a Florentine called Lorenzo. He is here referring to the astronomical clock made by Lorenzo della Volpaia[1] for Lorenzo de' Medici which contained representations of the planets. Such a figure of the world, says Ficino, is made not only to be gazed at but to be meditated upon in the soul. It is obviously a different kind of object to the one previously hinted at. It is a cosmic mechanism.

Finally, someone may construct, or will construct:

> on the domed ceiling of the innermost cubicle of his house, where he mostly lives and sleeps, such a figure with the colours in it. And when he comes out of his house he will perceive, not so much the spectacle of individual things, but the figure of the universe and its colours.[2]

I understand this to mean a painting on the ceiling of a bedroom, a painting which is also still a figure of the world, with perhaps still the figures of the Three Graces, the three fortunate planets, Sol, Venus, and Jupiter predominating, and their colours of blue, gold, and green as the leading colours of the painting or fresco.

These various forms of the "figure of the world" are thus artistic objects which are to be used magically for their talismanic virtue. They are attempting to influence "the world" by favourable arrangements of celestial images, so as to draw down favourable influences and exclude non-favourable ones. In short, these unfortunately so vaguely hinted at works of art are functional; they are made for a purpose, for magical use. By arranging the figure of the world and its celestial images with knowledge and skill, the Magus controls the influences of the stars. Just as Hermes Trismegistus arranged the images in the City of Adocentyn, which was planned as an image of the world, so as to regulate the astral

---

[1] See A. Chastel, *Marsile Ficin et l'Art*, Geneva–Lille, 1954, p. 95. Lorenzo della Volpaia's clock is referred to by Poliziano, Vasari and others (references in Chastel, *op. cit.*, pp. 96–7, note 16). Chastel thinks that the whole of the passage on making an image of the world in the *De vita coelitus comparanda* is a description of Della Volpaia's clock. I do not think that this is the case. Ficino is describing three different kinds of objects made to represent the figure of the world, one type being the cosmic mechanism of which Della Volpaia's clock is an example.

[2] Ficino, *loc. cit.*

influences on the inhabitants in such a way as to keep them healthy and virtuous, so Ficino's "figures of the world" would be calculated to regulate the influences in the direction indicated in the *Libri de Vita*, towards a predominance of Solar, Jovial, and Venereal influences and towards an avoidance of Saturn and Mars.

The point in the description of the "figures of the world" to which I want to draw particular attention in view of later developments in this book is that these figures are not only to be looked at but reflected or remembered within. The man who stares at the figure of the world on his bedroom ceiling, imprinting it and its dominating colours of the planets on memory, when he comes out of his house and sees innumerable individual things is able to unify these through the images of a higher reality which he has within. This is the strange vision, or the extraordinary illusion, which was later to inspire Giordano Bruno's efforts to base memory on celestial images, on images which are shadows of ideas in the soul of the world, and thus to unify and organise the innumerable individuals in the world and all the contents of memory.

In his article on "Botticelli's Mythologies", E. H. Gombrich quotes a letter from Ficino to Lorenzo di Pierfrancesco de' Medici, in which Ficino tells the young Lorenzo that he is giving him an "immense present".

> For anyone who contemplates the heavens, nothing he sets his eyes upon seems immense, but the heavens themselves. If, therefore, I make you a present of the heavens themselves what would be its price?[1]

Ficino goes on to say that the young man should dispose his "Luna", that is, his soul and body, in such a way as to avoid too much influence from Saturn and Mars, and to obtain favourable influences from the Sun, Jupiter, and Venus. "If you thus dispose the heavenly signs and your gifts in this way, you will escape the threats of fortune, and, under divine favour, will live happy and free from cares."

Gombrich discusses the "Primavera" (Pl. 2) in relation to such a

---

[1] Ficino, p. 805; cf. E. H. Gombrich, "Botticelli's Mythologies: a study in the Neoplatonic symbolism of his circle", *J.W.C.I.*, VIII (1945), p. 16.

disposition of the stars, suggesting that the Mercury on the extreme left is a planetary image, raising and dismissing the possibility that the Three Graces might be Sol, Jupiter, and Venus, and emphasising that the central figure is certainly a Venus. What I have now to suggest does not conflict with the general line of his approach.

Surely, the "immense present" which was a "present of the heavens themselves" which Ficino sent to Pierfrancesco was a construction of a similar nature to that described in chapter XIX of the *De vita coelitus comparanda* on "making a figure of the universe". It was an image of the world arranged so as to attract the favourable planets and to avoid Saturn. The "present" was probably not some actual object but advice as to how to make, internally in the soul or the imagination such a "figure of the world" and to keep the inner attention concentrated on its images, or possibly also how to have a real object or talisman designed to be used for reflection in the mind. Though painted earlier than the *De vita coelitus comparanda* was written, or at least published, Botticelli's "Primavera" is surely such an object, designed with such a purpose.

Far be it from me to attempt yet another detailed interpretation of the figures in the "Primavera". I want only to suggest that in the context of the study of Ficino's magic the picture begins to be seen as a practical application of that magic, as a complex talisman, an "image of the world" arranged so as to transmit only healthful, rejuvenating, anti-Saturnian influences to the beholder. Here, in visual form is Ficino's natural magic, using grouping of trees and flowers, using only planetary images and those only in relation to the "world", not to attract demons; or as shadows of Ideas in the Neoplatonic hierarchy. And, whatever the figures on the right may represent mythologically, is it not the *spiritus mundi* which blows through them, blown from the puffed cheeks of the aerial spirit, made visible in the wind-blown folds of the draperies of the running figure? The *spiritus* which is the channel for the influences of the stars has been caught and stored in the magic talisman.

How different is Botticelli's Alma Venus, with whom, as Ficino advises, we walk in the green and flowery meadows, drinking in the scented air, laden with *spiritus*—how different she is from the prim little talisman Venus, with an apple in one hand and flowers in the other! Yet her function is the same, to draw down the

Venereal spirit from the star, and to transmit it to the wearer or beholder of her lovely image.

Ficino's Orphic magic[1] was a return to an ancient *priscus theologus*, like his talismanic magic with its disguised, or revised, return to Hermes Trismegistus. Orpheus comes second after Trismegistus in the Ficinian lists of *prisci theologi*. The collection of hymns known as the *Orphica*, which was the main though not the only source of Orphic hymns known to the Renaissance, dates probably from the second or third century A.D., that is from roughly the same period as the *Hermetica*. They were probably hymns used by some religious sect of the period. Their content is usually to call upon a god, particularly the Sun, by his various names, invoking his various powers, and there is more than a touch of the magical incantation in them. Ficino and his contemporaries believed that the Orphic hymns were by Orpheus himself and were of extreme antiquity, reflecting the religious singing of a *priscus magus* who lived long before Plato. Ficino's revival of Orphic singing has deep importance for him because he believes he is returning to the practice of a most ancient theologian and one who foresaw the Trinity.[2] It thus has underlying it the same type of historical error as that which induced his profound respect for the *Hermetica*.

Ficino used to sing the Orphic songs, accompanying himself probably on a *lira da braccio*.[3] They were set to some kind of simple monodic music which Ficino believed echoed the musical notes emitted by the planetary spheres, to form that music of the spheres of which Pythagoras spoke. Thus one could sing Sun hymns, or Jupiter hymns, or Venus hymns attuned to those planets, and this, being re-enforced by the invocation of their names and powers, was a way of drawing down their influences. The *spiritus* theory also lies behind this vocal or aural magic, as it does behind the sympathetic and talismanic magic. The Orphic magic is thus exactly parallel to the talismanic magic; it is used for the same reasons, to draw down chosen stellar influences; its medium or channel is again the *spiritus*. The only difference between the two magics, and it is of course a basic one, is that one

---

[1] On Ficino's Orphic magic, see Walker, pp. 12–24.

[2] See Walker, "Orpheus the Theologian and the Renaissance Platonists", *J.W.C.I.*, XVI (1953), pp. 100–20.

[3] Walker (*Spiritual and Demonic Magic*), pp. 19, 22.

is visual, working through visual images (the talismans) whilst the other is aural and vocal, working through music and the voice.

Walker thinks that the incantatory and aural magic which is described in the *De vita coelitus comparanda* is really the same as the Orphic singing, though this is not expressly stated.[1] The two branches of Ficino's magic—sympathetic magic with natural groupings and talismans, and incantatory magic with hymns and invocations—are certainly both represented in that work.

The incantatory magic raises the same problem as the talismanic magic, namely, is it a natural magic, addressed to the gods as powers of the world, or a demonic magic, invoking the demons of the stars. The answer here is probably the same as in the case of the talismanic magic, namely that Ficino regarded his incantations as purely natural magic. At least we have Pico della Mirandola's word for it that the Orphic singing is natural magic for he calls it by this name in one of his *Conclusiones Orphicae*:

> In natural magic nothing is more efficacious than the Hymns of Orpheus, if there be applied to them suitable music, and disposition of soul, and the other circumstances known to the wise.[2]

And in another of his Orphic Conclusions, Pico definitely states that the names of the gods, of which Orpheus sings, are not those of deceiving demons but "names of the natural and divine virtues"[3] diffused throughout the world.

To complete our view of Ficino's natural magic, we thus have to think of him drawing down the stellar influences by musical incantations as well as by sympathetic arrangement of natural objects, talismans, exposing oneself to the air, and so on, for the *spiritus* is caught by planetary songs as well as in the other ways described. There may be an even closer connection between the Ficinian talismans and the Ficinian incantations, for in chapter XVIII, after his long and involved defence of his talismans, he seems to say that these are made "beneath a harmony similar to the celestial harmony"[4] which excites their virtue. I do not know whether this passage can be taken to mean that a Ficinian talisman or talismanic type of picture, was made, or painted, to the

---

[1] *Ibid.*, p. 23.
[2] Pico, p. 106; quoted by Walker, p. 22.
[3] Pico, p. 106. See below, p. 90.
[4] Ficino, p. 558.

accompaniment of suitable Orphic incantations which helped to infuse the *spiritus* into them.

In spite of all his precautions, Ficino did not avoid getting into trouble for the *Libri de vita*, as we learn from his *Apologia*[1] for that work. People had evidently been asking questions such as, "Is not Marsilius a priest? What has a priest to do with medicine and astrology? What has a Christian to do with magic and images?" Ficino counters by pointing out that in ancient times, priests always did medicine, mentioning Chaldean, Persian, and Egyptian priests; that medicine is impossible without astrology; that Christ Himself was a healer. But above all he emphasises that there are two kinds of magic, one demonic magic which is illicit and wicked, the other natural magic, which is useful and necessary. The only kind of magic which he has practised or advised is the good and useful kind—*magia naturalis*.[2]

How elegant, how artistic and refined is this modern natural magic![3] If we think of the Neoplatonic philosopher singing Orphic hymns, accompanying himself on his *lira da braccio* decorated with the figure of Orpheus taming the animals, and then compare this Renaissance vision with the barbarous mutterings of some invocation in *Picatrix*, the contrast between the new magic and the old is painfully evident.

> Beydelus, Demeymes, Adulex, Metucgayn, Atine, Ffex, Uquizuz, Gadix, Sol, Veni cito cum tuis spiritibus.[4]

How remote is the gibberish of this demonic invocation to Sol in *Picatrix* from Ficino and his "natural" planetary songs! Or if we think of the flowers, jewels, scents with which Ficino's patients are advised to surround themselves, of the charmingly healthy and wealthy way of life which they are to follow, and compare this with the filthy and obscene substances, the stinking and disgusting mixtures recommended in *Picatrix*, the contrast is again most striking between the new elegant magic, recommended by the fashionable physician, and that old dirty magic. Again, it would

---

[1] *Ibid.*, pp. 572–4. On the *Apologia*, see Walker, pp. 42 ff., 52–3.

[2] Ficino, p. 573; cf. Walker, p. 52.

[3] E. Garin (*Medioevo e Rinascimento*, p. 172) draws a contrast between mediaeval "bassa magia" and "magia rinascimentale".

[4] Sloane, 1305, f. 152 *verso*.

seem that the primitive talismanic image might be expanded by Renaissance artists into figures of immortal beauty, figures in which classical form has been both recovered and transmuted into something new.

And yet there is absolute continuity between the old magic and the new. Both rest on the same astrological presuppositions; both use in their methods the same groupings of natural substances; both employ talismans and invocations; both are pneumatic magic, believing in the *spiritus* as the channel of influence from the above to the below. Finally, both are integrated into an elaborate philosophical context. The magic of *Picatrix* is presented in a framework of philosophy; and Ficino's natural magic is fundamentally related to his Neoplatonism.

We have, in short, to think of Renaissance magic as both in continuity with mediaeval magic and also the transformation of that tradition into something new. The phenomenon is exactly parallel with that other phenomenon which Warburg and Saxl discovered and studied, namely how the images of the gods were preserved through the Middle Ages in astrological manuscripts, reached the Renaissance in that barbarised form, and were then reinvested with classical form through the rediscovery and imitation of classical works of art.[1] In the same way, astral magic comes down in the mediaeval tradition and is reinvested with classical form in the Renaissance through the rediscovery of Neoplatonic theurgy. Ficino's magic, with its hymns to the Sun, its Three Graces in an astrological context, its Neoplatonism, is closer in outlook, practice, and classical form to the Emperor Julian than it is to *Picatrix*. Yet the substance of it reached him through *Picatrix*, or some such similar text-books, and was transformed by him back into classical form through his Greek studies. One might say that the approach through the history of magic is perhaps as necessary for the understanding of the meaning and use of a Renaissance work of art as is the approach through the history of the recovery of classical form for the understanding of its form. The Three Graces (to take this perennial example) regained their classical form through the recovery and imitation of the true

[1] See Warburg's *Gesammelte Schriften*; Saxl's catalogues of illustrated astrological manuscripts and other writings (for bibliography, see F. Saxl, *Lectures*, Warburg Institute, University of London, 1957, I, pp. 359–62); and cf. J. Seznec, *The Survival of the Pagan Gods*, pp. 37 ff.

classical form of the group. They perhaps also regained their talismanic virtue through the renaissance of magic.

And yet, just as a pagan Renaissance work of art is not purely pagan but retains Christian overtones or undertones (the classical example of this being Botticelli's Venus who looks like a Virgin), so it is also with Ficino's magic. This cannot be regarded as a purely medical practice which he kept quite separate from his religion because, as D. P. Walker has emphasised, it was in itself a kind of religion. Walker has quoted a passage from Ficino's close disciple and imitator, Francesco da Diacetto in which this comes out most clearly.[1] Diacceto describes how one who wishes to acquire "solarian gifts", should robe himself in a mantle of solarian colour, such as gold, and conduct a rite, involving burning of incense made from solar plants, before an altar on which is an image of the sun, for example "an image of the sun enthroned, crowned, and wearing a saffron cloak, likewise a raven and the figure of the sun." This is the solar talisman in the *De vita coelitus comparanda* which we thought might be derived from *Picatrix*.[2] Then, anointed with unguents made from solar materials he is to sing an Orphic hymn to the Sun, invoking him as the divine Henad, as the Mind, and as the Soul. This is the Neoplatonic triad under which the Emperor Julian worshipped the Sun. As Walker says the triad is not actually mentioned in the *De vita coelitus comparanda*. But it is alluded to by Plotinus in that passage in the *Enneads* on which Ficino's work is a commentary, as the example of the hierarchy of the Ideas.[3] Diacceto's solar rites thus bring out something which is implicit in the *De vita coelitus comparanda* and they probably reflect Ficino's own practices. If so, Ficino's magic was a religious magic, a revival of the religion of the world.

---

[1] Francesco da Diacceto, *Opera omnia*, ed. Bâle, 1563, pp. 45–6; cf. Walker, pp. 32–3. On Diacceto, see Kristeller, *Studies*, pp. 287 ff.

[2] See above, p. 71. In this passage, the talismanic image of the sun is almost reverting to a "statue", worshipped with rites as in the *Asclepius*.

[3] "The sun of that sphere . . . is an Intellectual-Principle, and immediately upon it follows the Soul depending from it . . . the Soul borders also upon the sun of this sphere, and becomes the medium by which it is linked to the over-world"; Plotinus, *Ennead*, IV, 3, XI; McKenna's translation, p. 270.

I(*a*) The Zodiacal Sign Aries with its three Decans

I (*b*) The first Decan of Aries

Francesco del Cossa, Palazzo Schifanoja, Ferrara (p. 57)

2 Botticelli, "Primavera", Uffizi Gallery, Florence (p. 76)

How could a pious Christian reconcile such a revival with his Christianity? No doubt the Renaissance religious syncretism, by which the Neoplatonic triad was connected with the Trinity would account for regarding sun-worship theoretically and historically as a religion having affinities with Christianity, but this would hardly account for the revival of it as a religious cult. The moving force behind this revival was probably, as Walker has suggested, Ficino's deep interest in the Egyptian magical religion described in the *Asclepius*. It was on this, and only secondarily on Plotinus, that the *De vita coelitus comparanda* was a commentary, seeking to justify it by finding a "natural" and Neoplatonic basis for it.

By the time that the *Libri de vita* were published, in 1489 Hermes Trismegistus would have been safely ensconced inside the Duomo at Siena, proudly displaying the quotation from his *Asclepius* in which he prophesied the Son of God, and being urged to take up again the Egyptian laws and letters. Lactantius has much to answer for, for it was his interpretation of Trismegistus as a holy Gentile prophet which Ficino adopted, and which he thought that he found marvellously confirmed in the *Pimander*. And it is this which may have encouraged him to take up magical religion, which he did not do, as we have seen, without much fear and trembling and anxious avoidance of demons.

When Hermes Trismegistus entered the Church, the history of magic became involved with the history of religion in the Renaissance.

Chapter V

❖❖❖❖❖❖❖❖❖❖❖❖❖❖❖❖❖❖❖❖❖❖❖❖❖❖❖❖❖❖❖❖❖❖❖❖❖

PICO DELLA MIRANDOLA AND
CABALIST MAGIC

❖❖❖❖❖❖❖❖❖❖❖❖❖❖❖❖❖❖❖❖❖❖❖❖❖❖❖❖❖❖❖❖❖❖❖❖❖

PICO DELLA MIRANDOLA, contemporary of Ficino, though younger, began his philosophical career
under Ficino's influence and imbibed from Ficino his
enthusiasm for *magia naturalis* which he accepted and
recommended much more forcibly and openly than did Ficino.
But Pico is chiefly important in the history of Renaissance magic
because he added to the natural magic another kind of magic,
which was to be used with the *magia naturalis* as complementary
to it. This other kind of magic which Pico added to the equipment
of the Renaissance Magus was practical Cabala, or Cabalist
magic. This was a spiritual magic, not spiritual in the sense of
using only the natural *spiritus mundi* like natural magic, but in
the sense that it attempted to tap the higher spiritual powers,
beyond the natural powers of the cosmos. Practical Cabala in-
vokes angels, archangels, the ten sephiroth which are names or
powers of God, God himself, by means some of which are similar
to other magical procedures but more particularly through the
power of the sacred Hebrew language. It is thus a much more
ambitious kind of magic than Ficino's natural magic, and one
which it would be impossible to keep apart from religion.

For the Renaissance mind, which loved symmetrical arrangements, there was a certain parallelism between the writings of
Hermes Trismegistus, the Egyptian Moses, and Cabala which was
a Jewish mystical tradition supposed to have been handed down
orally from Moses himself. In common with all Cabalists, Pico

firmly believed in this extreme antiquity of the Cabalistic teachings as going right back to Moses, as a secret doctrine which Moses had imparted to some initiates who had handed it on, and which unfolded mysteries not fully explained by the patriarch in *Genesis*. The Cabala is not, I believe, ever called a *prisca theologia* for this term applied to Gentile sources of ancient wisdom, and this was a more sacred wisdom, being Hebrew wisdom. And since, for Pico, Cabala confirmed the truth of Christianity, Christian Cabala was a Hebrew-Christian source of ancient wisdom, and one which he found it most valuable and instructive to compare with Gentile ancient wisdoms, and above all with that of Hermes Trismegistus who particularly lent himself to Pico's essays in comparative religion because he was so closely parallel to Moses, as the Egyptian law-giver and author of the inspired Egyptian Genesis, the *Pimander*.

Looking at the Hermetic writings and at Cabala with the eyes of Pico, certain symmetries begin to present themselves to our enraptured gaze. The Egyptian law-giver had given utterance to wonderful mystical teachings, including an account of creation in which he seemed to know something of what Moses knew. With this body of mystical teaching there went a magic, the magic of the *Asclepius*. In Cabala, too, there was a marvellous body of mystical teaching, derived from the Hebrew law-giver, and new light on the Mosaic mysteries of creation. Pico lost himself in these wonders in which he saw the divinity of Christ verified. And with Cabala, too, there went a kind of magic, practical Cabala.

Hermetism and Cabalism also corroborated one another on a theme which was fundamental for them both, namely the creation by the Word. The mysteries of the *Hermetica* are mysteries of the Word, or the Logos, and in the *Pimander*, it was by the luminous Word, the Son of God issuing from the *Nous* that the creative act was made. In *Genesis*, "God spoke" to form the created world, and, since He spoke in Hebrew, this is why for the Cabalist the words and letters of the Hebrew tongue are subjects for endless mystical meditations, and why, for the practical Cabalist, they contain magical power. Lactantius may have helped to cement the union between Hermetism and Christian Cabalism on this point, for, after quoting from the Psalm "By the word of God were the heavens made", and from St. John, "In the beginning was the Word", he adds that this is supported from the Gentiles. "For

Trismegistus, who by some means or other searched into almost all truth, often described the excellence and the majesty of the Word", and he acknowledged "that there is an ineffable and sacred speech, the relation of which exceeds the measure of man's ability."[1]

The marrying together of Hermetism and Cabalism, of which Pico was the instigator and founder, was to have momentous results, and the subsequent Hermetic-Cabalist tradition, ultimately stemming from him, was of most far-reaching importance. It could be purely mystical, developing Hermetic and Cabalist meditations on creation and on man into immensely complex labyrinths of religious speculation, involving numerological and harmonic aspects into which Pythagoreanism was absorbed. But it also had its magical side, and here, too, Pico was the founder who first united the Hermetic and Cabalist types of magic.

It was in 1486 that the young Pico della Mirandola went to Rome with his nine hundred theses, or points drawn from all philosophies which he offered to prove in public debate to be all reconcilable with one another. According to Thorndike, these theses showed that Pico's thinking "was largely coloured by astrology, that he was favourable to natural magic, and that he had a penchant for such occult and esoteric literature as the Orphic hymns, Chaldean oracles, and Jewish cabala",[2] also the writings of Hermes Trismegistus. The great debate never took place, and theologians raised an outcry over some of the theses, necessitating an Apology or defence which was published in 1487 together with most of the oration on the Dignity of Man, with which the debate was to have opened. That oration was to echo and re-echo throughout the Renaissance, and it is, indeed, the great charter of Renaissance Magic, of the new type of magic introduced by Ficino and completed by Pico.

In the following pages I shall be using Pico's theses, or *Conclusiones*, his Apology, and also the Oration.[3] My objects are

---

[1] Lactantius, *Div. Inst.*, IV, ix; Fletcher's translation, I, p. 226.
[2] Thorndike, IV, p. 494.
[3] Pico's *Conclusiones*, absolutely fundamental though they are for the whole Renaissance, are available in no modern edition. The references to them and to the *Apologia* in this chapter are to the 1572 edition of Pico's works (abbreviated as "Pico", see Abbreviations). The references to the

strictly limited. First, I shall draw out what Pico says about *magia* or *magia naturalis*, endeavouring to determine what he means by this. Secondly, to show that Pico distinguishes between theoretical Cabala and practical Cabala, the latter being Cabalist magic. And, thirdly, to prove that Pico thinks that *magia naturalis* needs to be supplemented by practical Cabala without which it is but a weak force. These three objectives overlap with one another, and it may not always be possible to keep the different threads distinct. And I must add that, though I am certain that by "practical Cabala" Pico means Cabalist magic, I shall not be able to elucidate what procedures he used for this, since this is a matter for Hebrew specialists to investigate.

Amongst Pico's nine hundred theses there are twenty-six *Conclusiones Magicae*. These are partly on natural magic and partly on Cabalist magic. I select here some of those on natural magic.

The first of the magical conclusions is as follows:

> Tota Magia, quae in usu est apud Modernos, & quam merito exterminat Ecclesia, nullam habet firmitatem, nullum fundamentum, nullam ueritatem, quia pendet ex manu hostium primae ueritatis, potestatum harum tenebrarum, quae tenebras falsitatis, male dispositis intellectibus obfundunt.[1]

All "modern magic", announces Pico in this first conclusion is bad, groundless, the work of the devil, and rightly condemned by the Church. This sounds uncompromisingly against magic as used in Pico's time, "modern magic". But magicians always introduce their subject by stating that, though there are bad and diabolical magics, their kind of magic is not of that nature. And I think that by "modern magic" Pico does not mean the new-style natural magic, but mediaeval and unreformed magics. For his next conclusion begins:

> Magia naturalis licita est, & non prohibita. . . .[2]

[1] Pico, p. 104. [2] *Ibid., loc. cit.*

Oration are to the edition, with Italian translation, published by E. Garin (G. Pico della Mirandola, *De hominis dignitate, Heptaplus, De ente et uno, e scritti varii*, ed. E. Garin, Florence, 1942). An English translation of the Oration is included in *The Renaissance Philosophy of Man*, ed. E. Cassirer, P. O. Kristeller, J. H. Randall, Chicago, 1948, pp. 223 ff. On the first version of the Oration, see Garin, *Cultura*, pp. 231 ff.

There is then a good magic, an allowable magic which is not forbidden, and it is *magia naturalis*.

What does Pico understand by *magia naturalis*? In the third conclusion he states that:

Magia est pars practica scientiae naturalis

in the fifth that:

Nulla est uirtus in coelo aut in terra seminaliter & separata quam & actuare & unire magus non possit

and in the thirteenth that:

Magicam operari non est aliud quam maritare mundum.[1]

It is clear, I think, from these three conclusions that by the licit natural magic, Pico means the establishing of the "links" between earth and heaven by the right use of natural substances in accordance with the principles of sympathetic magic, and since such links would be inefficacious without the higher link of the talisman or the star image made efficacious with natural *spiritus*, the use of talismans must (or so I would think) be included in the methods by which Pico's natural Magus "unites" virtues in heaven with those on earth, or "marries the world" which is another way of putting the same notion.

That Pico's natural magic did not rest entirely on the arrangement of the natural substances is, moreover, proved from the twenty-fourth conclusion:

Ex secretioris philosophiae principiis, necesse est confiteri, plus posse characteres & figuras in opere Magico, quam possit quaecunque qualitas materialis.[2]

This is a definite statement that it is not the material substances which have most power, not the materials of which an object used in magic is made, but the actual magic "characters" and "figures" which are the most operative. He does not here use the word *imagines*, the correct term for talismanic images, but *characteres* are those magic characters (illustrated in works like *Picatrix*) and which are used as well as the talismanic image on some of the talismans quoted by Ficino. I am not sure whether "figures" can ever mean "images", or whether these too are in the nature of characters. But what is certain is that Pico is saying that it is the magical signs which are operative. Therefore his natural magic is

[1] *Ibid.*, pp. 104, 105.
[2] *Ibid.*, p. 105.

more than the arrangement of natural substances and includes such magical signs.

In his *Apologia*, Pico repeated the conclusions about the badness of bad magic and the goodness of his natural magic which is the uniting or marrying of things in heaven with things on earth, adding that these two definitions (about the "uniting" and "marrying") underlie, or are implied in, all his other magical conclusions, particularly the one about the characters and figures. He emphasised that the good natural magic which marries earth to heaven is all done naturally, by *virtutes naturales*, and that the activity of the magical characters and figures used is also a "natural" activity. In short, he is, I would think, trying to make it very clear that the Magia which he advocates is not a demonic magic but a natural magic.[1]

Pico's natural magic is therefore, it would seem, probably the same as Ficino's magic, using natural sympathies but also magical images and signs, though on the understanding that this is to attract natural power, not demonic power. It is indeed possible that there are echoes of Pico's apology for his natural magic in Ficino's apology for the *Libri de Vita*, published two years later.

Another link between Ficino's and Pico's magics is in the latter's recommendation of Orphic incantations, regarded as natural magic. In his second Orphic conclusion, Pico states as already quoted that:

> In natural magic nothing is more efficacious than the Hymns of Orpheus, if there be applied to them a suitable music, and disposition of soul, and the other circumstances known to the wise.[2]

---

[1] The passage is as follows: ". . . sicut dixi in prima conclusione, refellam omnem Magiam prohibitam ab Ecclesia, illam damnans et detestans, protestans me solum loqui de Magia naturali, et expressius per specialem conclusionem declarans: quod per istam Magicam nihil operamur, nisi solum actuando uel uniendo uirtutes naturales. Sic enim dicit conclusio undecima conclusionum Magicarum. Mirabilia artis Magicae, non sunt nisi per unionem & actuationem eorum, quae seminaliter & separate sunt in nature, quod dixi in 13 conclusione Quod Magiam operari non est aliud quam maritare mundum. Praedictam autem specificationem, & restrictionem intentionis meae, in conclusionibus Magicis, ad Magiam naturalem intendo esse applicandam, cuilibet conclusioni particulari, & ita cum dico, de actiuitate characterum & figurarum, in opere Magico loquor de uera actiuitate sua & naturali. Patet enim, quod talem habent secundum omnes philosophos tam in agendo, quam in modo agendi & patiendi." Pico, pp. 171-2 (*Apologia*).

[2] *Ibid.*, p. 106. See above, p. 79.

And in the third Orphic conclusion, he guarantees that this Orphic magic is not demonic:

> The names of the gods of which Orpheus sings are not those of deceiving demons, from whom comes evil and not good, but are names of natural and divine virtues distributed throughout the world by the true God for the great advantage of man, if he knows how to use them.[1]

It therefore seems that the Natural Magus, as envisaged by Pico, would use the same kind of methods as the Ficinian natural magic, natural sympathies, natural Orphic incantations, magic signs and images naturally interpreted. Amongst these procedures would almost certainly be the use of the talisman as Ficino interpreted it. Pico moved in the same world of imagery as Ficino, as his commentary on Benivieni's *Canzona de Amore* shows, and the Three Graces on his medal should perhaps be understood, at bottom, as in the nature of a Neoplatonised talismanic image against Saturn.[2]

In the oration on the Dignity of Man, which was to have opened the debate on the *Conclusiones* which never took place, Pico repeated all his main themes about magic: that magic is double, one kind being the work of demons, the other a natural philosophy[3]; that the good magic works by *simpatia*, through knowing the mutual rapports running through all nature, the secret charms by which one thing can be drawn to another thing, so that, as the peasant marries the vines to the elm, "so the Magus marries earth to heaven, that is to say the forces of inferior things to the gifts and properties of supernal things."[4] And this meditation on the marvellous powers of Man, the Magus, opens with the words of Hermes Trismegistus to Asclepius; "Magnum, o Asclepi, miraculum est homo."[5] That was the text for the whole sermon, and one which puts Pico's natural magic into the context of the magic of the *Asclepius*.

But, instead of muffling, like Ficino, the connection with the *Asclepius* under layers of commentary on Plotinus or rather mis-

---

[1] *Ibid., loc. cit.*

[2] In the commentary on Benivieni's poem (Pico, p. 742; *De hominis dignitate, etc.*, ed. Garin, pp. 508–9), Pico does not actually equate the Three Graces with the three "good" planets, but, as a disciple of Ficino, he would certainly have known of this.

[3] Pico, *De hominis dignitate, etc.*, ed. Garin, p. 148.

[4] *Ibid.*, p. 152. [5] *Ibid.*, p. 102.

leading quotations from Thomas Aquinas, Pico in those opening words boldly throws down the gauntlet, as though to say, "It is the magic of the *Asclepius* that I am really talking about, and I glory in Man the Magus as described by Hermes Trismegistus."

However, natural magic, according to Pico, is but a weak thing, and no really efficacious magic can be done with it, unless Cabalist magic is added to it.

> Nulla potest esse operatio Magica alicuius efficaciae, nisi annexum habeat opus Cabalae explicitum uel implicitum.[1]

So runs the fifteenth of the magical *Conclusiones*, a severe and uncompromising statement which really knocks out Ficino's magic as fundamentally ineffective because he did not use the higher forces.

> Nulla nomina ut significatiua, & in quantum nomina sunt, singula & per se sumpta, in Magico opere uirtutem habere possunt, nisi sint Hebraica, uel inde proxime deriuata.[2]

This twenty-second magical conclusion is hard on a poor magician who is weak in Hebrew, like Ficino who only knew a few words of that language.

> Opus praecedentium hymnorum (i.e. the Orphic Hymns) nullum est sine opere Cabalae, cuius est proprium practicare omnem quantitatem formalem, continuam & discretam.[3]

Even the Orphic singing, Ficino's pride and joy, is no good for a magical operation without Cabala, according to this twenty-first Orphic conclusion.

These cruel statements by the better-equipped young magician are at least, I think, an absolute guarantee that Ficino's natural magic was *not* demonic, as he claimed. Too pious and careful to attempt to use planetary or zodiacal demons, and too ignorant of Cabala to understand angelic magic, he was content with a natural magic which was harmless but weak. The Magus who combines natural magic with Cabala will be in a different position, for, as Pico explains in the Apology, there are two kinds of Cabala, and one of them is "the supreme part of Natural Magic".

---

[1] Pico, *Opera*, p. 105.　[2] *Ibid.*, *loc. cit.*　[3] *Ibid.*, p. 107.

The Cabala[1] as it developed in Spain in the Middle Ages had as its basis the doctrine of the ten Sephiroth and the twenty-two letters of the Hebrew alphabet. The doctrine of the Sephiroth is laid down in the Book of Creation, or *Sefer Yetzirah*, and it is constantly referred to throughout the *Zohar*, the mystical work written in Spain in the thirteenth century which embodies the traditions of Spanish Cabalism of that time. The Sephiroth are "the ten names most common to God and in their entirety they form his one great Name."[2] They are "the creative Names which God called into the world",[3] and the created universe is the external development of these forces alive in God. This creative aspect of the Sephiroth involves them in a connection with cosmology, and there is a relationship between the Sephiroth and the ten spheres of the cosmos, composed of the spheres of the seven planets, the sphere of fixed stars, and the higher spheres beyond these. A striking feature of Cabalism is the importance assigned to angels or divine spirits as intermediaries throughout this system, arranged in hierarchies corresponding to the other hierarchies. There are also bad angels, or demons, whose hierarchies correspond to those of their good opposites. The theosophical system of the universe on which the infinite subtleties of Cabalist mysticism are based is connected with the Scriptures through elaborate mystical interpretations of the words and letters of the Hebrew text, particularly the book *Genesis* (on which large parts of the *Zohar* are a commentary).

The Hebrew alphabet, for the Cabalist, contains the Name or Names of God; it reflects the fundamental spiritual nature of the world and the creative language of God. Creation from the point of view of God is the expression of His hidden self that gives Itself a name, the holy Name of God,[4] the perpetual act of creation. In contemplating the letters of the Hebrew alphabet and their configurations as constituents of God's name, the Cabalist is contemplating both God himself and his works through the Power of the Name.

The two branches of Spanish Cabalism are thus both based on the Name or Names; they are complementary to each other and

---

[1] On the Cabala, see G. G. Scholem, *Major Trends in Jewish Mysticism* Jerusalem, 1941.

[2] Scholem, *op. cit.*, p. 210.   [3] *Ibid.*, p. 212.   [4] *Ibid.*, p. 18.

intermingled. One branch is called the Path of the Sephiroth[1]; the other the Path of the Names.[2] An expert practitioner of the Path of the Names was the thirteenth-century Spanish Jew, Abraham Abulafia, who developed a most complex technique of meditation through a system for combining the Hebrew letters in endless varieties of permutations and combinations.

Though Cabala is primarily a mysticism, a way of trying to know God, there is also a magic which goes with it, which can be used mystically or subjectively on oneself, a kind of self-hypnosis, as an aid to contemplation, and G. Scholem thinks that this was how Abulafia used it.[3] Or it can be developed into an operative magic,[4] using the power of the Hebrew language, or the powers of the angels invoked by it, to perform magical works. (I am speaking, of course, from the point of view of a mystical believer in magic, like Pico della Mirandola.) The Cabalists evolved many angelic names unknown to the Scriptures (which mention only Gabriel, Raphael, and Michael) by adding to a root term describing the angel's specific function a suffix, such as "el" or "iah", representing the Name of God, and such angelic names invoked or inscribed on talismans had power. Abbreviations of Hebrew words, by the method of Notarikon, or transpositions or anagrams of words by the method of Temurah, were also potent. One of the most complicated of the methods used in practical Cabala, or Cabalist magic, was Gematria which was based on the numerical values assigned to each Hebrew letter involving a mathematics of extreme intricacy, and by which, when words were calculated into numbers and numbers into words the entire organisation of the world could be read off in terms of word-numbers, or the number of the heavenly hosts could be exactly calculated as amounting to 301,655,172. The word-number equation is, like all these methods, not necessarily magic and can be purely mystical; but it was an important feature of practical Cabala through its association with names of angels. There are, for example, seventy-two angels through whom the Sephiroth themselves can be approached, or invoked, by one who knows their names and numbers. Invocations must always be made in the Hebrew tongue, but there are also

---

[1] *Ibid.*, pp. 202 ff.   [2] *Ibid.*, pp. 122 ff.   [3] *Ibid.*, pp. 141-2.
[4] For a rudimentary account of "practical Cabala", or Cabalist magic, see K. Seligmann, *The History of Magic*, New York, 1948, pp. 346 ff.

silent invocations to be made merely by arranging or displaying Hebrew words, letters, signs or signacula.

Amongst the eager activities which Pico undertook for his total synthesis of all knowledge—made at the age of twenty-four—was the learning of Hebrew which he seems to have known quite well, or at least much better than any Gentile contemporary.[1] He had a number of learned Jewish friends, of some of whom we know the names—Elia del Medigo, for example, and Flavius Mithridates. These and others supplied him with the necessary books and manuscripts, and he had probably read the Hebrew Scriptures in their original language, together with many commentaries, including Cabalist commentaries and works. He seems to have had some knowledge of the *Zohar* and of the mystical commentary on the *Song of Solomon*. And G. Scholem has pointed out that he seems to refer to Abraham Abulafia's techniques of letter-combinations.[2] The pious and enthusiastic young man above all valued his Hebrew and Cabalist studies because he believed that they led him to a fuller understanding of Christianity, and certified the truth of the divinity of Christ and the doctrine of the Trinity. His seventy-two Cabalist *Conclusiones* are introduced as "confirming the Christian religion from the foundations of Hebrew wisdom".[3] The sixth conclusion states that the three great Names of God in Cabalist secrets, within the quaternary Name (the Tetragrammaton), refer to the Three Persons of the Trinity.[4] And the seventh conclusion affirms that "No Hebrew Cabalist can deny that the name of Iesu, if we interpret it according to Cabalistic principles

---

[1] For Pico and the Cabala the chief study was formerly J. L. Blau, *The Christian Interpretation of the Cabala in the Renaissance*, Columbia University Press, 1944. But see now the very important essay by G. Scholem, "Zur Geschichte der Anfänge der christlichen Kabbala", in *Essays presented to L. Baeck*, London, 1954; and F. Secret, "Pico della Mirandola e gli inizi della cabala cristiana", in *Convivium*, I, 1957. Of the many books on Pico, the one which concentrates most on Pico and the Cabala is E. Anagnine, *Giovanni Pico della Mirandola*, Bari, 1937.

[2] *Essays presented to L. Baeck*, p. 164, note.

[3] Pico, p. 107. There are two sets of Cabalist Conclusions: (1) a set of 48, said to be drawn straight from the Cabala (*ibid.*, pp. 80–3); (2) a set of 72, according to Pico's "own opinion" (*ibid.*, pp. 107–11). It is the latter set which I am using here.

[4] *Ibid.*, p. 108.

and methods, signifies God, the Son of God, and the wisdom of the Father through the divinity of the Third Person."[1]

Pico, both in his Cabalistic conclusions and in his Apology, distinguishes between different kinds of Cabala. In the first conclusion he says:

> Quicquid dicant caeteri Cabaliste, ego prima diuisione scientiam Cabalae in scientiam Sephirot & Semot, tanquam in practicam & speculatiuam distinguerem.[2]

In the next conclusion, he subdivides "speculative Cabala" into four divisions:

> Quicquid dicant alii Cabalistae, ego partem speculatiuam Cabalae quadruplicem diuiderem, correspondentes quadruplici partitioni philosophiae, quam ego solitus sum afferre. Prima est scientia quam ego uoco Alphabetariae reuolutionis, correspondentem parti philosophiae, quam ego philosophiam catholicam uoco. Secunda, tertia, et quarta pars est triplex Merchiana, correspondentes triplici philosophiae particularis, de divinis, de mediis & sensibilibus naturis.[3]

The first of these parts of speculative Cabala, described as "Catholic" philosophy done with revolving alphabets, is thought by Scholem to refer to letter-combinatory techniques of Abraham Abulafia and his school, the Path of the Names. The second with its allusion to the three worlds—the supercelestial world of the Sephiroth and the angels, the celestial world of the stars, and the sensible or terrestrial world—would presumably correspond to the Path of the Sephiroth.

In the third of the Cabalist conclusions, Pico gives a definition of practical Cabala:

> Scientia quae est pars practica Cabalae, practicat totam metaphysicam formalem & theologiam inferiorem.[4]

Fortunately, he explains himself a little more clearly about the different kinds of Cabala in his Apology. He now abandons the sub-divisions of the speculative Cabala, and makes only two classifications which he calls two sciences both of which are to be honoured with the name of Cabala. One is the *ars combinandi*,

---

[1] *Ibid., loc. cit.*   [2] *Ibid.*, pp. 107–8. Cf. Scholem, *essay cited, loc. cit.*
[3] Pico, p. 108.   [4] *Ibid., loc. cit.*

which would correspond to the Catholic philosophy done with revolving alphabets mentioned in the conclusion on speculative Cabala. And he now says that this art is like "that which is called amongst us the *ars Raymundi*" (that is the Art of Ramon Lull) though its procedures are not quite the same. And the second of the two sciences to be honoured with the name of Cabala is concerned with the powers of those higher things which are above the moon, and it is "the supreme part of natural Magic". He then repeats the two definitions. "The first of these two sciences is the *ars combinandi* which I called in my Conclusions a revolving alphabet; the second is about one way of capturing the powers of superior things, another way of doing which is by natural magic." He adds that Cabala in its original meaning does perhaps not quite apply to both these sciences, but through "transumption" they may both be given the name.[1]

So far as I am able to understand him, therefore, Pico divides Cabala into two main branches. One is the *ars combinandi* which is probably derived from the letter-combinatory mysticism of Abraham Abulafia and which Pico thinks is somewhat similar to the Art of Ramon Lull. This side of Pico's Cabalism I shall entirely exclude from all further discussion here, as it belongs into the history of the Art of Ramon Lull. Here we are solely concerned with Pico's second kind of Cabala, the kind which is a "way of capturing the powers of superior things another way of doing which is by natural magic", and which is "the supreme part of natural magic". Evidently this second kind is magic. It is related to natural magic, but higher. It must go high up beyond the

---

[1] The passage is as follows: "In uniuersali autem duas scientias, hoc etiam nomine honorificarunt, unam quae dicitur ars combinandi, & est modus quidam procedendi in scientiis, & est simile quid, sicut apud nostros dicitur ars Raymundi, licet forte diuerso modo procedant. Aliam quae est de uirtutibus rerum superiorum, quae sunt supra lunam, & est pars Magiae naturalis suprema. Utraque istarum apud Hebraeos etiam dicitur Cabala, . . . et de utraque istarum etiam aliquando fecimus mentionem in conclusionibus nostris: Illa enim ars combinandi, est quam ego in conclusionibus meis uoco, Alphebetariam reuolutionem. est ista quae de uirtutibus rerum superiorum, quae uno modo potest capi, ut pars Magiae naturalis, alio modo, ut res distincta ab ea: est illa de qua loquor in praesenti conclusione, dicens: Quod adiuuat nos in cognitione diuinitatis Christi ad modum iam declaratum, & licet istis duabus scientiis nomen Cabalae, ex primaria & propria impositione non conueniat, transumptiue tamen potui eis applicari." Pico, pp. 180–1 (*Apologia*).

stars, which is all that natural magic aims at, into the super-celestial spheres; or it must have a way of capturing the power of the stars which is stronger than that of natural magic, because it is as it were harnessed to higher forces.

That this kind of Cabala is magic is abundantly proved by Pico's further remarks on it in the Apology.[1] Just as there has been among us, says Pico, a bad form of Magia which is necromancy, and which is not the same thing as the natural magic which he advocates; so there has been among the Hebrews a bad form, a degradation of Cabala. There have been wicked Cabalist magicians, falsely claiming to derive their art from Moses, Solomon, Adam, or Enoch, who said that they knew the secret names of God, and by what powers to bind demons, and have said that it was by such means as this that Christ did his miracles. But of course it is not this wicked kind of false Cabalist magic which Pico is advocating as anyone can understand, for he has expressly pointed out in one of his conclusions that the miracles of Christ could not have been done by way of Cabala. (The seventh of the magical conclusions states that Christ's miracles were not done either by Magia or by Cabala.[2])

These excuses and disclaimers indicate pretty clearly that the methods of good practical Cabalists would be similar to those of the bad ones but used in a good way. They too would use the secret Hebrew names of God and names of angels, invoking them in the powerful Hebrew language or by magic arrangements of the sacred Hebrew alphabet. Bad Cabalists would raise bad angels or demons in this way; good ones would raise good angels. This would be a magic which would go beyond, and be far superior to, natural magic, for it would tap the powers in the supercelestial world, beyond the stars.

Examination of some of Pico's *Conclusiones* will bear out that his Cabalist magic was almost certainly of this kind.

Two of the sets of *Conclusiones* are important for this enquiry, namely the *Conclusiones Magicae* and the *Conclusiones Cabalistae*. The magical conclusions are partly about natural magic and partly about Cabalist magic, and some of them are about both. I have already quoted some of the ones on natural magic, and I

[1] *Ibid.*, p. 181.   [2] *Ibid.*, p. 105.

PICO DELLA MIRANDOLA AND CABALIST MAGIC

shall now quote some of those on Cabalist magic and on both of the magics.

> Quodcunque fiat opus mirabile, siue sit magicum, siue Cabalisticum, siue cuiuscunque alterius generis, principalissime referendum est in Deum. . . .[1]

This, the sixth magical conclusion, is interesting for its definition of the object of magic as doing a "wonderful work", that is a magical operation. It also specifies that such works can be done by different kinds of magic, by Magia (natural magic) or by Cabala, or by other kinds; the last clause would allow for the inclusion of, for example, Orphic magic and Chaldean magic on both of which Pico has something to say in other conclusions. And it solemnly recommends the spirit of piety towards God in which all good magical operations must be undertaken.

I have already quoted earlier the fifteenth magical conlusion which states that no magical operation is effective unless Cabala is added to it, and the twenty-second with its affirmation that no names are powerful for a magical work unless they are in Hebrew, or closely derived from Hebrew. I therefore go on to the twenty-fifth conclusion, which is as follows:

> Sicut characteres sunt proprii operi Magico, ita numeri sunt proprii operi Cabalae, medio existente inter utrosque & appropriali per declinationem ad extrema usu literarum.[2]

Natural magic uses characters, Cabalist magic uses numbers through its use of letters. This is a clear reference to the numerical values of Hebrew letters which are to be taken into account in doing Cabalist magic. There is also a very obscure reference to a connection between the characters of magic and the letter-numbers of Cabala.

> Sicut per primi agentis influxum si sit specialis & immediatus, fit aliquid quod non attingitur per mediationem causarum, ita per opus Cabale si sit pura Cabala & immediata fit aliquid, ad quod nulla Magia attingit.[3]

This, which is the twenty-sixth and last magical conclusion, is very important for the relation of Magia to Cabala. Natural magic

---

[1] *Ibid.*, p. 104. [2] *Ibid.*, pp. 105–6. [3] *Ibid.*, p. 106.

uses only intermediary causes, the stars. Pure Cabala goes immediately to the first cause, to God Himself. It can thus do works to which no natural magic can attain.

Of the Cabalistic conclusions, I have already quoted the first three which define the different kinds of Cabala, and I now select for quotation some of the others. In thinking about the Cabalist conclusions one cannot be quite sure that they are magical in purpose (as the magical conclusions certainly are) or whether some, perhaps most, of them are not purely mystical. Is Pico talking about a mystical ascent of the soul through the spheres to the Sephiroth and the mystical Nothing beyond them? Or does he envisage using magical means for this ascent or at gaining magical powers for operations from it? In a personality such as his, the fine line dividing mysticism from magic is difficult and perhaps impossible to trace.

> Modus quo rationales animae per archangelum Deo sacrificantur, qui a Cabalistis non exprimitur, non est nisi per separationem animae a corpore, non corporis ab anima nisi per accidens, ut contigit in morte osculi, de quo scribitur praeciosa in conspectu domini mors sanctorum eius.[1]

This, the eleventh conclusion, is certainly profoundly mystical. In a supreme trance, in which the soul is separated from the body, the Cabalist can communicate with God through the archangels, in an ecstasy so intense that it sometimes results, accidentally, in the death of the body, a way of dying called the Death of the Kiss. Pico was greatly preoccupied with this experience and mentions the *mors osculi* in his commentary on Benivieni's poem.[2]

> Non potest operari per puram Cabalam, qui non est rationaliter intellectualis.[3]

The operations of pure Cabala are done in the intellectual part of the soul. This immediately marks them off from the operations of natural magic, which are done only with the natural *spiritus*.

---

[1] *Ibid.*, pp. 108–9.

[2] Commentary on Benivieni's *Canzona de Amore*, Lib. III, cap. 8. (Pico, p. 753; *De hominis dignitate, etc.*, ed. Garin, p. 558.)

[3] Pico, p. 109.

Qui operatur in Cabala . . . si errabit in opere aut non purificatus accesserit, deuorabitur ab Azazale. . . .[1]

It is possible that this could refer only to mystical operations, attempts to reach the archangels which go wrong and encounter a bad angel instead. Or it could be one of the usual warnings to magicians of the preparations and purifications necessary before attempting to operate, and of the awful dangers which await a magician who makes a mistake in his magic or attempts to operate when not properly prepared.

The natural magic, which carefully avoided trying to reach star demons had taken precautions against such risks as these. For some of the star demons were good but others bad, hence it was better not to attempt to do anything more than *spiritus* magic. Although Pico's higher magic is angelic and divine, he is not altogether safe, for there are bad angels as well as good angels. Unpleasant though it might be to encounter face to face the tall dark man with red eyes, the Egyptian decan demon for the first face of Aries, it might be even worse to be devoured by this terrible Jewish bad angel, Azazael!

In the forty-eighth Cabalist conclusion, Pico shows that he fully understands that there is a relationship between the ten spheres of the cosmos—the seven spheres of the planets, the eighth sphere or the firmament of fixed stars, the empyrean, and the primum mobile—and the ten Sephiroth or Numerations of Cabala.

> Quicquid dicant caeteri Cabalisticae, ego decem sphaeras, sic decem numerationibus correspondere dico, ut ab edificio incipiendo, Jupiter sit quartae, Mars quintae, Sol sextae, Saturnus septimae, Venus octauae, Mercurius nonae, Luna decimae, tum supra aedificium firmamentum tertie, primum mobilae secundae, coelum empyreum primae.[2]

Though the way in which he is counting here is confusing,[3] Pico is thinking of correspondencies between the ten spheres and the ten Sephiroth such as are sometimes set out as follows:

	Sephiroth	Spheres
(1)	Kether	Primum mobile
(2)	Hokhmah	Eighth sphere
(3)	Binah	Saturn

---

[1] *Ibid., loc. cit.*   [2] *Ibid.*, p. 111.

[3] By starting with the empyrean, instead of the primum mobile, and by misplacing Saturn, Pico seems to confuse the normal order.

(4) Hesod	Jupiter
(5) Gevurah	Mars
(6) Rahimin	Sol
(7) Netsch	Venus
(8) Hod	Mercury
(9) Yesod	Luna
(10) Malkuth	Elements

It is this relationship of the Sephiroth with the spheres of the cosmos which makes of Cabala a theosophy related to the universe. And it is this relationship which makes it possible to speak of Cabalist magic as the completion of natural magic, or a higher form of natural magic, reaching higher spiritual forces which are yet organically related to the stars.

In the sixty-sixth Cabalist conclusion, Pico describes how he "adapts our soul" to the ten Sephiroth, describing them by their meanings, as follows:

Ego animam nostram sic decem Sephirot adapto, ut per unitatem suam fit cum prima, per intellectum cum secunda, per rationem cum tertia, per superiorem concupiscibilem cum quarta, per superiorem irascibilem cum quinta, per liberum arbitrium cum sexta, & per hoc totum ut ad superiora se conuertitur cum septima, ut ad inferiora cum octaua, & mixtum ex utroque potius per indifferentiam uel alternariam adhaesionem quam simultaneam continentiam cum noua, & per potentiam qua inhabitat primum habitaculum cum decima.[1]

This compares with the meanings of the Sephiroth as given by Scholem[2] as follows:

	Pico
Kether: the Supreme	Unity
Hokhmah: Wisdom	Intellect
Binah: Intelligence	Reason
Hesod: Love or Mercy	Superior concupiscence
Gevurah: Power and Wrath	Superior irascibility
Rahimin: Compassion	Free-will
Netsch: Eternity	That through which all converts to superiors
Hod: Majesty	That through which all converts to inferiors
Yesod: Basis	Mixtures, etc.
Malkuth: Kingdom or Glory	The power of the first

[1] Pico, p. 113.
[2] Scholem, *Major Trends*, p. 209.

Pico's meanings are, as can be seen, mostly the same, and he shows understanding of the circular arrangement, or movement, of the Sephiroth through which the last connects with the first.

It is no accident that there are seventy-two of Pico's Cabalist conclusions, for the fifty-sixth conclusion shows that he knew something of the mystery of the Name of God with seventy-two letters:

> Qui sciuerit explicare quaternarium in denarium, habebit modum si sit peritus Cabalae deducendi ex nomine ineffabili nomen 72 literarum.[1]

All that we need to retain of the mysteries of the Cabalist conclusions is that Pico knew in some form the outline of the Path of the Sephiroth and its connections with the cosmos, and that this was why Cabala connected with natural magic as its higher form. From the magical conclusions, we know that he did envisage doing practical Cabala, or Cabalist magic, though the details of the way in which he did this only the initiated can explain. More could doubtless be learned from Reuchlin's *De arte cabalistica* (1517)[2] in which several of Pico's Cabalist conclusions[3] are quoted and commented upon and in which the practitioner of Cabala could learn much that was not explained by Pico, for instance that angels, who are voiceless, are better communicated with by *signacula memorativa* (Hebraic mnemonic signs) than by speaking their names.[4] Reuchlin treats at length of the letter-number calculations, gives many names of angels, including those of the seventy-two who form the Name of God (Vehuiah, Ieliel, Sitael, Elemiah, and so on)[5] and instructions how to summon the more familiar Raphael, Gabriel, and Michael.[6] Through Reuchlin, Pico's Cabalist magic leads straight on to the angel magic of Trithemius or of Cornelius Agrippa, though these magicians were to work it in a more crudely operative spirit than the pious and contemplative Pico.

Pico's oration on the Dignity of Man echoes throughout with the words Magia and Cabala; these are the basic themes of his

---

[1] Pico, p. 112.

[2] Johannes Reuchlin, *De arte cabalistica*, Haguenau, 1517.

[3] For example, the 19th magical conclusion is quoted (*ed. cit.*, p. 58 *recto*) and the first Cabalist conclusion (p. 64 *recto*).

[4] *Ibid.*, p. 56 *verso*.   [5] *Ibid.*, p. 58 *verso*.   [6] *Ibid.*, p. 57 *recto*.

whole song. After the opening quotation from Trismegistus on man, the great miracle, comes the main eulogy of natural magic,[1] after which the speaker passes on to the mysteries of the Hebrews and the secret tradition stemming from Moses.[2] The oration is full of secrets not fully revealed. The Egyptians sculptured a sphinx on their temples to show that the mysteries of their religion must be guarded under a veil of silence.[3] The Cabala of the Hebrews contains mysteries handed on under a seal of silence.[4]

Sometimes he comes near to revealing a secret:

> And if it is permissible, under the veil of enigma, to mention in public something of the most secret mysteries . . . we invoke Raphael, the celestial doctor that he may liberate us with ethics and dialectics, like a salutary physician. In us, now restored to good health, will dwell Gabriel, the force of the Lord, who *leading us through the miracles of nature and showing us where dwell the virtue and power of God*, will present us to Michael, the high priest, who, after our service to philosophy, will crown us, as with a crown of precious stones, with the priesthood of theology.[5]

How do we invoke Raphael, Gabriel, and Michael, so that they dwell in us with all their powers and knowledge? Do we perhaps know their secret names and numbers? Is there a secret of practical Cabala at the core of this lofty mystical aspiration?

The praise of magic and of man as Magus in the oration is couched in general rhetorical terms, and only hints at the secrets of magical procedures. But it is certainly in praise of both Magia and Cabala, and it would therefore seem that the complete Renaissance Magus, as he burst upon the world for the first time in Pico's oration in his full power and Dignity, was a practitioner of both natural magic and also of its "supreme form", practical Cabala.

In his study of Ficino's magic, D. P. Walker has suggested that it was probably mainly subjective, that is to say he used it chiefly on himself.[6] It worked through the imagination, by conditioning the imagination through various ways of life and rituals towards receiving inwardly the divine forms of the natural gods. It was

---

[1] Pico, *De hominis dignitate etc.*, ed. Garin, pp. 102 ff., 152 ff., etc.
[2] *Ibid.*, pp. 155 ff., etc.   [3] *Ibid.*, p. 157.   [4] *Ibid.*, *loc. cit.*
[5] *Ibid.*, pp. 129, 131.   [6] Walker, pp. 82–3.

the magic of a highly artistic nature, heightening the artistic perceptions with magical procedures. The same is probably true of Pico's use of practical Cabala, that it was mainly a subjective use of Cabalist magic by a deeply religious and artistic nature. In what forms—perhaps more sublimely beautiful in his imagination than even the angelic forms painted by a Botticelli or a Raphael—did Raphael, Gabriel, and Michael come to dwell with Pico della Mirandola?

And perhaps it is also chiefly in this imaginative and artistic sense that we should understand the influence of the Renaissance magic of the type inaugurated by Ficino and Pico. The operative Magi of the Renaissance were the artists, and it was a Donatello or a Michelangelo who knew how to infuse the divine life into statues through their art.

The double magic of Pico brought magic quite inevitably within the sphere of religion. If even Ficino's mild cult of the natural gods as a kind of medical therapy involved him in difficulties with theologians, Pico's difficulties from the same quarter were bound to be much graver and deeper, for, by harnessing natural magic to Cabala, he took magic right up into the supercelestial world of divine and angelic powers. The cult which went with the religious magic, as compared with, for example, the solar rites of natural magic, was the religious cult itself. In the *Heptaplus* it is said that, in order to unite ourselves with the higher natures, we must follow the cult of religion with hymns, prayers, and supplications[1]; and in the Orphic conclusions, the "hymns of David", that is the Psalms, are spoken of as incantations as powerful for the work of Cabala, as the hymns of Orpheus are of value for natural magic.

> Sicut hymni Dauid operi Cabalae mirabiliter deseruiunt, ita hymni Orphei operi ueri licitae, & naturalis Magiae.[2]

Thus a practical Cabalist singing a psalm is performing a rite similar to the natural magician intoning an Orphic hymn—similar, but more powerful, because we are told in another Orphic conclusion, which I quoted above, that the Orphic hymns have no power unless "the work of Cabala" is added to them. It is difficult to understand how Cabala could be done at the same time as Orphic singing. Possibly Pico simply means that Psalm singing

[1] Pico, *De hominis dignitate*, etc., ed. Garin, pp. 319, 321.
[2] Pico, *Opera*, p. 106.

should alternate with Orphic singing. Or perhaps it is done with an *intentio animae* towards the true God above nature whilst singing the hymns to the natural gods. Or could it be through influence of religious chanting on the hymns to the natural gods, which would also work the other way, as a memory of the hymns to the natural gods within the religious hymns to the God of David sung in church? The problem is perhaps insoluble, but in thinking of it we are in the presence of a problem which was to agitate later controversies about religion in relation to magic, namely, should a religious reform involve putting more magic into religion, or taking the magic out of it? If one puts the problem, not only in these terms, but in terms of magical and wonder-working images in Christian churches the possible relevance of this tremendous Renaissance emphasis on religious magic to the Reformation and its iconoclasm is a question which begins to raise its head.

The connection between magic and Christianity in Pico's formulations is made even closer and more formidable by his extraordinary claim that Magia and Cabala help to prove the divinity of Christ. The seventh of the magical conclusions is as follows:

> Nulla est scientia, que nos magis certificet de diuinitate Christi, quam Magia & Cabala.[1]

What exactly he meant by this amazing statement is nowhere fully explained, but this was the conclusion to which most exception was taken, which raised a storm of protest, and which he concentrated on apologising for and defending in his Apology.[2] Some of the Cabalist conclusions refer to the power of Cabala for confirming the divinity of Christ.

> 7 Nullus Hebraeus Cabalista potest negare, quod nomen Iesu, si eum secundum modum & principia Cabalae interpretemur, hoc totum praecise & nihil aliud significat, id est Deum Dei filium patrisque sapientiam per tertiam diuinitatis personam, quae est ardentissimus amoris ignis, naturae humanae in unitate suppositi unitum.

> 15 Per nomen Iod, he uau, he, quod est nomen ineffabile, quod dicunt Cabalistae futurum esse nomen Messiae, euidenter cognoscitur futurum eum Deum Dei filium per spiritum sanctum hominem factum, & post eum ad perfectionem humani generis super homines paracletum descensurum.[3]

[1] *Ibid.*, p. 105.   [2] *Ibid.*, pp. 166 ff.
[3] *Ibid.*, pp. 108, 109. Cf. also Cabalist conclusions, 14, 16 (*ibid.*, p. 109).

It was thus, through Cabalistic letter-manipulations that the ecstatic young man perceived with rapture that IESU is indeed the name of the Messiah, the Son of God.

But how did Magia also prove the divinity of Christ? I have no explanation of this to offer, unless it is to be supposed that Pico thought of the Eucharist as a kind of Magia. Readers interested in this problem may be referred to Pico's treatise on the Eucharist,[1] in which I have not been able to find any definite use of the word Magia.

So, with the utmost confidence and boldness, the most devout Christian mystic, Pico della Mirandola, advanced to his defence Magia and Cabala. Far from being magics in which a Christian must not dabble, they are, on the contrary, magics which confirm the truth of his religion and lead him into a greater spiritual awareness of its mysteries. And yet, this was a double-edged tool which Pico was using in defence of his religion, and he was aware of its other dangerous cutting edge, which he guarded against in the seventh magical conclusion, repeated with great emphasis in his Apology:

> Non potuerant opera Christi, uel per uiam Magiae, uel per uiam Cabalae fieri.[2]

If Magia and Cabala have such power, was it by these means that Christ did his wonderful works? No, says Pico with the utmost emphasis. But later magicians were to take up this dangerous thought.

There is yet another aspect of Pico's crucially important position in the history of our subject. The Magia of the oration is ultimately derivable from the magic of the *Asclepius*, a derivation which Pico boldly emphasises when he begins the speech with Hermes Trismegistus on the great miracle of man. Thus, in yoking together Magia and Cabala, Pico was really marrying Hermetism to Cabalism, a union—which, as emphasised earlier in this chapter, Pico was the first to bring about—from which was to spring a progeny of Hermetic-Cabalists, composers of works of vast complexity and infinite obscurity as numerous as they are baffling.

[1] *Ibid.*, pp. 181 ff.
[2] *Ibid.*, p. 105; in *Apologia, ibid.*, pp. 166 ff., 181, etc.

In the last chapter, it was suggested that the mediaeval magic was reformed and superseded in the Renaissance by the new style philosophic magic. There was also a type of mediaeval magic which used names of angels, names of God in Hebrew, invocations in bastard Hebrew and curious magical arrangements of letters and diagrams. Magicians ascribed such magics as these to Moses, and more particularly to Solomon, and one of the most characteristic text-books of this type of magic was the work known as the *Clavis Salomonis*[1] which was widely circulated surreptitiously in variant forms. It is probably of this type of work that Pico is thinking when he says that his practical Cabala has nothing to do with wicked magics going under the name of Solomon, Moses, Enoch, or Adam, by which demons were conjured by bad magicians.[2] When seen in the context of the lofty philosophical mysticism of Cabala and from the stand-point of some real knowledge of Hebrew and the mystique of the Hebrew alphabet, those old magics were seen to be not only wicked, but also ignorant and barbarous. They are replaced by practical Cabala, the learned Hebrew magic which takes its place beside the learned Neoplatonic magic as one of the two disciplines which together make up the equipment of the Renaissance Magus.

We begin to perceive here an extraordinary change in the status of the magician. The necromancer, concocting his filthy mixtures, the conjuror, making his frightening invocations, were both out-casts from society, regarded as dangers to religion, and forced into plying their trades in secrecy. These old-fashioned characters are hardly recognisable in the philosophical and pious Magi of the Renaissance. There is a change in status almost comparable to the change in status of the artist from the mere mechanic of the Middle Ages to the learned and refined companion of princes of the Renaissance. And the magics themselves are changed almost out of recognition. Who could recognise the necromancer studying his *Picatrix* in secret in the elegant Ficino with his infinitely refined use of sympathies, his classical incantations, his elaborately Neo-platonised talismans? Who could recognise the conjuror, using the barbarous techniques of some *Clavis Salomonis*, in the mystical Pico, lost in the religious ecstasies of Cabala, drawing archangels to his side? And yet there is a kind of continuity because the

[1] Thorndike, II, pp. 280–1.
[2] Pico, p. 181 (*Apologia*).

techniques are at bottom based on the same principles. Ficino's magic is an infinitely refined and reformed version of pneumatic necromancy. Pico's practical Cabala is an intensely religious and mystical version of conjuring.

Just as the old necromancy was ultimately derivable from late antique types of magic which flourished in the context of the Hermetism, or pagan gnosticism of the early centuries A.D., so did the old conjuring go back to the same period and the same type of sources. Names of angels, names of God in Hebrew, Hebrew letters and signs, are a feature of gnostic magic in which pagan and Jewish sources are inextricably mingled. This mingling continues in the later tradition. There are, for example, names of Jewish angels in *Picatrix*, and the authorship of some "Keys of Solomon" is ascribed to "Picatrix".[1] Thus both the Renaissance Magia and its Cabala could be regarded as reformed revivals of magics ultimately derivable from pagan and Jewish gnosticism.

Moreover, the two theoretical contexts in which the two kinds of magic revive in the Renaissance—namely the *Hermetica* and Cabala—are both gnostic in origin. The *Hermetica* are collections of documents of pagan gnosticism of the early centuries A.D. in some of which (particularly the account of creation in *Pimander*) there is Jewish influence. And, as the researches of G. Scholem have recently emphasised, there is a strong gnostic influence in early Jewish Cabala,[2] and underlying the Neoplatonism with which it was mingled in the Spanish Cabalism of the Middle Ages. He has drawn attention, in particular, to one most interesting example of this. In the pagan gnostic theory of the ascent of the soul through the spheres, in which it casts off the influences of matter, its final regeneration takes place in the eighth sphere where the Powers and Virtues of God enter into it. I resumed an example of this doctrine in the second chapter, in the outline of "Egyptian Regeneration" from *Corpus Hermeticum* XIII with its description of the entry of the Powers into the regenerated soul in the eighth, or "ogdoadic" sphere, after which the Powers sing in the soul the "ogdoadic hymn" of regeneration.[3] Scholem has shown that in the

---

[1] Thorndike, II, p. 281, note 1.

[2] G. Scholem, *Jewish Gnosticism, Merkabah Mysticism, and the Talmudic Tradition*, New York, 1960; see also Scholem's *Major Trends* on gnostic influence on the Cabala.

[3] See above, pp. 28–30.

Hekhaloth literature (one of the predecessors of Cabala) there is exactly the same conception, the divine Glory and Power being thought of as in the eighth sphere, and even the word "ogdoas" is translated into Hebrew.[1]

Now, curiously enough, Pico della Mirandola saw a connection between Hermetism and Cabala, and what he saw is perhaps almost the same as what Scholem has arrived at by his scholarly methods. Pico draws ten *Conclusiones* from Hermes Trismegistus, which come just before the Cabalist conclusions. The ninth of these Hermetic conclusions is as follows:

> 9 Decem intra unumquemque sunt ultores, ignorantia, tristitia, inconstantia, cupiditas, iniustitia, luxuries, inuidia, fraus, ira, malitia.[2]

Pico is quoting from *Corpus Hermeticum* XIII as translated by Ficino where the twelve "punishments" of matter are translated as "ultores" and their names are translated[3] exactly as Pico gives them here, except that he has left out two of them, making only ten "punishments" or evil material forces, instead of twelve. It will be remembered that in *Corpus Hermeticum* XIII, the twelve "punishments", deriving from the zodiac and representing man under the power of the stars, are driven out by ten good forces or Powers and Virtues of God, and when the decade has driven out the dodecade, the soul is redeemed and sings the "ogdoadic" song. Pico had a reason for reducing the "ultores" to ten, for he wanted to make a comparison with Cabala in his following, and tenth, Hermetic conclusion.

> 10 Decem ultores, de quibus dixit secundum Mercurium praecedens conclusio, uidebit profundus contemplator correspondere malae coordinationi denariae in Cabala, & praefectis illius, de quibus ego in Cabalisticis conclusionibus nihil posui, quia est secretum.[4]

I believe that this means that Pico thinks that the Hermetic "punishments" correspond to ten evil things[5] in Cabala which are driven out by their good opposites—that is by the ten Sephiroth—in an experience of which he did not speak in the Cabalist con-

---

[1] Scholem, *Jewish Gnosticism*, pp. 65 ff.
[2] Pico, p. 80.   [3] See above, pp. 30–1.   [4] Pico, *loc. cit.*
[5] According to S. L. MacGregor Matthews, *The Kabbalah Unveiled*, London, 1951, the evil opposites of the Sephiroth would be the ten arch-devils, Satan, Beelzebub, and so on.

clusions, because it was too secret and holy to divulge. That is to say (or so I interpret it), Pico believes that the fundamental experience of the Cabalist, when the ten Sephiroth or Powers and Names of God, take up their abode in his soul, having driven out all evil forces, is the same as the experience of the Hermetist when the Powers, having driven out the Punishments, come to dwell in him and sing within him the "ogdoadic" hymn of regeneration.

If my interpretation of these Hermetic conclusions is correct, then it was not only on the level of their magics that Pico married together Hermetism and Cabalism, but on the very deep level of the actual structure of their religious experience, having perceived a basic similarity between the Hermetic system of the Powers and their opposites in a cosmic framework, and the Cabalist system of the Sephiroth and their opposites, also in a cosmic framework.

For Pico this remarkable essay in comparative religion would not take the critical form of a recognition of gnostic elements in Cabala comparable with Hermetic gnosticism. For him the comparison would be a rapturous realisation that what the Egyptian Moses, Trismegistus, teaches about the Powers and the Punishments is the same as what Moses, as reported by the Cabalists, teaches about the Sephiroth and their opposites.

The deepest root of the Renaissance revaluation of magic as a spiritual force allied to religion lies in the Renaissance interest in gnosticism and the *Hermetica*, to which, as we have just seen, Pico was able to relate his interest in Cabala. Much new work has been done in recent years on Hermetism in the Renaissance and it may eventually become apparent that both Ficino's Neoplatonism and Pico's attempted synthesis of all philosophies on a mystical basis are really, at bottom, an aspiration after a new gnosis rather than a new philosophy. At any rate, it was their immersion in the atmosphere of gnosis through their veneration for Hermes Trismegistus which led Ficino and Pico to their religious approach to magic and to their placing of the Magus on a lofty pinnacle of insight, a position very different from that held by the vulgar necromancers and conjurors in former less enlightened times.

Finally, it may be pointed out that the Dignity of Man the Magus in Pico's famous oration rests on a gnostic text, not on a patristic text. Pico does not quote the whole of the passage in the *Asclepius* on man the great miracle with which his oration opens, and which, in its context, claims that miraculous man is, in his origin, divine:

And so, O Asclepius, man is a *magnum miraculum*, a being worthy of reverence and honour. For he goes into the nature of a god as though he were himself a god; he has familiarity with the race of demons, knowing that he is of the same origin; he despises that part of his nature which is only human for he has put his hope in the divinity of the other part.[1]

The Fathers of the Church had placed man in a dignified position, as the highest of terrestrial beings, as spectator of the universe, as the microcosm containing within himself the reflection of the macrocosm. All these orthodox notions are in the oration on the Dignity of Man,[2] but the Dignity of Man as Magus, as operator, having within him the divine creative power, and the magical power of marrying earth to heaven rests on the gnostic heresy that man was once, and can become again through his intellect, the reflection of the divine *mens*, a divine being. The final revaluation of the magician in the Renaissance is that he becomes a divine man. Once again one is reminded of a parallel with the creative artists for this was the epithet which their contemporaries awarded to the great, of whom they often speak as the divine Raphael, or the divine Leonardo, or the divine Michelangelo.

Ficino, as we saw from his Apology, encountered difficulties from theologians because of his magic. Since Pico had been much bolder than Ficino, his difficulties were much more serious, and the Pico case became a theological *cause célèbre* which was long remembered. The main facts of the story can be very briefly resumed as follows.[3] Owing to serious murmurs among Roman theologians about the heretical character of some of Pico's theses, Pope Innocent VIII was obliged to appoint a commission to go into the matter. Pico appeared several times before this commission to answer for his views. Eventually, several of the theses were

[1] *C.H.*, II, pp. 301–2 (*Asclepius*); see above, p. 35.

[2] See E. Garin's study, "La 'Dignitas hominis' e la letteratura patristica", in *La Rinascita* (Florence, 1938), IV, pp. 102–46.

[3] See L. Dorez and L. Thuasne, *Pic de la Mirandole en France*, Paris, 1897. Particularly valuable for the bearing of Pico's case on the problem of magic is the discussion by Thorndike (VI, pp. 484–511) which I have largely followed.

categorically condemned, amongst them the magical conclusion
in which Pico states: *Nulla est scientia que nos magis certificet de
divinitate Christi quam magia et cabala.* Despite his condemnation,
Pico published his Apology, together with part of the oration on
the Dignity of Man. The edition is dated May, 1487, but this date
has been questioned. In the Apology, he defended his condemned
propositions. This publication naturally involved him in fresh
difficulties, and bishops with inquisitorial powers were appointed
to deal with his case. In July, 1487, Pico made a formal submission
and retraction to the commission, and in August the Pope issued
a bull condemning all the theses and forbidding their publication,
but exculpating Pico because of his submission. Nevertheless, when
Pico fled to France, papal nuncios were sent after him to obtain
his arrest, and he was for a time imprisoned at Vincennes, though
his case was viewed with a good deal of sympathy in France, both
in court and in university circles amongst whom his use of the
teachings of the Parisian schoolmen in many of the theses was
appreciated. He was allowed to return to Italy bearing French
royal letters in his favour, and he was constantly supported by
Lorenzo de' Medici who interceded for him with the Pope. He
was therefore allowed to live in Florence, though under rather a
cloud, and his way of life was one of extreme piety and asceticism,
under the influence of Savonarola. He died in 1494, on the day
that the French king's armies entered Florence.

In 1489, a long reply to Pico's Apology was published by Pedro
Garcia, a Spanish bishop who had been one of the commission
which examined Pico. Garcia's work has been analysed by Thorndike,[1] who has pointed out its great importance for the history of
the attitude to magic. A large part of the work is concerned with
refuting Pico's thesis that "there is no science which gives us more
assurance of Christ's divinity than magic and the Cabala." Garcia
is opposed to magic of any kind, all of which is evil and diabolical
and contrary to the Catholic faith. He does not deny astrological
theory and the consequent existence of occult sympathies, but
states that these cannot be known or used by man except by
diabolical assistance. He strongly condemns the use of astrological
images, that is talismans, and refutes a Spanish theologian who
has been trying to insinuate that Thomas Aquinas allowed their

[1] Thorndike, IV, pp. 497–507.

use. All this argument might, no doubt, be instructively compared with Ficino's tortuous attempts to draw in Thomas Aquinas in his defence of his talismans. The *De vita coelitus comparanda* was published in the same year as Garcia's book.

In connection with his condemnation of astrological images, Garcia has also to deal with those who have been saying that astrological magic can be as free from demonic influences as "ecclesiastical magic", such as the use of wax lambs blessed by the pope, or the blessing of bells. Garcia denies this, strongly affirming that Christian observances are not efficacious by virtue of the stars, but solely through the omnipotent power of the creator. Finally, Garcia denies the antiquity of Cabala.

Garcia's work is thus not only a condemnation of magic in itself but a refutation of the suggestion that "ecclesiastical magic" could have any connection with it.

In the next century, Archangelo de Burgo Nuovo wrote a defence of Pico against Garcia (printed at Venice in 1569),[1] and these two works—Garcia's and Archangelo's—may be said to epitomise the arguments for and against the connection of magic with religious practices which raged in the sixteenth century and to which D. P. Walker has drawn attention in his book.[2] The basic case for this controversy is the Pico case, and the arguments used by Pico's attackers and defenders.

In the last years of his life, Pico's situation was greatly eased by the advent to office in 1492 of a new pope. In that year, Innocent VIII was succeeded as the spiritual head of Christendom by Alexander VI, the Borgia pope, one of the most publicised and colourful characters of the Renaissance. Unlike his predecessor, the Borgia pope was not at all averse to astrology and magic, but, on the contrary, was deeply interested in those subjects, and he came most impressively to the rescue of Pico's orthodoxy. The bulls for Pico's absolution which Lorenzo de Medici had failed to obtain from Innocent VIII, in spite of repeated appeals, were promulgated by Alexander VI on June 18th, 1493, less than a year

---

[1] *Ibid.*, p. 507. Archangelo also wrote an exposition of Pico's Cabalistic Conclusions (*Cabalistarum delectiora . . . dogmata, a Ioanne Pico excerpta*, Venice, 1569).

[2] Walker, pp. 151, 153 ff.; 178–85, etc.

after his elevation to the Holy See.[1] Not only that, the Pope wrote a personal letter to Pico himself, beginning "Dilecte fili Salute & apostolicam benedictionem." In this letter, Alexander rehearses the whole history of Pico's case, mentioning the nine hundred theses, the *Apologia*, the commission which had accused Pico of heresy, his flight to France, and ends by completely absolving both him and his works from all taint from heresy. Pico is described as illuminated by a "divina largitas" and as a faithful son of the Church. This letter was printed in all the editions of Pico's works,[2] thus encouraging readers to accept, on the highest authority, the writer's views as of unimpeachable orthodoxy. And this would include the view which was the chief cause of the outcry against Pico, and of the commission which Alexander quashed, that Magia and Cabala are valuable aids to Christianity.

It was in this changed atmosphere that Pico wrote, about 1493–4, his *Disputationes adversus astrologiam divinatricem*. This work against astrology used to be taken as proof that Pico was free from astrological superstition. But its title alone shows that the kind of astrology which Pico is against is divinatory astrology, the normal astrology based on belief in the determination of man's fate by the stars and using calculations based on horoscopes to foretell the predestined future. And it has recently been pointed out[3] that Pico repeats in this book what is practically Ficino's theory of astral influences borne on a "celestial spirit". Further, Pico actually cites "our Marsilius" as one of those who have written against astrologers "following in the traces of Plotinus, in the interpretation and exposition of whom he has much aided Platonic studies, amplifying and enlarging them."[4] This could be an allusion to that commentary on Plotinus, the *De vita coelitus comparanda* and its *Magia naturalis* (including Plotinised talismans) as a work indirectly defended through being drawn in amongst those against

---

[1] Thorndike, IV, pp. 493, 560; Dorez and Thuasne, *Pic de la Mirandole en France*, p. 103; P. de Roo, *Material for a History of Pope Alexander VI*, Bruges, 1924, III, pp. 26–7. The letter which Pico wrote to Alexander in 1492 asking him to consider his case is printed in L. Dorez, "Lettres inédites de Jean Pic de la Mirandole", *Giornale storico della letteratura italiana*, XXV (1895), pp. 360–1.

[2] In the edition of Bâle, 1572, it is on the back of the title-page.

[3] Walker, pp. 54–5.

[4] Pico della Mirandola, *Disputationes adversus astrologiam divinatricem*, ed. E. Garin, Florence, 1946, p. 60.

3 Pinturicchio, Hermes Trismegistus with the Zodiac, Room of the Sibyls,
Appartamento Borgia, Vatican (p. 115)

4 Pinturicchio, Mercury killing Argus, Room of the Saints,
Appartamento Borgia, Vatican (p. 116)

5 Pinturicchio, Isis with Hermes Trismegistus and Moses, Room of the Saints, Appartamento Borgia, Vatican (p. 116)

6 (a) Pinturicchio, Egyptian worship of Apis, Room of the Saints, Appartamento Borgia, Vatican (p. 116)

6 (b) Apis bulls worshipping the Cross, Detail of frieze, Room of the Saints, Appartamento Borgia, Vatican (p. 116)

astrology.[1] In short, Pico is really defending the Ficinian "astral magic" (he does not use this expression) which, as emphasised in the last chapter, is quite a different thing from astrology proper being a way of escape from astrological determinism by teaching how to control and use the stellar influences. Written about 1493-4, that is at about the time that the Pope had exonerated Pico from all blame, the book against astrology is really a vindication of *Magia naturalis*.

It is into the context of the controversy about Pico, in which Alexander VI came out so strongly on the side of the Magus, that one should put the extraordinary "Egyptianism" in the frescoes painted by Pinturicchio for Alexander in the Appartamento Borgia in the Vatican. These frescoes were studied by F. Saxl,[2] who pointed out that within an orthodox programme there are strange allusions. In the first room are twelve Sibyls, uttering their prophecies of the coming of Christ, and twelve Hebrew prophets. I would suggest that Lactantius and the Siena pavement teach us to look for the greatest Gentile prophet, Hermes Trismegistus, as likely to be present in the Room of the Sibyls, and I think he is there, as the prophetic figure with the zodiac (Pl. 3) who ends the series of the planets, above the Sibyls. In the next room are twelve prophets with the twelve apostles; the Christianity foretold by Hebrew and Gentile prophets has arrived, represented by the apostles. In the following rooms come the seven liberal arts, with Astrology the most prominent, seven saints, and seven scenes from the life of the Virgin. It is, so far, a perfectly orthodox programme.

But very strange are the Egyptian scenes in the Room of the Saints. The emblem of the Borgia family was the bull, and the Borgia bull becomes identified in this series with Apis, the bull worshipped by the Egyptians as the image of Osiris, the sun god It is by a series of allusive shifts in meaning as the frescoes tell their story that the Egyptian Apis bull, or the sun, becomes identified with the Borgia bull, or the Pope as the sun. The Egyptian series begins with the story of Io, turned into a cow by

[1] But it could also refer to Ficino's criticisms of "bad" astrology in his commentaries on Plotinus; cf. Walker, p. 54. In any case, the point is that if Pico regards Ficino as a writer against astrology, then the kind of astrology which Pico is against cannot be the Ficinian type of Neo-platonised astral magic.

[2] F. Saxl, "The Appartamento Borgia", in *Lectures*, Warburg Institute, University of London, I, pp. 174-88; II, Pls. 115-24.

Juno, who set Argus to watch her. Argus was killed by Mercury, a scene shown in one of the paintings where Mercury, with drawn sword, is despatching Argus (Pl. 4). Having been rescued by Mercury from Argus, Io escaped into Egypt where she became the goddess Isis. After the scene with Mercury and Argus, there follows in the frescoes, a scene where Io-Isis is seated on a throne (Pl. 5), with a figure on her left identified by Saxl as Moses. The figure on her right is obviously the same person as the one shown with the zodiac in the Room of the Sibyls (Pl. 3). He is, I suggest, again Hermes Trismegistus, now shown with Moses.

The Mercury who killed Argus was, according to Cicero, Hermes Trismegistus who afterwards went into Egypt and gave the Egyptians their laws and letters. This is mentioned by Ficino in the *argumentum* before his *Pimander*:

> Hunc (i.e. Trismegistus) asserunt occidisse Argum, Aegyptiis prae-fuisse, eisque leges, ac litteras tradidisse.[1]

Hence, the Mercury in the fresco who kills Argus would be Hermes Trismegistus, and the next scene would show him in Egypt, as the lawgiver of the Egyptians, with, beside him, the law-giver of the Hebrews, Moses. This would be the usual Hermes-Moses comparison with which we have become so familiar in our study of Magia and Cabala.

Why did the Pope have such a programme painted early in his reign, a programme which glorifies the Egyptian religion (Pl. 6a), shows the Egyptian Apis bulls worshipping the Cross (Pl. 6b), associates Hermes Trismegistus with Moses? The answer to this question is, I believe, that the Pope wished to proclaim his reversal of the policy of his predecessor by adopting Pico della Mirandola's programme of using Magia and Cabala as aids to religion.

The profound significance of Pico della Mirandola in the history of humanity can hardly be overestimated. He it was who first boldly formulated a new position for European man, man as Magus using both Magia and Cabala to act upon the world, to control his destiny by science. And in Pico, the organic link with religion of the emergence of the Magus can be studied at its source.

---

[1] See above, pp. 2, 14.

Chapter VI

〜〜〜〜〜〜〜〜〜〜〜〜〜〜〜〜〜〜〜〜〜〜〜〜〜〜〜〜〜〜

PSEUDO-DIONYSIUS AND THE THEOLOGY OF A CHRISTIAN MAGUS

〜〜〜〜〜〜〜〜〜〜〜〜〜〜〜〜〜〜〜〜〜〜〜〜〜〜〜〜〜〜

SAINT DIONYSIUS the Areopagite was, for Ficino, both *culmen* of Platonism,[1] and the saint whom St. Paul had met at Athens, and whose vision of the nine angelic hierarchies, unquestioningly accepted by Thomas Aquinas and all the doctors of the Church, had become an integral part of orthodox Christian theology.[2] Saint Dionysius is constantly referred to in Ficino's *Theologia Platonica* and *De Christiana Religione*, the two works in which he set out his synthesis of Platonism with Christianity, and indeed, not only for Ficino but also for all later Christian Neoplatonists, Dionysius was one of the main Christian allies.

The author of the *Celestial Hierarchies* was, of course, not really the Areopagite with whom St. Paul spoke but an unknown writer who composed under strong Neoplatonic influence his work on nine orders of angels which he grouped into triads, each group of three representing one of the Persons of the Trinity. These nine angelic orders have their abode far above, or beyond the spheres of the universe, being orders of a purely spiritual or divine nature.

[1] See R. Klibansky, *The Continuity of the Platonic Tradition*, London, Warburg Institute, 1939, pp. 42 ff.

[2] Hence he was, for Ficino, not only the *culmen* of Platonism but the *columen* of Christian theology (Commentary on Dionysius' *Liber de Trinitate*; Ficino, p. 1013).

Nevertheless, though the Dionysian orders are not, strictly speaking, a cosmological religion, there is something in the whole idea of orders set out in this fashion which recalls the gnostic religion of the world, or religious experience in the setting of the cosmic orders. R. Roques has drawn attention to the parallels between the Dionysian mysticism and gnosticism, particularly of the Hermetic type, and has suggested a possible influence of Hermetism on the hierarchies.[1]

Thus, once again the phenomenon of misdating comes into play in the Renaissance synthesis, and the great Christian apologist who is believed to have been contemporary with St. Paul really belonged to nearly the same period as the misdated *prisci theologi*,[2] and came within the range of gnostic ways of thinking.

In the fourteenth chapter of the *De Christiana religione*, Ficino sets out the cosmic order completed by the nine spiritual orders, as follows:

The four elements, which are mutable in substance and quality.

The seven planets, which are not mutable in substance, but are so in quality and disposition.

The eighth sphere, whose movement is opposite to that of the planets and which has the qualities of *candor* and *splendor*.

The Chrystalline sphere, which has simple motion and the quality of *candor*.

The Empyrean, where all is stable and the *lumen* of which is a quality of light superior to *candor*.

In the stable and *lucens* Empyrean is accommodated the Trinity expressed in the nine orders of angels of Dionysius. There are legions of angels in the orders and their number exceeds the faculty of human computation. The nine orders are:

Seraphim, Cherubim, Thrones; the hierarchy of the Father.

Dominions, Virtues, Powers; the hierarchy of the Son.

Principalities, Archangels, Angels; the hierarchy of the Spirit.[3]

Ficino interprets Dionysius as having said that the first order drinks its liquor from the Trinity direct (*liquorem suum a sola*

---

[1] R. Roques, *L'univers dionysien*, Paris, 1954, pp. 240 ff.

[2] Recent scholarship is tending to put the Pseudo-Dionysian writings a good deal earlier than the sixth century A.D., the date formerly conjectured. See Eleuterio Elorduy, *Ammonio Sakkas. I. La doctrina de la creación y del mal en Proclo y el Ps. Areopagita*, Burgos, 1959, pp. 23 ff.

[3] *De Christiana religione*, cap. XIV (Ficino, p. 19).

haurit Trinitate), the second gets it through the first, and the third through the second and first. There is also a division of activities among the hierarchies, as follows:

Seraphim speculate on the order and providence of God.

Cherubim speculate on the essence and form of God.

Thrones also speculate, though some descend to works.

Dominions, like architects, design what the rest execute.

Virtues execute, and move the heavens, and concur for the working of miracles as God's instruments.

Powers watch that the order of divine governance is not interrupted and some of them descend to human things.

Principalities care for public affairs, nations, princes, magistrates.

Archangels direct the divine cult and look after sacred things.

Angels look after smaller affairs and take charge of individuals as their guardian angels.[1]

Ficino's notions on the celestial hierarchies have been modified by two intermediaries, namely Thomas Aquinas and Dante, and he has also introduced new modifications of his own. The differing activities of the hierarchies, which are not so specifically defined in Pseudo-Dionysius, he got from Thomas Aquinas.[2] The linking of the hierarchies with the spheres of the cosmos he got from Dante who, in his *Convivio* correlates the hierarchies with the spheres[3] and, above all, in the *Paradiso*, sets out the souls of the blest on the spheres of the seven planets; places the Apostles and the Church Triumphant in the eighth sphere; in the ninth sphere ranges the nine angelic hierarchies; and crowns all with the Trinity in the Empyrean.

Ficino was a great student of Dante, and was certainly thinking of the *Paradiso* in the passage on the hierarchies analysed above for he makes a reference to Dante's poem in it.[4] The analysis of the varying quality of the light, expressed by different words for

[1] *Ibid.*, *loc. cit.*

[2] *Summa Theologiae*, Pars I, quaest. 108, articles 5, 6. Cf. M. de Gandillac, "Astres, anges et génies chez Marsile Ficin", in *Umanesimo e esoterismo*, ed. E. Castelli, Padua, 1960, p. 107. Aquinas' source for varying activities of the hierarchies was Gregory, *Homil. 34 in Evang.* (Migne, *Patr. Lat.*, 76, cols. 1250–1) which Ficino might also have been using.

[3] Dante, *Convivio*, Lib. II, cap. 6.

[4] Dante is not mentioned by name, but the last words of the chapter on the grades of punishments of the wicked contrasted with the orders of the blessed in heaven refers to the *Inferno* and *Paradiso*. The opening of the chapter on souls returning to their star recalls *Paradiso*, IV, 49–54.

light, in Ficino's exposition may possibly be due to the influence of Dante. The notion that the supernal light is reflected down the angelic hierarchies, flashing as in mirrors from one to another, is a characteristically Dionysian conception, to which Dante had given a somewhat new turn by describing how, as he and Beatrice mount through the spheres of the planets, the light changes in quality at each ascent, reaching ever more dazzling degrees of intensity in the eighth sphere, the ninth sphere and the Empyrean. Ficino, in the passage analysed above, seems to be definitely using, *splendor* of light in the eighth sphere, *candor* of a more intense light in the chrystalline sphere, and *lumen* of the supreme light in the Empyrean (beyond which there is perhaps an even higher *lux* in the divine mind). He also uses such many varying terms for light in his *De sole*[1] and *De lumine*,[2] though I am not sure that the terms are always used consistently with the same degrees of meaning.

Ficino has intensified the continuity between hierarchies and spheres by introducing an almost astrological suggestion into the relationships between the hierarchies, which are said to "drink" the influences from the Trinity, a word which recalls the expression used in the *De vita coelitus comparanda* where the *spiritus* of the world is thought of as poured out through the stars and drunk by its recipients here below. And if we add one more term to the light series, the term "Sol" for the planet Sol or the Sun, the drinking in of *spiritus* from the Sun would connect with the higher series, the higher "liquor" drunk by the hierarchies, and the higher forms of light flashed down from the light supernal.[3]

Thus Ficino's natural or *spiritus* magic, aiming no higher than the planets and particularly at the Sun, would yet have an angelic continuation stretching out beyond and above it. Though Ficino, or so I believe, would make no attempt to "operate" with angels, beyond the normal Christian prayers and supplications, nor try to reach the Virtues which move the heavens in order to become a worker of miracles.

---

[1] Ficino, pp. 965–75.   [2] *Ibid.*, pp. 976–86.
[3] This transition is definitely made in the *De sole*, which first discusses the planet Sol and its central importance and, in the last chapter, compares the Sun to the Trinity and the nine orders of angels (*De sole*, cap. XII; Ficino, p. 973).

The angelic continuation beyond the stars was of course normal to Christian thought, and is, for example, exquisitely expressed in terms of music by Shakespeare's Lorenzo:

> Sit, Jessica. Look how the floor of heaven
> Is thick inlaid with patines of bright gold:
> There's not the smallest orb which thou beholdst
> But in his motion like an angel sings,
> Still quiring to the young-eyed cherubins. . . .[1]

Lorenzo, as he gazes at the night sky, is contemplating the marvellous fact that the harmony of the spheres connects with the celestial choirs of the angelic hierarchies.

As Pseudo-Dionysius was immensely important to Ficino for the synthesis of Neoplatonism with Christianity so, too, he helped Pico to build the bridge between Jewish Cabala and Christianity. Pico's *Heptaplus*, which is a commentary on *Genesis* in the Cabalistic manner, is full of references to Dionysius.

In this work, Pico frequently has occasion to mention the "three worlds" as understood by the Cabalists, who divided the universe into the elemental world or terrestrial world, the celestial world or the world of the stars, and the supercelestial world. Between all these worlds there was continuity of influences. Pico found no difficulty in linking this concept both with Neoplatonism and with the Christian or Pseudo-Dionysian mysticism.

He makes the link with Neoplatonism by identifying (as Ficino had also done) the angelic world with what the philosophers call the intelligible world. The highest of the three worlds is called "by the theologians angelic, and by the philosophers, intelligible"; then comes the celestial world, and last the sublunar world which we inhabit.[2] He then goes on to draw the parallel with the three worlds of the Cabalists, which Moses represented symbolically when he divided the tabernacle into three parts.[3] Particularly in the third book of the *Heptaplus* Pico devotes himself to assimilating the doctrines of the "ancient Hebrews" to those of Dionysius. Here he repeats the Thomistic definitions of the functions of the

---

[1] *Merchant of Venice*, V, i.
[2] Pico, *De hominis dignitate, Heptaplus*, etc., ed. Garin, p. 185.
[3] *Ibid.*, p. 187.

hierarchies and relates their three triadic groups to the three worlds, as follows:

> We read (that is in Cabalistic commentary on *Genesis*) that the firmament is placed in the midst of the waters; and here is indicated to us the three hierarchies of angels. . . . The first and the last (of the hierarchies) is indicated by the waters, those which are above the firmament and those which are below it; the intermediate zone between the two being the firmament. And if we ponder these things we find that they accord perfectly with the doctrine of Dionysius: the supreme hierarchy which, as he says, is given over to contemplation, is figured in the waters above the firmament which are above all action, whether celestial or terrestrial, and praise God with a perpetual music. The intermediate hierarchy, which has celestial functions, is most appropriately indicated by the firmament, that is the heaven itself. The last hierarchy, although by its nature it is above all bodies and above the heaven, yet it has the care of things below the heaven, since it is divided into Principalities, Archangels, and Angels, whose activities all refer to sublunar things, those of Principalities being directed towards states, kings, and princes; those of Archangels, to the mysteries and sacred rites; whilst Angels attend to private matters and each of them is assigned to an individual human being. Thus, with reason, the last hierarchy is figured by the waters below the firmament, since they preside over mutable and transient things. . . .[1]

By thus assigning the first hierarchy to the supercelestial world (waters above the firmament), the second hierarchy to the celestial world (firmament), and the third hierarchy to the elemental or sublunar world (waters below the firmament), Pico "astrologises" the celestial hierarchies even more strictly than Ficino, by allowing them these special influences in the three zones. There is no trace of such astrologising tendency in Pseudo-Dionysius himself, for whom the nine hierarchies both represent the Trinity and are solely devoted, in their several degrees, to the praise of the Trinity.

With Ficino's "hierarchising" of different qualities of light, may be compared Pico's hierarchical presentation of heat. "With us, *calor* is an elemental quality; in the heavens (that is in the stars) it is calorific virtue; in the angelic mind it is the idea of *calor*."[2]

It may well be, as E. Garin has suggested,[3] that in the proem to

---

[1] *Ibid.*, pp. 255, 257.   [2] *Ibid.*, p. 189.
[3] E. Garin, *Giovanni Pico della Mirandola*, Florence, 1937, pp. 194 ff.

the third book of the *Heptaplus*,[1] where he refers mysteriously to some perhaps deeper connection between the teachings of Dionysius and those of the "ancient Hebrews", Pico means to suggest a comparison of the Dionysian hierarchies with the Sephiroth. In the Sephiroth also, there is a certain gradation, the highest of them being concerned with pure contemplation of unutterable mysteries whilst the lower ones seem to have more connection with the affairs of men. There is a circular movement in the Sephiroth (which Pico shows that he has understood in Cabalist conclusion 66) by which the first can connect with the last; such a movement is also understood within the apparently Byzantine fixity of the angelic hierarchies, since these in their sum represent the Trinity. Pico nowhere, so far as I can discover, sets out a definite correlation between Sephiroth and angelic hierarchies, though this was certainly done in the later Hermetic-Cabalist tradition, for example by Robert Fludd, as can be seen in the diagram (Pl. 7a) in one of his works in which ten Cabalistic Names of God, the ten Sephiroth (the names of which are written on the verticals) and the ten spheres are put together with the nine celestial hierarchies, whose number is brought up to the necessary ten by adding to them *anima mundi*. It is possible that Pico might have given his blessing to some such correlation as this, though we cannot be sure that he would have made it in exactly this form. In another diagram (Pl. 8) Fludd correlates hierarchies and spheres with the twenty-two letters of the Hebrew alphabet.

The difference between Ficino and Pico within the angelic plus cosmological framework is that Pico, through practical Cabala, has a means of reaching and operating with the angelic world which was denied to Ficino. The Cabalistic angels would be for Pico fundamentally the same as the myriads of Pseudo-Dionysian angels,[2] the change being that Cabala gave more information about them and how to make contact with them.

---

[1] Pico, *De hominis dignitate, Heptaplus etc.*, ed. Garin, p. 247.

[2] In the second Cabalistic conclusion (in the set of 48), Pico says: "Nouem sunt angelorum hierarchiae, quarum nomina Cherubim, Seraphim, Hasmalim, Hagot, Aralim, Tarsisim, Ophanim, Thephrasim, Isim" (Pico, p. 81). These are the names of Cabalistic orders of angels (through whom the Sephiroth are approached, as the Trinity is approached through the Dionysian hierarchies) but Pico gives only nine of them

If we look (Pl. 9) at the frontispiece of a work published in 1646 by the Jesuit, Athanasius Kircher, who was a most notable descendant of the Hermetic-Cabalist tradition founded by Pico, we see there the Name in Hebrew surrounded by rays and clouds in which hosts of angels are indicated. Below them is the celestial world, with the zodiac; and below that is the sublunary world, over which rules the Archduke Ferdinand III. The fundamental conceptions outlined in this chapter have not changed, and the illustration shows how well the baroque style, with its sun-glories and swarms of angels goes with such conceptions.

Another way in which Pseudo-Dionysius was immensely important in the Renaissance synthesis was through his negative theology. Besides his positive adumbration of aspects of the God-head, in the nine hierarchies of angels in their relation to the Trinity, Dionysius also sets forth a "negative way". There are no words for God in His actual essence; no names for Him as He really is; therefore He is at the last best defined by negatives, by a kind of darkness, by saying that He is not goodness, not beauty, not truth, meaning by this that He is nothing that we can under-stand by those names. The mysticism of the Dionysian negative way brought forth some very beautiful spiritual fruits in the course of the ages, for example the English fourteenth-century *Cloud of Unknowing*, in which the unknown author, following the Hid Divinity of Denis,[1] puts himself under a cloud of unknowing within which, with a blind stirring of love,[2] he reaches forth towards the *Deus Absconditus*. And the learned philosopher Nicholas of Cusa found in the "learned ignorance" of Dionysius the only final solution, or mode of approach to the divine, as he expounds in his famous work the *De docta ignorantia*. The nega-tive theology or the idea of the negative way reached Ficino not only through Dionysius but also through Cusanus, of whom he was a great admirer, and whom he regarded as an important link in the great chain of Platonists.[3]

[1] *Deonise Hid Divinitie* (ed. P. Hodgson, Early English Text Society, 1955) is the title of a mystical treatise related to the *Cloud of Unknowing*.

[2] *Cloud of Unknowing*, ed. Justin McCann, London, 1925, p. 19.

[3] Klibansky, *op. cit.*, pp. 42, 47.

(there should be ten) and begins the list with Cherubim and Seraphim which do not come first in the Cabalistic order. His object must surely have been to bring the Cabalistic orders as close as possible to the nine Dionysian hierarchies.

Ficino made a new translation of Dionysius *On the Divine Names* in which there are various passages on the negative theology and on the thought that God is beyond all knowledge. God, says Dionysius, is above *Bonitas*, above *Essentia*, above *Vita*, above *Veritas*, above all his other names, so that in a sense he has no name. Yet in another sense he has innumerable names for he is the *Bonitas, Essentia, Vita, Veritas*, and so on in all things.[1] Ficino's commentary on this passage is as follows:

> These mysterious sayings of Dionysius are confirmed by Hermes Termaximus, who says that God is nothing, and yet that God is all. That God has no name, yet God has every name.[2]

He is thinking of the passage in the *Asclepius*, where Trismegistus says:

> It is impossible that the creator of the majesty of the All, the father and lord of all beings, should be designated by one or even by a multiplicity of names. God has no name, or rather he has all names, since he is at once One and All, so that one must either designate all things by his name, or give him the name of all things. . . . His will is entirely good, and the *bonitas* which exists in all things is issued from the divinity.[3]

The Hermetic writer is certainly here very close in spirit to the Syrian monk, and it is no wonder that Ficino was impressed by the way Hermes Trismegistus confirms Saint Dionysius on No Name yet All Names.

There is a negative theology also in the Hebrew Cabalistic mysticism, for the Ensoph, out of which the ten Sephiroth emerge, is the Nothing, the unnameable, unknown *Deus Absconditus*, and the highest and most remote of the Sephiroth, Keter or the Crown, disappears into the Nothing.[4] So that here, too, though there are as it were Ten Names in the Sephiroth, the highest is the Nothing or the No Name.

I cannot find that Pico anywhere relates the Ensoph to the Dionysian negative theology, though the fifteenth Orphic conclusion is significant:

---

[1] Pseudo-Dionysius, *Divine Names*, I.
[2] Ficino, p. 1034.
[3] *C.H.*, II, p. 321 (*Asclepius*, 30).
[4] See Scholem, *Major Trends in Jewish Mysticism*, pp. 12 ff.

Idem est nox apud Orpheum, & Ensoph in Cabala.[1]

It would be but a short step, in Pico's mind, from the Orphic *nox* to the Dionysian darkness. There is a similar mystical conception in the Platonic conclusions:

Ideo amor ab Orpheo sine oculis dicitur, quia est supra intellectum.[2]

This describes in terms of the blind Cupid the same "negative" experience as that of which Dionysius speaks.

It is the only clue to Pico's synthesis that he makes it on a mystical level, the many Names which he collects from all philosophies and religions being at bottom all one in the No Name. And the great Christian authority on the *via negativa* was Pseudo-Dionysius.

This chapter has not been specifically about the two magics, but an attempt to reconstruct the religious and cosmological framework into which they belong. It is most important for trying to understand the tenuous and delicate relations between religion and magic in the Renaissance to realise that there is at work a tendency towards astrologising mysticism, and, conversely, towards mysticising astrology. These are clumsy words to use of the Renaissance experience in which it is difficult to distinguish the moment when the supercelestial becomes merged with the celestial, and thence descends to the terrestrial. When does the supernal light drunk by the hierarchies from the Trinity become the light of the Sun, whence the whole heaven is illuminated, and which is drunk through *spiritus* in Magia? Or at what moment do the techniques of practical Cabala become ecstatic contemplation of Hebrew and Christian supercelestial hierarchies?

The problem can also be put in terms of Eros. In the Hermetic account, in *Pimander*, of the creation of the Magus Man, this half-divine being came down below because he loved beautiful nature and was united to her in a passionate embrace.[3] The erotic relation to nature is fundamental for sympathetic magic; the Magus enters with loving sympathy into the sympathies which bind earth to heaven, and this emotional relationship is one of the

[1] Pico, p. 107.
[2] *Ibid.*, p. 96 (sixth Platonic conclusion).
[3] *C.H.*, I, p. 11 (*Pimander*); see above, p. 24.

chief sources of his power. "Why is Love called a Magus?" asks Ficino in the commentary on the *Symposium*. "Because all the force of Magic consists in Love. The work of Magic is a certain drawing of one thing to another by natural similitude. The parts of this world, like members of one animal, depend all on one Love, and are connected together by natural communion. . . . From this community of relationship is born the communal Love: from which Love is born the common drawing together: and this is the true Magic."[1] In the Pseudo-Dionysian celestial hierarchies there is a current running between them all which he calls Eros and compares to a perpetual circle arising from the Good and returning to the Good.[2] M. de Gandillac has pointed out that, in another passage of the *Symposium* commentary,[3] Ficino has deformed this erotic current, giving it a sense quite absent in Pseudo-Dionysius where it is a gift of pure grace, and he sees in this deformation "the magical theme of universal sympathy".[4]

So, as with Light, again with Love, there is a kind of continuity between the operative love of the Magus and the divine love circulating amongst the celestial hierarchies. Once again, the point at which erotic magic might become participation in divine love, or at which the Magus might appear robed in supercelestial light and love, is not easy to distinguish. And the concept is immediately transferable into Neoplatonic terms, for the Neoplatonic *mens* is identified by Ficino and Pico with the "angelic mind". All these shades of meaning concur to give many complex undertones and overtones to such a work as Pico's commentary on the *Canzona de Amore* of Benivieni. Where is the magic in such a commentary on a love poem? Where is the Christian cum Cabalist mysticism? Where is the Neoplatonic mysticism? The guiding line in this maze is the poeticised astrology with which the commentary is full, and by which the transition is made from mystical magic to magical mysticism.

Those strange and deceptively simple conversations in the Hermetic treatises between Hermes and his son Tat, or with Asclepius

---

[1] *Commentarium in Convivium Platonis de amore*, oratio VI, cap. 10 (Ficino, p. 1348).

[2] Pseudo-Dionysius, *Divine Names*, IV, 14, 15; *Celestial Hierarchies*, I, 2.

[3] *In Convivium*, oratio III, cap. 2 (Ficino, p. 1329).

[4] M. de Gandillac, *article cited*, p. 99.

and other followers, convey a strong impression that a deep religious experience has been felt by the participants. And these religious experiences take place within the framework of the world, and are consummated in the eighth sphere when the Powers take possession of the soul. And the religion to which they belong is the "Egyptian" religion of astral magic. Believing as he did that the Hermetic dialogues strangely prophesied Christian truths, Ficino was encouraged to put Christian experience into the framework of the world. By real and perspicacious attempts at comparative religion, though made on a wrong chronological basis, Ficino and Pico perceived resemblances between the Hermetic religious scheme and the Neoplatonised Christianity of Pseudo-Dionysius, to which Pico was able to add comparisons with Cabalist theosophy. And they were in a sense right since all these three theosophic schemes are related to the religion of the world, or can be connected with the spheres of the universe.

The Hermetic treatises have been divided by Festugière into those representing an optimist type of gnosis in which the cosmos which is the setting for the religious experience is good and full of the divinity; and a pessimist or dualist type in which salvation must consist in escaping from the weight of matter permeated by influences which are in themselves evil. It is possible, as I suggested earlier,[1] that these distinctions were blurred for a Renaissance reader. How little Ficino understood dualism is indicated by the fact that he took Ormuzd, Mithras, and Ahriman to be the expression among the Magi of Persia of the truth pervading all religions that God is a Trinity,[2] whereas Ahriman is the evil principle in the uncompromisingly dualist Zoroastrian system. With this determination to find adumbrations of Christian truths everywhere, he would be likely to ignore, or to misunderstand as an "Egyptian" version of Christian asceticism, the dualist aspects of the *Hermetica*. Moreover, many of the most influential of the Hermetic treatises, including the *Asclepius*, are far from dualist and tend more in the direction of pantheism. The Cabala, in so far as it can be called a gnosis, is also optimist. Whilst Pseudo-

---

[1] See above, p. 33.

[2] *Theologia Platonica*, IV, 1 (Ficino, p. 130); *In Convivium*, II, 4 (*ibid.*, p. 1325). This extraordinary statement was repeated after Ficino in the later Renaissance; see below, p. 174.

Dionysius is surely the supreme type of a Neoplatonist illuminated by Christian optimism.

The word gnosis is applicable to the kind of experience which Ficino and Pico had, since it was a seeking of knowledge by religious methods. But it must be understood that when "gnosticism" is used in this book to describe the Renaissance experience, it is used without those irrevocably dualist or Manichaean implications with which it has become associated.

Chapter VII

❖❖❖❖❖❖❖❖❖❖❖❖❖❖❖❖❖❖❖❖❖❖❖❖❖❖❖❖

CORNELIUS AGRIPPA'S SURVEY
OF RENAISSANCE MAGIC

❖❖❖❖❖❖❖❖❖❖❖❖❖❖❖❖❖❖❖❖❖❖❖❖❖❖❖❖

HENRY CORNELIUS AGRIPPA of Nettesheim[1] is by no means the most important of the magicians of the Renaissance, nor is his *De occulta philosophia* really a text-book of magic, as it has sometimes been called. It does not fully give the technical procedures, nor is it a profound philosophical work, as its title implies, and Cardanus, a really deep magician, despised it as a trivial affair.[2] Nevertheless the *De occulta philosophia* provided for the first time a useful and—so far as the abstruseness of the subject permitted—a clear survey of the whole field of Renaissance magic. Since my book is not written by a really deep magician who fully understands the procedures, but is only a humble historian's attempt to outline those parts of the subject which affect the understanding of Giordano Bruno (who, incidentally, made great use of this trivial work) and his place in the sequence of magical thinking, I propose to devote a chapter to Agrippa's popular book on the occult philosophy.

[1] On Agrippa, see Thorndike, V, pp. 127 ff.; Walker, pp. 90 ff. Selections from Agrippa, including one chapter of the *De occulta philosophia*, are published by Paola Zambelli, with useful introduction and notes, in *Test. uman.*, pp. 79 ff. See also her article, in which further bibliography is given, "Umanesimo magico-astrologico" in *Umanesimo e esoterismo*, ed. E. Castelli, Padua, 1960, pp. 141 ff.

The *De occulta philosophia* was first published in 1533. I have used the edition in H. C. Agrippa, *Opera*, "Per Beringos fratres, Lugduni", s.d., Vol. I.

[2] Thorndike, V, p. 138.

He had completed the work by 1510, but did not publish it until 1533, that is several years after the publication of his *De vanitate scientiarum* (1530) in which he had proclaimed that all sciences are vain, including the occult sciences. Since Agrippa's major interest, up to the end of his life, was undoubtedly in the occult sciences, the publication of the book on the vanity of such sciences *before* the publication of his survey of those sciences in the *De occulta philosophia* can probably be regarded as a safety-device of a kind frequently employed by magicians and astrologers for whom it was useful, in case of theological disapproval, to be able to point to statements made by themselves "against" their subjects, by which, however, they usually mean that they are only against bad uses of such knowledge, not their own good uses.

The universe is to be divided, says Agrippa in the first two chapters of his first book, into three worlds, the elemental world, the celestial world, the intellectual world. Each world receives influences from the one above it, so that the virtue of the Creator descends through the angels in the intellectual world, to the stars in the celestial world, and thence to the elements and to all things composed of them in the elemental world, animals, plants, metals, stones, and so on. Magicians think that we can make the same progress upwards, and draw the virtues of the upper world down to us by manipulating the lower ones. They try to discover the virtues of the elemental world by medicine and natural philosophy; the virtues of the celestial world by astrology and mathematics; and in regard to the intellectual world, they study the holy ceremonies of religions. Agrippa's work is divided into three books; the first book is about natural magic, or magic in the elemental world; the second is about celestial magic; the third is about ceremonial magic. These three divisions correspond to the divisions of philosophy into physics, mathematics, and theology. Magic alone includes all three. Eminent magicians of the past have been Mercurius Trismegistus, Zoroaster, Orpheus, Pythagoras, Porphyry, Iamblichus, Plotinus, Proclus, Plato.[1]

Book I or Natural Magic

After chapters on the theory of the four elements, he comes to the occult virtues in things and how these are infused "by

[1] Agrippa, *De occult. phil.*, I, 1 and 2; *ed. cit.*, pp. 1–4.

the Ideas through the World Soul and the rays of the stars."[1]
This is based on the first chapter of Ficino's *De vita coelitus comparanda*, which is quoted verbally, and Agrippa has understood that Ficino is there talking about the star images as the medium through which the Ideas descend. "Thus all the virtues of inferior things depend on the stars and their images . . . and each species has a celestial image which corresponds to it."[2] In a later chapter on "The Spirit of the World as the Link between Occult Virtues"[3] he is again quoting Ficino and reproducing his *spiritus* theory.[4] Then follow chapters on the plants, animals, stones, and so on belonging to each planet, and to the signs of the zodiac, and on how the "character" of the star is imprinted in the object belonging to it, so that if you cut across the bone of a solar animal or the root or stem of a solar plant, you will see the character of the sun stamped upon it. Then come instructions on how to do natural magic by manipulations of the natural sympathies in things and thus through arrangements and correct uses of the lower things to draw down the powers of the higher things.[5]

So far, what Agrippa has been talking about is Ficino's natural magic as done in the elemental world that is through occult stellar virtues in natural objects. But, as D. P. Walker has pointed out,[6] Agrippa does not follow Ficino in taking care to avoid the demonic side of this magic by aiming only at attracting stellar influences and not the influences of spiritual forces beyond the stars. For you can draw down in this way, says Agrippa, not only celestial and vital benefits (that is benefits from the middle or celestial world) but also intellectual and divine gifts (that is benefits from the intellectual world). "Mercurius Trismegistus writes that a demon immediately animates a figure or statue well composed of certain things which suit that demon; Augustine also mentions this in the eighth book of his *City of God*."[7] Agrippa fails to add that Augustine mentions this with strong disapproval. "For such

[1] *Ibid.*, I, 11; *ed. cit.*, p. 18.
[2] *Ibid.*, *loc. cit.*; *ed. cit.*, p. 19.
[3] *Ibid.*, I, 14; *ed. cit.*, p. 23.
[4] He is quoting from *De vita coelitus comparanda*, 3 (Ficino, p. 534). This, and other borrowings from Ficino, are pointed out by Walker, pp. 89–90.
[5] Agrippa, *De occult. phil.*, I, 15–37; *ed. cit.*, pp. 24–53.
[6] Walker, p. 92.
[7] *De occult. phil.*, I, 38; *ed. cit.*, p. 53.

is the concordance of the world that celestial things draw super-celestial things, and natural things, supernatural things, through the virtue running through all and the participation in it of all species."[1] Hence it was that ancient priests were able to make statues and images which foretold the future. Agrippa is aiming at the full demonic magic of the *Asclepius*, going far beyond the mild Neoplatonised magic of Ficino which he has been describing in the earlier chapters. He knows that there is an evil kind of this magic, practised by "gnostic magicians" and possibly by the Templars, but adds that everyone knows that a pure spirit with mystical prayers and pious mortifications can attract the angels of heaven, and therefore it cannot be doubted that certain terrestrial substances used in a good way can attract the divinities.[2]

There follow chapters on fascination, poisons, fumigations (perfumes sympathetic to the planets and how to make them), unguents and philtres, rings,[3] and an interesting chapter on light.[4] Light descends from the Father to the Son and the Holy Spirit, thence to the angels, the celestial bodies, to fire, to man in the light of reason and knowledge of divine things, to the fantasy, and it communicates itself to luminous bodies as colour, after which follows the list of the colours of the planets. Then we have gestures related to the planets, divinations, geomancy, hydromancy, aeromancy, pyromancy, *furor* and the power of the melancholy humour. There is then a section on psychology followed by discussion of the passions, their power to change the body, and how by cultivating the passions or emotions belonging to a star (as love belonging to Venus) we can attract the influence of that star, and how the operations of the magician use a strong emotional force.[5]

The power of words and names is discussed in the later chapters of the book,[6] the virtue of proper names, how to compose an incantation using all the names and virtues of a star or of a divinity. The final chapter is on the relation of the letters of the Hebrew alphabet to the signs of the zodiac, planets, and elements

[1] *Ibid.*, *loc. cit.*
[2] *Ibid.*, I, 39; *ed. cit.*, pp. 54–5.
[3] *Ibid.*, I, 40–8; *ed. cit.*, pp. 55–68.
[4] *Ibid.*, I, 49; *ed. cit.*, pp. 68–71.
[5] *Ibid.*, I, 50–69; *ed. cit.*, pp. 71–109.
[6] *Ibid.*, I, 69–74; *ed. cit.*, pp. 109–17.

which give that language a strong magical power. Other alphabets also have these meanings but less intensely than the Hebrew.

Book II. Celestial Magic

Mathematics are most necessary in magic, for everything which is done through natural virtue is governed by number, weight, and measure. By mathematics one can produce without any natural virtue, operations which seem natural, statues and figures which move and speak. (That is, mathematical magic can produce the living statues with the same powers as those made by using occult natural virtues, as described in the *Asclepius* which Agrippa has quoted on such statues.) When a magician follows natural philosophy and mathematics and knows the middle sciences which come from them—arithmetic, music, geometry, optics, astronomy, mechanics—he can do marvellous things. We see to-day remains of ancient works, columns, pyramids, huge artificial mounds. Such things were done by mathematical magic. As one acquires natural virtue by natural things, so by abstract things— mathematical and celestial things—one acquires celestial virtue, and images can be made which foretell the future, as that head of brass, formed at the rising of Saturn.[1]

Pythagoras said that numbers have more reality than natural things, hence the superiority of mathematical magic to natural magic.[2]

There follow chapters on the virtues of numbers and number groupings, beginning with One which is the principle and end of all things, which belongs to the supreme God. There is one sun. Mankind arose from one Adam and is redeemed in one Christ.[3] Then come chapters on two to twelve,[4] with their meanings and groupings, as Three for the Trinity[5]; three theological virtues; three Graces; three decans in each sign; three powers of the soul; number, measure, and weight. The letters of the Hebrew alphabet have numerical values and these are most potent for number magic. Then follows an exposition of magic squares, that is numbers arranged in a square (either the actual numbers or their

[1] *Ibid.*, II, 1; *ed. cit.*, pp. 121–3.
[2] *Ibid.*, *loc. cit.*; *ed. cit.*, p. 123.
[3] *Ibid.*, II, 4; *ed. cit.*, pp. 125–7.
[4] *Ibid.*, II, 5–14; *ed. cit.*, pp. 127–62.
[5] *Ibid.*, II, 6; *ed. cit.*, pp. 129–31.

Hebrew letter equivalents) which are in accordance with planetary numbers and have power to draw down the influence of the planet to which they are related.[1]

Then comes a treatment of harmony and its relation to the stars, harmony in the soul of man, the effects of music rightly composed in accordance with universal harmony in harmonising the soul.[2]

After the long discussion of number in celestial magic, we have a very long discussion of images in celestial magic,[3] with long lists of such images, images for the planets, images for the signs, nor does Agrippa fear actually to *print* the images of the thirty-six decan demons.

First of all he explains the general principles of the making of talismans imprinted with celestial images. We need not go into this again and a few examples from his image-lists will suffice. One image of Saturn is "a man with a stag's head, camel's feet, on a throne or on a dragon, with a sickle in the right hand, an arrow in the left."[4] An image of Sol is "a crowned king on a throne, a crow at his bosom, a globe under his feet, robed in yellow".[5] An image of Venus is "a girl with loose hair wearing long white robes, holding in the right hand a branch of laurel or an apple or a bunch of flowers, in the left hand a comb."[6] The Saturn image correctly made on a talisman gives long life; the Sol image gives success in all undertakings and is good against fevers; the Venus image gives strength and beauty. The images of the thirty-six decans of the zodiac begin,[7] with the alarming first decan of Aries: "a black man, standing and dressed in a white robe, very huge and strong, with red eyes, and seeming angry." Agrippa also gives images for the mansions of the moon and for fixed stars other than those in the zodiac.[8] He thus provided a whole repertoire of images for talismans to be used in celestial magic. He also describes how images may be made, not to resemble any celestial figure, but to represent the wish and intention of the operator, for example, to procure love we might make an image of people embracing.[9] This opens up a wide field for original invention in talismanic imagery.

[1] *Ibid.*, II, 22; *ed. cit.*, pp. 174 ff.   [2] *Ibid.*, II, 24; *ed. cit.*, pp. 184 ff.
[3] *Ibid.*, II, 35–47; *ed. cit.*, pp. 212–25.   [4] *Ibid.*, II, 38; *ed. cit.*, p. 217.
[5] *Ibid.*, II, 41; *ed. cit.*, p. 219.   [6] *Ibid.*, II, 42; *ed. cit.*, p. 220.
[7] *Ibid.*, II, 37; *ed. cit.*, pp. 214–17.
[8] *Ibid.*, II, 46, 47; *ed. cit.*, pp. 221–5.
[9] *Ibid.*, II, 49; *ed. cit.*, pp. 227–8.

This is enough to say about images," concludes Agrippa, "for you can now go on for yourself to find others. But you must know that these kind of figures are nothing unless they are vivified so that there is in them . . . a natural virtue, or a celestial virtue, or a heroic, animastic, demonic, or angelic virtue. But who can give soul to an image, life to stone, metal, wood or wax? And who can make children of Abraham come out of stones? Truly this secret is not known to the thick-witted worker . . . and no one has such powers but he who has cohabited with the elements, vanquished nature, mounted higher than the heavens, elevating himself above the angels to the archetype itself, with whom he then becomes co-operator and can do all things.[1]

Which shows how far, far behind him Agrippa has left the timid and pious Ficino, who aimed only at doing natural magic in the elemental world, with just a spot of celestial magic from a few planetary talismans, used naturally. The Agrippan Magus aims at mounting up through all three worlds, the elemental world, the celestial world, the intellectual or angelic or demonic world, and beyond even that to the Creator himself whose divine creative power he will obtain. The door into the forbidden which Ficino had left only slightly ajar is now fully opened.

Agrippa's incantations also aim higher than Ficino's Orphic singing. Agrippa discusses the Orphic magic and how the divinities which he names in his hymns are not evil demons but divine and natural virtues established by God for the use of men and which are called upon in these hymns.[2] Agrippa gives lists of names, attributes, powers of the planets to be used in invocations to them, above all the Sun is to be called upon by "whoever wishes to do a marvellous work in this lower world". The ambitious Magus should attract the influence of the Sun in every possible way, praying to him not only with the lips but with a

[1] ". . . & haec de imaginibus dicta sufficiant, nam plura ejusmodi nunc per te ipsum investigare poteris. Illud autem scias, nihil operari imagines ejusmodi, nisi vivificentur ita, quod ipsi, aut naturalis, aut coelestis, aut heroica, aut animastica, aut daemonica, vel angelica virtus insit, aut adsistat. At quis modo animam dabit imagini, aut vivificabit lapidem, aut metallum, aut lignum, aut ceram? atque ex lapidibus suscitabit filios Abrahae? Certe non penetrat hoc arcanum ad artificem durae cervicis, nec dare poterit illa, qui non habet: habet autem nemo, nisi qui jam cohibitis elementis, victa natura, superatis coelis, progressus angelos, ad ipsum archetypum usque transcendit, cujus tunc cooperatur effectus potest omnia . . ." *Ibid.*, II, 50; *ed. cit.*, pp. 230–1.

[2] *Ibid.*, II, 58; *ed. cit.*, pp. 242–3.

religious gesture.[1] It is, in a manner, the Ficinian sun-worship and solar Orphic incantations, but now used to obtain power to do marvellous works.

The philosophy of magic in this book is important. Some of it is the usual material about the soul of the world, with the usual Virgil quotation on *mens agitat molem*,[2] but Agrippa is also using material from the *Corpus Hermeticum* from which he constantly quotes (of course in the form of opinions or sayings of Hermes Trismegistus). In relation to the world soul, he quotes from "Mercurius' Treatise *De communi*",[3] one of the Hermetic treatises which we analysed in our second chapter,[4] with its optimist gnosis of the divinity of the world and its animation, exemplified from the continual movement of the earth as things grow and diminish, which movement shows that the earth is alive. Agrippa was thus not only using the *Asclepius* and its magic, but other treatises of the *Corpus Hermeticum* the philosophy of which he incorporated into his magical philosophy.[5] His impressive description of the ascent of an all-powerful Magus through the three worlds is reminiscent of the ascents and descents of the Magus Man of the *Pimander*.[6]

Book III. Ceremonial or Religious Magic

In this book, Agrippa rises to yet higher flights, for it is concerned "with that part of Magic which teaches us to seek and know the laws of Religions", and how by following the ceremonies of religion to form our spirit and thought to know the truth. It is

[1] *Ibid.*, II, 59; *ed. cit.*, pp. 244–5.

[2] *Ibid.*, II, 55; *ed. cit.*, p. 239.

[3] "Et Mercurius in tractatu quem de Communi inscripsit, inquit, Totum quod est in mundo, aut crescendo, aut decrescendo movetur. Quod autem movetur, id propterea vivit: & cum omnia moveantur, etiam terra, maxime motu generativo & alterativo, ipsa quoque vivit." *Ibid.*, II, 56; *ed. cit.*, p. 240. Compare the following from Ficino's translation of the *De communi* (*Corpus Hermeticum*, XII); "Nunquid immobilis tibi terra uidetur? Minime, sed multis motibus agitata . . . .Totum . . . quod est in mundo, aut crescendo aut decrescendo mouetur. Quod uero mouetur, id praeterea uiuit. . . ." Ficino, p. 1854.

[4] See above, pp. 33–4.

[5] P. Zambelli has drawn attention to the many quotations from the *Hermetica* in the *De occulta philosophia*, and to Agrippa's development of Hermetic doctrines in a magical direction (*Test. uman.*, p. 108).

[6] See above, pp. 24–5.

the opinion of all the Magi that if spirit and thought are not in a good state, the body cannot be, and according to Hermes Trismegistus we cannot have firmness of spirit without purity of life, piety, and divine religion, for the holiness of religion purifies thought and renders it divine.[1] The reader is adjured to keep silence about the mysteries in this book, for, says Hermes, it is an offence to religion to propagate among the multitude a "discourse so full of the divine majesty".[2] (This is from the opening of the *Asclepius*.) Plato, Pythagoras, Porphyry, and Orpheus, and the Cabalists also enjoin secrecy in religious matters, and Christ hid the truth in parables. There is moreover a most necessary and secret thing which is absolutely necessary for a magician, and which is the key to all magical operations, and this is "the Dignification of man for such high virtue and power".[3] It is through the intellect, the highest faculty of the soul, that miraculous works are done, and it is by an ascetic, pure, and religious way of life that is to be achieved the dignification necessary for the religious Magus. Certain ceremonies, such as the laying on of hands, give this dignity. Whoever without the authority of office, or the merit of holiness and doctrine, or the dignity of nature and of education, presumes to do a magical work will achieve nothing.

Agrippa is evidently now taking us on from Ficino's type of magic, carried much further than Ficino took it, to Pico's type of magic. The mysterious allusions to Hermetic and Cabalist secrets, the dignification which the Magus at this level undergoes, are very much in the vein of Pico's oration on the Dignity of Man. But, again, Agrippa is going much further than Pico, for it is evident that the magic in the third or intellectual world which is now going to be discussed is really priestly magic, religious magic, involving the performance of religious miracles.

He next outlines a true divinely magical religion, based on faith, and a superstitious religion, based on credulity.[4] The two are not altogether unrelated, though the second is greatly inferior to the first. Miracles can be worked by the second kind, as well as by the

[1] Agrippa, *De occult. phil.*, III, 1; *ed. cit.*, p. 253.

[2] *Ibid.*, III, 2; *ed. cit.*, p. 254.

[3] *Ibid.*, III, 3; *ed. cit.*, pp. 256–8. With this chapter should be compared III, 36, "On man created in the image of God", which Zambelli has reprinted with notes on its sources many of which are Hermetic (*Test. uman.*, pp. 137–46).

[4] Agrippa, *De occult. phil.*, III, 4; *ed. cit.*, pp. 258–60.

first, provided that the credulity of the second kind is sufficiently strong. For works, both of divine and credulous magic,
demand above all things, faith. He is next careful to point out that
the religions of the old Magi, such as the Chaldeans, Egyptians,
Assyrians, Persians, were false as compared with the Catholic
religion and warns that all that he says about them is taken from
books and must not be taken too seriously. Nevertheless, there was
much that was good in those religions, and those who know how to
sift truth from falsehood can learn much from them.

The Three Guides in religion are Love, Hope, Faith, though
four is a Cabalist sacred number. Through these guides we can
sometimes dominate nature, command the elements, raise winds,
cure the sick, raise the dead. By the work of religion alone such
works can be done without the application of natural and celestial
forces. But whoever operates by religion alone cannot live long
but is absorbed by divinity. The magician must know the true
God, but also secondary divinities and with what cults they must
be served, particularly Jupiter whom Orpheus described as the
universe.[1]

The hymns of Orpheus and the ancient Magi are not different
from the Cabalist arcana and from the orthodox tradition. What
Orpheus calls gods, Denis (that is Pseudo-Dionysius) calls powers,
and the Cabalists call numerations (that is the Sephiroth). Ensoph
in Cabala is the same as *nox* in Orpheus (this is direct quotation
of one of Pico's conclusions). The ten numerations or Sephiroth
have names which act on all creatures, from the highest to the
lowest; first on the nine orders of angels, then on the nine celestial
spheres, then on men and the terrestrial world. Agrippa now gives
a list of the ten Hebrew Divine Names, of the names of the
Sephiroth and their meanings, with the angelic orders and the
spheres to which each are related.[2] We next have more on the
Hebrew divine names, a magical arrangement of Abracadabra and
pictures of talismans inscribed with names in Hebrew.[3] The influx
of virtue from the divine names comes through the mediation of

---

[1] *Ibid.*, III, 5–7; *ed. cit.*, pp. 260–5. The vaguely Trinitarian character
of the religion of the Magus is maintained by the numerological "three"
groupings. In chapter 8 (*ed. cit.*, pp. 265–7), the Trinity is said to be
foretold by ancient philosophers, particularly Hermes Trismegistus.

[2] *Ibid.*, III, 10; *ed. cit.*, pp. 268–72.

[3] *Ibid.*, III, 11; *ed. cit.*, pp. 272–89.

angels. Since the coming of Christ, the name IESU has all the powers, so that the Cabalists cannot operate with other names.[1]

There are three orders of intelligences or demons.[2] (1) super-celestial having to do only with the divinity; (2) celestial, the demons belonging to the signs, decans, planets, and other stars, all of which have names and characters, the former used in incantations, the latter engraved; (3) of the lower world, as demons of fire, air, earth, water.

The angels, according to the theologians, follow the same three groupings; Seraphim, Cherubim, Thrones for the supercelestial world; Dominions, Virtues, Powers, for the celestial world; Principalities, Archangels, Angels, for the terrestrial world. The Hebrew orders of angels correspond to these; there follow the names of the Hebrew orders, and of the Hebrew angels corresponding to the spheres. The Hebrew doctors draw many other names of angels from the Scriptures, such as the names of the seventy-two angels who bear the name of God.[3]

It is not necessary to go on with more of this. It is of course Cabalism which Agrippa derives partly from Reuchlin and Trithemius[4] but which is ultimately based on Pico. Agrippa is thinking on the lines which we studied in the last chapter; practical Cabala, or Cabalist magic, which puts the operator in touch with angels or Sephiroth or the power of divine names, also puts him in touch with the Pseudo-Dionysian angelic hierarchies, and thus becomes a Christian magic which is organically connected with celestial or elemental magic through the continuity linking all the three worlds.

In Agrippa, this magic is definitely connected with religious practices. He has much in his later chapters on religious ceremonies and rites,[5] on rich ritual with music, tapers and lamps, bells, altars. In a chapter on magic statues,[6] the examples given are mostly ancient but the reference to wonder-working images in

---

[1] *Ibid.*, III, 12; *ed. cit.*, pp. 279–81.

[2] *Ibid.*, III, 16; *ed. cit.*, pp. 287–90.

[3] *Ibid.*, III, 17–25; *ed. cit.*, pp. 291–309.

[4] Agrippa was in touch with both Reuchlin and Trithemius, both of whom specialised in practical Cabala.

[5] *Ibid.*, III, 58–64; *ed. cit.*, pp. 384–403. Walker (pp. 94–6) has discussed these chapters.

[6] *Ibid.*, III, 64; *ed. cit.*, pp. 399–403.

churches is obvious. As he says in his conclusion,[1] not everything has been said. The work is arranged to enable those who are worthy eventually to work out what is missing, and to prevent the unworthy from knowing too much. But the pious reader will feel the magical discipline penetrating into him and may begin to find himself in possession of powers formerly acquired by Hermes, Zoroaster, and Apollonius and other workers of marvels.

The theme of the *De occulta philosophia* is Magia and Cabala, Cabala and Magia, which was also Pico's theme. The Magia of Ficino has developed into a more powerful demonic magic which is however safeguarded (it is hoped) by the overlapping of demons with angels. The Cabala of Pico has developed into a powerful religious magic, which is in organic continuity with celestial and elemental magic, ties up with the angelic hierarchies, attempts to inform religious rites, images, ceremonial with magic, with the further suggestion that priests will be able to do miracles with it.

Agrippa is carrying to extreme lengths, or perhaps to their logical conclusion, the points which were at issue in the Pico controversy. Garcia's case that there is no connection between Magia and Cabala and Christianity was lost when the sacred Egyptian bull, Pope Alexander VI, gave his blessing to Pico.

Ficino's gentle, artistic, subjective, psychiatric magic, Pico's intensely pious and contemplative Cabalist magic, are quite innocent of the terrible power implications of Agrippa's magic. But they laid the foundations of this edifice, which is the direct result of the *prisca theologia*, which was always a *prisca magia*, and particularly of the alliance between the Egyptian Moses and the Moses of Cabala.

In its form and arrangement, and in its emphasis on the practical results to be obtained from the various kinds of magic, the first two books of the *De occulta philosophia* are reminiscent of *Picatrix*.[2] When one sees the Magia, or in the third book, the Cabala, set out in this technical way as recipes, the impression becomes strong that the magics which Ficino and Pico had seen in a lofty context of Neoplatonic philosophy or of Hebrew mysticism, are slipping back towards the old necromancy and conjuring. It is significant

[1] *Ed. cit.*, pp. 403–4.
[2] E. Garin suggests (*Medioevo e Rinascimento*, p. 172) that the *De occulta philosophia* is greatly indebted to *Picatrix*.

that a correspondent writes to Agrippa asking to be instructed in the mysteries, not of Magia and Cabala, but of "the *Picatrix* and the Cabala".[1]

Yet it is also not so simple as that. For Agrippa's necromancy and conjuring are not mediaeval in spirit, not the old hole-and-corner business of the persecuted mediaeval magician. They come invested with the noble robes of Renaissance magic, with the Dignity of a Renaissance Magus. Ficino's Neoplatonising of the talismans is quoted; the many references to the philosophy of the *Corpus Hermeticum* put the *Asclepius* magic into the context of Hermetic philosophy and mysticism, as Ficino saw it; above all, the advantages of practical Cabala in putting the conjuror in direct contact with the angelic, or intellectual world, come out very clearly as priestly magic, and the highest dignity of the Magus is seen to be the Magus as priest, performing religious rites and doing religious miracles. His "marrying of earth to heaven" with Magia, his summoning of the angels with Cabala, lead on to his apotheosis as religious Magus; his magical powers in the lower worlds are organically connected with his highest religious powers in the intellectual world.

In short, what we are arriving at here is something which is really very like the ideal Egyptian, or pseudo-Egyptian, society as presented in the Hermetic *Asclepius*, a theocracy governed by priests who know the secrets of a magical religion by which they hold the whole society together, though they themselves understand the inner meaning of those magical rites as being, beyond the magically activated statues, really the religion of the mind, the worship of the One beyond the All, a worship perceived by the initiated as rising beyond the strange forms of its gods, activated by elemental and celestial manipulations, to the intellectual world, or to the Ideas in the divine *mens*.

The problem of Renaissance Magic in relation to the religious problems of the sixteenth century is a vast question and one which cannot be tackled here,[2] or on the basis of the linking of magic with religious ceremonies by an irresponsible magician like Cornelius Agrippa. Its investigation would demand long study, starting from the Pico controversy and leading no one knows whither.

---

[1] Quoted from a letter to Agrippa by Thorndike, V, p. 132.
[2] The pioneer in seeing it as a problem is D. P. Walker in his *Spiritual and Demonic Magic*.

But certain obvious questions present themselves. Was some of the iconoclastic rage of the reformers aroused by there having been *more* magic put into religion in fairly recent times? The Middle Ages had, on the whole, obediently followed Augustine in banning the idolatry of the *Asclepius*. It was Lactantius, Ficino and Pico (the latter strongly approved of by Pope Alexander VI) who got Hermes Trismegistus into the Church, so that the issue between magic and religion was no longer the simple mediaeval one but very complex, arousing questions such as "What is the basis of ecclesiastical magic?" Or, "Should Magia and Cabala be accepted as aids to religion or rejected?" This question might also be put in the form "Does an increase of magic help a religious reform?" To which one answer might be the strong negative, "Let us get rid of all magic and break the images."

This is not, however, the form in which the question is put in Cornelius Agrippa's highly influential book. According to Agrippa, there are two kinds of religious magic, one good and leading to the highest religious insights and powers; the other bad and superstitious, as it were a bad copy of the good kind. This was how Giordano Bruno, the religious magician, saw the problem, and he got much—indeed most—of his material for his solution of it from Cornelius Agrippa.

❖❖❖❖❖❖❖❖❖❖❖❖❖❖❖❖❖❖❖❖❖❖❖❖❖❖❖❖❖❖❖❖❖❖

Chapter VIII

RENAISSANCE MAGIC AND
SCIENCE

❖❖❖❖❖❖❖❖❖❖❖❖❖❖❖❖❖❖❖❖❖❖❖❖❖❖❖❖❖❖❖❖❖❖

T HE cosmos, or the world-picture, within which the
Agrippan Magus operates is not different, in its main
outlines, from the mediaeval world-picture. The earth
is still at the bottom and at the centre, with next the
spheres of the other three elements, water, air and fire, then the
spheres of the planets in the Chaldean or Ptolemaic order with
the sun in the middle; then the sphere of fixed stars, and then
the divine sphere with the angels, and above them, God. There is
nothing strange in this; on the contrary it belongs into the long-
established order of things. What has changed is Man, now no
longer only the pious spectator of God's wonders in the creation,
and the worshipper of God himself above the creation, but Man
the operator, Man who seeks to draw power from the divine and
natural order. It may again be helpful at this point to look at an
illustration (Pl. 10) from one of Fludd's works which, though
much later than Agrippa, still belong into the same tradition. On
the central earth sits a monkey; around him is the elemental
world; he is linked by a chain to a woman representing the sun,
moon, and stars, the celestial world, the spheres of the planets and
the zodiac among which she stands. Outside the sphere of the
zodiac, or the sphere of fixed stars, are shown three spheres
inhabited by tiny angelic forms; a chain passing upward from the
woman's right arm reaches the Deity himself, beyond the angelic
spheres, represented by the Name in Hebrew within clouds of
glory. The monkey is Man, or rather Man's Art by which he

imitates Nature, with simian mimicry.[1] Man here seems to have lost some of his Dignity, but he has gained in power. He has become the clever ape of nature, who has found out the way that nature works and by imitating it, will obtain her powers. To use the terminology now so familiar, it may be said that by Magia man has learned how to use the chain linking earth to heaven, and by Cabala he has learned to manipulate the higher chain linking the celestial world, through the angels, to the divine Name.

An interesting example of applied magic, or power magic, is the *Steganographia* of Johannes Trithemius, Abbot of Sponheim, printed in 1606 but known in manuscript before that. Trithemius was the friend and teacher of Agrippa, and himself knew the work of Reuchlin. The *Steganographia* purports to be, and perhaps really is to some extent, about cryptography or ways of writing in cipher.[2] It is also, however, Cabalist angel magic. The first book is about summoning district angels, or angels which rule over parts of the earth; the second is about time angels who rule the hours of the day and night; the third is about seven angels higher than all these who rule the seven planets.[3] Trithemius aims at using this angelic network for the very practical purpose of transmitting messages to people at a distance by telepathy; he also seems to hope to gain from it knowledge "of everything that is happening in the world".[4] The technical side of this science is very complex, involving pages and pages of elaborate calculations, both astrological and in connection with the numerical values of the angelnames; for example, Samael, angel of the first hour, equals 4440, which is the sum of the numbers of his eight inferior angels.[5]

---

[1] Cf. H. W. Janson, *Apes and Ape Lore in the Middle Ages and Renaissance*, Warburg Institute, University of London, 1952, pp. 304 ff.

[2] See Walker, pp. 86 ff.

[3] The names of these are: Oriffiel (Saturn); Zachariel (Jupiter); Samael (Mars); Michael (Sol); Anael (Venus); Raphael (Mercury); Gabriel (Luna). (Johannes Trithemius, *Steganographia*, Frankfort, 1606, p. 162). One way of summoning these angels is by talismans imprinted with their image. For example: "fac imaginem ex cera vel pinge in chartam novam figuram Orifielis in modum viri barbati & nudi, stantis super taurum varii coloris, habentis in dextra librum & in sinistra calamum. . . ." (*Steganographia, ed. cit.*, p. 177; quoted by Walker, p. 87, note 3.)

[4] *Ed. cit.*, p. 179; quoted Walker, pp. 87–8.

[5] *Ed. cit.*, pp. 96–7.

How remote we are now from the contemplative piety with which Pico used Cabala! Trithemius lived too soon. He would be very happy in putting through a trunk-call to a friend at a distance, or in watching everything that is going on in the world with his television set. This is perhaps a little unfair, since there is a vast esoteric background to Trithemius' magic.

Operating with the talismans of Magia or with the angel-names of Cabala will not in itself lead to the practical achievements of modern applied science. There was, however, among Ficino's lists of *prisci theologi*, or *prisci magi*, the name of one who taught that number was the root of all truth—Pythagoras. Among Pico's nine hundred theses, there were fourteen conclusions "according to the mathematics of Pythagoras",[1] the first being that One is the cause of all other numbers. Others connect with his other theses through Pythagorean number symbolism. In his Apology, he connects Magia and Cabala with Pythagorean mathematics.[2] The combination of Cabalistic computation with Pythagoreanism is carried much farther by Reuchlin in his *De arte cabalistica*, and the concentration on number in the new magic is reflected in the long passages on number in Agrippa's guide, some of which we resumed in the last chapter. If we were to try to translate the tone of Agrippa's magic in terms of the "gifts" of the planets which it chiefly tries to attract, the answer might be that, whilst Ficino's magic avoids Saturn, Agrippa's magic seeks the Saturnian gifts of high abstract contemplation and pure mathematics. (Thus, as Botticelli's predominantly Venus talisman, the "Primavera", reflects the Ficinian type of magic, Dürer's predominantly Saturnian talisman, the "Melencholia" engraving, reflects the Agrippan type of magic.[3])

Thus the Renaissance magic was turning towards number as a possible key to operations, and the subsequent history of man's achievements in applied science has shown that number is indeed a master-key, or one of the master-keys, to operations by which the forces of the cosmos are made to work in man's service.

[1] Pico, p. 79. The Pythagorean numerology was also implicit in the *Hermetica*, particularly in the passage on the monas in *Corpus Hermeticum*, IV (*C.H.*, I, p. 53).

[2] Pico, pp. 172 ff.

[3] Agrippa is, in fact, one of Dürer's direct sources; see E. Panofsky and F. Saxl, *Dürer's Melencolia I, Studien der Bibliothek Warburg*, 2, 1923.

7 (*a*) Sephiroth, Angelic Hierarchies, and Spheres. From Robert Fludd, *Meteorologica cosmica*, Frankfort, 1626, p. 8 (p. 123)

pulcherrimo templolampadem hanc in alio uel meliori loco po neret,quàm unde totum simul possit illuminare? Siquidem non inepte quidam lucernam mundi,alij mentem, alij rectorem uocant. Trimegistus uisibilem Deum,Sophoclis Electra intuentê

7 (*b*) The Copernican System from N. Copernicus, *De revolutionibus orbium coelestium*, Nuremberg, 1543 (p. 154)

7 (*c*) The Ptolemaic and Copernican Systems from Giordano Bruno. *La cena de le ceneri*, 1584 (p. 241)

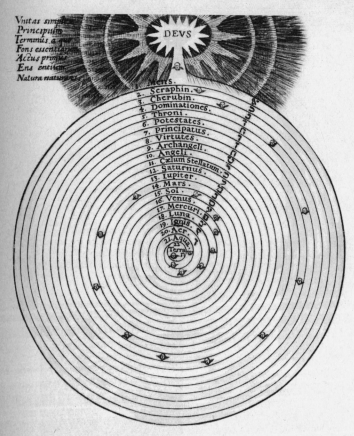

Vnitas simpl..
Principium
Terminus a quo
Fons essentia[...]um
Actus prim[us]
Ens entium
Natura natur[...]s

DEVS

Mens.
2. Seraphin.
3. Cherubin.
4. Dominationes.
5. Throni.
6. Potestates.
7. Principatus.
8. Virtutes.
9. Archangeli.
10. Angeli.
11. Cælum Stellatum.
12. Saturnus.
13. Iupiter.
14. Mars.
15. Sol.
16. Venus.
17. Mercuri.
18. Luna.
19. Ignis.
20. Aer.
21. Aqua.
22.
23. Terra.

8 Angelic Hierarchies, Spheres, and Hebrew Alphabet. From Robert
Fludd, *Utriusque cosmi, maioris scilicet et minoris, metaphysica, physica
atque technica historia*, Oppenheim, 1617, 1619, II (1), p. 219 (p. 123)

However, once again, neither Pythagorean number, organically wedded to symbolism and mysticism, nor Cabalistic conjuring with numbers in relation to the mystical powers of the Hebrew alphabet, will of themselves lead to the mathematics which really work in applied science. Yet it is important to notice that within the scheme of Magia and Cabala as formulated by Agrippa there was a place for genuine mathematical sciences and for their application to produce operations.

At the beginning of his second book, as we have seen, Agrippa emphasises that a magician must be versed in mathematics, for by mathematics there can be produced "without any natural virtue", that is by purely mechanical means, wonderful operations, such as the flying wooden pigeon made by Archytas, the moving statues made by Daedalus, the speaking statues of Mercurius (here we have the wonderful statues of the *Asclepius* regarded as marvels of applied science), and the like. A magician who knows natural philosophy and mathematics and also understands mechanics can do wonderful things, says Agrippa, and the Magus must know the sciences which produce such marvels as a necessary part of his training.[1]

That this inclusion of what appears to be genuine applied science based on a knowledge of genuine mathematics within the apparatus of a Magus was not forgotten can be shown by a quotation from Tommaso Campanella who, writing nearly a hundred years later, is recalling this passage in Agrippa. In his *Magia e Grazia*, a work chiefly devoted to religious magic, Campanella makes a classification of different kinds of magic, including a kind which he calls "real artificial magic".

Real artificial magic produces real effects, as when Archytas made a flying dove of wood, and recently at Nüremberg, according to Boterus, an eagle and a fly have been made in the same way. Daedalus made statues which moved through the action of weights or of mercury. However I do not hold that to be true which William of Paris writes, namely that it is possible to make a head which speaks with a human voice, as Albertus Magnus is said to have done. It seems to me possible to make a certain imitation of the voice by means of reeds conducting the air, as in the case of the bronze bull made by

[1] Agrippa, *De occult. phil.*, II, 1. Agrippa's source for the use of the mathematical sciences in magic may be *Picatrix*.

Phalaris which could roar. This art however cannot produce marvellous effects save by means of local motions and weights and pulleys or by using a vacuum, as in pneumatic and hydraulic apparatuses, or by applying forces to the materials. But such forces and materials can never be such as to capture a human soul.[1]

This passage may again suggest that a preoccupation with miraculous statues had its scientific side, and that mechanics and other "real artificial" magics could have been fostered by the general revival of magic in the Renaissance.

It is by putting "real artificial magic" in the context of Magia and Cabala that the apparently contradictory activities of a man like John Dee can be understood as all belonging quite naturally into the outlook of a Renaissance Magus. John Dee[2] (1527–1608) was a genuine mathematician of considerable importance, intensely interested in all mathematical studies, and in the application of mathematics to produce results in applied sciences. He himself was a practical scientist and inventor, his activities in this field being many and varied; they included a flying crab for a college stage-play. In his preface to H. Billingsley's English translation of Euclid's *Elements of Geometry*, Dee outlines the state of mathematical sciences in his time and fervently urges their prosecution and improvement, and he is certainly concerned with genuine mathematics and their application as genuine applied science. He bases this plea on "the noble Earl of Mirandula" who set up 900 theses in Rome, amongst them being, in his eleventh mathematical conclusion, the statement that "by numbers, a way is had, to the searching out, and understanding of euery thyng, hable to be knowen".[3] This is, indeed, as Dee says, an English translation of one of Pico's eighty-five mathematical conclusions, "Per numeros habetur uia ad omnis scibilis inuestigationem & intellectionem."[4]

Though on one side of his mind, Dee is interested in number as "real artificial magic" (he does not use this expression in the

---

[1] Tommaso Campanella, *Magia e Grazia*, ed. R. Amerio, Rome, 1957, p. 180.

[2] On Dee, see Charlotte Fell Smith, *John Dee*, London, 1909, and the valuable unpublished Ph.D. thesis by I. R. F. Calder, *John Dee, studied as an English Neoplatonist*, 1952, London University.

[3] H. Billingsley, *The Elements of . . . Euclide*, London, 1570, Dee's preface, sig. *i, *verso*.

[4] Pico, p. 101.

Billingsley preface)[1] he was also still more interested in the use of number in connection with Hebrew names of angels and spirits in the practical Cabala which he did with his associate, Edward Kelley. Dee and Kelley were close students of Agrippa's occult philosophy[2]; in Agrippa's third book there are elaborate numerical and alphabetical tables for angel-summoning of the type which Dee and Kelley used in their operations,[3] in the course of which Michael, Gabriel, Raphael and other angels and spirits appeared in the show-stone and spoke to Dee through Kelley, though Dee never saw them himself.[4] Kelley was a fraud who deluded his pious master, but the very nature of the fraud shows how well-versed they both were in Renaissance magic. What Dee chiefly wanted to learn from the angels was the secrets of nature[5]; it was a way of prosecuting science on a higher level. Like Pico della Mirandola, Dee was a most devout Christian man, and his attitude to the angel-visitants is like that of Pico in the oration on the Dignity of Man, full of awe and wonder.

Dee's ignorant contemporaries could not distinguish between practical Cabala and conjuring, in which they were perhaps not unjustified. But they also could not understand, as Dee

---

[1] But he lists under "Thaumaturgy" as an "Art Mathematicall", the brazen head made by Albertus Magnus, the wooden dove of Architas, and the mechanical fly made at Nüremberg (preface to Billingsley's *Euclid*, sig. A i *verso*), which shows that he was drawing upon a list of mechanical marvels similar to those given by Agrippa and Campanella.

Dee's mind passes rapidly from the pneumatics of Hero of Alexandria to the statues of the *Asclepius*, or "Images of Mercurie" as he calls them (*ibid.*, sig. A I *recto* and *verso*). I am inclined to think that some kind of mental association of miraculous Egyptian statues with the works of Hero on mechanics and automata may have stimulated interest in mechanics.

[2] Dee once speaks of Agrippa's book as lying open in his study, and therefore in constant use in the operations.

[3] These can be seen in Dee's manuscript "Book of Enoch", British Museum, Sloane MSS. 3189. Cf. the "Ziruph Tables" in Agrippa's *De occult. phil.*, III, 24. Agrippa was not Dee's and Kelley's only source for practical Cabala, but their minds run on these things within the Agrippan framework.

[4] The extraordinary story of these séances is told in Dee's spiritual diary, part of which was published by Meric Casaubon in 1659 with the title *A True and Faithful Relation of what passed for many years between Dr. John Dee . . . and some spirits . . .*, London, 1659.

[5] Cf. the *True and Faithful Relation*, p. 49, where a "Principal" comes who will reveal the secrets of nature.

bitterly complains in the Billingsley preface, that "Actes and Feates, Naturally, Mathematically, and Mechanically wrought"[1] are not done by wicked demonic magic but by a natural use of number.

John Dee has to the full the dignity, the sense of operational power, of the Renaissance Magus. And he is a very clear example of how the will to operate, stimulated by Renaissance magic, could pass into, and stimulate, the will to operate in genuine applied science. Or of how operating with number in the higher sphere of religious magic could belong with, and stimulate, operating with number in the lower sphere of "real artificial magic".

The Hermetic science *par excellence* is alchemy; the famous *Emerald Table*, the bible of the alchemists, is attributed to Hermes Trismegistus and gives in a mysteriously compact form the philosophy of the All and the One.[2] In the Renaissance, a new style "Alchymia" becomes associated with the new Magia and Cabala. Dee is an example of this, alchemy being one of his main interests. But the chief exponent of the new alchemy is Paracelsus.

The researches of W. Pagel have shown that the prime matter of Paracelsus, the basis of his alchemical thought, is related to the conception of the Logos, or the Word, as found in the *Corpus Hermeticum*, and also to Cabalistic interpretations of the Word.[3] The new Paracelsan alchemy thus derived its stimulus from the Renaissance Hermetic-Cabalist tradition. It can be said with certainty that Paracelsus was much influenced by Ficino and the Ficinian magic, his *De vita longa* having been inspired by the *De*

---

[1] Billingsley's *Euclid*, preface, sig. A i *verso*.

[2] "That which is above is like that which is below. . . . And as all things have been derived from one . . . so all things are born from this thing. . . ." (from a translation of the *Emerald Table*, or *Tablet*, in K. Seligmann, *History of Magic*, pp. 128–9). In the form *monas generat monadem*, this thought is constantly repeated by the Hermetists. On the origin and history of the *Emerald Table*, see J. Ruska, *Tabula Smaragdina*, Heidelberg, 1926.

[3] See W. Pagel, "The Prime Matter of Paracelsus", *Ambix*, IX (1961), pp. 119 ff.; see also the same writer's article "Paracelsus and the Neoplatonic and Gnostic Tradition", *Ambix*, VIII (1960), pp. 125 ff.; and his book, *Paracelsus: An Introduction to Philosophical Medicine in the Era of the Renaissance*, Bâle, New York, 1958.

vita coelitus comparanda.[1] In his use of magic in medicine he was following in the steps of Ficino, the doctor. The label "Hermetic-Cabalist" is thus a possible indication of the trend of Paracelsus' work, though he twists and alters the tradition in strange and original ways. He is the Magus as doctor, operating not only on his patients' bodies but on their imaginations, through the imaginative power on which he laid great stress, and this is recognisably a legacy from the Ficinian magic.

The *De harmonia mundi* (1525) of Francesco Giorgio, or Giorgi, a Franciscan friar of Venice, develops to the full a theme which is implicit in all types of the Hermetic-Cabalist tradition, namely the theme of universal harmony, of the harmonious relationships between man, the microcosm, and the greater world of the universe, the macrocosm. This theme was, of course, by no means new; on the contrary, it had been basic throughout the Middle Ages. But to the native Pythagorean mediaeval tradition, Hermetism and Cabalism added immense richness and complexity, swelling out the universal harmonies into a new symphony. Giorgi, who had learned Cabala and was in touch with Ficinian Florentine circles, was the first to make this new expansion. The profound influence on him of "Hermes Trismegistus", in Ficino's translation, has been studied by C. Vasoli, with many quotations from the *De harmonia mundi* and other of his works in proof of it.[2]

The intense concentration on the complexities of universal harmony, which is one of the most characteristic aspects of Renaissance thought from Giorgi onwards, though it used number in a Pythagorean or qualitative sense and not as mathematics proper, yet by so forcefully directing attention on number as the key to all nature it may be said to have prepared the way for genuine mathematical thinking about the universe. As is well known, Kepler still saw his new astronomy in a context of harmonies, and he was well aware that the Pythagorean theory was also implicit in the Hermetic writings, of which he had made a careful study.[3]

HELIOCENTRICITY

The cult of the *prisca theologia* laid a greatly increased em-

[1] See Pagel, *Paracelsus*, pp. 218 ff.
[2] C. Vasoli, "Francesco Giorgio Veneto" in *Test. uman.*, pp. 79 ff.
[3] See below, pp. 441–2.

phasis on the sun, and two of the *prisci thealogi* in Ficino's lists[1] had taught that the earth moves. These were Pythagoras and Philolaus; the latter had published the astronomical views of the Pythagorean school, which were that the earth, sun, and other bodies revolve around a central fire. The cult of Hermes Trismegistus also tended to suggest a different position for the sun to that which it held in the Chaldean-Ptolemaic system, universally accepted in the Middle Ages. The Egyptian order of the planets was different from the Chaldean order, for the Egyptians put the sun just above the moon, and below the other five planets, not in the middle of the seven. The difference between the two systems was emphasised by Macrobius—a Platonist much studied in the Middle Ages and Renaissance—who pointed out that the Egyptian order, in which the sun is much nearer to the earth, was the one which Plato accepted.[2] Ficino in his *De sole* mentions the Egyptian order,[3] soon afterwards remarking that the sun has been put nearer to the earth than the firmament by Providence in order to warm it with *spiritus* and *ignis*. The Egyptian position of the sun, only just above the moon which is the channel of all astral influences, would better suit Ficino's sun-centred *spiritus* magic than the Chaldean order. However, there is no evidence that he rejected the latter; both here and in other passages he accepts it.

Unquestioning belief in the Ptolemaic position of the sun was nevertheless somewhat shaken by the *prisci theologi*, but more important than this in fixing attention on the sun was the immense religious importance attached to it by the earliest (so Ficino believed) of the *prisci theologi*, Hermes Trismegistus, the Egyptian Moses. The sun, of course, is always a religious symbol and has always been so used in Christianity; but in some passages in the Hermetic writings the sun is called the demiurge, the "second god". In the *Asclepius*, Hermes says:

> The sun illuminates the other stars not so much by the power of its light, as by its divinity and holiness, and you should hold him, O

---

[1] See above, pp. 14–15.

[2] "Plato followed the Egyptians, the authors of all branches of philosophy, who preferred to have the sun located between the moon and Mercury . . ." (Macrobius, *In Somnium Scipionis*, XIX; trans. W. H. Stahl, New York, 1952, p. 162). Cf. Plato, *Timaeus*, 38 d 1–3; A. E. Taylor, *Commentary on Plato's Timaeus*, Oxford, 1928, pp. 192–3.

[3] *De sole*, cap. 6 (Ficino, pp. 968–9).

Asclepius, to be the second god, governing all things and spreading his light on all the living beings of the world, both those which have a soul and those which have not. (*Ipse enim sol non tam magnitudine luminis quam diuinitate et sanctitate ceteras stellas inluminat. secundum etenim deum hunc crede, o Asclepi, omnia gubernantem omniaque mundana inlustrantem animalia, siue animantia, siue inaminantia.*)[1]

There are also passages on the divinity of the sun in *Corpus Hermeticum* V[2] and X,[3] and above all, in XVI[4] (though the last-named sixteenth treatise did not influence Ficino since it was not in his manuscript; it was published, in Lazzarelli's translation, by Symphorien Champier in 1507).[5] The admired Egyptian religion included sun-worship, and the sun is among the list of the gods of the Egyptians given in the *Asclepius*.[6]

These Egypto-Hermetic sun-teachings undoubtedly influenced Ficino's sun-magic, and they connected philosophically with Plato on the sun as the intelligible splendour, or chief image of the ideas, and religiously with the Pseudo-Dionysian light symbolism. All these influences can be perceived, working together, in Ficino's *De sole* and *De lumine*. As we have tried to outline in previous chapters, the concentration on the sun in the astral magic, led upwards through the Christian Neoplatonism of Pseudo-Dionysius to the supreme *Lux Dei*, and in this way the sun very nearly is for Ficino what it is for Hermes or for the Emperor Julian, the "second god", or the visible god in the Neoplatonic series.

The *De revolutionibus orbium caelestium* of Nicholas Copernicus was written between 1507 and 1530, and published in 1543. It was not by magic that Copernicus reached his epoch-making hypothesis of the revolution of the earth round the sun, but by a great achievement in pure mathematical calculation. He introduces his discovery to the reader as a kind of act of contemplation of the world as a revelation of God, or as what many philosophers have called the visible god. It is, in short, in the atmosphere of the religion of the world that the Copernican revolution is introduced. Nor does Copernicus fail to adduce the authority of *prisci theologi* (though he does not actually use this expression),

---

[1] *C.H.*, II, pp. 336–7 (*Asclepius*, 29).   [2] *C.H.*, I, p. 61.
[3] *Ibid.*, I, pp. 114–5.   [4] *Ibid.*, II, pp. 233 ff.
[5] See below, p. 172.   [6] *C.H.*, II, pp. 336–7 (*Asclepius*, 29).

amongst them Pythagoras and Philolaus[1] to support the hypothesis of earth-movement. And at the crucial moment, just after the diagram showing the new sun-centred system (Pl. 7b), comes a reference to Hermes Trismegistus on the sun:

> In medio vero omnium residet sol. Quis enim in hoc pulcherrimo templo lampadem hanc in alio vel meliori loco poneret, quam unde totum simul possit illuminare? Siquidem non inepte quidam lucernam mundi, alii mentem, alii rectorem vocant. Trimegistus [sic] visibilem deum.[2]

There are perhaps echoes of Cicero's words for the sun[3] in that famous Dream, on which Macrobius commented, in this passage, but the main echo is surely of the words of Hermes Trismegistus in the *Asclepius*, which we have quoted above.

The teleological framework in which Copernicus presents his discovery has long been recognised,[4] but it is still not generally realised that this framework was the contemporary one. Copernicus is not living within the world-view of Thomas Aquinas but within that of the new Neoplatonism, of the *prisci theologi* with Hermes Trismegistus at their head, of Ficino. One can say, either that the intense emphasis on the sun in this new worldview was the emotional driving force which induced Copernicus to undertake his mathematical calculations on the hypothesis that the sun is indeed at the centre of the planetary system; or that he wished to make his discovery acceptable by presenting it within the framework of this new attitude. Perhaps both explanations would be true, or some of each.

At any rate, Copernicus' discovery came out with the blessing of Hermes Trismegistus upon its head, with a quotation from that

---

[1] N. Copernicus, *De revolutionibus orbium caelestium*, Thorn, 1873, pp. 16–17.

[2] *Ibid.*, p. 30.

[3] "mediam fere regionem Sol obtinet, dux et princeps, et moderator luminum reliquorum, mens mundi, et temperatio, tanta magnitudine, ut cuncta suâ luce illustret et compleat . . ." Cicero, *Somnium Scipionis*, cap. IV.

[4] Cf. A. Koyré, *La révolution astronomique*, Paris, 1961, pp. 61 ff. Koyré emphasises the importance for Copernicus of the sun in a religious and mystical sense, and speaks of the influence of the Neoplatonic and Neopythagorean renaissance on him, mentioning Ficino in this connection (p. 69). Cf. also E. Garin, "Recenti interpretazioni di Marsilio Ficino", *Giornale critico della filosofia italiana*, 1940, pp. 308 ff.

famous work in which Hermes describes the sun-worship of the Egyptians in their magical religion.

A recently discovered text[1] tells us that Giordano Bruno, when advocating Copernicanism at Oxford, did this in a context of quotations from Ficino's *De vita coelitus comparanda*. This famous philosopher of the Renaissance thus saw the Copernican sun in some close relationship to Ficinian sun magic. The analyses which I shall make in later chapters will show that Bruno was an intense religious Hermetist, a believer in the magical religion of the Egyptians as described in the *Asclepius*, the imminent return of which he prophesied in England, taking the Copernican sun as a portent in the sky of this imminent return. He patronises Copernicus for having understood his theory only as a mathematician, whereas he (Bruno) has seen its more profound religious and magical meanings. The reader must wait for the other chapters for proof of these statements which I anticipate here for a moment, because Bruno's use of Copernicanism shows most strikingly how shifting and uncertain were the borders between genuine science and Hermetism in the Renaissance. Copernicus, though not un-influenced by Hermetic mysticism about the sun, is completely free of Hermetism in his mathematics. Bruno pushes Copernicus' scientific work back into a prescientific stage, back into Hermetism, interpreting the Copernican diagram as a hieroglyph of divine mysteries.

This chapter has only hinted in a partial and fragmentary way, and with but a few examples, at a theme which I believe may be of absolutely basic importance for the history of thought—namely, Renaissance magic as a factor in bringing about fundamental changes in the human outlook.

The Greeks with their first class mathematical and scientific brains made many discoveries in mechanics and other applied sciences but they never took whole-heartedly, with all their powers, the momentous step which western man took at the beginning of the modern period of crossing the bridge between the theoretical and the practical, of going all out to apply knowledge to produce operations. Why was this? It was basically a matter of the will. Fundamentally, the Greeks did not *want* to operate. They regarded

[1] See below, pp. 208–9.

operations as base and mechanical, a degeneration from the only occupation worthy of the dignity of man, pure rational and philosophical speculation. The Middle Ages carried on this attitude in the form that theology is the crown of philosophy and the true end of man is contemplation; any wish to operate can only be inspired by the devil. Quite apart from the question of whether Renaissance magic could, or could not, lead on to genuinely scientific procedures, the real function of the Renaissance Magus in relation to the modern period (or so I see it) is that he changed the will. It was now dignified and important for man to operate; it was also religious and not contrary to the will of God that man, the great miracle, should exert his powers. It was this basic psychological reorientation towards a direction of the will which was neither Greek nor mediaeval in spirit, which made all the difference.

What were the emotional sources of the new attitude? They lie, it may be suggested, in the religious excitement caused by the rediscovery of the *Hermetica*, and their attendant Magia; in the overwhelming emotions aroused by Cabala and its magico-religious techniques. It is magic as an aid to gnosis which begins to turn the will in the new direction.

And even the impulse towards the breaking down of the old cosmology with heliocentricity may have as the emotional impulse towards the new vision of the sun the Hermetic impulse towards the world, interpreted first as magic by Ficino, emerging as science in Copernicus, reverting to gnostic religiosity in Bruno. As we shall see later, Bruno's further leap out from his Copernicanism into an infinite universe peopled with innumerable worlds certainly had behind it, as its emotional driving power, the Hermetic impulse.

Thus "Hermes Trismegistus" and the Neoplatonism and Cabalism associated with him, may have played during his period of glorious ascendance over the mind of western man a strangely important rôle in the shaping of human destiny.

Chapter IX

❖❖❖❖❖❖❖❖❖❖❖❖❖❖❖❖❖❖❖❖❖❖❖❖❖❖❖❖❖❖❖❖❖❖❖

AGAINST MAGIC
(1) THEOLOGICAL OBJECTIONS
(2) THE HUMANIST TRADITION

❖❖❖❖❖❖❖❖❖❖❖❖❖❖❖❖❖❖❖❖❖❖❖❖❖❖❖❖❖❖❖❖❖❖❖

(1) THEOLOGICAL OBJECTIONS

Though Pico gained the approval of Pope Alexander VI, the new magic did not go unchallenged by either Catholic or Protestant opinion in later years. On the contrary, there is a growing outcry of alarm, mounting in intensity throughout the sixteenth century, against the increase in magical practices. The Magi themselves always claim to be pious and good, both in act and in intention; they are doing only natural magic, not demonic magic; or if aiming at summoning higher spiritual powers, these are angels, not demons. Even Agrippa, the arch-magician, who seems to be calling on both demons and angels, crowns his work with religious magic and religious pretensions. But many people were asking when is an angel not an angel but a demon, and demanding that a check should be put on the whole movement, the religious aspects of which only made it the more dangerous. A valuable analysis of theological objections to Renaissance magic has been made by D. P. Walker, and there is also much relevant material in Thorndike's *History of Magic and Experimental Science*. My aim here is only to give a very brief impression of anti-magical opinion, based on these works.

Pico's nephew, Giovanni Francesco Pico, strongly disapproved of Ficino's talismans, and also of his uncle's magic, though he thinks, or pretends to think, that his distinguished relative had abjured all magic in his *Adversus Astrologiam*.[1] G. F. Pico's attack on magic and astrology shows how strongly both were bound up with the *prisca theologia*, which he regards as pagan idolatry. He also mentions *Picatrix* as a "most vain book".[2] He does not attack Ficino by name, but strongly reprobates the Orphic incantations which Ficino had used (and Pico had recommended as natural magic), and the remarks directed against a "certain man" who has written about astrological images must be meant for Ficino.[3]

The arguments of Pico's nephew were impressive, and many of them were repeated in 1583 by Johann Wier, a Protestant, who also regards the *prisca theologia* as wicked pagan superstition and as the source of magic.[4] "The visits of the Greek sages to Egypt resulted in their learning, not the Mosaic tradition of true theology, but bad Egyptian magic."[5] As a Protestant, Wier wants religion to be entirely free from magic, and a large part of his work is directed against Catholic practices which he regards as superstitious.[6] Erastus is another Protestant writer who strongly condemns magic, and in particular Ficino's magic, which he identifies with Egyptian abominations and with the Platonists. "Would you think this man a priest of God," he cries, "as he wished to appear, and not rather the patron and high priest of Egyptian mysteries?"[7] And he accuses Ficino of being addicted to "loathsome and clearly diabolical fables",[8] probably an allusion to the magic of the *Asclepius*. Erastus, too, wants to have religion entirely cleared of magic.[9]

---

[1] The chief of G. F. Pico's works against magic are the *Examen Vanitatis Doctrinae Gentium* and the *De Rerum Praenotione*; both are included in G. F. Pico, *Opera omnia*, Bâle, 1573.

[2] Walker, pp. 146–7; cf. also Thorndike, VI, pp. 466 ff.

[3] G. F. Pico, *Opera, ed. cit.*, p. 662; quoted by Walker, p. 147.

[4] Walker, pp. 147–9. G. F. Pico's attack on Peter of Abano whom he accuses of having used *Picatrix* could indirectly apply to Ficino, who mentions Abano as one of his sources, perhaps concealing a real debt to *Picatrix*. See above, pp. 50, 56.

[5] Quoted from Walker's summary (p. 152) of Wier's *De praestigiis daemonum* (first edition in 1566).

[6] Walker, pp. 153–6.

[7] Erastus, *Disputationem de medicina nova Philippi Paracelsi*, Bâle, n.d., p. 118. Quoted by Walker, p. 163.

[8] *Ibid., loc. cit.*

[9] Walker, pp. 156–66.

The Catholic views on magic were given authoritative pronouncement by Martin Del Rio, a Jesuit, in a weighty book published in 1599–1600.[1] Del Rio would allow some forms of natural magic and is not altogether unsympathetic to Ficino, but he firmly condemns his use of talismans. He denies that the Hebrew language has any special power. Thus both Ficino's Magia and Pico's practical Cabala would be rejected; Pope Alexander VI's views were not endorsed by the Counter Reformation. As to Agrippa, Del Rio regards him as an absolutely black magician, the worst of his kind. The Catholic writer defends Catholic practices from the charge of magic, as Garcia had done long ago when attacking Pico.

There were thus always strong bodies of theological opinion, both Catholic and Protestant, against the Renaissance magic throughout the period in which it flourished.

(2) THE HUMANIST TRADITION

I must first of all define what I mean by "the humanist tradition". I mean the recovery of the Latin texts, of the literature of Roman civilisation in the Renaissance, and the attitude to life and letters which arose out of that recovery. Though it had many antecedents in the Middle Ages, the chief initiator of this movement, so far as the Italian Renaissance is concerned, was Petrarch. The recovery of the Latin texts, the excitement about the new revelation of classical antiquity which they brought, belongs to the fourteenth century and continues into the fifteenth century. It was very well advanced and had reached a stage of sophistication *before* the next great experience of the Renaissance—the recovery of the Greek texts and their ensuing new philosophical revelation in the fifteenth century. It cannot, I think, be sufficiently emphasised that these two Renaissance experiences are of an entirely different order, using different sources in a different way, and making their appeal to different sides of the human mind. Let us draw up some comparisons.

There is, for example, the comparison with which we began the first chapter of this book. The Latin humanist's chronology is correct. He knows the correct date of the civilisation to which he

[1] Martin Del Rio, *Disquisitionum Magicarum, Libri Sex*, first edition Louvain, 1599–1600. See Walker, pp. 178–85.

wants to return, the golden age of Latin rhetoric as represented by Cicero, the proficiency in literary and historical studies which a Ciceronian speech represents, its exquisite Latin style, the dignified way of life in a well-organised society, which is its framework. This world really did exist at the date at which the Latin humanist thinks it existed. He is not transposing its date to some misty antiquity just before or just after the Flood, with a bogus chronology such as that by which the *prisca theologia* is given a false emphasis in the other tradition, and distorts the approach to Greek philosophy. This historical realism of the Latin humanist gives also a realism to his textual scholarship. Petrarch already has a feeling for the dating and genuineness of texts[1] which his successors rapidly carried to high standards of philological expertise. Lorenzo Valla was able to prove that the *Ad Herennium*, used throughout the Middle Ages as a text on rhetoric by "Tullius", was not really by Cicero.[2] Compare this with the unfailing gullibility with which Ficino swallows as *prisca theologia* texts which are really Hellenistic in date.

Then, the two traditions appeal to entirely different interests. The humanist's bent is in the direction of literature[3] and history; he sets an immense value on rhetoric and good literary style. The bent of the other tradition is towards philosophy, theology, and

[1] On Petrarch as a textual scholar, see G. Billanovich, "Petrarch and the Textual Tradition of Livy", *J.W.C.I.*, XIV (1951), p. 137 ff.

[2] Valla pointed out (in his invective against Bartolomeo Facio) that the *Ad Herennium* is not written in Cicero's style and therefore cannot be by him. Other bold feats of textual criticism by Valla were his exposure of the *Donation of Constantine* and his realisation that Dionysius the Areopagite was not the author of the writings traditionally ascribed to him.

[3] Or rather, he has chosen the subject which suits his bent. Two fundamental studies have clarified the meaning of the word "humanist" in the Renaissance. A. Campana has shown that "umanista" was originally university slang for a teacher of classical literature (A. Campana, "The Origin of the Word Humanist", *J.W.C.I.*, IX (1946), pp. 60–73). Kristeller has convincingly argued that humanistic studies were an expansion of the grammar and rhetoric of the mediaeval trivium, and quite distinct from the quadrivium subject of philosophy (see Kristeller, *Studies*, pp. 553–83; the chapter is a reprint of his article "Humanism and Scholasticism in the Italian Renaissance", first published in 1944). From this point of view, the tradition stemming from the *prisca theologia* is humanist only in the sense that it arose from a recovery of ancient texts. In every other sense it is non-humanist in the strict meaning of the word, dealing with the non-humanist subjects of philosophy, science or magic, and religion.

also science (at the stage of magic). The difference reflects the contrast between the Roman and the Greek mind. Again, in the Latin humanist tradition, the dignity of man has quite another meaning from that which it has in the other tradition. For Poggio Bracciolini, the recovery of dignity consists in casting off bad mediaeval Latin and dreary mediaeval and monastic ways of life, and the attempt to emulate in his person and surroundings the social pre-eminence, the sophisticated grandeur, of a noble Roman.[1] For Pico, the dignity of man consists in man's relation to God, but more than that, in Man as Magus with the divine creative power.

Again, the attitude to the Middle Ages is different in the two traditions. It is for the Latin humanist that the Middle Ages are "barbarous", using bad Latin and having lost the true sense of *Romanitas*. It is the humanist's mission to restore good Latin, which he thinks will in itself help to restore a universal *Romanitas*, and so to lead the world out of the ages of barbarism and into a new golden age of classical culture.[2] For the follower of the other tradition, the golden chain of *pia philosophia*, running from the *prisca theologia* to the present, threads its way through the Middle Ages and he finds some of his most revered Platonists in the ages of barbarism. Scholastic philosophy (for the other school the acme of barbarism) is for him an important source of *pia philosophia*, to be collated with his Neoplatonic and other sources. Ficino makes much use of Thomas Aquinas in his presentation of his Christian synthesis; and a large proportion of Pico's nine hundred theses are devoted to mediaeval philosophy. In his famous and oft-quoted letter to Ermolao Barbaro, Pico

---

[1] Poggio's *De nobilitate*, 1440, is a text in which the humanist (in the sense in which I am using the word) ideal of the dignity or nobility of man comes out clearly. For Poggio, the "noble" man is one who has become virtuous by imitating the antique virtues and who has gained fame and social prestige through his classical culture. It is entirely different from Pico's ideal, in which man's dignity consists in his lofty relation to God and, when he is a Magus, in the power which he can draw from the universe.

If one is going to use the word "humanism" in the vague sense of the Renaissance attitude to man, not in the precise sense of humanism as literary studies, it should be specified which kind of Renaissance attitude to man is meant.

[2] See W. K. Ferguson, *The Renaissance in Historical Thought*, Cambridge, Mass., 1948.

defended himself from the charge of having lost time over barbarous authors which he might have used for polite scholarship:

> We have lived illustrious, friend Ermolao, and to posterity shall live,
> not in the schools of the grammarians and teaching-places of young
> minds, but in the company of the philosophers, conclaves of sages,
> where the questions of debate are not concerning the mother of
> Andromache or the sons of Niobe and such light trifles, but of things
> human and divine.[1]

Pico is reproaching his humanist friend for remaining on the
childish level of the trivium, with his grammatical and linguistic
studies and cultivation of purely literary ornament, whereas he
himself is concerned with the loftier studies of the quadrivium.
Pico's letter marks very clearly the fundamental difference in aim
between the two traditions, which Giordano Bruno will express
more violently in his outcries against what he calls "grammarian
pedants" who fail to understand the higher activities of a Magus.
Here we may indulge in the curious reflection that if the Magi had
devoted more time to puerile grammatical studies and made
themselves into good philological scholars they might have seen
through the *prisci theologi*, and so never have become Magi.

Above all, it is in their relation to religion that the difference
between the two traditions is most profound. The humanist, if he
is a pious Christian like Petrarch, uses his humanist studies for
moral improvement, studying the great men of antiquity as examples of virtue from which the Christian may derive profit. If he
is not very Christian or pious, like Poggio, Valla, and other later
Italian humanists, he tends to be so obsessed with his admiration
for the pagan way of life that he looks down on Christianity. The
best authenticated examples of Renaissance paganism are to be
found amongst the later Latin humanists. In either case the issue
with religion is not an absolutely vital one; whether or not a
literary man uses his literary studies with a Christian moral intention is his own affair, not a major general religious issue. It is quite
otherwise with Neoplatonism which claimed to present a new
interpretation and understanding of Christianity. It is, above all,
quite otherwise with the Magus, who claimed to understand the
ways of God in the universe and to reproduce them in his magic.

---

[1] Pico, p. 352. The English translation is taken from a quotation in
J. A. Symonds's *Renaissance in Italy*, 1897, II, pp. 241-2.

Magic, as developed by Ficino and Pico was a major religious issue, as the objections to it quoted at the beginning of this chapter have shown.

Our theme here, however, is humanism as a force making against magic, and I think that it is such a force. Both by its critical scholarship and by its historical and social approach to man and his problems, an atmosphere of unadulterated humanism is not one which is congenial to the Magus and his pretensions. But the atmosphere very rarely was unadulterated and elements from the one tradition infiltrated into the other.

Perhaps the clearest case of such infiltration is that of the hieroglyphs. The history of the supposed Egyptian hieroglyphs of Horapollo, of the rage for them in the Renaissance, and of their development into the emblem, one of the most characteristic of Renaissance phenomena, is the aspect of Renaissance Egyptology which has been the most fully studied and explored.[1] The *Hieroglyphica* of Horapollo[2] was another of these supposedly ancient but really Hellenistic works; it explains the Egyptian hieroglyph as being a symbol with hidden moral and religious meanings, of course a misunderstanding of its true nature. The hieroglyph fashion is an offshoot of *prisca theologia*, for it owed much of its vogue to the deep respect for Egyptian wisdom as exemplified in Hermes Trismegistus. In the *argumentum* before his *Pimander*, Ficino attributes the invention of the hieroglyph to Hermes.[3] As compared with the talisman, the hieroglyph is not magical. It is a deep way of stating hidden truths in the sacred Egyptian writing. And it was immensely popular with the humanists, and therefore

[1] See Karl Giehlow, "Die Hieroglyphenkunde des Humanismus in der Allegorie der Renaissance", in *Jahrbuch der kunsthistorischen Sammlungen des allerhöchsten Kaiserhauses*, XXXII, pt. I, 1915; E. Iversen, *The Myth of Egypt and its Hieroglyphs*, Copenhagen, 1961.

[2] See *The Hieroglyphics of Horapollo*, translated by George Boas, Bollingen Series 23, New York, 1950.

[3] "Hunc (Hermes) asserunt occidisse Argum, Aegyptiis praefuisse, eisque leges, ac literas tradidisse. Literarum uero charracteres in animalium, arborumque figuris instituisse." (Ficino, p. 1836.) In one of the Plotinus commentaries he relates these figures used by the Egyptian priests to those described by "Horus", that is to the hieroglyphics of Horapollo (Ficino, p. 1768; cf. *Hieroglyphics of Horapollo*, ed. Boas, p. 28).

On the hieroglyphs as a medium for transmission of Hermetic philosophy, see below pp. 416–8.

an example of "Egyptian" infiltration into humanism.

Pure humanism could, however, turn in a religious direction, and towards a religious and theological attitude, and the clearest case of this is Erasmus. Erasmus is completely humanist in his whole outlook. He believes in polite learning, good letters, good Latinity, and he believes that a golden age will come when there is an international society of politely learned people all communicating easily with one another in an international language of good Latin. He is also a pious Christian, as Petrarch was, and the international society will be a piously Christian one, of well-educated people who have used their classical learning for its good moral teaching and moral examples of the virtuous men of old. He has absolutely no interest in dialectics, metaphysics, or natural philosophy, and he pours his amusing scorn, in the *Praise of Folly*, on the schoolmen, and their barbarous Latin. His dislike of mediaeval learning, below his aesthetic contempt for it and his contempt for its ignorance of polite learning, is really a temperamental dislike and incomprehension of the kind of subjects with which it deals.

His remedy for the decayed state of affairs which the decaying Middle Ages had brought with it is that of the humanist and literary man who is also a pious Christian. The remedy was to use the new invention of printing to make Christian literature available. Hence the labours of his life devoted to the publication and annotation of the New Testament and of the Greek and Latin Fathers of the Church. This was Erasmus' idea of a return to *prisca theologia*; the return to Christian sources by publishing the New Testament and the Fathers.

That he may even have thought of this as a contrast to the kind of *prisci theologi* to whom the Magi returned may perhaps be indicated by his extreme annoyance when an admirer addressed him as "Termaximus". George Clutton has suggested that Erasmus' otherwise rather incomprehensible anger at being addressed by an epithet which was meant as a fulsome flattery may be because "Termaximus" suggested "Hermes Trismegistus" and he did not like his work being compared to that kind of pristine theology.[1]

[1] George Clutton, "Termaximus: A Humanist Jest", *Journal of the Warburg Institute*, II (1938–9), pp. 266–8. In a letter to Erasmus, Ulrich Zasius addressed him as "ter maxime Erasme" (P. S. Allen, *Opus Epistolarum Des. Erasmi*, II, ep. 317). Clutton points out (*article cited*, p. 268) that "ter maximus" recalls "Trismegistus".

At any rate, as D. P. Walker has pointed out, Erasmus did not use *prisca theologia*, and in one passage may be throwing doubt on the authenticity of the Chaldean Oracles and the *Hermetica*:

> But if anything is brought from the Chaldeans or Egyptians, merely because of this we intensely desire to know it . . . and are often grievously disquieted by the dreams of some little man, not to say impostor, not only with no profit, but also with great waste of time, if not with some worse result, though this is already quite bad enough.[1]

Does "if not with some worse result" imply being led into magic? And how the great Hermes has sunk here to some dreaming little man, and perhaps an impostor!

Magia would not meet with the faith, or credulity, so necessary for its success in the Erasmian atmosphere. And Erasmus also several times indicates in his letters that he does not think much of Cabala,[2] although he was a friend of Reuchlin. Moreover, even the Christian basis of the synthesis of the Christian Magus is shaken when Erasmus in his New Testament Paraphrases, throws doubt on Dionysius the Areopagite as the author of the *Hierarchies*.[3] This critical impiety, in which Erasmus was following the bold Valla, greatly shocked the English Carthusians[4] and must also, one would think, have alarmed his friend John Colet, an ardent Dionysian.

Thus in the vicinity of Erasmus' critical (and also entirely non-scientific) mind, the whole set-up of the Renaissance Magus, as so impressively formulated by Ficino and Pico, would dwindle into vain dreaming based on doubtful scholarship. And, as a Christian, the Erasmian would repudiate *prisca theologia* as not the true,

---

[1] Erasmus, *Paraclesis* (1519), in *Opera omnia*, Leyden, 1703–6, col. 139; quoted as translated by D. P. Walker, "The *Prisca Theologia* in France", *J.W.C.I.*, XVII (1954), p. 254.

[2] "Mihi sane neque Cabala neque Talmud nunquam arrisit" (*Opus Ep.*, ed. cit. III, p. 589). He uses almost exactly the same phrase in another letter (*ibid.*, IV, p. 100). Cf. also *ibid.*, III, p. 253; IV, p. 379; IX, p. 300.

[3] See *Opus Ep.*, ed. cit., III, p. 482; XI, p. 111, and the note on this page pointing out that Erasmus queries the Areopagite as the author of the Dionysian writings in the paraphrases to Acts 17 (Erasmus, *N.T.*, 1516, p. 394) where he is following Valla.

[4] *Opus Ep.*, ed. cit., XI, p. III.

pristine, Gospel source to which the Christian should return.[1]

Huizinga has quoted the following words in an address by Erasmus to Anna of Borselen as an example of how Erasmus will flatter the "formal piety" of a patron in order to get money. "I send you a few prayers, by means of which you could, as by incantations, call down, even against her will, from Heaven, so to say, not the moon, but her who gave birth to the sun of justice."[2] If, as Huizinga probably rightly thinks, Erasmus is being ironical here, the irony is addressed, not at formal piety, but at the new astrological-religious fashions.

Thus if secular humanism is not favourable to the Magus, neither, certainly, is religious humanism of the Erasmian type. There is, however, one Egyptian product which Erasmus thinks valuable; namely the hieroglyphs. He uses them in the *Adagia*, and he thinks that they could help in furthering universal unity and good-will as a visual language which all could understand.[3] At this point, therefore, "Egyptian letters" join humanist Latin as, like it, making for universal tolerance and mutual understanding, the dearest dream of Erasmus. But this is a perfectly rational use of Egyptianism.

Terrible, in terms of destruction of art and learning, were the results in England when the egg which Erasmus had laid was hatched by the Reformation. The smashing of the "idolatrous" images in the churches was matched by the destruction of books and manuscripts in monastic and college libraries. When in 1550, in the reign of Edward VI, the government commissioners visited Oxford, bonfires were made of the contents of the libraries, and,

---

[1] The clouds of vagueness which hover over discussions of Renaissance humanism become even more dense when the writers' subject is "Christian humanism". Erasmus might, perhaps, with some truth be described as a Christian humanist, but not, in my opinion Ficino or Pico. Pico's attempt to prove the divinity of Christ by Magia and Cabala may be Christian but it is not humanist. It is more like Christian science, or, if we adopt Agrippa's expression, it is Christian occult philosophy. Ficino is not a Christian humanist but a Christian Hermetist and one who (in contrast to other Christian Hermetists to be discussed in the next chapter) did not exclude the magical side.

[2] J. Huizinga, *Erasmus of Rotterdam*, trans. F. Hopman, New York, 1952, p. 38.

[3] Erasmus, *Chiliades adagiorum* (1508), II, no. I.

according to Wood, particular suspicion was attached to works containing mathematical diagrams.

> Sure I am that such books wherein appeared Angles or Mathematical Diagrams, were thought sufficient to be destroyed because accounted Popish, or diabolical, or both.[1]

The humanist dislike of metaphysical and mathematical studies has turned into Reformation hatred of the past and fear of its magic. Where there is no understanding of such studies, there arises the ignorant dread of them as all magic.

A question which, I think, has never been asked, is how far the Renaissance revival of magic contributed to the suspicion of all philosophy as tinged with magic which inspired the devastating activities of the Edwardian reformers, products of the turning of Erasmian critical humanism against the Church with destructive fanaticism. It is a parallel question to the one asked previously, as to how far Reformation iconoclasm was aroused by attitudes to the magic of images some of which were relatively new.

After the brief interlude of the Marian reaction, the England of Elizabeth was officially a Reformation country, the reform being of an Erasmian type, and Erasmus' Paraphrases of the New Testament were placed in all churches. As regards learning at Oxford, this meant that the old pre-eminence of Oxford in philosophical and mathematical studies was not restored and was replaced by a different type of learning.

The central feature of Giordano Bruno's visit to England was the debate at Oxford when he expounded his "new philosophy", the reception of which by the Oxford "pedants" he bitterly complained of in his *Cena de le ceneri*, though he made some kind of apology in his *De la causa, principio e uno*. In an article published in 1938–9,[2] I analysed the historical setting of this episode, pointing out that Bruno's objection to the Oxford doctors is really that they are humanists, or "grammarian pedants" as he impolitely calls them, who do not understand philosophy, and who demonstrate their literary frivolity by quoting an Erasmian adage about madness at him when he insists that the sun is at the centre and the earth moves. I showed that his withdrawal of his abuse of

[1] Anthony à Wood, *The History and Antiquities of the University of Oxford*, ed. J. Gutch, Vol. II, part I (*Annals*), p. 107.

[2] "Giordano Bruno's Conflict with Oxford", *Journal of the Warburg Institute*, II (1938–9), pp. 227–42.

Oxford in the *De la causa* takes the form of a paean of admiration of pre-Reformation Oxford philosophy and science, and I compared the situation between Bruno and reformed, Erasmian Oxford with the situation between Pico della Mirandola and Ermolao Barbaro, where Pico defends his devotion to mediaeval and "barbaric" authors against the contempt of his humanist friend. I still think that these observations are quite correct, so far as they go, and I do not want to repeat here the detailed evidence with which I supported them in the article.[1]

We now know, however, from the most important discovery recently published by Robert McNulty, that Bruno at Oxford quoted long passages from memory from Ficino's *De vita coelitus comparanda*, with which he associated in some way the opinion of Copernicus.[2] In short, it was as a Ficinian Magus that Bruno presented himself at Oxford. This most valuable discovery, and its connection with what will be the theme of later chapters of this book—that Bruno's philosophy is basically Hermetic, and that he was a Hermetic Magus of a most extreme kind with a magico-religious mission of which Copernicanism was a symbol—will be analysed much more fully later.

I have anticipated the argument at this point, because the elucidation of the historical situation in which Bruno must be placed in order to understand him is so extremely complex that I have thought it better to prepare the reader for the future as we go along. At the end of chapter VIII we saw that Copernicus himself associated his discovery with Hermes Trismegistus, thus suggesting the possibility of the kind of use which Bruno was to make of it. And now, at the end of our analysis of the Magus in relation to humanism, we can see how the visit of a most extreme Magus to Oxford in 1583 could not fail to arouse violent reactions.

Madly impossible in a Protestant country which had been through the Erasmian reform, Bruno's philosophy also brought him to the stake in Counter Reformation Rome.

[1] Most of the points mentioned in this paragraph will, however, arise later.

[2] R. McNulty, "Bruno at Oxford", in *Renaissance News*, XIII (1960), pp. 300–5. See below, pp. 207–9.

Chapter X

RELIGIOUS HERMETISM IN THE SIXTEENTH CENTURY

THERE was a way of using the *Hermetica* which was purely religious and philosophical, without the magic, which was got rid of, either by approving of Hermes Trismegistus as a most religious writer but disapproving his lapses into bad magic, as in the passage on making the idols in the *Asclepius*, or by disposing of this passage by assuming that it was not really by Hermes but inserted by the magician, Apuleius of Madaura, when he made the Latin translation of the work. This left the way clear to admire Hermes without reserve for his remarkable insights into Old and New Testament truths. The most ancient Egyptian writes a *Genesis* which is close to the Hebrew *Genesis*; he speaks of the Son of God as the Word; he describes in a "Sermon on the Mount" (Discourse on the mountain of Hermes Trismegistus to his son Tat, *Corpus Hermeticum*, XIII) a religious experience which is like Christian regeneration; he seems to echo the beginning of St. John's gospel. All these Christian parallels, which had immensely struck Ficino, were free to be ecstatically pondered upon and developed, once the magic of the *Asclepius* was got rid of, by those who, unlike Ficino, were not willing to accept the magic.

Modern scholars, studying the *Hermetica* as Hellenistic gnosticism, have seen in them little or no trace of Christian influence.[1] For sixteenth-century religious enthusiasts, the Egyptian priest

[1] See above, p. 21, note 3.

seems to write almost as a Christian, as it were foreseeing Christianity from his remote position in time. It is significant that when Isaac Casaubon in 1614 pointed out for the first time for twelve centuries (Lactantius to Casaubon is about twelve centuries) that, though there may have been a man called Hermes Trismegistus of hoary antiquity, the *Hermetica* cannot have been written by any such person, he assumed that the works, or some of them were fakes by Christians.[1] So deeply had the Christian interpretation penetrated into the *Hermetica* that it was thus that they were seen in the first critical approach to them.

However, in the sixteenth century this discovery was not yet made, and even after it was made, Hermetism was not immediately dislodged, or only partially and in places dislodged from its powerful hold on religious thinking. Towards the end of the sixteenth century this influence reached a crescendo which pushed it forward into the seventeenth century where it long lingered. As J. Dagens has said, "La fin du XVIe siècle et le début du XVIIe siècle ont été l'âge d'or de l'hermétisme religieux."[2]

Religious Hermetism without magic was largely developed in France, where, as D. P. Walker has pointed out, the Neoplatonic movement imported from Italy was used with some caution, and the dangers of the *prisca theologia* as encouraging magic and heresy were recognised.[3] Lefèvre d'Etaples gave the lead in importing Hermetism into France and in warning against the magic of the *Asclepius*. Lefèvre had visited Italy, and met Ficino and Pico. He spoke of himself as a disciple and warm admirer of Ficino, and his edition of Ficino's *Pimander* was published in France, by the University of Paris, in 1494. A few years later, in 1505, Lefèvre brought together for the first time in one volume Ficino's *Pimander* and the *Asclepius*; he added a commentary by himself to the latter in which he condemned, as bad magic, the idol-making passage of the *Asclepius*.[4] The volume was dedicated

---

[1] See below, p. 400.

[2] J. Dagens, "Hermétisme et cabale en France de Lefèvre d'Etaples à Bossuet", *Revue de littérature comparée*, Janvier-Mars, 1961, p. 6.

[3] D. P. Walker, "The *Prisca Theologia* in France", *J.W.C.I.*, XVII (1954), pp. 204–59.

[4] This is the commentary which is printed with the *Asclepius* in collected editions of Ficino's works and was formerly thought to be by Ficino (see above, p. 40).

to a famous French bishop, Guillaume Briçonnet, thus inaugurating the ecclesiastical career of Hermetism without magic in France. Since Lefèvre d'Etaples was himself the author of a work on magic which he never published,[1] it is possible that his careful avoidance of the dangerous subject was due to repentance for, or concealment of, his own errors. Also, he included in the same volume with the *Pimander* and the *Asclepius*, a most extraordinary work which had been written before 1494 by Ludovico Lazzarelli, a most enthusiastic and exaggerated Hermetist. This was the *Crater Hermetis*, which was modelled on one of the regeneration treatises of the *Hermetica* (*Corpus Hermeticum* IV) and which describes in most excited language the passing on of the regenerative experience from a master to a disciple. In his valuable study of this work, P. O. Kristeller has suggested that it is meant to allude to Christ's inspiration of His disciples with His spirit, now interpreted as the Hermetic experience which can be repeated in modern times by an inspired Hermetist.[2] Thus, though Lefèvre banned the magic of the *Asclepius* in this volume, he included in it a work which is something like a magical interpretation of the psychology

[1] The manuscript of it exists: see Thorndike, IV, p. 513.

[2] Kristeller has been a pioneer in bringing to light documents on the extraordinary figure of Lazzarelli and his still more extraordinary mentor Joannes Mercurius da Corregio, who appears to have believed himself to be a kind of Hermetic Christ. He walked through the streets of Rome in 1484 wearing a crown of thorns with the inscription "Hic est puer meus Pimander quem ego eligi". On Lazzarelli and "Joannes Mercurius", see Kristeller, "Marsilio Ficino e Lodovico Lazzarelli", first published as an article in 1938, enlarged and revised in *Studies*, pp. 221–47; "Ancora per Giovanni Mercurio da Correggio", *Studies*, pp. 249–57; "Lodovico Lazzarelli e Giovanni da Corregio" in *Biblioteca degli Ardenti della Città di Viterbo*, 1961.

Extracts from Lazzarelli's *Crater Hermetis* and his *Epistola Enoch* (the latter is about Joannes Mercurius and his Hermetic mission) are published with introduction and notes by M. Brini in *Test. uman.*, pp. 23–77.

There are Cabalistic, as well as Hermetic, elements in the *Crater Hermetis* and its allied documents. It is possible that the phenomenon of Lazzarelli and "Joannes Mercurius" has not yet been put into its historical context. May it not be related to the controversy about Pico, which turned on the question of whether Magia and Cabala confirm the divinity of Christ which was so impressively answered in the affirmative by Pope Alexander VI? A sonnet by "Hermes Junior", almost certainly "Joannes Mercurius", is interpreted by the commentator as referring at one point to Alexander VI (see Kristeller, *Studies*, pp. 252, 255).

of religious experience.[1] A French translation of the *Crater Hermetis* was included in a French translation of the *Hermetica* dedicated to Cardinal Charles de Lorraine in 1549, which suggests that Hermetic religious enthusiasm was making headway in French ecclesiastical circles.

Symphorien Champier of Lyons was a leading apostle of Neoplatonism in France, and an admirer of Ficino. In his *De Quadruplici Vita* (Lyons, 1507) he is imitating Ficino's *Libri de Vita*, but without the talismans of the *De vita coelitus comparanda* against which he utters a warning. And it is Champier who first put forward the comforting view that the magical passage in the *Asclepius* was not by the holy Hermes himself but was interpolated into the Latin translation by the wicked magician Apuleius of Madaura.[2] This idea was repeated by later French writers on Hermetism and did much to help the general acceptance of religious Hermetism. Champier printed in his *De Quadruplici Vita* a Latin translation by Ludovico Lazzarelli of the *Definitiones*, namely the last treatise of the *Corpus Hermeticum*[3] which Ficino had not translated because it was not in his manuscript. The most striking feature of this Hermetic treatise, now published in Latin translation for the first time, is the tremendous passage on the sun and the "choirs of demons" surrounding it.

In 1554, Turnebus published at Paris the first edition of the Greek text of the *Corpus Hermeticum*, accompanied by Ficino's

---

[1] Walker suggests (pp. 70–1) that the experience described in the *Crater Hermetis* is somewhat like a magical operation by which the master provided his disciple with a good demon, and is analogous to the introduction of demons into idols described in the *Asclepius*. Lefèvre reports Lazzarelli as having interpreted the idol-making passage in the *Asclepius* "as if the idols were the Apostles and the man making them were Christ" (quoted by Walker, "The *Prisca Theologia* in France", p. 241, from Lefèvre's commentary on the *Asclepius*).

[2] Walker, "The *Prisca Theologia* in France", pp. 234–9.

[3] *Corpus Hermeticum* XVI (divided into three parts by modern editors); *C.H.*, II, pp. 231–55. Lazzarelli's Latin translation is reprinted from the edition of 1507 by C. Vasoli, "Temi e fonti della tradizione ermetica in uno scritto di Symphorien Champier", in *Umanesimo e esoterismo*, ed. E. Castelli, Padua, 1960, pp. 251–9. On the codex at Viterbo which contains the manuscript of Lazzarelli's translation, see Kristeller, *Studies*, pp. 227 ff. and his above-cited article in *Biblioteca degli Ardenti della Città di Viterbo*.

Latin translation, and Lazzarelli's translation of the treatise missing in Ficino. A preface by Vergerius stresses the resemblances of Hermetism to Christianity and states that Hermes the Egyptian lived before Pharaoh and consequently before Moses.[1] There seems to be a tendency by which the holier and more Christian Hermes Trismegistus becomes, the more his date is pushed back, now to *before* Moses.

François de Foix de Candale, Bishop of Aire, reaches new heights of ecstatic religious Hermetism. In 1574 he published another edition of the Greek text of the *Hermetica*, based on that of Turnebus with emendations suggested by Scaliger and others. He thinks that Hermes attained to a knowledge of divine things surpassing that of the Hebrew prophets and equalling that of the Apostles and Evangelists. He lived at an earlier date than Moses and must have been divinely inspired. The bad passages in the *Asclepius* were put in by Apuleius. In 1579, Foix published a French translation of the *Hermetica*, the preface to which repeats these statements and seems almost to elevate the works of Hermes Trismegistus to the level of canonical scriptures.[2]

In spite of this growing chorus of approval of a Hermes purged of magic, and consequently of Ficino's talismans, the magical current was also pretty strong in France. Jacques Gohorry, or "Leo Suavius" as he called himself, thought that Ficino had not gone far enough and that a much stronger Hermetic magic was needed. Gohorry lived in Paris until his death in 1576 and seems to have run a kind of medical-magical Academy, not far from the site of Baïf's Academy of Poetry and Music.[3]

The thought also occurs that the blame for the magic of the *Asclepius* which the pious Hermetists were casting on Apuleius of Madaura might have had the effect of attracting confirmed magicians to that author, whose romance of *The Golden Ass* had been extremely popular in the Italian Renaissance. The novel recreates for the reader with wonderful vividness the late antique society riddled with magic of all kinds. The experiences of the hero, turned into an ass by bad witches, suffering all the blows and

[1] Kristeller, *Studies*, p. 223; Walker, "The *Prisca Theologia* in France", p. 209; quotations from Vergerius' preface in Scott, I, pp. 33–4.

[2] Walker, "The *Prisca Theologia* in France", p. 209; Scott, I, pp. 34–6.

[3] Walker (*Spiritual and Demonic Magic*), pp. 96–106.

punishments of fortune in his asinine form, at last freed from that form in the ecstasy of his vision of Isis rising from the sea near the lonely shore to which he has wandered in despair, and finally initiated into the mysteries of Isis and becoming a priest of her cult, form a kind of odyssey of a suffering Magus. The story is written in a cruel and glittering style, facetious and obscene, yet with the Egyptian mysteries hidden within this ridiculous story of an ass. Such a style might have appealed to a modern magician as his model. I am thinking, of course, of Giordano Bruno.

Ficino and Pico had used *prisca theologia* and Neoplatonism as the basis of a Christian religious synthesis, in which all Gentile philosophy pointed towards Christianity. This theological or syncretistic use of *prisca theologia* is quite independent of magic and it is highly developed in many French theological writers of the sixteenth century. Pontus de Tyard, Bishop of Châlons, is an extreme example of it:

> From the holy Egyptian school . . . has descended to us the secret doctrine and salutary knowledge of the ternary number, so greatly reverenced that the essence of the World is entirely attributed to its disposition of number, weight, and measure. A secret which the Magi understood under the three Gods whom you have named. For by Oromasis they understood God, by Mitra, the understanding, or that which the Latins call *mens*, and by Araminis, the Soul.[1]

Most of this, and of similar arguments used by Pontus de Tyard, comes out of Ficino's *Theologia Platonica*.[2] In the passage quoted Egyptian and Zoroastrian material is not being used in any magical sense but simply as intimations in *prisca theologia* foreshadowing the Trinity, or indicating, as Tyard says later in the same passage "that the divine substance, spreading its power among all nations, has left no people in the world without some odour of the divinity."

The extreme Christian piety of Hermes Trismegistus, when purified of the bad aspects of the *Asclepius*, made him a useful *priscus theologus* to emphasise in these connections. Tyard speaks of Hermes' theology as the oldest of all, and after quoting a

---

[1] Pontus de Tyard, *Deux discours de la nature du Monde et de ses parties*, Paris, 1578, p. 98 *recto*; reprinted as *The Universe*, ed. J. C. Lapp, Columbia, 1950, pp. 148–9.

[2] Lib. IV, cap. 1 (Ficino, p. 130).

prayer from the *Pimander*, rhetorically asks whether anything can be found, even in the psalms of David, more pious and religious than this.[1] As a native of the Lyons region, Tyard would no doubt have been influenced by Symphorien Champier's purified version of Hermetism.

In his preface to Tyard's work, Jacques Davy Du Perron, afterwards Bishop of Evreux and eventually a cardinal, emphasises its syncretism and describes Tyard as embracing in it the Cabalist doctrine of the three worlds, the intelligible, the celestial, and the visible.[2] Here again, the Cabalism is not practical Cabala, but vague confirmation brought in from the Hebrew tradition of the prevailing syncretism.

I have examined at length in my book on *The French Academies of the Sixteenth Century* the bearings of the theological synthesis of writers like Tyard and Du Perron on the poetry of the French Pléiade and particularly on the Academy of Poetry and Music founded by one of its members, Baïf. This Academy was devoted to "measuring" together poetry and music after what was believed to be the antique fashion in order to produce the "effects" on the hearers attributed to ancient music. The Academy produced both profane songs, full of mythological allusions, and also Psalms, both set to music in the same manner. The question as to whether such products are "incantations" in the magical sense or incantatory for their artistic quality alone is a very difficult one, for the borderline between magic and art is as hard to trace in this period as the borderline between magic and religion. It is possible that the incantatory or magical intention varied with different people. A bishop, like Pontus de Tyard, might make cautious reservations in consonance with the Gallican caution about the magic of *prisca theologia*. But we have also to remember that at the centre of the French court, the moving spirit of its festivals in which the new artistic techniques were used, there was "the Italian woman", the Queen Mother, Catherine de' Medici, member of the great Florentine house which had encouraged Ficino and Pico and had certainly not discouraged their magic. Catherine was notorious for

[1] Pontus de Tyard, *Deux discours, etc.*, 1578, pp. 112 *verso*–113 *recto* (ed. Lapp, p. 169); cf. Walker, "The *Prisca Theologia* in France", p. 210.
[2] Pontus de Tyard, *Deux discours, etc.*, 1578, preface by Du Perron. sig. a iiii *verso*; cf. my book *The French Academies of the Sixteenth Century*, Warburg Institute, University of London, 1947, pp. 88–9.

her interest in talismans and her encouragement of magicians and astrologers, and it would be difficult to believe that there was not also something of a magical intention behind her festivals. When in the *Ballet comique de la reine* of 1581, the product of the festival tradition which she founded, Catherine saw Jupiter and Mercury descending from heaven in response to the incantatory music and singing, it is doubtful, great artist though she was, whether she saw this as a purely artistic representation. More probably, for her, such a performance was in the nature of an extended and complicated talisman, an arrangement of the planetary gods in a favourable order, invoked by favourable incantations, resulting, not only in a marvellous work of art, but in a magical action by which something was done, by which the favour of the heavens was actually drawn down in aid of the French Monarchy and for the pacification of the wars of religion.[1]

All the writers so far mentioned in this chapter have been Catholics, but in Philippe Du Plessis Mornay we have a Protestant author who is making a large use of Hermetism[2] in his *De la vérité de la religion chrétienne*, published at Antwerp by Plantin in 1581 with a dedication to the King of Navarre. In this dedication Mornay says that "in these miserable times" he is undertaking a work for religion through studying the world as a "shadow of the splendour of God", and man as made in the image of God. In this latter part of the century, in a Europe devastated by the awful wars and persecutions arising from the conflict between Reformation and Catholic reaction, Mornay is an example of how men were turning to the Hermetic religion of the world to take them above these conflicts, and as a possible way of escape from the agonies inflicted by fanatical use of force by both sides. Wise men of all ages have taught that God is one, says Mornay:

[1] On the *Ballet comique*, see my books *The French Academies of the Sixteenth Century*, pp. 236 ff., and *The Valois Tapestries* (Warburg Institute, University of London, 1959), pp. 82 ff. In my article, "Poésie et Musique au Mariage du Duc de Joyeuse" (in *Musique et Poésie au XVIe siècle*, Centre National de la Recherche Scientifique, Paris, 1954, pp. 241 ff.) I have suggested the magical aspects of such a performance, comparing (p. 255) the descent of Jupiter in the ballet with a Jupiter talisman said to have been in Catherine's possession.

[2] Walker ("The *Prisca Theologia* in France", p. 209, 211-2) and Dagens (*article cited*, p. 8) have drawn attention to Mornay's use of Hermetism.

Mercure Trismegiste, qui est (si vrayement ces liures sont de luy, &, pour le moins sont-ils bien anciens) la source de tous, enseigne par tout: Que Dieu est un; Que l'unité est la racine de toutes choses. . . . Qu'a luy seul appartient le nom de Pere, & de Bon. . . . Il l'appelle le Pere du monde . . . l'Action de toutes puissances, la Puissance de toutes actions. . . . Seul & luy-mesmes Tout; sans Nom, & meilleur que tout Nom.[1]

Mornay refers in the margin as sources for these sentiments both to the *Pimander*, II, III, IV, V, VI, IX, XI, XIII (that is to these treatises in the *Corpus Hermeticum*), and to the *Asclepius*.

In other passages he discusses the Hermetic "Son of God" as the Word and quotes the Hermetic account of creation, comparing it with *Genesis*.[2] And he draws from Pico della Mirandola mystical meditations on the Nothing in all religious teachings:

. . . les Egyptiens inuoquans le premier principe, qu'ils appeloyent Tenebres au dessus de toute cognoissance comme l'Ensoph des Hebrieux, ou la nuict d'Orphée.[3]

To Pico's conclusion on the Orphic *nox* being the same as Ensoph in Cabala, Mornay has added, as the same, the Egyptian (that is Hermetic) teaching on the darkness above reason, the No Name above the Names. He has a good deal more on Cabala, mentioning the *Zohar* of which he evidently has some knowledge.[4]

Mornay is making the familiar synthesis between Hermetism and Cabala, but it is emphatically not Magia and practical Cabala of which he is speaking. The synthesis is entirely mystical and theological. He states most emphatically later on that Cabala is not magic, that Moses was not a magician, and that all magic is wrong and vain.[5]

Mornay's work reflects the situation at Antwerp in 1581 where William of Orange was trying to establish the Southern Netherlands, now temporarily freed from Philip II of Spain, as a state in which religious toleration should be practised. In the following year, the French prince, François D'Anjou, was installed by

[1] Mornay, *De la vérité de la religion chrétienne*, Antwerp, 1581, p. 38.

[2] *Ibid.*, pp. 80, 98–100.

[3] *Ibid.*, pp. 101–2.

[4] *Ibid.*, pp. 106 ff., 740 ff. Dagens (*article cited*, pp. 9, 11) has pointed out that Mornay connects Hermetic and Cabalist teachings with the Pseudo-Dionysian mysticism.

[5] *Ibid.*, pp. 633 ff.

Orange as the titular head of this state, which had but a short life and soon succumbed to the pressure of many disasters.[1] The interesting thing is that those promoting this venture, and its efforts at religious toleration, were using the Erasmian tradition of tolerance as a basis. There is thus a point in the sixteenth-century longing for escape from religious dissension where the entirely different tradition of Erasmianism joins the Hermetic-Cabalist tradition.

This matter has a bearing on the problems of Giordano Bruno in England, where, according to himself he was better received by Sir Philip Sidney and his circle than by the Oxford "pedants". For Sidney was strongly in sympathy with the cause of the Southern Netherlands for which, in 1586, not long after Bruno's departure from England, he was to give his life. And Du Plessis Mornay was known to Sidney as a friend and was undoubtedly his favourite theologian, as evidenced by the fact that Sidney began to translate into English this very work from which we have been quoting. His death prevented him from completing the translation, which was carried on by Arthur Golding, who published it in 1587 as *A Woorke concerning the trewnesse of the Christian Religion*, with a dedication to the Earl of Leicester, then fighting against Spain in the Low Countries.

We can therefore quote again in what may be Sidney's English, the passage quoted above which comes fairly near the beginning of the work:

> Mercurius Trismegistus, who (if the bookes which are fathered uppon him bee his in deede, as in trueth they bee very auncient) is the founder of them all, teacheth eueriwhere, That there is but one God: That one is the roote of all things, and that without that one, nothing hath bene of all things that are: That the same one is called the onely good and the goodnesse it selfe, which hath uniuersall power of creating all things. . . . That unto him alone belongeth the name of Father, and of Good. . . . He calleth him the father of the world, the Creator, the Beginning . . . the worker of all powers, and the power of all workes.[2]

[1] In my book *The Valois Tapestries* (Warburg Institute, University of London, 1959) I have analysed Orange's abortive attempt to establish a tolerant state under Anjou, arguing that these tapestries reflect the hopes of that lost moment in history.

[2] *A Woorke concerning the trewnesse of the Christian Religion*, by Philip of Mornay . . . begun by Sir P. Sidney, finished at his request by Arthur

Thus Sidney knew the Hermetic teachings, in the form quite free from magic in which Mornay presented them.

What then did Sir Philip Sidney think of Giordano Bruno and his panacea for the religious situation of Europe, a return to *magical* Hermetism and *magical* Egyptianism? The message of the Magus also came out of the Hermetic tradition, yet it was very different in tone and content from the Protestant non-magical Hermetism of Mornay.

Another striking example of sixteenth-century religious Hermetism, is the commentary on the *Pymander Hermetis Mercurii Trismegistus*, in six huge volumes, by Hannibal Rosseli, an Italian Capucin, published at Cracow, 1585–90.[1] Rosseli is using Foix de Candale's text of the *Hermetica*, which puts him in the French tradition of religious Hermetism, and his commentary introduces the whole range of ancient writers used in Renaissance Neoplatonism. Rosseli is guarded in what he says about magic, and warns against it.[2] He devotes many pages to the hierarchies of Pseudo-Dionysius[3] before passing on to the "Seven Governors" mentioned in *Pimander*, which he identifies with angels.[4] He is, one might say, ecstatically aware of continuity between the celestial world and the supercelestial or angelic world but, since he does not mention Cabala, he is probably not attempting to do angelic magic. His approach to Hermetism is deeply religious and Christian, and his truly stupendous labours testify to the mounting religious excitement about Hermetism towards the close of the century. Since he was a Capucin, it may be assumed that religious

[1] There was another edition at Cologne in 1630. See Scott, I, p. 36; Dagens, *article cited*, p. 7.

[2] Hannibal Rosseli, *Pymander Hermetis Mercurii Trismegistus, cum commentariis*, Cologne, 1630, I, pp. 322 ff.

[3] *Ibid.*, I, pp. 241 ff.   [4] *Ibid.*, I, pp. 248 ff.

Golding, London, 1587, p. 27. Since this passage comes in chapter 3, and Golding says in his preface that Sidney had already translated certain chapters before he went to the war, it is possible that the passage quoted was translated by Sidney, though we cannot be sure of this. For a discussion of the question, and for an analysis of the use of *prisca theologia* in Mornay's work as a background to a passage in Sidney's *Arcadia*, see D. P. Walker, "Ways of Dealing with Atheists: a Background to Pamela's Refutation of Cecropia", *Bibliothèque d'Humanisme et Renaissance*, XVII (1955), pp. 252 ff.

Hermetism was making itself felt in this Counter Reformation order.

It has been said by J. Dagens that "cette influence de l'hermétisme religieux a touché les protestants et les catholiques, favorisant, chez les uns et les autres, les tendances les plus iréniques."[1] It is perhaps significant that, just as Mornay's Protestant treatise showing strong Hermetic influence was published at Antwerp, where William of Orange was trying to establish religious toleration, so also Rosseli's great effort of Catholic Hermetism was first published in Poland, a country which practised religious toleration. Such efforts need not have been aiming specifically at eirenism, or religious reunion, but merely at toleration or the avoidance of force for the settlement of religious problems, by creating an atmosphere of Christian tolerance through mutual return to the Hermetic religion of the world, understood in a Christian sense.

At the French court in the fifteen-eighties, the king, Henri III, was the centre of an intensive religious movement in which he was very much influenced by Capucins, an order which he greatly encouraged and to which his numerous penitent confréries were affiliated.[2] He was trying to deal with the situation with which he was faced in a religious way. Encouraged by Philip of Spain, Catholic extremists in France were bent on violent and dangerous courses; Protestant extremists were equally intransigent. The king was trying to find a middle course, and was endeavouring to foster a Catholic "politique" or tolerant religious movement which should be attached to himself and loyal to the French Monarchy. I have studied this atmosphere around Henri III in other books,[3] and in an article published in 1939–40 on "The Religious Policy of Giordano Bruno"[4] I showed that when, in 1582, Bruno came to

[1] Dagens, *article cited*, p. 8.

[2] A set of drawings in the Cabinet des Estampes represents a long religious procession winding through the streets of Paris and out into the country on a pilgrimage. Henri and his penitent *confrères* are taking part in it and the procession is led by Capucin friars. In my article, "Dramatic Religious Processions in Paris in the Late Sixteenth Century" (*Annales Musicologiques*, II, Paris, 1954, pp. 215–70) I published these drawings, analysing their meaning and pointing out (pp. 223 ff.) the importance of the Capucins in them and in Henri's religious movement generally.

[3] *The French Academies of the Sixteenth Century* and *The Valois Tapestries*.

[4] *Journal of the Warburg Institute*, III (1939–40), pp. 181–207. Cf. also *The French Academies*, pp. 225–9.

England from Paris, where he had received some encouragement from Henri III, it was on some kind of political mission, urging Henri's peaceable and religious intentions in contrast to the militant ambitions of Spain, with which England was equally threatened. Henri, says Bruno in his *Spaccio della bestia trionfante*,

> ... loves peace, he preserves his contented people as much as possible in tranquillity and devotion; he is not pleased with the noisy uproar of martial instruments which administer to the blind acquisition of the unstable tyrannies and principalities of the earth; but with all manner of justice and sanctity which show the straight road to the eternal kingdom.[1]

I suggested also, that Bruno's philosophy had a religious background to it and had behind it a conciliatory religious mission to Protestant England.

French religious Hermetism, and the Catholic religious Hermetism of a Capucin like Rosseli, is something which Bruno would have known in the Parisian atmosphere from which he came. Nevertheless his own Hermetism, his own "new philosophy" which he preaches as a palliative for the religious situation, is not the Christian, Pseudo-Dionysian and angelic type of Hermetism which we find in Rosseli, though this writer ought to be carefully studied in connection with Bruno.

In this rapid survey of the tremendous subject of Hermetism in the sixteenth century I have picked out only a few examples, chosen with a view to assisting the estimate, to be made in the next chapters, of Bruno's position as a Hermetic philosopher. I now come to an example, which is in many ways the most important of all from this point of view, namely Francesco Patrizi.

As Scott has said, "Patrizi seems to have been impelled by a genuine enthusiasm to take upon himself the task of bringing about a restoration of true religion; and he regarded the *Hermetica* as one of the most effective instruments that could be used in this design."[2] He outlined his scheme in his *Nova de universis philosophia*, first published at Ferrara in 1591 (second edition, Venice, 1593), with a dedication to Pope Gregory XIV. With his "New

---

[1] Giordano Bruno, *Spaccio della bestia trionfante*, dial. 3 (*Dial. ital.*, p. 826). Cf. "The Religious Policy of G. Bruno", p. 224; *The French Academies*, pp. 227–8; and below, pp. 228–9.

[2] Scott, I, p. 37.

Universal Philosophy", Patrizi published the *Corpus Hermeticum*, using the Greek text of Turnebus and Foix de Candale and giving a new Latin translation, also the *Asclepius*, also some of the *Hermetica* preserved by Stobaeus, with Latin translations of these. Patrizi thus made available in this volume, as the foundation of his new philosophy, a larger collection of *Hermetica* than had hitherto been assembled together. This was a labour of enthusiastic devotion; Patrizi believed that Hermes Trismegistus was a little earlier than Moses[1]; that Moses' account of creation must be supplemented by the account in *Pimander*; that Hermes spoke much more clearly of the mystery of the Trinity than Moses.[2]

In his dedication to Gregory XIV of the *Nova de universis philosophia*, Patrizi says that a philosopher nowadays is thought to be one who does not believe in God. The reason for this is that the only philosophy studied is that of Aristotle which denies the omnipotence and providence of God. Yet Hermes said that without philosophy it is impossible to be pious, and therefore Patrizi has tried to discover a truer philosophy by which we might return to God. He hopes that the Pope and his successors will adopt this religious philosophy and cause it to be taught everywhere. He asks why those parts of Aristotle's philosophy which are hostile to God are studied, when a Hermetic treatise contains more philosophy than all the works of Aristotle put together. Many of Plato's dialogues should also be taught publicly; also Plotinus, Proclus and the early Fathers. But the scholastics are dangerous, being too Aristotelian.

> I would have you then, Holy Father, and all future Popes, give orders that some of the books which I have named (prominent among these was the *Hermetica*) shall be continually taught everywhere, as I have taught them for the last fourteen years at Ferrara. You will thus make all able men in Italy, Spain, and France friendly to the Church; and perhaps even the German Protestants will follow their example, and return to the Catholic faith. It is much easier to win them back

[1] "Videtur Hermes hic Trismegistus coetanus quidem fuisse Mosy, sed paulo senior. . . ." Introduction to the *Hermetica* in Patrizi's *Nova de universis philosophia*; cf. Scott, I, p. 40.

[2] "Poemander creationem mundi et hominis, cum Mosaica fere eandem complectitur. Et Trinitatis mysterium longe apertius quam Moses ipse enarrat." Dedication to Gregory XIV of Patrizi's *Nova de universis philosophia*. Cf. Scott, I, p. 39.

in this way than to compel them by ecclesiastical censures or by secular arms. You should cause this doctrine to be taught in the schools of the Jesuits, who are doing such good work. If you do this, great glory will await you among men of future times. And I beg you to accept me as your helper in this undertaking.[1]

Here we have the pious philosophy, based on Hermetism, in a clearly Counter Reformation setting. The Jesuits are advised to use it, and it is a peaceful way of attracting Protestants, without persecution and force of arms.

Patrizi's "new philosophy" as expounded in the *Nova de universis philosophia* is much more in the tradition of Italian Hermetism, going back to Ficino and Pico, than in the French tradition with its careful avoidance of magic. Patrizi quotes Plato as having said that magic is the cult of the gods,[2] and "John Picus" who said that Magus among the Persians means the same thing as philosopher among the Greeks.[3] Elsewhere he repeats that the true meaning of the word Magus is one who cultivates God, and that the most ancient part of magic, or *prisca magia*, is true religion.[4] In the first book,[5] he sets out a light series, running from the supercelestial light, through the stars, to the light of the sun in this world, referring in this connection to Hermes and Dionysius.[6] Rosseli also has something of the same kind, but in Patrizi we are closer to the original Ficinian exposition, and some kind of magic is certainly implied. Patrizi devotes much space to questions of natural philosophy, such as the position of the sun, mentioning that Hermes puts it above the moon[7]; he does not mention Copernicus, nor adopt heliocentricity. He discusses at length universal animation,[8] in which he believes (though not in the

---

[1] Patrizi, dedication of the *Nova de universis philosophia*; quoted as translated by Scott, *loc. cit.*

[2] *Zoroaster*, separately paged work in Patrizi, *Nova de universis philosophia*, p. 4 *verso*.

[3] *Ibid., loc. cit.*

[4] *Ibid.*, p. 5, and in other passages.

[5] Patrizi, *De luce*, separately paged work with which the *Nova de universis philosophia* begins.

[6] *Ibid.*, p. 11, etc.

[7] Patrizi, *De spacio physico* (separately paged work in *Nova de universis philosophia*), p. 109.

[8] Patrizi, *Pampsychia* (separately paged work in *Nova de universis philosophia*), pp. 54 ff. (*an mundus sit animatus*).

movement of the earth), and in his chapter "on the One", he expatiates on the theme of the One and the All.[1]

In Patrizi, we have an expounder of a "new philosophy" strongly influenced by Hermetism and going back, behind the more recent attempts to purify Hermetism of magic, to the Ficinian atmosphere with its belief in *prisca magia*. This philosophy is anti-Aristotelian, in the sense that it claims to be more religious than Aristotle. Its author hopes that the Pope will use it in the Counter Reformation effort, as a means of reviving religion and converting the Protestants.

In 1592, Patrizi was called to Rome by Pope Clement VIII to teach the Platonic philosophy in the university. He must have gone to Rome full of hopes that this summons meant that he was to be allowed to teach and preach there the Hermetic Counter Reformation which he had outlined in his "New Universal Philosophy". But critical voices were raised against his ideas, he got into trouble with the Inquisition,[2] and consented to revise and retract whatever was thought heretical in his book. But the book was eventually condemned, and though Patrizi was not otherwise punished (he seems to have retained his chair until his death in 1597) he was, in effect, silenced, and his effort to put "Hermes Trismegistus, contemporary of Moses" back into the Church, as at Siena, did not receive official encouragement. His story illustrates the mental confusion of the late sixteenth century and how it was not easy, even for a most pious Catholic Platonist like Patrizi, to realise how he stood theologically (the position about magic was being drawn up by Del Rio[3] when Patrizi was in Rome but was not yet published).

Giordano Bruno was also the preacher of a "new philosophy" which he expounded in Protestant England and which was, as will be demonstrated in later chapters, basically Hermetic. In 1591, Bruno returned to Italy hoping to interest Pope Clement VIII in his philosophy. But Bruno had taken the appalling step of abandoning the Christian interpretation of Hermetism, which was the

---

[1] Patrizi, *Panarchios* (separately paged work in *Nova de universis philosophia*), pp. 9 ff.

[2] For an account of Patrizi's troubles, see Luigi Firpo, "Filosofia italiana e Controriforma", *Rivista di Filosofia*, XLI (1950), pp. 150–73; XLII (1951), pp. 30–47.

[3] See above, p. 159.

whole foundation of pious religious Hermetism, whether Protestant or Catholic. Hence his fate as a Hermetic philosopher with a universal reforming mission was very much worse than that of Patrizi.

As compared with the intense preoccupation with religious Hermetism on the continent of Europe in the sixteenth century, England was in a curious position of isolation, owing to the religious convulsions through which she passed. The adaptation of Catholic theology and philosophy to Neoplatonism and the *prisca theologia* made a beginning in England with Thomas More, John Colet, and their circle. Colet was certainly touched with Ficinian influences, and his treatise on the Pseudo-Dionysian angelic hierarchies is an adaptation of English pre-Reformation Dionysian mysticism to the new Dionysianism.[1] More greatly admired Pico della Mirandola, whose biography by G. F. Pico he translated into English for the edification of a nun.[2] This biography contains references to Pico's interests, translated by More as the "secrete misteryes of the hebrewes, caldyes and arabies" and "ye olde obscure philosophye of Pythagoras, trismegistus, and orpheus".[3] Thus, at the very dawn of the sixteenth century (More's *Life of Picus* was printed in 1510 and he is thought to have made the translation five years earlier) the names of the *prisci theologi* are enunciated by an Englishman.

In More's *Utopia*, first published in Latin in 1516, the religion of the Utopians is thus described (in Ralph Robinson's English translation):

[1] In particular, Colet's treatise on the celestial hierarchies reveals dependence on Ficino's view of the nine angelic hierarchies as "drinking" the divine influences which thence pass down into the nine-fold order of the world, that is the *primum mobile*, zodiac, and seven planets. "Nam quod novem hauriunt angelorum ordines, id novenario progressu in universa diffunditur . . ." (John Colet, *Two Treatises on the Hierarchies of Dionysius*, published with English translation by J. H. Lupton, London, 1869, p. 180). Colet's Dionysian mysticism is affected here by the Ficinian "astrologising" of mysticism (see above, pp. 118–20). Colet also knew Pico's praises of Cabala, from which he quotes in this work.

[2] R. W. Chambers, *Thomas More*, London, 1935, pp. 93–4.

[3] *The Life of John Picus, Earl of Mirandula*, in *The English Works of Sir Thomas More*, ed. W. E. Campbell, A. W. Reed, R. W. Chambers, etc., 1931, I, p. 351.

Some worship for God the sonne: some the mone: some, some other of the planettes. There be that give worship to a man that was ones of excellente vertue or of famous glory, not only as God, but also as the chiefest and hyghest God. But the moste and the wysest parte (rejectynge al these) beleve that there is a certayne Godlie powre unknowen, everlastinge, incomprehensible, inexplicable, farre above the capacitie and retche of mans witte, dispersed throughout all the worlde, not in bignes, but in vertue and power. Him they call the father of al. To him alone they attribute the beginninges, the en-creasinges, the procedinges, the chaunges, and the endes of al thinges. Neither they geve any divine honours to any other then to him.[1]

I would suggest that there is Hermetic influence in this description of the religion practised by the wisest of the Utopians, which prepared them to receive Christianity.

But after they hearde us speake of the name of Christ . . . you will not beleve with howe gladde mindes, they agreed unto the same: whether it were by the secrete inspiration of God, or elles for that they thought it nieghest unto that opinion, which among them is counted chiefest.[2]

The converted Utopians are then, perhaps, Christian Hermetists. At any rate they already display the distinctive badge of religious Hermetism in the sixteenth century, the disapproval of the use of force in religious matters. When a Utopian, converted to Christianity, grew bigoted and began to condemn all other religions, he was sharply rebuked and banished.

For this is one of the auncientest lawes amonge them: that no man shall be blamed for resininge in the maintenance of his owne religion. For kyng Utopus . . . made a decree, that it should be lawfull for everie man to favoure and folow what religion he would, and that he mighte do the best he could to bring other to his opinion, so that he did it peaceablie, gentelie, quietly and soberlie, without hastie and contentious rebuking and invehing against other. If he could not by faire and gentle speche induce them unto his opinion yet he should use no kinde of violence, and refraine from displesaunte and sedi-tious woordes. To him that would vehemently and ferventlye in this cause strive and contende was decreed banishment or bondage.[3]

Thus did Thomas More enunciate the principles of religious toleration *before* the disasters of the sixteenth century had begun—

---

[1] More's *Utopia*, Robinson's translation, Everyman edition, p. 100.
[2] *Ibid.*, pp. 100–1. [3] *Ibid.*, pp. 101–2.

before his own execution, before the fires had been lighted at Smithfield under Mary, before the torturing of Catholic missionaries under Elizabeth, before the French wars of religion and the Massacre of St. Bartholomew, before the appalling cruelties of the Spaniards in the Netherlands, before the burning of Servetus by Calvin, before the burning of Giordano Bruno by the Inquisition. And, if I am right in suggesting that the Utopians were *prisci theologi* who carried on some of their earlier wisdom into Christianity, More indicates, before the disasters, the palliative to which the late sixteenth century turned—religious Hermetism.

These beginnings of a development of pre-Reformation English Catholicism in new directions under the new Italian influence were cut short by the sinister turn of events in the latter part of the reign of Henry VIII. With the death of More on the scaffold, a chapter in the history of thought which had only just begun was prematurely closed. The violently intolerant Protestant break with the past in the reign of Edward VI, with its destruction of books and libraries, was followed by the equally violent Spanish-Catholic intolerance of the reign of Mary. Under Elizabeth, the Reformation was established with an extreme party, the Puritans, in the ascendant. Puritan Anglicanism had quite lost the Erasmian tolerance. Bitterly resenting the persecutions of Mary's reign, and dreading a repetition if Philip II should win the upper hand in Europe and regain hold of England, Puritan thought ran on narrowly theological and drearily historical lines—dreary in the sense that history reduced itself to a long tale of the wickedness of the popish past and justification for the break of the English crown and Church with Rome. Foxe's "Book of Martyrs", with its ghastly pictures of the Marian martyrs in this historical setting, is characteristic of the attitude. There is little trace of philosophy of any kind in Foxe's book. No talk of *prisca theologia* went on in this atmosphere, nor was there any English ecclesiastical figure corresponding to a French bishop such as Pontus de Tyard, imbued with Neoplatonism and in touch with poets and musicians, or to an enthusiastic friar, like Hannibal Rosseli, immersed in Hermetism. If there was any interest in such things in England, it was not in officially established circles in Church or University, but in private circles, such as Sir Philip Sidney's group of courtiers studying number in the three worlds with John Dee, or in survivals of the More-Colet tradition.

As a Renaissance Magus, Dee needed the mediaeval traditions on which to build and these, in England, were broken and dispersed. The destruction of the monastic libraries caused Dee great anguish and he tried to rescue as much of their contents as possible, which made him suspected not only as a "conjuror" but as in sympathy with the papist past. An isolated and lonely figure, the modern Magus collects the spiritual, and also the scientific, treasures from those great ruins which towered in broken majesty over the Elizabethan scene. He enjoyed the favour of Queen Elizabeth to whom he was astrologer in chief—though she never gave him the endowed position for the prosecution of his studies for which he pleaded—and a set of intellectual courtiers, led by Philip Sidney, chose him as their teacher in philosophy.

Dee was not in England during the greater part of Bruno's stay; he left for his travels on the continent in the latter part of the year (1583) in which Bruno arrived. In 1585, when Bruno was in England, Dee was at Cracow where he met the Hermetist, Hannibal Rosseli. "I took Ghostly Council of Doctor Hannibal the great divine, that had now set out some of his commentaries upon *Pymander Hermetis Trismegisti*", writes Dee in his spiritual diary, and, on the following day, "I received Communion at the Bernardines where that Doctor is Professor."[1] This shows us where lay Dee's true spiritual home—in religious Hermetism. Dee was preparing himself by these religious practices for a bout of practical Cabala with Kelley, and he would need, to keep himself safe, that Christian angelic continuation in the celestial hierarchies which was the constant theme of "Doctor Hannibal's" enthusiastic Dionysian-Hermetic meditations, as his book shows.

Sidney thus knew at least two types of Hermetism; he knew the non-magical type expounded by Du Plessis Mornay; he knew Dee, who was a Magus, but a Christian one, also a genuine scientist having a genuine mathematical understanding of the Copernican theory.[2] Bruno was to present him with yet another brand of Hermetism.

We are at last ready for the eruption of Giordano Bruno into

---

[1] *A True and Faithfull Relation of what passed . . . between Dr. John Dee and some Spirits*, p. 397.

[2] See F. R. Johnson, *Astronomical Thought in Renaissance England*, Baltimore, 1937, pp. 134–5.

this book. We have been preparing for him all along, for it is only by putting him into the context of the history of Hermetism in the Renaissance that one can begin to understand this extraordinary man.

Chapter XI

GIORDANO BRUNO:
FIRST VISIT TO PARIS

GIORDANO BRUNO[1] was born at Nola, a small town on the foot-hills of Vesuvius, in 1548. He never lost traces of this volcanic and Neapolitan origin, and was proud to call himself "the Nolan", born under a kindly sky. He entered the Dominican Order in 1563, and became an inmate of the great Dominican convent in Naples, where Thomas Aquinas is buried. In 1576, he got into trouble for heresy, and fled, abandoning his Dominican habit. Thereafter began his life of wandering through Europe. After trying Calvin's Geneva which he did not like, nor was he liked by the Calvinists, and lecturing on the *Sphere* of Sacrobosco for about two years at Toulouse, Bruno reached Paris some time late in 1581. Here he gave public lectures, amongst them thirty readings on thirty divine attributes,[2] and he attracted the attention of the king, Henri III. And here he published two books on the art of memory which reveal him as a magician.

As was explained in the Preface, the present book aims at placing Bruno within the history of Renaissance Hermetism and magic. I hope to write another volume, similar in plan to the present one, the aim of which will be to place Bruno within the history of the classical art of memory. The two strands converge,

[1] The literature on Giordano Bruno is vast (see the *Bibliografia*). The best biography is V. Spampanato, *Vita di Giordano Bruno*, Messina, 1921.

For the abbreviations which I am using for editions of Bruno's works, and for the documentary sources, see the list of abbreviations on pp. xiii–xiv.

[2] *Documenti*, p. 84.

190

for Bruno's art of memory is a magical art, a Hermetic art. It is this aspect of the mnemonic works of which I treat in this volume, reserving for the other book the fuller discussion of how the magic became absorbed into the mnemonic tradition. It is, however, necessary to say something about the classical art of memory[1] as an introduction to this chapter.

The Roman orators used a mnemonic which is described in the *Ad Herennium* and referred to by Cicero and Quintilian. It consisted in memorising a series of places in a building, and attaching to these memorised places, images to remind of the points of the speech. The orator when delivering his speech, passed in imagination along the order of memorised places, plucking from them the images which were to remind him of his notions. Not only buildings could be used as a memory place system: Metrodorus of Scepsis is said to have used the zodiac as the foundation of his memory-system.

This classical art, usually regarded as purely mnemotechnical, had a long history in the Middle Ages and was recommended by Albertus Magnus and Thomas Aquinas. In the Renaissance, it became fashionable among Neoplatonists and Hermetists. It was now understood as a method of printing basic or archetypal images on the memory, with the cosmic order itself as the "place" system, a kind of inner way of knowing the universe. The principle is already apparent in the passage in Ficino's *De vita coelitus comparanda* in which he describes how the planetary images or colours, memorised as painted on the vaulted ceiling, organised for the man who had so memorised them, all the individual phenomena which he perceived on coming out of his house.[2] The Hermetic experience of reflecting the universe in the mind[3] is, I believe, at the root of Renaissance magic memory, in which the classical mnemonic with places and images is now understood, or

---

[1] For a brief account of it, see my article "The Ciceronian Art of Memory" in *Medioevo e Rinascimento, studi in onore di Bruno Nardi*, Florence, 1955, II, pp. 871–903; a recent book on the subject, which includes a chapter on Bruno, is that by Paolo Rossi, *Clavis Universalis arti mnemoniche e logica combinatoria da Lullo a Leibniz*, Milan–Naples, 1960; see also C. Vasoli, "Umanesimo e simbologia nei primi scritti lulliani e mnemotecnici del Bruno", in *Umanesimo e Simbolismo*, ed. E. Castelli, Padua, 1958, pp. 251–304, and P. Rossi's article in the same volume (pp. 161–78).

[2] See above, pp. 75–6.   [3] See above, p. 31–2.

applied, as a method of achieving this experience by imprinting archetypal, or magically activated, images on the memory. By using magical or talismanic images as memory-images, the Magus hoped to acquire universal knowledge, and also powers, obtaining through the magical organisation of the imagination a magically powerful personality, tuned in, as it were, to the powers of the cosmos.

This amazing transformation, or adaptation, of the classical art of memory in the Renaissance has a history before Bruno, but in Bruno it reached a culmination. The *De umbris idearum* and the *Cantus Circaeus*, which we discuss in this chapter, are his two first works on magic memory. They reveal him as already a magician before he came to England.

The *De umbris idearum*, published at Paris in 1582, is dedicated to Henri III. The dedication is preceded and followed by poems warning readers of the difficulty of the work which they are about to study, the entrance to which is rough and hard but it promises a great reward. It may be compared to the statue of Diana at Chios which showed a weeping face to those entering the temple but a smiling face to those going out.[1] Or to the riddle of Pythagoras on *bicornis*, one side rough and unwelcoming, the other leading to better things. This face and this riddle now seem hard, but those who immerse themselves in the depths of these shadows will find something to their advantage. A poem attributed to Merlin's wisdom describes the unsuitability of various animals to various actions, for example pigs are not well adapted by nature for flying. The reader is therefore warned not to attempt the present work unless he feels equal to it.[2] The combination of mysteriousness and bombast in these poetic sign posts to the book sets a tone which it follows throughout.

The book opens with a dialogue between Hermes, Philothimus, and Logifer.[3] Hermes describes the knowledge or art about to be revealed as a sun. At its rising the workers of darkness retreat into their lairs, but man and the creatures of light go out to their work. Dark creatures, sacred to night and to Pluto, are witches, toads, basilisks, owls: these are banished. Creatures of light are the cock, the phoenix, the swan, the goose, the eagle, the lynx, the ram, and

[1] Bruno, *Op. lat.*, II(i), pp. 1 ff.
[2] *Ibid.*, p. 6.   [3] *Ibid.*, pp. 7 ff.

the lion; these are awake and working. The herbs and flowers of light—such as the heliotrope or the lupin—banish the growths of night.

Hermes describes the illumination contained within the art, not only in these terms of animals and plants astrologically affiliated to the planet Sol, but also in terms of a philosophy which is based on the "unerring intellect", rather than on "fallacious sense". He now speaks of "circuits" and "hemicycles"; of the "movement of worlds" which many think to be "animals" or "gods"; of the power of the sun in this philosophy.[1]

Philothimus asks what is the book which Hermes holds in his hand, and he is told that it is the book *On the Shadows of Ideas*,[2] the contents of which its author is in doubt whether or not to make known. Philothimus points out that no great work would be produced if such hesitations were allowed to prevail. The providence of the gods does not cease, as the Egyptian priests used to say, because of statutes promulgated at various times by repressive Mercuries. The intellect does not cease to illuminate, and the visible sun does not cease to illuminate, because we do not always all turn towards it.

Logifer now enters the conversation, adducing a large number of learned doctors, Magister Adhoc, Magister Scoppet, and so on, who think nothing of the art of memory. He cites the opinion of Magister Psicoteus that nothing useful can be learned from the mnemonics of a Tullius, a Thomas (Aquinas), or an Albertus (Magnus).[3] Logifer is very well-informed about medical recipes for improving the memory, what diet is best for it, what regimen of life. Information such as this he regards as much more useful than that empty and deceptive art of memory which uses images and figures. The reaction of Philothimus to Logifer's speech is to remark that thus do crows caw, wolves howl, horses whinney, and so on. It is clear that Logifer is one of those who ought to heed the warning of Merlin and not attempt to discuss things which are beyond him.

In these seven or eight opening pages of dialogue in *De umbris idearum*, written in Paris before coming to England, we already have the outline which the dialogues to be written in England will follow, both as to *dramatis personae* and as to imagery. The sage

[1] *Ibid.*, pp. 8–9.   [2] *Ibid.*, p. 9.   [3] *Ibid.*, p. 14.

who expounds the new Copernican philosophy in the dialogues published in England is called either Filoteo or Teofilo, and stands for the Nolan himself; he has both admiring disciples and criticising opponents, pedants who attack him. The pervading imagery of the dialogues published in England is already present here, the rising sun of mysterious revelation with which is associated a "Copernican" natural philosophy, the creatures of light and the creatures of darkness ranged for and against the revelation, just as here the pedants with their non-solar characteristics are ranged against the sages.

And the dialogue in the *De umbris idearum* makes it quite clear that the instructor of Philothimus—and therefore of Filoteo or Teofilo, of the Nolan, of Giordano Bruno—is Hermes Trismegistus. It is Hermes who hands the book with the new philosophy and the new art in it to Philothimus; and this is the book on the Shadows of Ideas by Giordano Bruno, which is, in fact, written by Hermes—that is to say it is a book about magic, about a very strong solar magic. The allusion to the Lament in the *Asclepius*, describing how the magical religion of the Egyptians came in late, bad times, to be forbidden by legal statutes,[1] relates this new Hermetic revelation vouchsafed to Giordano Bruno to the Egyptian religion, the religion of the intellect, or of the mind, reached beyond the worship of the visible sun. Those who forbade that religion by

---

[1] Bruno's actual words are as follows: "Non cessat prouidentia deorum (dixerunt Aegyptii Sacerdotes) statutis quibusquam temporibus mittere hominibus Mercurios quosdam. . . . Nec cessat intellectus, atque sol iste sensibilis semper illuminare, ob eam causam quia nec semper, nec omnes animaduertimus)" (*ibid.*, p. 9). He is thinking of the passage in the Lament (*C.H.*, II, p. 327, see above, p. 38) which prophesies that the Egyptian religion will be forbidden by legal statutes. Augustine (see above, p. 10) interpreted the Lament as a prophecy of the suppression of the false Egyptian religion by Christianity. Bruno uses this interpretation, but takes it to mean that the Christian suppressors ("Mercurios quosdam") legislated against the true Egyptian solar religion which, beyond the sensible sun, penetrated to the divine *mens*. In spite of the suppression, that true religion did not cease and Bruno is reviving it.

Though the grammar of the above passage is not very clear, I believe that this interpretation of its meaning is correct. It needs to be compared with other passages where Bruno speaks of false "Mercuries", pretending to be teachers of true religion, but really suppressing the truth and introducing confusion and discord (*Dial. ital.*, p. 32; *Op. lat.*, I (iii) p. 4; cf. below, pp. 236–8, 314–5).

law, were, in the Augustinian interpretation of the Lament, the Christians, whose purer religion superseded that of the Egyptians. But, according to Bruno, the false Christian "Mercuries" have suppressed the better Egyptian religion—an anti-Christian interpretation of Hermetism of which much more evidence will be adduced from Bruno's works later on.

Though most heedful of Merlin's warning, and very doubtful whether we can claim to be a solar animal or bird, let us nevertheless attempt to penetrate a little further into the mysterious Shadows of the Ideas.

The book is arranged in groupings of thirty. First, there are thirty short paragraphs or chapters about *intentiones*, or seeking the light of the divinity through having an intention of the will towards shadows or reflections of it.[1] There are some references in this to the Cabalists and to the imagery of Solomon in his Canticle. It is illustrated by a wheel divided into thirty lettered divisions, with a sun at the centre of it.[2] All the "intentions" are towards the sun, not merely the visible sun, but the divine intellect of which it is an image. The lettered wheel is certainly a Lullist element in the book, and reflects the Lullist principle of basing an art upon divine attributes, represented by letters. It probably connects, too, with those lectures on "thirty divine attributes" which Bruno gave in Paris and of which we do not have the text.[3]

Then come thirty short chapters on "concepts of ideas"[4]; these are vaguely Neoplatonic, with several mentions of Plotinus. Without making direct quotations from it, the work which Bruno chiefly has in mind is Ficino's *De vita coelitus comparanda*. He is really here alluding, though in a confused way, to Ficino's "Plotinising" of celestial images, and preparing the way for the lists of such images upon which the magic memory system is based.

The lists of these images take up a considerable part of the book.[5] They are arranged in thirty groups, each subdivided into sets of five, making one hundred and fifty images in all.

First come the images of the thirty-six decans, beginning, of course,

There ascends in the first face of Aries a dark man, of immense

---

[1] *Op. lat.*, II(i), pp. 20 ff.   [2] *Ibid.*, p. 54.   [3] See above, p. 190.
[4] *Op. lat.*, II(i), pp. 41 ff.   [5] *Ibid.*, pp. 135–57.

stature, with burning eyes, angry face, and clothed in a white garment.[1]

The fearless Bruno does not hesitate to inscribe on his memory the images of the Egyptian decan demons. As E. Garin has pointed out,[2] Bruno has taken the list, ascribed to Teucer the Babylonian, of the thirty-six decan images almost entirely from Cornelius Agrippa's *De occulta philosophia*.[3]

Then come forty-nine images of the planets, seven for each planet. For example:

First image of Saturn. A man with a stag's head, on a dragon, with an owl which is eating a snake in his right hand.[4]

Bruno's planet images are close to those given by Agrippa,[5] though with some variations. Next come twenty-eight images for the mansions of the moon, and one image of the *Draco lunae*[6]; all these correspond very closely indeed to those given by Agrippa.[7] Finally, Bruno gives thirty-six images which he associates with the twelve houses into which a horoscope is divided.[8] These images are peculiar and have not yet been traced to any known type. Probably Bruno invented them (Agrippa, his chief authority, says that one can make up astrological images for special purposes).[9]

[1] *Ibid.*, p. 135. The decan images run from p. 135 to p. 141. They are grouped with the twelve signs of the zodiac of which they are "faces"; the signs are illustrated by cuts.

[2] Garin, *Medioevo e Rinascimento*, p. 160, note.

[3] Agrippa, *De occult. phil.*, II, 37. Detailed analysis of Bruno's decan images has shown that 17 of them are the same as in Agrippa; 17 are close to Agrippa but with slight variations; one (Pisces, 2) is more like the image given by Peter of Abano (in his *Astrolabium planum*) than the Agrippa image; one (Capricorn, 3) is quite different from the image given by either Agrippa or Abano.

[4] *Op. lat.*, II(i), p. 144. The planet images are on pp. 144–51, illustrated by cuts of the planets.

[5] Agrippa, *De occult. phil.*, II, 37–44.

[6] *Op. lat.*, II(i), pp. 151–3.

[7] Agrippa, *De occult. phil.*, II, 46.

[8] *Op. lat.*, II(i), pp. 154–7.

[9] See above, p. 135. I am inclined to think that these 36 invented images may be intended to complement the decan images by images composed to obtain universally favourable influences. In short, that the set of 150 images may be something corresponding to a favourable model of the heavens.

He was an expert in the composition or invention of magic images, for the last book which he published, in 1591, is about the composition of images, by which he means talismanic or magic images.[1]

Bruno has returned to Ficino's use of talismans with a vengeance, and without any of Ficino's Christian inhibitions, for he believes in Hermetic Egyptianism as better than Christianity. And, to those familiar with the literature of magic, the very title of his book would have suggested magic, for Cecco d'Ascoli, a famous magician of the fourteenth century who was burned at the stake, cites in his necromantic commentary on the *Sphere* of Sacrobosco a book called *Liber de umbris idearum* which he attributes to Solomon.[2] By his rejection of Christianity, and his enthusiastic adoption of Hermetic Egyptianism, Bruno moves back towards a darker, more mediaeval necromancy, whilst at the same time retaining the elaborate "Plotinising" by Ficino of the talismans. Extraordinary though this may seem, I believe that Bruno's "shadows of ideas" *are* the magic images, the archetypal images in the heavens which are closer to the ideas in the divine mind than things here below. And it is even possible that Ficino, in his frequent uses of the word "shadows" may sometimes mean this too.

The magic images were placed on the wheel of the memory system to which corresponded other wheels on which were remem-

---

[1] See below, pp. 331-4.

[2] Cecco d'Ascoli's commentary is published by Lynn Thorndike in *The Sphere of Sacrobosco and its Commentators*, Chicago, 1949, pp. 344 ff.; the quotations from Solomon *in libro de umbris idearum* are on pp. 397, 398, in this edition. Cf. also Thorndike (*History of Magic and Experimental Science*), II, pp. 964-5.

Bruno knew Cecco d'Ascoli's work, for he mentions it in one of the commentaries in his *De immenso et innumerabilibus*: "Nec mentitus est Cicco Aesculano Floron spiritus, qui de umbra lunae interrogatus quid esset, respondit: *ut terra terra est . . .*" (*Op. lat.*, I (I), p. 377). Cecco in fact mentions the spirit Floron "who is of the hierarchy of the Cherubim" precisely in one of his quotations from Solomon's *Liber de umbris idearum* (*The Sphere, etc.*, ed. Thorndike, p. 398).

Since Bruno mentions his own lost work on the Sphere in the context of these quotations from Cecco d'Ascoli (see below, p. 323, note 1) it seems not impossible that he may have used Cecco's necromantic commentary in his lectures on the sphere at Toulouse, and found in it the suggestion for the title for his book on magic memory.

bered all the physical contents of the terrestrial world—elements, stones, metals, herbs and plants, animals, birds, and so on—and the whole sum of human knowledge accumulated through the centuries through the images of one hundred and fifty great men and inventors.[1] The possessor of this system thus rose above time and reflected the whole universe of nature and of man in his mind. I believe, as already suggested, that the reason why such a memory system as this is a Hermetic secret may be because of allusions in the *Corpus Hermeticum* to gnostic reflection of the universe in the mind, as at the end of *Pimander* when the initiate engraves within him the benefit of Pimander,[2] or as in *Corpus Hermeticum* XI, resumed in chapter II of this book as "Egyptian Reflection of the Universe in the Mind". I quote now again from the concluding paragraph of that résumé:

> Unless you make yourself equal to God, you cannot understand God: for the like is not intelligible save to the like. Make yourself grow to a greatness beyond measure, by a bound free yourself from the body; raise yourself above all time, become Eternity; then you will understand God. Believe that nothing is impossible for you, think yourself immortal and capable of understanding all, all arts, all sciences, the nature of every living being. Mount higher than the highest height; descend lower than the lowest depth. Draw into yourself all sensations of everything created, fire and water, dry and moist, imagining that you are everywhere, on earth, in the sea, in the sky, that you are not yet born, in the maternal womb, adolescent, old, dead, beyond death. If you embrace in your thought all things at once, times, places, substances, qualities, quantities, you may understand God.[3]

By engraving in memory the celestial images, archetypal images in the heavens which are shadows near to the ideas in the divine

---

[1] The great men and inventors (*Op. lat.*, II(i), pp. 124–8) are in thirty groups with five subdivisions lettered by the five vowels. The other lists (*ibid.*, pp. 132–4) are grouped and lettered in the same way. The magic images (*ibid.*, pp. 135–7) are also grouped and lettered in the same way. When all the lists are set out on concentric wheels one has the complete system, based on the 150 magic images in groups of 30, to which the groupings of the great men and inventors and of the contents of the universe correspond.

The system will be dealt with more fully in the book on the art of memory, and the mad method in its magic will be better understood when seen in the context of other memory systems.

[2] See above, p. 25.   [3] See above, p. 32.

mens on which all things below depend, Bruno hopes, I believe, to achieve this "Egyptian" experience, to become in true gnostic fashion the *Aion*, having the divine powers within him. By imprinting the figures of the zodiac on the fantasy "you may gain possession of a figurative art which will assist, not only the memory, but all the powers of the soul in a wonderful way."[1] When you conform yourself to the celestial forms "you will arrive from the confused plurality of things at the underlying unity". For when the parts of the universal species are not considered separately but in relation to their underlying order—what is there that we may not understand, memorise, and do?[2]

Bruno's magic memory system thus represents the memory of a Magus, one who both knows the reality beyond the multiplicity of appearances through having conformed his imagination to the archetypal images, and also has powers through this insight. It is the direct descendant of Ficino's Neoplatonic interpretation of the celestial images,[3] but carried to a much more daring extreme.

The "Egyptian" character of the art described in *De umbris idearum* was strongly emphasised by Bruno's Scottish disciple, Alexander Dicson, who published in London in 1583[4] an imitation of it prefaced by a dialogue in which "Mercurius" and "Theut" are speakers, both names of Hermes Trismegistus, the Egyptian.

The other book on magic memory published in Paris has for its heroine that great sorceress Circe, the daughter of the Sun. The title of it is *Cantus Circaeus*,[5] and it is dedicated by Jean Regnault

---

[1] *Op. lat.*, II(i), pp. 78–9.

[2] *Ibid.*, p. 47.

[3] This has been seen by E. Garin, who, in the article in which he discusses the *De vita coelitus comparanda*, makes the following remark: "Che Bruno . . . si serva nella sua arte della memoria delle *facies* astrologiche di Teucro babilonese non è nè un caso nè un capriccio: è la continuazione di un discorso molto preciso intorno agli *esemplari* della realtà." ("Le 'Elezioni' e il problema dell'astrologia", in *Umanesimo e esoterismo*, ed. E. Castelli, Padua, 1960, p. 36.)

[4] Alexander Dicson, *De umbra rationis & iudicii, siue de memoriae virtute Prosopopaeia*, London, 1583, dedicated to Robert, Earl of Leicester. That Dicson, or Dickson, was Scottish is stated by Hugh Platt, *The Jewell House of Art and Nature*, London, 1594, p. 81. He appears as "Dicsono", a disciple, in some of Bruno's Italian dialogues.

[5] *Op. lat.*, II(i), pp. 179 ff.

to Henri d'Angoulême, Grand Prieur de France, an important personage at the French court for he was semi-royal, being the illegitimate son of Henri II. Regnault says that Bruno had given him the manuscript and asked him to edit it for publication. Published in 1582, the same year as the *De umbris idearum*, it is later than that work which is referred to in the preface as having been dedicated to the Most Christian King.[1]

It opens with a terrific incantation to the Sun by Circe,[2] mentioning all his names, attributes, animals, birds, metals, and so on. From time to time, her assistant, Moeris, has to look out to inspect the line of the sun's rays and to see if the incantation is working. There is a distinct though slightly garbled reference to Ficino's *De vita coelitus comparanda* in this incantation, on the sun as the vehicle of inscrutable powers reaching us from the "ideas" through "reasons" in the soul of the world, and on the power of herbs, plants, stones, and so on to attract *spiritus*.[3] Circe then makes equally terrific, though not quite so long, incantations to Luna, Saturn, Jupiter, Mars, Venus, and Mercury, finally adjuring all the seven rulers to listen to her.[4] She is at the same time doing magic with arrangements of plants, stones, etc., and holding out "writings of the sacred gods" on a plate, drawing characters in the air, whilst Moeris is instructed to unfold a parchment on which are most potent *notae*, the mystery of which is hidden from all mortals.[5]

Bruno's main source for the incantations in this work, as for his celestial images in the *De umbris*, is the *De occulta philosophia* of Cornelius Agrippa.[6] I quote, for comparison, parts of the incantation to Venus from Bruno and Agrippa:

---

[1] *Ibid.*, p. 182. [2] *Ibid.*, pp. 185–8.
[3] "Sol qui illustras omnia solus. . . . Cuius ministerio viget istius compago vniuersi, inscrutabiles rerum vires ab ideis per animae mundi rationes ad nos vsque deducens & infra, vnde variae atque multiplices herbarum, plantarum caeterarum, lapidumque virtutes, quae per stellarum radios mundanum ad se trahere spiritum sunt potentes." (*Ibid.*, p. 185.)
[4] *Ibid.*, pp. 188–92.
[5] *Ibid.*, p. 193.
[6] Cf. Agrippa, *De occult. phil.*, II, 59, on the various names and epithets with which to invoke "the seven governors of the world, as Hermes calls them".

Bruno.

Venus alma, formosa, pulcherrima, amica, beneuola, gratiosa, dulcis, amena, candida, siderea, dionea, olens, iocosa, aphrogenia, foecunda, gratiosa, larga, benefica, placida, deliciosa, ingeniosa, ignita, conciliatrix maxima, amorum domina. . . .[1]

Agrippa.

Venus, vocatur domina, alma, formosa, siderea, candida, pulchra, placida, multipotens, foecunda, domina amoris et pulchritudinis, seculorum progenies, hominumque parens initialis, quae primis rerum exordiis sexuum diversitatem geminato amore sociavit, et aeterna sobole hominum, animaliumque genera, quotidie propagat, regina omnium gaudiorum, domina laetitiae. . . .[2]

This, and other planetary incantations in Bruno and Agrippa are not identical, but Bruno has based himself on Agrippa's versions, adding or changing at will, just as he based himself on the Agrippan star images, with variations.

The Circean incantations or *Cantus* is said to be *ad Memoriae praxim ordinatus*[3] and is followed by an Art of Memory.[4] If we think back for a moment to the solar rites described by Ficino's disciple, Diacceto, in which the solar talisman was cultivated with rituals and Orphic hymns, until the imagination was emotionally disposed to receive a "kind of imprint",[5] it may seem that the planetary incantations of Circe were disposing the imagination to receive imprints of planetary images. The adept would then proceed to the Art of Memory with an imagination already stamped with celestial images, the necessary preliminary for magic memory. I am not sure if this is the right explanation of the unexplained connection between the incantations and the following Art of Memory, but it is a possible one.

The comparison with genuinely Ficinian magic, with its elegance, its graceful and learned incantations in the form of Orphic hymns, brings out the reactionary and barbaric character of Bruno's wild magic in the *Cantus Circaeus*. This may have been intentional, in order to get a stronger magic. Addressing the Sun, Circe says:

Adesto sacris filiae tuae Circes votis. Si intento, castoque tibi adsum animo, si dignis pro facultate ritibus me praesento. En tibi faciles

---

[1] *Op. lat.*, II(i), p. 191.   [2] Agrippa, *De occult. phil.*, *loc. cit.*
[3] *Op. lat.*, II(i), p. 185.   [4] *Ibid.*, pp. 211 ff.
[5] See above, p. 82, and Walker, p. 33.

aras struximus. Adsunt tua tibi redolentia thura, sandalorumque rubentium fumus. En tertio susurraui barbara & arcana carmina.[1]

Here are the altar and the fumigations, as in the Ficinian solar rite, but the incantations, instead of being Orphic hymns to the Sun, are "barbara & arcana carmina".

There is some kind of moral reform implied in Circe's magic. She asks where is Astraea, the justice of the Golden Age,[2] threatens evil-doers, calls on the gods to restore virtue.[3] As a result of her magic, men are turned into beasts,[4] and this (quite contrary to the usual interpretation of the Circe story) is a good thing because wicked men are less harmful in their true animal forms.[5] There are, however, beautiful and virtuous animals and birds which fly from the night of evil. The cock is a most beautiful, tuneful, noble, generous, magnanimous, solar, imperial, almost divine creature, and when it has vanquished evil cocks in conflict it shows its supremacy in song.[6] The cock, of course, represents the French Monarchy. There are, as F. Tocco pointed out,[7] curious anticipations of the *Spaccio della bestia trionfante* in Circe's reform movement (though like all the nineteenth-century liberal admirers of Giordano Bruno, Tocco was quite oblivious of the magic).

Bruno was a magician who was sympathetically receptive to the influences of the milieu in which he found himself. As will be shown later, he picked up when in England some of the more abstruse aspects of the courtly cult of Queen Elizabeth I. He might have arrived in Paris in 1581 in time to see that great court festival, the *Ballet comique de la reine*, or at least to hear about it, and the text of the *Ballet* was printed in 1582, the same year as his *Cantus Circaeus*. In the *Ballet*, Circe represents the evil enchantment of the French wars of religion which are turning men into beasts. She is vanquished by the good magic of the performance, and, at the end, the victory is typified by her being led in triumph to King Henri III, to whom her magic wand is presented, thus transforming bad Circe magic into good French Monarchy magic. It is thus possible that Bruno might have picked up the idea of a magical solar reform connected with the French Monarchy from notions circulating at the French court.

[1] *Op. lat.*, II(i), p. 186.   [2] *Ibid., loc. cit.*
[3] *Ibid.*, pp. 186–7, etc.   [4] *Ibid.*, pp. 193 ff.   [5] *Ibid.*, p. 194.
[6] *Ibid.*, pp. 209–10.
[7] F. Tocco, *Le opere latine di Giordano Bruno*, Florence, 1889, p. 56.

Let us recall the last chapter, and the care taken by French religious Hermetists to dissociate Christian Hermetism from the magic of the *Asclepius* and from Ficino's talismanic magic. And now, into this world where Catholic Christian Hermetism was flourishing in French ecclesiastical circles, and perhaps in the Capucin movement around Henri III, there erupts Giordano Bruno proclaiming a deeply magical Hermetism, rejoicing in the magic of the *Asclepius*, carrying Ficinian magic to lengths of which Ficino never dreamed. Yet Bruno and his magic were also to become involved in the larger issues of religious Hermetism.

Bruno's relations with Henri III are only documented from what Bruno himself told the Venetian inquisitors. He said, that hearing of his lectures, the French King sent for him, and asked him whether the art of memory which he taught was natural or done by magic art. Bruno says that he proved to the King that it was not magical. This, of course, is untrue. He then says that he dedicated a book called *De umbris idearum* to the King, who thereupon made him a reader.[1] If Henri looked at the *De umbris idearum* he would certainly have recognised its magic images, for we saw, in an earlier chapter, that at one time this king sent to Spain for magic books, which he allowed D'Aubigné to see when they arrived, and one of which was *Picatrix*.[2] It is also incredible in view of his mother's addiction to magicians and astrologers, that Henri should not have known a good deal about magic. The more probable version of the story would be that Henri was attracted by the rumour about magic in connection with Bruno, and this was why he sent for him.

Bruno also told the inquisitors that when he went into England he had with him letters of introduction from the French king to the French ambassador in England, Michel de Castelnau de Mauvissière, with whom he stayed during the whole time that he

---

[1] ". . . il re Enrico terzo mi fece chiamare un giorno, ricercandomi se la memoria che avevo e che professava, era naturale o pur per arte magica; al qual diedi sodisfazione; e con quello che li dissi e feci provare a lui medesmo, conobbe che non era per arte magica ma per scienzia. E doppo questo feci stampar un libro de memoria, sotto titolo *De umbris idearum*, il qual dedicai a Sua Maestà e con questo mi fece lettor straordinario e provisionato. . . ." (*Documenti*, pp. 84–5.)

[2] See above, p. 51.

was in the country.[1] We have only Bruno's word for these letters of introduction but I think that it is probably true. We know that he did stay with the ambassador the whole time, and we know too, from one of Bruno's books, that the ambassador protected him from the tumults aroused by his writings and behaviour. In some of those books published in England, Bruno said things which no native of the country in that time of strict censorship and supervision would have been allowed to say. That he published what he did, and was not imprisoned or punished in some way, strongly suggests, I think, that he had some kind of diplomatic protection, such as a letter of introduction to the French ambassador from the French King himself would have provided.

It is therefore possible that it was Henri III who, by sending Bruno into England on some mission, albeit *sub rosa*, changed the course of his life from that of a wandering magician into that of a very strange kind of missionary indeed.

The English ambassador in Paris, Henry Cobham, warned the ever watchful Francis Walsingham, in a despatch dated March, 1583, of Bruno's impending arrival: "Doctor Jordano Bruno Nolano, a professor in philosophy, intends to pass into England, whose religion I cannot commend."[2] Note that it is Bruno's religion, not his philosophy, which the ambassador feels that he cannot commend—perhaps an understatement.

If the reader feels somewhat aghast at the state of mind of a noted philosopher of the Renaissance as revealed in this chapter, and is inclined to agree rather strongly with the ambassador, I cannot blame him. But if we want the truth about the history of thought, we must omit nothing. Giordano Bruno, Hermetic magician of a most extreme type, is now about to pass into England to expound his "new philosophy".

[1] ". . . con littere dell'istesso Re andai in Inghilterra a star con l'Ambasciator di Sua Maestà, che si chiamava il Sr. Della Malviciera, per nome Michel de Castelnovo; in casa del qual non faceva altro, se non che stava per suo gentilomo." (*Documenti*, p. 85.)

[2] *Calendar of State Papers, Foreign*, January–June 1583, p. 214.

Chapter XII

GIORDANO BRUNO IN ENGLAND: THE HERMETIC REFORM

RUNO opened his campaign in England with a volume, dedicated to the French ambassador, containing an Art of Memory which is a reprint from the one in the *Cantus Circaeus*, and two other works entitled *Explicatio Triginta Sigillorum* and *Sigillus Sigillorum*.[1] The "thirty" grouping of the "seals" shows that he is still moving in the mystico-magical realms of the *De umbris idearum*, and, in fact, the whole volume is a further development of the exploration of memory as a major instrument in the formation of a Magus which he had begun in the two books published in Paris. There, he had gained a lectureship and the attention of the King by such efforts, and he hoped to achieve similar results in England, for, after the dedication to the ambassador, there is an address "to the most excellent Vice Chancellor of Oxford University and to its celebrated doctors and teachers", which opens as follows:

[1] *Ars reminiscendi et in phantastico campo exarandi, Ad plurimas in triginta sigillis inquirendi, disponendi, atque retinendi implicitas nouas rationes & artes introductoria; Explicatio triginta sigillorum . . .; Sigillus sigillorum. . . .* No date or place. The volume is almost certainly the first of the works of Bruno published in England, and is not later than 1583; see *Bibliografia*, p. 68. It is now established that the publisher both of this work and of Bruno's Italian dialogues published in England was John Charlewood; see G. Aquilecchia, "Lo stampatore londinese di Giordano Bruno", in *Studi di Filologia Italiana*, XVIII (1960), pp. 101 ff.

Philotheus Jordanus Brunus Nolanus, doctor of a more abstruse theology, professor of a purer and more innocuous wisdom, noted in the best academies of Europe, an approved and honourably received philosopher, a stranger nowhere save amongst the barbarous and ignoble, the waker of sleeping souls, tamer of presumptuous and recalcitrant ignorance, proclaimer of a general philanthropy, who does not choose out the Italian more than the Briton, the male more than the female, the mitred head more than the crowned head, the man in the toga more than the armed man, the cowled man more than the man without a cowl, but him who is the more peaceable-minded, the more civilised, the more loyal, the more useful; who regards not the anointed head, the forehead signed with the cross, the washed hands, the circumcised penis, but (where the man may be known by his face) the culture of the mind and soul. Who is hated by the propagators of foolishness and hypocrites, but sought out by the honest and the studious, and whose genius the more noble applaud. . . .[1]

This certainly arrests the attention, and if any of the doctors addressed in so striking a manner by this rather threateningly tolerant writer looked into the book, he would have seen at once that it is about some extremely obscure kind of magic. In fact, to discover this, he need have looked no further than the title-page, on which the reader is informed that he will find here whatever he is seeking through "logic, metaphysics, Cabala, natural magic, arts long and short".[2] The book, indeed, sets forth Bruno's appallingly complex combination of Magia and Cabala with Lullism and the art of memory.

In June, 1583, the Polish prince Albert Alasco, or Laski, visited Oxford and, by order of the Queen, was sumptuously entertained with banquets, plays, and public disputations.[3] From John Dee's diary, it would appear that Sir Philip Sidney accompanied the prince to Oxford, for Dee says that Sidney brought Alasco to visit him at Mortlake on their way back from Oxford.[4] Bruno states in

[1] *Op. lat.*, II (ii), pp. 76–7.

[2] "hic enim facile invenies quidquid per logicam, metaphysicam, cabalam, naturalem magiam, artes magnas atque breves theorice inquiritur" (*ibid.*, p. 73). The "artes magnas atque breves" refer to the arts of Ramon Lull.

[3] Anthony à Wood, *History and Antiquities of the University of Oxford*, ed. J. Gutch, 1796, II (I), pp. 215–8.

[4] *Private Diary of Dr. John Dee*, ed. J. O. Halliwell, Camden Society, 1842, p. 20.

his *Cena de le ceneri* that he took part in the disputes organised at Oxford for the entertainment of Alasco:

> . . . go to Oxford and get them to tell you what happened to the Nolan when he disputed publicly with the doctors of theology in the presence of the Polish prince Alasco, and others of the English nobility. Learn how ably he replied to the arguments; how the wretched doctor who was put forward as the leader of the Academy on that grave occasion came to a halt fifteen times over fifteen syllogisms, like a chicken amongst stubble. Learn how roughly and rudely that pig behaved and with what patience and humanity the Nolan replied, showing himself to be indeed a Neapolitan, born and bred beneath a kindlier sky. Hear how they made him leave off his public lectures on the immortality of the soul and on the quintuple sphere.[1]

Apart from some vague references by Gabriel Harvey, John Florio, and Samuel Daniel's friend "N.W.",[2] we have hitherto only had Bruno's own account of his experiences at Oxford, indicating, as the above quotation shows, that the magician was not satisfied with his reception there.

Entirely new evidence from the Oxford side about Bruno's lectures was published in 1960 in an article by Robert McNulty in *Renaissance News*.[3] In 1604, George Abbot, later to be Archbishop of Canterbury, and who was at Balliol at the time of Bruno's visit to Oxford in 1583, published a doctrinal work which was a Protestant reply to the arguments of a Catholic writer whose book had been secretly printed and distributed in England. The Catholic writer was the Benedictine, Thomas Hill, whose *A Quartron of Reasons of Catholike Religion*, printed in 1600, was having a considerable influence. Hill's book largely reproduced the arguments in an earlier Catholic propagandist work, Richard Bristow's *A Briefe Treatise of Diuerse Plaine and Sure Ways to Finde Out Truths in This . . . Time of Heresie* first printed in 1574 and several times

---

[1] *La cena de le ceneri* (1584), dial. 4 (*Dial. ital.*, pp. 133–4).

[2] Gabriel Harvey, *Marginalia*, ed. G. C. Moore Smith, 1913, p. 156; Florio's address to the reader before his translation of Montaigne's essays; preface by "N.W." before Samuel Daniel's *The Worthy Tract of Paulus Iouius* (1585).

[3] Robert McNulty, "Bruno at Oxford", *Renaissance News*, 1960 (XIII), pp. 300–5.

reprinted.[1] The Catholics give a series of reasons why their faith is the true one, as compared with the Protestants. For example, they have the authority of tradition and the Fathers; heresy is no new thing, and modern heresies are but repetitions of ancient heresies; by those of their faith, miraculous works are done, but not by the Protestants; Catholics see visions and Protestants do not; Catholics are all agreed as one in their faith, whereas heretics are divided amongst themselves.

George Abbot, whose leanings were definitely Calvinist and Puritan, took up the task of replying to Hill (and to Bristow, on whom Hill was founded) in a work published in 1604 by Joseph Barnes, Printer to the University, and entitled, *The Reasons Which Doctour Hill Hath Brought, for the Upholding of Papistry, Which is Falselie Termed the Catholike Religion; Unmasked, and Shewed to Be Very Weake, and Upon Examination Most Insufficient for That Purpose*. Who would have dreamed of looking in a work with such a title as this for new light on Giordano Bruno? Yet this is the book in which R. McNulty made his remarkable discovery. Here is the passage:

When that Italian Didapper, who intituled himselfe *Philotheus Iordanus Brunus Nolanus, magis elaborata Theologia Doctor, &c* (margin: Praefat, in explicatio triginta sigillorum) with a name longer then his body, had in the traine of *Alasco* the Polish Duke, seene our Vniversity in the year 1583, his hart was on fire, to make himselfe by some worthy exploite, to become famous in that celebrious place. Not long after returning againe, when he had more boldly then wisely, got vp into the highest place of our best & most renowned schoole, stripping vp his sleeues like some Iugler, and telling vs much of *chentrum & chirculus & circumferenchia* (after the pronunciation of his Country language) he vndertooke among very many other matters to set on foote the opinion of Copernicus, that the earth did goe round, and the heavens did stand still; wheras in truth it was his owne head which rather did run round, & his braines did not stand stil. When he had read his first Lecture, a graue man, & both then and now of good place in that Vniversity, seemed to himselfe, some where to haue read those things which the Doctor propounded: but silencing his conceit till he heard him the second time, remembered

[1] On Hill's and Bristow's books see A. F. Allison and D. M. Rogers, *A Catalogue of Catholic Books in English Printed Abroad or Secretly in England*, Bognor Regis, 1956, nos. 146–9, 400–1; and cf. McNulty, *article cited*, p. 302.

himselfe then, and repayring to his study, found both the former and later Lecture, taken almost verbatim out of the workes of *Marsilius Ficinus* (margin: De vita coelitus comparanda). Wherewith when he had acquainted that rare & excellent Ornament of our land, the Reverend Bishop of Durham that now is, but then Deane of Christs-Church, it was at the first thought fit, to notifie to the Illustrious Reader, so much as they had discovered. But afterward hee who gaue the first light, did most wisely intreate, that once more they might make trial of him; and if he persevered to abuse himselfe, and that Auditory the thirde time, they shoulde then do their pleasure. After which, *Iordanus* continuing to be *idem Iordanus*, they caused some to make knowne vnto him their former patience, & the paines which he had taken with them, & so with great honesty of the little man's part, there was an end of that matter.[1]

What a marvellous scene! There is the Magus announcing the Copernican theory in the context of the astral magic and sunworship of the *De vita coelitus comparanda*. There is the grave man thinking that he has read something like this somewhere and going to his study to fetch his Ficino. Do they understand what it is all about? Perhaps not, but the word "juggler" is significant, suggesting the magician.

Abbot introduces Bruno into his rampantly anti-Catholic book when he is replying to the Bristow-Hill argument that the Catholics have "Unitie and Consent" whilst the heretics quarrel. He wants to underline that Hill is unoriginal, only repeating Bristow's material, and Bruno is drawn in as another example of cribbing, detected at Oxford in the act of delivering lectures which were all out of Ficino. This is so flimsy a pretext for dragging in the Bruno episode that there must be more behind it. Abbot evidently knew something of one of Bruno's books; he had seen the address to the Oxford doctors in the *Explicatio Triginta Sigillorum*. If he had delved deeper into that work, he would have found in it a defence of "good" magical religion, based on Cornelius Agrippa's *De occulta philosophia*. This alone might account for his including an attack on the Italian "juggler" in his attack on the Catholics who had defended their religion for its power to do miracles. Moreover, in his *Cena de le ceneri*, ostensibly about the Copernican theory, Bruno had referred to his experiences at Oxford, violently abusing the "pedants" who had interrupted his lectures there; an

[1] Abbot, *The Reasons*, etc., pp. 88–9; quoted McNulty, *article cited*, pp. 302–3.

example of his language has been given in the quotation already made. In his *De la causa, principio e uno*, Bruno makes some apology for his attack on Oxford, but this takes the form of comparing pre-Reformation Oxford with the university of the present day, to the disadvantage of the latter:

> Neither is the memory passed away of those who flourished in this place (Oxford) before speculative studies were to be found in other parts of Europe; although their language was barbarous and they were friars by profession, from the principles of metaphysics which they laid down was derived the splendour of a most rare and noble part of philosophy (now in our times almost extinct) which was diffused to other academies in the non-barbarian provinces. But what has disquieted me and caused me both annoyance and amusement is that, although I have found no purer Latin and Greek than here (in Oxford), for the rest (I speak of the generality) they make a boast of being totally different from their predecessors, who, caring little for eloquence and the niceties of grammar, were all intent on those kind of speculations which these men call Sophisms. But I esteem much more highly the metaphysics of those bygone students, in which respect they went far beyond their lord and master Aristotle . . . than anything that these of the present age have to show, for all their Ciceronian eloquence and rhetorical art.[1]

This apology really apologises for nothing, for though it expresses deep admiration for the friars of the old Oxford, it really complains again that those who have replaced them are "grammarian pedants", which was what he called the Oxford doctors in the abuse in the *Cena*. Bruno would have preferred to meet one of the old barbarous friars at Oxford, rather than the Ciceronians of the present day. Perhaps the Prince Alasco was also not quite satisfied, since Sidney took him to see Dee, the "conjuror", after his visit to Oxford.[2]

---

[1] *De la causa, principio e uno* (1584), dial. I (*Dial. ital.*, pp. 209–10). For an English translation of this work, see S. Greenberg, *The Infinite in Giordano Bruno*, New York, 1950, pp. 77 ff.

[2] These events may well have been in the mind of Robert Greene when he wrote (about 1587 or later) his play on *Friar Bacon and Friar Bungay*, set in mediaeval Oxford which is visited by distinguished foreigners, the Emperor and others, accompanied by a foreign doctor who has won great triumphs in all the universities of Europe when disputing on magic but who is defeated at Oxford in a conjuring match in which Friar Bacon's magic proves the stronger. As A. W. Ward noticed years ago, some of the foreign magician's remarks about Oxford in Greene's play echo phrases

Though allowance must be made for Abbot's natural animus against the magician who had attacked Oxford, I see no reason to doubt his evidence that Bruno in his lectures there associated Copernicus on the sun with Ficino's *De vita coelitus comparanda*—a priceless piece of information. It confirms what we should expect from our study of the magical works published in Paris. And Abbot's inclusion of his attack on Bruno in his anti-Catholic controversial work suggests that he had also seen a religious meaning in Bruno's Ficinian Copernicanism.

The works in the form of dialogues written in Italian which Bruno published in England are usually classified as moral and philosophical. In the following pages I hope to show that both Bruno's proposed moral reform and his philosophy are related to his Hermetic religious mission—a mission in which Ficino's magic becomes expanded into a projected full restoration of the magical religion of the pseudo-Egyptians of the *Asclepius*. Since the full "Egyptian" character of Bruno's message comes out very clearly in one of the so-called moral dialogues, the *Spaccio della bestia trionfante*, I shall discuss this first, passing in the next chapter to the *Cena de le ceneri*, a so-called philosophical dialogue, in which the message is translated into terms of the Copernican philosophy.

A basic theme of Bruno's *Spaccio della bestia trionfante* (1584) is the glorification of the magical religion of the Egyptians. Their worship was really the worship of "God in things":

> For . . . diverse living things represent diverse spirits and powers, which beyond the absolute being which they have, obtain a being communicated to all things according to their capacity and measure. Whence God as a whole (though not totally but in some more in some less excellently) is in all things. For Mars is more efficaciously in natural vestiges and modes of substance, in a viper or a scorpion, nay even in an onion or garlic, than in any inanimate picture or statue. Thus one should think of Sol as being in a crocus, a daffodil, a sunflower, in the cock, in the lion; and thus one should conceive of each of the gods through each of the species grouped under the divers genuses of the *ens*. For as the divinity descends in a certain manner inasmuch as it communicates itself to nature, so there is an ascent

in the *Cena de le ceneri* (Marlowe, *Tragical History of Dr. Faustus* and Greene, *Honourable History of Friar Bacon and Friar Bungay*, ed. A. W. Ward, Oxford, 1887, pp. 254-5).

made to the divinity through nature. Thus through the light which shines in natural things one mounts up to the life which presides over them. . . . And in truth I see how the wise men by these means had power to make familiar, affable and domestic gods, which, through the voices which came out of the statues, gave counsels, doctrines, divinations and superhuman teachings. Whence with magical and divine rites they ascended to the height of the divinity by that same scale of nature by which the divinity descends to the smallest things by the communication of itself. But, what seems to me most deplorable, is that I see some senseless and foolish idolaters, who no more imitate the excellence of the cult of Egypt than the shadow approximates to the nobility of the body; and who seek the divinity, of which they know nothing, in the excrements of dead and inanimate things; and who not only mock at those divine and deep-seeing worshippers, but also at us, reckoning us to be no better than beasts. And what is worse, they triumph at seeing their foolish rites in such repute whilst those of others are vanished and annulled.

Let not this trouble you, Momus, said Isis, since fate has ordained a vicissitude of darkness and light.

But the worst of it is, said Momus, that they hold it for certain that they are in the light.

And Isis replied that darkness would not be darkness to them, if they knew it.

Those wise men, then, in order to obtain certain benefits and gifts from the gods, by means of a profound magic, made use of certain natural things in which the divinity was latent, and through which the divinity was able and willing to communicate itself for certain effects. Whence those ceremonies were not vain fancies, but living voices which reached the very ears of the gods. . . .[1]

Needless to say, this is based on the "god-making" passage in the *Asclepius*,[2] explained as done by profound magic, and as belonging to the magical religion of the Egyptians which Bruno states that he prefers to any other religion. He further expands his view of the Egyptian religion on some later pages:

Thus crocodiles, cocks, onions and turnips were never worshipped for themselves, but the gods and the divinity in crocodiles, cocks and other things, which divinity was, is and will be found in diverse subjects in so far as they are mortal at certain times and places, successively and all at once, that is to say, the divinity according as it

---

[1] *Spaccio della bestia trionfante*, dial. 3 (*Dial. ital.*, pp. 777–8).
[2] See above, p. 37.

is near and familiar to these things, not the divinity as it is most high, absolute in itself, and without relation to the things produced. You see, then, how one simple divinity which is in all things, one fecund nature, mother and preserver of the universe, shines forth in diverse subjects, and takes diverse names, according as it communicates itself diversely. You see how one must ascend to this One by the participation in diverse gifts; for it would be in vain to attempt to catch water in a net, or fish in a plate. Hence, in the two bodies which are nearest to our globe and divine mother, the sun and the moon, they conceive is the life which informs things according to the two principal reasons. Then they understand life according to seven other reasons, distributing it to seven wandering stars, to which, as to the original principle and fecund cause, they reduce the differences in species in each genus, saying of plants, animals, stones and influences, and other things, that these belong to Saturn, these to Jupiter, these to Mars, and so on. And so also parts and members, colours, seals, characters, signs, images are distributed under seven species. But notwithstanding all this, they were not ignorant that One is the divinity which is in all things, which, as it diffuses and communicates itself in innumerable ways, so it has innumerable names, and by innumerable ways, with reasons proper and appropriate to each one, it is to be sought, whilst with innumerable rites it is honoured and cultivated, by which we seek to obtain innumerable kinds of favours from it. For this is needed that wisdom and judgment, that art and industry and use of the intellectual light, which is revealed to the world from the intelligible sun, sometimes more strongly, sometimes less strongly. Which habit is called Magia: and this, when it is directed to supernatural principles is divine; when towards the contemplation of nature and scrutiny of her secrets, it is called natural; and it is called middle or mathematical as it consists in reasons and acts of the soul, which is on the horizon between corporeal and spiritual, spiritual and intellectual.

And, to return to our purpose said Isis to Momus, the stupid and senseless idolaters had no reason to laugh at the magic and divine cult of the Egyptians, who in all things and in all effects, according to the proper reasons of each, contemplated the divinity; and knew how through the species which are in the womb of nature, to receive those benefits which they desired from her. For, as she gives fish to the sea and rivers, deserts to wild animals, metals to the mines, fruits to the trees, so they give certain lots, virtues, fortunes and impressions to certain parts of certain animals, beasts, and plants. Hence the divinity in the sea was called Neptune, in the sun, Apollo, in the earth Ceres, in the deserts, Diana, and diversely in all other species which, like diverse ideas, were diverse divinities in nature, all of which referred to one deity of deities and fountain of the ideas above nature.[1]

What is Giordano Bruno doing here? It is quite simple. He is taking Renaissance magic back to its pagan source, abandoning the feeble efforts of Ficino to do a little harmless magic whilst disguising its main source in the *Asclepius*, utterly flouting the religious Hermetists who tried to have a Christian Hermetism without the *Asclepius*, proclaiming himself a full Egyptian who, like Celsus in his anti-Christian arguments quoted by Origen,[2] deplores the destruction by the Christians of the worship of the natural gods of Greece, and of the religion of the Egyptians, through which they approached the divine ideas, the intelligible sun, the One of Neoplatonism.

Hence he can quote in full the Lament from the *Asclepius*, translating its moving cadences into Italian:

Non sai, o Asclepio, come l'Egitto sia la imagine del cielo . . . la nostra terra è tempio del mondo. Ma, oimè, tempo verrà che apparirà l'Egitto in vano essere stato religioso cultore della divinitade. . . . O Egitto, Egitto, delle religioni tue solamente rimarrono le favole. . . . Le tenebre si preponeranno alla luce, la morte sarà giudicata più utile che la vita, nessuno alzarà gli occhi al cielo, il religioso sarà stimato insano, l'empio sarà giudicato prudente, il furioso forte, il pessimo buono. E credetemi che ancora sarà definita pena capitale a colui che s'applicarà alla religion della mente; perché si trovaranno nove giustizie, nuove leggi, nulla si trovarà di santo, nulla di religioso: non si udirà cosa degna di cielo o di celesti. Soli angeli perniciosi rimarrano, li quali meschiati con gli uomini forzaranno gli miseri all'audacia di ogni male, come fusse giustizià; donando materia a guerre, rapine, frode e tutte altre cose contrarie alla anima e giustizià naturale: e questa sarà la vecchiaia ed il disordine e la irreligione del mondo. Ma non dubitare, Asclepio, perché, dopo che saranno accadute queste cose, allora il signore e padre Dio, governator del mondo, l'omnipotente proveditore . . . senza dubbio donarà fine a cotal macchia, richiamando il mondo all'antico volto.[3]

[1] *Spaccio*, dial. 3 (*Dial. ital.*, pp. 780–2).   [2] See above, pp. 59, 68.

[3] *Spaccio*, dial. 3 (*Dial. ital.*, pp. 784–6). Cf. the *Asclepius* in *C.H.*, II, pp. 326–30, and above, pp. 38–40.

It has been known that this passage comes from the *Asclepius*, but it has not been realised that the preceding passages, quoted above, are all derived from the description of the Egyptian religion in that work, expanded and Neoplatonised by Bruno after the manner which Ficino had made fashionable.

The marvellous magical religion of the Egyptians will return, their moral laws will replace the chaos of the present age, the prophesy of the Lament will be fulfilled, and the sign in heaven proclaiming the return of Egyptian light to dispel the present darkness was (as we shall see in the next chapter) the Copernican sun.

The Ficinian Neoplatonising of the Asclepian magic is very clear in some of the passages quoted above, particularly in the use of the word "reasons" for basic stellar influences which recalls the opening of the *De vita coelitus comparanda*.[1] There is also an influence of Cornelius Agrippa in the classification of Magia into divine or supernatural, middle or mathematical, and natural.[2] To know more of, for example, the colours, seals, characters, signs, images, belonging to the seven planets the reader would naturally turn to Agrippa's useful book. Bruno's Egyptianism is thus that of a complete Modern Magus, deriving ultimately from Ficino but having passed through the Agrippa stage. And Bruno openly proclaims his Egyptianism as a religion; it is the good religion which was overwhelmed in darkness when the Christians destroyed it, forbade it by statutes, substituted worship of dead things, foolish rites, bad moral behaviour and constant wars, for the Egyptian natural religion with its Neoplatonic basis, and the Egyptian good moral laws. "Mercurio Egizio sapientissimo" is for Bruno the name of the divine wisdom itself,[3] and the *Spaccio della bestia trionfante* outlines a coming religious and moral reform.

The peculiarity of the reform in the *Spaccio* is that it begins in the heavens; it is the images of the constellations of the zodiac and of the northern and southern constellations which are reformed or cleansed through a council of the planetary gods which is summoned by Jupiter for this purpose. Amongst the speakers in this celestial council conducting the celestial reform are the divine Sophia, Isis, and Momus. The idea of a reform beginning in the heavens with the rearranging or cleansing of the celestial images (whence the lower world is reformed through the reform of the celestial influxes upon it) might have been suggested to Bruno by a Hermetic treatise, not one of the familiar ones in the *Corpus Hermeticum* but one of those preserved by Stobaeus in his anthology. This is the treatise known as the *Koré Kosmou*,[4] or

[1] See above, p. 64. [2] See above, p. 131.
[3] *Spaccio*, dial. 3 (*Dial. ital.*, p. 780).
[4] *C.H.*, IV, pp. 1–22 (Stobaeus Excerpt XXIII).

"Daughter (or Virgin) of the World", or, in Patrizi's Latin translation as the *Minerva Mundi*. It is in the form of a dialogue between Isis and her son Horus in which Momus is also one of the speakers. Isis begins by describing the creation, an early stage of which was the arrangement of the celestial images on which all things below depend.[1] The things of the lower world were then created, but this lower nature was unsatisfactory. God therefore decided to create man, so he called an assembly of the gods who offered to help, each planetary god giving man its distinctive gifts.[2] But things still went from bad to worse, so God again convoked the gods in a plenary assembly[3] (just as Jupiter convokes the gods in Bruno's *Spaccio* to conduct a reform). Ignorance which had reigned supreme was driven out; the pollution of the elements was cleansed and they received a second efflux of the divine nature.[4] The treatise ends with the praises of Isis and Osiris; who have put an end to slaughter and have restored justice; who having learned from Hermes that things below must be kept in sympathy with things above have instituted on earth the sacred functions vertically linked with the mysteries of heaven.[5]

This treatise is very obscure[6] and I have picked out from it only certain points for comparison with Bruno's *Spaccio* in which the divine Sophia, Isis, and Momus (but not Horus) are among the speakers; which is concerned with the convoking of an assembly of the gods to reform themselves and the celestial images; whence there is to come a general reform of mankind involving a return of Egyptian religion and ethics. There is, further, a curious vein of Lucianic familiarity in the treatment of the gods in the Hermetic treatise (Momus is a character much used by Lucian)[7] which is also typical of the *Spaccio*.

The *Koré Kosmou* was first published in 1591, grouped with the

---

[1] *Ibid.*, p. 7. [2] *Ibid.*, pp. 8–9.
[3] *Ibid.*, p. 17. [4] *Ibid.*, pp. 18–20.
[5] *Ibid.*, pp. 21–2. I have only mentioned a few items in the litany.
[6] For a discussion of it, see Festugière, III, pp. 37–41, 83 ff.
[7] He is mentioned in Lucian's *Vera historia*, which was well known to Bruno and is referred to in the *Cena de le ceneri*, dial. 3 (*Dial. ital.*, p. 111). Bruno certainly knew Lucian's works directly, but the point is that in the *Koré Kosmou* there is a Momus in a Hermetic context. "Hermes was pleased at hearing the words of Momus for they were said to him in a familiar tone" (*C.H.*, IV, p. 16).

other Hermetic writings, and with a Latin translation by Patrizi.[1] If Bruno knew it before 1584, the date of the publication of the *Spaccio*, he must therefore have known it, either through manuscript translations circulating amongst Hermetists, or he must have read it in the original Greek in Stobaeus.[2]

Up, up, O ye gods! and remove from heaven all these spectres, statues, figures, images, pictures, histories of our avarice, lusts, thefts, hatreds, contempts, and shames. May this dark and gloomy night of our errors pass away, for the dawn of a new day of justice invites us. And let us place ourselves in such a manner that the rising sun does not disclose our uncleanness. We must purify ourselves and make ourselves beautiful. . . . We must place ourselves, I say, first in the intellectual heaven which is within us, and then in this sensible and corporeal heaven which presents itself to our eyes. Let us remove from the heaven of our minds the BEAR of Deformity, the ARROW of Detraction, the HORSE of Levity, the DOG of Murmuring, the LITTLE DOG of Flattery. Let us banish the HERCULES of Violence, the LYRE of Conspiracy, the TRIANGLE of Impiety, the BOOTES of Inconstancy, the CEPHEUS of Cruelty. May the DRAGON of Envy be far from us, and the SWAN of Imprudence, the CASSIOPEIA of Vanity, the ANDROMEDA of Laziness, the PERSEUS of Vain Anxiety. Let us chase away the OPHIUCHUS of Evil-Speaking, the EAGLE of Arrogance, the DOLPHIN of Lust, the HORSE of Impatience, the HYDRA of Concupiscence. Let us put far from us the CETUS of Gluttony, the ORION of Ferocity, the RIVER of Superfluities, the GORGON of Ignorance, the HARE of Timidity. Let us no longer carry in our breast the ARGO of Avarice, the CUP of Insobriety, the BALANCE of Iniquity, the CANCER of Slowness, the CAPRICORN of Deception. Let not the SCORPIO of Fraud come near us, nor the CENTAUR of Animal Affection, the ALTAR of Superstition, the CROWN of Pride, the FISH of Unworthy Silence. May the TWINS of Indecent Familiarity fall with them, and the BULL of Concern for Mean Things, the RAM of Inconsiderateness, the LION of Tyranny, the AQUARIUS of Dissoluteness, the VIRGIN of Fruitless Conversation, and the SAGITTARIUS of Detraction.

[1] In the *Nova de universis philosophia*, Ferrara, 1591, and Venice, 1593. See above, p. 182. On Patrizi's publication of the Stobaeus fragments, see Scott, I, p. 40.

[2] The *Anthologium* of Stobaeus, compiled *circa* A.D. 500, is a collection of extracts from Greek writers amongst which are several *Hermetica*. Some of these are the same as some in the *Corpus Hermeticum*; others are otherwise unknown and one of these is the *Koré Kosmou*. The *editio princeps* of the anthology (Bks. I and II) was at Antwerp in 1575. See Scott, I, pp. 82 ff.

If we thus purge our habitations, O ye gods, if we thus renew our heaven, the constellations and influences shall be new, the impressions and fortunes shall be new, for all things depend on this upper world. . . .[1]

These words are part of a speech made by Jupiter in the *Spaccio* to an assembly, or General Council, of the celestial gods. The Almighty Thunderer feels that he grows old, and he is in a mood of penitence. Casting his eye around the heavens he perceives that the images of the forty-eight constellations are either in the ugly forms of animals, like that great deformed Bear, the Ursa Major, or like Aries and Taurus and other animal forms of the zodiac, or their images recall shameful actions of the gods, like the Lyre which reminds of the thefts of Mercury, or Hercules and Perseus, who are his own bastards. The assembled gods in their conclave are therefore to consider each in turn the images of the constellations, beginning with the Bear and the other northern constellations, passing along the twelve signs of the zodiac, and concluding with a survey of the southern constellations.[2] Jupiter had perhaps provided each member of the celestial board with a copy of one of those illustrated editions of Hyginus, which have cuts of the constellation images beside the letterpress describing their shameful mythological associations. (One of Bruno's later mnemonic works is illustrated by cuts of the gods of the planets which are identical with those of an edition of Hyginus published in 1578 in Paris.)[3] At any rate, the student of the *Spaccio* will find it useful to have an illustrated Hyginus beside him, for Bruno has taken much of his mythology from that work, and it is to the images of the constellations, reviewed in their order, that he attaches the theme of his amazing work, which is about a universal religious and moral reform.

As each constellation image is discussed, vices associated with it are deplored and the virtues opposite to these vices are praised. More than that, there is an active movement of ascent and descent going on; the vices are thrown out by the gods, cast out of the heavens, and to their places ascend the opposite virtues. Thus, in the end, the Triumphant Beast is fully expelled. And the Triumphant Beast is not the Pope, as used sometimes to be thought. It

[1] *Spaccio*, dial. 1 (*Dial. ital.*, pp. 611–2).
[2] *Ibid.* (*Dial. ital.*, pp. 595 ff.).
[3] Hyginus, *Fabularum liber*, Paris, 1578. See below, p. 328.

is the sum of all the vices which are opposite to the virtues. This is stated by Bruno in the dedication of the work to Philip Sidney: "Then the triumphant beast is driven out, that is the vices which predominate, and oppose the divine part (of the soul).[1]

The list of the constellations and of the virtues and vices he connects with them is given twice by Bruno, first in the dedication to Sidney, and again in the dialogues where the reform movement is described in detail as the gods work through the heavens. In the second dialogue, where he is discussing the triumphant virtues in the abstract, he is still following the order he has assigned to them in the constellations. It has to be realised that he has absolutely clearly imprinted on his memory, after the manner of a magic memory system, the order of the constellation images, and on this the whole argument depends.

The following are some examples of the virtue–vice movements, the ascent of virtues and descent of vices, which take place as the gods reform the heavens.

To Ursa Major and Minor there ascend Truth, Being, Goodness, which drive out Deformity, Falsehood, and Defect.[2] In Cephus, Wisdom (Sophia) replaces Ignorance and Foolish Faith.[3] Natural and Human Law rise in Bootes (Arctophylax) in place of Crime.[4] In the Corona Borealis, Justice replaces Iniquity.[5] In the Triangulum, Faith, Love and Sincerity drive out Fraud.[6] In the Pleiades (which Bruno places amongst the zodiacal signs, as in some editions of Hyginus) Union, Civility, Concord are found instead of Sect, Faction, and Party.[7] In Scorpio, Sincerity and Truth drive out Fraud and Treason.[8] Capricorn, with which, in Hyginus, is told the story of the Greek gods turning themselves into animals in Egypt, is the point in the heavenly review at which are inserted the praises of the Egyptian religion, quoted above, and the Lament from the *Asclepius*.[9] Rapine and Falsehood leave Orion, to

---

[1] *Spaccio*, dedication (*Dial. ital.*, p. 561).
[2] *Spaccio*, dedication and dial. 1 (*Dial. ital.*, pp. 562 ff., 617 ff.).
[3] *Ibid.* (*Dial. ital.*, pp. 562, 611.)
[4] *Ibid.* (*Dial. ital.*, pp. 562, 621).
[5] *Ibid.* (*Dial. ital.*, pp. 563, 622).
[6] *Spaccio*, dedication and dial. 3 (*Dial. ital.*, pp. 565, 755).
[7] *Ibid.* (*Dial. ital.*, pp. 566, 765–6).
[8] *Ibid.* (*Dial. ital.*, pp. 567, 774).
[9] *Ibid.* (*Dial. ital.*, pp. 567, 775 ff.).

which mount Magnanimity, and Public Spirit.[1] In Corvus, Magia
Divina replaces Imposture.[2]

We can already begin to see, in part, what the Brunian reform
of the heavens means. The prophecy at the end of the Lament is
coming true; the old age of the world after the collapse of the
Egyptian religion and the Egyptian moral laws is over; the magical
religion mounts up again into the sky and so do the virtues of the
Egyptian society. Some of the vices overcome are the same as
those mentioned in the Lament, for example, Fraud.[3] And with
the Lament, Bruno is associating another "Egyptian" work, namely
Corpus Hermeticum XIII, with its description of how, in the
regenerated soul, the decade of the Powers replaces the dodecade
of the vices, associated with bad influences of the stars.[4] He is not
following this numbering, but the idea of the moral regeneration
taking place in the cosmological setting can now be recognised as
undoubtedly Hermetic in origin.

The names of the gods who attend the reforming council and
conduct the reform of the heavens are nowhere listed, but we
know who they are from the names of the speakers in the delibera-
tions of the council. Summoned by Jupiter, the council was
attended by Apollo, Mercury, Saturn, Mars, Venus, Diana. These
are, of course, the planetary gods, with Sol and Luna under their
Olympian names. Others present were Juno, Minerva, Neptune,
and Isis, the latter being a very prominent speaker.

In the dedication to Sidney, Bruno explains that the gods
represent "the virtues and powers of the soul",[5] and that, since "in
every man . . . there is a world, a universe",[6] the reform of the
heavens is the reform, or the production, of a personality. Jupiter
says, in the speech already quoted, that the reform begins in the
minds of the gods themselves, who are to "place themselves in the
intellectual heaven" within them, to "drive from the heaven of
their minds"[7] the bad qualities and replace them with good qualities. It is this interior reform of the gods themselves which is
reflected all round the vault of heaven as the virtues rise to replace
the vices in the forty-eight constellations. It is thus a personality

---

[1] *Ibid.* (*Dial. ital.*, pp. 568, 803 ff.).
[2] *Ibid.* (*Dial. ital.*, pp. 569, 817 ff.).
[3] See above, p. 39. [4] See above, pp. 28–31.
[5] *Spaccio*, dedication (*Dial. ital.*, pp. 561–2).
[6] *Ibid.* (*Dial. ital.*, p. 560). [7] See above, p. 217.

which is being formed in the *Spaccio*, a personality whose powers are being formed into a successful whole.

What kind of personality? That we can know by looking round the heavens and reading off the victorious good qualities in the constellations. It is a predominantly solar personality, for Apollo is the patron of magic and divination, and this personality is the prophet and leader of a revival of magical religion. The triumph of good solar characteristics is witnessed in, for example, Draco, where Apollo with his magic charms the dragon,[1] and in Corvus in which Magia Divina triumphs over bad forms of magic.[2] Another most important influence in this character is that of Jupiter. The Jovial characteristics of benevolent law-giving and tolerance are seen to prevail in the constellations Bootes,[3] Aquila,[4] Aries,[5] Libra,[6] and others. There is also a strong Venus influence, making for friendship and love, harmonising of discords, and the tempering of Mars, or of forces making for war. Venus triumphs in the Pleiades[7] and in Gemini,[8] and in Delphinus,[9] she overcomes Mars. Good Saturnian qualities, such as deep study and contemplation are preserved, for example in Perseus,[10] but the Saturnian unsociability and other disagreeable qualities are tempered by Jupiter or Venus influences in other constellations. Mars is everywhere kept down, being particularly snubbed by Jupiter in Cassiopeia.[11]

Such, at least, is the kind of explanation which I would proffer of the curious lists of good and bad qualities given in the *Spaccio*, which are something other than straightforward lists of virtues and vices. I suggest that they represent good and bad influences of the stars. The personality is mastering the stars by choosing out their good gifts, the good side of their influences (taking for example from Venus, love and benevolence, not lasciviousness, and so on

---

[1] *Spaccio*, dedication (*Dial. ital.*, pp. 619–20).

[2] *Ibid.*, dedication and dial. 3 (*Dial. ital.*, pp. 569, 817–8).

[3] *Ibid.*, dedication and dial. 1 (*Dial. ital.*, pp. 562, 621).

[4] *Ibid.*, dedication and dial. 3 (*Dial. ital.*, pp. 565, 751).

[5] *Ibid.* (*Dial. ital.*, pp. 565, 761–3).

[6] *Ibid.* (*Dial. ital.*, pp. 567, 771).

[7] *Ibid.* (*Dial. ital.*, pp. 566, 765–6).

[8] *Ibid.* (*Dial. ital.*, pp. 566, 766–7).

[9] *Ibid.* (*Dial. ital.*, pp. 565, 753–4).

[10] *Ibid.* (*Dial. ital.*, pp. 564, 711).

[11] *Spaccio*, dedication and dial. 2 (*Dial. ital.*, pp. 563, 705–6).

for the good and bad sides of the other planetary influences) and also by tempering the predominantly bad planets, Mars and Saturn, by attracting strong Solar, Jovial or Venereal influences. I shall return to this aspect of the *Spaccio* in a later chapter when discussing a later work by Bruno in which he gives lists of good and bad moral characteristics, which are of the same type as those used in the *Spaccio*, in a context where these are quite definitely related to astral psychology.[1]

If my interpretation of the ethics of the *Spaccio* is correct, it means that Bruno has developed the Ficinian magic, directed towards the formation of a personality in which Solar, Jovial, and Venereal influences predominate and the bad influences of the stars are kept at bay, into a fully "Egyptian" or Hermetic ethic or religion, in which reformation or salvation is achieved in the cosmological setting, the "triumphant beast" of the sum of the vices, the bad influences coming from the stars, is cast out by their good opposites, and the divine virtues or powers predominate in the reformed personality.

Animal form or the form of the "beast" is used in a strangely ambivalent manner in the *Spaccio*. Sometimes the animal forms in the sky, that is in the constellation images in animal form, seem to represent the vices which are being expelled from the reformed personality. But when the gods are discussing Capricorn, they allow this animal to remain in heaven to testify to the truth of the religion of natural magic which worships "the divine in things".[2] Elsewhere it is said that though the celestial images in animal form may seem to signify vices yet they are also not without divine virtue; hence the Egyptians from the natural forms of beasts ascended to the penetration of the divinity.[3] Thus, though the animal forms of some of the constellation images signify vices contrary to the virtues which the reform proclaims, yet animal form itself as the representative of *Deus in rebus* is vindicated by the celestial animal forms, and particularly by that of Capricorn. The ethical reform drives the beast images out of heaven when those beasts are understood as allegories of vices. The religious reform maintains the beasts in heaven as representative of Egypt

[1] See below, pp. 328–9.
[2] *Spaccio*, dial. 1 (*Dial. ital.*, p. 602).
[3] *Ibid.*, dial. 3 (*Dial. ital.*, pp. 795-6).

and its animal worship. The "Expulsion of the Triumphant Beast" thus has a double meaning; the beast is expelled on one level and triumphs on another. One wonders whether Pope Alexander VI thought along these extremely difficult lines about Apis.[1]

For his meditations on Greek and Egyptian forms of the gods, it is possible that Bruno had been studying Cartari's *De gli immagini degli dei*, the plates of which often show Greek and Egyptian forms together. The gods of the *Spaccio* almost, as it were, tremble between the two forms as the Egyptian power grows. The Appartamento Borgia frescoes, showing the Greek cow, Io, turning into Isis in Egypt, perhaps move within a similar frame of reference, though they are orthodox in showing the Egyptian bulls worshipping the Virgin and saints, like proper *prisci theologi*.

Bruno's views on the history of *prisca theologia*, or *prisca magia*, are made abundantly clear:

> Do not suppose that the sufficiency of the Chaldaic magic derived from the Cabala of the Jews; for the Jews are without doubt the excrements of Egypt, and no one could ever pretend with any degree of probability that the Egyptians borrowed any principle, good or bad, from the Hebrews. Whence we Greeks own Egypt, the grand monarchy of letters and nobility, to be the parent of our fables, metaphors and doctrines. . .[2]

So the grand controversy of the relative dates of Moses and Hermes the Egyptian is resolved by Bruno. The Egyptians are earlier than Greeks and Hebrews (and, of course, Christians) and had the best religion and the best magic and the best laws of them all. He uses the familiar counters, but shifts them round into appallingly unorthodox positions.

Apart from the basic influences upon the *Spaccio* of Hermetic treatises, read by Bruno as records of the ancient Egyptian religion and ethic which he is reviving, there was another certain influence, namely that of the *Zodiacus vitae* (first published in 1534)[3] of

---

[1] See above, p. 115.

[2] *Spaccio*, dial. 3 (*Dial. ital.*, pp. 799–80).

[3] The work was very popular, particularly in Protestant countries, because of its satire on monks. In England, it was used as a school text-book; see Foster Watson, *The Zodiacus Vitae*, London, 1908, p. 5. There was an English translation by Barnabe Googe (reprinted with an introduction by R. Tuve, Scholars' Facsimiles and Reprints, New York, 1947).

Palingenius. In this didactic Latin poem, Palingenius goes through in order the twelve signs of the zodiac attaching to them his moral teaching, the overcoming of vices by virtues. Since the poem is punctuated by outbursts of enthusiasm or *furor* in which the *mens* makes ascensions into the heavens, it seems to me that the writer has been influenced by Hermetic teachings,[1] and that these are also reflected in his presentation of his ethics in the cosmological setting of the zodiac. The ethic of Palingenius, the kind of moral virtue which he teaches, is supposedly Epicurean. Epicurus is introduced as the supreme moral teacher, and the Epicurean doctrine of pleasure is inculcated, not in any lascivious or degenerate way but with the gravity and restraint of true Epicureanism. Palingenius derived his knowledge of Epicurus from the poem of Lucretius, some of the cosmology of which also influenced him. Yet Palingenius' Epicureanism is singularly combined with Neoplatonic and Hermetic influences, and there are also many references to magic in his poem. Obviously, this Renaissance Epicureanism must be a very different matter from the Epicureanism of Lucretius.

As E. Garin has pointed out,[2] the newly rediscovered poem of Lucretius influenced Ficino; and in some Renaissance writers the

---

[1] There is only one actual mention of Hermes, as follows:

> Hei mihi! quam vere dixit ter maximus Hermes,
> Congeries mundus cunctorum est iste malorum,
> Nimirum quoniam daemon, qui praesidet orbi
> Terrarum, malus est, saevaque tyrannide gaudet.

(*Zodiacus Vitae*, ed. of Rotterdam, 1722, p. 251). I have not been able to trace this quotation which seems to ascribe a position of extreme pessimism to Hermes. In the following passage, the writer continues to deplore that the world is given over to the rule of an evil demon called Sarcotheus. This seems to imply dualism which would explain the pessimism of the poem and its pre-occupation with evil. (R. Tuve in her introduction to Googe's translation suggests an almost Manichaean outlook.) This is difficult to reconcile with the Pythagoro-Platonic interpretation of Epicureanism. In fact it seems to me impossible to make sense of Palingenius' outlook on normal philosophical grounds. A possible explanation might be that Palingenius totally misunderstood Lucretius, interpreting his pessimism and his deep interest in "the world" as some kind of dualist gnosis (this would account for the setting of the Epicurean ethics in the zodiac, and the magic) which he then proceeded to combine with his Pythagoreanism and Neoplatonism.

[2] Garin, Ricerche sull'epicureismo del quattrocento" in *Cultura*, pp. 72–86.

Epicurean teaching on pleasure as a good becomes merged with the cosmic significance of *amor* as the intrinsic vital force in universal nature. As an example of this, Garin quotes[1] the lines on Venus from Palingenius' *Zodiacus vitae*, lines which are influenced by Lucretius' invocation to Venus at the beginning of the *De natura rerum*, but in which the "natural" Venus is connected with the soul of the world in a Neoplatonising manner.

The moral teaching which Bruno associates with his "Egyptian" reform is non-ascetic and partially Epicurean. The clue to it is perhaps provided by Palingenius' extraordinary compound of Hermetism and Epicureanism, and Palingenius, too, uses his naturalist Epicurean ethic as the basis for his satire on the unnatural lives and moral depravity of monks and priests with which the poem is full (hence its popularity in Protestant countries), thus leading the way towards the *Spaccio* and its religious satire.

Nevertheless, there is nothing in Palingenius like Bruno's elaborate reform of the heavens or his advocacy of the holy Egyptian religion; and Bruno's religious satire in the *Spaccio*, though it envisages some forms of Catholicism, is mainly anti-Protestant. As some remarks in a later work show, Bruno was not entirely in agreement with Palingenius.[2] Yet for his ethics, for the type of liberal ethical reform which he associates with his "Egyptianism", the Epicureanism of Palingenius in the setting of the zodiac is suggestive.

Bruno's "Egyptian" or Hermetic reform is envisaged by him as having a close relevance to the times in which he lived. The *Spaccio* contains a politico-religious message which is announced in the heavens, that is, in the discussions about the images of the forty-eight constellations and their reform.

In the constellation Bootes, in its reformed state, there rises the law. This law is based on what is useful for human society. It should protect the poor and weak, control tyrants, encourage arts,

---

[1] *Ibid.*, pp. 83–4.

[2] In Book VIII of the *De immenso*, Bruno cites Palingenius as one with whom he partially agrees and partially disagrees (*Op. lat.*, I (ii), pp. 292 ff.). The passage explicitly about Palingenius leads on to a passage against the "Gnostica secta" who posit two principles, one good and one evil, the world being given over to the evil principle (*ibid.*, pp. 302 ff.). It is possible that he is here dissociating himself from Palingenius' dualism.

learning and sciences to be applied for the benefit of the community. Jupiter, in his reform, is violently opposed to "pedants" who teach that good works are valueless:

> Whilst no one works for them, and they work for no one (for they do no other work except to speak evil of works), yet they live on the works of others who worked for others beside them, and who for others instituted temples, chapels, inns, hospitals, colleges, and universities; wherefore they are open robbers and occupiers of the hereditary goods of others; who, if not perfect nor as good as they ought to be, yet will not be (as these men are) perverse and pernicious to the world; but rather necessary to the commonwealth, skilled in the speculative sciences, careful of morality, solicitous for increasing zeal and care for helping one another and maintaining society (for which all laws are ordained) by proposing certain rewards to well-doers and threatening criminals with certain punishments.[1]

And in a later passage, Jupiter orders Judgment to enquire into the behaviour of these "grammarians who in our times flourish all over Europe".

> Let him see what success they have, and what customs they arouse and provoke in others as to that which concerns the acts of justice and mercy, and the conservation and increase of the public good; let him enquire whether through their doctrine and rule academies, universities, temples, hospitals, colleges, schools and places of discipline and art are raised; or whether, where these are to be found, they are not the same and endowed with the same faculties as they were before the advent of these men and their appearance among the peoples. Next, whether by their care these things are augmented, or whether by their negligence they are diminished, brought to ruin, dissolved, and dispersed. Also whether they are occupiers of the goods of others, or enlargers of their own goods; and finally whether those who take their part, increase and establish the public good, as did their predecessors who were of an opposite way of thinking, or whether they unite with these men to dissipate, squander and devour it, and whilst they discourage works, extinguish all zeal both to perform new works and to conserve old ones.[2]

In these and other passages against the "pedants" who despise good works (the reference, of course, is to the doctrine of justification by faith) and destroy the good works of their predecessors,

---

[1] *Spaccio*, dial. 1 (*Dial. ital.*, pp. 623–4).
[2] *Ibid.*, dial. 2 (*Dial. ital.*, p. 662).

there rises, by a curious kind of double reference, a vision of the pre-Reformation English past as nearer to the "Egyptian" ideal of law than the present, and the ruins of its temples, hospitals, colleges are lamented almost in the tones of the Lament of the *Asclepius*. Bruno's quarrel with the "Oxford pedants", found less satisfactory than earlier barbarous friars, takes on a new meaning in this context, and George Abbot's inclusion of him in his anti-Catholic propaganda becomes quite understandable.

The argument on law continues under the next two constellations, Corona Borealis and Hercules. The Crown is to be given to the prince who will crush the pernicious pedants who decry good works,[1] and Hercules, though his image is banished from heaven because it recalls Jupiter's fault, will go down to earth to do new good works.[2]

When the constellation Cassiopeia comes under review, before the other gods have had time to determine anything about her, Mars jumps up and demands furiously that her image shall remain in the sky because her character so much resembles the Spanish character. (Cassiopeia was punished by Neptune for boasting of being fairer than the Nereids.) But her Pride, Arrogance, and Falsehood are made to go down out of heaven, in spite of pro-Spanish Mars's plea for her, and Simplicity ascends in her place.[3] It is clear, by implication, that Catholic Spain represents another kind of pedantry, making for war and social disruption.

In contrast, under Gemini, Cupid, Apollo, Mercury, Saturn, Venus speak in favour of Love, Friendship, and Peace which are to replace Partiality.[4] Under Libra, we learn that the Balance must go down to look into injustices on earth, amongst other things to correct the violence done to nature in Vestal edifices.[5]

The ethic which Bruno advocates is that of a rule of law and order which encourages peaceful and useful activities and from which warring between sects is banished. In its private aspect, this ethic encourages good Venereal, Jovial, and Solar characteristics and it is non-ascetic, as instanced in the protest against "Vestal edifices" just mentioned. All the failures of the Christian

---

[1] *Ibid.*, dial. 1 (*Dial. ital.*, p. 622).
[2] *Ibid.* (*Dial. ital.*, pp. 627 ff.).
[3] *Ibid.*, dial. 2 (*Dial. ital.*, pp. 705 ff.).
[4] *Ibid.*, dial. 3 (*Dial. ital.*, pp. 766 ff.).
[5] *Ibid.* (*Dial. ital.*, p. 771).

sects are to be healed by the return to the Egyptian religion and the kind of moral law which Bruno associates with it. Yet this reform he envisages as remaining in some manner associated with the Church, for the Altar, discussed under the constellation of that name, is to remain in heaven with the Centaur, half beast (in the Egyptian sense of god) and half man beside it.[1] The Centaur is admired for having healed the sick and shown a way to mount up to the stars. He is to remain in heaven, for where there is an altar, there must be a priest for the altar.

Under the Corona Australis, Apollo asks what is to be done with this Crown?

> That, (replied Jupiter), is the crown which, by the high decree of fate and the inspiration of the divine spirit and as a reward for high merit, awaits the invincible Henri III, king of the magnanimous, powerful, and warlike realm of France, which he promises himself after the crown of France and the crown of Poland, as he testified at the beginning of his reign, when he ordained his celebrated device, the body of which consists of two lower crowns surmounted by another more eminent and more beautiful, and to it is added as a soul the motto: *Tertia coelo manet*. This most Christian king, holy, religious, and pure, may securely say: *Tertia coelo manet*, for he well knows that it is written: Blessed are the peacemakers, blessed are the pure in heart, for theirs is the kingdom of heaven. He loves peace, he preserves his contented people as much as possible in tranquillity and devotion; he is not pleased with the noisy uproar of martial instruments which administer to the blind acquisition of the unstable tyrannies and principalities of the earth; but with all manner of justice and sanctity which show the straight road to the eternal kingdom. Let not the bold, tempestuous and turbulent spirits among his subjects hope that whilst he lives (the tranquillity of whose spirit does not encourage warlike fury) he will give assistance to those who, not in vain, seek to disturb the peace of other countries on the pretext of acquiring other crowns and other sceptres; for *Tertia coelo manet*. In vain shall the rebel French forces against his will disturb the boundaries and coasts of others; for by no proposal of unstable counsels, by no hope of changeable fortune, by no occasion of external administrations or suffrages will he be induced, on a pretence of investing him with mantles and adorning him with crowns, to give up (otherwise than by force of necessity) the blessed care of tran-

---

[1] *Ibid.*, dial. 3 (*Dial. ital.*, p. 825). Cf. also what is said under the constellation Centaur (*ibid.*, pp. 823 ff.). The Centaur is Christ, understood as a Hermetic Christ, or a benevolent Magus.

quillity of spirit, for he is more liberal of his own goods than greedy for those of others. Let others, therefore, make attempts on the vacant kingdom of Portugal; let others be solicitous over the Belgian dominion. Why should you break your heads and busy your brains, you other princes? Why should you fear and suspect that other princes and kings will come to dominate your forces and rob you of your crowns? *Tertia coelo manet*. Let the crown remain then (Jupiter concluded), awaiting him who shall be worthy of so magnificent a possession. . . .[1]

All the gods approved in chorus that the crown would belong to Henri III, and they concluded their reforming labours by going to a great banquet in Piscis Australis.

Bruno is here offering to Englishmen, and particularly, one supposes, to Philip Sidney to whom the book is dedicated, the friendship of a Catholic king who disclaims the ambitions of Spain and of the Catholic League, who renounces all aggressive projects against other states, whether of open war or of subversive intrigue. Those turbulent spirits amongst his subjects who follow the Spanish-Guise faction are as much enemies of the French king as they are of the English queen. Let us transcend these broils, says Bruno in Henri's name, and return to the old spiritual union of Europe.

Written by an inmate of the French embassy, who had dedicated other works to the French ambassador, the *Spaccio* would appear to English readers to have some weight of French authority behind it. Mauvissière does not seem to have disapproved in any way of the publication of this book which seems to carry with it a message from the French king. And the magical religious Hermetism which is the theme of the *Spaccio* is not inconsistent with the magical works which Bruno had published in France.

Though written in an apparently light vein of Lucianic irony, the *Spaccio* belongs into the context of sixteenth-century religious Hermetism, a most strange and aberrant form of which it is preaching.

As we saw in chapter X, the forms of religious Hermetism are very varied, and these later years of the sixteenth century were the

---

[1] *Ibid.* (*Dial. ital.*, pp. 826–7). "Tertia coelo manet" refers to Henri III's device of the Three Crowns of which it is the motto; see my *French Academies of the Sixteenth Century*, pp. 227–8.

time when religious Hermetism of all types was reaching its climax of influence. When Bruno wrote the *Spaccio*, Du Plessis Mornay had already written his theological work, which Sidney was translating, with its appeal to a Protestant type of Christian Hermetism, entirely non-magical, as a palliative for religious differences. Rosseli, the Capucin, was probably already engaged on his enormous Hermetic labours. In a few years time, Patrizi would address to a pope a work in which he urged a philosophy based on Hermetism as a way of winning the Protestants of Germany, and recommended the Jesuits to take up Hermetism. Patrizi's type is nearer to that of Bruno than the other two, as it may contain some Ficinian magic, yet it is also very different. Patrizi does not abandon the Christian interpretation of. Hermetism, as Bruno does. Bruno takes a radical step, which puts him outside the pale of normal Christian Hermetism, by abandoning the Christian interpretation, and above all, by going wholeheartedly for the magic as the chief thing, the core of Hermetism. Instead of avoiding, or disguising, the magical passage in the *Asclepius*, he openly makes this the basis of both his proposed religious and moral reforms. He thus cannot be called a Christian Hermetist (it is as a beneficent Magus that he would retain Christ in the magical religion), though he thought of his magical reform, or of his prophecy of the approaching return of Egyptianism, as developing within a Catholic framework.

On his return to Paris, after his momentous stay in England, Bruno used to read in the library of the Abbey of St. Victor, the librarian of which kept a diary in which he recorded some of his conversations with Bruno. He reports Bruno as having said that he greatly admired Thomas Aquinas but condemned the subtleties of scholastics "about the Sacraments and the Eucharist, saying that St. Peter and St. Paul did not know of these (subtleties) knowing only that *hoc est corpus meum*. He says that the troubles in religion could be easily taken away if these questions were taken away, and he says that he hopes that soon there will be an end of them. But above all he detests the heretics of France and England, because they despise good works and preach the certitude of their faith and justification; for the whole of Christianity tends to goodness of life (toute la chrestienté tend à bien vivre)."[1] This accords perfectly well with the teaching of the *Spaccio* and its

[1] *Documenti*, p. 40.

condemnation of the "pedants" who despise good works, and in which, under the constellations Fluvius Eridanus and Ara there are obscure remarks which evidently refer to the Eucharist, or to some magical interpretation of it.[1]

Mocenigo, in one of his reports about Bruno to the Venetian inquisitors in 1592, reports him as having said: "that the Church to-day does not proceed as the Apostles used to proceed, for they converted men by their preaching and the example of a good life, but to-day whoever wishes not to be a Catholic must endure punishment and pain, for force is used and not love; that the Catholic religion pleases him better than any other, but that this too has need of much reformation; that this is not good, but that soon the world would see a general reform of itself, for it was impossible that such corruptions should go on; and that he hoped great things of the King of Navarre."[2] This, also, accords perfectly well with the teaching of the *Spaccio*.

Thus Giordano Bruno, magician, had a Hermetic religious mission. He is an *enfant terrible* among religious Hermetists, and yet he *is* a religious Hermetist. By putting him in that context he is at last placed among the movements of his century.

Though the vitally important fact of Bruno's connection with Hermetism has not been known, it has long been recognised by Italian scholars that magic plays a part in Bruno's thought. Corsano drew attention to this in a book published in 1940, and he further noted that there is some element of religious reform behind Bruno's magical thinking.[3] Elaborating Corsano's views on Brunian magic and Brunian reform, Firpo suggested that these were connected, that Bruno believed that he could make the reform come by magic.[4]

And something of this kind may indeed be the last secret of the *Spaccio della bestia trionfante*, that the magician is manipulating

---

[1] *Spaccio*, dial. 3 (*Dial. ital.*, pp. 808, 825).

[2] *Documenti*, p. 66.

[3] A. Corsano, *Il pensiero di Giordano Bruno nel suo svolgimento storico*, Florence, 1940, pp. 281 ff.

[4] L. Firpo, *Il processo di Giordano Bruno*, Quaderni della Rivista Storica Italiana, Naples, 1949, pp. 10 ff. Both Corsano and Firpo are concerned with Bruno's late period and of his return to Italy as a magical reformer. That all Bruno's works from the start are full of magic was not realised by Corsano. The magic in the *Spaccio* has never been discussed.

the celestial images on which all things below depend in order to make the reform come. "If we thus renew our heaven," says Jupiter, "the constellations and influences shall be new, the impressions and fortunes shall be new for all things depend on this upper world."[1] So, in the *Koré Kosmou* when the gods met in a plenary assembly to reform a degenerated world there was a "second efflux of the divine nature" upon the mundane elements.[2] It is in the context of this kind of thinking that the *Spaccio* should be read. The constellation images are not merely a literary device to which is attached an amusing satire on religious and social conditions in the late sixteenth century. In the reforming magician's mind, the reform begins in heaven, with the rearrangement or purification of the celestial images, of the shapes of the celestial gods who reform the zodiac and the northern and southern constellations.

And what does this remind us of? Surely of the magical City of Adocentyn in *Picatrix*, built by Hermes Trismegistus, and who placed around the circumference of the city "engraved images and ordered them in such a manner that by their virtue the inhabitants were made virtuous and withdrawn from all wickedness and harm."[3] This, as we suggested in chapter IV, provides the connection between Hermes Trismegistus as magician and Hermes Trismegistus as the law giver of the Egyptians, who gave them their good moral laws and kept them in it. And this, I believe, may be also the connection in the *Spaccio* between the manipulation or reform of the celestial images and the universal religious and moral reform.

As will be remembered, Hermes Trismegistus is also described in *Picatrix* as having built a temple of the sun and we thought that students of the magical text-book might have connected this, and the City of Adocentyn, with the mysterious remark in the *Asclepius*, in the prophecy after the Lament of the eventual restoration of the Egyptian religion and laws: "The gods who exercise their dominion over the earth will be restored one day and installed in a City at the extreme limit of Egypt, a City which will be founded towards the setting sun and into which will hasten, by land and sea, the whole race of mortal men."[4] That Bruno's

---

[1] See above, p. 218. [2] See above, p. 216.
[3] See above, p. 54. [4] See above, pp. 55–6.

mind was running on magical cities of the sun is indicated from a remark in the useful diary of the librarian of the Abbey of St. Victor, who reports in one entry that "Jordanus told me that he knew nothing of the town built by the Duke of Florence where only Latin would be spoken, but he has heard it said that this duke wished to build a *Civitas solis*, in which the sun would shine every day of the year, as it does in other cities, such as Rome and Rhodes."[1]

It is also in these strange magical realms that Campanella's ideal republic or City of the Sun, must be placed, with its astral religion and sun-worship. In a later chapter we shall attempt to compare the Campanellian City of the Sun with the *Spaccio* with which it has much in common, particularly in that ethic of social utility and public service, and the use of learning and invention for the public good which both Bruno and Campanella teach as a necessary part of their reformed societies.

And here yet another, and a very unexpected, comparison for the *Spaccio* suggests itself, namely Thomas More's *Utopia*. More's ideal republic has been universally admired for its ethic of social utility. And what was the religion of the Utopians like? They had very large, dark churches, dimly lighted by tapers, into which the priests made a spectacular entry clothed in vestments of "chaungeable colours" made of bird's feathers arranged in a manner which contained "certaine divine misteries".[2] The dress of the Utopian priests reminded an early critic of "conjuring garments",[3] and there is certainly rather a strange atmosphere about the religion of More's communists. The *Utopia* may reflect reform notions entertained by More before Henry VIII's break with Rome.

The English reader of the *Spaccio* might perhaps have been reminded of the famous book by the man who had died on the scaffold rather than agree that the good works of those who had worked for others should go into private hands.

At any rate, Bruno's magical Hermetism offered to sub-Catholics, discontented intelligentsia, and other secretly dissatisfied

---

[1] *Documenti*, p. 44.

[2] Thomas More, *Utopia*, Everyman edition, p. 109.

[3] Quotation in Strype, *Life of Parker*, 1821, I, p. 301; cf. R. W. Chambers, *Thomas More*, p. 264. Another curious feature, suggesting *prisca magia*, in the *Utopia*, is that a word which looks like "gymnosophists" occurs twice in the poem in the Utopian language at the end of the book (*ed. cit.*, p. 119).

elements in Elizabethan society, a new outlet, quite independent of the hated Spanish Catholicism, for their secret yearnings. Written in a bold, dramatic style, powerful in its imagery and with a highly original kind of Lucianic or celestial humour, the *Spaccio della bestia trionfante* may have been an operative work on the formation of the Elizabethan Renaissance. For it contained in a potent and unexpurgated form, that charge of dynamite at the heart of Renaissance Neoplatonism, the magic of the *Asclepius*.

Chapter XIII

✦✧✦✧✦✧✦✧✦✧✦✧✦✧✦✧✦✧✦✧✦✧✦✧✦✧✦✧✦✧✦✧✦

GIORDANO BRUNO IN ENGLAND:
THE HERMETIC PHILOSOPHY

✦✧✦✧✦✧✦✧✦✧✦✧✦✧✦✧✦✧✦✧✦✧✦✧✦✧✦✧✦✧✦✧✦

BEFORE "the philosophy which suits you so well arose," cries Bruno to the pedant doctor in the *Cena de le ceneri* (published in 1584, that is in the same year as the *Spaccio*, but probably before it), "there existed that of the Chaldeans, of the Egyptians, of the Magi, of the Orphics, of the Pythagoreans and other early thinkers which is more to our liking."[1] The satire on the pedants in the *Cena* reflects his quarrel with the Oxford doctors, and these words proclaim to them and to all readers of his work that Bruno's philosophy is a *prisca magia*. Fourteen years later in an address to the doctors of Wittenberg University he was to give a similar genealogy of *prisca magia*, or of the "temple of wisdom" which was built first by the Egyptians and Chaldeans, who were followed by the Magi, Gymnosophists, Orphics, and so on, and in more modern times by Albertus Magnus, Nicholas of Cusa, and Copernicus "who understood more than Aristotle and all the Peripatetics" in the contemplation of the universe.[2] Similarly, in the *Cena de le ceneri*,

---

[1] *Cena de le ceneri*, dial. I (*Dial. ital.*, p. 41). This work is dedicated to Mauvissière, the French ambassador. The Supper at which Bruno disputed with the pedant doctors about the Copernican theory is stated in the text to have taken place at the house of Fulke Greville, but Bruno afterwards told the Inquisitors that it was really held in the French embassy (*Documenti*, p. 121). I have discussed some aspects of the work in my article, "The Religious Policy of Giordano Bruno", *J.W.C.I.*, III (1939–40), pp. 181–207. The best edition of the *Cena de le ceneri* is that by G. Aquilecchia, Florence, 1955.

[2] *Oratio valedictoria*, Wittenberg, 1588 (*Op. lat.* I (i), pp. 16–17).

Copernicus is highly praised:

> To him (Copernicus) we owe our liberation from several false pre-
> judices of the commonly received philosophy, which I will not go so
> far as to call blindness. Yet he himself did not much transcend it; for
> being more a student of mathematics than of nature he was not able
> to penetrate deeply enough to remove the roots of false and mis-
> leading principles and, by disentangling all the difficulties in the way,
> to free both himself and others from the pursuit of empty enquiries
> and turn their attention to things constant and certain.[1]

That is to say, Copernicus has made a beginning, but, being only
a mathematician, he has not understood the profound meaning of
his discovery. He is a precursor of the dawn of truth and of its
prophet, the Nolan, to whom nevertheless gratitude is due for his
preparatory labours:

> Who then would treat this man (Copernicus) and his labours with
> such ignoble discourtesy as to forget all his achievements and his
> divinely ordained appearance as the dawn which was to precede the
> full sunrise of the ancient and true philosophy after its agelong
> burial in the dark caverns of blind and envious ignorance, and to
> judge him by reason of some omissions in his work as being on the
> same level as the vulgar herd which is swayed hither and thither by
> brutal superstition? Should he not rather be counted in the number
> of those whose good wits have enabled them to raise themselves and
> to stand upright under the faithful guidance of the eye of the divine
> intelligence?
>
> And now, what shall I say concerning the Nolan? Perhaps it
> becomes me not to praise him since he is so near to me, as near,
> indeed, as I am to myself. Yet no reasonable man would reprove me
> for so doing, since it is sometimes not only convenient but necessary
> to speak well of oneself. . . . If in days of old Tiphys was to be
> praised who invented the first ship and voyaged across the ocean with
> the Argonauts . . . if in our times Columbus receives honour . . . what
> then shall be said of him who has found a way to mount up to the
> sky. . . .? The Nolan . . . has released the human spirit, and set
> knowledge at liberty. Man's mind was suffocating in the close air of a
> narrow prison house whence only dimly, and, as it were, through
> chinks could he behold the far distant stars. His wings were clipped,
> so that he might not soar upwards through the cloudy veil to see
> what really lies beyond it and liberate himself from the foolish
> imaginations of those who—issuing from the miry caverns of earth

[1] *Cena*, dial. I (*Dial. ital.*, p. 28).

as though they were Mercuries and Apollos descending from heaven —have with many kinds of deceit imposed brutal follies and vices upon the world in the guise of virtues, of divinity and discipline, quenching the light which rendered the souls of our fathers in antique times divine and heroic whilst confirming and approving the pitch dark ignorance of fools and sophists. Therefore during all this long while oppressed human reason, bewailing from time to time in her lucid intervals her base condition and turning herself to that divine prophetic mind whose voice murmurs always in her inner ear, cried out in words like these:

> Mistresse, who shall for me to heau'n vp fly,
> To bring again from thence my wandring wit . . .[1]

Behold now, standing before you, the man who has pierced the air and penetrated the sky, wended his way amongst the stars and over-passed the margins of the world, who has broken down those imaginary divisions between spheres—the first, the eighth, the ninth, the tenth or what you will—which are described in the false mathematics of blind and popular philosophy. By the light of sense and reason, with the key of most diligent enquiry, he has thrown wide those doors of truth which it is within our power to open and stripped the veils and coverings from the face of nature. He has given eyes to blind moles, and illuminated those who could not see their own image in the innumerable mirrors of reality which surround them on every side; he has loosened the mute tongues which cared little for intricate discussion; he has strengthened the crippled limbs which were too weak to make that journey of the spirit of which base matter is incapable. . .[2]

These are the passages which used to throw the nineteenth-century liberals into ecstasies as the cry of the advanced scientific thinker breaking out of mediaeval shackles, and they are indeed very striking, very thrilling words. What do they mean?

Forms of heliocentricity had been known in antiquity and Copernicus himself had cited some antique predecessors.[3] But this ancient truth now reviving of which the Nolan is the prophet is not heliocentricity in an astronomical sense, or as a mathematical hypothesis. Bruno has himself explained that he sees far more in

---

[1] Ariosto, *Orlando furioso*, XXXV, I. Quoted in Sir John Harington's translation.

[2] *Cena*, dial. I (*Dial. ital.*, pp. 29–33).

[3] See above, pp. 153–4.

it than the mere mathematician had done. Yet even Copernicus had not been purely mathematical, for he had quoted, near his diagram of the new system, Hermes Trismegistus in the *Asclepius* on the sun as the visible god. This is the clue; the vision which the Nolan is developing is a new Hermetic insight into the divinity of the universe, an expanded gnosis.

The Copernican sun heralds the full sunrise of the ancient and true philosophy after its agelong burial in dark caverns. Bruno has here in mind the image of *Veritas Filia Temporis*, Time bringing Truth to Light, which had been used in England of the return of Catholic Truth from Protestant darkness under Mary, and *vice versa*, of the return of Protestant Truth from Catholic darkness under Elizabeth.[1] The Truth of which Bruno speaks had been imprisoned in the dark caverns by "Mercuries and Apollos" pretending to descend from heaven. The meaning of this is clear when compared with the similar passage in the *De umbris idearum* on the providence of the gods which does not cease, as the Egyptian priests used to say, because of statutes promulgated at various times by repressive Mercuries. The intellect does not cease to illuminate, and the visible sun does not cease to illuminate, because we do not always all turn towards it.[2] The truth which is coming to light is the truth which was suppressed by false Mercuries, (that is by the Christians), magical truth, Egyptian truth, the sun as the visible god, as Hermes Trismegistus called it, the truth lamented in the lament of the *Asclepius*. Another passage in the *Cena de le ceneri* describes the dawning sun of truth as follows:

> The question which we ought to ask ourselves is whether we are in the daylight with the light of truth rising above our horizon, or whether the day is with our adversaries in the antipodes; whether the shadows of error are over us or over them; whether we who are beginning to revive the ancient philosophy are in the dawn which ends the night or in the evening of a day which is closing. And this is not difficult to decide for these two schools of thought can be roughly judged by their fruits.

[1] See F. Saxl, "Veritas Filia Temporis", *Philosophy and History*, essays presented to E. Cassirer and edited by R. Klibansky and H. J. Paton, Oxford, 1936, pp. 197–222.

[2] See above, p. 193.

Let us now consider the differences between them. The one produced men who were temperate in their lives, expert in the arts of healing, judicious in contemplation, remarkable in divination, having miraculous powers in magic, wary of superstitions, law-abiding, of irreproachable morality, penetrating in theology, heroic in all their ways. This is shown in the length of their lives, the greater strength of their bodies, their most lofty inventions, their prophecies which have come true; they knew how to transform substances and how to live peacefully in society; their sacraments were inviolable, their executions most just, they were in communion with good and tutelar spirits, and the vestiges of their amazing prowess endure unto this day.

But as to these others, their opponents, I leave them to the examination of any man of good sense.[1]

Bruno's truth is neither orthodox Catholic nor orthodox Protestant truth; it is Egyptian truth, magical truth. Yet, since the whole of the *Cena de le ceneri*, with its two grammarian-pedant doctors, Manfurio and Prudenzio, reflects Bruno's quarrel with the Protestant doctors of Oxford, the Egyptian truth, by a similar kind of double vision which we noted in the *Spaccio*, could also refer to their predecessors, those "others" with whom the great magical, Hermetic reform has something in common.

Bruno claims to be qualified as prophet and leader of the new movement because he has made an ascent through the spheres. Under the impression that the Copernican discovery has abolished the spheres to which the stars were formerly thought of as attached, he sees this as a breaking of those envelopes by which the Hermetic gnostic ascended and descended through the spheres, as described in the *Pimander*, when the Magus man "leant across the armature of the spheres, having broken through their envelopes."[2] Bruno has made the gnostic ascent, has had the Hermetic experience, and so has become divine, with the Powers within him.

Even more significant for comparison with Bruno's description of himself in this passage as, to give the phrase in the original Italian, "quello ch'ha varcato l'aria, penetrato il cielo, discorso le stelle, trapassato gli margini del mondo",[3] is the description in Cornelius Agrippa's *De occulta philosophia* of the experience which

---

[1] *Cena*, dial. 1 (*Dial. ital.*, pp. 43–4).
[2] See above, p. 24.   [3] *Cena*, dial. 1 (*Dial. ital.*, p. 33).

the magician must have had before he can impart power into celestial images. After the chapters in which Agrippa has described the talismanic magic, given the lists of astrological images, described how such images can be invented for special purposes, there comes the passage which we quoted earlier on the experience which is the necessary prerequisite for obtaining magical powers. It is a kind of ascent.

> . . . no one has such powers but he who has cohabited with the elements, vanquished nature, mounted higher than the heavens, elevating himself above the angels to the archetype itself, with whom he then becomes co-operator and can do all things.[1]

These words are almost exactly the same as those in which Bruno describes his ascent, except that Bruno leaves out the angels.

It is characteristic of Bruno's extraordinary style, with its mixture of magic, philosophy, and poetry, that he chooses to express the gnostic trance, in which the soul leaves the body which is left asleep in the ligature of the senses (as described in *Pimander*) in terms of the experience of ecstatic love described in Ariosto's *Orlando furioso*:

> Chi salirà per me, madonna, in cielo,
> A riportarne il mio perduto ingegno?

What could the Oxford doctors have made of this man? What can anyone make of him? The megalomania of the magician is combined with a poetic enthusiasm of appalling intensity. The lunatic, the lover, and the poet were never all of imagination so compact as in Giordano Bruno.

We know from George Abbot's valuable evidence that one of the Oxford doctors went to fetch Ficino's *De vita coelitus comparanda* to confront him with his source.[2] The *Cena* reflects the Oxford debate in its theme of a discussion on Copernicanism between Bruno and two "pedants", natives of the country, which is now supposed to take place in London in the presence of Fulke Greville and other gentlemen. The episode of sending for a book also looms large in Bruno's story. Bruno had been arguing against the "pedants"—both sides drawing diagrams in support of their

---

[1] Agrippa, *De occult. phil.*, II, 30. See above, p. 136.
[2] See above, pp. 208–9.

views—that Copernicus has said, not that the moon revolves about the earth, but that both revolve in the same epicycle.[1] To settle the question "the gentlemen who were present provided that the book of Copernicus should be brought".[2] Bruno was confronted with the diagram, but still maintained that he was right and that the point which Torquato, the pedant, (correctly) thought indicated the earth, was really "the point made by the foot of the compass in delineating the epicycle of the earth and the moon which are one and the same."(Pl. 7c)[3] It is possible that the episode of fetching a book has been deliberately altered by Bruno in the version of the Oxford debate which he gives in the *Cena*—the book fetched being now, not a Ficino, but a Copernicus.

The truth is that for Bruno the Copernican diagram is a hieroglyph, a Hermetic seal hiding potent divine mysteries of which he has penetrated the secret. To understand the true import of the argument about the diagram in the *Cena* one should read those masterly pages in which, in 1621, Kepler analysed the difference between his own and Fludd's use of diagrams in their respective works on harmony. His own diagrams, says Kepler, are truly mathematical; those of Fludd are Hermetic. "Tu tractas Mathematica more Hermetico", he cries to Fludd.[4] So does Bruno read the Copernican diagram "more Hermetico", encouraged thereto by Copernicus' own reference to Hermes Trismegistus near the diagram in his book.

In the heliocentric hypothesis the earth *moves*, for Copernicus, according to Bruno, "with his mathematical rather than natural reasoning", has rehabilitated the theory of the earth's motion, hitherto covered with ridicule and scorn.[5] Earth movement is enthusiastically welcomed by Bruno, not on the inferior mathematical grounds, but as follows:

[1] *Cena*, dial. 4 (*Dial. ital.*, pp. 139 ff.).

[2] *Ibid.* (*Dial. ital.*, pp. 140–1).

[3] *Ibid.*, *loc. cit.* I pointed out Bruno's mistake in my article on "The Religious Policy of G. Bruno", and in my book, *The French Academies of the Sixteenth Century*, pp. 102–3, note 3, and Plate 6.

[4] J. Kepler, *Harmonice mundi* (*Gesammelte Werke*), ed. M. Caspar, Munich, 1940, Band VI, p. 432. See below, p. 443.

[5] *Cena*, dial. 1 (*Dial. ital.*, p. 29).

It (the earth) moves that it may renew itself and be born again, for it cannot endure for ever in the same form. For those things which cannot be eternal as individuals . . . are eternal as a species; and substances which cannot be everlasting under the same aspect, change themselves into other appearances. For the material and substance of things is incorruptible and must in all its parts pass through all forms. . . . Therefore, since death and dissolution are unfitted to the whole mass of which this globe, this star, consists, and complete annihilation is impossible to all nature, the earth changes all its parts from time to time and in a certain order and so renews itself. . . . And we ourselves and the things pertaining to us come and go, pass and repass; there is nothing of our own which may not become foreign to us, and nothing foreign to us which may not become our own. . . . And nothing is of itself eternal, save the substance and material of which it is made, and this is in constant mutation. Of the supersubstantial substance I speak not at present, but I return to reason more especially concerning this great individual, our perpetual nurse and mother, of which you asked what was the cause of its motion. And I say that the cause of its motion, not only its motion as a whole but the movement of all its parts, is in order that it may pass through vicissitudes, so that all may find itself in all places and by this means undergo all forms and dispositions. . . .[1]

I would place beside this the passage in *Corpus Hermeticum* XII, "Hermes Trismegistus to Tat on the Common Intellect":

Do not the living beings in the world die, O father, although they are parts of the world?
Hush, my child, for you are led into error by the denomination of the phenomenon. For living beings do not die, my child, but, being composite bodies they are dissolved: now this dissolution is not death but the dissolution of a mixture. And if they are dissolved, it is not to be destroyed but to be renewed. What in fact is the energy of life? Is it not movement? Or what is there in the world which is immobile? Nothing, my child.
But the earth, at least, does it not seem to be immobile, O father?
No, child: on the contrary alone of all beings, it is both subject to a multitude of movements and stable. Would it not be ridiculous to suppose that this nurse of all beings should be immobile, she who causes to be born and gives birth to all things? Without movement, indeed, it is impossible for that which gives birth to give birth to anything. It is quite absurd to ask, as you do, if the fourth part of the world can be inert: for to be immobile, for a body, can have no

<hr/>

[1] *Ibid.*, dial. 5 (*Dial. ital.*, pp. 154–6).

other meaning than to be inert. Know then, child, that all that is in the world, without exception, is in movement, either diminishing or increasing. And that which is in movement is also in life, but there is no necessity that every living being should conserve its identity. For, no doubt, considered in its totality the world is immobile, my child, but the parts of this world are all in motion, yet nothing perishes or is destroyed.[1]

Bruno had only to change the Hermetic argument, that the earth is both subject to a multitude of movements and stable, to the mobility of the earth as a whole, as well as of its parts, and then to reproduce the feeling and in some places the words of the Hermetic passage, as he does, to arrive at the passage on earth movement which we have quoted from the *Cena de le ceneri*.

Moreover, Cornelius Agrippa had quoted the Hermetic passage in his chapters on the world soul and on universal animation. It is unreasonable, says Agrippa, to suppose that the stars which give life and animation to all should themselves be without life and animation, and the earth, too, is alive:

Mercurius in the treatise which he wrote *De communi* says: *All that is in the world moves by increasing or diminishing. And since everything which moves is alive*, even the earth through the movement of generation and alteration, it too is alive.[2]

The passage italicised is direct quotation from Ficino's Latin translation of the *De communi*; Agrippa has added that the earth, too, is alive. In Bruno, this becomes:

The interior principle in things is the cause of their movement. . . Therefore the earth and the heavenly bodies move in accordance with individual differences in their intrinsic principle which is their soul. . . .[3]

Going far beyond the "merely mathematical" arguments by which Copernicus put forward the hypothesis of earth-movement, Bruno has seen that it confirms Hermes Trismegistus and Cor-

---

[1] *C.H.*, I, pp. 180–1; Ficino, p. 1854. For a *résumé* of the whole treatise in which this passage occurs, see above, pp. 33–4.

[2] Agrippa, *De occulta philosophia*, II, 56. For the comparison with Ficino's translation, see above, p. 137, note 3.

Pico della Mirandola's fifth and sixth Hermetic conclusions ("Nihil est in mundo expers uitae. Nihil est in uniuerso passibile mortis uel corruptionis") are drawn from the Hermetic *De communi*. See Pico, p. 80.

[3] *Cena*, dial. 3 (*Dial. ital.*, p. 109).

nelius Agrippa, or, in other words, it confirms the magical philosophy of universal animation.

Bruno is chiefly celebrated in histories of thought and of science, not only for his acceptance of the Copernican theory, but still more for his wonderful leap of the imagination by which he attached the idea of the infinity of the universe to his Copernicanism, an extension of the theory which had not been taught by Copernicus himself. And this infinite universe of his, Bruno peopled with innumerable worlds all moving through the infinite space—thus finally breaking down the closed mediaeval Ptolemaic universe and initiating more modern conceptions. Readers familiar with a more usual approach to Bruno than that pursued in this book will know that antecedents for Bruno's ideas of infinity have been found in Nicholas of Cusa; that it has been suggested that he might have come across in England the work of Thomas Digges in which Copernicanism is associated with the infinity of the universe[1]; that it has been convincingly demonstrated that Bruno's belief in infinity and innumerable worlds is based on the principle of plenitude, that an infinite cause, God, must have an infinite effect and there can be no limit to his creative power.[2]

Yet it has also been observed that "Bruno's world-view is vitalistic, magical; his planets are animated beings that move freely through space of their own accord like those of Plato or Patrizi. Bruno's is not a modern mind by any means."[3] To this it may be added that, as we have just seen, Bruno's acceptance of Copernican earth movement was based on magical and vitalistic grounds, and that, not only the planets, but also the innumerable worlds of his infinite universe move through space like great animals, animated by the divine life.

He . . . made his affirmation that the universe is infinite; that it consists of an immense ethereal region; that it is like a vast sky of space in whose bosom are the heavenly bodies . . . that the moon, the

---

[1] Thomas Digges, *A Perfit Description of the Caelestiall Orbes*, first edition in 1576. On Digges and Bruno, see F. R. Johnson, *Astronomical Thought in Renaissance England*, Baltimore, 1937, pp. 168 ff.

[2] See A. O. Lovejoy, *The Great Chain of Being*, Harvard University Press, 1942 (second edition), pp. 116 ff.

[3] A. Koyré. *From the Closed World to the Infinite Universe*, New York, 1958 (second edition), p. 54.

sun, and innumerable other bodies are in this ethereal region, and the earth also; that it is not to be believed that there is any firmament, base, or foundation to which are fixed these great animals which form the constitution of the universe, the infinite material of the infinite divine potency.[1]

This is a characteristic passage on the infinite universe and the innumerable animated worlds from the *Cena de le ceneri*. In the *De l'infinito universo e mondi*[2] the same message is many times repeated, with variations which show that it is as an image of his conception of the divinity that Bruno needs such a picture of the world:

Needs must indeed that there should be an infinite image of the inaccessible divine countenance and that there should be in this image as infinite members thereof, innumerable worlds. . .[3]

Now, though Bruno would not have found in the Hermetic writings the conception of an infinite universe and innumerable worlds, the spirit in which he formulates such a conception is to be found in them. For example:

The amplitude of the Good is as great as the reality of all beings, both corporeal and incorporeal, sensible and intelligible. That is what the Good is; that is what God is.[4]

And in the *Asclepius*, there are the following words:

For as the space outside the world, if it exists (which I do not believe) must be, in my opinion full of intelligible beings, that is beings like the divinity of that space, so the sensible world is absolutely full of living beings. . .[5]

To increase his awareness of the divine, Bruno had but to add to this that there *is* an infinite space outside the world and it *is* full of divine beings and he would have his extended Hermetic gnosis of the infinite and the innumerable worlds. And in a remarkable

[1] *Cena*, dial. 4 (*Dial. ital.*, pp. 130–1).

[2] Published in England in 1584, with a dedication to the French ambassador. An English translation of this work by Dorothea Waley Singer is available in her book *Giordano Bruno, His Life and Thought*, London, 1950, pp. 225 ff.

[3] *De l'infinito*, dial. 1 (*Dial. ital.*, p. 377); quoted in D. W. Singer's translation, *op. cit.*, p. 257.

[4] *C.H.*, I, p. 38 (*Corpus Hermeticum*, II).

[5] *C.H.*, II, p. 343 (*Asclepius*).

passage in the *De immenso, innumerabilibus et infigurabilibus* one can actually watch how it is the Hermetic spring upwards, the Hermetic ascent, which lands Bruno, so to speak, in the infinite. The opening chapter of that poem is on the ascent of the *mens* whence a new vision of the world is to be revealed. In the commentary on that chapter, there are these words:

> Miraculum magnum a Trismegisto appellabitur homo, qui in deum transeat quasi ipse sit deus, qui conatur omnia fieri, sicut deus est omnia; ad objectum sine fine . . . contendit, sicut infinitus est deus, immensus, ubique totus.[1]

Bruno has slightly altered the famous passage on the miraculous and godlike power of man to know the world, extending it into a power to know an infinite god and an infinite universe. Thus it is as man the great miracle, knowing himself to be of divine origin, that Bruno soars into the infinite to grasp and draw into himself the newly revealed reflection of infinite divinity in a vastly expanded universe.

As to the immediate source of the new vision there can be no doubt. Bruno found the conceptions of infinite space and innumerable worlds, inhabited like our own, in Lucretius' *De natura rerum* from which he frequently quotes on these points in the *De l'infinito universo e mondi*[2] and elsewhere. But he absolutely transforms the Lucretian notions (themselves derived, of course, from the Epicurean philosophy) by imparting to the innumerable worlds magical animation, totally absent from Lucretius' cold universe, and to the infinite and its contents the function of being an image of the infinite divinity—again a notion totally foreign to the agnosticism of Lucretius. Thus the godless universe of Lucretius, in which that pessimistic man took refuge from the terrors of religion, is transformed by Bruno into a vast extension of Hermetic gnosis, a new revelation of God as magician, informing innumerable worlds with magical animation, a vision to receive which that great miracle, the Magus man, must expand himself to an infinite extent so that he may reflect it within.

At the beginning of this chapter, I quoted a genealogy of wisdom

[1] *De immenso*, Bk. I, cap. 1 (*Op. lat.*, I (I), p. 206).

[2] Particularly in the last dialogue. On the importance of Lucretius for Bruno, see D. W. Singer, *op. cit.*, A. Koyré, *op. cit.* Koyré thinks that Bruno was the first to take the Lucretian cosmology seriously.

expounded by Bruno in a speech at Wittenberg to show the sequence of *prisca magia*, or occultism, within which he placed Copernicus. It is highly significant that Lucretius also comes into that genealogy, though I omitted him in the earlier quotation which I now give more fully. The Temple of Wisdom, says Bruno, was built first among the Egyptians and Chaldeans; secondly among the Persian Magi, with Zoroaster; thirdly by the Indian gymnosophists; fourthly in Thracia with Orpheus; fifthly among the Greeks with Thales and others of the Wise; sixthly amongst the Italians by, amongst others, LUCRETIUS; seventhly among the Germans by Albertus Magnus, Cusanus, Copernicus, Palingenius.[1] To my mind, this genealogy shows that—just as he interpreted Copernicanism as heralding the return of "Egyptianism", so, to him, the Lucretian universe seemed a kind of extended Egyptian wisdom, whence he adopted the Lucretian infinite universe and innumerable worlds into his Copernicanism as all part of an expanded Hermetic vision.

Of the others in the genealogy, Albertus Magnus he certainly thought of as a Magus. Cusanus, whom he greatly admired, had used a type of geometrical symbolism in his teaching which Bruno probably thought was Hermetic. The famous saying that God is "a sphere of which the centre is everywhere and the circumference nowhere" is, in fact, first found in a pseudo-Hermetic treatise of the twelfth century,[2] and was transferred by Cusanus to the universe,[3] as a reflection of God, in a manner which is Hermetic in spirit. This concept was basic for Bruno, for whom the innumerable worlds are all divine centres of the unbounded universe.

In Palingenius, who also appears in the genealogy of the Wise, Bruno had met with an Epicurean ethic, derived from Lucretius,

---

[1] *Oratio valedictoria*, Wittenberg, 1588 (*Op. lat.*, I (I), pp. 16–17).

[2] The *Liber XXIV philosophorum*, published by Clemens Baeumker, *Das pseudo-hermetische Buch der XXIV Meister*, Beiträge zur Geschichte der Philosophie und Theologie des Mittelalters, fasc. xxv, Münster, 1928. The second proposition in this work describes God as a "sphaera infinita cuius centrum est ubique, circumferentia nusquam". Cf. Koyré, *op. cit.*, pp. 18, 279 (note 19).

Ficino attributes this saying to Hermes. "Disse Mercurio: Iddio è spera intelligibile, il cui centro è in ogni loco, la circumferentia in nessuno (Ficino, *De Deo et anima*, in Kristeller, *Suppl. Fic.*, II, p. 134). So also does Robert Fludd (see Garin, *Cultura*, p. 145, note).

[3] Cusanus, *De docta ignorantia*, II, cap. 2; cf. Koyré, *op. cit.*, pp. 10 ff.

and some features of the Lucretian cosmology, combined with Hermetism[1] and with magic in the peculiar manner suggested in the last chapter. Though Bruno did not entirely approve of Palingenius, yet that author would have encouraged him in his misunderstanding of Lucretius.

Thus that wonderful bound of the imagination by which Bruno extended his Copernicanism to an infinite universe peopled with innumerable worlds, all moving and animated with the divine life, was seen by him—through his misunderstandings of Copernicus and Lucretius—as a vast extension of Hermetic gnosis, of the magician's insight into the divine life of nature.

And this infinitely extended All was still One, which is, as we have seen, a basic tenet of Hermetism. The unity of the All in the One is Bruno's constant theme; some of the most striking passages on this are in the *De la causa, principio e uno* which becomes something in the nature of a Hermetic hymn:

> The *summum bonum*, the supremely desirable, the supreme perfection and beatitude consists in the unity which informs the all. . . . May the gods be praised and may all living beings magnify the infinite, the most simple, the most one, the most high, the most absolute cause, beginning and one.[2]

The unity of the All in the One is, cries Bruno in an earlier passage in the *De la causa*,

> a most solid foundation for the truths and secrets of nature. For you must know that it is by one and the same ladder that nature descends to the production of things and the intellect ascends to the knowledge of them; and that the one and the other proceeds from unity and returns to unity, passing through the multitude of things in the middle.[3]

This is the philosophy conducive to magic, that the All is One, and that the Magus can depend on the ladders of occult sympathies

---

[1] This phenomenon needs further study. Is it possible that there are some Epicurean influences in the Hermetic writings (which do reflect, as discussed in Chapter I, a mixture of the philosophies current in late antiquity) and that enthusiasts for that ancient Egyptian, Hermes Trismegistus, were able to recognise some of his teachings in Lucretius? Just as the Platonists could also find the source of Platonism in Hermes. Some historical explanation is needed of the, apparently impossible, combination of Hermes and Lucretius in Palingenius and Bruno.

[2] *De la causa, principio e uno*, dial. 5 (*Dial. ital.*, pp. 341–2).

[3] *De la causa*, dial. 5 (*Dial. ital.*, p. 329).

running through all nature. And when this philosophy is not only a magic but a religion, it becomes the religion of the Hermetic pseudo-Egyptians who, as Bruno says in the *Spaccio*,

> with magic and divine rites . . . ascended to the height of the divinity by that same scale of nature by which the divinity descends to the smallest things by the communication of itself.[1]

Bruno's philosophy and his religion are one and the same, and both are Hermetic. One has to see his message as a whole to realise the connections. The expanded universe is related to the expanded non-ascetic Epicurean ethics. The huge extension of Hermetic gnosis connects with his dissatisfaction with organised forms of religion. Lucretius' dislike of the forms of religion current in his time, his direction of attention towards "the world" as an escape from superstitious terrors, was no doubt most congenial to Bruno. Yet Bruno was certainly not an atheist, like Lucretius. The infinite universe and the innumerable worlds are for him new revelations, intense accentuations of his overpowering sense of the divine. Or they are ways of figuring the infigurable, of grasping and holding within, the infinite divine reality. For Bruno uses thought in a Hermetic way, a semi-magical way, as a mode of reaching intuitive knowledge of the divine.

His peculiar point of view liberated Bruno from the scruples of the Christian Hermetists in their approach to the Hermetic literature, and allowed him to choose out the more pantheist and optimist treatises of the *Corpus Hermeticum* as the basis of his philosophy, treatises such as *Corpus Hermeticum* XII, *De communi*, or *Corpus Hermeticum* V, *Quod Deus latens simul et patens est* (I am giving the treatises their Ficinian titles).

It also allowed him to accept unchristian doctrines, which had been carefully avoided by the Christian Hermetists, for example, metempsychosis (to be found particularly in the *Asclepius* and in *Corpus Hermeticum* X[2]) which Bruno openly accepts in his *Cabala del Cavallo Pegaseo*[3] and implies in some passages of the *Cena* and elsewhere.[4] Also, the gnostic ascent through the spheres had been

---

[1] See above, p. 212.
[2] *C.H.*, I, p. 116; II, p. 311.
[3] *Cabala del cavallo pegaseo*, dial. 2 (*Dial. ital.*, pp. 892 ff.).
[4] See particularly *Eroici furori*, Pt. I, dial. 4 (*Dial. ital.*, pp. 1026 ff.).

avoided, though Ficino may have had some hankerings after it in his interest in the doctrine of the astral body,[1] and, as we have seen, the magician Agrippa has it.

Another result is, that all the elaborate arguments used in other types of Hermetism, in which Hermes is accepted as having fore-seen the Trinity, as in Ficino's Christianising commentaries on the *Corpus Hermeticum*, are entirely ignored by Bruno. This must have been deliberate, since he was certainly using Ficino's Latin trans-lation of the *Corpus* and must have seen the commentaries. Those sets of threes collected from early theologies and philosophies as foreshadowings of the Trinity, such as are to be found in Ficino's *Theologia Platonica*, Tyard's dialogues, and indeed almost every-where among Christian Neoplatonists, are conspicuous by their absence from Bruno's works. This differentiates his religious Her-metism from, for example, that of Patrizi, who may be using a little Ficinian magic but is full of Trinitarianism. It even differen-tiates him from his beloved *De occulta philosophia* of Agrippa which, at the end, assumes the Pseudo-Dionysian and Trinitarian framework of the magic.[2] Bruno himself is aware of the absence of theology in his work and explains it by saying that he does not attempt to go above nature, and speaks as a pure natural philo-sopher. He does not want to be contrary to theology, but he seeks his divinity in the infinite worlds.[3]

Through this approach, Bruno's Hermetism perhaps almost does interpret the Hermetic writings in their true sense, as expres-sions of the gnostic "religion of the world", which he has expanded to infinite worlds, and, in the case of the *Asclepius*, as a late antique Neoplatonised Egyptian mystery cult. Yet Bruno, like everyone else, has no idea of the true date of the *Hermetica*, and thinks that he is returning to an Egyptian philosophy and religion earlier than Moses.

The question of Bruno's philosophy is immensely complicated by the fact that, like Ficino and Pico, he, too, is a syncretist, and draws in out of a vast reading other philosophies and literatures which are accreted to the Hermetic core. He knew the works of

---

[1] See D. P. Walker, "The Astral Body in Renaissance Medicine", *J.W.C.I.*, XXI (1958), p. 123.

[2] See above, p. 140.

[3] *De la causa*, dial. 4 (*Dial. ital.*, pp. 300 ff.).

Plato and the Neoplatonists in Ficino's translations. Averroist philosophy (also used in Pico's synthesis) would be important to him, since the *intellectus agens* would be a confirmation and expansion of the Hermetic *De communi*. The *Fons vitae* of Avicebron is an influence. And Bruno, the ex-Dominican who was very proud of his Order, was deeply read in that difficult author Albertus Magnus; he also always expressed great admiration for that brightest luminary of his Order, Thomas Aquinas, though I fear that it was not at all after the manner of a modern Thomist philosopher that the magician revered one whom he thought of as a great Magus and a noble heroic enthusiast.[1]

Apart from his constant deep devotion to the occult philosophy of Cornelius Agrippa, other modern influences upon him included Telesio and, more important, Paracelsus—who appears in the genealogy of the Wise, after Palingenius.

Bruno's anti-Aristotelianism is not quite what it has seemed to those who have admired him as the thinker in advance of his times, the enlightened defender of the Copernican theory against the hide-bound Aristotelianism of the Middle Ages. For Bruno, Aristotle is the type of the pedant, the literal-minded person who cannot or will not see occult truths, fails to understand the Copernican theory as a Hermetic seal, like the doctors in the *Cena de le ceneri*, who qualify as both "grammarian" and "Aristotelian" pedants. In another work, "poor Aristotle" is to be pitied for his inability to grasp "profound magic".[2] Sometimes this attitude leads Bruno into remarkable insights, as when he dismisses the Aristotelian order of the elements as not a "natural" conception, but "logical".[3]

On another level, Aristotle himself, unlike the stupid Aristotelians his followers, was one who did see deep truths but veiled them in obscure language. In a moment of divination, Aristotle half guessed that the earth moves when he used in the *Meteorologica* the words "propter solem et circulationem". Here Aristotle was not speaking as a philosopher, but "as a diviner, or as one who understood but did not dare to say what he understood, or as one who saw but did not believe what he saw."[4]

[1] See below, p. 272.
[2] *De la causa*, dial. 5 (*Dial. ital.*, p. 340).
[3] *De l'infinito universo*, dial. 5 (*Dial. ital.*, pp. 524–5).
[4] *Cena*, dial. 5 (*Dial. ital.*, p. 160).

For Bruno, mathematics can also be a kind of pedantry, a stopping short of deepest truth. The Copernican mathematics have to be transcended by the further insights of the Nolan.

But Bruno's greatest enemy, his nightmare obsession, is the "grammarian pedant". This kind of pedant can be combined with the Aristotelian type, but his pedantry consists, not merely in a narrow-minded philosophy, but in a contempt for philosophical studies altogether, which he has abandoned for minute attention to Latin style, dictionaries of words and phrases, with which he is so absorbed that he has lost all sense of using language to express a meaning. The hatred of the grammarian pedant expresses Bruno's hatred of humanist studies, and their usurpation of the primacy formerly belonging to philosophical studies. His grammarian pedant is, in his literary ancestry, the stock pedant of comedy. Bruno had written a comedy with a pedant in it, the *Candelaio* (published in Paris before he came to England), who exhibits his pedantry by quoting strings of Erasmian adages.[1] The pedant doctor in the *Cena* hurls the Erasmian adage "Anticyram navigat" at Bruno,[2] meaning to say in his pedantic manner, "You are mad". We need not suppose that the Oxford doctors actually shouted "Anticyram navigat" at Bruno when he was expounding his Copernican-Ficinian magic, but we know from George Abbot that they thought that he was mad: "in truth it was his owne head which rather did run round, & his braines did not stand stil."[3]

Bruno expressed his hatred of humanism and humanist Latin by himself using a Latin which is resolutely monkish and also all his own in its astonishing and peculiarly Brunian vocabulary; only those who (like myself) are not proper classical scholars can bear to read it.

Bruno's satires on grammarian pedantry are, in a manner, a reversal of Erasmus' satires on scholastic pedantry. Bruno, looking in quite a different direction from Erasmus, sees humanism, not as the new learning which has superseded mediaeval barbarism, but as the destroyer of the philosophical tradition. We know that what he objected to in the new Oxford was that its doctors "make

---

[1] G. Bruno, *Candelaio*, ed. V. Spampanato, Florence, 1923, pp. 130 ff.

[2] *Cena*, dial. 1 and 4 (*Dial. ital.*, pp. 37, 132). Cf. Erasmus, *Adagia*, chiliade I, centuria VIII, no. 51. Anticyra was renowned for its hellebore, a herb supposed to cure madness.

[3] See above, p. 208.

a boast of being totally different from their predecessors",[1] the barbarous friars. Very likely the ex-Dominican noted with annoyance that the great Magi of his Order were not now studied in Oxford.

All this, however, does not quite get to the bottom of Bruno's objection to grammarian pedants. Such a pedant is a childish person who has not gone beyond elementary stages to reach the deeper insights; and from this it follows that his use of language is trivial and superficial, and without magical and incantatory power. These finer points will perhaps come out more clearly in later chapters.

Just as Bruno's Hermetic or "Egyptian" natural philosophy cannot be separated from his Hermetic or "Egyptian" natural religion, so the pedants of the philosophical dialogue, the *Cena de le ceneri*, cannot be separated from the pedants of its companion piece, the *Spaccio della bestia trionfante*, where pedantry obviously has a religious application, referring to those who despise good works and have destroyed the good works of their predecessors, that is to the religious intolerance of the Protestants or Puritans. As we have seen, Bruno's Hermetism, however strange, yet belongs into the movements of religious Hermetism of the sixteenth century, tending towards religious toleration or some kind of eirenic solution of the religious difficulties.

I see clearly that we are all born ignorant and willing to acknowledge our ignorance; then, as we grow, we are brought up in the disciplines and habits of our house, and we hear disapproval of the laws, rites, faith and manners of our adversaries and of those who are different from ourselves, whilst they hear the same about us and our affairs. Thus, just as there are planted in us by the natural forces of breeding the roots of zeal for our own ways, so in others an enthusiasm for their own different customs is instilled. Thence it easily becomes axiomatic that we should esteem the oppression and slaughter of the enemies of our faith as a pleasing sacrifice to the gods; as they do also, when they have done the like by us. And they render thanks to God for having vouchsafed to them the light which leads to eternal life with no less fervour and conviction than we feel in rejoicing that our hearts are not blind and dark as theirs are.[2]

[1] See above, p. 210.
[2] *Cena*, dial. I (*Dial. ital.*, pp. 46–7).

So does one of the speakers in the *Cena* describe the sixteenth-century religious situation, and the words have their application to what has been said just previously about the rising sun of the Nolan's philosophy which heralds the dawn of a better day, though its opponents take an opposite view of it. How can such persons be corrected?

> By weakening with arguments their conviction that they know, and in a subtly persuasive manner drawing them away as much as possible from their bigotry. . .[1]

The irritable magician regarded himself as a missionary of conciliation.

I have suggested elsewhere[2] that the curious title of *Cena de le ceneri* or "Ash Wednesday Supper", which Bruno gives to the work describing the Supper (which took place, so he told the Venetian Inquisitors, not really at Fulke Greville's house as the text says but at the French embassy)[3] in which he expounded his philosophy to knights and pedants, may imply a religious meaning for this Supper, perhaps some version of the Sacrament such as he seems to allude to in the *Spaccio*, and of which he spoke to the librarian of St. Victor.[4] But all is so confused about this Supper, and its setting, and the journey to and from it through the London streets (an imaginary journey if the Supper really took place at the embassy where Bruno was living) that it is best to regard it as a kind of magical and allusive picture, as Bruno himself suggests in the dedication to the French ambassador.

The mysteries of the *Cena de le ceneri*, whatever they may be, were to be associated with the King of France, described in the dedication to the ambassador as a beneficent solar lion, "who when he roars with anger, like a lion in his den, strikes mortal fear into the other predatory beasts of the jungle; and when he is calm and in repose he sends forth such a flame of liberal and courteous love that it warms the tropics, heats the frozen Bear, and dissolves

---

[1] *Ibid.*, p. 44.

[2] "The Religious Policy of Giordano Bruno", *J.W.C.I.*, III (1939–40), p. 189.

[3] It should be remembered in this connection that in Elizabethan England it was only at the foreign embassies that the Mass could be openly celebrated.

[4] See above, p. 230.

the arctic ice which lies under the eternal sway of proud Bootes."[1]
This connects the *Cena de le ceneri* with the equally celestial
appearance of Henri III in the *Spaccio della bestia trionfante*. It
may also connect with the royal palace which appears in the
strange picture in which, in the dedication of the *Cena* to the
ambassador, Bruno summarises the contents of that most strange
work:

> (In the second dialogue) you will see, first of all the original cause of
> the supper party; secondly a description of walks and wanderings,
> which readers may possibly take to be poetical and figurative, rather
> than historically true; thirdly, he, as it were, confusedly plunges into
> moral topography, through which as he takes his way he looks about
> him with the penetrating eyes of Lynceus, not lingering the while,
> and as he contemplates the great structures of the universe he seems
> to trip over every tiny thing, every stone and stumbling-block in his
> path. And in this he is imitating a painter, who, not satisfied with
> confining himself to a simple picture of his subject, puts in stones,
> mountains, trees, springs, rivers, hills, in order to fill the canvas and
> bring his art in conformity with nature. Here he will display to you
> a royal palace, there a wood, there a strip of sky, on that side the half
> disc of the rising sun, and from time to time a bird, a boar, a stag, an
> ass, a horse, of which animals it suffices to show the head only, or a
> horn, or part of their hind quarters, or an ear, with, perhaps, a com-
> plete description of one of them; and each one has its own distinctive
> look and attitude, so that he who examines the picture again and
> again with judgment, can, as they say, tell himself the whole story
> of what is represented to his own great satisfaction. In the same
> manner, you are to read and to visualise what I have to say.[2]

The Elizabethan reader, unless he had travelled abroad, would
hardly have seen a picture painted in this style, though he no
doubt understood the allusions in it much better than we can.

Bruno attempted a partial apology for his strictures on pedants
in the *Cena* in the first dialogue of the *De la causa, principio e uno*,
in which another remarkable picture is added to the Brunian
gallery:

> The task which you have undertaken, O Filoteo, is a most unusual
> and difficult one, for you wish to lead men out of their abyss of blind-
> ness into the clear and tranquil light of those stars, which we now

[1] *Cena*, dedication (*Dial. ital.*, pp. 17–18).
[2] *Cena*, dedication (*Dial. ital.*, pp. 10–11).

see scattered over the dusky-blue mantle of heaven in all their beautiful variety. Although it is to men, and not to animals, that you have stretched forth hands in eagerness to help, nevertheless you must expect to meet with as many different varieties of ingratitude as there are different kinds of animals. . . Some men, resembling the dim-eyed mole, who, the moment he feels upon him the open air of heaven, rushes to dig himself back again into the ground, desire to remain in their native darkness; others are like those birds of night which, because of the weakness of their eyes, retreat into their shadowy haunts as soon as they see in the brightening east those bars of crimson which are the sun's ambassadors. All those creatures who may not gaze upon the lights of heaven but are destined to dwell in the infernal circles of Pluto's dark prison-house, when they hear the dread summons of Alecton's furious horn, spread wide their wings and veer away in rapid flight toward their abodes. But those who were born to see the sun, being full of thanksgiving when they come to the end of loathsome night, dispose themselves to receive in the very centre of their eyes' crystal globe the long-expected rays of the glorious sun, and, with unaccustomed gladness in their hearts, they lift up hands and voices to adore the east. . .[1]

This is a companion picture to the one about the pedants and the Copernican theory in the *Cena* dedication. What a painter the magician would have made! It was a part of his philosophy that (by an extension of the *ut pictura poesis* theory), poetry, painting, and philosophy were all one.

Whence philosophers are in some ways painters and poets; poets are painters and philosophers; painters are philosophers and poets. Whence true poets, true painters, and true philosophers choose one another out and admire one another.[2]

[1] *De la causa*, dial. 1 (*Dial. ital.*, pp. 192–3).
[2] *Explicatio triginta sigillorum* (*Op. lat.*, II (ii), p. 133).

Chapter XIV

~~~~~~

GIORDANO BRUNO AND THE
CABALA

~~~~~~

THE Renaissance Magus, in his full dignity as described
by Pico della Mirandola, combined Magia with Cabala,
adding to the natural magic of the Ficinian type, with
its Hermetic basis, the practical Cabala which brought
the Magus into contact with the higher spiritual and angelic world,
and which the Christian Magus connected with the Pseudo-Dionysian angelic hierarchies. We have already seen that, as a Renaissance Magus, Bruno is abnormal in his Hermetism through his
rejection of the Christian interpretation of the Hermetic writings
and his total "Egyptianism". We should expect to find that his
attitude to the Cabala would also be abnormal, and so it is, though
in spite of his alarming departures from the norm, Bruno can still
be described as belonging into the Hermetic-Cabalist tradition. In
his *Cabala del Cavallo Pegaseo* he appears to be totally rejecting
Cabala for his purely Egyptian insights, an attitude which accords
with his highly unorthodox view of the history of *prisca theologia*,
or *prisca magia*, in which, according to him, the Egyptians are not
only earliest but best, and the Jews and Christians later and worse.
Nevertheless, he did not quite consistently maintain this attitude,
or rather, just as he thought that his "Egyptianism", though unchristian, could still be the basis of a reform within the Church, so
also he would retain in it something of Cabala, of the inferior
Jewish revelation and magic.

It is probable that Bruno knew very little Hebrew.[1] He knew the alphabet which he uses on some of his diagrams. But when he speaks of the structure of Cabalism, of the Names, Sephiroth, orders of angels, and so on, he is getting his material direct from his bible, that is to say from the occult philosophy of Cornelius Agrippa. He also knew Trithemius's *Steganographia*, and possibly Reuchlin's *De arte cabalistica*, and he may have known something of the *Zohar*.[2] He knew the works of Pico della Mirandola, no doubt, but the librarian of St. Victor confided to his valuable diary that Bruno (who must have held forth a good deal to that man) had said that he "despises Picus Mirandulanus and all the philosophy of the Jesuits"[3] (rather a curious combination).

The sources of Bruno's magic may have been somewhat meagre, for it is curious to see what intense faith he placed in Agrippa's second-hand compilation. The Noroff manuscript[4] contains extracts from magical texts which were copied out for Bruno by his amanuensis, Besler. At that time Bruno was making great efforts to intensify the magic of his personality before his return to Italy in 1591, with the manuscript of a book in his baggage for dedication to the Pope whom he hoped to interest in his reform movement.[5] And what was Besler so busily copying out? Chiefly long extracts from the *De occulta philosophia*. This book must have made an immense impression on Bruno. He did not follow it slavishly, but it was his *point de départ* for most of his magic, and, as we have seen, some of the major points of the Hermetic philosophy had been incorporated by Agrippa in his magical text-book, and could have struck Bruno in that context, as well as in his reading of the Ficino translations.

[1] McIntyre thought that it is unlikely that Bruno read Hebrew and that he probably derived most of his knowledge of Cabala from Agrippa and, perhaps, Reuchlin. See J. L. McIntyre, *Giordano Bruno*, London, 1903, p. 131, note.

[2] Probably only indirectly.

[3] *Documenti*, p. 40.

[4] The Noroff manuscript in Moscow contains magical works by Bruno and notes and transcripts from magical texts. Most of the Noroff manuscript was published in 1891 as Vol. III in the edition of Bruno's Latin works; the notes from Agrippa and Trithemius (*Op. lat.*, III, pp. 493–506) are only indications of the passages copied, not the full transcripts as they are in the manuscript.

[5] See below, p. 341.

In his *Cabala del Cavallo Pegaseo*, printed in England in 1585, with the false imprint "Paris",[1] Bruno reveals his attitude to the Cabala, to its Christian extension to the Pseudo-Dionysian hierarchies, and to that religious syncretism, based on the negative theology of Pseudo-Dionysius, the ultimate sources of which are Ficino and Pico. He outlines the Cabalist-Pseudo-Dionysian system, giving the names of the ten Sephiroth, their meanings, the Hebrew orders of angels which go with them, and the nine celestial hierarchies to which they correspond. He makes up the number of the hierarchies to the necessary ten, by putting with Malkuth, the tenth Sephiroth, and its corresponding Hebrew angelic order, the Issim, an order of "separated souls or heroes".[2] All this he took straight out of the *De occulta philosophia*.[3]

The mystical Nothing beyond the Cabalist Sephiroth he symbolises by the Ass, and this Ass of negative theology or Unknowing is the strange hero of the work. In spite of appearances, I do not think that Bruno really means to be as blasphemous as he sounds in this. The ass which carries the Sacraments, Christ entering Jerusalem on the ass, had been allegorised in this sense as humble negation. Bruno knows and refers to such allegories.[4] Bruno is not insincere, nor does he mean to be flippant. He just had an ex-

---

[1] All the works by Bruno printed in England by John Charlewood (see above, p. 205, note 1) have false imprints, either Venezia or Parigi, except the *Triginta Sigilli* which has no imprint. These clandestine publications by an inmate of the French embassy must surely have been connived at by the Ambassador, to whom several of them are dedicated.

The *Cabala del Cavallo Pegaseo* is in dialogue form, like the other Italian works written by Bruno in England and is followed by a shorter dialogue called *L'Asino cillenico del Nolano*.

[2] *Cabala*, dial. 1 (*Dial. ital.*, pp. 865–6).

[3] Agrippa, *De occult. phil.*, III, 10.

[4] See the address to the "devout and pious reader" before the *Cabala* (*Dial. ital.*, pp. 851 ff.) on the theme of the choice of the ass for the entry into Jerusalem. One of Alciati's emblems (no. 7) shows—with an Egyptian adaptation of the sacred rôle of the ass—an ass with a statue of Isis on its back. The ass is being ignorantly worshipped by those who mistake the bearers of holy things for the holy things themselves. The emblem is interpreted by Mignault and Whitney as a satire on the presumption of the clergy. It is not, however, in this sense, that Bruno is using the ass, though there may be a *double entendre*. On the ass symbol, including its use by Bruno and Agrippa, see John M. Steadman, "Una and the Clergy: the Ass Symbol in *The Faerie Queene*", *J.W.C.I.*, XXI (1958), pp. 134–6.

tremely strange religion which he expounds under extremely strange allegories.

The Hebrews, continues Bruno after his exposition of the Cabalist system, derived their wisdom from the Egyptians, and he then takes a story out of Plutarch's *De Iside et Osiride* to symbolise Hebrew corruption of Egyptian wisdom, when the Egyptians were made to turn "their bull Opin or Apin" (the Apis bull) into an Ass, which then became for them a symbol of wisdom.[1] The Ass, in short, symbolises all negative theology, whether Cabalist or Pseudo-Dionysian and Christian,[2] but Bruno has a new, or rather an old Egyptian, Cabala, which is his religion and which is expounded in *L'Asino Cillenico del Nolano*, the dialogue which follows the first part of the work.

One of the speakers in this is actually an Ass which speaks, and it describes itself as a "naturalissimo asino".[3] It contemplates the "works of the world and the principles of nature" and its nature is "physical".[4] It becomes a member of a Pythagorean academy devoted to the "physical", because

> It is not possible to understand supernatural things, except through their shining in natural things; for only a purged and superior intellect can consider them in themselves.[5]

There is no metaphysics in this academy, for "what others boast of as metaphysics is only a part of logic."[6]

Bruno has swept away as "metaphysics" the Cabalistic system of the Sephiroth, the Pseudo-Dionysian hierarchies, the whole superstructure which the Christian Magus had erected upon his natural Magia, to guarantee it from demonic influences, returning to the "natural religion" of the Egyptians, and the natural philosophy or natural religion of the world which he had extracted from Hermetism. It is explicitly said that this "natural Ass" is the same as the Triumphant Beast of the *Spaccio*.[7]

---

[1] *Cabala*, dial. I (*Dial. ital.*, pp. 867–8).

[2] *Cabala*, dial. I (*Dial. ital.*, pp. 875–6). It also symbolises (*ibid.*, p. 876) the total scepticism of the "Pirronians and ephetics".

[3] *L'asino cillenico* (*Dial. ital.*, p. 915). The epithet "cillenico" connects the ass with Mercury, born in a cave on Mount Cyllene. He is also conflated with the horse Pegasus, hence the title *Cabala del Cavallo Pegaseo*.

[4] *L'asino cillenico* (*Dial. ital.*, p. 917).   [5] *Ibid., loc. cit.*   [6] *Ibid., loc. cit.*

[7] *L'asino cillenico* (*Dial. ital.*, pp. 842, 862). Since we have also been told that the Egyptians were made to turn their bull, Apis, into an ass, it

The MLA Style
        Sheet
$1.25

MLA
    Materials Center

62 Fifth Ave
        NY, 10011

Cordially without reservs

Enrico Campelli

The origin of Bruno's Egyptian Ass is quite clear. We need only recall the *Golden Ass of Apuleius*, the romance by Apuleius of Madaura about the man turned into an ass who had the vision of Isis on the lonely seashore and became a priest of the Egyptian mysteries. Apuleius of Madaura, it will be remembered, was supposed to have been the Latin translator of the *Asclepius*, and was accused by the Christian Hermetists of having fraudulently inserted the bad magical passage into that work.[1] The non-christian Hermetist, the wild magician, Giordano Bruno, proclaims his admiration of Apuleius, the magician, and of the full magic of the *Asclepius*, by taking the Apuleian Ass as his hero.

Moreover, the Apuleian Ass as a natural philosopher was almost certainly suggested to Bruno by his great hero, Cornelius Agrippa of Nettesheim, the magician. As F. Tocco pointed out, some of Bruno's passages about the ass are taken from Agrippa's *De vanitate scientiarum* in which he had expounded the occult sciences, in the end rejecting them as vanity, using the ass of ignorance symbol.[2] In the dedication of this work, Agrippa describes himself as having been turned into a "philosophical ass", like those described by Lucian and Apuleius.

We have to see Bruno in the framework of the *Cabala del Cavallo Pegaseo* and its sequel, in order to realise the full abnormality of his position in the tradition of the Renaissance Magi. By outlining the system of the Sephiroth and the related Christian celestial hierarchies, Bruno is consciously evoking the position of the Christian Renaissance Magus and consciously departing from it. Not only was Bruno's Magia entirely without the safeguards with which Ficino's hesitations had surrounded natural magic, his Magia stood alone, without those angelic superstructures through which (it was hoped) the demons were controlled by higher spiritual forces.

Yet this is not the whole story, for the Renaissance revaluation of magic basically affects Bruno. On the one hand it had promoted

[1] See above, pp. 172–3.

[2] Cornelius Agrippa, *De vanitate scientiarum*, cap. 102, *Ad Encomium Asini digressio*. Cf. V. Spampanato, *Giordano Bruno e la letteratura dell'asino*, Portici, 1904; Steadman, *article cited*, pp. 136–7.

might follow that the Triumphant Beast was really Apis, representing not, as for Pope Alexander VI, a precursor of Christianity, but the true religion which Jews and Christians suppressed and perverted.

magic to being an adjunct of important philosophies, a tradition most notably continued by Bruno. And, on the other hand, the intense religious feeling which had inspired Pico to welcome Magia and Cabala as aids to religious insight, persists very strongly in Bruno, who pursues his philosophical religion, or his religious philosophy, or his philosophical-religious magic, with the deepest earnestness and believes that it can become the instrument of a universal religious reform. Bruno's own definition of his new "cabala" is that it is "a cabala of theological philosophy, a philosophy of cabalistic theology, a theology of philosophical cabala."[1]

He thus retains the word "cabala" to describe his position, and indeed, as we shall shortly see, his attitude both to Cabalist and to Pseudo-Dionysian mysticism is not, in practice, so radically adverse as the *Cabala del Cavallo Pegaseo* would lead one to suppose. He uses elements from both in other works, and thus still qualifies as a Renaissance Magus, though a most extraordinary one.

There are several works by Bruno explicitly devoted to the magic of which his mnemonic and philosophical works are also full. The chief of the works explicitly on magic are the *De magia* and the *De vinculis in genere*, both probably written about 1590 to 1591, though they were not published until the late nineteenth century, in the collected edition of Bruno's Latin works.[2] It was his study of the *De magia* and the *De vinculis* which brought home to A. Corsano the realisation of Bruno's interest in magic,[3] though Corsano thought that Bruno did not take this up seriously until the late period, whereas, in fact, the magic is present from the start of Bruno's career.

As we should expect, Bruno's *De magia* is based on Agrippa's *De occulta philosophia* and follows in the main the general cadres and classifications of the subject which Agrippa had laid down. Yet there are also some very significant differences. It will be remembered that Agrippa's book is divided into three parts, on elemental magic, celestial magic, and supercelestial or religious magic, corresponding to the three worlds of the Cabalists. These

---

[1] *Cabala*, dedication (*Dial. ital.*, p. 837).

[2] *Op. lat.*, III, pp. 395 ff. and 653 ff. Both these works are in the Noroff manuscript. They will be mentioned again later on in the context of Bruno's career in Germany (see below, p. 317).

[3] A. Corsano, *Il pensiero di Giordano Bruno*, pp. 281 ff.

divisions are also perceptible in Bruno's *De magia*, but when Bruno comes to religious magic, he significantly omits all mention of the antiquity, sanctity and power of the Hebrew language, of the Sephiroth, and of the Hebrew and Pseudo-Dionysian orders of angels.[1] It is true that the Cabalists occur in the list of *prisci magi* with which the *De magia* opens, where it is stated that the Magus is the wise man, as were Hermes Trismegistus among the Egyptians, the Druids among the Gauls, the Gymnosophists among the Indians, the Cabalists among the Hebrews, the Magi among the Persians, the Sophi among the Greeks, the Sapientes among the Latins.[2] Still, to a magician familiar with the correct tradition, it would be rather noticeable that Bruno nowhere mentions the superior power in magic of the Hebrew language. On the contrary, he devotes a significant passage to praise of the Egyptian language and its sacred characters:

> . . . the sacred letters used among the Egyptians were called hiero-glyphs . . . which were images . . . taken from the things of nature, or their parts. By using such writings and voices (*voces*), the Egyptians used to capture with marvellous skill the language of the gods. After-wards when letters of the kind which we use now with another kind of industry were invented by Theuth or some other, this brought about a great rift both in memory and in the divine and magical sciences.[3]

This reminds one of the praise of the Egyptian language in *Corpus Hermeticum* XVI (the so-called "Definitions" treatise) in which Asclepius tells king Ammon that the treatise should be preserved in the original Egyptian, and should not be translated into Greek, for the Greek language is diffuse and empty, and the "efficacious virtue" of the original Egyptian would be lost in a Greek transla-tion.[4] If Bruno had read this passage, it would probably have been in Ludovico Lazzarelli's Latin translation (it will be remembered that this treatise was not translated by Ficino)[5] in which the point that it is the magical power of the Egyptian language which would be lost in translation into a language lacking in this power comes

---

[1] There is one mention of angels (*De magia, Op. lat.*, III, p. 428) but this is only a passing allusion. As a whole, the angelic superstructure of normal Renaissance magic is entirely omitted.

[2] *De magia* (*Op. lat.*, III, p. 397).

[3] *De magia* (*Op. lat.*, III, pp. 411–2).

[4] *C.H.*, II, p. 232.   [5] See above, p. 172.

out very clearly.¹ This passage would, it might be supposed, surely have attracted Bruno, for it really gets to the root of his whole objection to "pedants". The Greeks use language, like pedants, merely as empty words to argue with; the Egyptian, or magical, use of language or signs is for communicating directly with divine reality, "capturing the language of the gods" as Bruno puts it, and for operating. By substituting the invention of the normal alphabet, which has brought about the use of language "with another kind of industry" for the "Greeks" who stand in the Hermetic passage for the non-magical use of language, Bruno has turned the whole issue into a general one, between "Egyptians" who use language and signs magically and intuitively and (as he would probably say) "pedants" who do not.²

For magic it is axiomatic, says Bruno, in every work to have before the eyes the sequence of influence from God to the gods, from the gods to the stars, from the stars to the demons, who are cultivators of the stars and of whom one is the earth, from the demons to the elements, from the elements to the sense and to the "whole animal" and this is the descending scale. The ascending scale is from sense to elements, demons, stars, gods, thence to the soul of the world or the spirit of the universe, and from thence "to the contemplation of the one simple Optimus Maximus, incorporeal, absolute, sufficient in itself."³ Obviously a vital stage in

¹ "Etenim ipsa vocis qualitas et egyptiorum nominum lingua in seipsa habet actum dictorum. Quantum igitur possibile est, o rex, omnem (ut potes) sermonem serva inconversum, ne ad grecos perveniant talia misteria, neve grecorum superba locutio atque dissoluta ac veluti calamistrata debilem faciat gravitatem, validitatem atque activam nominum locutionem. Greci enim, o rex, verba habent tantum nova demonstrationum activa. Et hec est grecorum philosophia verborum sonus. Nos autem non verbis utimur, sed vocibus maximis operum." From the Latin translation of the Hermetic *Definitiones* by Ludovico Lazzarelli published in Symphorien Champier's *De quadruplici vita*, Lyons, 1507, and reprinted by C. Vasoli, "Temi e fonti della tradizione ermetica", in *Umanesimo e esoterismo*, ed. E. Castelli, Padua, 1960, pp. 251–2.

² Bruno may, however, also have been thinking of the passage in Plato's *Phaedrus* (274 C–275 B) in which the Egyptian king Thamus objects to Theut's invention of writing on the ground that this will destroy memory. Both the Platonic passage and the Hermetic passage are reflected in the dialogue between Thamus, Mercurius, and Theutates, which Bruno's disciple, Alexander Dicson, prefixed to his imitation of Bruno's mnemonics (A. Dicson, *De umbra rationis, etc.*, London, 1583. See above, p. 199).

³ *De magia* (*Op. lat.*, III, pp. 401–2).

this ascent would be to reach the demons, and Bruno's magic is quite frankly demonic. He knows the basis of the natural *spiritus* magic[1] but entirely abandons Ficino's reservations. Bruno *wants* to reach the demons; it is essential for his magic to do so; nor are there any Christian angels within call in his scheme to keep them in check. Bruno, of course, like all magicians, regards his magic as good magic[2]; only other people's magics are ever bad to the magician. And from his point of view and with his belief in the Egyptian religion as the right one, this would be the right magic, since, as we all know, it was the demons which the Egyptian priests knew how to manipulate and to draw down into their statues.

Bruno's practical magic therefore consists in drawing spirits or demons through "links". The linking-with-demons method was mentioned by Ficino at the beginning of the *De vita coelitus comparanda*, with quotations from Neoplatonist authors on it,[3] though he protested that he was not using it. Agrippa has a chapter on the links, and this is Bruno's basis[4] though he greatly elaborates it. One way of linking is "through words and song",[5] that is incantations, now no longer regarded as purely natural magic as by

[1] Cf. *De magia* (*Op. lat.*, III, pp. 414 ff., 434 ff. (in the second passage the inevitable "Spiritus intus alit" passage from Virgil is quoted); *De rerum principiis, elementis et causis* (*Op. lat.*, III, pp. 521 ff.). But Bruno's belief in Lucretius as a natural magician and his introduction of Lucretian atoms into his natural magic (see for example, *Op. lat.*, III, p. 415) gives his magic a different slant.

[2] There is, he says, a bad kind of demonic magic, which is called the "magia desperatorum", and of this kind is the *Ars notoria* (The *Ars Notoria* was a magic current in the Middle Ages, attributed to Solomon and using invocation of demons; see Thorndike, II, pp. 279–89). But there is another kind of this magic which aims at ruling through inferior demons with the authority of the head of the superior demons, and this is transnatural, or metaphysical magic or theurgy. Bruno's demonic magic is of this superior type (*De magia, Op. lat.*, III, p. 398).

[3] See above, p. 64.

[4] Agrippa, *De occult. phil.*, III, 33, *De vinculis spiritum*. Bruno is also sometimes using Trithemius. (For example in *Steganographia*, I, 15, Trithemius gives the names of spirits which rule the four cardinal points, and their numbers. Cf. Bruno's third "link" which is through the rulers of the four cardinal points, *De magia, Op. lat.*, III, p. 436.) The passages from Agrippa and Trithemius which Besler copied for Bruno (see above, p. 258) were those which he needed for his conjuring.

[5] *De magia, Op. lat.*, III, pp. 443–6.

Ficino, but invoking demons. Another way is by attracting demons with images, seals, characters, and so on.[1] Another way is through the imagination,[2] and this was Bruno's chief magical method, the conditioning of the imagination or the memory to receive the demonic influences through images or other magical signs stamped on memory. In the *De magia*, Bruno relates his magical psychology of the imagination to the terminology of normal faculty psychology which, however, he transforms by making the imagination, and more particularly the magically animated or excited imagination, when joined to the cogitative power, the source of psychic energy. This magically animated imagination is "the sole gate to all internal affections and the link of links".[3] Bruno's language is excited and obscure as he expounds this, to him, central mystery, the conditioning of the imagination in such a way as to draw into the personality spiritual or demonic forces which will unlock its inner powers. This was what he was always trying to do with the magic memory-systems,[4] and the object was, as is quite clear from the concluding pages of *De magia*, to achieve the personality and powers of a great Magus or religious leader.

We have indeed come a long way from the Magia and Cabala system of the Christian Magus, with its safeguards in natural magic and its Hebrew-Christian angels as guarantees for religious magic. Nevertheless Giordano Bruno is the direct and logical result of the Renaissance glorification of Man as the great Miracle, man who is divine in his origin and can again become divine, with divine Powers residing in him. He is, in short, the result of the Renaissance Hermetism. If man can obtain such powers through Hermetic experiences, why should not this have been the way in which Christ obtained his powers? Pico della Mirandola thought to prove the divinity of Christ through Magia and Cabala. Bruno interpreted the possibilities of Renaissance Magic in another way.

---

[1] Link IX is through "characteres et sigilla" (*De magia, Op. lat.*, III, p. 437.

[2] *De magia, Op. lat.*, III, pp. 449 ff.

[3] *De magia, Op. lat.*, III, p. 453.

[4] In the other work on "links" in the Noroff manuscript, the *De vinculis in genere*, the linking-with-demons methods are expounded under thirty heads, indicating connection with the "thirty" systems in the mnemonic works, *De umbris* and *Triginta Sigilli* (see *De vinculis in genere, Op. lat.*, III, pp. 669–70).

Though "Egyptianism" and Hermetism are primary in Bruno's outlook, the connections of Hermetism with Cabala in the earlier tradition do, in a manner, persist in his scheme, though with a different relative emphasis. One example of this is his acceptance of the traditional *Genesis-Pimander* equation, or the equation of Mosaic wisdom about the creation with Hermetic wisdom. In the *De immenso et innumerabilibus*, published in Germany in 1591, he discusses Moses' use of the word "waters" in *Genesis* which, he says, Moses is deriving from the Egyptian wisdom, quoting Mercurius Trismegistus (that is, the *Pimander*) on the "humid nature" which was 'activated by the light. Moses is here in his usual Brunian position as inferior to and later than the Egyptians, and getting the best of his wisdom from them, but Bruno does use the Mosaic *Genesis* as well as the Egyptian one, and in the next phrase he speaks of the "Egyptians and the Cabalists" (note the order) who agree in not putting *ignis* among the primal substances.[1] I quote, from another part of the *De immenso*, this agreement between Mercurius and Moses about the primal matter of creation as water-light and not fire:

> Quare et nonnullis humens substantia dicta est,
> Mercurio nempe et Mosi, qui corpora prima
> Inter non numerant ignem, quem compositorum
> In genere esse volunt, quod constat lumine et unda.[2]

Similarly, in the *De triplici minimo et mensura* (also published in Germany in 1591) Moses, Trismegistus, and "other Chaldeans and Egyptians" are found to be in agreement about the creation,[3] and a good many other Moses-Hermes references could be collected from the Latin works, which may perhaps mean that Bruno did know some Cabalistic commentaries on *Genesis*.

The persistence of Cabalistic ideas in Bruno's mind, though secondary to his primary Hermetism and Egyptianism, can also be studied in the *Spaccio della bestia trionfante*. After his exposition of the Egyptian religion, and its power of reaching the unity beyond the multiplicity of things, he expounds a Cabalistic scheme of unity in multiplicity. In order to show the sequence of the latter in relation to the "Egyptianism" I shall quote here again the

---

[1] *De immenso et innumerabilibus*, *Op. lat.*, I (i), p. 376.
[2] *Ibid.*, *Op. lat.*, I (ii), p. 33.
[3] *De triplici minimo et mensura*, *Op. lat.*, I (iii), p. 171.

Egyptian passage (already quoted in chapter XII). I do this without apology because the Egyptian passage expresses so well Bruno's fundamental outlook and it is essential constantly to return to it and to grasp it. He is describing how the Egyptian worship ascended through the multiplicity of things, distributed among the astrological relationships, to the One beyond things.

> . . . they (the Egyptians) conceive that the life, which informs things according to two principal reasons, is owing to the two principal bodies which are next to our globe and maternal deity; that is, the sun and moon. Then they conceive life according to seven other reasons, derived from the seven wandering stars; to which, as to an original principle and fruitful cause, they reduce the differences of species in any genus you please; saying of plants and animals, of stones and influences, and many other sorts of things, these belong to Saturn, these to Jupiter, these to Mars, these and others to this and the other planet. Thus also of parts, of members, of colours, of seals, of characters, of signs, of images distributed into seven species. But notwithstanding all this, they were not ignorant of the unity of the divinity, which is in all things, which as it diffuses and communicates itself in innumerable ways, so it has innumerable names, and is sought after by innumerable ways and reasons suited and appropiated to each of these names, whilst it is worshipped and honoured with innumerable rites. . . . Wherefore in this is required that wisdom and judgement, that art industry and use of the intellectual light, which is sometimes less, and sometimes in greater abundance revealed to us by the intelligible sun, which habit is called magic. . . .
>
> . . . the stupid and senseless idolaters had no reason to laugh at the magical and divine worship of the Egyptians, who contemplated the divinity in all things . . . and knew, by means of the species in the womb of nature, how to receive those benefits which they desired of her . . . which (species) like diverse ideas, were diverse divinities in nature, who all centered at last in one Deity of deities, and fountain of ideas above nature.

From hence I believe is derived that Cabala of the Jews, the wisdom of which (of whatsoever kind it be) hath proceeded from the Egyptians, among whom Moses was educated. In the first place it gives an ineffable Name to the first principle, from whence secondarily proceed four, which are afterwards resolved into twelve, and these never rest till they come to seventy-two in a direct line, which again go in a direct and oblique line till they come to a hundred and forty-four, and so on by fours and twelves till they become innumerable, according to the innumerable species of things. And in this manner they name, according to their proper idioms, by fit names, a god, an angel, an intelligence, a power that presides over one species; so that in the end, the whole Deity is reduced to one fountain, as all light to the first and of itself lucid principle; and the images which are in diverse and numerous mirrors, as in so many particular subjects, all centre in one formal and ideal principle, the fountain of them.

It is so. So that God, considered absolutely, has nothing to do with us, but only as He communicates Himself by the effects of nature, to which He is more nearly allied than nature itself; so that if He is not nature itself, certainly He is the nature of nature, and the soul of the soul of the world, if He is not the very soul itself.[1]

In this passage, he is talking about the Tetragrammaton, the sacred four-lettered Name of God, and of the seventy-two "Semhamaphores", or light-bearing angels, who bear the sacred name. These angels all had names drawn by the Hebrew doctors from the Scriptures[2] and by celestial arithmetical progression the numbers of the angels expanded from the four in the way which Bruno describes. He could have been getting this information from no more recondite source than Agrippa's *De occulta philosophia*,[3] though he may also have seen Reuchlin on the subject.[4] But in the Cabalist mysticism, these angels, progressively expanding from the sacred name, belong into the super-celestial world, and the mystic who learns through profound knowledge of the Hebrew alphabet to get into touch with them, and through them with the Name itself, is moving in realms of the absolute far above the world of nature and penetrating into the mysteries of the life of God within himself. Bruno sweeps away these "metaphysics" but uses the system "naturally", bringing the metaphysical down into the physical, yet using its unifying method to help in his constant aim of unifying multiplicity, or relating the All to the One. As far as practical magic is concerned, I think he would have interpreted the angel-summoning Cabalist magic as really demon summoning. This transformation is easily suggested by study of

---

[1] *Spaccio*, dial. 3 (*Dial. ital.*, pp. 781–3). The passage is here quoted in the eighteenth-century translation attributed to W. Morehead, hence the variation of the phrasing from the form in which the first part of it is quoted above, pp. 213–4.

[2] See above, p. 102.

[3] Agrippa, *De occult. phil.*, III, 25.

[4] Reuchlin, *De arte Cabalistica*, Hagenau, 1517, pp. lvii ff.

Agrippa whose chapter on demons,[1] some of which also expand arithmetically, as 12 for the signs, 36 for the decans, 72 for the quinarians, comes just before his angel chapters. In fact the physical or demonic application of angel magic is probably implied in Trithemius' angel magic, which Bruno certainly knew and used (Besler copied out parts of the *Steganographia* for him).[2]

So, in Bruno's religion and magic, the best way is the Egyptian way, described in the first part of the passage quoted from the *Spaccio*. But the way of the Jews and the Cabalists (which they got from the Egyptians but spoiled by making it "metaphysical") can also be used, provided that it is understood "naturally". I think that this is what Bruno means when, in the work which we were studying at the beginning of this chapter, he describes his Cabala as that of the "asino naturalissimo". In his usual way, this man is working with the old, familiar counters, but shifting them round to make a new pattern.

The most essential thing, in Bruno's outlook, was to find the living "voices", signs, images, seals, to heal the rift in the means of communication with divine nature introduced by pedantry, and when these living means of communication were found (or imprinted on consciousness in some trance-like experience) to unify through them the universe as reflected in the psyche and thereby obtain the Magus' powers and to live the life of an Egyptian priest in magical communion with nature. Within the context of this incredibly strange outlook, such a procedure as we find in the *De umbris idearum*—the imprinting on memory of decan demons— becomes, not exactly intelligible, but at least logical within the outlook.

More important for Bruno in his unifying aim than the residue of Cabalism, was his use of Lullism; but we are deliberately excluding here the Lullian side of Bruno, in order not to over-complicate the historical exposé.

If Cabalism is subservient to Egyptianism in Bruno's view of the Renaissance Magus, what then becomes of the connection with the Pseudo-Dionysian mysticism, the Christian angelic hierarchies by which the Magia and Cabala of the Christian Magus were kept

---

[1] Agrippa, *De occult. phil.*, III, 16.

[2] See *Op. lat.*, III, p. 496 (Besler's transcripts from the *Steganographia* in the Noroff manuscript).

within a Christian scheme? Here again traces of the former synthesis remain—as when Bruno speaks with admiration of the Areopagite in the *Eroici furori*[1]—though the balance is profoundly altered. And, once again, Bruno starts from Agrippa's *De occulta philosophia* to reach new conclusions about religious magic.

One of Bruno's strangest and most interesting works is the *Thirty Seals*,[2] the first book which he published in England, in 1583, and the one which contains the challenging address to the doctors of Oxford[3] which relates to his highly controversial visit to Oxford. The "thirty seals" are thirty mysterious disquisitions, accompanied by diagrams, in which he expounds the principles of his magic mnemonics. There is also in this work another version of his remarkable theory of the imagination[4] on which we have touched in the discussion of *De magia* and in what has just been said of his aim of inner unification. The ultimate object of the magic memory was the formation of the religious personality, or the personality of the good Magus. Hence, after the mysteries of the thirty mnemonic "seals",[5] Bruno enters upon a discussion of religion. This he does under the heading of different "contractions",[6] by which he means different kinds of religious experience, some of which are good and some bad. In nearly all of these he is following, expanding, turning for his own purposes, the treatment of similar themes by Agrippa. Thus Agrippa had discussed solitude and tranquillity of life as necessary for the religious experience, quoting Moses' vision in solitude, and Proclus on rising to the vision of the intelligible essence in solitude.[7] This becomes the basis of Bruno's first "contraction" mentioning among those who in solitude have achieved the vision and gained marvellous powers, Moses, Jesus of Nazareth, Ramon Lull, and the leisured contemplators amongst the Egyptians and Babylonians, and he introduces attacks on those who have destroyed the leisure and peace necessary for the con-

[1] See below, pp. 284–5.

[2] I give the work this title to cover its three parts; see above, p. 205, note 1.

[3] See above, p. 206.

[4] It will be treated more fully in the book which I hope to write on the art of memory.

[5] These are a combination of mnemonic "place" systems with magical figures.

[6] *Sigillus Sigillorum*, *Op. lat.*, II (ii), pp. 180 ff.

[7] Agrippa, *De occult. phil.*, III, 55.

templative life.[1] Other "contractions" on bad and superstitious religious magic and experience, and the good kinds,[2] are based on Agrippa's discussion of a truly divine magical religion, based on truth, and a superstitious and credulous kind.[3] As an example of one who achieved the good kind of "contraction", Bruno greatly admires Thomas Aquinas, most eminent for contemplation, and who was rapt in imagination to heaven, as were also Zoroaster and Paul.[4]

Agrippa had tried to preserve at least an appearance of Trinitarianism in his expositions of religious magic, stating, for example, that the three guides in religion are Love, Hope, Faith, the orthodox three theological virtues.[5] Bruno, as he takes a wandering course through Book III of the *De occulta philosophia*, picking out some material, altering, rearranging to suit his purposes, always avoids the "threes", and his guides in religion become four, Love, Art, Mathesis, and Magic.[6] It is in following these four that the religious Magus reaches the highest heights of perfection and power. All are connected with magic combined with Platonic *furor*. Love is the living virtue in all things, which the magician intercepts and which leads him from the lower things to the supercelestial realm by divine *furor*.[7] Art is the knowledge of how to become joined to the soul of the world.[8] By mathesis we learn how to abstract from matter, motion, and time and to reach intellectual contemplation of the intelligible species. Magic is of two kinds, one bad, the other very good. The good kind, by regulated faith and other laudable kinds of "contractions", corrects the erring, strengthens the weak, and, through the greatest demon, which is love, joins the soul to the divine power.[9] The magical love is then related to Ficino's theory of the two Venuses[10] (though

---

[1] *Op. lat.*, II (ii), pp. 180–2.   [2] *Ibid.*, pp. 189–93.

[3] Agrippa, *De occult. phil.*, III, 4.   [4] *Op. lat.*, II (ii), pp. 190–1.

[5] Agrippa, *De occult. phil.*, III, 5.

[6] "De quatuor rectoribus", *Op. lat.*, II (ii), pp. 195 ff.

[7] *Ibid.*, p. 195.   [8] *Ibid.*, p. 196.

[9] *Ibid.*, pp. 197–9. The power of the good magical religion which ". . . errantem corrigat, imbecillem et obtusum roborat et acuat" (*ibid.*, p. 198) may be compared with the powers which the Nolan claims for himself in the *Cena de le ceneri* (see above, p. 237).

[10] It would appear that the magician uses both the Venuses, both the vulgar one concerned with things of sense and the celestial one (*ibid.*, pp. 198–9). This is not inconsistent with Ficino's teaching but in Bruno becomes more "naturalist".

Bruno does not mention Ficino by name), thus making it possible for the religious magician to transform (as he does in the *Eroici furori*) into the Neoplatonising love poet.

What then is the answer from all this to our question as to what becomes of the Christian side of the Renaissance Magus in Bruno's outlook ? The answer is that it has disappeared, with the Christian and Trinitarian interpretation of the *Hermetica*, which Bruno abandoned. Nevertheless, Christ is a good and beneficent Magus, and Bruno feels a strong sense of solidarity with the Catholic Middle Ages, which encouraged great philosophers and contemplators, and gave them leisure and opportunity to reach the highest heights of heroic *furor*, the supreme "contractions", with their attendant magical insight and magical powers.

Thus Ficino's whole effort of Christian *Theologia Platonica*, with its *prisci theologi* and *magi* and its Christian Platonism, furtively combined with some magic, was as nothing in the eyes of Giordano Bruno, who, fully and boldly accepting the magical Egyptian religion of the *Asclepius* (and disregarding the supposed intimations of Christianity in the *Corpus Hermeticum*) saw the Egyptian magical religion as really Neoplatonic theurgy and ecstasy, the ascent to the One. And this was what it really was, for the Hermetic Egyptianism was Egyptianism interpreted by late antique Neoplatonists. However, the Bruno problem is not solved by simplifying him into a late antique Neoplatonist following an Egyptian mystery cult, for the whole great apparatus set in motion by Ficino and Pico had reached him, with all its emotional force, its Cabalist and Christian associations, its syncretism of all philosophies and religions, mediaeval as well as antique, and its magic.

Moreover—and this is to my mind one of the most significant aspects of Giordano Bruno—he came at the end of that sixteenth century with its terrible exhibitions of religious intolerance, in which men were seeking in religious Hermetism some way of toleration or union between warring sects. We saw in chapter X that there were many varieties of Christian Hermetism, Catholic and Protestant, most of them avoiding the magic. And then comes Giordano Bruno, taking full magical Egyptian Hermetism as his basis, preaching a kind of Egyptian Counter Reformation, prophesying a return to Egyptianism in which the religious difficulties will disappear in some new solution, preaching, too, a moral reform with emphasis on social good works and an ethic of social utility. As he stands in post-Reformation Oxford, the ex-Dominican has behind him the great ruins of the mediaeval past, and he deplores the destruction of the good works of those others, the predecessors, and the contempt for their philosophy, their philanthropy, and their magic.

Where is there such a combination as this of religious toleration, emotional linkage with the mediaeval past, emphasis on good works for others, and imaginative attachment to the religion and the symbolism of the Egyptians ? The only answer to this question that I can think of is—in Freemasonry, with its mythical link with the mediaeval masons, its toleration, its philanthropy, and its Egyptian symbolism. Freemasonry does not appear in England as a recognisable institution until the early seventeenth century, but it certainly had predecessors, antecedents, traditions of some kind going back much earlier, though this is a most obscure subject. We are fumbling in the dark here, among strange mysteries, but one cannot help wondering whether it might have been among the spiritually dissatisfied in England, who perhaps heard in Bruno's "Egyptian" message some hint of relief, that the strains of the Magic Flute were first breathed upon the air.

9 Title-page of Athanasius Kircher, *Ars Magna Lucis et Umbrae*,
Rome, 1646 (p. 124).

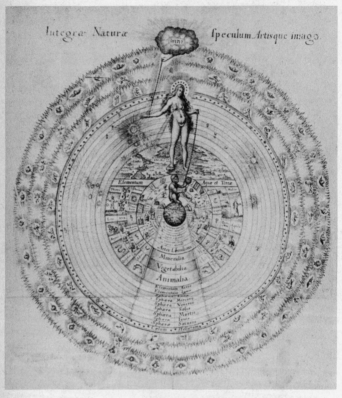

10   Nature and Art. From Robert Fludd, *Utriusque cosmi—
historia*, I, p. 3 (p. 144).

Chapter XV

GIORDANO BRUNO: HEROIC
ENTHUSIAST AND ELIZABETHAN

RUNO'S *De gli eroici furori*,[1] published in England in 1585 with a dedication to Philip Sidney, consists of a series of love poems, using Petrarchan conceits, accompanied by commentaries in which the poems are interpreted as referring to a philosophical or mystical love. In the dedication to Sidney,[2] Bruno explains that his Petrarchism is not of the ordinary kind, directed towards the love of a woman, but of a higher kind, belonging to the intellectual part of the soul. He is not against the "vulgar loves", and indeed recommends them in their proper place, but it is towards the "higher Cupid" that his loves are addressed. It is clear that he is referring to Ficino's commentary on Plato's *Symposium*, with its theory of the two Venuses, or the two Cupids, one higher and one lower.

To underline yet more clearly the mystical aim of his love poems, Bruno in the dedication compares them to the *Canticle*.[3] The divine light which is always present in things and which beats on the door of our senses was described by Solomon when he said: "Behold he standeth behind the wall, he looketh forth at the windows, shewing himself through the lattice."[4]

---

[1] There is an English translation by L. Williams, *The Heroic Enthusiasts*, London, 1887–9; and a French translation by Paul-Henri Michel, *Des fureurs héroiques*, Paris, 1954.

[2] *Eroici furori*, dedication (*Dial. ital.*, pp. 927–48).

[3] *Ibid.* (*Dial. ital.*, p. 932).

[4] *Ibid.*, quoting the *Canticle*, II, 9 (*Dial. ital.*, p. 937).

The use of love poetry to express philosophical or mystical aims has a vast tradition behind it. It may have been implied in the *amour courtois* from the start, though this is a much debated question; cases in which we know from the commentaries accompanying the poems that the aim is mystical are Dante's *Convivio* and Pico's commentary on the *Canzona* of Benivieni, both of which Bruno may have used.[1] And the *Canticle* attributed to Solomon was so interpreted both in the Christian mystical tradition and in Cabalist mysticism.[2]

The *Eroici furori* is arranged in sections, each section usually consisting of an emblem or device which is described in words, this description taking the place of what would be a plate in an illustrated emblem-book[3]; a poem, generally in sonnet form, using the conceits shown visually in the description of the emblem; and a commentary in which the meanings latent in the emblem and the poem are expounded.

The following is an example of the method.[4] The emblem consists of two stars in the form of two radiant eyes, with the motto *Mors et vita*. The accompanying sonnet is built round one of the commonest clichés of Petrarchist poetry, that of the lady's eyes as stars which the lover prays may be turned upon him although he knows that their glance has power to kill him. This central convention is supported by other equally conventional ideas. There is the worn face of the lover on which his sufferings are written:

> Writ by the hand of love may each behold
> Upon my face the story of my woes ...

There is the pride and cruelty of the lady who seems to torment her lover:

> But thou, so that thy pride no curb may know
> ... Thou dost torment ...

[1] See J. C. Nelson, *Renaissance Theory of Love: The Context of Giordano Bruno's "Eroici furori"*, Columbia University Press, 1958, pp. 15 ff.

[2] Bruno refers to such interpretations by "gli mistici e cabalistici dottori" (*Dial. ital.*, p. 932).

[3] I have compared some of Bruno's emblems with illustrations reproduced from emblem-books in my article "The Emblematic Conceit in Giordano Bruno's *De gli eroici furori* and in the Elizabethan sonnet sequences", *J.W.C.I.*, VI (1943), pp. 101–21 (also published in *England and the Mediterranean Tradition*, Oxford University Press, 1945, pp. 81–101).

[4] *Eroici furori*, pt. II, dial. 1 (*Dial. ital.*, pp. 1092 ff.).

This leads up to the image which is the foundation of the whole poem, that of the lady's eyes as lights or stars:

> Thou dost torment, by hiding from my view
> Those lovely lights beneath the beauteous lids.
> Therefore the troubled sky's no more serene . . .

Finally, there is the prayer to the lady, as to a goddess, to relent and turn her eyes upon the suffering lover even though her glance may kill him:

> Render thyself, O Goddess, unto pity!
> Open, O lady, the portals of thine eyes,
> And look on me if thou wouldst give me death![1]

The conceit dominating the whole sonnet, which is a tissue of Petrarchist phraseology, is that of the stars-eyes which had already been presented in the emblem.

In the commentary, the meanings are explained. The face upon which the story of the lover's woes is written is the soul seeking God. Here Bruno quotes metaphors from the Psalms: "My soul thirsteth after thee as a weary land", and, "I opened my mouth wide and panted; for I longed for thy commandments".[2] The pride of the lady is a metaphor, as God is sometimes said to be jealous, angry or asleep, signifying how often he withholds the vision of himself. "So the lights are covered with the eyelids, the troubled sky of the human mind does not clear itself by the removal of metaphors and enigmas."[3] By praying that the eyes should open, the lover is praying that the divine light should show itself. And the death which the glance of the eyes can give signifies the mystical death of the soul "which same is eternal life, which a man may anticipate in this life and enjoy in eternity."[4]

Standing by itself, without the commentary, the stars-eyes poem would look like a sonnet in a normal sonnet-sequence. With the commentary, we understand that the love poem is Bruno's prayer to his divinity.

And what is the divinity sought with so intense an aspiration

[1] *Ibid.* (*Dial. ital.*, p. 1093); Williams, II, p. 28.
[2] Psalm 143, v. 6, and Psalm 119, v. 131.
[3] *Eroici furori*, pt. II, dial. 1 (*Dial. ital.*, pp. 1093-4); Williams, II, p. 29.
[4] *Eroici furori*, ibid. (*Dial. ital.*, p. 1094): Williams, II, p. 30.

by the heroic enthusiast? It is, as he tells Sidney in the dedication, a religion of "natural contemplation" by which the divine light, which shines in things, "takes possession of the soul, raises it, and converts it into God."[1] The darts which wound the heart of the lover are "the innumerable individuals and species of things, in which shine the splendour of the Divine Beauty."[2] There are theologians who have taught how to

> seek the truth of nature in all her specific natural forms in which they contemplate the eternal essence, the specific substantial perpetuator of the eternal generation and vicissitude of things which are called after their founders and fabricators, and above them all presides the form of forms, the fountain of light, the truth of truths, the God of gods, for all is full of divinity, truth, being, and goodness.[3]

The sun, the universal Apollo, the absolute light, is reflected in its shadow, its moon, its Diana which is the world of universal nature in which the enthusiast hunts for the vestiges of the divine, the reflections of the divine light in nature, and the hunter becomes converted into what he hunts after, that is to say, he becomes divine. Hence the wonderful image of Actaeon and his dogs, hunting after the "vestiges", which recurs again and again in the *Eroici furori*, until, by progressive insights, the dogs, thoughts of divine things, devour Actaeon and he becomes wild, like a stag dwelling in the woods, and obtains the power of contemplating the nude Diana, the beautiful disposition of the body of nature. He sees All as One. He sees Amphitrite the ocean which is the source of all numbers, the monad, and if he does not see it in its essence, the absolute light, he sees it in its image, for from the monad which is the divinity proceeds this monad which is the world.[4]

The religion which is cultivated under the marvellously complex and beautiful imagery of the *Eroici furori* is the same as the Egyptian religion of the *Spaccio della bestia trionfante* which contemplated the divine in all things and knew how to rise through the innumerable species, in their astral groupings, to the unity of the divinity, and to the fountain of ideas above nature.

---

[1] *Eroici furori*, dedication (*Dial. ital.*, p. 937).
[2] *Ibid.*, pt. II, dial. 1 (*Dial. ital.*, p. 1107).
[3] *Ibid.*, pt. II, dial. 2 (*Dial. ital.*, p. 1123); Williams, II, pp. 65–6.
[4] *Ibid.* (*Dial. ital.*, pp. 1123–6); Williams, II, pp. 66–9. On *monas generat monadem*, see above, p. 150, note 2.

We have also, in the *Eroici furori* again the prophecy of the imminent return of the Egyptian religion through the revolution of the "great year of the world".

> The revolution of the great year of the world is that space of time in which, through the most diverse customs and effects, and by the most opposite and contrary means, it returns to the same again. . . . Therefore now that we have been in the dregs of the sciences, which have brought forth the dregs of opinions, which are the cause of the dregs of customs and of works, we may certainly expect to return to the better condition.[1]

For since the states of the world go by contraries; when it is in a very bad state it may expect to return to the good state. When it is in a very good state, as once in Egypt, the fall into darkness is to be expected.

> As in the case of Hermes Trismegistus, who, seeing Egypt in all the splendour of sciences and divinations, through which he considered that men were consorting with demons and gods and were in consequence most religious, he made that prophetic lament to Asclepius, saying that the darkness of new religions and cults must follow, and that of the then present things nothing would remain but idle tales and matter for condemnation. . . . And as in these days there is no evil nor injury to which we are not subject, so there is no good nor honour which we may not promise ourselves.[2]

The implication is that the world being now at its lowest ebb of "opinions" and "works", the nadir of that fall into darkness prophesied in the Lament, it may now expect to return back into such light and splendour as Egypt enjoyed in the days of Hermes Trismegistus when men consorted with gods and demons and were most religious.

With this should be compared the passage in the *Cena de le ceneri*[3] in which the Nolan announces himself as one who has had an experience of a kind now repressed (and we saw by comparison with a similar passage in *De umbris idearum* that the reference is to the repression of the Egyptian religion by statutes as described in the Lament), though this was "the light which rendered the souls of our fathers in antique times divine and heroic" and is to

---

[1] *Ibid.*, pt. II, dial. 1 (*Dial. ital.*, pp. 1072–3); Williams, II, p. 2.
[2] *Ibid.* (*Dial. ital.*, p. 1074); Williams, II, pp. 4–5.
[3] See above, p. 237.

be likened to the trance of the "furious" lover in the *Orlando furioso* whose "wit" has become separated from his body in the frenzy:

> Chi salirà per me, madonna, in cielo
> A riportarne il mio perduto ingegno.

In this passage we have both elements of the title, *De gli eroici furori*, of Bruno's book of mystical love poetry; an experience which makes the soul "divine and heroic" and can be likened to the trance of the *furor* of passionate love.

In the supreme Hermetic experience, as described in *Pimander*, in which the soul was transformed into the light of the divine *mens*, in the likeness of which it was created, the body "slept" during the whole vision, the senses being bound whilst the soul left the body to become divine.[1] The Hermetic trance is described by Milton in *Il Penseroso*, his poem on melancholy:

> Or let my lamp at midnight hour
> Be seen in some high lonely tower,
> Where I may oft outwatch the Bear,
> With thrice great Hermes, or unsphere
> The spirit of Plato, to unfold
> What worlds or what vast regions hold
> The immortal mind *that hath forsook*
> *Her mansion in this fleshly nook;*
> And of those daemons that are found
> In fire, air, flood, or under ground,
> Whose power hath a true consent
> With planet, or with element.

These lines (which to my mind have a Brunian ring through the mention of the Bear, where the reform of the heavens begins in the *Spaccio*) brilliantly suggest the atmosphere of the Hermetic trance, when the immortal mind forsakes the body, and religiously consorts with demons, that is to say, gains the experience which gives it miraculous or magical powers.

The trance is several times described or alluded to in the *Eroici furori*, as for example in the commentary on the emblem and poem on a boat without a pilot, where Iamblichus is referred to on the power of contemplation being sometimes so great that the soul leaves the body. Bruno here refers the reader to what he has

---

[1] See above, p. 23.

said about "contractions" in the book of the "thirty seals", on there being different "methods of contraction, of which some infamously, others heroically operate".[1] In another place he classifies the good kinds of enthusiasts, or enthusiastic contractions as being of two kinds. In one kind the divine spirit may enter an ignorant person who becomes inspired without himself understanding his inspiration. In the other kind, persons "skilful in contemplation and possessing innately a clear intellectual spirit . . . come to speak and act, not as vessels and instruments, but as chief artificers and experts." Of these two "the first are worthy, as is the ass which carries the sacraments; the second are as the sacred thing", that is they are divine.[2]

In short, I think that what the religious experiences of the *Eroici furori* really aim at is the Hermetic gnosis; this is the mystical love poetry of the Magus man, who was created divine, with divine powers, and is in process of again becoming divine, with divine powers.

The Hermetic core is, however, veiled under the apparatus of Neoplatonism. Where can one find Hermetism associated with the Neoplatonic *furores*? If one could find such an association explicitly made, this would explain Bruno's *Eroici furores* as Neoplatonic love frenzies directed towards Hermetic gnosis. And one can find such a passage, and it is where one would expect, namely in Cornelius Agrippa, the authority whom we have found to have been so constantly consulted by our magician.

The four degrees of *furor*, or enthusiasm, by which the soul re-ascends to the One, had been drawn up by Ficino, from Platonic sources, in his commentary on Plato's *Symposium* and elsewhere, as being, first the *furor* of poetic inspiration, under the Muses; second, religious *furor*, under Dionysius; third, prophetic *furor*, under Apollo; fourth the *furor* of love, under Venus. In this last and highest of the four degrees of inspiration, the soul is made One and recovers itself into the One. Agrippa in the *De occulta philosophia*[3] goes through the *furores*, in this order, and when he reaches the fourth and highest one, this is what he says:

As for the fourth *furor*, coming from Venus, it turns and transmutes the spirit of man into a god by the ardour of love, and renders him

[1] *Eroici furori*, pt. II, dial. 1 (*Dial. ital.*, p. 1091); Williams, II, p. 26.
[2] *Ibid.*, pt. I, dial. 3 (*Dial. ital.*, pp. 986–7); Williams, I, pp. 69–70.
[3] Agrippa, *De occult. phil.*, III, 46–9.

entirely like God, as the true image of God. Whence Hermes says: "O Asclepius, man is a great miracle, an animal to be admired and adored, for he passes into the nature of God, as though he were himself God. He has familiarity with the race of demons knowing himself to be of the same origin. He despises that part of his nature which is only human for he has put his hope in the divinity of the other part." The soul thus changed into God receives from God so great a perfection that it knows all things, by an essential contact with the divinity. . . . Changed into God by love . . . it can sometimes do works greater and more marvellous than nature itself, and such works are called miracles. . . . For man is the image of God, at least he who by the furor of Venus has been made like to God and lives only in the *mens*. . . . The Hebrew and Cabalist doctors say that the soul of man is the light of God, created in the image of the Word, first pattern of the cause of causes, substance of God, marked with a seal of which the character is the eternal Word. Having understood this, Hermes Trismegistus said that man is of such a kind that he is higher than the inhabitants of heaven, or at least possessing with them an equal fate.[1]

I think that this gives the answer as to the real meaning of the heroic love *furores* of the *Eroici furori*, they are the *furor* of Venus interpreted as the means whereby man becomes the *magnum miraculum* of the *Asclepius*, having miraculous powers and living in consort with the race of demons to which he himself belongs in his origin. We have also in the Agrippa passage the usual *Pimander-Genesis* equation about the creation of man, which explains why Cabalist, as well as Neoplatonic, mysticism may be used in describing the mystical loves of the *Eroici furori*, the real nature of which is that they are at bottom "Egyptian" loves, the loves of that *magnum miraculum* the Hermetic man, or the Magus.

One of the most striking and mysterious passages in the *Eroici furori* is that in which Actaeon, the hunter after the divine, sees a face of divine beauty mirrored in the waters of nature:

Here, amongst the waters, that is in the mirrors of similitude, in those works where shines the brightness of divine goodness and splendour, which works are symbolised by the waters superior and inferior, which are above and below the firmament, he sees the most beautiful bust and face . . . that it is possible to see.[2]

[1] *Ibid.*, III, 49.
[2] *Eroici furori*, pt. I, dial. 4 (*Dial. ital.*, p. 1007); Williams, I, p. 92.

Possibly an explanation of this might be that it reflects the wonderful description in *Pimander* of how the Magus man, having leant across the armature of the spheres, came down to the Nature which he loved and saw his own face, the image of her divine creator, mirrored in her waters.[1]

Agrippa might have quoted the words which come immediately after the *magnum miraculum* passage in the *Asclepius*, in which it is said that man "attaches all living beings, to which he knows himself to be linked by the celestial plan, to himself by the knot of love."[2] The love of the Magus man is operative love, the final basis of his magic, as is explained in the *Thirty Seals* where Bruno puts Love and Magic among the chief guides in the magical religion.

Thus, though there is not much overt magic in the *Eroici furori*, the work is, as it were, the spiritual record of one who aspired to be a religious Magus. And where one can, I think, detect the influence of Bruno's inner magics is in the Petrarcan love emblems themselves, those precise and clearly visualised descriptions of the darts, eyes, fires, tears and so on of the common Petrarcan conceits, which are distributed throughout the work, like a chain of beads in a rosary, and to which the poems and their commentaries are attached. Those familiar with the memory systems in which Bruno tries to unify the universal contents of memory by basing it on magic or talismanic images, will recognise the familiar pattern of his mind in the basing of the *Eroici furori* on the visual emblems. It may be suggested that the Petrarcan conceits as emblems are here being used as hieroglyphs (thus reverting to the origin of the emblem), or as images, signs, seals, characters, voices, in living, magical contact with reality—in contrast to the empty pedant language.

Just as the reform of the *Spaccio* really took place within a personality, so too the experiences of the *Eroici furori* are inward experiences. When Actaeon had "absorbed the divinity into himself" it was not necessary to search outside himself for it. For "divinity dwells within through the reformed intellect and will."[3] For Bruno, the Dignity of Man as Magus lies within, and it is

---

[1] See above, p. 24.

[2] *Asclepius*, in *C.H.*, II, p. 302. See above, pp. 35–6.

[3] *Eroici furori*, pt. I, dial. 4 (*Dial. ital.*, p. 1008); Williams, I, p. 93.

within that he applies on the imagination the magical techniques which induce the gnosis.

We have seen that Bruno always puts the Hermetic or Egyptian revelation first, but this does not mean that the other ingredient of the personality of the Renaissance Magus, Cabala, does not come in. In the *Eroici furori*, too, the element of Hebrew mysticism is not lacking. The dedication states, as we have seen, that the loves are to be likened to the mysticism of the Song of Songs, and in the text, Bruno twice alludes to the mystical "death of the kiss" of the Cabalists as an experience comparable to those which he is describing.[1] The *Eroici furori* is thus still, in a manner, within hail of Pico della Mirandola's synthesis, though the balance has been radically altered.

Moreover the Christian, or at least the Pseudo-Dionysian, element in the Renaissance Magus, is also not lacking in Bruno's work. There is a Christian influence in his mysticism when he speaks, as he often does, of the divine influences as "divine love". This, with his frequent quotations from the Psalms, lends an accent to his mysticism which is not to be found in the pagan gnosis of the *Hermetica*. And he compares his ineffable experiences to the negative teaching, not only of Pythagoras, but also of Dionysius (the Areopagite):

. . . the most profound and divine theologians say, that God is more honoured and loved by silence than by words; as one sees more by shutting the eyes to the species represented, than by opening them, therefore the negative theology of Pythagoras and of Dionysius is more celebrated than the demonstrative theology of Aristotle and the scholastic doctors.[2]

Thus the negative theology of Pseudo-Dionysius, which was so important to Ficino and to Pico in their efforts to achieve a Christian synthesis in their outlook, is not absent from the mysticism of the *Eroici furori*, though used with a difference (as a "negative" attitude to the divine revelation in the species or in nature). And the mention of the Areopagite comes within the curious episode of the "nine blind men" which is the conclusion

---

[1] *Ibid.*, pt. I, dial. 4, and pt. II, dial. 1 (*Dial. ital.*, pp. 1010, 1094); Williams, I, p. 96; II, p. 30.

[2] *Ibid.*, pt. II, dial. 4 (*Dial. ital.*, p. 1164); Williams, II, pp. 111–12.

and the culmination of the whole work.[1] These nine blind men bewail their blindness in nine poems, and then, when a sacred urn is opened by nymphs, they receive their sight, and as nine illuminati, sing nine songs to the accompaniment of nine different instruments of music. Beyond the obvious allusion to the nine spheres, there is in the nine illuminati, so Bruno explains in the dedication to Sidney,[2] a reference to the "nine orders of spirits" of the Christian theologians, that is, to the Pseudo-Dionysian celestial hierarchies. Thus Bruno's work builds up at its close to the angelic harmonies as the apex of the edifice, reflecting the scheme of the Christian Magus, in which Magia and Cabala are included within the Pseudo-Dionysian angelic hierarchies. Nevertheless, as usual, Bruno is not using the scheme in the normal way. The nine blind men who become the illuminati seem to be, not a system of external "metaphysics", like the angelic hierarchies, but all ingredients of one personality who becomes illumined with their illumination. Bruno, however, makes his concession to the normal scheme by putting the highest and final illumination of the heroic enthusiast in this form.

The experience which led to the illumination of the nine (who are the Nolan who has left with them his home in the "happy Campanian country") came when they visited the fane of Circe, where they prayed that "it might please heaven that in these days, as in past more happy ages, some wise Circe might make herself present who, with plants and minerals working her incantations, would be able to curb nature."[3] In answer to their prayer, Circe, daughter of the Sun, herself appeared "at whose appearance they saw vanish all the figures of the many other deities who ministered to her."[4] Thus, the supreme illumination was magical, which brings us back to the interpretation of the *Eroici furori* as the

---

[1] *Ibid.*, pt. II, dials. 4 and 5 (*Dial. ital.*, pp. 1140 ff.); Williams, II, pp. 88 ff.

[2] *Ibid.*, dedication (*Dial. ital.*, pp. 943–4). The "nove ciechi", he says, allude to the "nove sfere" which by Cabalists, Chaldeans, Magi, Platonists, and Christian theologians are distinguished into nine orders. Later (p. 944) he says that the Christian theologians speak of them as "nove ordini di spiriti".

[3] *Ibid.*, pt. II, dial. 5 (*Dial. ital.*, p. 1197); Williams, II, p. 114.

[4] *Ibid.* (*Dial. ital.*, p. 1168); Williams, II, p. 115. As always, Circe as presented by Bruno has completely discarded her traditional bad character and represents good magic.

experiences of a Magus, and one who was at bottom primarily a Hermetic optimist gnostic, though touched with infinitely complex influences of Neoplatonism, Cabalism, Pseudo-Dionysianism, and the traditions of Catholic philosophy which he had learned in his Dominican training.

Thus once again, Bruno appears as a Renaissance Magus, proceeding from the Ficino-Pico synthesis (via the *De occulta philosophia* of Agrippa) but shifting the balance so that the Hermetic element is predominant, with the Cabalist and Pseudo-Dionysian elements subservient to the leading Egyptian naturalism. Yet, it was not for nothing that Hermes Trismegistus had been inside the Church, as we saw him at Siena. Hermetism had been profoundly Christianised through its supposed prophetic allusions to Christianity. Religious Hermetism had been, and was being, fervently used by both Catholic and Protestant Christians of the sixteenth century, who, weary of the crimes and wars generated in the name of religion, were seeking a way of toleration and of union. Though Bruno's religion is purely "Egyptian" these strong religious feelings enter into the *Eroici furori*, giving to these love enthusiasms tones and accents which are often nearly Christian and are always inspired with a profound religious feeling. Christian religious Hermetists had tended to avoid the magic. Bruno, the full Egyptian Hermetist, stresses the magic, and in his message it is the love of the Magus which is the unifying power. The *Eroici furori* are the religious experiences of the reformer of the *Spaccio della bestia trionfante*, in which, in the Pleiades or in Gemini, all the gods, all the powers of the personality, speak in praise of love[1]; the intolerant "pedants", whether Catholic or Protestant, with their wars and persecutions, are driven from heaven; and a new age of new magical insights dawns for the individual and for the world. Such was the Reformation propounded by Giordano Bruno under the image of the return of the Egyptian religion.

Bruno's use of love emblems with mystical meanings in the *Eroici furori* is remarkably similar in its method to the transposition of "profane" love emblems into emblems of "sacred" love in the Jesuit religious emblem-books of the early seventeenth century. I have pointed this out elsewhere by studying, in connection with

---

[1] See above, p. 221.

Bruno's emblems, profane love emblems from the Vaenius collection, showing lovers wounded by darts from the eyes of the lady, or from Cupid's bow, together with sacred love emblems showing arrows of divine love wounding the heart, or rays from divine love penetrating the soul.[1] It is in exactly the same kind of way that Bruno uses the Petrarcan conceits in the *Eroici furori*, save that, with him, the darts of divine love, the rays from the divine light, which penetrate the heroic enthusiast reach him from God in nature. In view of his strong criticisms of the results of the Protestant Reformation in England, it might not have been difficult, in the confused Elizabethan atmosphere to confuse Bruno's message with the orthodox Counter Reformation, as George Abbot, afterwards Archbishop of Canterbury, perhaps did when he included his unfavourable presentation of the little Italian "juggler" at Oxford in his book entitled *The Reasons which Doctor Hill hath brought for the upholding of Papistry, which is falselie termed the Catholike Religion; Unmasked, and shewed to be very weake, and upon examination most insufficient for that purpose*, in which he combated at length the Catholic claim to superiority through superior power in working "miracles".[2]

Certainly basically different in doctrine from the orthodox Counter Reformation, Bruno's message carried with it a distinctive political outlook. The political message of the *Spaccio* is one of proffered friendship from France to England in the face of the menace from the Catholic reaction as represented by Spain which threatened both the French King, hemmed in by the Spain-inspired Catholic League, and the English Queen, constantly threatened by Spain-inspired "Popish Plots". Whether or not Bruno actually had a mandate from Henri III for this message, it is certain that he did live in the French embassy during the whole time of his visit to England, dangerous years full of fears, with the great crisis of the Spanish Armada not far ahead. Politically, Bruno is strongly anti-Spanish (this comes out particularly in passages in the *Spaccio* against the Spanish rule in Naples)[3] and

[1] In my article cited above, p. 276, note 1.
[2] See above, p. 208.
[3] In the "Regno Partenopeo", that is, in the Kingdom of Naples, Avarice rules "under the pretext of maintaining religion" (*Spaccio*, dial. 2; *Dial. ital.*, pp. 719–20).

he expresses unbounded admiration for Queen Elizabeth and her wise counsellors who are steering a way through many perils. In fact, Giordano Bruno joins in that strange and many-sided phenomenon, the Elizabeth cult, and may even have helped to shape some of its forms of expression, which is why I have called him in the title to this chapter "Heroic Enthusiast and Elizabethan".

> Where will you find one of the masculine gender who is the superior, or the equal, of this divine Elizabeth ("diva Elizabetta") who reigns in England and whom Heaven has so endowed and favoured, so firmly maintained in her seat, that others strive in vain to displace her with their words and actions? None in all her realm is more worthy than this lady herself; amongst the nobles, none is more heroic than she, amongst doctors, none more learned, amongst counsellors none have a wiser head.[1]

In after years, Bruno retracted this praise of a "heretic prince" to the Venetian Inquisitors:

> *Interrogatus*—whether he had ever praised any heretic or heretic princes, since he had been in contact with them for so long; what did he praise them for and what was his intention in this.
> *Respondit*—I have praised many heretics and also heretic princes; but I have not praised them as heretics, but solely for the moral virtues which they had, neither have I ever praised them as religious and pious, nor used such kind of religious epithets. And in particular in my book *De la causa, principio ed uno* I praise the Queen of England and call her "diva", not as a religious attribute, but as that kind of epithet which the ancients used to give to princes, and in England where I then was and where I composed this book, this title of "diva" used to be given to the Queen. And I was the more induced to name her thus because she knew me, for I was continually going with the ambassador to court. And I know that I erred in praising this lady, she being a heretic, and above all in attributing to her the name of "diva".[2]

More significant, however, than the passage in *De la causa*, and which he did not mention to the Inquisitors, are the praises of Elizabeth in the *Cena de le ceneri* where some vast, mystical universal empire is promised to the Queen of England. Bruno here joins in that mystical imperialism in the worship of the Virgin

---

[1] *De la causa*, dial. 1 (*Dial. ital.*, pp. 222–3).
[2] *Documenti*, pp. 121–2.

Queen, of which her name "Astraea", the Virgin of the Golden
Age, was a symbol:

> Of Elizabeth I speak, who by her title and royal dignity is inferior to
> no other monarch in the world; who for her wisdom and skill in
> sound government is second to none of those who hold the sceptre. . . .
> If her earthly territory were a true reflection of the width and
> grandeur of her spirit, this great Amphitrite would bring far horizons
> within her girdle and enlarge the circumference of her dominion to
> include not only Britain and Ireland but some new world, as vast as
> the universal frame, where her all-powerful hand should have full
> scope to raise a united monarchy.[1]

The use of the name "Amphitrite" of Elizabeth as the One, in the
sense of an imperial or universal ruler, might associate her mystical
empire with the Amphitrite seen in the vision of "natural" divinity
in the *Eroici furori* as the ocean of the fountain of ideas, the All
as One.

The *Eroici furori* is, indeed, bound up with the Elizabethan cult
in most curious and subtle ways. In the dedication to Sidney, the
Queen appears as "that unique Diana" and the vision of the nine
blind men is described as having taken place in a country "penitus
toto divisus ab orbe" that is in the British Isles, described as
situated "in the bosom of Ocean, of Amphitrite, of the divinity".[2]
In the actual description in the text of the vision in which the nine
became illuminated, the connection with England and with Elizabeth is made even more strikingly. When the nine, after all their
wanderings, come to the British Isles they meet with "lovely
graceful nymphs of Father Thames" of whom One is the chief,
and it is in the presence of this One that the urn opens of its own
accord, the vision is seen, the nine become the nine Illuminati.[3]
It is clear that the One in whose presence the mystic truth unveils
itself, is the unique Diana, the Amphitrite, in short, the "diva
Elizabetta" (the suspicions of the Inquisitors were justified about
this), who thus becomes the earthly ruler whom Bruno expects to
bring in his extraordinary new dispensation.

[1] *Cena*, dial. 2 (*Dial. ital.*, pp. 67–8). I have discussed this passage in
relation to the mystical imperialism surrounding Elizabeth in my article
"Queen Elizabeth as Astraea", *J.W.C.I.*, X (1947), pp. 80–1.

[2] *Eroici furori*, dedication (*Dial. ital.*, p. 496).

[3] *Ibid.*, pt. II, dial. 5 (*Dial. ital.*, pp. 1168–9, 1173); Williams, II, pp.
115–16, 119–20.

I also think that the *Eroici furori* reflects the cult of the Queen in the great revival of chivalry in her reign of which the Accession Day Tilts, in which the knights presented shields with devices on them to Elizabeth, were a manifestation. In the *Eroici furori*, a set of emblems or *imprese* is in the form of shields which the heroic enthusiasts come in bearing.[1] As I have suggested elsewhere, if one wishes to study the kind of abstruse meanings which might be drawn out of an *impresa* shield at an Accession Day Tilt "one cannot do better than read what Bruno has to say on, for example, a shield bearing a Flying Phoenix with the motto *Fata obstant*; or on one which showed an oak, with the words *Ut robori robur*; or, still more profound, on the one on which there was nothing but a sun and two circles with the one word *Circuit*."[2] The Accession Day Tilt imagery was formed at the Woodstock Entertainment of 1575, a theme of which was that the Hermit Hemetes, who was blind, received his sight when he came to the best country of the world and into the presence of the best ruler.[3] The Woodstock Entertainment was published in 1585,[4] the same year as the *Eroici furori*. As I have said, "Bruno, who elsewhere shows himself in sympathy with the Elizabeth cult, may have been intentionally linking his philosophical dialogues with the chivalrous romance woven around the Virgin Queen."[5]

Bruno's attitude to English knights, courtiers, and the English Queen, seems to be very different from his attitude to the Oxford "pedants" who had dispossessed their predecessors, suggesting that he saw Elizabethan society as divided, finding himself at home and understood in the innermost recesses of the Queen cult but antagonistic to some aspects of the Elizabethan world. That his reception into inner courtly circles was not entirely an invention of his own is indicated by the fact that some of the most recondite productions of Elizabethan poetry use his imagery.

The whole question of Bruno's influence in England will have to be studied afresh and from entirely new angles.

---

[1] *Ibid.*, pt. I, dial. 5 (*Dial. ital.*, pp. 1030 ff.); Williams, I, pp. 121 ff.
[2] See my article "Elizabethan Chivalry: The Romance of the Accession Day Tilts", *J.W.C.I.*, XX (1957), p. 24.
[3] "Elizabethan Chivalry", p. 11.
[4] *The Queen's Majesty's Entertainment at Woodstock*, 1575, London, 1585 (edited by A. W. Pollard, Oxford, 1910).
[5] "Elizabethan Chivalry", p. 24.

Chapter XVI

<hr style="border-top: dotted;">

GIORDANO BRUNO:
SECOND VISIT TO PARIS

<hr style="border-top: dotted;">

BRUNO was never to write again as he wrote in England. For one thing, he never again wrote in Italian, which suited him better than Latin. G. Aquilecchia has suggested that it may have been the influence of the new school of philosophical and scientific writing in England,[1] which used the vernacular, which led Bruno to write in Italian when in England. And the dialogue form which he used in the works written in England (except in the *Thirty Seals* which is the only one of these which is in Latin) suited his remarkable dramatic gifts. He felt such gifts stirring strongly within him and describes himself as hesitating between the Tragic and the Comic Muse.[2] Though he wrote no plays in England, some of the scenes in the dialogues—for example between the Pedants and the Philosopher in the *Cena*—are inimitable though scurrilous. Bruno's genius is developing towards poetic and literary expression in England, perhaps encouraged by happier conditions than he was ever to meet with again. He had during his English period a sense of backing and support, whether or not actually from the French king, certainly from the French ambassador who seems to have been very kind to him, and with whom he lived in a decent household probably for the only time in his life. And there was also, one feels sure, a mounting excitement in response to his message.

[1] See G. Aquilecchia, "L'adozione del volgare nei dialoghi londinesi di Giordano Bruno", *Cultura Neolatina*, XIII (1953), fascs. 2–3.

[2] *Eroici furori*, pt. I, dial. 1 (*Dial. ital.*, p. 956).

Further, with all its drawbacks in the way of rude people in the streets,[1] it was more peaceful in England than anywhere else in Europe, which was another reason why he admired the "diva Elizabetta":

> The fortunate success of her reign is the wonder of the present age; for, whilst in the heart of Europe the Tiber runs angrily, the Po looks threatening, the Rhone rages with violence, the Seine is full of blood, turbulent is the Garonne, the Ebro and the Tagus pursue their course with fury, the Moselle is disturbed, and unquiet flows the Danube, she with the splendour of her eyes for the space of five lustres and more has tranquillised the great Ocean which peacefully receives into the ample ebb and flow of its vast bosom her dear Thames, after it has taken its winding way past grassy banks in happiness and safety, secure from all alarms.[2]

In October, 1585, Mauvissière, the French ambassador, left England, having been recalled, and Bruno went with him in his suite. The channel crossing was not fortunate as the ship was attacked and robbed by pirates.[3] And when the travellers arrived in Paris, it was clear that the Seine would indeed soon again be full of blood. The situation was ugly in the extreme. Guise had already mobilised his forces, with Spanish assistance; in July, Henri III had been forced to conclude the Treaty of Nemours which annulled the liberties formerly enjoyed by the Huguenots and showed that he had practically given up to Guise and the Spain-inspired extreme reaction of the Catholic League. In September, the pro-Spanish Pope, Sixtus V, had launched his bull against Henry of Navarre and the Prince of Condé, proclaiming that as heretics these princes could never succeed to the throne of France, a move which made war inevitable. The League preachers were in full voice in Paris with their frightful sermons, and the unfortunate King had retreated more and more into his devotions, only emerging for those weird penitent processions. This situation, immensely changed for the worse since Bruno was last in Paris,

---

[1] See the amusing descriptions in the *Cena* of the imaginary journey along the Strand from the French embassy to Fulke Greville's house.

[2] *De la causa*, dial. 1 (*Dial. ital.*, p. 223). The "sanguinosa" Seine refers to the Massacre of St. Bartholomew.

[3] See the letters from Mauvissière to Florio quoted in my *John Florio, The Life of an Italian in Shakespeare's England*, Cambridge, 1934, pp. 71–2.

would mean that he could no longer count on any royal support, and indeed it accounts for the recall of Mauvissière, and his replacement as ambassador in England by Châteauneuf, who was a Guisard.[1] There would be no more Suppers at the French embassy, no more mysterious love poetry emanating from its occupants, and Philip Sidney, to whom that mysterious love poetry had been dedicated, left England a month after Bruno to fight against Spain in the Low Countries, where he was killed in the following year.

Bruno told the Venetian Inquisitors that on this second visit to Paris he lived for the most part at his own expense and in the society of "gentlemen whom I knew".[2] This meagre information has been supplemented by the discovery of the mentions of Bruno in the letters of Jacopo Corbinelli to Gian Vincenzo Pinelli.[3] Corbinelli, an accomplished scholar, was employed by Henri III in various capacities and was perhaps on more intimate terms with that monarch than any other Italian.[4] He was employed by Pinelli to send him reports of political and literary news from Paris and to procure him books and manuscripts for the magnificent library which he was forming at Padua. Corbinelli was a loyal member of the group round Henri III and strongly anti-Guise and anti-League. His correspondence with Pinelli is not only rich in literary and learned matters but represents a certain current of political and religious feeling running in the late sixteenth century between some circles in the Veneto and some circles in France. These circles, though Catholic, looked to Henry of Navarre for some solution of the European *impasse*. Closely in touch with Corbinelli, and constantly mentioned in his letters, was Piero Del Bene, Abbot of Belleville, who worked as an agent for Navarre.[5] Now, two of the books which Bruno published in Paris in 1586

[1] *Ibid.*, p. 84.

[2] *Documenti*, p. 85.

[3] See my article "Giordano Bruno: Some New Documents", *Revue internationale de philosophie*, XVI (1951), fasc. 2, pp. 174–99. I here published the hitherto unknown references to Bruno in the Corbinelli-Pinelli correspondence and endeavoured to put them into the historical setting.

[4] See my *French Academies of the Sixteenth Century*, p. 175.

[5] See E. Picot, *Les Italiens en France au XVIe siècle*, Bordeaux, 1901–18, pp. 91 ff., and my "Giordano Bruno: Some New Documents".

are dedicated to this Del Bene,[1] and this fact, together with the friendly mentions of Bruno in Corbinelli's letters, makes it fairly certain that the "gentlemen whom I knew" with whom he was on friendly terms during his second visit to Paris were probably Corbinelli, Del Bene and their circle—that is to say, a group of Italians faithful to Henri III, interested in Henry of Navarre and his destiny, and in contact with Pinelli at Padua. As we shall hear later, Bruno seems to have placed hopes in Navarre as a possible channel through which the hoped for new liberal and tolerant dispensation might come.

An amazing feature of Bruno's second stay in Paris—which, however, should not amaze the reader too much if I have succeeded in putting across to him that Giordano Bruno is not like other people—was the episode of Fabrizio Mordente and his compass.[2] Fabrizio Mordente had invented a new kind of compass, which by adjustment of a device on its arms, could produce "wonderful results necessary for Art which is the imitator of Nature" as Mordente claims in the short description, illustrated with a picture of it and a diagram, which he published in Paris in 1585.[3] Mordente's compass has been suggested as a possible fore-

---

[1] The *Figuratio Aristotelici physici auditus*, Paris, 1586 (*Op. lat.*, I (iv), pp. 129 ff.), and the dialogues about Fabrizio Mordente recently published by G. Aquilecchia (see next note).

[2] Two dialogues by Bruno about Fabrizio Mordente's compass have long been known (*In Mordentium* and *De Mordentii circino*, published as *Dialogi duo de Fabricii Mordentis*, Paris, 1586) and were published in the edition of the Latin works (*Op. lat.*, I (iv), pp. 223 ff.). Two others (*Idiota Triumphans* and *De somnii interpretatione*) have been located in an edition of 1586, dedicated to Piero Del Bene, of which one copy only exists. (See John Hayward, "The Location of First Editions of Giordano Bruno", *The Book Collector*, V, 1956, p. 154.) All four dialogues have now been published together by G. Aquilecchia (Giordano Bruno, *Due dialoghi sconosciuti e due dialoghi noti*, Rome, 1957). In his introduction, Aquilecchia relates the newly discovered dialogues to the information about Bruno's quarrel with Mordente which I found in the Corbinelli-Pinelli correspondence. Aquilecchia's volume thus brings together all the material about the extraordinary compass episode.

[3] *Il Compasso, & Figura di Fabritio Mordente di Salerno: con li quali duoi mezzi si possono fare un gran numero di mirabili effetti, al tutto necessarij all'Arte, imitatrice della Natura. . .* , Paris, 1585. Cf. Aquilecchia, *Due dialoghi*, introduction, p. xvii.

runner of Galileo Galilei's invention of the proportional compass.[1] Bruno knew Mordente who was in Paris at the time and was immensely struck by the compass. He mentioned it to his patient listener, the librarian of the Abbey of St. Victor, describing Mordente as the "god of geometricians", and adding that, since Mordente did not know Latin, he, Bruno, would publish his invention in Latin for him.[2] This he did with a vengeance, for he wrote four dialogues about Mordente's compass, in which he patronised the inventor for not having seen the full meaning of his divine invention, as he, Bruno, has seen it. We know from Corbinelli's letters that Mordente, not unnaturally, "fell into a brutal rage"[3]; that he bought up the edition of the dialogues and destroyed them[4] (missing the two copies, one complete and the other incomplete, which have reached us); and further that he "went to the Guise" for support against Bruno.[5] The last item in this news was pretty frightening, in a Paris full of Guisards armed to the teeth.

To understand this episode, we should remind ourselves of Bruno and Copernicus in the *Cena de le ceneri*; how that worthy man, Copernicus, had indeed made a great discovery without himself fully understanding it, for he was only a mathematician; how the Nolan saw the true meaning of the Copernican diagram, saw it blazing with divine significance, a hieroglyph of divine truth, a hieroglyph of the return of Egyptianism, mysteries which were hidden from the poor, blind Oxford pedants. I think that something of the same sort happened when the Nolan saw Mordente's compass and its diagram.

In one of the dialogues by Bruno about the compass, Mordente is praised to the skies for having found something which even "curious Egypt, grandiloquent Greece, operative Persia, and

---

[1] A. Favaro, *Galileo Galilei e lo studio di Padova*, Florence, 1883, I, p. 226.

[2] *Documenti*, p. 43.

[3] "contro al Nolano e in una collera bestiale il nostro Fabritio". Corbinelli to Pinelli, February 16th, 1586 (Ambrosiana, T.167 sup., f. 180).

[4] "A Fabritio costa parecchi scudi per comparar et far abbruciar il Dialogo del Nolano." Corbinelli to Pinelli, April 14th, 1586 (Ambrosiana, T.167 sup., f. 183).

[5] "Il Mordente andò al Guisa et vuole ch'ei pigli il mondo co suoi ingegni." Corbinelli to Pinelli, August 4th, 1586 (Ambrosiana, T.167 sup., f. 187).

subtle Arabia"[1] did not know, a collection of ancient wisdoms which shows the way Bruno's mind is working; and in the strange *Insomnium* added to these dialogues it is clear from the opening phrase that he thinks that the invention has to do with "wandering stars" and is a "divine mathesis".[2] This word "mathesis" is also used in the dialogue so strangely called *Idiota Triumphans* and it is highly significant. For "mathesis", as we know from the *Thirty Seals*, is not mathematics, but one of the four "guides in religion" of which the others are Love, Art, and Magic.[3] The theme of the *Idiota Triumphans* is that Mordente has spoken from "inspired ignorance"; it is he who is the "Triumphant Idiot", and this is worked out with an analysis of the kind of inspiration which can come to simple people who speak in an inspired way without fully understanding what they are saying, as compared with the higher types who have a full conscious grasp of their inspired message.[4] We have already met this argument in a passage in the *Eroici furori* where the simple type of inspired person was likened to the Ass which carries the Sacraments.[5] Here the comparison is with Balaam's ass, and it is clear that this is the kind of ass which Mordente is. Bruno then passes straight on to the sacred theme of the holy worship of Egyptians, how this was a worship of God in things, and how they passed up beyond it to the divinity itself.[6]

---

[1] *Op. lat.*, I (iv), p. 255; *Due dialoghi, etc.*, ed. Aquilecchia, p. 55.

[2] *Op. lat., vol. cit.*, p. 256; *Due dialoghi, ed. cit.*, p. 57.

[3] The meanings of the word *mathesis* seem somewhat variable. The Greek μάθησις means learning or education in general. The Latin *māthēsis* can mean, according to Lewis and Short: (1) mathematics; (2) astrology. It is in the latter sense that the late Latin astrologer Julius Firmicus Maternus uses it. According to John of Salisbury (*Policraticus*, I, 9; II, 18, ed. Webb, pp. 49, 101–2) a lot depends on how the word is accented; *máthesis*, pronounced with the penultimate syllable short, is the foundation of astrology; *mathésis*, with the penultimate long, is magic.

Since Bruno does not accent the word, John of Salisbury's rule for the identification of its meaning cannot be applied. It is quite clear, however, that in the passage referred to above where he takes *mathesis* as one of his Four Guides he is associating the word with magic.

[4] *Idiota Triumphans* in *Due dialoghi, etc.*, ed. Aquilecchia, pp. 6–7.

[5] See above, p. 281.

[6] *Idiota Triumphans, ed. cit.*, pp. 6–7. As Aquilecchia points out (*Due dialoghi*, introduction, p. xxi), the *Idiota Triumphans* connects with the *Spaccio* and the *Cabala* through the appearance in all three works of the personage "Saulino" or "Savolinus", supposed to refer to a maternal relative of Bruno's.

It is most understandable that Mordente objected to being called a triumphant idiot, or Balaam's ass, but (I believe) that Bruno means that he has shown forth a divine truth which he does not understand himself but which those with deeper insight—such as the Nolan—can acclaim as a wonderful revelation. Later on it is said quite clearly that by "mathesis" Mordente's figure is to be mystically interpreted, after the manner of the Pythagoreans and the Cabalists.[1] In short, Mordente's compass has become what Kepler calls Hermetics, or mathematical figures used, not mathematically, but with "Pythagorean intentions".

The Pythagorean and numerological approach to the diagram was traditional in the Middle Ages and this was a tradition which the Renaissance occultism not only sanctioned but enlarged and elaborated with Hermetics and Cabalism. It was not until the next century that people began to react consciously from this kind of thing and in Bruno's time it was rampantly fashionable, as can be illustrated from George Peele's description of the studies of the Wizard Earl of Northumberland:

> Renowmed (*sic*) lord, Northumberland's fair flower,
> The Muses' love, patron, and favourite,
> That artisans and scholars dost embrace,
> And clothest Mathesis in rich ornaments;
> That admirable mathematic skill,
> Familiar with the stars and zodiac,
> To whom the heaven lies open as her book;
> By whose directions undeceivable,
> Leaving our schoolman's vulgar trodden paths,
> And following in the ancient reverend steps
> Of Trismegistus and Pythagoras,
> Through uncouth ways and unaccessible,
> Dost pass into the spacious pleasant fields
> Of divine science and philosophy.[2]

What is amazing is the incredible boldness with which Bruno throws out such maddeningly provocative publications as the *Cena de le ceneri* against the Oxford doctors (Copernicus might well have bought up and destroyed all copies of the *Cena* had he been alive) and these Mordente dialogues. Or did he think, as with the

[1] *Idiota Triumphans*, ed. cit., p. 12.
[2] George Peele, *The Honour of the Garter*, in Peele, *Works*, ed. A. H. Bullen, 1888, II, pp. 316–20.

Copernican diagram in the *Cena*,[1] that the mathesis of Fabrizio's compass was a prophecy that the period of pedantry was coming to an end and that the Catholic League would shortly disappear in the return of Egyptianism? At any rate, Mordente "went to the Guise", a most terrifying pedant.

I do not pretend to have fully solved here the mysteries of the Bruno-Mordente controversy. As I pointed out in my article, Corbinelli's reports to Pinelli about the quarrel come in the context of his reports on the politico-religious situation and particularly of reactions to the papal bull against Navarre.[2] When the Corbinelli-Pinelli correspondence is fully published,[3] we may be able to see Bruno's activities in Paris at this time in a clearer light.

Bruno's other great exploit during this second period in Paris was the public debate in the Collège de Cambrai to which he summoned the doctors of Paris to hear him propound "one hundred and twenty articles on nature and the world against the Peripatetics." These articles were published in Paris in 1586 by the author, under the name of his disciple, Jean Hennequin, and with a dedication to Henri III and a letter to the Rector of the University of Paris, Jean Filesac.[4] This letter is, for Bruno, rather mild and almost modest, compared, for example, with his address to the Vice-chancellor and doctors of Oxford. He thanks Filesac for the past kindness of the University of Paris to him, presumably referring to that readership which he had held on his previous

---

[1] It is rather curious to remember now that Bruno's interpretation of the diagram turns on his mistaken belief that the point representing the earth is really a mark made by the foot of the compass in describing the circle in which both earth and moon revolve (see above, p. 241).

[2] "Giordano Bruno: Some New Documents", pp. 188 ff. G. Aquilecchia adds some interesting new points to the background of the quarrel, for example that it appears from one of Corbinelli's letters that Mordente was a Leaguer (*Due dialoghi, etc.*, introduction, p. xxii, note).

[3] Only fragments of it have been published, chiefly by R. Calderini De-Marchi, *Jacopo Corbinelli et les érudite français*, Milan, 1914.

[4] *Centum et viginti articuli de natura et mundo . . . per Ioh. Hennequinum . . . sub clipeo & moderamine Iordani Bruni Nolani*, Paris, 1586. Only the title is given in *Op. lat.*, II (ii), p. 221, for the work was reprinted at Wittenberg in 1588 with another title, namely *Camoeracensis Acrotismus*, Wittenberg, 1588. This edition is published in *Op. lat.*, I (i), pp. 53 ff.

visit to Paris, and tells him that he is about to leave Paris.[1] Apparently the publication of the *Centum et viginti articuli* took place before the debate, as a programme of the proposed proceedings. The work was published again, substantially in the same form, two years later at Wittenberg, where Bruno then was, with the title *Camoeracensis Acrotismus*.[2]

The worthy Cotin (this was the name of the librarian of the Abbey of St. Victor) was much interested in this public appearance of the striking habitué of his library and from his diary we learn that the dates on which Bruno summoned "les lecteurs royaux et tous à l'ouïr dedans Cambray" were the 28th and the 29th of May (1586), which were "les mercredy et jeudy de la semaine de Pentecoste".[3] The theses were sustained by H... ...Bruno's disciple, who was in the "great chair", whilst B... ...f was in "a little chair, near the door into the gard... ...was possibly a precautionary measure, in case it becam... ...o escape—which it did.

The opening oration, read by Hennequin, contai... which are almost word for word the same, except that ... Latin, as passages in the *Cena de le ceneri*. We have been imp... in a dark dungeon, whence only distantly could we see the ... stars.[5] But now we are released. We know that there is one heave... a vast ethereal region in which move those flaming bodies which announce to us the glory and the majesty of God.[6] This moves us to contemplate the infinite cause of the infinite effect; we see that the divinity is not far distant but within us, for its centre is everywhere, as close to dwellers in other worlds as it is to us. Hence we should follow not foolish and dreamy authorities but the regulated sense and the illuminated intellect. The infinite universe is a conception more worthy of God's majesty than that it should be finite.[7] The most ingenious professors of the sciences are summoned to judge of these matters in the presence of the majesty of truth, acting not wickedly and rigidly, but in an equable and pacificatory spirit.[8]

---

[1] *Op. lat.*, I (1), pp. 56–8.
[2] "Camoeracensis" refers to Cambrai, that is to the Collège de Cambrai where the debate was held.
[3] *Documenti*, p. 44. [4] *Ibid.*, p. 45.
[5] *Op. lat.*, I (i), pp. 66–7. [6] *Ibid.*, pp. 68–9.
[7] *Ibid.*, p. 70. [8] *Ibid.*, p. 71.

According to Cotin, when this speech was over, Bruno arose in his place, calling for anyone to defend Aristotle and attack him. No one said anything and so he shouted more loudly, as though he had gained the victory. But then arose a young advocate called "Rodolphus Calerius", who in a long speech defended Aristotle from the calumnies of Bruno, having prefaced this by remarking that the "lecteurs" had not spoken before because they deemed Bruno unworthy of a reply. He called upon Bruno to reply and defend himself, but Bruno was silent and left the place. The students caught hold of him, saying that they would not let him go unless he renounced his calumnies against Aristotle. Finally he escaped from their hands, on condition that he should return the next day to reply to the advocate. The latter put up notices announcing that he would be there the next day. And on the next day "Rodolphus Calerius" took the chair, and pursued very gracefully the defence of Aristotle against the impostures and the vanity of Bruno, calling upon him again to reply. "But Brunus did not appear, and has not since then been seen in this town."[1]

> I have never taught anything directly against the Catholic Christian religion," said Bruno to the Venetian Inquisitors, "though I was judged to have done so indirectly in Paris; where, however, I was allowed to treat of certain disputations under the title of *A Hundred and Twenty Articles against the Peripatetics* and other vulgar philosophers, printed with the permission of the superiors, as it was allowable to treat of these according to the way of natural principles, not prejudicial to the truth according to the light of faith. In this way one can read and treat the works of Aristotle and Plato, which are also indirectly contrary to the faith, and much more contrary to it than the articles philosophically propounded and defended by me.[2]

One of the most significant features of the scene in the Collège de Cambrai is the part played in it by this "Rodolphus Calerius" who looks as though he had been "inspired" (not in the sense of heroic *furor*) to silence Bruno. Cotin adds a note giving the information that this "Calerius" is at present "retired with Monsieur Du Perron, who is the king's orator and chronicler".[3] Jacques Davy Du Perron was an intimate member of the King's circle and gave admired spiritual discourses, full of *prisca theologia* and religious Hermetism at the spiritual academy at Vincennes, one of those religious groups into which Henri III

[1] *Documenti*, pp. 45–6.   [2] *Ibid.*, p. 92.   [3] *Ibid.*, p. 46.

retreated more and more in these anguished years.[1] The "Rodolphus Calerius" who is retired with Du Perron must be Raoul Cailler, also one of the Vincennes group and who wrote the following admiring sonnet about a spiritual discourse by Du Perron which he had heard there:

> Quand je t'oy discourir de la Diuinité,
> J'admire en ton esprit une grandeur Diuine,
> Qui tout le monde embrasse, & qui ne se termine
> Que par les larges fins de son infinité.
>
> J'admire tes discours remplis de verité,
> Qui font qu'à l'immortel le mortel s'achemine,
> Par les diuers degrez de ceste grand'machine,
> Où tu nous vas guidant à l'immortalité.
>
> Comme l'Ame du monde en ce grand tout enclose
> Fait viure, fait sentir, fait mouuoir toute chose:
> Tout de mesme ton Ame infuse en ce grand corps,
>
> Void tout ce qui se fait en la terre & en l'onde,
> Void les effects des cieux & leurs diuers accords:
> Puis fait en nos esprits ce que Dieu fait au monde.[2]

This seems to present Du Perron somewhat as a religious Magus who has become one with the soul of the world. The fact that it was the author of this sonnet, and the friend of Du Perron, who intervened against Bruno at the Cambrai debate, shows that that intervention was inspired, not by the Guise or the Leaguers, but by the King's own group. Henri III, as it were, resigns his celestial seat in the Corona Australis as leader of the reform of the heavens—too dangerous a position—and it must be made clear to his enemies that Bruno is disowned. As I have suggested in my book on *The French Academies of the Sixteenth Century*, Bruno's activities in England from the French embassy may have done Henri no good with his virulent enemies—if news of them got abroad in France—who were always on the look-out for material with which to discredit him in the eyes of his Catholic subjects.[3]

---

[1] See my *French Academies of the Sixteenth Century*, pp. 162 ff.

[2] Poem by Raoul Cailler in Jacques Davy Du Perron, *Discours spirituel*, Leyden, 1600. The *Discours spirituel* had been delivered before Henri III at Vincennes. See *The French Academies*, pp. 170, 230.

[3] *French Academies*, pp. 231 ff.

Bruno must have known from Cailler's intervention that the French royal support which he had had, or had fancied that he had, was no longer there.

Bruno's action in provoking this debate cannot have been from the motive of trying to reinstate himself in some position, either with the university or with the King, for he had already planned to leave Paris, having no doubt realised that a Paris preparing to become Paris under the League was no place for him. And he would have known from Corbinelli, who was very much in the know about the situation, that Henri's position was hopeless and that he could do nothing for him. Why then did he provoke the debate, very dangerous to himself? Partly, perhaps, from constitutional inability ever to keep still or silent. Bruno's character is a most difficult one to assess; on the one hand there is the constant self-advertisement and bombast, but on the other hand there is also a sense of mission which was certainly genuine. To suggest, as I think he means to do, at such a time and in such a place, that the "religion of the world" might be a better religion than Christianity as interpreted by the Catholic League was a very brave thing to do—even if he did sit near the door into the garden and failed to turn up on the next day. The explanation of that failure might well be that he had not expected opposition from the quarter from which it came.

The indefatigable man also published during this year (1586) in Paris a long work entitled *Figuratio Aristotelici Physici Auditus*,[1] dedicated to Piero Del Bene, to whom the dialogues about Mordente's compass were also dedicated. This Aristotelian *Figuratio* is one of the most obscure of all Bruno's works—and that is saying a great deal. It is a kind of mnemonics; fifteen principles of Aristotelian physics are subsumed under images, such as Arbor Olympica, Minerva, Thetis, Natura or the Superior Pan, and so on; and these are to be arranged on a diagram, which is certainly not mathematical but "mathesis". It has something of the appearance of the square in which the houses of a horoscope are drawn, but gone mad, and breaking up into all kinds of irregular geometrical figures.[2] We have here some sort of combination of classical mnemonics using images on places on a building, with "mathesis"

---

[1] *Op. lat.*, I (iv), pp. 129 ff.
[2] *Ibid.*, p. 139.

and heaven knows what other complexities invented with crazy ingenuity. I suspect this work of containing the "message" in some form or other.

The output in Paris thus corresponds roughly to the output in England. There is a strange mnemonics corresponding to the *Thirty Seals*. The dialogues about Mordente, particularly the *Idiota Triumphans* carry on themes of the *Cabala del Cavallo Pegaseo* and of the *Spaccio*. The Collège de Cambrai debate with the Parisian doctors corresponds to the brush with the Oxford doctors and repeats the themes of the *Cena de le ceneri*. But the Parisian output is much more obscure and crabbed in form; there is nothing corresponding to the marvellous imagery which Bruno bequeathed to Elizabethan poetry in the *Eroici furori*, nor to the brilliant drama, with bursts into lyricism, with which the contest with the English pedants (Protestant intolerance) is presented in the *Cena*. The atmosphere of Catholic pedantry rife in Paris was perhaps so dire that it quenched the genius, at least for the time being.

That all the works published in Paris at this time were dedicated to the agent of Navarre, Piero Del Bene (except the dedication of the programme of the Cambrai debate to Henri III, which drew a blank) may suggest that Bruno was looking towards Navarre, like his friend Corbinelli and his correspondent in Padua, as the prince to support in these times. Henri III and his mother were also looking towards Navarre, and secret emissaries were being sent down into the south to try to persuade him to ease the situation by becoming a Catholic. In later times, when Henri was dead and when Navarre finally came out victorious after those frightful wars of the League which destroyed the Renaissance civilisation of France, it was actually Jacques Davy Du Perron, Bishop of Evreux, and eventually a cardinal, who played the major part in the conversion of Navarre and in the negotiations for his reception into the Church as Henri IV, the Most Christian King of France.[1] This has a bearing on Bruno's life and death because it was almost certainly, as Corsano has pointed out, because of the universal European hopes aroused by the accession of Henry IV to the crown of France that Bruno took the fatal step of returning to Italy.[2]

[1] See *The French Academies*, pp. 193 ff.
[2] See A. Corsano, *Il pensiero di Giordano Bruno*, pp. 290 ff.

One other event of this Parisian period must be mentioned, for it is an important piece in the complex Bruno problem. During this time he made an effort to be received back into the Catholic Church. He approached Mendoza whom he had known in London and who was now in Paris, and also the papal nuncio, the Bishop of Bergamo, with this intention, but to no effect. He wanted to return to the Church and to be absolved so that he could partake of the sacrament of the Mass; but he was not willing to return into his Order.[1] Was this move on Bruno's part merely calculation, since he was once more in a Catholic country? It seems to me that Bruno never calculated; it was not in his nature to do so; all his actions throughout his life were rash and spontaneous. This wish to return to the Church was therefore probably perfectly spontaneous and sincere, and fits in with his views. He disliked heretics and their contempt for "works"; he had an entirely Catholic formation of temperament to which Protestantism could never be congenial. And the great reform was to come somehow or other within a Catholic framework, when difficulties about the Sacrament had been removed, which could be "easily done" as he explained to the librarian of St. Victor. I therefore think that this attempt to return to the Church at this time in Paris was quite in character and quite sincere. The new dispensation was to be an Egyptianised and tolerant Catholic and universal religion, reformed in its magic and reformed in its ethics.

Bruno was still in Paris on August 4th, 1586, the date of Corbinelli's letter to Pinelli in which he says that Giordano fears "some affront for having scolded poor Aristotle so much",[2] adding

---

[1] *Documenti*, p. 104; cf. Spampanato, *Vita di Giordano Bruno*, p. 392.

[2] "il Giordano s'ando con Dio per paura di qualche affronto, tanto haveva lavato il capo al povero Aristotele". Corbinelli to Pinelli, August 4th, 1586 (Ambrosiana, T.167 sup., f. 187). See "Giordano Bruno: Some New Documents", p. 185. In a previous letter of June 6th, Corbinelli says, after mentioning the Cambrai debate, "I think he (Bruno) will be stoned by this university. But soon he is going to Germany. Enough that in England he has left very great schisms in those schools. He is a pleasant companion, an Epicurean in his way of life" (Ambrosiana T.167 sup., f. 190; cf. "Giordano Bruno; Some New Documents", p. 181). Apart from the interesting side-light on Bruno's personality, it is valuable to know that Corbinelli was under the impression that Bruno's mission in England had been rather successful.

Corbinelli was a collector of works by Bruno, copies of which, ultimately deriving from his library, are in the Biblioteca Trivulziana at

that Mordente has "gone to the Guise". It must have been soon after this that Bruno left Paris. He told the Venetian Inquisitors that he left "because of the tumults",[1] which was true enough.

He went to Germany.

[1] *Documenti*, p. 85.

Milan. Amongst them is a copy of the *Cena* inscribed in a late sixteenth-century hand "Al Sr. Corbinello". See R. Tissoni, "Lo sconosciuto fondo bruniano della Trivulziana", *Atti della Accademia delle Scienze di Torino*, Vol. 93 (1958–9).

Chapter XVII

GIORDANO BRUNO IN GERMANY

EACH of Bruno's periods needs a separate study, relating the works which he published in each place to the conditions prevailing in the place at the time. In the foregoing chapters, I have tried to do something of the kind, though not in sufficient detail, for the first Parisian period, the English period, and the second Parisian period. The German period I shall have to pass over even less adequately, doing little more than indicate what seem to me the points of major importance.

At Wittenberg, where Bruno stayed for two years (1586–8) we see him in the rôle of university teacher or professor, for the doctors of Wittenberg, to his unbounded delight and gratitude, accepted him and allowed him to teach in their schools. In a dedication to the Wittenberg senate, he says that though he was "a man of no name or authority among you, escaped from the tumults of France, supported by no princely commendation . . . you thought me worthy of the kindliest welcome, enrolled me in the album of your academy, and gave me a place in a body of men so noble and learned that I could not fail to see in you, neither a private school nor an exclusive conventicle, but, as becomes the Athens of Germany, a true university."[1] Luther's university passed the severe test of a visit from the Nolan with honours and he has nothing but good to say of it. He evidently liked the Lutherans

[1] Dedication of the *De lampade combinatoria*, *Op. lat.*, II (ii), pp. 230–1. Quoted as translated by McIntyre, *Giordano Bruno*, pp. 53–4. Bruno did, however, have a friend at Wittenberg, namely Alberico Gentile, the great jurist, whom he had known in England and who recommended him to the university (*Documenti*, pp. 85–6).

(a) "Figura Mentis"

(b) "Figura Intellectus"

(c) "Figura Amoris"

(d) "Zoemetra"

11 Figures from Giordano Bruno, *Articuli centum et sexaginta adversus huius tempestatis mathematicos atque philosophos*, Prague, 1588 (p. 313 ff.)

12 (*a*) Figure from Giordano Bruno, *Articuli adversus mathematicos*, Prague, 1588 (p. 313)

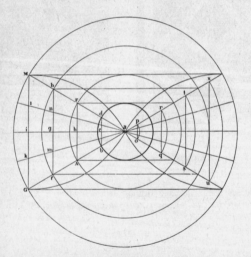

12 (*b*) This figure as reproduced in Giordano Bruno, *Opere latine*, I (iii), 1889, p. 84 (p. 313)

(a) "Theuti Radius"

(b) Unnamed Figures

(c) "Speculum Magorum"

(d) "Expansor"

13 Figures from Giordano Bruno, *Articuli adversus mathematicos*, Prague, 1588 (pp. 313, 324)

14 (a), (b) Figures from Giordano Bruno, *De triplici minimo et mensura*,
Frankfort, 1591 (p. 320)

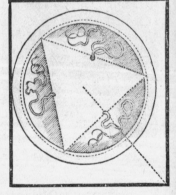

14 (c), (d) Figures from Giordano Bruno, *De monade numero et figura*,
Frankfort, 1591 (pp. 322, 324)

very much better than the Calvinist heretics of France or the Puritan Anglicans. Unfortunately, whilst he was there a Calvinist party gained the upper hand over the party which favoured him, and this was why he left, at least that is what he told the Venetian inquisitors.[1] Owing to his happiness under the Lutheran encouragement during this period, the mission was in abeyance and we hear nothing of pedants. On the contrary, in the same dedication, he goes through the staff of the university by name with admiring mention of their studies.[2]

Bruno's huge production whilst at Wittenberg probably, in the main, consists of his lectures there. Among the works actually published at Wittenberg were the *De lampade combinatoria lulliana*,[3] and the *De progressu et lampade venatoria logicorum*.[4] To these must be added as belonging to the teaching of the Wittenberg period the *Artificium perorandi*[5] published by J. H. Alsted in 1612, after Bruno's death; and the *Liber physicorum Aristotelis*,[6] first published in the edition of the Latin works. These works are all important for the student of Bruno, particularly for his Lullism. But they are dull indeed compared with those marvellous dialogues which he wrote in England because his lectures at Oxford were stopped.

The magician's extraordinary inner life was burning intensely during the Wittenberg period, as is revealed by the *Lampas triginta statuarum*,[7] first published from the Noroff manuscript in the edition of the Latin works but probably written at Wittenberg. As its title shows, this work belongs into the same group as the "Thirty Shadows",[8] published during the first visit to Paris, the "Thirty Seals", published in England, and the "Thirty Links"[9] in the Noroff manuscript. Bruno is here continuing his efforts to

---

[1] *Documenti*, p. 86.

[2] *Op. lat.*, II (ii), pp. 239–40.

[3] *Op. lat.*, II (ii), pp. 225 ff.

[4] *Op. lat.*, II (iii), pp. 1 ff.

[5] *Ibid.*, pp. 336 ff.; cf. *Bibliografia*, p. 160.

[6] *Op. lat.*, III, pp. 259 ff.; cf. *Bibliografia*, p. 165. There is another ms. copy of the work with which the editors collated the one in the Noroff. ms.

[7] *Op. lat.*, III, pp. 1 ff.; cf. *Bibliografia*, p. 164.

[8] That is the *De umbris idearum* in which the images are arranged under thirty groupings; see above, p. 195.

[9] That is the *De vinculis in genere* in which the "links" are subsumed under thirty heads; see above, p. 266, note 4.

form a memory, or a psyche, which is unified through being based on images or signs which bring the psyche into direct contact with reality. The astrological images on which the memory was based in the "Thirty Shadows" are here replaced by "statues", or interior images constructed on talismanic principles. "We are not the first inventor of this way of teaching, but we are reviving it; as in nature we see vicissitudes of light and darkness, so also there are vicissitudes of different kinds of philosophies. Since there is nothing new as Aristotle says in his book *De coelo*, it is necessary to return to those opinions after many centuries."[1]

Now, since it is always in the context of vicissitudes of light and darkness that he speaks in other works of the approaching return of the Egyptian religion, I believe that these inner "statues" are a transference into inner imagery of those statues which formed so essential a part of the religion of the Egyptians, as described in the *Asclepius*, which they knew how to animate by introducing demons into them. As we know from the *De magia*, Bruno believed that the most important and powerful of all ways of "linking" with demons was through the imagination. It follows, I think, that the thirty statues are thirty imaginative links with demons through which the Magus is forming a Magus personality. The same idea, as already suggested, lay behind the use of the Egyptian decan demons in memory in the "Thirty Shadows", and the work on linking with demons (the *De vinculis in genere*) which, like the "Thirty Statues" comes from the Noroff manuscript, is subsumed under "Thirty Links".

The "Thirty Statues" is a basic work for the understanding of Bruno. It cannot be tackled as a whole until Bruno's mnemonic works have been placed within the context of the history of the art of memory,[2] and until his Lullism has been placed within the context of the history of the Art of Ramon Lull.[3] The partial

[1] *Op. lat.*, III, pp. 8–9.

[2] The Hermetic adaptation of the use of mental images belongs into the history of the use of images in the classical art of memory.

[3] The "thirty" grouping is related to Lullism, as can be seen in the *De umbris idearum*, where the first "thirty" is a grouping of concepts on a wheel which is taken directly from Lullism, or rather, Pseudo-Lullism (we omitted discussion of this, above, p. 195). Lull's Arts were based on divine attributes as creative causes, and these basic concepts varied in number in different arts (see my article, "Ramon Lull and John Scotus Erigena", *J.W.C.I.*, XXIII (1960), pp. 1 ff.). It is in one of his Lullist

treatment of it which I shall attempt here is from the point of view of his place in the history of Hermetism which is the theme of the present book.

Before coming to the formed "statues", Bruno considers three "infigurables", of which no image can be formed. These are Chaos, Orcus, and Nox. Chaos has no statue or figure and cannot be imagined; it is space which can only be known through the things in it, and it contains the infinite universe. Orcus follows Chaos as a son to the father; he is called Orcus, or Abyss, because his amplitude corresponds to the amplitude of his father, Chaos; he is infinite appetite, an unending abyss of need seeking after the infinity of his father. Nox is the daughter of Orcus and so one of the three infigurables; but through reason she becomes the most ancient of the gods, and in this aspect is figurable. She stands for the *materia prima*, and as a goddess can have a figurable statue, an old woman, wearing black clothes, with black wings of immense extent.[1]

To this lower triad of Chaos, Orcus, Nox, there is opposed a "supernal triad", consisting of the Father, or mind, or plenitude; of the Son, or the primal intellect; of Light which is the spirit of all things, or the *anima mundi*. There is no statue of the Father, but infinite light is the type of him; or an infinite sphere the centre of which is everywhere; or absolute unity. By finite intelligences like ours, the nature of the Father can only be seen as reflected in a mirror, as in Plato's cave they look at the shadows, not at the light itself; not at the species and ideas but at the shadows of species and ideas. That face we can only contemplate in vestiges and effects.[2]

"Ancient theologians," Bruno continues, understand by the Father, mind or *mens*, who generates intellect, or the Son, between them being *fulgor*, or light or love. Hence one may contemplate in the Father, the essence of essences; in the Son the beauty and love of generating; in *fulgor*, or light, the spirit pervading and vivifying all.[3] Thus a triad may be imagined; "pater, mens; filium verbum; et per verbum, universa sunt producta".[4] From *mens*

[1] *Op. lat.*, III, pp. 9–37. [2] *Ibid.*, pp. 37–43.
[3] *Ibid.*, p. 44. [4] *Ibid.*, pp. 51–2.

works that Bruno discusses his choice of "thirty" (*De compendiosa architectura artis Lullii*, *Op. lat.*, II (ii), p. 42). Bruno adapts Lullism to his own purposes.

proceeds *intellectus*; from *intellectus* proceeds *affectus* or love. *Mens* sits above all; *intellectus* sees and distributes all; love makes and disposes all. This last is light or *fulgor* which fills all things and is diffused through all. Whence it is called the *anima mundi* and *spiritus universorum,* and is that of which Virgil spoke when he said "spiritus intus alit".[1]

I think that what has happened is this. Bruno's triad comes from the *Corpus Hermeticum,* with its frequent description of the *mens* as Father; its mention of "Filius Dei" as the Word proceeding from him, and of the light or spirit or *anima mundi.*[2] These concepts, interpreted by Ficino, with the approbation of Lactantius, as prophecies or prefiguration of the Christian Trinity, lie at the heart of Ficino's Christian Neoplatonism, much of the terminology of which Bruno is here repeating. But Bruno, the "Egyptian", rejects the Christian interpretation and reverts to the Hermetic gnosticism.

After the "infigurables" come the "figurables", the magic inner statues.

First is the statue of Apollo or the monad. He stands in his chariot to signify the absolute one; he is naked to signify the one simplicity; the constancy and solidity of his rays signify the one pure truth. One crow flying before his face signifies unity by the negation of multitude. He denotes one genus because he illuminates all the stars; one species because he illuminates the twelve signs; one number through the lion his sign; one congregation through the chorus of the Muses over which he presides; one harmony or consonance, one symphony of many voices, denoted by the lyre of Apollo which is called the spirit of the universe.[3]

This sounds like a fairly normal statue of Apollo, but its magical or talismanic nature is indicated by some of the ingredients, for instance the "one crow" which flies before his face, suggesting the talisman with a crow in it which Ficino had used.[4]

The statue of Saturn, or the beginning, is constructed on similar principles; he is the usual old man with a sickle; has a chariot drawn by stags as in the magic image of Saturn used by Bruno in the *De umbris.*[5]

---

[1] *Ibid.,* pp. 53–4, 60.   [2] See above, pp. 7 ff., 23 ff.
[3] *Op. lat.,* III, pp. 63–8.   [4] See above, p. 71.
[5] *Op. lat.,* III, pp. 68–73; see above, p. 196.

Among other statues are those of Prometheus, Vulcan, Thetis, Sagittarius, Mount Olympus, Coelius, Demogorgon, Minerva (an important statue for she represents "ecstasy" or a "kind of continuation of human reason with divine or demonic intelligence"[1]), Venus, Arrow of Cupid (this statue connects with imagery in the *Eroici furori*), and Aeon. The order of the series is not an astrological order, but is based on an order of concepts.

In this extraordinary work one sees perhaps more clearly than in any of the others how Bruno's cult of the Egyptian religion with its magical statues was transferred by him within, into the imaginative life. It was an inner cult, not an outer cult with temples and rites. This inner or individual character of Hermetism permeates the Hermetic writings themselves which always emphasise the reflection within, in man's mind which is made in the image of the creator, of the divine universe as the core of religious experience. Further, the "Thirty Statues" reveal how Bruno's philosophy of an infinite universe and innumerable worlds, which we have earlier called an extension of gnosis, is in fact used by him in a Hermetic manner. It is to be reflected within, as in the Hermetic reflection of the world within the mind, so that it becomes an extended inner spiritual experience, filling the infinite need of the soul for infinity.

Thus, though the university teacher of Wittenberg did not write a *Spaccio* or an *Eroici furori* he was intensely cultivating the inner life and the inner imagery which gives those works their power.

Bruno took an affectionate farewell of the University of Wittenberg in an *Oratio valedictoria*.[2] He told the assembled doctors that he, unlike Paris, had made Minerva his choice from among the three goddesses. To see Minerva is to become blind, to be wise through her is to be foolish, for she is Sophia, Wisdom itself, beautiful as the moon, great as the sun, terrible as the marshalled ranks of armies, pure because nothing of defilement can touch her, honourable because the image of goodness itself, powerful because being one she can do all things, kind because she visits the nations that are sacred to her and makes men friends to God and prophets.

---

[1] *Ibid.*, p. 142. Bruno may be using the *Mythologia* of Natalis Comes (which he certainly knew, see *Bibliografia*, p. 167), but his analyses and interpretations of his "statues" are staggering in their complexity and profundity.

[2] *Op. lat.*, I (i), pp. 1 ff.

Her have I loved and sought from my youth, and desired for my spouse, and have become a lover of her form . . . and I prayed . . . that she might be sent to abide with me, and work with me, that I might know what I lacked, and what was acceptable to God: for she knew and understood, and would guide me soberly in my work and would keep me in her charge.[1]

The genealogy of wisdom which has been quoted earlier comes in this speech; and the list of the German builders of the temple of wisdom ends with a resounding eulogy of Martin Luther, as was inevitable in an address to Luther's university.[2]

It was a marvellous speech, in the course of which he brought in the *Deus pater*, the *mens*, dwelling in light inaccessible, but who could be seen in his shadows and vestiges, in the infinite universe and the innumerable worlds, and ending with the suggestion that it is here, in Wittenberg, whither come all the nations of the world in search of truth, that the truth will be found.[3] Just as he had suggested in England, when the urn opened amongst the nymphs of Thames, that perhaps here it would be found.[4]

In Mocenigo's delation to the Inquisition against Bruno, he reports him as having said that he had intended to found a new sect under the name of philosophy.[5] Other informers made the same insinuation, adding that Bruno had said that the sect was called the "Giordanisti" and appealed particularly to the Lutherans in Germany.[6]

It has occurred to me to wonder whether these rumoured

---

[1] *Ibid.*, p. 12. Parts of this speech are translated by McIntyre in his *Giordano Bruno*, pp. 55–7.

[2] *Op. lat.*, I (i), pp. 20 ff. On this genealogy of wisdom, and its inclusion of Lucretius and Palingenius, see above, p. 247.

[3] *Ibid.*, pp. 21 ff. At least, such is my interpretation of the confused and excited imagery in which Bruno expresses his gratitude to Wittenberg and calls down blessings upon her.

[4] See above, p. 289. There is nymph and river imagery at the end of the Wittenberg speech.

[5] "He revealed a plan of founding a new sect under the name of philosophy . . ." (*Documenti*, p. 60).

[6] "He (Bruno) said that formerly the works of Luther were much prized in Germany, but that after they had tasted of his (Bruno's) works they sought for no others, and that he had begun a new sect in Germany, and if he could get out of prison he would return there to organise it better, and that he wished that they should call themselves Giordanisti . . ." (*Sommario*, p. 61; cf. also *ibid.*, pp. 57, 59).

"Giordanisti" could have any connection with the unsolved mystery of the origin of the Rosicrucians who are first heard of in Germany in the early seventeenth century, in Lutheran circles.[1]

Early in 1588, Bruno left Wittenberg for Prague where he stayed for about six months.[2] Here the Emperor Rudolph II held his court and gathered under his wing astrologers and alchemists from all over Europe to assist in his melancholy search for the philosopher's stone. Bruno was not a practising alchemical Hermetist, but he tried to interest the Emperor in his "mathesis", dedicating to him a book, which was published at Prague, and which had the provocative title of *Articuli adversus mathematicos*.[3] It may be only a curious coincidence that Fabrizio Mordente happened to be in Prague at this time, in the position of imperial astronomer![4]

The book "against mathematicians" is illustrated with an intriguing collection of diagrams, a selection from which I here reproduce (Pls. 11–13).[5] They are erratically geometrical in appearance, though with occasional intrusion of interesting objects, such as serpents or lutes. One, which has the Egyptian title of "Theuti Radius" (Pl. 13 a), is decorated with a design of zigzags and dots which looks like variations on some theme based on the characters of the planets. Another, equally decorative, is called "Theuti circulus". Even the apparently more geometrical diagrams are enlivened with queer floral and other designs which have been omitted in the reproductions of them in the edition of 1889,[6] (Pl. 12 a, b) where they have a thin and staid nineteenth-century appearance which is quite foreign to the temperamental ebullience of the originals.[7] It seems to me probable that Bruno cut the

[1] See further below, pp. 407–14.

[2] *Documenti*, p. 86.

[3] *Op. lat.*, I (iii), pp. 1 ff. Bruno also published, or rather republished, a Lullian work in Prague.

[4] Spampanato, *Vita di Giordano Bruno*, p. 429.

[5] They are photographed from the copy in the Bibliothèque Nationale (Rés. D² 5278) which is the only known copy containing all the diagrams (see *Bibliografia*, p. 138).

[6] In *Op. lat.*, I (iii), edited by Tocco and Vitelli.

[7] The same editing of the diagrams towards a more normal appearance was done by Tocco and Vitelli in the case of the diagrams in the *De triplici minimo*, a work published in the same volume of the *Op. lat.* See below, p. 320–1.

blocks for these diagrams himself for they resemble in style those in the *De triplici minimo* which the printer of that work states to have been cut by Bruno's own hand.[1]

I have found it difficult to relate the "mathesistical" text to these diagrams except in the case of the first three (Pls. 11 a, b, c),[2] which are variations on the theme of intersecting circles. The text definitely states that the first of these is a figure representing the universal *mens*; the second represents the *intellectus*; and the third is the "figure of love", concording contrarieties and uniting many in one.[3] These three figures are said to be most "fecund", not only for geometry but for all sciences and for contemplating and operating.[4] These three figures thus represent the Hermetic trinity, as defined by Bruno in the "Thirty Statues". The third one, the one which is the *amoris figura* (Pl. 11 c). actually has the word MAGIC written in it in letters on the diagram. It is further stated that these three figures are referred to in the text under the following abbreviations:

Figurae Mentis nota ☉
Figurae Intellectus ☽
Figurae Amoris ★

The first two of these are signs for the sun and moon, and the third is a five-pointed star. These figures do in fact appear in the pages of the "mathesistical" text which follow, dotted about here and there amidst the talk of lines and circles, spheres and angles, and so on. It therefore seems possible that this book may be written in a cipher of some kind.

Whether or not the Emperor Rudolph could read the message concealed in the "mathesis", the drift of the preface dedicating the work to him is clear. There are vicissitudes of light and darkness and the present time of darkness is afflicted by quarrelling sects. Breaking the *ius gentium* and consequently the order instituted by the true God, these dissolve the bonds of society, being moved by misanthropic spirits, ministers to the infernal furies, who put the sword of discord between the peoples, as though they were Mercuries descending from heaven, imposing all kinds of impostures. They set man against man and break the law of love, which belongs not to one kind of cacodaemonical sect, but comes from God, the Father of all, who pours out his gifts upon the just and

---

[1] See below, p. 320. [2] *Op. lat.*, I (iii), pp. 78–80.
[3] *Ibid.*, pp. 20–1. [4] *Ibid.*, p. 21.

the unjust and ordains a general philanthropy. True religion should be without controversy and dispute, and is a direction of the soul. No one has the right to criticise or control the opinions of others, as to-day, as though the whole world were blind under Aristotle or some such leader. But we raise our heads towards the lovely splendour of light, listening to nature who is crying aloud to be heard and following wisdom in simplicity of spirit and with an honest affection of the heart.[1]

The Nolan's message in its application to the times in which he lived is nowhere more clearly set out than in this dedication to Rudolph II. Here are all his usual themes, the vicissitudes of light and darkness, the "Mercuries descending from heaven" who, as we know from this familiar phrase in other contexts, destroyed the religion of the Egyptians, the natural religion which he himself follows and which does not break the *ius gentium* and the universal law of love as the fanatical sectaries do, the "Aristotelians" who want to impose their prejudices on others. Was he perhaps mainly thinking now of Paris under the League, of which the presence of Fabrizio Mordente in Prague might have reminded him? In England, he had been mainly thinking of repressive English Protestants. All religious persecution and all war in the name of religion breaks the law of love. Strange though Bruno's magical religion was, extraordinary and indeed frightening though his inner Egyptianism was, yet it did not break the law of love as the sectaries did. This is the noble side of the heroic enthusiast.

The Emperor gave Bruno money for his mathesis "against mathematicians",[2] but he did not give him any employment or position. He went on to Helmstedt.

"Iordanus Brunus Nolanus Italus" matriculated at the Julian university of Brunswick, at Helmstedt, on January 13th, 1589.[3] This university had been founded only twelve years previously, on liberal principles, by Duke Julius of Brunswick-Wolfenbüttel.

---

[1] *Ibid.*, pp. 3–7.

[2] *Documenti*, p. 86. John Dee's associate, Edward Kelley, was at Prague at the time of Bruno's visit, and in very high favour with the Emperor (see C. Fell Smith, *John Dee*, 1909, pp. 179 ff.).

[3] *Documenti*, p. 51. On the situation at Helmstedt at the time of Bruno's visit, see Spampanato, *Vita di Giordano Bruno*, pp. 431 ff.; W. Boulting, *Giordano Bruno*, London, 1914, pp. 214 ff.

Julius died shortly after Bruno's arrival and was succeeded by his son, Henry Julius. The religious situation at Helmstedt was fairly fluid; the old duke had been a Protestant; his son and successor was nominally Catholic. Bruno got into difficulties with a Protestant pastor at Helmstedt who excommunicated him,[1] but the young Duke Henry Julius seems to have been rather kind to him, and allowed him to deliver an oration to the university on the death of his father, Duke Julius, the founder of the university. Once again the Nolan is in his element, and about to deliver one of his highly original addresses to the doctors of a university.

The *Oratio consolatoria*[2] at Helmstedt is not so brilliant as was the *Oratio valedictoria* at Wittenberg, but it is interesting for the indications that Bruno had moved into a more radically anti-Catholic and anti-Papal position than he had held when in England. He now speaks of a tyranny by which a vile priesthood destroys the natural order, the *ius gentium,* and the civil law, in Italy and Spain, whilst Gaul and Belgia are destroyed by wars of religion, and some regions in Germany are most unhappy.[3] In the *Spaccio* he had emphasised the importance of a restoration of law in the reform of the heavens, but his strong interest, both here and in the Prague dedication to the Emperor, in the *ius gentium,* perhaps suggests an influence of his friend Alberico Gentile, the founder of international law,[4] whom he had known in England and met again at Wittenberg, where it was through Gentile's introduction that he obtained his lectureship in the university.

The rhetorical praises of the late Julius take a particularly Brunian turn when the speech starts to go through the northern and southern constellations into which the virtues of Julius are mounting whilst vices descend.[5] There is some definite anti-papalism here, as when the snakey-haired head of Gorgon represents the monster of perverse papal tyranny which has tongues more numerous than the hairs of the head, all blasphemous against God, nature, and man, infecting the world with the rankest poison of ignorance and vice.[6] The speech thus outlines a reform of the

[1] *Documenti,* p. 52.
[2] *Op. lat.,* I (i), pp. 27 ff.
[3] *Ibid.,* p. 33.
[4] Through his famous work, the *De legationibus.*
[5] *Op. lat.,* I (i), pp. 47 ff.
[6] *Ibid.,* p. 49; cf. McIntyre, *Giordano Bruno,* pp. 60–1.

constellations which has been made through the virtues of the late Lutheran Duke and which is definitely anti-papal and anti-Catholic.

To appreciate this shift in emphasis in the celestial reform as compared with the *Spaccio* we must remember the situation of Europe in 1589 as compared with 1585. The Catholic League with its violent propaganda and violent actions had been in control of Paris since 1586 (soon after Bruno left); Henri III was assassinated in 1589; in this terrible year Navarre's siege of Paris was in its last stages; in the preceding year, 1588, England had won the Armada victory. The still Catholic colouring of the *Spaccio della bestia trionfante* presupposed a leadership of the reform by a liberal and tolerant Catholic monarch, Henri III. That leadership is now no longer possible and the reform shifts in a more Protestant and anti-papal direction. With a more ordinary character, allowance would have to be made for the fact that Bruno was being paid to flatter the late Protestant duke, but the Nolan was not an ordinary character and always spoke from conviction.

Duke Julius of Brunswick-Wolfenbüttel brackets with the "diva Elizabetta" as one of those heretic princes whom Bruno had praised and about whom the Inquisitors were suspicious.

To the nominally Catholic son, Henry Julius, Bruno dedicated the Latin poems which he had been writing for years. Though these poems were not published in Helmstedt, as the *Oratio consolatoria* was, but in Frankfort, the dedications[1] belong into the atmosphere of the Helmstedt period. In one of them Bruno reminds Henry Julius, who was both a duke and a bishop, that in the time of Hermes Trismegistus, priests were kings, and kings priests.[2]

It was probably whilst in Helmstedt that Bruno wrote several of the works on magic preserved in the Noroff manuscript, including the *De magia* with its examination of ways of "linking" with demons and its magical psychology of the imagination, and the *De vinculis in genere*, also on linking. It may have been here, too, that the passages from Agrippa, from Trithemius, and other magical texts were copied out for Bruno by Jerome Besler.[3]

---

[1] *Op. lat.*, I (i), pp. 193–9, and *Op. lat.*, I (iii), pp. 123–4.

[2] *Op. lat.*, I (i), p. 193.

[3] See *Op. lat.*, III, introduction, pp. xxvii–xxix.

With the money which Henry Julius gave him for the oration on the death of his father, Bruno went on to Frankfort "in order to get two books printed".[1] He got into touch with the printer John Wechel[2] and busied himself with the publication of the long Latin poems which he had perhaps begun in England and had been writing during all his wanderings. Enthusiasts for Bruno's philosophy have often mainly confined themselves to the Italian dialogues written in England,[3] which, when read in isolation from their English context and without understanding of Bruno's position in the line of the Renaissance Magi, can be so strangely misunderstood. The Latin poems repeat the whole message but in a form much less attractive than the Italian dialogues. There is perhaps another of Bruno's tragedies here, for he was a poet, though not a good Latin poet, and magical imagery is at the root of his message. The magic of the imagery does do its work on the reader of the Italian dialogues, and the same enthusiasm and fire are in these vast Latin poems. But it demands indeed a heroic enthusiasm to read through from beginning to end the *De immenso, innumerabilibus et infigurabilibus*,[4] the *De triplici minimo et mensura*,[5] and the *De monade numero et figura*.[6]

The poems are in imitation of Lucretius. The *De immenso* repeats in its fullest form the philosophy of the infinite universe and the innumerable worlds which Bruno had derived from Lucretius, animating it with the universal animation of the magical philosophy and using it in the Hermetic manner, to reflect in the *mens* the universe in this immensely extended form and so to absorb the infinite divinity. I quoted earlier[7] the words from the commentary to the beginning of the poem in which the *magnum miraculum est homo* passage from the *Asclepius* is expanded to include the infinite which man, the great miracle, must now

---

[1] *Documenti*, p. 86.

[2] Spampanato, *Vita di Giordano Bruno*, pp. 446 ff.

[3] Some of Bruno's admirers, on the other hand, have considered that the *De immenso* is his *chef d'œuvre*.

[4] *Op. lat.*, I (i), pp. 191 ff., and *Op. lat.*, I (ii), pp. I ff.

[5] *Op. lat.*, I (iii), pp. 119 ff.

[6] *Op. lat.*, I (ii), pp. 319 ff. Manuscripts of two short works by Bruno, which are closely related to the *De triplici minimo* and the *De monade*, have recently been discovered at Jena. They are published by G. Aquilecchia in *Atti dell' Accademia dei Lincei*, vol. XVII, 1962.

[7] See above, p. 246.

expand himself to receive. The immense and the innumerable are those "infigurables" which, in the "Thirty Statues" are reflected within to satisfy the infinite need of the soul for the infinite.[1]

In the *De minimo* Bruno reflects upon the infinitely small, the *minima* of which the world is composed. These minima or monads are related to the Democritean atoms, his knowledge of which Bruno is again deriving from Lucretius' poem. In the *De magia*[2] he introduces the atoms when discussing *spiritus*, also in the *De rerum principiis elementis et causis*.[3]

There is something else in the two Latin poems on the Immense and the Minute, something which one cannot but think is almost deliberately hidden in inconspicuous places amongst the philosophy. In the *De immenso* there is a particularly violent attack on those who have destroyed the Egyptian religion, whence "sepulta est lux" and cruelty, schisms, evil customs and contempt for law are spread through the world.[4] In the mysterious heading to the passage the prophecy of Mercurius in *Pimander* is mentioned, leaving no doubt that we have here once again the familiar Bruno interpretation of the Lament as the destruction by the Christians of the good religion. The reader of the *De minimo*, towards the end is jerked into attention when he finds himself confronted by three figures called "Atrium Apollinis", "Atrium Minervae", and "Atrium Veneris", which are described as most fecund figures, and "seals" of the archetypes of things.[5] If the reader is a devoted disciple of Giordano he will remember that he has seen those figures before, or figures almost exactly like them, namely in the *Articuli adversus mathematicos* where they were seals of the trinity *mens, intellectus, amor* (Pl. 11 a, b, c), seals "against the mathematicians" who seem to be explained in the preface to the Emperor Rudolph as the warring Christian sects who should be replaced by a religion of love and a cult of nature. If the disciple is such a devoted Giordanist that he has been with Bruno in Paris he will wonder when he sees the two diagrams labelled "Plectrum Mordentii"

---

[1] See above, pp. 309, 311.

[2] *Op. lat.*, III, p. 416.

[3] *Ibid.*, p. 535. D. W. Singer (*Giordano Bruno, etc.*, p. 71) speaks of Bruno's "cosmic metabolism" in connection with the eternal motion of the *minima*.

[4] *Op. lat.*, I (ii), pp. 171–2.

[5] *Op. lat.*, I (iii), pp. 277–83.

and " Quadra Mordentii"[1] whether these may not have something to do with the controversy about a compass in Paris under the League. The whole of the book *De mensura* appended to the *De triplici minimo* seems to me very peculiar. Though he does seem to be going through the different types of geometrical figures, why should such figures "give a way for the Charites (Graces) of Hermes"?[2] Or why should a "Charitis domus" be found in a triangle formed of Bacchus, Diana, and Hermes?[3]

When the diagrams in the three Latin poems published by Wechel at Frankfort are examined in the original editions, the discovery is made that the diagrams in the *De triplici minimo et mensura* differ greatly from those in the other two works, being sprinkled with large numbers of stars, flowers, leaves, and other fantasies (Pl. 14 a, b). The editors of Bruno's Latin works in their reproductions of these diagrams showed only their basic geometrical forms,[4] omitting the stars and other addenda which they may have thought were only meaningless decorations (just as they also pruned the diagrams of the *Articuli adversus mathematicos*). Yet the printer Wechel in the dedication of the *De triplici minimo* to Henry Julius states that Bruno cut these diagrams with his own hand.[5] Bruno himself must therefore have attached importance to the many stars and other peculiarities in them. A possible explanation of these mysteries might be that Bruno did found some Hermetic sect in Germany (the "Giordanisti" of which there are rumours in the *Sommario*) and such figures are symbols of the sect. One wonders whether the lettering on some of the diagrams

[1] *Op. lat.*, I (iii), pp. 253, 256.

[2] *Ibid.*, p. 323. [3] *Ibid.*, p. 333.

[4] The *De triplici minimo et mensura*, is in *Op. lat.*, I (iii), ed. Tocco and Vitelli, Florence, 1899. Since many of the diagrams in this work appear in other works without the stars and other additions, Tocco and Vitelli presumably felt justified in regarding these as unnecessary freaks which could be omitted.

[5] "non schemata solum ipse (i.e. Bruno) sua manu sculpsit, sed etiam operarum se in eodem correctorem praebuit" (*Op. lat.*, I (iii), p. 123). It is not impossible that Wechel might have been a printer favourable to a secret society. A printer of the same name, Andreas Wechel, had formerly made his house in Frankfort a rendezvous for travellers from all over Europe (see, J. A. Van Dorsten, *Poets, Patrons and Professors*, Leiden, 1962, p. 30). As is well known, Philip Sidney stayed with Andreas Wechel, on his first continental tour. The John Wechel who prints Bruno's books is, however, not the same man.

may contain messages in cipher. The plethora of stars in these diagrams is very striking. In the work "against mathematicians", Bruno used the star with the meaning of "amor".[1]

The third Latin poem published at Frankfort, the *De monade numero et figura*,[2] is a study of numbers and their meanings, beginning with the monas, then the two, the three, and so on. It is based on the chapters on these numbers in Cornelius Agrippa,[3] as was pointed out long ago.[4] But Bruno alters the Agrippan schemes. Agrippa being still ostensibly in the orthodox descent from the Christian Magi gives the numbers Christian Trinitarian, Pseudo-Dionysian and Cabalist meanings. Bruno leaves these out and his numbers become purely "Egyptian" or Hermetic or Pythagorean. It is the same development in the numerology as that which we studied in the *Spaccio* or the *Eroici furori*, a change of balance by which the Hermetic-Egyptian becomes dominant.

With each number, Agrippa gives a scale for the number in which he sets out its meanings on different levels. For example, in the scale for three,[5] the highest or archetypal meaning is the three-lettered name of God (in Hebrew) signifying the Father, the Son, and the Holy Spirit, the Christian Trinity. In the intellectual world this number signifies the three hierarchies of angels, that is the nine Pseudo-Dionysian hierarchies grouped into three representing the Trinity. In the celestial world, three refers to the three quaternations of the signs (of the zodiac), the three quaternations of the houses (of a horoscope), and the three triplicities; in the elemental world it refers to three degrees of elements; in the minor world, that is the microcosm or man, it refers to the three main parts of man's body, the head, the breast, and the belly. In the infernal world, it becomes three infernal furies, three infernal judges, and three degrees of the damned.

In the chapter on three in Bruno's poem, we hear nothing of the Trinity, and the three are *Mens, Intellectus, Amor*, which can be expressed as other threes, for example, *Veritas, Pulchritudo, Bonitas*, the Three Graces. He also has *Unitas, Veritas, Bonitas*,

---

[1] See above, p. 314.

[2] *Op. lat.*, I (ii), pp. 319 ff.

[3] Agrippa, *De occult. phil.*, II, 4–13.

[4] F. Tocco, *Le fonti più recenti della filosofia del Bruno*, Rome, 1892, p. 71.

[5] Agrippa, *De occult. phil.*, II, 5.

as a three. And his figure illustrating three is three suns (Pl. 14 c) corresponding to *Vita*, *Intellectus* (which can be compared to the Word), *Generatio*, which are said to be within a rainbow of three colours.[1] I have greatly abbreviated here what Bruno says about three, but it is sufficient to make the point that, as compared with Agrippa, it is not Trinitarian in a Christian sense, but only in a Neoplatonic or Hermetic sense.

A good way to approach the study of Bruno's numerology would be, first of all to master the relevant chapters in Agrippa; then to compare these carefully with Bruno's *De monade*; and then to go on to Robert Fludd on the "Divine Numbers".[2] Fludd is doing the same thing, going through the numbers and their meanings and within the same macrocosm-microcosm framework, but he has reverted to the Christian interpretation of the *mens*, *intellectus*-Word, *anima mundi*, as representing the Christian Trinity. Fludd mentions Hermes Trismegistus, whom he worships, with nearly every breath he takes, but the Trinity, the Angels, Cabalism are once again correctly related into the framework from which a Christian Magus operated and within which he thought. Studied within this sequence, placed between Agrippa and Fludd, the eccentricity of Bruno's numerology comes out clearly and is seen to be due—as indeed was his whole position as a Renaissance Magus—to his non-acceptance of the Christian interpretation of the *Hermetica* and the alteration in balance in favour of an all out "Egyptianism" which this implied.

A remarkable feature of the *De monade* is the use which Bruno makes in it of Cecco d'Ascoli's necromantic commentary on the *Sphere* of Sacrobosco. As I suggested earlier,[3] Bruno probably took the title of his magic-memory book published during the first visit to Paris, the *De umbris idearum*, from Cecco who mentions a magical book by Solomon with this title. In the *De monade*, there are long quotations from Cecco who is actually mentioned by

---

[1] *Op. lat.*, I (ii), pp. 358–69. A very similar arrangement of three suns within a rainbow appears as a "portent" in a woodcut in one of William Lilly's prophecies (W. Lilly, *An Astrological Prediction of the Occurences in England, Part of the years 1648, 1649, 1650*, printed by T. B., 1648).

[2] R. Fludd, *Utriusque cosmi historia*, part 2 (*Microcosmi historia*), Oppenheim, 1619, pp. 19 ff.

[3] See above, p. 197.

name as "Ciccus Asculanus (born in the time of light)",[1] showing
what a high opinion Bruno had of this necromancer who was
burned by the Inquisition in 1327. The longest quotation from
Cecco comes when Bruno is discussing ten, the number sacred to
the ten Sephiroth. He mentions these, but later describes orders
of demons or spirits whose hierarchies can be contemplated in the
intersection of circles. "These (the orders of demons) are contemplated in the intersection of circles, as Astophon says in *libro
Mineralium constellatorum*. O how great, he says, is the power in
the intersection of circles."[2] This is a quotation of Cecco's quotation from this Astophon who is to be heard of nowhere else and
was probably invented by Cecco.[3] It throws a light on why intersecting circles are such a prominent feature in the diagrams by
which Bruno represents his Hermetic trinity (Pl. 11 a, b, c), and indeed in many of the other of the diagrams in his works. Bruno is also very
interested in the demon Floron, mentioned according to Cecco, in
the *Liber de umbris* by Solomon as a ruler of the north. Floron is
summoned by magic mirrors and seems formerly to have belonged
to the order of the Cherubim. All this is repeated by Bruno after
Cecco.[4]

This is the type of magic which was carefully suppressed and
superseded by Pico when he introduced practical Cabala, the new,
safe, learned kind of conjuring with angels. Bruno's return to an

---

[1] "Ciccus Asculanus (tempus lucis nactus) . . ." *Op. lat.*, I (ii), p. 467.
The whole of pp. 466–8 here is closely based on Cecco's commentary as is
revealed when these pages are compared with Lynn Thorndike, *The
Sphere of Sacrobosco and its Commentators*, Chicago, 1948, Commentary
by Cecco d'Ascoli, pp. 396–9. It is therefore significant that Bruno mentions in this context his own lost book on the sphere ("Et ego, in libro de
sphaera", p. 466). In all probability, therefore, this lost book was based
on Cecco.

[2] *Op. lat.*, I (ii), p. 466.

[3] Thorndike, *Sphere*, p. 405; cf. Thorndike's introduction, p. 54, on
Astophon being an invention of Cecco's.

[4] *Op. lat.*, I (ii), pp. 467–8; cf. Thorndike, *Sphere*, pp. 398–9, 407–8,
and *History of Magic and Experimental Science*, II, p. 965. According to
Cecco, the demon Floron was confined in a steel mirror by a major
invocation and knew many of the secrets of nature. This is referred to by
Bruno in the *Spaccio* (dial. I) under the northern constellation of the
Bear; "there where the magicians of the steel mirror seek for the oracles
of Floron, one of the great princes of the arctic spirits" (*Dial. ital.*, p.
617).

all-out "Egyptianism" means that he returns to an old style frankly "demonic" conjuring. The final figure in Bruno's *De monade* (Pl. 14 d)[1] is a triangle tilted sideways, with three curious looking curly things, rather like worms, outside the triangle. I am inclined to think that these may be intended to represent "links" with demons. There is another little curly one in one of the figures in the *Articuli adversus mathematicos* (Pl. 13 b).[2]

Compare this with John Dee's conjuring with Kelley, in which they are so nervous about demons and so careful only to have dealings with good and holy angels. Compare this with the profound piety of Pico della Mirandola. Even Agrippa, one feels, would have been shocked.

I believe that the crazy diagrams in Bruno's works are what he calls "mathesis". It will be remembered that in the *Thirty Seals* he says that the four guides in religion are Love, Magic, Art, Mathesis. By Art, I think he means his entirely unorthodox interpretation of the Lullian Art. In defining "Mathesis", he says that Pythagoras and Plato knew how to insinuate profound and difficult things by mathematical means. This is normal Pythagorean or symbolic attitude to number. But then he says that between the "mathemata" and physical things there is a place where the natural forces of things can be drawn, as is done by the Magi. Heraclitus, Epicurus, Synesius, Proclus confirm this and necromancers use it much.[3] (Note the curious company in which Bruno places Epicurus.)

Neither Pythagorean symbolic number, nor "mathesistical" use of number is the "real artificial magic" which can produce mechanical doves and crabs. Bruno is not at all in the line of the advance of mathematical and mechanical science. Rather he is a reactionary who would push the Copernican diagram or a compass invention back towards "mathesis".

But the scientific or the genuinely philosophical approach to Giordano Bruno is not the only approach. As one follows him on his wanderings, the conviction grows ever stronger that the new philosophy was a religious message, and that some of the diagrams in his works may allude to the symbols of a sect.

[1] Bruno, *Op. lat.*, I (ii), p. 473.
[2] *Op. lat.*, I (iii), p. 87.
[3] *Sigillus sigillorum*, *Op. lat.*, II (ii), pp. 196–7.

❖❖❖❖❖❖❖❖❖❖❖❖❖❖❖❖❖❖❖❖❖❖❖❖❖❖❖❖❖❖

Chapter XVIII

GIORDANO BRUNO:
LAST PUBLISHED WORK

❖❖❖❖❖❖❖❖❖❖❖❖❖❖❖❖❖❖❖❖❖❖❖❖❖❖❖❖❖❖

BRUNO'S stay in Frankfort, where the three Latin poems were printed, falls into two parts. He went there about the middle of 1590, paid a visit to Switzerland during 1591, after which he returned to Frankfort.[1]

A curious character called Hainzell (Johannes Henricius Haincelius), native of Augsburg, had recently acquired an estate at Elgg, near Zurich. This man was interested in alchemy and in various kinds of occultism and magic, and he liberally entertained at Elgg those who had a reputation for proficiency in such arts.[2] Bruno stayed with him for several months, and it was for the strange lord of Elgg that he wrote a work which he himself regarded as very important. This is the *De imaginum, signorum et idearum compositione*,[3] dedicated to Hainzell and published at Frankfort by Wechel in 1591. Bruno probably wrote it at Elgg, or at Zurich where he stayed for a while, and took the manuscript back with him to Frankfort. It was the last book that he published.

It is a magic memory system which has points in common with the *De umbris idearum*, published during the first visit to Paris and dedicated to Henri III. That system, as will be remembered,[4] was

---

[1] Spampanato, *Vita di Giordano Bruno*, pp. 446 ff.; McIntyre, *Giordano Bruno*, pp. 62 ff.

[2] Spampanato, *op. cit.*, pp. 449–50; McIntyre, *op. cit.*, p. 64.

[3] *Op. lat.*, II (iii), pp. 85 ff.

[4] See above, pp. 195 ff.

based on 150 magic or talismanic images; these were the images of the Egyptian decan demons, images of the planets, and other made up images. Around them, on concentric circles, were placed images of animals, plants, stones, etc., the whole world of physical creation, and on the outer circle, all arts and sciences under the images of 150 inventors and great men. The central magic images formed as it were the magical power-station informing the whole system. The system was attributed to "Hermes" and we thought that it related to the experience, described in one of the Hermetic treatises, of the initiate who reflects within his mind the whole universe in the ecstasy in which he becomes one with the Powers.

In the *De imaginum, signorum et idearum compositione* we have a similar idea but in a more elaborate form. The central magical power-station is now represented by twelve "principles". These are the powers or forces of one personality. The contents of the universe, arts and sciences, and so on, are arranged, or rather incoherently jumbled, in a madly elaborate series of rooms, atria, divisions. This arrangement is related to classical mnemonics in which notions are remembered through images placed in order on places memorised in buildings. But the mnemonic architecture itself has been "magicised" in Bruno's wild scheme, for some of the various plans of memory places in the book are obviously related to the Hermetic "seal" as can be seen by comparing these supposed mnemonic schemes with "seals" in other works. I shall not bewilder the reader by taking him through these magic memory rooms, but the twelve central "principles" or powers on which the whole scheme centres are interesting because they remind us of the gods in the *Spaccio della bestia trionfante*.

The twelve "principles" of the *De imaginum compositione*, some of which have other principles with them, or in the same "field", are as follows: Jupiter, with Juno; Saturn; Mars; Mercury; Minerva; Apollo; Aesculapius, with whom are grouped Circe, Arion, Orpheus, Sol; Luna; Venus; Cupid; Tellus, with Ocean, Neptune, Pluto.[1]

If these twelve principles are set out in a column, and in a parallel column are listed the gods who are the speakers in the *Spaccio*, the gods who hold the council by which the heaven is reformed, the result is as follows:

[1] *Op. lat.*, II (iii), pp. 200–77.

THE TWELVE PRINCIPLES of G. Bruno's *De imaginum, signorum et idearum compositione*, 1591			THE GODS of G. Bruno's *Spaccio della bestia trionfante*, 1585
I	JUPITER	(18 images)	JUPITER
	JUNO		JUNO
II	SATURN	(4 images)	SATURN
III	MARS	(4 images)	MARS
IV	MERCURY	(7 images)	MERCURY
V	MINERVA	(3 images)	MINERVA
VI	APOLLO	(8 images)	APOLLO
VII	AESCULAPIUS	(6 images)	with his magicians
	CIRCE	(1 image)	CIRCE and MEDEA
	ARION	(1 image)	with his physician
	ORPHEUS	(3 images)	AESCULAPIUS
VIII	SOL	(1 image)	
IX	LUNA	(6 images)	DIANA
X	VENUS	(10 images)	VENUS and CUPID
XI	CUPID	(2 images)	
XII	TELLUS	(3 images)	CERES
	OCEAN	(1 image)	NEPTUNE
	NEPTUNE	(1 image)	THETIS
	PLUTO	(1 image)	MOMUS
			ISIS

As can easily be seen by comparing the two lists, there is a marked similarity between the gods of the *Spaccio* and the "principles" of *De imaginum compositione*. Many, indeed most of them, are the same. There is a general similarity, too, in the fact that both lists contain the seven planetary gods and also other non-planetary principles. Even these non-planetary principles are somewhat similar in both lists; Minerva is in both; if we include with Apollo in the *Spaccio* list, Circe, Medea, Aesculapius who support Apollo in the council, we have something corresponding to the curious Aesculapius group in the *De imaginum compositione*; if we remember that Isis can mean the earth or nature, we have something corresponding to the Isis of the *Spaccio* in the Tellus group of the other work.

One naturally thinks, in connection with these "principles", of the twelve Olympian gods whom Manilius associates with the signs of the zodiac, namely Minerva, Venus, Apollo, Mercury

Jupiter, Ceres, Vulcan, Mars, Diana, Vesta, Juno, Neptune. It is possible that Bruno has these in mind but is, as usual, adapting and altering a conventional scheme to suit his own purposes. The astrological aspect of Bruno's "principles" is certainly strong, for the seven which correspond to the seven planets (Jupiter, Saturn, Mars, Mercury, Apollo-Sol, Luna, Venus) are actually illustrated by cuts showing the planetary gods riding in their chariots which are taken from an edition of Hyginus.[1]

Not only are the principles of the *De imagnum compositione* of a rather similar character to the gods of the *Spaccio*, but we also have in the former work elaborate lists of epithets applied to each principle, and these epithets are very like those virtues and vices, good and bad qualities, which ascend into, and descend from, the constellations as the heaven is reformed by the central group of gods. For example, the first principle, Jupiter, in the *De imaginum compositione* is preceded by Cause, Principle, Beginning; surrounding him are Fatherhood, Power, Rule; crowning him are Counsel, Truth, Piety, Rectitude, Candour, amiable Cult, Tranquillity, Liberty, Asylum; on the right side of his chariot are Life, incorrupt Innocence, erect Integrity, Clemency, Hilarity, Moderation, Toleration; on its left side are Pride, Display, Ambition, Dementia, Vanity, Contempt for others, Usurpation.[2] With amazing exuberance, Bruno proliferates epithets like these for all the principles, and the above is only a small selection from the Jupiter epithets. Readers of the *Spaccio* will recognise at once that these are of the same type as those in which the reform of the heavens is described in that work. If we were to use the above Jupiter epithets in the *Spaccio* manner, we would say that to such and such a constellation were ascending Candour, amiable Cult, Tranquillity and so on, displacing the descending opposites of Pride, Dementia, Contempt for others, Usurpation and so on. In the *De imaginum compositione*, Bruno does not describe the constellations, nor use the idea of ascent and descent from them of all these brilliantly expressed notions, but it is clear that he is thinking on the same lines as in the *Spaccio* and that the epithets attached to the principles are the raw material for just such a reform as the one described in the *Spaccio*.

In fact, the *De imaginum compositione* gives the clue to the way

[1] Hyginus, *Fabularum liber*, Paris, 1578.
[2] *Op. lat.*, II (iii), pp. 202–5.

the epithets are being used in the *Spaccio*. In the above Jupiter example, we can see that the good epithets belong to Jupiter both as a philosophic principle (Cause, Principle, Beginning) and as the planetary god whose characteristics are "jovial" and benevolent, and who is the special planet of rulers. The good Jupiter epithets describe a good, jovial, benevolent type of rule, with Clemency, Hilarity, Moderation, Toleration. The bad Jupiter epithets belong to the bad side of the planet and to the bad ruler; Pride, Ambition, Contempt for Others, Usurpation.

It was from study of the epithets in *De imaginum compositione*. and how these relate to good and bad sides of planetary influences, that I based the statement which I made in the earlier chapter on the *Spaccio* that the reform really represents a victory of good sides of astral influences over bad ones.[1] The way to study the *Spaccio* is to correlate the epithets in it with those in the *De imaginum compositione* which reveals to what planet the epithets belong.

Further, in the *De imaginum compositione* the epithets for Saturn are nearly all bad, things like Squalor, Moroseness, Severity, Rigidity; and so are the epithets for Mars, such as Ferocity, rabid Rigidity, implacable Truculence.[2] Reading round the constellations in the *Spaccio* and noting what bad things are driven down, it becomes evident, when these are compared with Saturn and Mars epithets in the *De imaginum compositione*, that in the celestial reform, Saturn and Mars are downed by the influence of the good planets, Jupiter, Venus, Sol. Lovely indeed are some of the epithets for Venus and Cupid in the *De imaginum compositione* —sweet Unanimity, placid Consent, holy Friendship, innocuous Geniality, Concordance of things, Union[3]—and concepts like these, together with Jovial concepts, will be found in the celestial reform of the *Spaccio* replacing the miseries of Mars and Saturn.

As in the *Spaccio*, the Sun is of central importance in the *De imaginum compositione*. The centre of the list of principles is taken up by a group all of which are solar in character. First, there is Apollo himself,[4] Wealth, Abundance, Fertility, Munificence. Then there is Aesculapius,[5] son of Apollo, with Circe, daughter of the Sun, and Orpheus and Arion.[6] This group is all magical, represent-

[1] See above, pp. 221–2. [2] *Op. lat.*, II (iii), pp. 207 ff.; pp. 221 ff.
[3] *Ibid.*, pp. 261 ff. [4] *Ibid.*, pp. 243 ff.
[5] *Ibid.*, pp. 247–8. [6] *Ibid.*, pp. 248–50.

ing benevolent magic. Aesculapius is acceptable Healing, vigorous Salubrity, among other things. Circe is magic, very powerful she is, and her power can be used benevolently or malevolently. Orpheus and Arion, represent, I think, solar incantations. Finally, in this group, there is Sol[1] himself as Time, Duration, Eternity, Day and Night.

As in the *Spaccio*, the central principles in the *De imaginum compositione* are solar and magical. We are in the presence of the magical reform, which Bruno is going over again in his mind, more or less as he had thought of it years ago in England.

And further, the application of the magical reform to the present-day situation is also perfectly apparent in the way the epithets are used in the *De imaginum compositione*, just as it is in the *Spaccio* where the "pedants" of intolerance are overcome by the Jovial, Solar, and Venereal reform. In the *De imaginum compositione*, the incantations of Orpheus and Arion overcome the miseries of Saturn, which here have obvious reference to bad forms of religion, Lamentation and Wailing, torn out hair, dust and ashes sprinkled on the head, horrible Squalor, mad Tenacity.[2] The evil Mars[3] has reference to religious wars and persecution. And the "grammarian pedants" are represented by the bad side of Mercury, whose splendid good sides are Eloquence, Refining Culture, perverted by grammarian pedantry (actually mentioned here) to Garrulity, Scurrility, sinister Rumour, biting Vituperation.[4]

Of the non-planetary principles of the *De imaginum compositione* list, Minerva is Truth, Candour, Sincerity[5]; whilst the last group with Tellus at their head represent the philosophy of nature. Tellus is Nature, Maternity, Fecundity, Generation[6] (corresponding to the Isis of natural religion among the gods of the *Spaccio*).

Though in the *De imaginum compositione* these remarkable notions are buried beneath the appalling intricacies of a most unattractive, difficult and daunting work apparently about mnemonics, they are in fact the same as those developed with great literary skill and thrilling imagery in the *Spaccio della bestia trionfante*.[7] Bruno is presenting to the eccentric owner of the castle

---

[1] *Ibid.*, pp. 250 ff.   [2] *Ibid.*, p. 250.   [3] *Ibid.*, pp. 221–2.

[4] *Ibid.*, pp. 227–9.   [5] *Ibid.*, p. 241.   [6] *Ibid.*, p. 270.

[7] There are also connections in the *De imaginum compositione* with others of the works published in England; with the *Asino cillenico* (see *ibid.*, pp. 237 ff.), and with the *Thirty Seals* (see *ibid.*, pp. 93, 163 ff., etc.).

of Elgg the same panacea for the times, the same magical reformation, as he had presented to Philip Sidney in London six years
earlier.

Interesting and important though this is, it is still not the most
interesting and revealing aspect of the *De imaginum, signorum et
idearum compositione*. For the book is really about, as its title
states, "the composition of images, signs and ideas", and by this is
meant, the composition of magic or talismanic images, signs and
ideas, an "idea" being here the equivalent of a talismanic image.
To each of the principles, there are attached a number of talismanic or magic images which have been made up, or composed,
for a special purpose. This purpose is, or so I believe, to attract
into the personality through imaginative concentration on these
images, these twelve principles or powers (only the good aspects
of them) and so to become a Solar, Jovial and Venereal Magus,
the leader of the magical reformation. The number of images
attached to each principle varies very greatly. In the list (see above),
the number of images with each principle is stated, so that one
can see at a glance that whilst Jupiter (with Juno) has eighteen
images; Apollo (if one counts with him the Aesculapius group and
Sol) has twenty; and Venus and Cupid have twelve; Saturn and
Mars have only four each. The personality which has captured
powers through these images will thus be mainly Solar, Jovial,
and Venereal, with only a little of Martial or Saturnian qualities.

Extraordinary and strange though this may seem, it is not really
more strange than the methods taught by Ficino in his *De vita
coelitus comparanda*. Ficino's object was to avoid melancholy and
the bad influences of Saturn and Mars, by cultivating the good
planets, Sol, Jupiter and Venus. He did this by his mild little
astral cults which involved the use of talismans, and he intended
it as a medical therapy, to cure melancholy in students. Nevertheless it was really more than this; it was, even with Ficino, a kind
of religion with a cult which he managed somehow or other to
reconcile with his Christian conscience. He did not aim at becoming a Magus or wonder-worker through it. But he did aim at
changing the personality, from a melancholy Saturnian one into a
happier and more fortunate Jovial-Solar-Venereal type.

Giordano Bruno, as we know from George Abbot, knew
Ficino's *De vita coelitus comparanda* by heart and he has developed

Ficino's sub-Christian supposedly medical cult into an inner technique for the formation of a religious Magus. It is really quite a logical development from Ficino; once you start a religion, there is no knowing what it may become. And we have also always to remember to see Bruno in the context of that Christian Hermetism which was such a major force in the sixteenth century and through which many Catholics and Protestants were trying to ease the religious antagonisms. Bruno always goes much further than the Christian Hermetists for he accepts the magical religion of the *Asclepius* as the best religion. Transferred into the inner life, that religion becomes Ficino's talismanic magic used inwardly to form a Magus aiming at being the leader of a magical religious movement.

In composing his images, Bruno has been influenced by astrological talismans, but diversifies these with normal mythological figures, or combines the talismanic with classical figures, or invents strange figures of his own. I can give only a few examples. Here are some of the images of Sol.

> Apollo with a bow and without the quiver, laughing.
> A man with a bow, killing a wolf, above him a crow flying.
> A young and beautiful man with a lute. . .
> An unfamiliar image . . . a bearded and helmeted man riding on a lion, above his helmet a gold crown . . . On the helmet a great cock with a conspicuous crest and ornamented with many colours.[1]

As can be seen here, ordinary classical images are varied with more magical ones, and this kind of mixture is found in all the lists of images. Bruno often introduces the more magical type of image with the remark that this is an "unfamiliar" image. One has a very curious impression of a mixture of the classical with the barbarous in Bruno's images, when one finds strange, dark and violent forms in close juxtaposition to the classical forms. A striking example of this is Orpheus, the first image of whom is the beautiful young man with the lute taming the animals, but his second image is a black king on a black throne before whom a violent sexual scene takes place[2] (there is possibly an alchemical meaning in this).

In composing these images, is Bruno behaving in a highly original way, peculiar to himself? Or is he leaving a door ajar

---

[1] *Ibid.*, p. 243.   [2] *Ibid.*, p. 249.

through which we can peer into something which may lie behind much Renaissance imagery? When a man of the Renaissance "composes" an image to be used on his medal, does he compose it in this kind of talismanic way? What is strange about these images of Bruno's is that he would seem to be reversing the process of the early Renaissance by which the more archaic images achieved a classical form. He seems to be deliberately pushing the classical images back towards a more barbarous form. Why? This could be a part of his general "Egyptianism". He wants to gain more magical power from them, or to recover their magical power.

The curious mixture of classical and barbarous or talismanic forms is strangely apparent in this selection from the Venus images:

> A girl rising from the foam of the sea, who on reaching dry land wipes off the humour of the sea with her palms.
>
> The Hours place garments on that naked girl and crown her head with flowers.
>
> A less familiar image, A crowned man of august presence most gentle of aspect, riding on a camel, dressed in a garment the colour of all flowers, leading with his right hand a naked girl, moving in a grave and venerable manner. . . . from the west with a benignant zephyr comes an assembly (? *curia*) of omniform beauty.[1]

The first two images here might be something like Botticelli's "Birth of Venus"; the third, with its crowned man on a camel, is talismanic in type, but softened by notions and forms—the garment the colour of all flowers, the benignant zephyr coming in from the west—such as could never find expression in the fixed rigidity of an ordinary talisman.

Was it something after this manner that Ficino himself composed images, in which the basic magical or talismanic power was softened by expansion into Renaissance classical forms? In an earlier chapter we suggested that Botticelli's "Primavera" is basically a talismanic Venus, expanded in just such a way into a richer classical form, and that the whole picture reflects Ficino's astral cult. In Giordano Bruno's Venus images, composed with a definite magical intention, there is perhaps some confirmation of this suggestion.

There is, too, in Ficino's *De vita coelitus comparanda* a precedent for Bruno's practice of reflecting the magic images within,

[1] *Ibid.*, pp. 259–61.

in the imagination and in the magic memory. We saw that in the curious chapter "On making a figure of the universe", that the figure and its images was to be "reflected in the soul". And there also seemed to be a hint that such remembered images unified the multiplicity of individual things, so that a man coming out of his house with such images in his mind saw, not so much the spectacle of individual things, as the figure of the universe and its colours.[1] This was exactly Bruno's aim, in his eternal efforts to find the images, signs, characters in living contact with reality which, when established in memory, would unify the whole contents of the universe.

It is thus possible that—although it comes so late in time—Bruno's *De imaginum, signorum et idearum compositione* may be an important key to the way in which the Renaissance composed images, and also to the way in which it used images.

Bruno's method was still known and being used by Robert Fludd who in the second part of his *Utriusque cosmi . . . historia* of 1619 has a memory system with a celestial basis to which is attached a series of mnemonic places in a theatre[2]—an arrangement like that of the two parts of the *De imaginum compositione* which I think that Fludd must have known. It is interesting that Fludd, too, uses "ideas" not in the usual Platonic sense but as meaning spiritual things, angels, demons, the "effigies of stars" or the "images of gods and goddesses attributed to celestial things".[3]

In the dedication to Hainzell of the *De imaginum compositione*, Bruno states that the twelve principles are "the effecters, signifiers, enlargers (?) of all things under the ineffable and infigurable optimus maximus".[4] They are thus divine Powers, and the object of the whole system is (I believe) to become identified with such Powers. Once again we are back to a Hermetic notion, the effort

---

[1] See above, pp. 75–6.

[2] R. Fludd, *Utriusque cosmi . . . historia*, Part II (Microcosmus), Oppenheim, 1619, pp. 48 ff. On Fludd and Bruno see further below, pp. 406–7.

[3] "nec enim vocabulo ideae hic utimur tali modo quo Plato . . . sed . . . pro Angelis, Daemonibus, stellarum effigiebus, & Deorum vel Dearum imaginibus, quibus coelestia attribuuntur . . .", Fludd, *op. cit.*, p. 50. The title of Bruno's book, "On the composition of images, signs, and ideas" refers to "ideas" in this sense.

[4] *Op. lat.*, II (iii), p. 92.

of the initiate to become identified with Powers, and so to become divine.

Bruno once more expounds in the first part of the *De imaginum compositione* his theory of the imagination as the chief instrument in religious and magical processes. He had given the theory in the *Explicatio Triginta Sigillorum*, written in England, and gives it most fully of all in the *De magia*, written about 1590 or 1591 (that is at about the same time as the *De imaginum compositione*) and which we used in an earlier chapter. The theory can be interestingly studied in the *De imaginum compositione* where is revealed a curious confusion in Bruno's mind. He cites Aristotle on "to think is to speculate with images".[1] Aristotle's statement is used by Bruno as support for his belief in the primacy of the imagination as the instrument for reaching truth. Later, he quotes Synesius' defence of the imagination in his work on dreams (using Ficino's translation).[2] Synesius is defending imagination because of its use by divine powers to communicate with man in dreams. Bruno seems to fail to realise how totally opposite are the Aristotelian and the Synesian defences of the imagination. Aristotle is thinking of images from sense impressions as the sole basis of thought; Synesius is thinking of divine and miraculous images impressed on the imagination in dreams. Having cited Aristotle on images from sense impressions as the basis of thought, Bruno then goes right to the other extreme of the classical tradition and uses the arguments of a late Hellenistic Neoplatonist in favour of imagination in quite another sense from the Aristotelian, as the most powerful of the inner senses because through it the divine communicates with man.

This confusion belongs to Bruno's transformation of the art of memory from a fairly rational technique using images, theorists on which—amongst them Thomas Aquinas himself—had used the Aristotelian dictum, into a magical and religious technique for training the imagination as the instrument for reaching the divine and obtaining divine powers,[3] linking through the imagina-

---

[1] Aristotle, *De anima*, 431 a, 17. Quoted in the Latin translation *Op. lat.*, II (iii), p. 103, also in the dedication to Hainzell, *ibid.*, p. 91.

[2] *Op. lat.*, II (iii), pp. 120–1. Bruno is here compressing and adapting Synesius' *De somniis*, using Ficino's translation (Ficino, pp. 1970–1).

[3] I hope to study the change in theory of the imagination in relation to the Renaissance development of the use of images in memory in my book on the art of memory.

tion with angels, demons, the effigies of stars and inner "statues" of gods and goddesses in contact with celestial things.

In an extraordinary passage in the *De imaginum compositione*, Bruno mentions the golden calf and the brazen image described in *Genesis* (which he interprets as magic images used by Moses, referring for this astonishing statement to "the doctrine of the Cabalists"), and the clay figures made by Prometheus, as all examples of the power of the simulachrum for drawing down the favour of the gods through occult analogies between inferior and superior things "whence as though linked to images and similitudes they descend and communicate themselves."[1] With the last phrase, we reach the familiar ground of the Egyptian statues, linked with demons, which Bruno has here related to the magic of Moses and Prometheus to produce a truly amazing Hermetic-Cabalist justification for the inner magics in his arts of memory.

Light, says Bruno, is the vehicle in the inner world through which the divine images and intimations are imprinted, and this light is not that through which normal sense impressions reach the eyes, but an inner light joined to a most profound contemplation, of which Moses speaks, calling it "primogenita", and of which Mercurius also speaks in *Pimander*.[2] Here the *Genesis-Pimander* equation, so characteristic of the Hermetic-Cabalist tradition, is applied by Bruno to creation in the inner world.

There are words and passages in the *De imaginum compositione* about the frenzy or *furor* with which the enthusiast hunts after the vestiges of the divine which are very like passages in the *Eroici furori*; and he gives another formulation of his belief that poetry, painting, and philosophy are all one, to which he now adds music. "True philosophy is music, poetry or painting; true painting is poetry, music, and philosophy; true poetry or music is divine sophia and painting."[3]

It is in such contexts as these, which have been little studied by the philosophers who have admired Giordano Bruno, that one should see the philosophy of the infinite universe and the innumerable worlds. Such concepts are not with him primarily philosophical or scientific thinking, but more in the nature of hieroglyphs of the divine, attempts to figure the infigurable, to be

[1] *Op. lat.*, II (iii), p. 102.
[2] *Op. lat.*, II (iii), p. 117.
[3] *Ibid.*, p. 198.

imprinted on memory through imaginative effort to become one with the universe, which was the Hermetic aim pursued throughout his life by this intensely religious magician.

Why, I say, do so few understand and apprehend the internal power? .... He who in himself sees all things, is all things.[1]

[1] *Ibid.*, p. 90 (dedication to Hainzell of the *De imaginum compositione*).

Chapter XIX

GIORDANO BRUNO:
RETURN TO ITALY

GIOVANNI BATTISTA CIOTTO was a book-
seller who kept a shop in Venice. Among his clients
was Zuan Mocenigo, scion of an ancient and noble
Venetian family, who bought a book, or books, by
Bruno of him, and asked him if he knew where the author was as
he would like to learn "secrets of memory" and other matters
from him. Ciotto knew Bruno, having met him in Frankfort
whither he went for the book-fairs, and he transmitted to him an
invitation from Mocenigo to come to Venice. Bruno accepted, and
in August 1591 he appeared in Venice.[1] Why did he take that fatal
step of returning to Italy, apparently oblivious of its danger?

For years, now, he had been crossing and recrossing frontiers,
brushing aside the ideological curtains, passing from Protestant
England to Paris under the League, thence to Lutheran Wittenberg and on to Catholic Prague, making for the centres of learning
in each country where he delivered his message. He seems to have
thought that he could continue such a career with impunity in
Italy, for he got into touch in Venice with a Dominican whom he
had known long ago in Naples, informing him that he was writing
a book for presentation to the Pope and mentioning that he would
like to have the opportunity of taking part in some literary exercise
in Rome, to show his powers and perhaps to gain some lecture-

---

[1] *Documenti*, pp. 69 ff.; Spampanato, *Vita di Giordano Bruno*, pp. 456
ff.; McIntyre, *Giordano Bruno*, pp. 66 ff.

15 (*a*) The "Monas Hieroglyphica". From the title-page of John Dee, *Monas Hieroglyphica*, Antwerp, 1564 (p. 420, note)

15 (*b*) Kircher's version of the "Monas Hieroglyphica". From Athanasius Kircher, *Obeliscus Pamphilius*, Rome, 1650, p. 371 (p. 420, note)

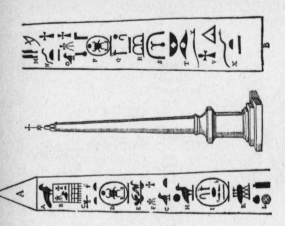

16 (b) "Obeliscus Heliopolitanus". From Athanasius Kircher, *Obeliscus Pamphilius*, Rome, 1650, p. 371 (p. 420)

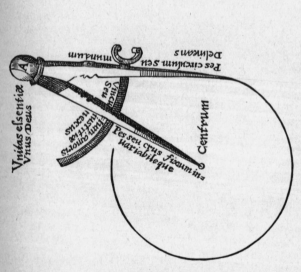

16 (a) The Mystical Compass. From Robert Fludd, *Utriusque cosmi—historia*, II (1), p. 28 (p. 407)

ship.[1] I think that the very madness of this plan indicates that Bruno had never thought of himself as anti-Catholic. The Catholic religion "pleased him more than any other"[2] but there was a great deal that was wrong with it. It needed reformation and it was the Nolan's mission to assist in that reformation. The best centre from which to start on this would be Rome itself where he would get into touch with the Pope.

People like Giordano Bruno are immunised from a sense of danger by their sense of mission, or their megalomania, or the state of euphoria bordering on insanity in which they constantly live. "Although I cannot see your soul", he makes an English admirer say of him, "from the ray which it diffuses I perceive that within you is a sun or perhaps some even greater luminary."[3] When he was an infant in Nola, a huge serpent of very ancient appearance came out of an aperture in the wall of the house.[4] Serpents in the cradle are a sign of a heroic destiny, as we know from the history of Hercules. There is little doubt that Bruno thought of himself as a Messiah, an illusion not uncommon in the Renaissance. A remarkable example is the case of the man who called himself "Mercurius" and who thought that he was a kind of Christ.[5] The divinising Hermetic experience, thought to be transmitted in a miraculous way, like the way in which Christ transmitted experience to the Apostles, is described by Ludovico Lazzarelli, who was a disciple of the "Mercurius-Christ", in his *Crater Hermetis*. This work was published by Symphorien Champier in the same volume as Lazzarelli's Latin translation of the sixteenth treatise of the *Corpus Hermeticum*. We have thought earlier that Bruno knew the sixteenth treatise in Lazzarelli's translation, and if so it is likely that he would also have seen the *Crater Hermetis*. Hermetism, with its belief in a "divinising" experience, is conducive to religious mania of this kind.

As A. Corsano and L. Firpo have pointed out,[6] Bruno in his last years of liberty seems to have been working up towards taking action. There is the feverish production, the intense concentration

[1] *Documenti*, pp. 88–9.

[2] See below, p. 340.

[3] *De l'infinito universo e mondi*, dial. 1 (*Dial. ital.*, p. 392).

[4] *Sigillus sigillorum* (*Op. lat.*, II (ii), pp. 184–5).

[5] See above, pp. 117–2, for the references about Mercurius and Lazzarelli.

[6] A. Corsano, *Il pensiero di Giordano Bruno*, Florence, 1940, pp. 267 ff.; L. Firpo, *Il processo di Giordano Bruno*, Naples, 1949, pp. 10 ff.

on magical techniques of the late works in the Noroff manuscript. The time was coming for a new mission, like the one on which he was sent into England by Henri III. We have seen that in the *De imaginum, signorum et idearum compositione* the notions behind the *Spaccio della bestia trionfante* are rising with renewed force in the inner life. The prior of the Carmelite monastery at which Bruno stayed in Frankfort told Ciotto that he was always writing and dreaming and astrologising about new things ("se occupava per il più in scriver ed andar chimerizando e strolegando cose nove")[1]; that he said that he knew more than the Apostles, and that, if he had a mind to it, he could bring it about that all the world should be of one religion ("egli dice, che sa più che non sapevano li Apostoli, a che gli bastava l'animo de far, se avesse voluto, che tutto il mondo sarebbe stato d'una religione").[2]

Most important of all in influencing Bruno's return to Italy was the turn which events in Europe had taken by the middle of 1591. Henry of Navarre was the hero of the hour; victorious over the Catholic League and its Spanish backing, he had won his right, the crown of France, and there was already talk in the air that he would become a Catholic. For Bruno this meant renewed possibility of the universal reform within a Catholic framework.

> The procedure which the Church uses to-day is not that which the Apostles used: for they converted the people with preaching and the example of a good life, but now whoever does not wish to be a Catholic must endure punishment and pain, for force is used and not love; the world cannot go on like this, for there is nothing but ignorance and no religion which is good; the Catholic religion pleases him more than any other, but this too has need of great reform; it is not good as it is now, but soon the world will see a general reform of itself, for it is impossible that such corruptions should endure; he hopes great things of the King of Navarre, and he means to hurry to publish his works to gain credit in this way, for when the time comes he wishes to be "capitano", and he will not be always poor for he will enjoy the treasures of others.[3]

So Mocenigo reported, in one of his delations to the Venetian Inquisition (May, 1592), what he had heard Bruno say. We can recognise here the familiar theme that the world is at its lowest

---

[1] *Documenti*, p. 74. [2] *Ibid.*, p. 75.
[3] *Documenti*, p. 66; *Sommario*, p. 55.

ebb of corruption, which means that it is about to return to a better "Egyptian" state. The mixed motives of the prophet of the return, who expects to become a "capitano" in the new dispensation of love and magic, may well be fairly correctly reported by Mocenigo, also the feverish haste to publish and so "gain credit" sounds very much in character. I would not have thought that the Nolan was greedy for wealth, as Mocenigo insinuates, but he would certainly want spiritual recognition, and acknowledgement of his prophetic rôle.

The new book which it was so necessary to publish quickly was on "The Seven Liberal Arts" and was to be dedicated to the Pope, Clement VIII. He was about to go back to Frankfort to get this printed when, through Mocenigo's efforts, he was put into the prisons of the Inquisition in Venice. He explained it all to the Inquisitors, how he had meant to get this book printed at Frankfort and then take it and other of his printed works "which I approve of" and present himself at the feet of His Beatitude, who, so he has heard, "loves virtuosi", and explain to him his case, asking for absolution and permission to live in a clerical habit "outside of Religion" (that is, without returning into his Order).[1] This is the plan which he had discussed with the Dominican, as he also mentions to the Inquisitors.

The Inquisitors questioned him about the King of Navarre. Did he know him? Did he expect aid or favour from him?

> I do not know the King of Navarre nor his ministers, nor have I ever seen him. In speaking of him I have said that I did not think that he was a Calvinist or a heretic except from necessity of reign, for if he did not profess heresy he would not have followers. I also said that I hoped that when he had pacified the kingdom of France he would confirm the orders of the late King, and that I would have of him the favours that I had from the late King concerning public lectures.[2]

So he tried to pass off Mocenigo's report that he had hoped great things of the King of Navarre. But the Inquisitors were not satisfied with this explanation, and asked whether in speaking of the King of Navarre he had said that he hoped great things of him, and that the world had great need of reform, inferring that the Christian religion pleased him more than any other but that a great reform was needed.

[1] *Documenti*, pp. 86–7, 131. [2] *Ibid.*, p. 122.

I did not say such a thing; and when I praised the King of Navarre, I did not praise him because he was an adherent of the heretics, but for the reason which I have already given, the belief that he was not otherwise a heretic, but that he lived as a heretic from desire of ruling.[1]

He also denied that he had said that he wanted to be a "capitano".[2] Clearly this matter of the expected "great reform", and the connection of this with Navarre, was a point of special interest to the Inquisitors.

Bruno did know more than he told them about Henry of Navarre and his inner confidants, for he had known Corbinelli and Piero Del Bene in Paris, and to the latter he had dedicated the Mordente dialogues and another book.[3] Del Bene was considerably in the know about Henry of Navarre and his inner mind. In a letter from Corbinelli to Pinelli of August, 1585, Pinelli is told of Del Bene's recent visit to the court of Navarre in Gascony; where his efforts are vaguely hinted at in mythological language as greater than those of Nessus; and a hint of Navarre's possible conversion is dropped.[4] Thus in the circle which Bruno was frequenting in Paris in 1586 such matters would have been knowledgeably discussed. It is also perhaps interesting that it was Alessandro Del Bene, brother of Piero, who actually brought the document of the absolution from Rome to Henri IV in 1595.[5] This whole question of the relations of the Del Bene family with Henry of Navarre, afterwards Henri IV, is very important and much light would be thrown on it (and perhaps indirectly on Bruno's politico-religious position) by a full publication of the Pinelli-Corbinelli correspondence.

If in the impossible event of Bruno's conception of a general reform having been realised, we were to imagine the impossible celebration of that event in the form of some vast mannerist painting on the lines of the *Spaccio della bestia trionfante*, which would lend itself well to pictorial representation, the form and

---

[1] *Ibid.*, pp. 122–3. [2] *Ibid.*, p. 123. [3] See above, pp. 293–4, 302.

[4] Ambrosiana T.167 sup., ff. 170 *v.*–171; quoted in R. Calderini De-Marchi, *Jacopo Corbinelli et les érudits français*, Milan, 1914, pp. 237–8; cf. my article "Giordano Bruno: Some New Documents", *Revue internationale de philosophie*, 1951, pp. 195–6.

[5] H. C. Davila, *Historia delle guerre civili di Francia*, ed. Lyons, 1641, p. 972; cf. my article cited in preceding note, *loc. cit.*

face of Henri IV, wearing his perpetual grin, fit rather well into that picture—better than poor melancholy Henri III—enthroned among the gods who have carried out the Jovial, Solarian, and Venereal reform.

Vast and vague hopes of some religious settlement following on Navarre's victory and conversion were aroused throughout Europe, and particularly in Venice, as Agrippa d'Aubigné ironically reports:

> Divines . . . were finding by the figures of geomancy, by oracles, by the fatal name of Bourbon, that this prince was destined to convert the hierarchies to the Empire, the pulpit into a throne, the keys into swords, and that he would die Emperor of the Christians. The Venetians were adoring this rising sun with such devotion that when a French gentleman passed through their town they would run to greet him. At the Court of the Emperor and in Poland one heard public prayers that the Empire might be confided into his fortunate hands, together with disputes concerning the reunion of religions, or the toleration of them all, and many discourses to induce Italy to this point of view.[1]

Giordano Bruno was thus not alone in hoping great things of the King of Navarre.

The hopes for the reunion and reform of Christendom which were stirring in Europe at this time, and which centred on Navarre, have not yet been fully studied as a whole, though recent researches have drawn attention to individuals who were working in this direction.[2] The most important of these, from the point of view of comparison with Bruno, is Francesco Pucci.[3] Like Bruno, Pucci

---

[1] Agrippa d'Aubigné, *Confession Catholique du Sieur de Sancy*, in *Œuvres complètes*, ed. Réaume et de Caussade, II, p. 327; cf. my *French Academies of the Sixteenth Century*, p. 224.

[2] See, for example, the study of the Italian Huguenot and Navarrist, Jacopo Brocardo, by Delio Cantimori; "Visioni e speranze di un ugonotto Italiano", *Rivista storica italiana*, 1950, pp. 199 ff. Or the study of Francesco Maria Vialardi, a Navarrist political agent who was in the prisons of the Inquisition at the same time as Bruno, by Luigi Firpo; "In margine al processo di Giordano Bruno, Francesco Maria Vialardi", *Rivista storica italiana*, 1956, pp. 325 ff. Bruno denied any connection with Vialardi or with the "parole orrende contro Dio, la religione e la Chiesa" which he had heard him speak (*Sommario*, p. 84).

[3] Delio Cantimori drew attention to the importance of F. Pucci in his *Eretici italiani del cinquecento*, Florence, 1939, pp. 370 ff., and published some of his writings in *Per la storia degli eretici italiani del secolo XVI in*

had wandered much in foreign heretical lands (he had been in England and had influential friends there). In Prague, in 1585, he returned to the Catholic church; and there he was also in contact with Dee and Kelley, some of whose spirit-raising séances he attended.[1] He was a Navarrist, and in 1592 he returned to Italy, only a few months after Bruno's return, after writing a number of letters to important personages, amongst them Navarre, Elizabeth of England, and Pope Clement VIII.[2] His reception in Italy was probably not what he expected, for he was put into the prisons of the Inquisition in Rome, and in 1597 he suffered the death penalty (he was not actually burned alive, like Bruno, but beheaded in prison and his corpse was burned on the Campo de' Fiori) having refused to abjure his errors. There was almost certainly some kind of Hermetism in Pucci's line of thinking. It is indeed possible, though detailed research would be needed before definite statements can be made, that the whole Navarrist movement drew largely for its eirenic hopes on different brands of Hermetism among its adherents. At any rate, it coincides in date with that end of the sixteenth century which J. Dagens has called "l'âge d'or de l'hermétisme religieux".[3]

By the time that Bruno returned to Italy, the enthusiastic Hermetist, Hannibal Rosseli, whom John Dee consulted as his religious adviser,[4] had published at Cracow (1585–90) his vast

---

[1] The angel Uriel appeared at the séances (of course seen only by Kelley) and addressed inspiring speeches to Pucci. Pucci seems to have tried to induce Dee to go to Rome to tell the Pope about his experiences with the angels. See *A True and Faithfull Relation of what passed for many years between Dr. John Dee . . . and some spirits*, ed. Meric Casaubon, London, 1659, pp. 409 ff. Pucci's own subsequent fate would seem to prove that he was acting in good faith in urging Dee to go to Rome, and not as an *agent provocateur*, though Dee suspected him at the time.

[2] See Firpo, *Gli Scritti di Francesco Pucci*, pp. 114, 124, 134. To Navarre's secretary, Louis Revol, Pucci wrote that he was going to try "whether in Italy I can do some good office with this Pope Clement for the public good" (*ibid.*, p. 120).

[3] See above, p. 170.   [4] See above, p. 188.

Europa, Rome, 1937. Luigi Firpo has studied Pucci's life and trial in his article "Processo e morte di Francesco Pucci", *Rivista di Filosofia*, 1949 (XL) and has compiled a bibliography of his writings, *Gli Scritti di Francesco Pucci*, Turin, 1957.

"scritture" by Bruno.[1] And Pinelli, as the tenor of his correspondence shows, belonged to the Venetian liberals and would, in all probability, at this time have been hoping things from Navarre. There is, however, no evidence that Bruno got into touch with Pinelli at Padua, and we know little about his time there, except that he was very busy with his secretary, Besler, dictating to him and having copies made of various works. It was here that he dictated to Besler the *De vinculis in genere*,[2] his ripest thought on magical "linking", particularly links through love or sexual attraction. Here Besler made a copy of the "Thirty Statues", written in Wittenberg.[3] And here was transcribed, from a copy in Besler's possession, a work called *De sigillis Hermetis et Ptolomaei*, which was found among the "conjuring books" in Bruno's possession when he was arrested, and which seems to have excited a good deal of interest and alarm.[4] Bruno stated that it was not written by himself, but was copied for him at Padua, adding, "I do not know whether as well as natural divination there may be some other condemned thing in it; I had it transcribed to use in judicial (astrology); but I have not read it yet, and I procured it because Albertus Magnus in his book *De mineralibus* mentions it, and praises it in the place where he treats *De imaginibus lapidum*."[5] The careless remark that he had not yet read this work on his favourite subject of Hermetic seals does not carry conviction.

Thus the magician was busily working at his magic in Padua, endeavouring to acquire the magical personality with its powers of "linking" through love, working at Hermetic seals and links with demons. As L. Firpo has suggested, the time at Padua should probably be regarded as a time of preparation for the mission.[6]

---

[1] The "scritture" were sent with the letter of February 16th, 1586, describing Fabrizio's anger against Bruno (Ambrosiana, T.167 sup., f. 180); cf. my article "Giordano Bruno: Some New Documents", p. 178.

[2] *Op. lat.*, III, introduction, p. xxviii.

[3] *Ibid.*, *loc. cit.*

[4] *Documenti*, pp. 64, 90–1, 127–8; *Sommario*, pp. 100, 110.

[5] *Documenti*, pp. 127–8. Bruno is probably referring to the remarks about seals in *De mineralibus*, II, 3 (Albertus Magnus, *Opera*, ed. P. Jammy, Lyons, 1651, II, p. 226). The *De mineralibus* also contains lists of magic images of the stars, and would altogether be a useful work of reference for a Dominican magician. Hermes Trismegistus is frequently mentioned in it. Cf. *Sommario*, p. 100, note; Thorndike, II, pp. 556 ff.

[6] Firpo, *Il Processo di Giordano Bruno*, p. 14.

The same writer has also acutely pointed out[1] that Bruno was most unsuited by character and temperament for such a difficult, delicate, and dangerous task. Irritable, quarrelsome—indeed, more than that, subject to pathological accesses of rage in which he said terrible things which frightened people—he did not have the magical charm of personality which he sought after and he undid the work of his message by his strange outbursts. Tommaso Campanella, who was also a magician with a message, was yet of a very different calibre, with some degree of realism in his make-up, and with a certain massive grasp of situations—qualities in which the poor Nolan was totally lacking.

Bruno left Padua for Venice in March, 1592,[2] and began to live with Mocenigo and to teach him as originally agreed when he accepted the invitation transmitted by Ciotto. It has been said that the invitation was from the first a trap and that Mocenigo always intended to hand him over to the Inquisition. There is, however, no real evidence about this trap. Again it has been said that Mocenigo was irritated and disappointed with Bruno's teaching and in spite about this delated him to the Inquisition. Possibly, in view of what has been suggested concerning Bruno's real intentions in coming to Italy, it might now be possible to take another view of Mocenigo's delation. Perhaps, having had Bruno under observation for some two months in his house, he saw something of the mission, and as a non-liberal Venetian, who was not hoping for more liberty from Navarre, he did not approve of it. Also, Bruno seems to have given way to some of his more alarming outbursts whilst in Mocenigo's house. Probably because he had grown distrustful of his host, Bruno made arrangements to leave and to return to Frankfort, which Mocenigo prevented by force, shutting him up in a room in the house, whence he was transported to the prisons of the Holy Office in which he was incarcerated on May 26th, 1592.[3] On that day began for Bruno eight years of imprisonment ending in death.

[1] *Ibid.*, pp. 12, 114.

[2] In his delation of May 25th, 1592, Mocenigo said that Bruno had been in his house about two months (*Documenti*, p. 64); this may, however, not be reliable (see Spampanato, *Vita di Giordano Bruno*, p. 468).

[3] *Documenti*, pp. 68–9, 77–9. It may be significant that the book by Bruno which Mocenigo bought of Ciotto, and which led to the invitation to come to Venice, is described by Ciotto as the *De minimo, magno et men-*

The documents of the Venetian Inquisition on Bruno's case have long been known, also some Roman documents, and are available in Vincenzo Spampanato's publication, *Documenti della vita di Giordano Bruno* (1933). In 1942, a large addition to the evidence was made by Cardinal Angelo Mercati who published in that year *Il Sommario del Processo di Giordano Bruno*. This *Sommario*, a summary of the evidence drawn up for the use of the Roman Inquisitors, was discovered by Mercati among the personal archives of Pope Pius IX.[1] This document repeats much that was known from the Venetian archives but adds a great deal of new information. It is not, however, the actual *processo*, the official report on the case giving the sentence, that is to say stating on what grounds Bruno was finally condemned. This *processo* is lost for ever, having formed part of a mass of archives which were transported to Paris by the order of Napoleon, where they were eventually sold as pulp to a cardboard factory.[2]

At the end of the Venetian trial, Bruno fully recanted all the heresies of which he was accused and threw himself in penitence on the mercy of the judges.[3] He had, however, by law to be sent to Rome where the case dragged on. In 1599 an effort was made to clarify the situation by the famous Jesuit, Robert Bellarmine, who, assisted by Tragagliolo, drew up eight heretical propositions taken from his works which Bruno was required to abjure, and he said that he was prepared to do so.[4] But later in that year he withdrew all his retractions, obstinately maintaining that he had never written or said anything heretical and that the ministers of the Holy Office had wrongly interpreted his views.[5] He was therefore sentenced as an impenitent heretic and handed over to the secular arm for punishment. He was burned alive on the Campo de' Fiori in Rome on February 17th, 1600.

[1] *Sommario*, introduction, p. 21.

[2] *Ibid.*, pp. 1–4.

[3] *Documenti*, pp. 135–6.

[4] *Documenti*, p. 191; cf. Mercati's introduction to the *Sommario*, pp. 41 ff.; Firpo, *Il processo di Giordano Bruno*, pp. 90 ff.

[5] *Documenti*, pp. 183, 186; cf. *Sommario* (introduction), pp. 43 ff.; Firpo, *op. cit.*, pp. 92 ff.

---

sura (*Documenti*, p. 70). If the *De triplici minimo* contains allusions to a sect or secret society, as suggested in chapter XVII, and Mocenigo recognised these, the theory that his invitation was a trap might become more probable.

In one of the earlier interviews with the Venetian Inquisitors,[1] Bruno gave a very full and frank account of his philosophy, rather as though he were addressing the doctors of Oxford, Paris, or Wittenberg. The universe is infinite, for the infinite divine power would not produce a finite world. The earth is a star, as Pythagoras said, like the moon and other planets and worlds which are infinite in number. In this universe is a universal providence in virtue of which everything in it lives and moves, and this universal nature is a shadow or vestige of the divinity, of God, who in his essence is ineffable and inexplicable. The attributes of the divinity he understands—together with theologians and the greatest philosophers—to be all one. The three attributes of Power, Wisdom, and Goodness ("Potenzia, Sapienza e Bontà"), are the same as *mens*, *intellectus*, and *amor* ("mente, intelletto ed amore").

In speaking of this according to faith, and not philosophically, the wisdom, or son of the *mens*, called by philosophers *intellectus*, and by theologians, the Word, must be believed to have taken on human flesh, but he (Bruno) has always had doubts about this, holding it doubtfully and with inconstant faith. And concerning the divine spirit, as a third person, he has held this in the Pythagorean manner, or in the manner of Solomon when he says: "Spiritus Domini replevit orbem terrarum, et hoc quod continet omnia"; or after the manner of Virgil when he said:

> Spiritus intus alit totamque infusa per artus
> mens agitat molem. . .

It seems that Bruno's faith is that of a Renaissance Neoplatonic Hermetist, except—and this makes all the difference between a Christian Hermetist and a non-Christian Hermetist—that he does not accept the *intellectus* or *Filius Dei* of the *Hermetica* as referring to the Second Person of the Trinity, as Lactantius did, and as is shown in the representation of Hermes Trismegistus on the Siena pavement. His view of the Third Person as the *anima mundi* or the Virgilian "spiritus intus alit" was an interpretation frequently made in the Renaissance. To give only one example, it was expounded at length by Bishop (later Cardinal) Jacques Davy Du Perron in a Whit Sunday sermon.[2]

---

[1] *Documenti*, pp. 93–8.

[2] "He (the Holy Spirit) it is of whom the Pagans themselves said, speaking of the constitution of the world, *Spiritus intus alit*." Jacques

Bruno's faith as he emphasises later to the Inquisitors, he considers to be Catholic and orthodox as concerning the Father or the *mens*; he confesses that he is unorthodox as regards the Son[1]; his view of the Third Person as the *anima mundi* would have been orthodox to many Christian Renaissance Neoplatonists.

It is this attitude to the Hermetic *Filius Dei* as not the Second Person of the Christian Trinity which is the root theological reason why Bruno's Hermetism becomes purely "Egyptian", with the Hermetic Egyptian religion not as a *prisca theologia* foreshadowing Christianity but actually as the true religion.

Very important, among the new documents in the *Sommario* are the indications of Bruno's view of the cross as really an Egyptian sacred sign. A fellow-prisoner reports him as having said that the cross on which Christ was crucified was not in the form shown on Christian altars, this form being in reality the sign which was sculptured on the breast of the goddess Isis, and which was "stolen" by the Christians from the Egyptians.[2] In reply to an inquisitorial question about this, Bruno acknowledged that he had said that form of the cross on which Christ was crucified was different from the way in which it is usually "painted", adding these significant words:

> I think that I have read in Marsilio Ficino that the virtue and holiness of this character ("carattere", by which he means the cross) is much more ancient than the time of the Incarnation of Our Lord, and that it was known in the time in which the religion of the Egyptians flourished, about the time of Moses, and that this sign was affixed to

[1] *Documenti*, p. 96.

[2] "Vedendo ch'io e gl'altri ci segnavamo con la croce disse (i.e. Bruno disse) che non occorea fare questo segno perchè Christo non fu messo sopra la croce, ma fu confitto sopra dui legni, sopra li quali si solevano sospendere i condannati e che quella forma di croce che hoggidi si tiene sopra l'altari era un carattere e segno ch'era scolpito nel petto della Dea Iside, e che quel segno dagl'antichi era sempre tenuto in veneratione, e che i Christiani l'haveano rubbato da gl'antichi fingendo che in quella forma fosse il legno sopra il quale fu affisso Christo . . ." *Sommario*, pp. 70–1.

Davy Du Perron, *Diverses œuvres*, Paris, 1622, p. 684. Cf. my *French Academies of the Sixteenth Century*, p. 169, note 5. Du Perron's views on the point are of particular interest since he was one of the chief converters of Henry of Navarre; see above, p. 303.

the breast of Serapis, and that the planets and their influences have more efficacy . . . when they are at the beginning of the cardinal signs, that is when the colures intersect the ecliptic or the zodiac in a direct line, whence from two circles intersecting in this manner is produced the form of such a character (that is the form of the cross). . . .[1]

There is indeed such a passage in Ficino, in the *De vita coelitus comparanda*,[2] where he explains that the form of the cross is a powerful form for capturing the influences of the stars; and that it was sculptured on the breast of Serapis. Ficino thinks, however, that the form of the cross was revered among the Egyptians, not only as a testimony to the "gifts of the stars", but also as a presage of the coming of Christ.

One wonders whether this passage in the *De vita coelitus comparanda* might be a major source of Bruno's Egyptianism. He had only slightly to change Ficino's argument, that the Egyptian cross powerful in magic was a presage of Christianity, into the argument that the Egyptian cross was the true cross, representing the true religion, powerful in magic, which the Christians had

[1] "Ho ben detto (Bruno is speaking) che la croce non havea quattro rami eguali secondo l'uso che si pinge, et è usurpato il sacro carattere di quella perchè altrimente si pratticava ne la punitione de rei anticamente, e che ne la croce di Christo il quarto ramo fu posticcio cioè il superiore palo per commodità di affigervi il titolo, e confessando che il carattere della croce ha virtù della morte di nostro signore in quella ho detto quello che mi pare haver letto in Marsilio Ficino, che la virtù e riverenza di quel carattere è molto più antica che non è il tempo dell'incarnatione di nostro Signore e ch'è stata riconosciuta dal tempo che fioriva la Religione de gl'Egittij circa i tempi di Moise, e che quel segno era affisso nel petto di Serapide, et all'hora li pianeti et influssi di essi hanno più efficacia oltre il principio, e fondamento quando sono nel principio de segni cardinali cioè dove i colori intersecano l'eclitica o il zodiaco per linea retta, onde da dui circoli in questo modo intersecanti viene prodotta la forma di tale carattere, li quattro segni cardinali sono li dui equinottiali e li dui solstitiali circa li quali la morte, natività et incarnatione di Nostro Signore sempre fu intesa essere, e fu celebrata." *Sommario*, pp. 72–3. I gather from this that Bruno thought that Christ was crucified on a "tau" cross, the cross used by the Christians being really the Egyptian "character".

There are some representations of the Crucifixion in which the form of the cross is the "tau" or T form. On this question, see G. Miccoli, "La 'Crociata dei Fanciulli' del 1212", *Studi medievali*, 3e serie, II, 2 (1961), pp. 421 ff. and the references there given. See below, pp. 419–20, on Athanasius Kircher on the cross.

[2] See above, p. 72.

changed and weakened its magic (which appears to be what he said to the fellow-prisoner who reported him as saying that the Christians had "stolen" the Egyptian sign), and the Egyptian cross would become the sign, the "character", the "seal" of his own message. Perhaps this was one of the reasons why he thought it would be so easy to incorporate his message into a reformed Catholicism, since it was the form of the true Egyptian cross which was on the altars!

The Nolan's mind was evidently continuing to work in the same extraordinary way in prison—a way, be it noted, very like the way in which Ficino's mind worked on the cross, save for the one basic difference that Ficino's Egyptian cross is a presage of Christianity, whilst for Bruno the Christians have stolen and spoiled the true Egyptian cross (for one feels pretty sure that the fellow prisoner correctly reported what Bruno had said).

It was this basic difference which made it possible, and indeed right and religious, for Bruno to go all out for every sort of magic, in contrast to Ficino, who had to be so extremely careful to keep his magic natural and non-demonic.

Bruno expressed his views on good and bad magic in the course of answers to questions about why he had the book *De sigillis Hermetis* in his possession. Magic, he said, is "like a sword, which can be used ill in the hands of a wicked person, but in the hand of a good man who fears God and knows the licit and the illicit effects which can proceed from it, and knows how to work it well through the virtues of the dispositions of the stars, and through the work of images and of characters", it can be used for good.[1]

Moses was a great Magus (this is the report of a fellow-prisoner on Bruno's talk in prison, not his own words in answer to interrogation), who had learned magic from the Egyptians to such good effect that he was able to overcome Pharaoh's magicians.[2]

In reply to interrogation as to what was his view of Christ's miracles, Bruno said that they were a testimony to his divinity, but he thought that a still greater testimony was the gospel law. When others, such as the Apostles, did miracles this was in virtue of Christ; so that, although externally the miracles of Christ and of an Apostle or a Saint were the same, nevertheless Christ's miracles

[1] *Sommario*, p. 101.
[2] *Sommario*, pp. 86–7.

were done through his own power, those of others by the power of another.[1]

We unfortunately do not have the report of Bellarmine and Tragagliolo on the eight heretical propositions which Bruno was required to recant, but there is in the *Sommario* a summary of a reply by "Frater Jordanus" to censures on propositions drawn from his works,[2] which possibly (though we cannot be quite sure of this) is some indication of what Bellarmine's censures were. I find this document very confused and confusing, but it touches on God's infinity implying an infinite universe, on the mode of creation of the human soul, on the motion of the earth, on the stars being angels, on the earth as animated by a sensitive and rational soul, on there being many worlds. These seem to be mainly philosophical points, but, as Mercati has pointed out, the interrogations very rarely raise philosophical or scientific points and are concerned mainly with theological queries, matters of discipline, his contacts with heretics and heretic countries, and the like.[3]

Since Bruno in his final refusal to recant anything included all that he had ever said or written, the final sentence may have included the many and various points in all the interrogations over the years of imprisonment, as well as the eight points, whatever these were exactly. Gaspar Scioppius who witnessed the death of Bruno and may have heard the sentence read out at the time, gives a very mixed list of points for which he was condemned; that there are innumerable worlds; that magic is a good and licit thing; that the Holy Spirit is the *anima mundi*; that Moses did his miracles by magic in which he was more proficient than the Egyptians; that Christ was a Magus.[4] There are others, equally incoherent. The fact is that we do not have enough evidence (the

---

[1] *Documenti*, pp. 101–2. Here he is not expressing his true opinion, for which see above, p. 228.

[2] *Sommario*, pp. 113–9.

[3] *Sommario*, pp. 12–13. It is most certainly true, as Mercati states (*ibid.*, p. 12) that Bruno was prosecuted for matters of *faith*. Firpo agrees (*Il processo di Giordano Bruno*) that the trial was strictly legal.

[4] Scioppius' letter is printed in Spampanato, *Vita di Giordano Bruno*, pp. 798–805; his list of Bruno's errors is given in *Sommario*, p. 9.

processo being lost) from which to reconstruct Bruno's trial and condemnation.[1]

If the movement of the earth was one of the points for which Bruno was condemned, his case in this respect is not at all the same as that of Galileo who was made to retract his statement that the earth moves. Galileo's views were based on genuine mathematics and mechanics; he lived in a different mental world from Giordano Bruno, a world in which "Pythagorean intentions" and "Hermetic seals" played no part, and the scientist reached his conclusions on genuinely scientific grounds. Bruno's philosophy cannot be separated from his religion. It *was* his religion, the "religion of the world", which he saw in this expanded form of the infinite universe and the innumerable worlds as an expanded gnosis, a new revelation of the divinity from the "vestiges". Copernicanism was a symbol of the new revelation, which was to mean a return to the natural religion of the Egyptians, and its magic, within a framework which he so strangely supposed could be a Catholic framework.[2]

Thus, the legend that Bruno was prosecuted as a philosophical thinker, was burned for his daring views on innumerable worlds or on the movement of the earth, can no longer stand. That legend has already been undermined by the publication of the *Sommario*, which shows how little attention was paid to philosophical or scientific questions in the interrogations, and by the writings of Corsano and Firpo, laying stress on Bruno's religious mission. The present study has, I hope, brought out even more clearly the fact of the mission and its nature, and has also emphasised that the philosophy, including the supposedly Copernican heliocentricity, belonged to the mission. Completely involved as he was in Hermetism, Bruno could not conceive of a philosophy of nature, of number, of geometry, of a diagram, without infusing into these

[1] Cf. Firpo, *Processo di Giordano Bruno*, p. 108.

[2] Firpo (*op. cit.*, p. 112) notes a "grave sense of injustice" in Bruno at the end, as though his intentions had not been understood. We have to remember that there was a general sense in this *fin de siècle* of vast impending religious changes and when this historical situation has been more fully reconstructed the Bruno problem will be more fully understood. Too often, the mistake is made in judging people of the sixteenth century as if they knew, what we know, that no great, general, religious change was about to come.

divine meanings. He is thus really the last person in the world to take as representative of a philosophy divorced from divinity.

The Church was thus perfectly within its rights if it included philosophical points in its condemnation of Bruno's heresies. The philosophical points were quite inseparable from the heresies.

Yet, on moral grounds Bruno's position remains strong. For it was the descendant of the Magi of the Renaissance who stood for the Dignity of Man in the sense of liberty, toleration, the right of man to stand up in any country and say what he thought, disregarding all ideological barriers. And Bruno, the Magus, stood for love, as against what the pedants, of both sides, had made of Christianity, the religion of love.

> For valour, is not Love a Hercules,
> Still climbing trees in the Hesperides?
> Subtle as Sphinx, as sweet and musical
> As bright Apollo's lute, strung with his hair;
> And, when Love speaks, the voice of all the gods
> Make heaven drowsy with the harmony.[1]

These images in praise of love are uttered by Giordano Bruno's namesake, Berowne, in Shakespeare's *Love's Labour's Lost*. A long line of writers, amongst them myself, have argued that the character of Berowne must be an echo of Bruno's visit to England, but we have none of us known what to look for in the play, having failed to understand what it was that Bruno was talking about. It now seems to me absolutely clear that Berowne's great speech on love is an echo of the *Spaccio della bestia trionfante*, in which all the gods speak in praise of love in one of the constellations. Further, the fact that the setting of the play is a French court—the court of the King of Navarre—in which Berowne is the leader of the poets and lovers, is now seen to be highly significant, connecting Berowne-Bruno with a message from the French court, and with the general European atmosphere of "hoping things" from Navarre.

The foils of the poets and lovers in the play are the two pedants, one a Spanish soldier (Don Armado), the other "grammarian" (Holofernes). Once again the *Spaccio* with its two types of pedantry, the truculence and ambition of Catholic Spain and the "grammarian" Protestants who despise good works provides the

[1] *Love's Labour's Lost*, IV, 3, 337–42.

answer to this. All kinds of minor points will bear out this interpretation. They are too detailed to discuss here, though it may be mentioned that Berowne enters a hospital at the end of the play, to look after the sick. Hospitals were amongst the "works" of the predecessors the suppression of which by their successors Bruno deplored.

An entirely new approach to the problem of Bruno and Shakespeare will have to be made. The problem goes very deep and must include the study, in relation to Bruno, of Shakespeare's profound preoccupation with significant language, language which "captures the voices of the gods"—to use one of Bruno's marvellous expressions—as contrasted with pedantic or empty use of language. Shakespeare's imagination is full of magic, which often seems to become a vehicle for imaginative solutions of the world's problems. Was it not Shakespeare who created Prospero, the immortal portrait of the benevolent Magus, establishing the ideal state?[1] How much does Shakespeare's conception of the rôle of the Magus owe to Bruno's reformulation of that rôle in relation to the miseries of the times?

The Navarre from whom things were hoped did, after his conversion to Catholicism and accession to the throne of France, do something towards toleration in France in the Edict of Nantes by which freedom of worship, under certain conditions, was allowed to the Huguenots. But if English sub-Catholic loyalists were hoping for anything of the kind from Navarre's supremacy in Europe they were disappointed for there was no Edict of Nantes for English Catholics.[2] And as for Italy, the confidence which prompted Bruno to return to his native land hoping in Navarre led him to the stake.

Though Bruno's voice appears to have been so quickly stifled in Italy I have wondered whether there may not be an echo of it in Traiano Boccalini's *Ragguagli di Parnaso* (1612–13) with its ironical discussion of contemporary affairs in the setting of a

[1] Prospero has been thought to reflect John Dee which may also be true, but as we have seen, Dee and Bruno are both variations on the Renaissance theme of Magia and Cabala.

[2] When Bruno's influence in England has been fully explored, it may turn out to be one of the major ironies of history that his mission in England looked to the natives something like an occult Counter Reformation.

meeting on Parnassus under the presidency of Apollo. This work is, to my mind, reminiscent of Bruno's *Spaccio* in the Lucianic touch with which it uses mythology to present a similar political attitude. Boccalini was a Venetian liberal and strongly anti-Spanish, and the hero of his work is Navarre (Henri IV). The "News from Parnassus" seems to me to use a number of Bruno's themes, discussing grammarians who are starting a reformation, and also Spanish enormities. When news of the assassination of Henri IV was brought to Parnassus, Apollo veiled his face under a thick cloud and was heard to say, amidst deep sighs, "That the world was come to the point of being ready to return to its first principles, since the wickedness and perfidiousness of some was grown to that height of impiety.[1]

Galileo accepted the movement of the earth on entirely different grounds from Bruno, yet it is rather curious to notice that the *Dialogo dei due massimi sistemi del mondo* (1632) is, in its *literary* form, not unlike the *Cena de le ceneri*. The hide-bound Aristotelian in Galileo's dialogue is represented by Simplicius, called after one of Aristotle's commentators, the name also being chosen for its suggestion of "simpleton", and the argument takes place in the presence of two noblemen, Francesco Sagrado and Filippo Salviati, in Sagrado's palace in Venice. If for Francesco Sagrado is substituted Fulke Greville, at whose house in London the Copernican debate described by Bruno is supposed to have taken place, and for Filippo Salviati is substituted Philip Sidney, the Venetian gathering corresponds quite closely to the London gathering, with its knights, its pedants, and its philosopher—the latter now not Bruno but Galileo. Galileo is transposing the great debate on the Copernican and Ptolemaic systems of the universe to a rational and scientific level, but the setting in which he places it is strangely reminiscent of that earlier debate on a Pythagorean and Hermetic level.[2] Had Galileo read the *Cena de le ceneri*?

[1] Traiano Boccalini, *Ragguagli di Parnaso*, Centuria I, Ragguaglio 3. Quoted from the English translation by Henry, Earl of Monmouth, *Advertisements from Parnassus*, second edition, London, 1669, p. 5.

On the use of Boccalini's work by the Rosicrucians, see below, pp. 408–12.

[2] Galileo carefully repudiates Pythagorean numerology in a passage on which a modern editor of his great work has commented as follows: "These remarks are meant by Galileo to dissociate him explicitly from

Galileo was in Padua from 1592 onwards (very soon after the time that Bruno was there) and he was on intimate terms with Pinelli and used his collections.[1]

One wonders whether the use which Bruno had made of Copernicanism might have raised in the inquisitorial mind the idea that there might be something else behind Galileo's support of the movement of the earth.

[1] A. Favaro, *Galileo Galilei e lo studio di Padova*, Florence, 1883, I, p. 226.

the current trend of pseudo-Pythagorean occult science and mystical rationalism, of which there had been an extraordinary revival in the late Renaissance, climaxed by the tragic fate of Bruno" (Galileo Galilei, *Dialogue on the Two Great World Systems*, in the Salusbury translation, revised and annotated by G. De Santillana, Chicago, 1953, p. 15 note). This note is remarkably perceptive about Bruno.

Chapter XX

GIORDANO BRUNO AND TOMMASO CAMPANELLA

TOMMASO CAMPANELLA[1] was the last of the line of Italian Renaissance philosophers, of whom Giordano Bruno was the last but one. Like Bruno, Campanella was a magician-philosopher, in the line of the Renaissance Magi descending from Ficino. Campanella is known to have practised the Ficinian magic up to the end of his life. Like Bruno, too, Campanella was a Magus with a mission. This huge man, who believed that he had seven bumps on his head representing the seven planets,[2] had colossal confidence in himself as in touch with the cosmos and destined to lead a universal magico-religious reform. Unlike Bruno, Campanella was not burned at the stake, though he was several times tortured and spent more than twenty-seven years of his life in prison. Yet—also unlike Bruno—Campanella very nearly succeeded in bringing off the project of magical reform within a Catholic framework, or, at least, in interesting a number of very important people in it.

[1] On Campanella, see L. Amabile, *Fra Tommaso Campanella, la sua congiura, i suoi processi, e la sua pazzia*, Naples, 1882, and the same writer's *Fra Tommaso Campanella ne' Castelli di Napoli, in Roma ed in Parigi*, Naples, 1887; L. Blanchet, *Campanella*, Paris, 1920; Paolo Treves, *La filosofia politica di Tommaso Campanella*, Bari, 1930; A. Corsano, *Tommaso Campanella*, second edition, Bari, 1961.

The indispensable tool for unravelling the complexities of Campanella's opus is L. Firpo's *Bibliografia degli scritti di Tommaso Campanella*, Turin, 1940.

[2] Blanchet, *op. cit.*, p. 37.

Campanella's notions are near to those of Bruno, with variations; his career resembles that of Bruno, with variations; and these resemblances and differences throw a retrospective light on Bruno and help to explain him.

Campanella's career falls roughly into three periods. First of all there is his early life as a heretical Dominican friar and agitator, constantly in and out of prison, culminating in the Calabrian revolt. This was a revolutionary movement aimed at throwing off the Spanish rule in the Kingdom of Naples and substituting for it a wildly utopian republic, a magical City of the Sun, of which Campanella was to be head priest and prophet. The advent of this new era in world affairs was, according to Campanella, heralded by portents in the sky. This revolution, though preached with mad enthusiasm by Campanella and his supporters, was almost entirely without serious practical preparation and naturally failed totally against the might of Spain and the organised Spanish rule in southern Italy. Then begins the second period of Campanella's life which he spent in prison in Naples, writing with amazing determination huge philosophical and theological works and conducting a propaganda in which he switched the magical reform from its revolutionary manifestation into what were, seemingly, more orthodox channels. The Spanish Monarchy, or the Papacy, were now to provide the framework within which the universal reform would come. Though without ever abandoning the foundation in naturalism and magic of his philosophy and theology, Campanella succeeded in making himself more respectable, and was at last released from the prisons in Naples, in which he had spent the whole of the prime of his life. Then comes his third period. He went to France, and there transferred to the French Monarchy the honour of being the channel through which the universal reform would manifest itself, of being the sun centre in the coming City of the Sun. He was encouraged by Richelieu and by the court, and lived to hail the birth of the dauphin, who was afterwards to reign as Louis XIV, as destined to be the Sun King in a reformed world.

Thus, through a kind of savoir-faire, or, perhaps, cunning, which Bruno entirely lacked, Campanella, who was, I believe, in his first period, following very closely in Bruno's tracks, managed to avoid Bruno's fate, and in his last period to achieve in Paris an apotheosis as prophet of that French Monarchy which, in the persons of Henri III and Henri IV, Bruno had also expected to lead a universal reform.

The pre-Bruno chapters in this book were written with an eye to preparing for Bruno by building up the context in the history of Renaissance magic and of religious Hermetism into which he belongs. This post-Bruno chapter has a similar aim; it is written with an eye to Bruno retrospectively through Campanella. Out of the vast and appallingly complex material on Campanella, I shall select only certain points with this end in view.

Campanella was born at Stilo, in Calabria, in 1568; Bruno was born at Nola, near Naples, in 1548. They thus both came from the south, from that Kingdom of Naples in which the heavy hand of the Hapsburg-Spanish tyranny was strongest upon the Italian peninsula. Campanella was twenty years younger than Bruno, and this age gap means that Campanella follows the earlier steps of Bruno's career but at later dates. Bruno entered the Dominican Order and the Dominican convent in Naples in 1563. Nineteen years later, in 1582, Campanella entered the Dominican Order, in convents farther south. In 1576 Bruno left the Order and the convent in Naples, having been proceeded against for heresy, and began his wanderings in many lands. Thirteen years later, in 1589, Campanella left his convent and came to Naples, where he was proceeded against for heresy and imprisoned. Campanella seems to be having the same experiences as Bruno in his early years, gaining his first impressions from those curiously unruly Dominicans of the south.

There was a point at which these two lives very nearly touched one another. As we saw in the last chapter,[1] when Bruno returned to Italy, he spent about three months in Padua, preparing himself for his mission. He would no doubt have been in a high state of incandescence at this time, working with every kind of magic, both demonic and natural, to heighten the power of his personality with which he hoped to impress Pope Clement VIII in favour of the great reform. When, in March 1592, he left Padua for Venice, and soon afterwards through the good offices of Mocenigo disappeared into the prisons of the Inquisition, this would almost certainly have been known in Padua and well noted by Pinelli and his circle in that town.

[1] See above, pp. 346–7.

In October, 1592, Campanella came to Padua,[1] six months after Bruno had left it. He stayed there for a year or two and met Galileo there. Campanella, too, seems to have been in an excited state of mind when in Padua. Various accusations were made against him and he was imprisoned. Whilst in prison in Padua in 1593 and 1594 he wrote works addressed to Clement VIII.

It seems in itself significant that Campanella arrived in Padua so shortly after Bruno had left it to go into his fatal imprisonment. The two magician-philosophers, universal reformers, and heretical Dominicans just missed one another. Yet may not Bruno have left behind him in Padua an atmosphere, or a circle, or a reputation, which affected Campanella?

At the end of 1594, Campanella was transferred to the prisons of the Inquisition in Rome; amongst the charges against him were that he had taught in his *De sensitiva rerum facultate* a heretical doctrine of the world soul, and had written an impious sonnet. He addressed to the Pope a treatise assigning to him universal monarchy and outlining a vast plan for world union. He also wrote a treatise advising Italian princes not to oppose the projects of the Spanish monarchy.[2] It is difficult to believe that he was sincere in the latter, since a few years later he was to lead the Calabrian revolt against Spain. Campanella, unlike Bruno, was sometimes willing to dissimulate to gain his ends. At any rate, he was released from prison at the end of 1595,[3] probably through the influence of a powerful protector, Lelio Orsini, whose sympathy he had gained by these works.

How close together again ran the lives of Bruno and Campanella, without meeting! For Bruno, too, was in the prisons of the Roman Inquisition at this time, in some different dungeon.

At the end of 1597, Campanella left Rome for Naples where he conferred with an astrologer and with the geographer, Stigliola, who had been in prison in Rome with him and who was an enthusiastic adherent of the Copernican astronomy.[4] Probably these conferences confirmed Campanella in the view, to which he so often gave utterance during the Calabrian revolt, that signs in the heavens were announcing the imminence of far-reaching political and religious changes. In 1598 he left Naples to go farther

[1] Amabile, *Congiura*, I, pp. 63 ff.; Blanchet, *op. cit.*, pp. 24–7.
[2] Blanchet, *op. cit.*, pp. 25–9. [3] *Ibid.*, p. 29. [4] *Ibid.*, p. 32.

south, into his native country of Calabria, where, in 1598 and 1599, he organised the revolt against the Spanish government.

The astonishing story of the Calabrian revolt has been well told by Léon Blanchet, in his life of Campanella[1]; Blanchet's account is based on the rich fund of documentary evidence, collected by the authorities after the suppression of the revolt, which was discovered and published by Luigi Amabile.[2] In impassioned discourses, Campanella and his followers, many of whom were also Dominicans, announced that great changes were at hand. The decline of charity among men, and the growth of discord and heresies, witnesses to the need of a new dispensation, the coming of which is presaged by celestial portents. Amongst the latter is the "descent of the sun", that the sun is coming nearer to the earth. (Campanella in many later writings was constantly to insist on this portent.[3]) The year 1600 will be particularly important, owing to the numerological significance of nine and seven, the sum of which is sixteen. In the coming dispensation there will be established a better religious cult and better moral laws, both based on nature and natural religion. Calabria must prepare for the new age by throwing off the Spanish tyranny and establishing a republic embodying the new religion and ethic. Campanella is the Messiah of the new age, designated both by astrological prediction and by religious prophesy to lead the world into another era.

The part of Christianity in this new era will remain important. Christianity has had its prophets, its thaumaturges, its experts in the art of divination, its miracle workers. Christ was a great and inspired Magus and legislator. Therefore a *rapprochement* can be made between Catholic mysteries and the religion of natural magic. Hence Christian sources and prophecies, particularly those of St. Catherine, St. Brigit, and St. Vincent Ferrer, are cited by Campanella, also Savonarola, the Abbot Joachim, Petrarch, and Dante. Above all the Sibyls are the prophetesses to whom Campanella most frequently appeals, and he sees them in the Lactantian setting.[4]

---

[1] *Ibid.*, pp. 33–41.

[2] The documents on the Calabrian revolt are published in the third volume of Amabile's *Congiura*.

[3] See, for example, Campanella's *Lettere*, ed. V. Spampanato, Bari, 1927, pp. 23, 219.

[4] Amabile, *Congiura*, III, p. 490.

In this strange revolution, heretical Dominicans, or ex-Dominicans, were very prominent. Not only was Campanella's right-hand man, Dionisio Ponzio, a Dominican friar but so were many others of his adherents.[1] It is possible that one should connect the Calabrian outbreak of 1599 with the wild behaviour of Dominicans in Naples four years earlier, in 1595, when armed resistance was made by the friars of the Convent of S. Domenico to a party of reformers sent from Rome to enforce a more regular way of life upon them.[2] There was evidently much disturbance among Dominicans in south Italy, and may not this have been because the revolutionary ideas of Bruno and Campanella were not peculiar to those philosophers but grew out of some way of thinking which was generally fermenting in the Order in the south? The Calabrian revolt may have been the final ebullition of those forces which impelled both Bruno and Campanella upon their dangerous careers.

Campanella seems to have relied mainly on the power of his inspired personality for the success of this extraordinary movement, and on belief in the portents and prophecies. Almost the only practical steps seem to have been arrangements with disaffected southern Italian noblemen and with the Turks who were to send, and actually did send, but too late, a detachment of galleys to aid the insurgents. The whole thing was easily crushed and by the end of 1599 the prisons of Naples were full of rebellious Dominicans and their friends being examined, often with torture, to extract the evidence about the movement which Amabile found and published in 1882.

No one, either in 1882 or, I believe, since, has seen any connection between this movement and Giordano Bruno. But surely it now leaps to the eye that this Calabrian revolution is very like a putting into action of Bruno's programme of reform which he, too, believed to be imminent because a new era in world affairs was at hand. The rash confidence of Campanella's action in Calabria, born of belief in miraculous powers and in the signs of the times, is like the rashness of Bruno's return to Italy in a similar state of over-confidence. Obviously, it would be going too

---

[1] The strong Dominican element in the revolt is apparent in the documents published by Amabile, but this has not been emphasised by later writers.

[2] Amabile, *Congiura*, I, pp. 25–8.

far to view Campanella's movement as resulting solely from the impact of Bruno's return to Italy. Other factors have to be reckoned with; the apparent similarity may be due, as already suggested, to the impulse of both Bruno and Campanella having been derived from this strange southern Dominican discontent of which the Calabrian revolt gives us a glimpse. Moreover, in this *fin de siècle* these notions of imminent change and reform seem to have been much in the air, and the prisons of the Inquisition in Rome were populated with unhappy visionaries with disappointed hopes. One such was Francesco Pucci, who had been in England, who had a scheme for a universal Christian republic, who returned to Italy in 1592, at about the same time as Bruno with a moving appeal to Clement VIII, and who, also like Bruno, hoped in Henry IV of France for a solution.[1] Pucci's fate was again like Bruno's; he went into prison in Rome in 1594 and in 1597 suffered the death penalty. As Luigi Firpo has pointed out, it seems almost certain that Pucci, with whom he had talked in prison in Rome, influenced Campanella.[2]

But when due allowance has been made for other influences, and precaution taken against over-statement, it does look very much as though a torch may have passed from Bruno to Campanella. In letters written by Campanella in later years, there are many notions, and even phrases, which are strangely reminiscent of passages in Bruno's Italian dialogues, particularly the *Cena de le ceneri*, suggesting that Campanella had read at least some of Bruno's works.

The date of Bruno's death gains new significance when seen in the context of the Calabrian revolt and its sequel. Why was it that, after eight years of imprisonment Bruno was at last brought out, in February, 1600, to die his terrible death publicly in Rome? In November, 1599, Campanella went into prison in Naples; in February, 1600, he was undergoing tortures. The execution of Bruno, the rebellious Dominican, at the time when the Calabrian revolt, led by another rebellious Dominican, had just been quelled, may well have seemed like a warning. Campanella narrowly escaped dying the same death as Bruno, an escape which was apparently due to his having had the presence of mind to simulate madness.

[1] See above, pp. 343–4.
[2] Firpo, "Processo e morte di F. Pucci", p. 23.

So opened the auspicious year 1600, composed of the nine and the seven, with the death of Bruno and with Campanella going into prison for twenty-seven years. In the fate of these two descendants of Ficino, in whom still worked the ferment of the Renaissance is typified the suppression in Italy of those Renaissance forces which in other countries were to turn into new channels in the new era of the seventeenth century.

In his most famous work, the *Città del Sole*, or the City of the Sun, Campanella outlined his Utopia, his idea of the ideal state. When Amabile made his discoveries about the Calabrian revolt, he realised that the aims of that revolt, as revealed in the documentary evidence about it, were close to the views expressed in the City of the Sun, that, in fact, the object of the revolt was to establish a state very like the City of the Sun. In a chapter in his book on Campanella, Blanchet resumed these findings and further analysed the connection between the revolt and Campanella's ideal city.[1]

The *Città del Sole* was probably written about 1602, that is in the very early years in prison. This earliest version of the work, written in Italian, remained unpublished (it was not published until 1904).[2] Campanella later made a Latin translation of the work, which is not quite the same as the original, and it was this revised and modified Latin version which was published in his lifetime, first in Germany in 1623, and later in Paris in 1637, the Parisian edition being slightly different from the German one.

The City of the Sun was on a hill in the midst of a vast plain, and was divided into seven circular divisions (*giri*) called after the seven planets. The houses, palaces, cloisters of the City were built along these *giri*, which were separated from one another by walls. Four roads traversed the City, starting from four outer gates, the points of the compass, and running towards the centre.

In the centre, and on the summit of the hill, there was a vast temple, of marvellous construction. It was perfectly round, and its great dome was supported on huge columns. On the altar, the only objects were a great "mappamondo" on which all the heaven

---

[1] Amabile, *Congiura*, I, pp. 220 ff.; Blanchet, *op. cit.*, pp. 66 ff.

[2] Campanella, *Città del Sole*, ed. E. Solmi, Modena, 1904. References are to this edition.

was depicted and another showing all the earth. On the ceiling of the dome were depicted all the greatest stars of heaven, with their names and the powers which they have over things below, with three verses for each; the representations on the dome were in correspondence with the globes on the altar. In the temple hung seven lamps, which were always lighted, called after the seven planets. On the outer walls of the temple, and on its curtains, every star in its order was also represented with three verses for each.[1]

It is clear that the temple was a detailed model of the world, and that the cult celebrated in it must have been a cult of the world.

The walls of the *giri* also had representations on them, on both their inner and their outer sides. On the inner side of the first *giro* (the one nearest to the temple) were shown all mathematical figures, more than those described by Euclid and Archimedes; on its outer side, the map of all the earth with all its provinces, with descriptions of the rites, customs, and laws of each, and the alphabets of their languages, co-ordinated with the alphabet of the Solarians.

The next *giro* had representations of all precious stones and minerals on its wall; and on the outer side, lakes, seas, rivers, wines, and all liquids; here were jugs full of many different liquors with which sicknesses were cured. The wall of the third circle was devoted, on one side, to the vegetable world, with pictures of all kinds of trees and herbs, their virtues and correspondencies with the stars; on the other side were shown all manner of fishes and their correspondencies with celestial things. On the fourth wall were birds and reptiles; and on the fifth animals.

Finally, on the outermost *giro* were displayed, on the inner side of the wall, all the mechanical arts and their inventors, and the different ways in which these are used in different parts of the world. And on its outer side were images of inventors of sciences and laws. There were Moses, Osiris, Jupiter, Mercury, Mahomet, and many others.

In a higher and more honourable place on this wall were placed images of Christ and the twelve apostles, whom the Solarians greatly venerated.

[1] *Città del Sole, ed. cit.*, pp. 3–5.

The City was thus a complete reflection of the world as governed by the laws of natural magic in dependence on the stars. The great men were those who had best understood and used those laws, inventors, moral teachers, miracle workers, religious leaders, in short, Magi, of whom the chief was Christ with His apostles.

The ruler of this City was the chief priest whose name meant the Sun (in the manuscripts, the name is represented by the symbol of the sun, a circle with a dot in the centre), and, in our language, Metaphysics. The Sun Priest was the head in all things, both spiritual and temporal. He was assisted by three collaborators, Power, Wisdom, and Love. Power had charge of all military matters; Wisdom of all the sciences; and Love directed the processes of generation, of uniting masculine and feminine, in such a way as to secure a good race; education and medicine were also under his care.

Under this rule, the people of the City lived in brotherly love, having all things in common; they were intelligent and well-educated, the children beginning at an early age to learn all about the world and all arts and sciences from the pictures on the walls. They encouraged scientific invention, all inventions being used in the service of the community to improve the general well-being. They were healthy and well skilled in medicine. And they were virtuous. In this City, the virtues had conquered the vices, for the names of its magistrates were Liberality, Magnanimity, Chastity, Fortitude, Justice, Ingenuity (Solertia), Truth, Beneficence, Gratitude, Pity, and so on. Hence, among the Solarians, there was no robbery, murder, incest, adultery, no malignity or malevolence of any kind.

As in every Utopia, there is clearly an influence of Plato's *Republic* on the City of the Sun, particularly in its communism. But Campanella's republic is saturated through and through with astrology; its whole way of life is directed towards achieving a beneficial relationship with the stars. The aim of producing a good human stock by selective breeding, which is one of the daring innovations for which Campanella's work is most famous, has really nothing to do with genetics as we understand it. It is concerned with choosing the right astrological moment for conception, and with mating males and females in accordance with their astrological temperaments. The work is entirely misunderstood if it is viewed as a blue-print for a well-governed state in any modern sense. The City is arranged so as to be right with the stars, and thence flows all its happiness, health, and virtue.

It is surely clear that the head priest, and his assistants, who governed the City of the Sun were Magi, who understood the world, knew how to "draw down the life of heaven", to use Ficino's phrase, for the benefit of mankind. Campanella does not describe how the stars were represented in the temple. The star-images on the dome, which were in correspondence with the globes on the altar, with its seven planetary lamps—may not these have included magic images of the thirty-six decans of the zodiac? Was it not by a good magic that the City was ruled, so that the good influences of the heaven predominated over the bad? Various sources have been suggested for Campanella's *Città del Sole*, such as an influence of Thomas More's *Utopia*, particularly in the fiction that the City has been discovered in the New World by a traveller; or an influence of other Renaissance city plans. But such influences are, I believe, secondary. To find the ultimate source one must dig deeper down and uncover those hidden magical springs from which the Renaissance was fed. For, to my mind, the closest parallel to Campanella's City is none other than the City of Adocentyn in *Picatrix*.[1]

In that magical city there was a castle with four gates, on which were images into which Hermes Trismegistus had introduced spirits. Compare this with the four gates and roads of the City of the Sun. On the summit of the castle was a lighthouse which flashed over the city the colours of the seven planets. Compare this with the seven planetary lamps always burning in the temple of the City of the Sun. Around the circumference of Adocentyn, Hermes had placed magic images, "ordered in such a manner that by their virtue the inhabitants were made virtuous and withdrawn from all wickedness and harm." Compare the celestial images in the City of the Sun which, we have suggested, had a similar function. In the midst of Adocentyn was a great tree which bore the fruit of all generation. Compare the control of generation in the City of the Sun.

And, in the passage in *Picatrix* describing the City of Adocentyn, Hermes Trismegistus is also said to have built a temple to the Sun. If we relate (as I suggested in an earlier chapter) the Hermetic City of Adocentyn and Temple of the Sun in *Picatrix* to

[1] See above, p. 54.

the account of the "natural" Egyptian religion, and the lament for its decay in the *Asclepius*, we find there, among the prophecies of the future restoration of the Egyptian religion and laws the words

> The gods who exercise their dominion over the earth will be restored one day and installed in a City at the extreme limit of Egypt, a City which will be founded towards the setting sun, and into which will hasten, by land and sea, the whole race of mortal men.[1]

Here, surely, in that foundation text for Renaissance magic, the *Asclepius*, is a prophecy of Campanella's universal City of the Sun.[2]

Once one sees this, it becomes obvious that Campanella's white-robed Solarians are really Egyptians, that is to say, Hermetic pseudo-Egyptians. The Sun priest must know all sciences and the "grades of being and their correspondencies with celestial things".[3] Such was the wisdom of the Hermetic Egyptian priests, and such the wisdom of Hermes Trismegistus in his triple rôle of priest, philosopher, and king and law-giver. So is the Sun priest in the City of the Sun both the wise man, the priest, and the ruler.

Of course he is also the ideal philosopher-king of Platonism. But in the Renaissance historical perspective, Plato learned from Egypt, and the Hermetic writings were a wisdom earlier than the Greek wisdom. Moses, too, learned his wisdom in Egypt. Campanella's City is in this perspective; there are Hebrew influences, echoes of Solomon's temple in the temple of the Sun; there are Platonic influences; but, hidden away behind these is the Egyptian influence. The deepest, the primary layer of influence behind the City of the Sun is, I suggest, Hermetic; and its first model, to which many later influences have been superadded, is, I believe, the magical city of Adocentyn described in *Picatrix*: and the description in the *Asclepius* of the religion of the Egyptians.

Campanella's City thus takes its place as one among the

---

[1] See above, pp. 55–6.

[2] This view of the source of the City of the Sun does not conflict with the suggestion made by Paolo Treves who pointed to Isaiah, XIX, 18, as the source: "In die illa erunt quinque civitates in terra Aegyptii, loquentes lingua Chanaan, et jurantes per Dominum exercituum; Civitas Solis vocabitur una." (Paolo Treves, "The Title of Campanella's City of the Sun", *J.W.C.I.*, III, 1939–50, p. 251.) The *Civitas Solis* of which the Hebrew prophet speaks is *in Egypt*.

[3] Campanella, *Città del Sole*, ed. cit., p. 11.

infinitely rich and varied products of Renaissance religious Hermetism. It is of the extreme magical type of religious Hermetism, but, owing to the pervasive Christianising of the Hermetic writings, Campanella still believes that their "natural" religion and laws are close to Christianity, can easily be completed with the Christian sacraments, and, with Christ revered as a Magus, can form the new universal religion and ethic for which the world is waiting.

> If these people (the Solarians) who follow the law of nature are so close to Christianity, their natural laws needing nothing but the addition of the Sacraments, I draw from this the conclusion that the true law is Christian, and that, when its abuses are taken away, it will rule the world.[1]

The City of the Sun is heliocentric in a religious and magical sense, being ruled by the Sun priest. Is its plan also heliocentric in an astronomical sense, that is to say, is it Copernican? The *giri* are called after the planets, but it is not specified whether the earth is one of them, with the sun at the centre, or whether the sun is among them, with the earth at the centre. The Solarians were interested in both theories.

> They (the Solarians) praise Ptolemaeus and admire Copernicus, although Aristarchus and Philolaus were before him (in teaching heliocentricity). . . . They search into this matter with subtlety, for it is important to know the structure of the world ("la fabrica del mondo"), and if it will perish and when. And they believe that what Christ said about signs in the stars, the sun, and the moon is true . . . and that the end of things will come, like a thief in the night. Whence they expect the renovation of the age (the millennium before the end of the world) and perhaps its end. . . . They are enemies of Aristotle, whom they call a pedant.[2]

It would thus seem that, though not quite decided about Copernicus, their minds ran on immediately from astronomical theory to "portents", and they disliked Aristotle, the "pedant". We are close here to the atmosphere in which Bruno in the *Cena* defends Copernicanism against Aristotelian pedantry as a portent of the rising sun of the return to Egyptianism. The millenarianism of the Solarians is unlike Bruno and there are some other differences. Nevertheless I would think that the City of the Sun represents something like the magical and Ficinian reform of religion and

[1] *Ibid.*, p. 43.   [2] *Ibid.*, p. 38.

morals of which Bruno foresaw the imminent return through Copernicanism as a portent, a sign in the sun.

Bruno's exposition of Hermetic reform in the *Spaccio* can be illuminatingly compared with the *Città del Sole*. In the *Spaccio*, too, Christ remains in heaven, revered as a Magus. The reform of the heavens is also centred on the sun; the good planetary influences, Venus, Jupiter, Mercury, unite under Apollo to bring about universal good will. In the gods who reform the constellations a beneficent relationship between planets and zodiac and other constellation of the heaven is established, typified in the City of the Sun by the relationship between the star images on the dome of the temple and the altar with its planetary lamps. Virtue triumphs over vice in the *Spaccio* as the good sides of astral influences rise as virtues, and the bad sides are thrown out, as vices. So in the City of the Sun, the inhabitants are maintained in virtue and vices are expelled. The nature of the reform too is similar with, in both cases, a direction of ethics towards social utility. In spite of the extremely different literary form of the two works there is concordance between them at a deeper level.

It may be recalled, too, that Bruno in one of his conversations with the librarian of the Abbey of St. Victor is reported to have used the words "City of the Sun" of some fabled city.[1]

Campanella's revolt to establish his City of the Sun can thus be seen as not altogether dissimilar in aim from Bruno's Hermetic mission.

Campanella's literary output during his long imprisonment was enormous and this huge opus has not even yet been co-ordinated or fully published. Some of his manuscripts were taken to Germany, whilst he was still in prison, by his German disciple, Tobias Adami, and there published. Amongst these was the first Latin version of the *Civitas Solis*, published at Frankfort in 1623. Many works were published in Paris during Campanella's last, or French, period; their late publication is not an indication of their being a late development in his thought for he wrote little that was new in France; he was publishing his prison output. Other works have only begun to see the light in recent years; for example the enormous *Theologia*, in many volumes, written in prison, for which authority to publish was never given in Campanella's life-

---

[1] See above, p. 233.

time, is now being brought out.[1] Other of Campanella's manuscripts are still unpublished. These curious circumstances mean that one cannot follow variations in Campanella's thought in the normal way from the chronological order of his publications. Another, and even more serious, difficulty, is that Campanella revised and reshaped his works in his efforts to gain orthodox support from some quarter or other, modifying his more extreme earlier views; for example, the third version of the *Civitas Solis*, published in France in 1637, adapted the Sun City with Richelieu's ambitions for the French Monarchy in mind. All this makes Campanella a difficult author to study, though his actual thought is really less difficult and less subtle than that of Bruno.

Only one writer, of the many who have written on Campanella, has brought out the importance of his use of Ficino's magic; this is D. P. Walker to whose book I shall be much indebted in what follows.[2]

In his *Metaphysica*,[3] first published in Paris in 1638 but at which he had probably been working nearly all his life, Campanella gives a complete summary of Ficino's magic in a detailed analysis of the *De vita coelitus comparanda* which can be used with advantage by modern students of that difficult work; he refers also to many of his own works in which he has taught Ficino's magic, "what odours, tastes, colours, temperature, air, water, wine, clothes, conversations, music, sky, and stars are to be used for breathing in the Spirit of the World."[4] This exposition of Ficino's magical theory and practice is preceded by summaries of Iamblichus, Porphyry, Proclus, on magic, and above all by a full account of the magic in the *Hermetica*. Campanella here quotes the passage in the *Asclepius* on the Egyptian religion and on the magical processes by which celestial demons were introduced into idols.[5] He also

[1] Campanella, *Theologia libro primo*, ed. R. Amerio, Milan, 1936; other volumes, all edited by Amerio, have been published in subsequent years at Rome by the *Centro internazionale di studi umanistici*.

[2] Walker, pp. 203–36.

[3] Campanella, *Universalis philosophiae seu metaphysicarum rerum, iuxta propria dogmata, Libri* 18, Paris, 1638. On the vicissitudes of this work, of which Campanella perhaps wrote the first version about 1590, see Firpo, *Bibliografia di Campanella*, pp. 119–22.

[4] Campanella, *Metaphysica*, Pars III, XV, vii (2), pp. 179–183; cf. Walker, pp. 210–11.

[5] Campanella, *Metaphysica*, III, XV, iii (1), pp. 167–70.

says that Hermes Trismegistus "taught how to see in the heavens the forms of things, as though in seals"[1]; this of course refers to astrological images and he mentions in the same passage the images of the thirty-six decans.

When he introduces his account of Ficino's magic, Campanella states that "all this doctrine" is derived from Hermes Trismegistus.[2] Walker interprets this to mean that "Ficino's astrological magic consists of the same kind of operation as that described in the *Asclepius*, the idol becoming either a talisman or a human being (the operator)." It is thus quite certain that Campanella knew very thoroughly the Ficinian magic and was also fully aware of its source in Hermes Trismegistus.

We know that Campanella actually practised this magic at Rome in 1628 and for Pope Urban VIII who was afraid of some eclipses which his enemies (particularly his Spanish enemies, for this Pope was anti-Spanish) had prophesied would cause his death. Campanella did magic with him to ward off the evil. They sealed a room against the outside air, hung it with white cloths, and burned certain herbs in it. Two lamps (*luminaria*) and five torches were lit, representing the planets, and the signs of the zodiac were imitated in some way "for this is a philosophical procedure, not superstitious as the vulgar think." There was Jovial and Venereal music; stones, plants, colours belonging to the good planets were used, and they drank astrologically distilled liquors. This procedure is described by Campanella in an appendix to his *Astrologica* (Lyons, 1629).[3]

He also practised the same kind of magic just before his own death. Fearing that an eclipse in 1639 would be fatal to him he went through, for his own benefit, in his cell in the Dominican convent of the Rue St. Honoré, the proceedings which are described in the *Astrologica*.[4]

This magic, as Walker has pointed out,[5] aimed at artificially

---

[1] *Ibid.*, p. 169.   [2] *Ibid.*, p. 179; cf. Walker, pp. 211–12.

[3] Campanella, *Astrologicorum Libri VI. In quibus Astrologia, omni superstitione Arabum, & Iudaeorum eliminata, physiologice tractatur, secundum S. Scripturas, & doctrinam S. Thomae, & Alberti*, Lyons, 1629, Lib. VII, *De siderali Fato vitando*, IV, I, pp. 11–13; cf. Walker, pp. 206–10.

[4] Quétif & Echard, *Scriptores Ordinis Praedicatorum*, Paris, 1721, II, p. 508; cf. Walker, p. 210.

[5] Walker, p. 223.

creating favourable heavens as a substitute for the real heavens which are going wrong in the eclipse. It is done privately and for individuals. But if there were an organised state in which the priesthood knew how to do this magic and did it constantly, that state would be permanently preserved, free from all evil celestial influences, both as regards health and as regards morals. This was what the pseudo-Hermetic Egyptians knew how to do in their natural religion, as described in the *Asclepius*. Such an ideal state was the City of Adocentyn which Hermes Trismegistus built, as described in *Picatrix* with its light-house perpetually flashing the colours of the planets, and its celestial images around the circumference. And such, it is quite clear, was Campanella's ideal City of the Sun, with its sun-altar and seven planetary lamps in correspondence with the images on the dome, an altar perpetually served by a priesthood of trained Magi.

Campanella must have hoped that Urban VIII, with his interest in astrology, might be going to adopt the magical reform into the papacy, always the right and best centre for it in his eyes. And he certainly hoped, during his last triumphant period in Paris, that Richelieu was getting interested in it in relation to the French Monarchy. In the dedication to Richelieu of his *De sensu rerum et magia* (the Paris edition of 1637), Campanella appeals to the great cardinal to build the City of the Sun. The Paris edition of the *Civitas Solis* (1637) revises the City in a slightly more orthodox direction; Mahomet is left out; Christ and the Apostles are put into a much higher place; Aristotle is called a logician, instead of a pedant. But another change is that the Solarians are described as actually practising the magic.[1]

How was it that Campanella could believe that the magical reform could come within a Catholic framework? One way was through the continuity of the stars with the Pseudo-Dionysian hierarchies of angels, and here, again, Campanella was in straight line of descent from Ficino. In our chapter of "Pseudo-Dionysius and the Theology of a Christian Magus" we showed how, in Ficino's thought, the hierarchies of angels pass down divine influences, almost in an astrological manner, and that these pass

[1] These variants from the original version in the Paris edition are quoted in *Città del Sole, ed. cit.,* notes to pp. 7, 38, 44–5; cf. Walker, p. 209.

into the celestial influences, so that there is a continuity up and down, and the cult of the stars leads up into the angelic world. Since the angelic hierarchies represent the Trinity it was St. Dionysius, the Christian Platonist, who most helped Ficino to Christianise his so-called "Neoplatonism", with its core in Hermetic magic.

Campanella was thinking along similar lines. Walker has pointed out that Campanella's magic connects with angels; and it is certain that these angels were specifically the Pseudo-Dionysian hierarchies, for, in his *Metaphysica*, just before his accounts of Hermes Trismegistus and of Ficino's magic, Campanella has a long section on the angelic hierarchies, detailing their various functions in a manner strongly reminiscent of Ficino.[1] Even in the first version of the *Città del Sole*, the continuity of the celestial world with the angelic world was clearly stated, for on the columns at the door of the temple there was an exposition of the scale of being. Here was written, or perhaps shown in images, "che cosa è Dio, che cosa è angelo, che cosa è mondo, stella, uomo . . .".[2] This made it quite clear to the worshippers that they were ultimately approaching the angels and God through the stars.

In Renaissance magic, as studied in this book, the Magia, ultimately based on Hermes, which Ficino had made fashionable was complemented with Cabala by Pico della Mirandola. This re-enforced the continuity of Magia with the angelic world through the power of Cabala to reach the angels and, through them, the Sephiroth and the highest divine mysteries enclosed in the Hebrew Name of God. The double process of Magia, in continuity with the Christian angelic hierarchies, and Cabala with its angelic magic, made very strong the connection of the Hermetic cult of the world with religion. In Campanella, I do not find much trace of the Cabala branch of Renaissance magic; there is no mention of the Sephiroth in his discussion of the Pseudo-Dionysian hierarchies in the *Metaphysica*; in the correct scheme of Magia *cum* Cabala, these should be placed with the hierarchies (as in the Fludd diagram Pl. 7 a). And in at least one passage I have found

---

[1] Campanella, *Metaphysica*, III, XV, ii (1 and 2); cf. Walker, pp. 224–9.
[2] Campanella, *Città del Sole, ed. cit.*, pp. 34–5.

Campanella deprecating Cabalist mysticism.[1] These observations corroborate what Walker has observed of Campanella, that he did not believe in the Cabalist scheme of Francesco Giorgi.[2] We may compare this negative attitude to Cabala with what we noted in Giordano Bruno, with whom Cabala, though not entirely without influence upon him, is definitely relegated to a place secondary to that of the primary Hermetism and Egyptianism.

Upon his intense belief in the Hermetic cult of the world, Campanella built a detailed theology. In this he is unlike Bruno, who did not concern himself with theology but only with "nature", though he believed that the natural religion could be the basis of a reformed Catholicism.

When the volumes of Campanella's *Theologia* have been fully studied we shall gain a better understanding of his natural theology; merely the titles of some of them, such as *Magia e Grazia*,[3] are significant enough. As one would expect, religious Hermetism plays a very important part in Campanella's theology. In the *De Sancta Monotriade*, Campanella states that Trismegistus, who was a king in Egypt, spoke of nearly all the Christian mysteries.[4] He knew that God was a Trinity; that he created the world through his Word, crying *Germinate et pullulate omnia opera mea*, just as God says *Crescite et multiplicamini* in *Genesis*.[5] Campanella is quoting from *Pimander* in Ficino's translation,[6] giving the parallel with Moses as Ficino gives it in his commentary.[7] This one example must suffice to show that Campanella is deep in

[1] Campanella, *Magia e Grazia*, ed. R. Amerio, Rome, 1957, p. 45. Cf. also Campanella's deprecation in one of his letters of Pico's devotion to Cabala (Campanella, *Lettere*, ed. Spampanato, p. 134).

[2] Walker, p. 218.

[3] *Magia e Grazia* is, however, the title given to this volume of the *Theologia* by the editor.

[4] Campanella, *De Sancta Monotriade* (*Theologia*, Liber II), ed. R. Amerio, Rome, 1958, p. 14.

[5] "Trismegistus autem non loquitur de mundo, sed de Deo trino mundi creatore: nam Verbo suo omnia creasse docet et clamasse *Germinate et pullulate omnia opera mea*, sicuti Moyses dixi *Crescite et multiplicamini*. Item docet quod Deus Verbo genuit tertiam mentem, quae Deus est et Spiritus et Numen, et semper in divinis ista considerat." Campanella, *op. cit.*, *loc. cit.*

[6] "Ex templo Deus uerbo sancto clamauit pullulate, adolescite, propagate universi germina, atque opera mea." Ficino, p. 1838.

[7] Ficino, p. 1839. See above, pp. 25–6.

religious Hermetism, that for him, as for Ficino, the piety of Trismegistus and his foreknowledge of Christian mysteries, makes of him almost a Christian and authorises his magic.

On an earlier page in the same work, Campanella makes some very significant remarks. Thomas Aquinas, he says, teaches that we cannot in any natural way know the Trinity, which is not reflected in the creatures. But St. Thomas "had not read the Platonists nor Trismegistus, whose works in his time had not been translated into Latin."[1] The inference is that Thomist theology needs revision in the light of the Platonists and Trismegistus. And indeed it is, I believe, precisely this that Campanella sets out to do in prison, using his Dominican theological training to produce a revised *Summa Theologica*, using the new light from the Platonists and Trismegistus to produce a more "natural" theology of the Trinity, a more "natural" Christology, and a more "natural" view of the Sacraments in which Grace is a kind of Magia Divina, following on naturally from Magia Naturalis. The philosophy going with this new theology will be, of course, not scholastic Aristotelianism, but the animist philosophy of the Renaissance and its magical interpretation of nature.

We cannot follow Campanella into this stupendous effort; it would require a book, or several books to do so. For Campanella's theology needs to be put into the context of the history of Thomism in the Renaissance, a history which has not yet been written. It should begin with Ficino and his devious efforts to implicate Thomas Aquinas into approval of the use of talismans. These efforts seem less strange when it is found, as Walker has pointed out, that Cardinal Caietano in his edition of the works of Aquinas, published in 1570, defends in his commentaries the legitimacy of talismans.[2] Campanella used Caietano's edition, since he appealed to it when defending his astral magic.[3] (The attempt to turn the other great Dominican, Albertus Magnus, into a supporter of

---

[1] ". . . Thomas, cum non viderit Platonicos neque Trismegistus suo tempore nondum redditos latinos, ut patet ex sua confessione *super Ethicam Aristot.*, et ex historiis, nihil mirum si glossas dat textui non convenientes", Campanella, *De Sancta Monotriade*, p. 12.

[2] Walker, pp. 43, 214–15, 218–19, 222–3. The defence of talismans is in Thomas Aquinas, *Opera omnia*, Rome, 1570, XI, Pars Altera, folios 241 r.–242 r., commentary by Tommaso de Vio, Cardinal Caietano.

[3] Walker, p. 214.

magic was much easier, since Albertus probably was a magician.)
There was a Renaissance Thomism which would be anathema to
the modern Thomist, and Campanella's theology (unpublished
and unapproved in his time) is its culmination. His *Theologia* was
intended to be a new Dominican *Summa*, formulated in the hope
of providing a theological basis for Renaissance magic as a Counter
Reformation force.

In those many works by Campanella in which he is speaking
solely as a natural philosopher, as Bruno always did, he teaches
that the world is alive and sentient, and to this animism or panpsychism he related his Magia. We are always told that the two chief
influences on Campanella were the animist philosophy of Telesio,
with its insistence on conflict between hot and cold as a basic
principle, and the organisation of magic into a science by Giovanni
Battista Porta.[1] It is certainly true that Campanella was heavily
influenced by these two contemporary south Italian thinkers. But
two quotations will serve to suggest that Campanella himself
thought of these influences as secondary to, and ultimately derived
from, the basic influence of Hermetism. In the first book of the
Theologia, Campanella speaks of the living world as follows:

> ... docet Virgilius, Lucanus et poetae omnes, et Platonici mundum
> esse animal, quod Trismegistus apprime docet. ... Propterea con-
> tendit Trismegistus non esse mortem, sed transmutationem, quam
> vocat transmutationem. Nos quoque asserimus non esse mortem, nisi
> detur annihilatio caloris et frigoris et sensu illorum.[2]

That the world is a living animal was, says Campanella "first
taught by Trismegistus" and he proceeds to quote from *Corpus
Hermeticum* XII on there being no death, but only change. He
then modifies this statement with Telesian hot and cold theory.
But the fundamental fact of animism was "first taught by Trismegistus". Therefore I would say that, as in the case of Bruno
whose animism is Hermetic in origin as we showed in an earlier
chapter, using this very passage from the *Hermetica*,[3] so is Campanella's animism, though he is modifying the Hermetic animism
with Telesianism. The passage is an important confirmation of the

[1] Blanchet, *Campanella*, pp. 138 ff., 201 ff.
[2] Campanella, *Theologia*, *Libro Primo*, ed. Amerio, 1936, p. 189.
[3] See above, pp. 342–3.

truth of our contention that Renaissance animism is ultimately Hermetic in origin, of course also using Plato and the Platonists, Virgil and so on, as here. But the tremendous authority of Trismegistus as much the more ancient and the one who first taught that the world is an animal would lend great weight to the theory of universal animation, which is the basis of magic.

In the case of the influence of Porta's magic on Campanella, we read in the *Del senso delle cose e della magia*, immediately after some pages on Porta's improvements in magic, the following words:

> Trismegisto sapientissimo dice che l'uomo è un miracolo del mondo e più nobile delli Dei o eguale, e che però abbia potestà tanta nel suo senno che può far Dei di marmo e di bronzo e dargli anima sotto a certe costellazioni e ricever risposta da loro. E questo crede Porfirio e Plotino, aggiundendo che vi siano Angeli buoni e perversi, come ogni dì si vede esperienza e io n'ho visto manifesta prova non quando la cercai, ma quando pensava ad altro.[1]

Here Campanella goes back behind the contemporary magician, Porta, about whom he has just been talking, to the gospel text of Renaissance magic, the *Asclepius* on man as the great miracle and on the Egyptian power of making gods, connecting this in the correct manner with Neoplatonic theurgy ("Porfirio e Plotino").

Hence it is clear that both Campanella's animism and his magic are ultimately Hermetic, like Bruno's, and the influence of Telesio and Porta are secondary to this. (There is also an influence

---

[1] Campanella, *Del senso delle cose e della magia*, ed. A. Bruers, Bari, 1925, p. 223. The original version of this work was written in Latin about 1590–92, but the manuscript was stolen from Campanella by some friars when he was at Bologna in 1592, on his way to Padua, and was used against him in the trial for heresy for which he was taken from Padua to Rome. This original version has been sought for in vain amongst the archives of the Holy Office. He wrote the book again in Italian, from memory, probably about 1604 when he was in prison in Naples. Afterwards he wrote it again in Latin, and this Latin version was taken to Germany by Adami and published at Frankfort in 1620; it was published again at Paris in 1637.

The Italian version from which we quote here is thus perhaps the nearest to Campanella's original thought, though not so near as the lost original Latin version which was confiscated by the emissaries of the Holy Office. See Bruers' introduction to his edition of the Italian version, and Firpo, *Bibliografia di Campanella*, pp. 67–72.

of Porta on Bruno, particularly of the animal physiognomy which is in some way connected with magic, and some influence of Telesio though less strong than in Campanella.)

After his quotation from the *Asclepius*, Campanella goes on to say that there is a "magia divina" which man cannot operate without grace, and it was through this that Moses and the saints did miracles, also a "magia naturale", and a "magia diabolica", done through devils. The natural magic when rightly operated can go on into the divine magic. "Chi ben la esercita (natural magic) con pietà e riverenza del Creatore merita spesso esser levato alla sopranaturale con li superi."[1] We are here not far from those divine and magical rites of Bruno's Egyptians, through which they rose up to the divinity above nature.

One sometimes fancies that one can hear verbal echoes of Bruno in Campanella, as, for example, the following in the *Del senso delle cose*:

> Ecco che quando l'uomo va cogitando, pensa sopra il sole e poi più di sopra, e poi fuor del cielo, e poi più mondi infinitamente. . . . Dunque di qualche infinita causa ella (the race of man) è effetto. . . . Dice Aristotile ch'è vana imaginazione pensar tanto alto; e io dico con Trismegisto ch'è bestialità pensar tanto basso; et è necessario ch'egli mi dica d'onde avviene questa infinita. Se si risponde che da un simile mondo un altro simile si pensa, e poi un altro, poi in infinito, io soggiongo che questo caminare di simile in simile senza fine, è atto di cosa partecipe dell'infinito.[2]

Here is something very like Bruno's leap out beyond the margins of the world into an infinity in which are innumerable other worlds. The power of man's mind to do this shows that it is akin to the infinite. To Campanella, these thoughts suggest "Trismegisto", whom he contrasts with the petty Aristotle.

Thus Campanella, in his natural philosophy is moving on very similar lines to Bruno, though with differences and reservations. He does not, for example, approve the Hermetic doctrine of metempsychosis,[3] which Bruno accepted. We have to remember, however, that the *Del senso delle cose*, as we have it, may be a modification of his earliest views.

If we could know those earliest views in unexpurgated form it is probable that the resemblance to Bruno might be even closer, and

[1] *Op. cit., ed. cit.*, p. 224.   [2] *Ibid.*, p. 119.
[3] *Ibid.*, p. 138. But the passage is somewhat ambiguous.

that what Campanella really aimed at in the beginning, and in the revolt, was the full "Egyptian" reform of the Brunian type, using the extremes of demonic magic. As Walker has pointed out, in the early days in prison, Campanella was using very dangerous forms of magic.[1] In the *Quod Reminiscentur* he seems to be expressing repentance for his earlier dabblings in demonic magic.[2]

It is possible that in later years Campanella consciously tried to avoid being connected with Bruno's reputation. The only work, so far as I know, in which Campanella actually mentions Bruno by name is concerned with the subject of which Bruno had made notorious use, namely Copernican heliocentricity. In 1622 Campanella published an apology for Galileo in which, when speaking of others who have defended Copernican heliocentricity and the movement of the earth, Campanella mentions Bruno as one of these other defenders, adding that he was heretical. "Nolanus, & alii, quos heresis nominare non permittit."[3] Campanella is being careful to dissociate himself from the full implications of Bruno's Copernicanism. This was all the more necessary since, both in the apology and in letters to Galileo, Campanella speaks of heliocentricity as a return to ancient truth and as portending a new age, using language strongly reminiscent of Bruno in the *Cena de le ceneri*. "Queste novità di verità antiche di novi mondi, nove stelle, novi sistemi . . . son principio di secol novo", writes Campanella in a letter to Galileo of 1632.[4] And in other letters he assures Galileo that he is constructing a new theology which will vindicate him.[5] It had therefore to be made clear that heliocentricity as a portent of a new age, and as integrated into a new theology did not mean for Campanella at this stage in his career, acceptance of all Bruno's heresies.

Everything goes to show that Campanella modified his earlier extreme views, either because he really repented of having gone to such lengths, or because, after the revolt had failed, he realised that it was impossible to put them into practice. His *Theologia* was

[1] Walker, pp. 228–9.

[2] Campanella, *Quod reminiscentur . . .*, ed. R. Amerio, Padua, 1939, pp. 23 ff.; cf. Blanchet, *op. cit.*, pp. 90 ff.; Walker, p. 213.

[3] Campanella, *Apologia pro Galileo*, Frankfort, 1622, p. 9.

[4] Campanella, *Lettere*, ed. Spampanato, p. 241. All Campanella's letters to Galileo remind one strongly of Bruno, and particularly of the *Cena de le ceneri*; see *Lettere, ed. cit.*, pp. 163 ff.; 176 ff.; 240 ff.

[5] Campanella, *Lettere, ed. cit.*, p. 177; letter to Galileo in 1614.

written to cover a modified Hermetism, which accepted the Christian interpretation of the *Hermetica*—after the manner of the more orthodox traditions of religious Hermetism—and used less frightening forms of magic, leading on to "magia divina". In *Magia e Grazia*, Campanella warns against Agrippa's error in keeping the magic which is of the devil[1]; whereas of Ficino's three ways of obtaining divine life he says that, though very difficult to put into practice, they are not heretical as some people say.[2] Thus Campanella's *summa* was formed to cover less extreme forms of "Egyptianism" than that of Bruno who scrupled not to use the most demonic of Agrippa's magic, and even that of Cecco d'Ascoli of dangerous memory.

It would have been far harder to produce a *summa* to cover Bruno's magic, and his Hermetism which rejected the Christian interpretation of the *Hermetica*. Yet even this, Bruno thought to be possible. Otherwise why should he have appealed to Pope Clement VIII and tried to go to Rome? Perhaps he hoped to do magic for the Pope, as Campanella was later to do for Urban VIII. That he believed that his views could be adapted to Thomism is indicated by his constant mention of his great respect for Thomas, whom he revered as a Magus. Though Bruno cast off the Dominican habit and wandered in foreign heretical lands, neither of which things Campanella ever did, the Dominican theologian is still apparent in him, in his veneration for Thomas and Albertus. Campanella's efforts to make the magical reform respectable theologically show us that Bruno's mission—within the context of the times—was not quite so improbably wild as it seems to us.

We have to see Bruno and Campanella within the sequence which we have tried to build up in this book. Ficino revives Hermetic magic, apologises for it as compatible with Christianity, tries to implicate Thomas Aquinas in his use of talismans. Pico della Mirandola thinks that Magia and Cabala confirm the divinity of Christ. Pope Alexander VI has a fresco painted in the Vatican, full of Egyptianism, to mark his protection of Magia. The fact is that Hermes Trismegistus had been received into the Church by Lactantius, and this momentous step, never accepted by all,

---

[1] Though Agrippa, says Campanella, rejected the magic which subjects man to the devil, he kept the magic by which man subjects the devil and constrains him to do his will. Campanella, *Magia e Grazia, ed. cit.*, p. 206.

[2] *Ibid.*, p. 202.

always subject to severe criticism by the orthodox, eventually led to Giordano Bruno and Tommaso Campanella.

The publication of Del Rio's book against magic in 1600 (again that important year 1600) marks the alarm of the Counter Reformation and its awareness of the danger.[1] Nevertheless, Hermes Trismegistus was too deeply infiltrated into Renaissance religion to be easily expelled, as the career of Campanella shows.

When the revolt had failed to cast off Spain in Calabria and to build the City of the Sun there, Campanella turned to other political ways of establishing his ideas, one of these being an appeal to the very political power against which the revolt had been directed. In his *Monarchia di Spagna*, first published in 1620, he prophesies that the Spanish Monarchy will become a universal world monarchy, in which One alone will reign and thus universal peace and justice will be secured. This universal monarchy will be Catholic with the Pope as its spiritual head. In other works, such as the *Discorsi universali del Governo ecclesiastico* and the *Monarchia Messiae*, Campanella prophesied for the papacy a universal world monarchy by which the Pope would become both spiritual and temporal head of the whole world, all religions would be converted into one, and there would be a world-wide religious and political unity.[2]

How was it that Campanella was able to switch from the revolt to these visions of a universal Spanish Monarchy or a universal theocracy under the Pope? Campanella's political ideas were entirely mediaeval and mystical. The ideal is the return of the Empire in a new golden age, the ideal to which Dante gave classical expression in his *Monarchia* with its vision of universal peace and justice under One ruler. Campanella seeks for a contemporary representative of ideal universal empire, finding this either in the Spanish Monarchy or in the papacy as a universal monarchy. When he goes to France, and switches now to the French Monarchy, prophesying for the French King a universal empire in a new golden age, it is not in the sense of French nationalism that he thinks of this mission but in the sense of the French Monarchy as representing mystical empire, the Dantesque rule of the

---

[1] See Walker, pp. 178–85.
[2] See Blanchet, *op. cit.*, pp. 44 ff.; 59 ff., etc.

One.[1] In Campanella's vision, there must be an organised world state under One ruler, who will be either himself both temporal and spiritual head, as in a papal theocracy, or the Spanish, or the French, Monarchy working in unison with the Pope as spiritual head of the world state. Campanella needs such a world state for the full expansion of his City of the Sun, for the universal establishment of the magical reform in which a priesthood of Catholic Magi keep the City in permanent happiness, health and virtue, and the religion of the City is in perfect accord with its scientific view of the world, that is to say with natural magic.

When we look at the propaganda for the Calabrian revolt, we find that it is full of mystical imperialism, of prophecy of the return of an imperial golden age,[2] such as Lactantius and the Sibyls speak of, combined with apocalyptic prophecy, Joachimism, and the like. Campanella believed from the portents that the hour had struck for such a renewal of the age; the Calabrians and the Dominicans were to prepare for it by establishing the ideal city in Calabria, whence it was to spread to the rest of the world. When the revolt failed, he did not think that the portents had deceived him (he went on talking of them for the rest of his life, particularly the descent of the sun) but that he must modify his ideas and find some Monarch who would build the City within his monarchy, either the Spanish Monarch, the Pope as Monarch (that is as both spiritual and temporal head of the world), or the French Monarch. This is Blanchet's interpretation of Campanella's political evolution after the revolt, and I believe that he is right.

I would add to it, however, the following suggestions. First, that the idea of establishing an ideal imperialist state in southern Italy which was to spread to the rest of the world was not a new one. In the thirteenth century, the Emperor Frederick II had established in the Kingdom of Sicily (which included Naples) a model autocratic state,[3] which he hoped to extend eventually to

[1] I have studied Campanella's mystical imperialism in relation to the French Monarchy in my article "Considérations de Bruno et de Campanella sur la monarchie française", *L'Art et la Pensée de Léonard de Vinci, Communications du Congrès International du Val de Loire*, 1952, Paris–Alger, 1953–4, pp. 409 ff.

[2] See Campanella's *Articuli profetales*, printed in Amabile, *Congiura*, III, pp. 489–98.

[3] See E. Kantorowicz, *Frederick II*, trans. E. Lorimer, London, 1931, pp. 234 ff.

the rest of his empire. It was probably this state which was one of the inspirations of Dante's *Monarchia*. Is it, perhaps, not impossible that memories of this imperialist experiment in southern Italy lay behind the Calabrian revolt, in his propaganda for which Campanella made constant allusion to Dante, as one of its prophets?

Secondly, it is now clear that to the Roman ideal of universal empire returning in a new golden age, to the Platonic ideal of a state in which philosophers ruled, Campanella added a third ideal, that of the Egyptian state kept intact and eternal by priestly magic. The Sun ruler of the City of the Sun is both priest and king, supreme in both the spiritual and the temporal domains, in short, he is Hermes Trismegistus, priest, philosopher, and king.

Campanella was thus in no sense a liberal revolutionary. His ideal was an all powerful theocracy like that of Egypt, so powerful that it regulated by scientific magic the celestial influences and through them the whole life of the people. Its apparently liberal side is that it encouraged scientific enquiry and invention; the Solarians are interested in the Copernican theory for it is important to know the "fabrica del mondo"; they are also expert in mechanical devices which are used for the general well-being. But this advanced Solarian science was in the hands of the supreme priesthood and regulated by it—as in ancient Egypt.

Campanella's astounding determination and pertinacity gradually had their reward; the monarchs of the world began to take an interest in the prisoner, and the man who, in 1599, had gone into prison in imminent danger of death for dangerous heresies and revolt against Spain was, in 1626, released from prison through Spanish influence. He was again in prison in Rome for a while but again released and then began a short period during which he fancied that he was on the brink of success. In his *Quod reminiscentur et convertentur ad Dominum universi fines terrae* he had outlined a plan for a vast missionary effort. Missions were very much to the fore in Rome, and it has even been rumoured that the establishment of the Congregation *De propaganda fide* might have been, in part, suggested by Campanella. This rumour seems, however, to depend only on words of Campanella in his dedication of the *Quod Reminiscentur*[1] to Popes Paul V, Gregory XV, and

[1] Blanchet, *op. cit.*, pp. 52–3. This dedication is in one of the manuscripts of the work, and was published by J. Kvacala, *Thomas Campanella, ein Reformer der ausgehenden Renaissance*, Berlin, 1909, p. 152. On the

Urban VIII in which he offers his book for the use of that Congregation. And, in letters written in France in 1635 he says that his *Reminiscentur* is a great demand for missionaries, and that he is intending to write to the Congregation *De propaganda fide* about how to convert French heretics.[1] That he should even have thought of himself in connection with such a famous Catholic work is extraordinary enough in view of his past history. And the faith which Campanella wanted to propagate throughout the whole world was, of course, the Catholicised natural religion. As Blanchet points out, in the *Atheismus Triumphatus*, another book associated with the missionary plans to all heretics, Mohammedans, Jews, and all peoples of the world, the philosopher reproduces the visions and the conception of natural religion which had inspired his enterprise of 1599.[2] It was in 1628, in Rome, that Campanella did his anti-eclipse magic for Pope Urban VIII; Walker sees this effort as, in part, an effort to obtain this astrologically-minded Pope's favour for his schemes. "If he could convince the Pope of the sun's slow approach and the events this portended, then missionaries, trained by Campanella, would go forth from Rome to convert the whole world to a reformed, 'natural' Catholicism, which would introduce the millennium, the universal City of the Sun."[3] And it does seem that for a time, and through the favour of Urban VIII, Campanella was exercising some influence on policy in Rome.

[1] Campanella, *Lettere, ed. cit.*, pp. 328, 330.

[2] Blanchet, *op. cit.*, p. 53. The *Atheismus Triumphatus* was published at Rome in 1631, but was sequestrated because of ecclesiastical censure; it was published again at Paris in 1636. See Firpo, *Bibliografia di Campanella*, pp. 101–3.

[3] Walker, p. 205; Blanchet, *op. cit.*, pp. 56–7.

In his letter to Urban VIII of 1628, Campanella describes the descent of the sun, said to be now much lower than in the time of Ptolemy, and other portents (*Lettere, ed. cit.*, pp. 218–25), repeating similar statements which he had made at the time of the Calabrian revolt (Amabile, *Congiura*, III, pp. 480, 495, etc.). Cf. also *Lettere*, pp. 23, 65, and the eclogue on the birth of the Dauphin (see below, p. 390).

The descent of the sun and associated portents are described by Spenser, *Faerie Queene*, V, Introduction, 5–8.

complicated history of the *Quod Reminiscentur*, permission to publish which was nearly given by Bellarmine and then withdrawn, see Firpo, *Bibliografia di Campanella*, pp. 153–7. The first volume of it was published in 1939, edited by R. Amerio.

That Campanella should have had even a partial and fleeting success in Rome, for it was only partial and fleeting, is little short of astounding when we think of Giordano Bruno "astrologising" in Frankfort with schemes to reduce all the world to one religion, going to Italy with his mission and his book dedicated to a pope, in Padua just before Campanella was there, constantly prophesying the return of the world to better things through solar portents. Bruno was of course much more extreme, much more violent than Campanella in his penitent later period; yet the basic idea of a "natural" reform within a Catholic framework is common to both.

Nevertheless, great care must be taken not to exaggerate Campanella's success. There were very many who very strongly disapproved of him; amongst these strong disapprovers was the general of the Dominican Order, Ridolfi.[1] It appears, too, that the publication of the account of his magical practices with Urban VIII, which is inserted at the end of the *Astrologica*, published in France in 1629, was done without the knowledge of Campanella himself and through the instrumentality of highly placed Dominicans who wished to prevent him from exercising influence in Rome by discrediting him through exposing his magic.[2] Campanella's credit in Rome was short-lived and sank rapidly during the years 1630 to 1634, and his position became dangerous.

In 1634, he left Rome and went to Paris.

He had already begun to switch to the French Monarchy as the channel for the universal reform, had been publishing works to that effect, and was in contact with the French ambassador in Rome. In Paris, almost the only newly written works which he published were on the sacred imperial destiny of the French Monarchy, such as the *Aphorismi politici* (1635) in which he announces that signs in the heavens foretell that the power of the Spanish Monarchy is weakening whilst that of the French Monarchy is growing. Other works to similar effect circulated in manuscript amongst French érudits and politicians, such as the *Documenta ad Gallorum nationem* which is a glorification of Louis XIII, who, with his noble minister Richelieu, will free Europe from the Spanish tyranny, like a new Charlemagne with his

[1] Blanchet, *op. cit.*, p. 57.

[2] L. Firpo, *Ricerche Campanelliane*, Florence, 1947, pp. 155 ff., and *Bibliografia di Campanella*, pp. 98–100; Walker, p. 208.

knights.[1] He also republished earlier works adding to them the new French Monarchy slant, such as the *De sensu rerum et magia* (1637) with the dedication to Richelieu,[2] already mentioned, urging him to build the City of the Sun; and the Paris edition (1637) of the *Civitas Solis* itself.

In Paris he was still strongly supported by his sense of universal mission, busy converting French Protestants. In his letters he says that he is also making many English converts.[3] And he was trying to get the Church to make concessions about the Sacrament to conciliate Protestants.[4]

Think of Giordano Bruno in Paris, attaching himself to the French Monarchy in the person of Henri III, putting that French king in the *Spaccio della bestia trionfante* as leader of the reform of the heavens; talking to the librarian of St. Victor on his return to Paris of how the difficulties about the Sacrament will soon be done away with, and of some "City of the Sun". History again seems to be repeating itself, with Campanella as a more successful Bruno.

Yet once again Campanella's success must not be exaggerated even in Paris and with powerful court favour. Protests about his unorthodoxy were constantly coming from Rome, and though many of Campanella's major philosophical works, written in prison, and including the *Metaphysica* with its account of Ficino's magic, were published in France, the Sorbonne never gave permission for the publication of his *Theologia*.[5]

In September, 1638, a son was born to the French Monarch, and was saluted by Campanella in an eclogue, modelled on the Messianic Virgilian Fourth Eclogue, as the French Cock destined to rule with a reformed Peter a united world. In this coming dispensation, labour will be a pleasure amicably shared by all; all will recognise one God and Father and love will unite all; all kings and peoples will assemble in a city which they will call Héliaca, the City of the Sun, which will be built by this illustrious

---

[1] Campanella, *Opuscoli inediti*, ed. L. Firpo, Florence, 1951, pp. 57 ff. (*Documenta ad Gallorum nationem*).

[2] This dedication is printed in the *Lettere, ed. cit.*, pp. 372–4.

[3] *Ibid.*, pp. 309, 403, etc.

[4] Blanchet, *op. cit.*, p. 62.

[5] See Amerio's introduction to his edition of the *Theologia*, Lib. I, p. xviii; Firpo, *Bibliografia di Campanella*, p. 161.

hero.[1] In this prophecy, the return of an imperial golden age is combined with the Egyptian strain of the City of the Sun into which all the peoples of the earth will run, as foretold in the *Asclepius*. Even the so-called communism of the original *Città del Sole* is faintly recalled in the promise that labour will be amicably shared by all. The Calabrian revolt has been transformed into an anticipation of the Age of Louis XIV.

Giordano Bruno had hoped great things of Henry of Navarre, the French Monarch who ruled as Henri IV. Campanella hopes great things of Navarre's grandson, the infant who will reign as "le roi Soleil".

In the following year, Campanella, fearing that an approaching eclipse boded ill for him, did the same anti-eclipse magic in his cell in the Dominican convent in Paris as he had done for Urban VIII in Rome. Shortly afterwards he died, assisted at the end with Christian rites.[2] A great concourse of the noble and the learned attended his funeral.

Campanella's end was very different from that of Giordano Bruno.

In this amazing story one hardly knows which to wonder at most —the persistence in history of a symbol, or the spectacle of how an individual man, Campanella, himself transformed a symbol, the City of the Sun, in such a manner as eventually to bring victory

---

[1] "The Cock will sing; Peter will spontaneously reform himself; Peter will sing; the Cock will fly over the whole world, but will submit it to Peter and be guided by his reins. Work will become a pleasure amicably divided among many, for all will recognise one Father and God. . . . All kings and peoples will unite in a city which they will call 'Heliaca', which will be built by this noble hero. A temple will be built in the midst of it, modelled on the heavens; it will be ruled by the high priest and the senates of the monarchs, and the sceptres of kings will be placed at the feet of Christ." From the *Ecloga Christianissima Regi et Reginae in portentosam Delphini . . . Nativitatem*, Paris, 1639. The eclogue is accompanied by notes by Campanella himself. The best modern edition is that in Campanella, *Tutte le opere*, ed. L. Firpo (Classici Mondadori), 1954, Vol. I, pp. 281 ff.; the above quotations are on pp. 308, 310, in this edition. The eclogue opens with portents, descent of the sun, Copernicus, etc., and repeats much of the language used in the Calabrian revolt; since Campanella's notes give sources, the whole is of prime value for his eschatology.

[2] Quetif and Echard, *Scriptores Ordinis Praedicatorum*, Paris, 1721, II, p. 508; cf. Blanchet, *op. cit.*, p. 65; Walker, p. 210.

and honour out of total defeat. Or should one look at it more simply? Was the French Monarchy always Campanella's ideal channel for the reform, as it was Giordano Bruno's? Was the cult of the Spanish Monarch never anything but a safety device, a lever for getting out of prison, and it was only at the last, with the French Monarchy, that he really felt at home?

There is a point at which the parallel between Bruno and Campanella breaks down. Campanella never lived in Protestant and heretical countries, never joined in the cult of their monarchs, as Bruno did. In England, Bruno joined with the courtiers in calling the anti-Spanish Virgin Queen "diva Elizabetta". He prophesied for her some Dantesque united monarchy in which this One Amphitrite should reign supreme.[1] The atmosphere of imperialist mysticism surrounding Elizabeth I, which I have analysed in my study of her symbol of Astraea,[2] the just virgin of the golden age, is a transfer to the Tudor Monarchy of the sacred imperial theme. Uniting, as it did, the spiritual and temporal headship, this monarchy might well have qualified as "Egyptian". Bruno knew of the mystical cult of the English queen in the revival of chivalry and joins in it in the *Eroici furori*.[3]

And if, after a stay in Paris at the time of the height of Campanella's influence at the French court, some traveller should have passed on into England (as Bruno had done so many years before), he might have been privileged to see a masque at court, with sets designed by Inigo Jones, the plot and much of the actual language of which was taken straight out of Bruno's *Spaccio della bestia trionfante*. The masque *Coelum Britannicum*, given at court in 1634, has for its theme Jupiter's reform of the heavens; the words are by Thomas Carew, with many verbal borrowings from Bruno,[4] and the changing celestial scenery gave opportunities for a great

[1] See above, p. 289.

[2] "Queen Elizabeth as Astraea", *J.W.C.I.*, X, 1947, pp. 27 ff. On the transfer of imperialist mysticism to the national monarchies see also my article "Charles Quint et l'idée d'empire" in *Fêtes et Cérémonies au temps de Charles Quint*, Centre National de la Recherche Scientifique, Paris, 1960, pp. 57 ff.

[3] See above, p. 290.

[4] The influence of Bruno on this masque is well known; see Thomas Carew, *Poems, with his Masque Coelum Britannicum*, ed. R. Dunlap, Oxford, 1949, pp. 275–6.

artist (Inigo Jones) to realise the artistic possibilities of Bruno's work. "At this the Scaene changeth, and in the heaven is discovered a Spheare, with Starres placed in their severall Images."[1] At the conclusion of the revels, when the King (Charles I) and his French Queen (Henrietta Maria, daughter of "Navarre") were seated in state, theatrical clouds dissolved over them, disclosing Religion, Truth, and Wisdom triumphant in the heavens, or Eternity in the firmament surrounded by a troop of stars "expressing the stellifying of our British Heroes; but one more great and eminent than the rest, which was over his head, figured his Majesty. And in the lower part was seene a farre off the prospect of Windsor Castell, the famous seat of the most honourable Order of the Garter."[2]

So King Charles the Martyr ascends into the heavens, successor of Henri III as leader of the celestial reform, and the masque does imaginative and artistic magic to bring him success. Through the undoubted influence on both works of Bruno's *Spaccio*, the *Coelum Britannicum* has the honour of being linked with Shakespeare's *Love's Labour's Lost*. And it proves that Bruno's influence was still very much alive in England in the early seventeenth century.

Like Bruno, Campanella was a poet, who expressed his religious cult of the world in a series of sonnets and other poems interspersed with prose commentaries, after the manner of the *Eroici furori*. Part of Campanella's "Canticle" as he called it (just as Bruno called the *Eroici furori* a Canticle)[3] was published in Germany in 1622[4] under the pseudonym of "Settimontano Squilla", alluding to the seven bumps on Campanella's head representing the seven planets; the rest is lost. These poems and commentaries are closely related in some of their themes to the *Eroici furori*, but lack the richness of imagery so characteristic of Bruno. Campanella's avoidance of imagery was deliberate.[5] Yet in the *Epilogo Magno* where Campanella speaks of the world as a statue of God, and that the true philosophy is to seek the vestiges of the divine in nature as a lover contemplates the image of a beloved,[6] he is

[1] *Ibid.*, p. 158. [2] *Ibid.*, pp. 182–3. [3] See above, p. 275.

[4] See Firpo, *Bibliografia di Campanella*, pp. 43 ff. The best edition is that in Campanella, *Tutte le opere*, ed. Firpo, I, 1954.

[5] *Tutte le opere, ed. cit.*, p. 9.

[6] Campanella, *Epilogo magno*, ed. C. Ottaviano, Rome, 1939, pp. 181–2.

opening up the theme which, when developed by Bruno in Petrarcan conceits and with his marvellous Actaeon imagery, becomes the *Eroici furori*, the Hermetic cult of the world expressed in a work of great poetic power. Dedicated to Sir Philip Sidney, leader of the Elizabethan poets, and with its allusions to the chivalrous Queen cult, the *Eroici furori* is integrated into Elizabethan literature.

And at Wittenberg, Bruno identified himself sympathetically with the Lutherans. His praise of heretic princes told heavily against him at his trial. These left-wing tendencies sharply differentiate Bruno from Campanella.

One other comparison between Bruno and Campanella must be mentioned, though it cannot be developed here for it belongs to the history of the art of memory which I hope to treat in another book. We have seen that the chief form which Bruno's magic takes is his adaptation of the Hermetic theme of reflection of the world in the mind to the techniques of classical mnemonics. In the *De umbris idearum* he gives a world memory system based on magic images.

Campanella also knew this tradition well, and in fact the City of the Sun itself can be reflected within, as "local memory".[1] As a memory system, the City will have to be compared and contrasted with Bruno's systems. And in the *Monarchia di Spagna*, Campanella recommends that a plan of constellations should be made, with the princes of the House of Austria placed in the heavens, and which is also to serve for "local memory":

> Let him (the Monarch) send able astrologers abroad into the New World; that there they may give an account of, and describe all the new Stars that are in that Hemisphere; from the Antarctick Pole to the Tropick of Capricorn, and may describe the Holy Crosse, whose figure is at that Pole, and about the Pole itself they may place the Effigies of Charles V and of other Princes of the House of Austria; following herein the Example of the Grecians and the Egyptians,

[1] In the list of works which Campanella offered to do, when in prison in Naples, he says that he can "make a City in such a wonderful way that only by looking at it all the sciences may be learned", and that he can teach "local memory" with the world as book. See *Lettere, ed. cit.*, pp. 27, 28, 160, 194, and the other versions of these lists of marvellous works which Campanella promised to perform which L. Firpo has published in *Rivista di Filosofia*, 1947, pp. 213–29.

who placed in the Heavens the Images of their Princes and Heroes. For by this meanes both Astrology and Local Memory will be both learnt together. . . .[1]

Written in Campanella's pro-Spanish Monarchy period, this sounds like instructions for making a mappamondo which will do magic for the House of Austria by placing their princes in the heavens; and at the same time it is a memory system. If we can throw light on this, in the context of the whole history of the art of memory and its use for Hermetic magic in the Renaissance, we may better understand the *Spaccio della bestia trionfante*, a mappamondo made in the interests of Henri III, and perhaps of Elizabeth, and which is also to be reflected within and bears some relation to Bruno's memory systems.

Thus at almost every point, Bruno and Campanella seem like close relations, of differing temperament and character whose ways through life repeat one another with variations and differing fortunes. They shot out into the world, the one twenty years later than the other, impelled by a tremendous impetus, religious Hermetism in an extreme magical form. That difference of twenty years in their age is important for it means that, whilst Bruno's life was passed in the period in which Hermetism reached a crescendo, when it was at the root of the dominant philosophy and had deeply infiltrated into the religious problems of the age, Campanella lived on into a time when it was on the wane. Whilst Campanella was in prison, the Hermetic writings had at last been accurately dated; the supposed extreme antiquity of Hermes Trismegistus had been the foundation upon which the whole vast edifice of Renaissance Hermetism, with all its ramifications into magic and religion, had rested; when that foundation was cut away by textual criticism, the edifice was doomed. For the new school of Cartesian philosophy, Renaissance animist philosophies, with their Hermetic basis, were utterly outmoded ways of approaching the world. Science replaced magic in the great seventeenth-century advance.

When Campanella came to Paris his favourable reception by "les grands" and the court was probably due to the fact that his

[1] Quoted from the English translation of Campanella's *Monarchia di Spagna* by E. Chilmead, *Discourse touching the Spanish Monarchy*, London, 1654, p. 48.

French Monarchy cult suited Richelieu's ambitions and his anti-Hapsburg policy. There was, however, still a strong survival of the old ways of thinking and many French savants were interested in him, for he had acquired a great reputation. There is no doubt that his books aroused much interest and perhaps revived the Renaissance atmosphere.

But to those with whom the future lay, to those who were advancing into the new era, to Mersenne, Descartes, and their circle, Campanella meant nothing. Writing to Peiresc, who had strongly recommended Campanella to him, Mersenne says, "I saw the reverend Father Campanella for about three hours and for the second time. I have learned that he can teach us nothing in the sciences. I had been told that he is very learned in music but when I questioned him I found that he does not even know what the octave is; but still he has a good memory and a fertile imagination."[1] The last remark, thrown in for politeness' sake, is perhaps even more damning than the rest. Mersenne wrote to Descartes to enquire whether he would like Campanella to come to Holland to see him, but the great man's reply was that he knew enough about Campanella not to want to see any more of him.[2] As Lenoble remarks, "les temps sont révolus"; we are now in the modern world, and though Campanella was triumphantly received at the court and drew the horoscopes of great personages, the learned had abandoned such dreams.

And, in the modern world now dawning, the dream of a universal religion in which science interpreted as "natural magic" should blend indissolubly with religion interpreted as "divine magic", was obviously doomed to fade. Always of very doubtful orthodoxy, it was its consonance with the dominant Renaissance philosophies which had given the dream its power. That Campanella should have been able to revive it so late, and with a good deal of success, testifies to the strength of the foothold which Hermes Trismegistus had gained within religion. But now, science and philosophy will join hands with orthodoxy in driving him out of the Church; Mersenne's great campaign against magic was also a campaign against natural theology.

[1] Mersenne, letter to Peiresc of 1635; cited by R. Lenoble, *Mersenne et la naissance du mécanisme*, Paris, 1943, p. 41.
[2] Letters of Descartes to Huyghens and Mersenne, 1638; cited *ibid.*, p. 43.

Born twenty years too late, Campanella in Paris seems like a mammoth survivor of a nearly extinct race, the race of the Renaissance Magi. The indomitable power of this man, even in the most daunting circumstances, testifies to the strength which the Renaissance Magus drew from his natural religion. Let us end this chapter with one of those sonnets which Campanella wrote in his dungeon in Naples:

The Way to Philosophise

The world's the book where the eternal Sense
    Wrote his own thoughts; the living temple where,
    Painting his very self with figures fair
    He filled the whole immense circumference.
Here then should each man read, and gazing find
    Both how to live and govern, and beware
    Of godlessness; and, seeing God all-where,
    Be bold to grasp the universal mind.
But we tied down to books and temples dead,
    Copied with countless errors from the life,
    These nobler than that school sublime we call.
O may our senseless souls at length be led
    To truth by pain, grief, anguish, trouble, strife!
    Turn we to read the one original.[1]

[1] Quoted in the English translation by J. A. Symonds, *Sonnets of Michael Angelo Buonarrotti and Tommaso Campanella*, London, 1878, p. 123. For the Italian original, see Campanella, *Tutte le opere*, ed. Firpo, I, p. 18. Symonds' translation is moderately faithful except for the fourth line, "He filled the whole immense circumference" which, in the original reads, "He ornamented the lower and upper (worlds) with living statues."

Chapter XXI

❖❖❖❖❖❖❖❖❖❖❖❖❖❖❖❖❖❖❖❖❖❖❖❖❖❖❖❖❖❖❖❖❖❖❖❖

AFTER HERMES TRISMEGISTUS
WAS DATED

❖❖❖❖❖❖❖❖❖❖❖❖❖❖❖❖❖❖❖❖❖❖❖❖❖❖❖❖❖❖❖❖❖❖❖❖

SOME discoveries of basic importance for the history of thought seem to pass relatively unnoticed. No one speaks of the "pre-Casaubon era" or of the "post-Casaubon era" and yet the dating by Isaac Casaubon in 1614 of the Hermetic writings as not the work of a very ancient Egyptian priest but written in post-Christian times, is a watershed separating the Renaissance world from the modern world. It shattered at one blow the build-up of Renaissance Neoplatonism with its basis in the *prisci theologi* of whom Hermes Trismegistus was the chief. It shattered the whole position of the Renaissance Magus and Renaissance magic with its Hermetic-Cabalist foundation, based on the ancient "Egyptian" philosophy and Cabalism. It shattered even the non-magical Christian Hermetic movement of the sixteenth century. It shattered the position of an extremist Hermetist, such as Giordano Bruno had been, whose whole platform of a return to a better "Egyptian" pre-Judaic and pre-Christian philosophy and magical religion was exploded by the discovery that the writings of the holy ancient Egyptian must be dated, not only long after Moses but also long after Christ. It shattered, too, the basis of all attempts to build a natural theology on Hermetism, such as that to which Campanella had pinned his hopes.

Casaubon's bomb-shell did not immediately take effect and there were many who ignored it, or refused to believe it, and clung obstinately to the old obsessions. Nevertheless, though other factors were working strongly against the Renaissance traditions in the seventeenth century, Casaubon's discovery must, I think, be reckoned as one of the factors, and an important one, in releasing seventeenth-century thinkers from magic.[1]

Isaac Casaubon,[2] born at Geneva of Protestant parents in 1559, was one of the most brilliant Greek scholars of his time, profoundly erudite in all branches of classical learning and also in church history. His friend Joseph Scaliger thought him the most learned man in Europe. In 1610 he was invited to England, and was encouraged by James I to embark on his criticism of Baronius' *Annales Ecclesiastici*, in which his attack on the legend of the hoary antiquity of the *Hermetica* is embedded. He died in 1614 and is buried in Westminster Abbey.

The twelve huge volumes of the *Annales Ecclesiastici* of Cesare Baronius had appeared between 1588 and 1607; they were a Counter Reformation reply to the Protestant view of church history.[3] Baronius used all the old romantic legends and the old sources with sincere enthusiasm and quite uncritically. In his first volume, he has a long section on Gentile prophecy of the coming of Christ, based on Lactantius, whom he cites in the margin. The Gentile prophets were, he states, following Lactantius, Mercurius Trismegistus, Hydaspes and the Sibyls.[4] This is all that he actually says about Trismegistus, but in the Lactantian context, with the Sibyls, it implied the whole elaborate interpretation of the Hermetic writings as Gentile prophecy of the coming of Christ. This was evidently how Casaubon saw it, for he delivered a full attack on the authenticity and supposed antiquity both of the Sibylline oracles and of the *Hermetica*.

Casaubon's work has the somewhat forbidding title of *De rebus*

---

[1] In a brilliant short essay, "Nota sull'Ermetismo", E. Garin has pointed out the importance, in relation to seventeenth-century thought, of Casaubon's dating of the *Hermetica*; see Garin, *Cultura*, pp. 143 ff.

[2] On Casaubon, see the article in the *Dictionary of National Biography* and Mark Pattison, *Isaac Casaubon*, Oxford 1892 (second edition).

[3] On Baronius, see the article in the *Enciclopedia italiana*; there is no modern monograph on this important Counter Reformation figure, one of the first disciples of St. Philip Neri, and confessor to Clement VIII from 1594 onwards, a crucial period. He died in 1607.

[4] "Erant hi (i.e. the Gentile prophets) Mercurius Trismegistus, Hydaspes, atque Sibylla", with reference to Lactantius I, 6, in the margin. C. Baronius, *Annales Ecclesiastici*, edition of Mainz, 1601, I, p. 10.

sacris et ecclesiasticis exercitationes XVI. It goes through Baronius' text in order pointing out the errors in the first half of the first volume. Casaubon intended to go through the whole twelve volumes in this way, but was interrupted by death. When he comes to Baronius on the Gentile prophets, he expresses his deep suspicion of the genuineness of these writings.[1] There is not a word, he says, about Hermes Trismegistus or about the Sibylline oracles in Plato, Aristotle, or in any of the other main pagan authors.[2] Casaubon believes them to have been forged in early Christian times to make the new doctrine palatable to the Gentiles.[3] The writings ascribed to Trismegistus are, he states, by Christian or semi-Christian authors, forgeries made for a good purpose, yet detestable because untrue. There was, he allows, probably a real person of great antiquity called Hermes Trismegistus,[4] but he cannot have been the writer of the works ascribed to him. These do not contain the doctrines of an ancient Egyptian but are made up partly from the writings of Plato and the Platonists and partly from Christian sacred books.[5] The *Pimander* contains echoes of Plato, particularly the *Timaeus*; of *Genesis*; and of St. John's Gospel.[6] The Powers in *Corpus Hermeticum* XIII recall St. Paul's Epistle to the Romans.[7] Many of the hymns are from old liturgies, particularly those of St. John Damascene, or from the Psalms.[8] The "regeneration" treatises are suggested by St. Paul, Justin Martyr, Cyril, Gregory Nazianzenus, and others.[9]

Detailed proof that the *Hermetica* cannot be of the antiquity supposed is brought forward by pointing out that they mention, for example, Phidias, and the Pythian games; also the many later Greek authors which they quote. Finally, there is the question of their style. They are not written in an early Greek style but a late style with late vocabulary.[10] Therefore, concludes Casaubon after his long and detailed analysis, it is most false to say that

---

[1] Isaac Casaubon, *De rebus sacris et ecclesiasticis exercitationes XVI. Ad Cardinalis Baronii Prolegomena in Annales*, London, 1614, pp. 70 ff. Some discussion of Casaubon's critique can be found in Scott, I, pp. 41–3, and Pattison, *op. cit.*, pp. 322 ff. Scott points out that Casaubon puts the date of the *Hermetica* a little too early and is wrong about their being Christian forgeries.

[2] Casaubon, *op. cit.*, p. 73. [3] *Ibid.*, pp. 73–5.
[4] *Ibid.*, p. 75. [5] *Ibid.*, p. 77. [6] *Ibid.*, pp. 77–9.
[7] *Ibid.*, p. 82. [8] *Ibid.*, pp. 82–3. [9] *Ibid.*, p. 83.
[10] *Ibid.*, pp. 85–7.

these works were written by Mercurius Trismegistus, an ancient Egyptian, or were translated from his writings.[1]

The actual copy of the *Hermetica* which Casaubon used when making his devastating exposure is in the British Museum, with his signature on the title page and many manuscript notes by him in the margins. It is a copy of the Greek text published at Paris by Turnebus in 1554,[2] together with Ficino's Latin translation of the first fourteen treatises of the *Corpus Hermeticum* and Lazzarelli's translation of the "Definitiones". Holding this little book in one's hand one realises, with a certain awe, that it represents the death of the Hermes Trismegistus of the Renaissance, the imaginary Egyptian priest who as the leader of the *prisci theologi* had exerted such a tremendous influence for so long.

The uncritical Baronius, who was no Greek scholar, had repeated the old Lactantian view of Gentile prophecy, the view which, as we have seen, played such a large part in the Christianising of Hermes Trismegistus. Casaubon's allegation that the *Hermetica* are Christian forgeries shows what a strong hold the Christian interpretation of them had taken. The Christian influence in the writings seems to him so obvious that he accounts for it through his theory that they are Christian forgeries—a theory which, though he does not state this, might even implicate Lactantius for passing off such forgeries. As at the beginning of this study, we saw that Lactantius' view of Hermes as a Gentile prophet, grouped with the Sibyls, played a large part in establishing his influence, so at the end, when Hermes is demolished by modern textual criticism, it is within the Lactantian setting, repeated by Baronius, that his execution takes place. And here we cannot but reflect with astonishment that it was so late before a critical approach to the *Hermetica* was made. The weapons of textual criticism which Casaubon uses for his dating—the approach both from content and from style—had been developed long ago by the Latin humanists and used with effect for the dating

[1] *Ibid.*, p. 87.

[2] Ἑρμοῦ τοῦ Τρισμεγίστου Ποιμάνδρης . . . Ἀσχληπιου Ὅροι πρὸς Ἀμμονα βασιλεα: *Trismegisti Poemander, seu de potestate ac sapientia divina. Aesculapii Definitiones ad Ammonem Regem*, Paris, 1554, A. Turnebus. British Museum Press Mark 491. d. 14. The commentaries in this edition are those of Lefèvre d'Etaples, not those by Ficino. See Kristeller, *Suppl. Fic.*, I, p. lviii; Walker, "The *Prisca Theologia* in France", p. 209, note.

of Latin authors. Yet the whole of the sixteenth century had to pass, witnessing the most extraordinary developments based on the misdating of Hermes, before Casaubon appeared to apply these well-known tools to the dating of the Greek text of the *Corpus Hermeticum*. Of the *Asclepius* there was, of course, no Greek text. Nevertheless the *Asclepius* which had always been read in the Renaissance in close association with the *Corpus Hermeticum* as by the same very ancient Egyptian writer, naturally also fell from its status and with it there fell a major ally in the justification for magic, from Ficino onwards.

Tucked away as it was within Casaubon's elaborate criticism of Baronius' history, the de-bunking of Hermes Trismegistus could be, and was, disregarded and ignored by those who, though living in the seventeenth century with its entirely new movements of thought, still clung to the Renaissance traditions.

First and foremost among such *retardataires* must be reckoned Campanella. Bruno was burned fourteen years before Casaubon's exposure was published; Campanella was in prison at the time, and conducted all his subsequent campaigns in total ignorance of it. To men like Bruno and Campanella, the modernist critical approach to the sacred ancient texts of *prisca theologia* would have been unthinkable. Both came of a tradition which was entirely non-humanist, in which "Hermes" and the "Platonici" had been grafted on to mediaevalism without the slightest admixture or tincture of humanist philological scholarship. We may be sure that if Bruno had been still living in the earlier seventeenth century, however much his mission might have varied from that of the later Campanella, he would have resembled him in never losing faith in the extreme antiquity of Hermes Trismegistus.

Nor were Campanella, and the ghost of Bruno, alone in such an attitude in the seventeenth century. Renaissance Neoplatonism was slow in dying, and lingered on in various forms contemporaneously with the new philosophy and the new science. Whilst those who, like Marin Mersenne, were actively combating the Renaissance animistic and magical conceptions in order to clear a way for the new times, and using the new dating of the *Hermetica* as one of the tools in their warfare, others like Robert Fludd and Athanasius Kircher maintained the full Renaissance attitude to Hermes Trismegistus, completely ignoring Casaubon. Others again, though still in the Renaissance Platonist tradition to a large extent, were affected by the Casaubon discovery.

In this chapter I shall discuss Fludd and the Rosicrucians and Kircher as representing full survival of the Renaissance attitude to Hermes Trismegistus in the post-Casaubon era; and More and Cudworth as Platonists in the Renaissance tradition whose attitude to the *Hermetica* is profoundly modified by Casaubon's discovery.

REACTIONARY HERMETISTS: ROBERT FLUDD

It was in 1614 that Casaubon's volume containing his critique of the *Hermetica* was published in England and with a dedication to James I. Three years later the Englishman, Robert Fludd, dedicated to the same monarch the first volume, published in Germany, of his *Utriusque cosmi . . . historia.*[1] A more total contrast than that exhibited by these two works, published within a few years of one another and both dedicated to the King of England could hardly be imagined. Casaubon, using humanistic tools on Greek scholarship, had convincingly demolished the early dating of the *Hermetica* and had shown that parallels between these writings and the Old and New Testament and the works of Plato and the Platonists were to be explained as borrowings by later writers from earlier ones. Fludd, totally ignoring the new dating both in this work and in all his other voluminous writings,[2] lives in a world in which Casaubon might never have been born, the

---

[1] Robert Fludd, *Utriusque cosmi, maioris scilicet et minoris, metaphysica, physica atque technica historia*, Vol. I, Oppenheim, 1617; Vol. II, Oppenheim, 1619.

Another interesting date in connection with Casaubon's exposure of Hermes is that it was published whilst Sir Walter Raleigh was a prisoner in the Tower writing his *History of the World*, which is peppered with quotations from Ficino's *Pimander* and contains a whole section on Hermes Trismegistus (Part I, Book II, Chap. 6, paragraph VI), whom Raleigh thinks probably more ancient than Moses and venerates profoundly, taking the line that the idolatry of the *Asclepius* must be a corruption introduced into the writings of this holy man. We have, therefore, at about the same time under James I, (1) Casaubon critically exposing Hermes Trismegistus, (2) a survivor from the Elizabethan age, Raleigh, still deeply under his spell, (3) the young Fludd preparing to carry the cause of Hermetism into the new age.

[2] A bibliography of these is given by R. Lenoble, *Mersenne ou la naissance du mécanisme*, Paris, 1943, pp. xlvi–xlvii.

world of religious Hermetism with its profound respect for Hermes Trismegistus as the very ancient Egyptian whose sacred writings are of practically canonical authority. Again and again Fludd quotes the sayings of the holy Hermes as of equal weight with those of *Genesis* or of St. John's Gospel and as teaching the same religious truths, or as the utterances of a *priscus theologus* long prior to Plato and the Platonists who absorbed his teachings.

It is hardly an exaggeration to say that on nearly every page of Fludd's works there will be found a quotation from Ficino's Latin translation of the *Corpus Hermeticum*. He also uses the *Asclepius* freely and some other Hermetic writings, but Ficino's *Pimander* was his chief stand-by. Comparisons of Fludd's quotations with Ficino's text suggest that Fludd knew the latter by heart and is quoting from memory, always pretty closely but sometimes freely. He also sometimes quotes from Ficino's commentaries, and he had completely absorbed from these and from the subsequent Christian Hermetic tradition the attitude which regarded Hermes Trismegistus as in agreement with Moses on the creation and as foreshadowing the Trinity.

It would be tedious to illustrate these statements in detail, and I take as an example the dedication to the reader of the first volume of the *Utriusque cosmi . . . historia*. Here Fludd quotes from "Trismegistus, the most divine of all philosophers and near to Moses", who has said in his *Pimander* that man was given the powers of the Seven Governors (the passage is quoted in Ficino's Latin), whence he may not only know the nature of the stars and their action on things below but may rise to the highest heights and understand all truth. Man's *mens* being made of life and light, in the image of God, when man knows himself he becomes like God (again quoted in Ficino's Latin).[1] It is thus on this Hermetic basis of man as the Magus Man[2] that Fludd proceeds to his account of the two worlds, the macrocosm and the microcosm, in his *Utriusque cosmi . . . historia*.

The account of the creation, with which he begins his first volume and which is illustrated by De Bry's remarkable plates,

---

[1] Fludd, *Utriusque cosmi . . . historia*, I, pp. 11–12; cf. Ficino, *Pimander*, cap. I (Ficino, pp. 1837–8).

[2] The "magnum miraculum est homo" passage is, of course, constantly quoted by Fludd; see for example, *Utriusque cosmi . . . historia*, II, pp. 72; *ibid.*, second section, p. 23, etc.

is based on the usual conflation of the Hermetic *Pimander* with *Genesis*, with copious quotation from both. A later work, the *Philosophia Moysaica*,[1] is also Mosaic-Hermetic; the hieroglyphic figure on its title-page is explained in the text opposite as referring to: "Tenebrae fuerunt super faciem abyssi. Genesis I. Et Hermes, Erat umbra infinita in abysso, aqua autem & Spiritus tenuis in abysso inerant." In fact, as in the Renaissance, Fludd sees Hermes as the Egyptian Moses, and as the almost Christian Trinitarian.

Like Pico della Mirandola, whom he frequently refers to with respect,[2] to this Ficinian type of Hermetism, with which he is absolutely saturated, Fludd adds Cabalism. I cannot make it my business here to discuss how much about the Cabala, or how much Hebrew, Fludd actually knew. When I say that he adds Cabala to the Ficinian Hermetism, I mean that in Fludd's cosmos above the spheres of the elements and the spheres of the planets, there is ascent to the higher spheres of the Pseudo-Dionysius hierarchies of angels, as in Ficino, and these are equated, or ranged together with, the Sephiroth of the Cabala. This is the scheme which resulted from Pico's addition of Cabala to Magia, and I used plates from Fludd's work in an earlier chapter[3] to illustrate it. The scheme is set out and discussed in the text of the first volume of the *Utriusque cosmi . . . historia* in the chapters on demons and angels, where the Pseudo-Dionysian angelic hierarchies are related to the star demons, or angels[4]; in the *De philosophia moysaica* in the chapter on the Sephiroth, for which Fludd is using Reuchlin, *De arte cabalistica*, the Sephiroth are related to the Pseudo-Dionysian hierarchies.[5]

Thus Fludd is living entirely within the scheme within which the Renaissance Magus operated with Magia and Cabala—a scheme which was kept vaguely Christian through its connection with the Christian hierarchies of angels. Was Fludd an "operator", that is to say a practising Magus? His frequent quotation from Agrippa's *De occulta philosophia*, makes it pretty certain, to my

[1] R. Fludd, *Philosophia Moysaica*, Gouda, 1638.
[2] He uses Pico's *Conclusiones*; cf. for example, *Utriusque cosmi . . . historia*, II, p. 55.
[3] See Pls. 7a, 8, 10.
[4] Fludd, *Utriusque cosmi . . . historia*, I, pp. 108 ff.
[5] Fludd, *De philosophia Moysaica*, pp. 84 ff.

mind, that he was. Mersenne certainly thought so and accused him firmly of being a magician.[1]

In this very brief sketch of Fludd, I aim at no more than putting him in a place in the context of this history in general. That place seems to me to be, roughly, as follows. At a very late date, after the *Hermetica* have been dated and when the whole Renaissance outlook is on the wane and about to give way before the new trends of the seventeenth century, Fludd completely reconstructs the Renaissance outlook. He might be living in the full flood of that intense mystical enthusiasm aroused by Ficino's translations of the *Hermetica*, or just after Pico had completed Magia with Cabala. This is, of course, an exaggeration since there are many later influences. For example, Fludd knows the useful text-book of Renaissance magic compiled by Agrippa. I would say, too, that he knew something of the traditions of sixteenth-century religious Hermetism of the purely mystical and non-magical type, such as that of Foix de Candale. As a firm believer in the *Hermetica* as canonical books of equal value with the Scriptures, Fludd's enthusiasm knows no bounds. Writing in England in the seventeenth century, he is giving expression, by a kind of delayed action, to sixteenth-century religious Hermetism of the most intense kind.

Fludd (1574–1637) is almost exactly contemporary with Campanella (1568–1639). Both might be described as late religious Hermetists, but they do not come out of the same stream. Campanella belongs into the original Italian tradition which was still alive and developing; by their lack of emphasis on Cabala and the intense naturalism of their Hermetic cult, Bruno and Campanella make something different of the Renaissance tradition; compared with them, Fludd is a reactionary towards the origins, towards Ficino and Pico. Moreover, Fludd does not have that Dominican formation, which makes the two Dominican Magi so formidable and forceful, both as philosophers and as missionaries. Nevertheless there are points at which the student of Fludd might find help through comparison with Campanella and Bruno. Campanella's *De Sancta Monotriade* is based on a similar type of Hermetic Trinitarianism to that which Fludd is using, though the book could not have actually influenced Fludd, since Campanella's *Theologia*, of which it forms a part, was never published. Comparison of Fludd with Bruno might be even more revealing. As

[1] See below, pp. 437–8.

already pointed out,[1] though Fludd is certainly not like Bruno in the latter's avoidance of Trinitarianism and in his general extreme attitude, there are points in Fludd's works at which one feels that he is near to Bruno. At least one of Bruno's works, the *De imaginum compositione*, was I think, certainly known to Fludd, for it is reflected in Fludd's memory system,[2] which helps to explain it. And some of Bruno's magical diagrams, particularly those in the Latin poems, might possibly have been seen by Fludd. Fludd's mystical interpretation of the compass (Pl. 16a)[3] might also be examined in connection with Bruno's mysterious controversy with Fabrizio Mordente.

In his earliest works, Fludd announced himself as a disciple of the Rosicrucians, the mysterious sect, or secret society, or group, which seems to have originated in Germany, and apparently in a Lutheran milieu. The evidence as to the views of the Rosicrucians is tantalisingly vague, nor is it by any means certain that they were an organised sect. The Rosicrucians represent the tendency of Renaissance Hermetism and other occultisms to go underground in the seventeenth century, transforming what was once an outlook associated with dominant philosophies into a preoccupation of secret societies and minority groups.[4]

The connection with the Rosicrucians places Fludd within such tendencies. His late revival of the outlook of the Renaissance Magus comes at a time when the Renaissance Magus—driven by the dominant thought of the seventeenth century from the high position in which Ficino and Pico had placed him—is going underground and turning into something like a Rosicrucian.

REACTIONARY HERMETISTS: THE ROSICRUCIANS

Since the object of a secret society is to keep itself secret, it is not easy to uncover the secrets of the Rosicrucians; even the manifestoes explicitly concerned with them are couched in veiled and mysterious language, and nothing is known of their organisa-

[1] See above, p. 322.
[2] Fludd, *Utriusque cosmi . . . historia*, II, section II, pp. 54 ff. See above p. 334.
[3] *Ibid.*, II, pp. 28–9.
[4] As E. Garin has put it, Renaissance Hermetism in this period descends "sul terreno dell'occultismo e delle confraternite ed associazioni variamente caratterizzate"; "Nota sull'ermetismo", in *Cultura*, p. 144.

tion, or even whether they had an organisation or were actually formed into a sect.[1] However, when Marin Mersenne, who disliked them intensely, emphasises in one of his works how much he is opposed "aux magiciens et aux charlatans qu'on appelle Frères de la Rose-Croix, lesquels se vantent d'entendre Trismégiste et tous les cabalistes de l'Antiquité",[2] this is enough to place them as belonging in some way within our Hermetic-Cabalist tradition.

The first document in the Rosicrucian mystery is the manifesto published at Cassel in 1614.[3] This peculiar publication falls into two strangely ill-matched parts; the "General Reformation" is nothing but a translation into German of chapter 77 of Traiano Boccalini's *Ragguagli di Parnaso*; the "Fama Fraternitas" is the Rosicrucian manifesto.

I had occasion to mention Boccalini's *Ragguagli di Parnaso* in chapter XIX where I suggested that this satire by the Venetian liberal who was a great admirer of Henry of Navarre and strongly anti-Spanish, and which is cast in a mythological setting, at the court of Apollo. is somewhat reminiscent of Giordano Bruno's *Spaccio* which Boccalini might have known, since Bruno's books were distributed in Venice.[4] Published at Venice in 1612–13, Boccalini's work promulgates the pro-French, anti-Spanish, liberal line of thinking, under an extremely thin mythological

---

[1] P. Arnold, *Histoire des Rose-Croix et les origines de la Franc-Maçonnerie*, Paris, 1955, pp. 166–7, thinks that the "fraternity" had no real existence. This book gives the myths about the Rosicrucians in a critical spirit, together with much valuable new research about the German circles in which they originated.

[2] M. Mersenne, *La vérité des sciences*, Paris, 1625, pp. 566–7; cf. Mersenne, *Correspondance*, ed. Waard and Pintard, Paris, 1932, I, pp. 154–5.

[3] *Allgemeine und General Reformation der gantzen weiten Welt. Beneben der Fama Faternitas, dess Löblichen Ordens des Rosencreutzes, an alle Gelehrte und Haüpter Europas geschrieben*, Cassel, 1614. The German original of this and the other Rosicrucian manifestoes will be found in *De Manifesten der Rosekruisers*, ed. A. Santing, Amersfoort, 1930; and in *Chymische Hochzeit Christiani Rosencreutz*, etc., ed. F. Maack, Berlin, 1913 (reprints the manifestoes as well as the "Chemical Wedding"). English translation in A. E. Waite, *The Real History of the Rosicrucians*, London, 1887, pp. 36 ff.; critical discussion as to authorship, etc., in Arnold, *op. cit.*, pp. 23 ff.

[4] See above, p. 338.

disguise, a bold thing to do in view of the political situation in Italy. The author was a friend of Galileo, and belonged to the Venice-Padua liberal group. When he died rather suddenly in 1613, assassination or poison were rumoured, though there seems to be no proof of this.[1]

The chapter from Boccalini's book which the German Rosicrucians chose to have translated into German, and which they prefixed to their first manifesto, is entitled "By order from Apollo, a general Reformation of the World is published by the Seven Wise Men of Greece, and by the other Literati."[2] The state of the Age being found to be so terrible that many commit suicide to be out of it, Apollo orders a Universal Reformation of which the Seven Wise Men of Greece are to be in charge. The wise men make speeches giving their views as to what ought to be done. Thales is of the opinion that hypocrisy and dissembling is the main cause of the present evils, and advises that a little window should be made in men's breasts to enforce candour. This seemed a good idea to Apollo and he gave orders that the little windows should be made. But when the surgeons took their instruments in hand, some of the Literati pointed out how awkward the business of governing would become if everyone could see into the governors' breasts; so the plan was given up. The opinion of Solon is that what

> hath put the present Age into so great confusion is the cruel hatred, and spiteful envie which in these days is seen to reign generally amongst men. All help then for these present evils, is to be hoped for from infusing Charity, reciprocal Affection, and that sanctified Love of our Neighbour, which is God's chiefest Commandment, into mankind; we ought therefore to employ all our skill in taking away the occasions of those hatreds, which in these days reign in men's hearts . . .[3]

[1] See A. Belloni, *Il Seicento, Storia letteraria d'Italia*, Milan, ed. of 1955, p. 471.

[2] Traiano Boccalini, *Ragguagli di Parnaso*, Centuria I, Ragguaglio 77 (in the edition of Venice, 1669, pp. 214 ff.); in the English translation by Henry, Earl of Monmouth, *Advertisements from Parnassus*, London, 1669, pp. 119 ff.; original of the German translation published with the Rosicrucian *Fama*, in *Chymische Hochzeit*, etc., ed. Maack, separately paged at end; English translation, based on Monmouth's translation, in Waite, *op. cit.*, pp. 36 ff.

[3] Monmouth's translation, *ed. cit.*, p. 121; Waite's translation, *op. cit.*, p. 41.

Solon thinks that this can best be done by making a new division of the world's goods, so that all have equal shares. But the many inconveniences which would arise from this were pointed out by others, and Solon's opinion was set aside. The bright ideas of the other wise men were also all found to be impracticable, and in the end, the Age was dressed up again in a gay jacket to hide his rotten carcase, and the Reformers abandoned their larger plans for a general reformation of the whole world and confined themselves to regulating the price of cabbages, sprats, and pumpkins.

In striking contrast to the sophisticated disillusion, the bitter irony, of the weary Venetian liberal is the "Fama Fraternitas", or the Rosicrucian manifesto which follows the German translation of the extract from Boccalini. The latter is as naïve and incoherent as the former is experienced and lucid. We gather that the Fraternity of the Rosy Cross was founded by one Christian Rosencreutz, a German, who was educated in a monastery and afterwards travelled widely, particularly in the east.[1] The Magia and Cabala of the wise men with whom he conferred at Fez was not altogether pure "but notwithstanding, he knew how to make good use of the same, and found still better grounds for his faith, altogether agreeable with the harmony of the whole world, and wonderfully impressed in all periods of time."[2] He also admired the way in which the learned of Fez communicated to one another new discoveries in mathematics, physics, and magic and wished that the magicians, Cabalists, physicians, and philosophers of Germany were equally co-operative.[3] Much of the "Fama" is quite unintelligible; no doubt it is intended to be so; mysterious "rotae" are alluded to; vaults covered with geometrical diagrams, and the like.[4] The brethren possess some of the books of Paracelsus.[5] Amongst the articles to which they agree are that none of them should profess any other thing than to cure the sick, and that gratis; that they should not wear a distinctive habit but follow the custom of the country they are in; that the word R.C. should be their seal mark and character; that the Fraternity should remain secret for one hundred years.[6]

---

[1] Waite's translation, *op. cit.*, pp. 66 ff. Christian Rosencreuz is here alluded to as "Brother C.R.C.".

[2] *Ibid.*, p. 68.   [3] *Ibid.*, p. 67.

[4] *Ibid.*, pp. 75–7.   [5] *Ibid.*, p. 78.   [6] *Ibid.*, p. 73.

The only thing which seems to connect the "Fama" with the translation from Boccalini with which it is yoked is that the Rosicrucians, too, are expecting a general reformation of the world.

> Howbeit we know after a time there will now be a general reformation, both of divine and human things, according to our desire and the expectation of others; for it is fitting, that before the rising of the Sun there should appear and break forth *Aurora*, or some clearness, or divine light in the sky.[1]

It is also intimated near the beginning of the "Fama" that man is about "to understand his own nobleness and worth, and why he is called *Microcosmus*, and how far his knowledge extendeth into nature".[2]

The Rosicrucian general reformation of the world would appear to be a mystical and magical development, perhaps something like that rising sun of magical reform which Bruno hailed. Linked as it is, through the extract from Boccalini, to the liberal Italian viewpoint which Bruno, on his political level, also represented, the thought at which I hinted in a preceding chapter[3] again arises in the mind. Could the Rosicrucians be in any way connected with the sect of Giordanisti which Bruno is said to have founded in Germany?

This placing of the extract from Boccalini before the "Fama" is extremely curious. The Rosicrucian who is said to have instructed Fludd, Michael Meier, said that there was no connection between the two documents, the inclusion of the "General Reformation" of Boccalini with the "Fama" being purely fortuitous.[4] This is extremely unlikely, and in any case is disproved by what appears to be a sympathy with Boccalini shown in other writings connected with the Rosicrucian movement.[5]

Bruno had been through Germany preaching a coming magical reform movement which he associated politically with Henry of Navarre. Henri IV was assassinated in 1610, ending the hopes which the liberals had placed upon him. In 1612–13, Traiano Boccalini published his *Ragguagli di Parnaso*, full of praises and laments for the French king, of hatred of Spain, of ironical attacks

[1] *Ibid.*, pp. 80–1.   [2] *Ibid.*, p. 65.
[3] See above, pp. 312–3.   [4] Waite, *op. cit.*, p. 271.
[5] Arnold, *op. cit.*, pp. 66–7. The Rosicrucians were anti-Spanish.

on pedantry and tyranny. In 1613, Boccalini, like Bruno before him, is dead. In 1614, the German Rosicrucians come out with their "Fama" associated with Boccalini on general reformation. This sequence does not prove anything; it is merely suggestive.

Other Rosicrucian publications were the *Confessio Fraternitatis* (Cassel, 1615) and the *Chymische Hochzeit Christiani Rosencreutz* (Strasbourg, 1616), the latter certainly by Johann Valentin Andreae, a Lutheran pastor, who may also be the author of the translation from Boccalini and the other manifestoes, though this is not certain.[1] It would seem that Rosicrucianism, as it emerges in Germany in the early seventeenth century, has Lutheran connections; one explanation of the Rosicrucian emblem of the cross and the rose which has been put forward is that it is an imitation of Luther's emblem.[2] "Christian Rosencreutz", the founder, seems entirely mythical; perhaps this name, too, is an allusion to Luther. But the Rosicrucians were magical, Hermetic, Cabalistic Lutherans and particularly addicted to alchemical symbolism of which "The Chemical Wedding of Christian Rosencreutz"[3] is an elaborate and incomprehensible example.

The Lutheran flavour of Rosicrucianism is not against the hypothesis of a connection with Bruno, since we know that Bruno found favour with the Lutherans of Wittenberg and, in his stirring address to the university, prophesied that truth would be found among them.[4]

In the *Summum bonum* which purports to reflect the Magia, Cabala, and Alchymia of the Rosicrucians, there is an epilogue stating that the divisions of Christendom into Romans, Lutherans, and Calvinists are unreal and to be disregarded since all are at bottom the same and tend to the same end.[5] We thus have in

[1] On this question, see Arnold, *op. cit.*, pp. 85 ff.

[2] Luther's emblem, a cross within a rose, is reproduced in the *Chymische Hochzeit*, ed. Maack, p. XLVIII, as the explanation of the "Rosy Cross". Other interpretations relate the name to the meanings of the rose in alchemy (see C. G. Jung, *Psychology and Alchemy*, London, 1953, pp. 74–5). The Lutheran flavour of Rosicrucianism as it appears in the manifestoes may be due to these being a Lutheran adaptation of an earlier movement.

[3] English translation in Waite, *op. cit.*, pp. 99 ff.

[4] See above, p. 312.

[5] *Summum bonum*, Frankfort, 1629, epilogue. This work, which passed under the name of R. Frizius, was almost certainly partly by Fludd; see Arnold, *op. cit.*, p. 236.

Rosicrucianism a survival or continuation of those eirenist and liberal tendencies which were a feature of sixteenth-century religious Hermetism, and which Bruno put into practice as he wandered from country to country preaching against "pedantry" wherever he found it. The Rosicrucians perhaps hoped to avert the Thirty Years War by magic, perhaps hoped to find when they came to Paris a liberal French King.[1] If so, they were disappointed. The French Monarchy was now under the management of Richelieu who would help to destroy Germany in the Thirty Years War.

There is much that reminds of Bruno in this Rosicrucian movement but there is also much that is different. If Fludd represents their views, his version of Magia and Cabala is not the same as that of Bruno, as has been pointed out before. Bruno is both less Christian and less alchemical than Fludd and the Rosicrucians seem to be; nor is Fludd's system heliocentric,[2] like Bruno's. Whilst no definite statement can be made, nevertheless it may be broadly speaking true that the latter are continuing the reform motive in a Hermetic context which was so characteristic of Bruno.

Though I do not think that Giordano Bruno has ever been mentioned before in connection with the Rosicrucians, Tommaso Campanella has been so mentioned, and here the link seems certain. It will be remembered that Campanella's German disciple, Tobias Adami, took some of Campanella's manuscripts to Germany and eventually published them there.[3] It was to Tübingen that he took them, between about 1611 and about 1613, where lived Johann Valentin Andreae, who, whether or not actually the author of the Rosicrucian manifestoes, was certainly connected with the group whence they emanated. It seems undoubted that Campanella's ideas reached Andreae in this way, and also through another German, his close friend Wense, who visited Campanella in Naples in 1614. Wense suggested that Andreae's proposed Christian union should be called the City of the Sun, and further, Andreae's published work on an ideal republic is heavily

---

[1] On the visit of the Rosicrucians to Paris, see below, p. 446.

[2] Fludd is against heliocentricity; see *Utriusque cosmi . . . historia*, I, pp. 156 ff.

[3] See above, p. 373.

influenced by Campanella's *Civitas Solis*.[1] There is thus, a link between Campanella and the Rosicrucians through those German disciples who visited him in prison and carried some of his works to Germany.

This link between Campanella and Rosicrucian reform notions does not, to my mind, cancel out the Bruno suggestion but rather re-enforces it. If Bruno had earlier sown the seed in Germany by establishing groups of "Giordanisti", the soil would have been prepared for the Campanella influence, since, as we argued in the last chapter, Bruno's reform movement runs on into the earlier Campanella and his Calabrian revolt.

To take leave of this difficult and misty subject, I would say that the Rosicrucians represent the Hermetic-Cabalist tradition of the Renaissance in some form, and strongly associated with religious ideas. If Fludd is to be taken as characteristic of their views (which is by no means certain), their Magia and Cabala were more of a return to Renaissance origins, perhaps preserved in German Lutheran circles, as at the University of Wittenberg with its intense interest in those subjects, than representative of the more recent developments of the tradition by Bruno and Campanella. Nevertheless rumours of the reform movement of one of those missionaries, Campanella, had certainly reached them, and possibly that of the other, Bruno, who had actually preached his mission in Germany. It may therefore be suggested that Rosicrucian aspirations after a universal reform in a Hermetic context may well owe something to Bruno as well as to Campanella.

Is there, or is there not, a connection between the Rosicrucians and the origins of Freemasonry? Some people think that there is; others think that Freemasonry came out of a stream of thinking similar in its tendencies to that of the Rosicrucians but different in its immediate origins.[2]

[1] On Campanella's influence on Andreae and his friends, see Arnold, *op. cit.*, pp. 60 ff. The book by Andreae which shows the influence of the *Civitas Solis* is his *Reipublicae Christianopolitanae descriptio*, Strasburg, 1619. Andreae also published German translations of some of Campanella's poems; see Firpo, *Bibliografia di Campanella*, p. 43.

[2] For a discussion, with references to some of the immense literature on this subject, see Arnold, *op. cit.*, pp. 229 ff.; for a Masonic point of view, see B. E. Jones, *Freemason's Guide and Compendium*, London, 1950, pp. 117 ff.

Freemasonry is first heard of as an institution in England in the seventeenth century, and Elias Ashmole is an important figure in connection with it. Ashmole states in his diary that he was made a mason in a lodge at Warrington in 1646.[1] There were certainly earlier traditions and origins in England upon which Ashmole and his group were drawing, but about these very little is known. Speculative Freemasonry claims, of course, to be descended from the guilds of the mediaeval masons, but all these matters are wrapped in mystery.

May it not be of significance that Giordano Bruno preached, not only to the Lutherans in Germany, but also to the courtiers in Elizabethan England? I made the very tentative and allusive suggestion in an earlier chapter that Bruno's mission in England, with its appeal to pre-Reformation social and mystical ideas, his lament at the destruction of great abbeys and monasteries, might have something in common with the attitudes to the past of Free-masonry.[2] Bruno attached his Hermetism to royalism, to the chivalrous cult of Elizabeth I by her knights. The interests of the first known Freemason, Ashmole, would not conflict with the idea of a stream of influence having reached him from courtly circles of the time of Elizabeth. Ashmole was a fervent royalist with a strong interest in the history of chivalry. That Bruno's influence had persisted in court circles is indicated by the *Coelum Britannicum*, produced at court only twelve years before Ashmole was made a Freemason. It is a not impossible supposition that the influence of the importation of Rosicrucian ideas into England on Fludd, Vaughan, and Ashmole, may have crossed with an earlier courtly stream, perhaps influenced by Bruno, to produce Free-masonry.

In any event, our new understanding of the nature of Bruno's influence in England and in Germany makes of him a key figure for the exploration of those impulses through which Renaissance Hermetism passed underground into the channels of esoteric societies.

We are told that Mozart's *Magic Flute* embodies some of his beliefs as a Freemason. If so, we might have in this opera a translation into poetic and musical imagery of the theme of the good religion of the Egyptians, of the mysteries of Isis and Osiris into

[1] Quoted Jones, *op. cit.*, p. 99.   [2] See above, p. 274.

which the good are initiated, of the magical atmosphere through which human souls make their way to a Hermetic-Egyptian salvation.[1] The name "Zarastro" of the head priest would reflect the equation of Zoroaster with Hermes Trismegistus in Renaissance genealogies of wisdom.

REACTIONARY HERMETISTS: ATHANASIUS KIRCHER

Leaving these abstruse themes of the "confraternite ed associazioni variamente caratterizzate", as E. Garin[2] has called those esoteric channels within which Hermetism continued after "Hermes Trismegistus" was dated, we come now to a solid mass of published work in which, as in the publications of Robert Fludd, the dating of Trismegistus is completely ignored and the Renaissance Hermetic-Cabalist synthesis is maintained on a quite unimpaired foundation.

> To thee belongs the fame of Trismegist
> A righter Hermes; th'hast outgone the list
> Of's triple grandure . . .

These verses addressed to the Jesuit, Athanasius Kircher, by an English admirer and prefixed to his vast work on the hieroglyphs, the *Oedipus Aegyptiacus*,[3] published in 1652, indicate the nature of his reputation and prepare us for the innumerable quotations from Ficino's *Pimander*, and from the *Asclepius* with which the huge tomes are sprinkled. Kircher dates Hermes Trismegistus in the time of Abraham,[4] and implicitly believes him to be the true author of the works ascribed to him. He had foreknowledge of the Trinity which, however, he did not quite well define, though it cannot be denied that he spoke of it first and better than any subsequent Gentile.[5]

Kircher's great passion is for the Egyptian hieroglyphs[6] and

[1] It was, of course, with continental Freemasonry that Mozart was in contact (see E. Iversen, *The Myth of Egypt and its hieroglyphs*, Copenhagen, 1961, p. 122). But all continental Freemasonry ultimately derived from England; and it was in Elizabethan England that Giordano Bruno had so fervently preached the revival of the Egyptian religion.

[2] Garin, *Cultura*, p. 144.

[3] A. Kircher, *Oedipus Aegyptiacus*, Rome, 1652.

[4] *Op. cit.*, I, p. 103. [5] *Ibid.*, II (2), p. 506.

[6] Like Ficino (see above, p. 163) Kircher holds that Hermes Trismegistus invented the hieroglyphs.

their meanings. He continues the Renaissance tradition of interpretation of the hieroglyphs as symbols containing hidden divine
truths, expanding it with enormous labour and pseudo-archaeology.
These vast labours in which Renaissance hieroglyphic lore finds
a last full flowering come at so late a date that they will soon be
utterly superseded by the discovery of the true nature of the
hieroglyphs.[1] In order to think on Renaissance lines about the
hieroglyphs it was absolutely necessary to keep up the belief in
Hermes Trismegistus, for, as the ancient Egyptian priest, it was
his kind of wisdom, the wisdom of the *Hermetica*, which was
hidden in the Egyptian hieroglyphs and in the images of their gods.
Kircher has interesting pages in which he explicitly relates
definitions of God in the *Corpus Hermeticum* to Egyptian symbols.
Thus after quoting the beginning of *Corpus Hermeticum* IV on
God, the creator immanent in the world which is, as it were, his
body, and from *Corpus Hermeticum* V, also on God latent in the
world, he goes on to exclaim in the customary admiring manner
of the religious Hermetist that no Christian and no theologian
could have spoken more profoundly of God than this, and adds
that these things will be found hidden in the hieroglyphs.[2] Both
quotations are made from Ficino's Latin translation,[3] which was no
doubt used in a similar manner by the Renaissance hieroglyphists.
The Renaissance hieroglyphic tradition, with its interpretations of
hieroglyphs as truths about God and the world, is a channel
through which the Hermetic religion of the world is carried
throughout the entire period—reaching a very late climax in the
works of Athanasius Kircher. In the final outburst of Hermetism
at the end of his *Oedipus Aegyptiacus*, Kircher gives expression
to the belief which inspires his whole work on the hieroglyphs.

Hermes Trismegistus, the Egyptian, who first instituted the hieroglyphs, thus becoming the prince and parent of all Egyptian theology
and philosophy, was the first and most ancient among the Egyptians

---

[1] Champollion's discovery, which at last enabled the hieroglyphic
inscriptions to be deciphered, was published in 1824. For the history of
the discovery, see Iversen, *The Myth of Egypt*, pp. 137 ff.

Champollion represents the second phase of the break-up of the
Egyptian myth, the first phase of which was Casaubon's dating of the
Hermetica.

[2] Kircher, *op. cit.*, II (2), pp. 504–5.

[3] Cf. Ficino, *Opera*, pp. 1842, 1843–4.

and first rightly thought of divine things; and engraved his opinion
for all eternity on lasting stones and huge rocks. Thence Orpheus,
Musaeus, Linus, Pythagoras, Plato, Eudoxus, Parmenides, Melissus,
Homerus, Euripides, and others learned rightly of God and of divine
things. . . . And this Trismegistus was the first who in his *Pimander*
and *Asclepius* asserted that God is One and Good, whom the rest of
the philosophers followed.[1]

Thus the hieroglyphs and the *Hermetica* were both writings of
Hermes Trismegistus in which he made the same statements
about divine things in which he was followed by all the poets and
philosophers of antiquity. In the light of this profound belief,
Kircher interprets all Egyptian monuments and obelisks, as
having written on them in the hieroglyphs the truths of Ficinian
Hermetism.

Kircher is much preoccupied with Isis and Osiris as the chief
gods of Egypt. In one of his discussions of their meanings he says:

The divine Dionysius testifies that all created things are nothing else
but mirrors which reflect to us the rays of the divine wisdom. Hence
the wise men of Egypt feigned that Osiris, having given charge of all
things to Isis, permeated invisibly the whole world. What else can
this signify save that the power of the invisible God penetrates
intimately into all?[2]

Here "Egyptian" divine immanence combines with Pseudo-
Dionysian light mysticism to produce that acute sense of the
divine in things so characteristic of Renaissance Hermetism. For
Kircher, Isis and Osiris have a meaning which, when found
among philosophers of the Renaissance such as Giordano Bruno, is
called "panpsychism".

Kircher's passion for Egypt leads him into elaborate geographi-
cal researches, in the course of which he comes to the Egyptian
city called Heliopolis, or "civitas Solis", the City of the Sun. He
says that the Arabs called this city "Ainschems", that is "the eye
of the sun", and that in the Temple of the Sun in it there was a
marvellous mirror, constructed with great art to flash back the
rays of the sun.[3] We seem to be here in the miraculous atmosphere
of the City of Adocentyn, the Arabic version of the City of the

---

[1] Kircher, *op. cit.*, III, p. 568.

[2] *Ibid.*, I, p. 150.

[3] *Ibid.*, I, pp. 29–30. Cf. also III, p. 331, on the "solarian" obelisk at
Heliopolis.

Sun in *Picatrix*, though Kircher does not name that work nor make any connection between Heliopolis and the prophecies of the *Asclepius*. Nevertheless his remarks confirm the view that Campanella's *Città del Sole* was ultimately Egyptian in origin.

Kircher discusses the priesthood of Egypt (basing himself mainly on quotation from Clement of Alexandria),[1] the laws of the Egyptians,[2] the love of the people for their kings and how the Egyptian monarchy represented the idea of the universe,[3] the philosophy of the Egyptians and how the Platonic doctrine of the ideas originated with them (using Hermes),[4] the "mechanics" of the Egyptians,[5] or their applied science, and, finally, the magic of the Egyptians.[6] And this brings one to the question whether, within this late continuation of Renaissance "Egyptianism", ultimately derived from Ficino's cult of the *Hermetica*, there was still room for magic.

There is a quotation from Ficino's *De vita coelitus comparanda* in the *Oedipus Aegyptiacus*,[7] and it is the passage in which Ficino discusses the Egyptian form of the cross. Kircher introduces the quotation by stating that Hermes Trismegistus invented the Egyptian form of the cross, the *crux ansata* which he calls the "crux Hermetica". The quotation from Ficino is followed by a long and most elaborate discussion[8] of the relation of the Hermetic cross to the world and its power of drawing into it the celestial influences. The Egyptian or Hermetic cross, says Kircher, was a "most potent amulet"; it was a "character" fabricated with marvellous skill after the pattern of nature and showing the way to the

---

[1] *Ibid.*, I, pp. 115 ff.

[2] *Ibid.*, pp. 118 ff.

[3] *Ibid.*, pp. 119, 137, etc.

[4] *Ibid.*, p. 148 (Plato, Pythagoras, Plotinus as followers of Hermes Trismegistus); II (2), p. 523 (doctrine of the ideas originated with the Egyptians and Chaldeans, with references to *Pimander* and *Asclepius*).

[5] *Ibid.*, II (2), pp. 280 ff. (on mechanical devices used by the Egyptians for building, for producing seemingly miraculous effects in their temples, and so on). The Egyptians are regarded as the inventors of mechanics, from whom the Greeks learned all that they knew (*ibid.*, p. 322).

[6] *Ibid.*, II (2), pp. 436 ff.

[7] *Ibid.*, II (2), p. 399; cf. Ficino, p. 556 (the passage is quoted above, p. 72, note 3).

[8] Kircher, *op. cit.*, II (2), pp. 400 ff.

one light; and Marsilius Ficino has described its power.[1] Kircher is thus in agreement with Ficino about the magical power of the Egyptian cross, and his own learned and astrological exposition of it is a development, or a further explanation, of Ficino's words in the work which Kircher calls, by rather a curious slip of the tongue, the *De vita coelitus propaganda*. He makes no comparison in this passage with the Christian cross, nevertheless such a comparison is made very clearly in some of his interpretations of Egyptian monuments.

For example, the hieroglyphs on the obelisk of Heliopolis,[2] which include several representations of what Kircher calls the Egyptian cross, are explained as having the meaning of the obelisk shown in the centre, on which there is a Christian cross and sun. (Pl. 16b). Kircher's interpretation of the hieroglyphs on the obelisk[3] is permeated by the influence of Ficino's *De vita coelitus comparanda*. By elaborate developments he succeeds in making his Hermetic-Ficinian interpretation of the hieroglyphs fit with the Christian cross with the sun and trinity shown in the centre. The whole interpretation is but the expression in terms of hieroglyphs of religious Hermetism; "Hermes Trismegistus" has written in hieroglyphs on the obelisk dedicated to the sun the same truths which he wrote in the Hermetic writings with their foreknowledge of Christianity and of the Trinity, and with the Egyptian magical cross foreshadowing the Christian cross, as in Ficino's *De vita coelitus comparanda*.

It will be remembered that Giordano Bruno had views about the Egyptian and the Christian forms of the cross, which he based on the passage in Ficino's *De vita coelitus comparanda* and about which he was questioned by the Inquisitors.[4]

---

[1] *Ibid.*, II (2), p. 399. Kircher has another long passage on the Egyptian cross in his *Obeliscus Pamphilius*, Rome, 1650, pp. 364 ff., again quoting Ficino (*ibid.*, pp. 377–8).

In the passage on the Egyptian cross in this work, Kircher also quotes at length from John Dee's *Monas hieroglyphica*, 1564, and reproduces a glorified form of Dee's "monas" diagram which he seems to regard as a form of the Egyptian cross (Pl. 15a, b) (Kircher, *Obeliscus Pamphilius*, pp. 370–73).

[2] Kircher, *Oedipus Aegyptiacus*, III, pp. 332 ff.

[3] *Ibid.*, p. 334.

[4] See above, p. 351. Bruno, as usual, had it the wrong way round.

The great test for magic is the passage in the *Asclepius* describing how the Egyptians introduced demons into their idols by magical practices. Kircher twice quotes this passage; the first time in full, including part of the Lament, without any disapproval[1]; this is in the part of the book in which he is describing Egypt and its life as an archaeologist or a historian. The second quotation, now a paraphrase or abridgement of the idol making passage only, comes in the section on Egyptian magic and here Kircher expresses very strong disapproval of these practices as bad, diabolic magic, labelling them very clearly in the margin "Trismegisti impia doctrina".[2]

In view of this strong condemnation, it is to be assumed that when Kircher gives his list of the magic images of the decans,[3] which he relates to the passage in the *Asclepius* on the decans,[4] his interest in these images is purely academic and harmless. It is not easy to assess Kircher's point of view. He had the instincts of a historian and an archaeologist,[5] yet, living as he does so intensely within the Hermetic atmosphere, his approach to these matters cannot be quite detached. He does definitely disapprove of diabolic magic. On the other hand, he is very interested in Egyptian mechanical means for giving statues an animated appearance, by means of pulleys and other devices,[6] suggesting a strong and admiring interest in Egyptian priestcraft.

Kircher certainly did some kind of natural magic. In his *Ars magna lucis et umbrae*,[7] of which we earlier reproduced the title-page[8] there is a section on *Magia lucis et umbrae*; this magic is

[1] Kircher, *op. cit.*, I, pp. 142–5.

[2] *Ibid.*, II (2), pp. 442–3. He has also earlier condemned Egyptian magic, citing Delrio (*ibid.*, pp. 436–7).

[3] *Ibid.*, II (2), pp. 182–6. Kircher's list of the decan images is discussed in Gundel, *Dekane und Dekansternbilder*, pp. 370–2.

[4] Kircher, *op. cit.*, II (2), p. 182; cf. also *ibid.*, p. 519; "Nam in Pimandro & Asclepio Hermes varios deorum ordines, uti sunt Usiarchae Horoscopi, Decani, Pantomorphi . . . varios choros assignat . . ." (cf. above, pp. 36–7, on the order of the Egyptian gods in the *Asclepius*).

[5] Kircher's work as an archaeologist, particularly his Coptic studies, is not to be despised; cf. Iversen, *op. cit.*, pp. 92 ff.

[6] Kircher, *op. cit.*, II (2), pp. 280 ff.

[7] Kircher, *Ars magna lucis et umbrae*, Rome, 1646.

[8] See Pl. 9.

described as, not a diabolic, but a natural magic.[1] The section concludes with the ecstatic chapters on Pseudo-Dionysius and Trismegistus on light[2] which are somewhat reminiscent of similar developments of light themes in Patrizi.[3]

Kircher was also a Cabalist of vast learning, and he sets out, as Pico della Mirandola did in his *Conclusiones*, to make a synthesis between Cabalism and Hermetism; the section on Cabala in the *Oedipus Aegyptiacus* is headed "De Allegorica Hebraicorum veterum Sapientia, Cabalae Aegyptiaca & hieroglyphicae parallela".[4] He gives an elaborate plan of the arrangement of the Sephiroth.[5] But he sharply condemns Cabalist magic.[6] Kircher was thus a Hermetist-Cabalist in the full Renaissance tradition, but one who was careful about Magia and practical Cabala.

Kircher's passion for everything Egyptian, combined with his intense religious Hermetism, makes him an interesting figure in our series. Giordano Bruno's Egyptianism was demonic and revolutionary, demanding a full restoration of the Egyptian-Hermetic religion. In the Egyptianism of the Jesuit, Kircher, diabolic magic is severely condemned and Christianity is supreme, yet Egypt, and the Egyptian magical cross, play a rôle behind Christianity which depends in some way upon that momentous entry of Hermes Trismegistus into the Church.

That Hermetism is still so deeply engrained in the mind of a pious Jesuit as late as the mid-seventeenth century, may suggest that Patrizi's advice to the Jesuits to take up Hermetism was not out of place.[7]

At the end of the *Oedipus Aegyptiacus*, just after the hymn from the *Pimander* with which he concludes, Kircher places a hieroglyph enjoining secrecy and silence concerning these sublime doctrines. And, in effect, in this survival in seventeenth-century Jesuitism of the most enthusiastic type of Renaissance religious

---

[1] *Op. cit.*, p. 769. Kircher's position may thus be that of the Jesuit Del Rio, whom he frequently cites, who condemned diabolic magic but allowed the natural kind; see Walker, pp. 178–85.

[2] Kircher, *op. cit.*, pp. 919 ff.   [3] See above, p. 183.

[4] Kircher, *Oedipus Aegyptiacus*, II (1), p. 209. Kircher is aiming at making a synthesis of all mystical traditions. He is a seventeenth-century Pico della Mirandola in this respect, but he includes areas unknown to Pico, such as Mexico and Japan, which had been covered by the Jesuit missions.

[5] *Ibid.*, II (2), p. 480.   [6] *Ibid.*, II (1), p. 358.   [7] See above, *loc. cit.*

Hermetism we have something like another of those esoteric channels through which the Hermetic tradition is carried on, which perhaps explains why Mozart could be a Freemason as well as a Catholic.

As is well known, the school of English thinkers known as the Cambridge Platonists, of whom the chief were Henry More and Ralph Cudworth, continued in the seventeenth century many of the themes and traditions of Renaissance Platonism. But, unlike Fludd and Kircher, both More and Cudworth knew of and accepted Casaubon's critique of the *Hermetica*, and this deprived them of Hermes Trismegistus as a *priscus theologus* and so of one of the main foundations of the Renaissance synthesis. I believe that this has never been noticed, nor has its bearing on More's and Cudworth's adaptations of Renaissance thought been examined. This is an important matter which cannot be explored in the few pages devoted to More and Cudworth in this chapter. I can only point out, very briefly, certain facts, and leave it to others to investigate the matter further.

When discussing the pre-existence of the soul in his work on the immortality of the soul, More says:

> In Egypt, that ancient Nurse of all hidden sciences, that this Opinion (i.e. that the soul pre-exists) was in vogue amongst all the wise men there, those fragments of Trismegist do sufficiently witness. For though there may be suspected some fraud and corruption in several passages of that Book, in reference to the interest of Christianity; yet this Opinion of the Praeexistency of the Soul, in which Christianity did not interest itself, cannot but be judged, from the Testimony of those Writings, to have been a Branch of the Wisdome of that Nation: of which Opinion not only the Gymnosophists and other wise men of Egypt were, but also the Brachmans of India, and the Magi of Babylon and Persia; as you may plainly see by those Oracles that are called either Magical or Chaldaical, which Pletho and Psellus have commented upon. To these you may adde the abstruse Philosophy of the Jews, which they call their Cabbala, of which the Soul's Prae-existence makes a considerable part; as all the learned of the Jews do confess. And how naturally applicable this Theory is to those

three mysterious chapters of Genesis, I have, I hope, with no contemptible success, endeavoured to shew in my *Conjectura Cabbalistica*.[1]

More had certainly studied Casaubon's *Exercitationes* very carefully; for he quotes from it in his *Conjectura Cabbalistica*, naming Casaubon as the author.[2] It was therefore certainly from Casaubon that he derived the view expressed in the above quotation that the "Book" containing the "fragments of Trismegist" (i.e. the *Corpus Hermeticum*) is to be suspected of being a pious fraud by Christians. His argument is that, since the pre-existence of the soul is not a Christian doctrine, the passages in the *Corpus Hermeticum* which teach this may be genuinely "Egyptian wisdom", untampered with by those who made the fraud. He then proceeds to make a synthesis of this genuinely Egyptian teaching of the *Hermetica* with the Chaldean Oracles and with Cabala after the manner of the Renaissance tradition. But if one has to pick and choose like this for genuine Egyptian passages in the *Hermetica*, this is a very different matter from seeing them as ancient Egyptian prophetic writings which concord with *Genesis* and which foretell the Trinity in passages now suspected by More, following Casaubon, "of fraud and corruption in the interest of Christianity".

How radically More was affected by this new view of the *Hermetica* can be readily recognised by some examination of his *Conjectura Cabbalistica* in which he "interprets the mind of Moses in the three first chapters of Genesis" according to a threefold Cabala, literal, philosophical, and mystical. More was convinced, like Pico della Mirandola and all the Renaissance Cabalists, that "the Jewish Cabala is conceived to be a Traditional doctrine or exposition of the Pentateuch, which Moses received from the mouth of God while he was on the Mount with him".[3] He further believes that philosophical Cabala contains mysteries that are "the same that those eximious philosophers, Pythagoras and Plato,

---

[1] Quoted from *A Collection of Several Philosophical Writings of Henry More*, second edition, London, 1662, *The Immortality of the Soul* (separately paged), p. 113.

[2] Henry More, *Conjectura Cabbalistica*, in the above-cited *Collection* (separately paged), p. 102.

[3] *Ibid.*, p. 1. More was, however, also influenced by later types of Cabala than those available in the Renaissance; see R. J. Z. Werblowsky, "Milton and the *Conjectura Cabbalistica*," *J.W.C.I.*, XVIII, 1955, pp. 94, 96.

brought out of Egypt and the parts of Asia into Europe. And it is generally acknowledged by Christians that they both had their Philosophy from Moses."[1] More therefore conflates his Cabalistic commentary on *Genesis*—for that is what the *Conjectura Cabbalistica* is—with Pythagorean number mysticism and with the teachings of Plato and the Neoplatonists. Once again, this is the Renaissance tradition of combining a *priscus theologus* like Pythagoras with ancient Cabalistic tradition going back to Moses. With this return to Pythagorean-Mosaic antiquity, More connects his Platonism, and he finds that the whole tradition leads up to Christianity, or rather to his form of Christian Platonism, which it confirms.

Now the new thing about More's *Conjectura Cabbalistica* is, not so much what is in it, but what is not in it. For there is an enormous omission, namely that Hermes Trismegistus is never mentioned. This means that More never makes the usual conflation of the Egyptian Genesis, *Pimander*, with the Mosaic *Genesis*; nor does he ever use the Hermetic Trinitarian passages to support his Christian Platonism. The reason for these omissions must be that More has been led by Casaubon to believe that the "Mosaic" and "Christian" passages in the *Hermetica* are not most ancient Egyptian wisdom concording with Moses and prefiguring Christianity, but "frauds and corruptions" inserted by late Christian writers. Though he believes in general that Moses learned from the Egyptians, he has ceased to believe in the *Hermetica* as reliable evidence about Egyptian wisdom and its concordance with *Genesis* and with St. John's Gospel.

The enormous difference which this made can best be realised by comparing More with Fludd and Kircher. Fludd's *Philosophia Moysaica* is also a kind of Cabalistic commentary on *Genesis* but one in which Hermes Trismegistus holds equal authority with Moses, and the *Pimander* in Ficino's translation is constantly quoted as parallel to *Genesis*. Also the Hermetic Trinitarianism is joined with Pythagorean and Cabalist number mysticisms to produce Fludd's ecstatic mystical diagrams. The same observation is also roughly speaking true of the work of Kircher's which we discussed, the *Oedipus Aegyptiacus*, in which *Genesis* is buttressed with Ficino's *Pimander*, and the Hermetic Trinitarianism is

[1] *Ibid.*, p. 3.

freely used as authoritative. Fludd's life overlaps with that of
More, for he died when More was twenty-three; Kircher was
More's slightly older contemporary. Yet they are separated from
him by a great gulf, for they refused to admit Casaubon's criticism
of the *Hermetica*, whilst he accepted it. The result is, that whilst
Fludd and Kircher are still Hermetic-Cabalists, attaching to this
double basis their approach to Platonism, More is not a Hermetist
but a Cabalist only, and his Mosaic-Pythagoro-Platonic synthesis
is freed from the heavy, overpowering influences of Christian
Hermetism which he recognised as spurious.

What this fact (for it is a fact) may mean for the understanding of
More's Platonism, as compared with that of Ficino or of Pico and
the Renaissance tradition generally, must be left for future in-
vestigators to determine. Perhaps it may mean that Henry More
really was what Ficino used to be thought to be, a pious Christian
interpreting Platonism mystically to re-enforce his Christianity,
and free from that core of magical theory, and magical practice,
which the cult of Hermes Trismegistus imparted to Ficinian
Platonism and its influence.

More was also touched by quite modern influences, being a
student and an admirer of the work of Descartes whose mechanistic
philosophy of nature he accepted, though with some reservations.
He was able to accord, at least to his own satisfaction, the new
mechanical philosophy with his own outlook in which so much of
the Renaissance tradition persisted. One of the ways in which he
managed to do this was by regarding the Cartesian mechanism as a
truth anciently known to Moses and preserved in Cabalist tradition
which Descartes had rediscovered by divine inspiration.[1] More,
however, did not entirely accept the mechanistic interpretation of
nature, pointing out that there are some natural phenomena which
it does not cover. He therefore wished to modify it by the concept
of a "spirit of nature". More's modification of the Cartesian
mechanism in this direction has been analysed by E. A. Burtt.[2]
And here it is interesting to notice that in one of the passages in
his book on *The Immortality of the Soul* in which he is defending
his "spirit of nature" against the Cartesian mechanism and the
Cartesian dualist view of matter and mind, More falls back upon

[1] *Ibid.*, p. 104.
[2] E. A. Burtt, *The Metaphysical Foundations of Modern Physical Science*,
London, 1932, pp. 127–36.

what is evidently a survival of Ficinian Hermetism in his outlook.
The Cartesian first and second elements are, says More, really the
same as:

> that true Heavenly or Aethereal Matter which is everywhere, as
> Ficinus somewhere saith Heaven is; and is that Fire which Tris-
> megist affirms is the most inward vehicle of the Mind, and the
> instrument that God used in the forming of the world, and which the
> Soul of the world, wherever she acts, does most certainly still use.[1]

The reference in the margin for this quotation is "Trismegist.
Poemand. cap. 10 *sive Clavis*" that is to chapter 10 of Ficino's
Pimander (really *Corpus Hermeticum* X.)[2]

Thus More's acceptance of Cartesian mechanism is really
Cabalistic, and his criticism of it is, at least in part, Hermetic,
using an appeal to Ficino's *Pimander* which thus evidently still
had some considerable validity for him, in spite of Casaubon.

More's friend and fellow Cambridge Platonist, Ralph Cudworth,
wrote his *True Intellectual System of the Universe* (1678) to confute
atheists by bringing together beliefs in the existence of God at all
times and in all places and in the great philosophical traditions—a
method which bears upon it obvious marks of the influence of
Renaissance syncretism. He intends to demonstrate that the
doctrine of the pagan polytheists was always the same, that
besides their many gods there was one supreme omnipotent Deity.

> And this we shall perform, not as some have done, by laying the
> chief stress upon the Sibylline oracles, and those reputed writings
> of *Hermes Trismegist*, the authority whereof hath been of late so
> much decried by learned men; nor yet upon such oracles of the
> Pagan deities, as may be suspected to have been counterfeited by
> Christians; but upon such monuments of Pagan antiquity, as are
> altogether unsuspected and indubitate.[3]

Cudworth then proceeds to go through what are really, in effect,
the old *prisci theologi*, but basing his account of Zoroaster[4]

---

[1] *Immortality of the Soul*, p. 96 (in the *Collection* cited).

[2] See Ficino, p. 1849.

[3] Ralph Cudworth, *The True Intellectual System of the Universe*, second
edition, London, 1743, p. 281.

[4] *Ibid.*, pp. 285 ff.

on other texts beside the *Chaldean Oracles* (though these he considers to be fairly authentic); his account of Orphism[1] on better authorities than the *Orphica*, which he thinks highly suspect; and his account of the theology and philosophy of the ancient Egyptians[2] on Iamblichus, Plutarch, the Fathers, and so on, rather than on the writings of "Hermes Trismegist", which, like the Sibylline Oracles which he dismisses almost entirely as Christian forgeries,[3] have been tampered with by late Christian writers. For it seems that some pretended Christians of former times have

> endeavoured to uphold the truth of Christianity by figments and forgeries of their own devising. Which, as it was a thing ignoble and unworthy in itself, and argued that those very defenders of Christianity did themselves distrust their own cause; so may it well be thought, that there was a policy of the devil in it also, there being no other more effectual way than this, to render all Christianity (at least in after-ages) to be suspected. Insomuch that it might perhaps be questioned, whether the truth and divinity of Christianity appear more in having prevailed against the open force and opposition of its professed enemies, or in not being at last smothered and oppressed by these frauds and forgeries of its seeming friends and defenders.[4]

How far we have travelled, in the company of the New Criticism, from Ficino's commentaries on the *Pimander*, from Hermes Trismegistus among the Sibyls in the cathedral of Siena, from the religious Hermetism of the sixteenth century, and also from seventeenth-century reactionary Hermetists like Fludd and Kircher, the latter of whom was still alive when Cudworth's book was published!

On later pages in his book, Cudworth examines Casaubon's criticism of the *Hermetica* in detail. Isaac Casaubon, he says, was the first discoverer of the Christian frauds in the Sibylline and "Trismegistic" writings, and has pointed out many spurious, because Christian, passages

> in that first Hermetick book, entitled, *Poemander*; some also in the fourth book, inscribed *Crater*, and some in the thirteenth called the *sermon in the mount, concerning regeneration*; which may justly render those three whole books, or at least the first and last of them, to be suspected. We shall here repeat none of *Casaubon's* condemned

---

[1] *Ibid.*, pp. 294 ff. [2] *Ibid.*, pp. 308 ff.
[3] *Ibid.*, pp. 282 ff. [4] *Ibid.*, pp. 281-2.

passages, but add one more to them out of the thirteenth book, or *sermon in the mount*, which, however omitted by him, seems to be more rankly Christian than any other . . . *Tell me this also, who is the cause or worker of regeneration? The son of God, one man by the will of God*. Wherefore, though *Ath. Kircherus* contend with such zeal for the sincerity of all these Trismegistick books; yet we must needs pronounce of the three forementioned, at least the *Poemander* properly so called, and the *sermon in the mount*, that they were either wholly forged and counterfeited by some pretended Christians, or else had many spurious passages inserted into them. Wherefore it cannot be solidly proved from the Trismegistick books after this manner, as supposed to be all alike genuine and sincere, that the Egyptian Pagans acknowledged one universal Numen.[1]

It is curious to observe in all this how deeply influenced Casaubon and Cudworth have been by the Christian Hermetist tradition. Modern scholars who, naturally, have not been brought up in that tradition and are not reacting from it, though they are convinced of the post-Christian dating of the *Hermetica*, do not regard them as Christian forgeries, as some of the Sibylline Oracles undoubtedly are.[2] Indeed, they see little or no Christian influence in them.[3] But to Cudworth, emerging from centuries of intensively Christian interpretation of the "Trismegistick" writings as the work of the ancient Egyptian *priscus theologus* and prophet of Christianity—an attitude which he knew to be still very much alive in his contemporary world as his reference to Kircher shows[4] —the books and passages which he mentions can seem "rankly Christian", and therefore forged.

Cudworth, however, is not in agreement with Casaubon that the Hermetic books are entirely valueless as sources for Egyptian wisdom. Even if they were all forged, yet because they were written "before the Egyptian paganism and their succession of priests were yet extinct" their writers would have known something of those priests and "their arcane and true theology" and so the books are not to be discarded as without information about

[1] *Ibid.*, pp. 319–20.

[2] For references to literature in the Sibylline Oracles as forgeries, see above, p. 8, note 4.

[3] See above, p. 21, note 3.

[4] In another passage, Cudworth again refers to Kircher as having asserted the genuineness of those writings "commonly imputed to Hermes Trismegist" (*op. cit.*, p. 285).

this.[1] Further, he thinks that Casaubon is wrong in labelling all the Hermetic books as spurious because some of them have been proved to be so.[2] He points out that Casaubon falls into the error of thinking that what Ficino published under the title *Pimander* was all one book,[3] whereas this includes several distinct books, not all of which need be spurious. And he thinks that the other books which Patrizi published, and above all the *Asclepius*, should not fall under condemnation as Christian forgeries since no signs of spuriousness (i.e. of Christianity) can be discovered in them[4]

Another of his objections to Casaubon is that the latter assumes that "Platonical and Grecanical" opinions in the *Hermetica* were all inserted by Christian writers skilled in Greek learning. But since we know that "Pythagorism, Platonism, and the Greek learning in general was in great part derived from the Egyptians" why should not such learning in the Hermetic books have come straight from the Egyptian priests, its true source?[5] This circular argument shows how strong a hold Renaissance respect for Egypt as the fount of wisdom still had on Cudworth's mind. The example he gives is that the dogma in Trismegistic books "That nothing in the world perisheth, and that death is not the destruction, but change and translation of things only" though Pythagorean, was derived by Pythagoras from the Egyptians and fits very well with another doctrine in these books that the world is a "second god" and therefore immortal. This may therefore well be some of the old Egyptian learning preserved in these books.[6]

That the *Asclepius* cannot be a Christian forgery is sufficiently proved, for Cudworth, by the passage on god-making, the spirit of which is "not at all Christian, but rankly Pagan".[7] He cannot understand why Lactantius thought that the "Son of God" passage in the *Asclepius* meant the second person of the Trinity, since it clearly refers to the visible world.[8] And he suggests that the Lament may describe the destruction of the Egyptian religion by the Christians written after the event, not as a prophecy of it, though he is not sure of this.[9]

The upshot of Cudworth's argument is:

that though some of the Trismegistick books were either wholly counterfeited, or else had certain supposistitious passages inserted

---

[1] Cudworth, *op. cit.*, p. 320. [2] *Ibid.*, *loc. cit.* [3] *Ibid.*, *loc. cit.*
[4] *Ibid.*, p. 321. [5] *Ibid.*, p. 326. [6] *Ibid.*, pp. 326–7.
[7] *Ibid.*, p. 328. [8] *Ibid.*, p. 331. [9] *Ibid.*, p. 329.

into them by some Christian hand, yet there being others of them originally Egyptian, or which, as to the substance of them, do contain Hermaical or Egyptian doctrines (in all which one supreme Deity is every where asserted) we may well conclude from thence, that the Egyptians had an acknowledgement of one supreme Deity.[1]

That so much anxious labour was required to rescue something from the wreck of "Hermes Trismegistus" as the safe authority on Egypt shows what a jolt Casaubon had given to pious Christian Platonists who were still otherwise, to a large extent, working within the Renaissance tradition.

It is interesting to note that what Cudworth saves as genuinely Egyptian from the *Hermetica* (the eternity and divinity of matter, the *Asclepius* and its magical religion) is representative of Bruno's Egyptianism which he arrived at by his refusal—so painfully unorthodox and shocking—to admit the Christian interpretation of these writings.

These four examples of what happened after Hermes Trismegistus was dated must suffice to give an impression of Hermetism in the seventeenth century. It was slow in losing its grip. Fludd, the Rosicrucian, and Kircher, the Jesuit, both maintained Renaissance Hermetic-Cabalist attitudes by ignoring or forgetting that Hermes Trismegistus was not still the ancient *priscus theologus* that he was to Ficino. The Cambridge Platonists accepted Casaubon's criticisms in the main, with the result that Cambridge Platonism, bereft of the Hermetic foundation, must be a very different matter from Renaissance Platonism. Nevertheless, they are reluctant to abandon the *Hermetica*, and find ways and means of keeping something of their influence.

And the *Hermetica* were not, and are not, invalidated as profoundly important documents of religious experience by being at last correctly dated. Nor are modern scholars even yet in agreement as to how much, or how little, of genuinely Egyptian teachings they may contain.[2]

[1] *Ibid.*, p. 333.
[2] The Egyptian approach may be strengthened by the recent discovery of a version of the *Asclepius* in Coptic; see J. Doresse, *The Secret Books of the Egyptian Gnostics*, London, 1960, pp. 255 ff.

Chapter XXII

━━━━━━━━━━━━━━━━━━━━━━━━━━━━━━━━━━━━━━━

HERMES TRISMEGISTUS AND
THE FLUDD CONTROVERSIES

━━━━━━━━━━━━━━━━━━━━━━━━━━━━━━━━━━━━━━━

IN the last chapter, we examined the attitude to Casaubon's critique of the *Hermetica* amongst those who, in one way or another, were still attached to Renaissance traditions, whether as Magi, like Fludd, as Egyptologists, like Kircher, or as Christian Platonists, innocent of magic, like More and Cudworth. We have now to turn to the use made of Casaubon's discovery by those who have emerged from Renaissance traditions, who are, indeed, actively ranged against them and bent on destroying them, particularly their magical and animistic aspects, in order to clear the way for a changed attitude to the world, that of the Cartesian mechanical philosophy of nature, and for genuinely scientific and non-magical ways of operating with its powers in the tremendous development of the mechanical sciences. Though much had gone before to prepare the way for it, no one will deny that the seventeenth century represents that momentous hour in the history of man in which his feet first began to tread securely in the paths which have since led him unerringly onwards to that mastery over nature in modern science which has been the astonishing achievement of modern European man, and of him alone, to this extent, in all the annals of mankind.

The attack on Renaissance magic, with its associated so-called Neoplatonism and its animistic philosophies of nature was led in France in the early seventeenth century by "le bon père" Marin Mersenne, of the Order of the Minimes. Mersenne, a most devout Christian and an eager scientific enquirer, friend of Descartes and of Gassendi, admirer of Galileo, played an important part in encouraging the new movement, by putting enquirers into touch with others working on similar lines through his vast correspondence with all the savants of Europe. As Lenoble has succinctly pointed out,[1] the issue was not seen by those, like Mersenne, who were actively engaged in the conflict, as solely an issue between the new philosophical and scientific attitudes and the old scholastic tradition. Descartes broke the Aristotelian physics finally, but he also despised, ignored, brushed aside, Renaissance naturalism which he saw to be more incompatible with his own views, in spite of an apparent resemblance in the anti-Aristotelianism of some Renaissance thinkers. And for Mersenne the chief enemy, both of orthodox Christianity and of true science, was Renaissance naturalism with all its associated magics.[2] He therefore devoted his energies to dethroning the Renaissance Magus from his seat and to attacking the efflorescence of base magics of all kinds which the long prevalent Hermetism and Cabalism had brought in their train.

In the opening years of that momentous seventeenth century, every kind of magic and occultism was rampant. The authorities were deeply alarmed. In France, hundreds of sorcerers were being burned every year,[3] which, as Lenoble has said, is an indication not only of the prevalence of magic but of belief in its powers. There can be little doubt that the esoteric and demon-ridden atmosphere of this period was the final outcome—as it were, the decadence—of the revaluation of magic ultimately deriving from Ficino and Pico and which, extravagantly continued by such descendants of theirs as Cornelius Agrippa, had received support from the animistic interpretations of nature of the Renaissance philosophers. As Koyré has said, "Pour les gens du XVIe et du XVIIe siècle tout est naturel et rien n'est impossible, parce que tout est compris en fonction de la magie et la nature elle-meme n'est qu'une magie avec un Dieu magicien suprême."[4] It was into such a world as this that Mersenne and Descartes were born, and Mersenne saw it as his mission to fight it with every weapon he possessed. The scientific weapons were not, as yet, very strong. We

[1] R. Lenoble, *Mersenne ou la naissance du mécanisme*, Paris, 1948, pp. 5 ff.

[2] *Ibid.*, p. 7.   [3] *Ibid.*, pp. 30 ff.

[4] Quoted by Lenoble, *op. cit.*, p. 85.

are inclined to forget, dazzled as we are by the immense advance in the acquisition of exact scientific knowledge made in the course of this century, how little there was of it at the start, and how slight was the armour with which Mersenne advanced to attack the prevailing magical view of nature as the only scientific explanation of its phenomena.

Mersenne's *Quaestiones in Genesim* (1623)[1] is an awkward book to grasp, not only because of its immense length, but also because the contents seem confusingly arranged. The sections, which are of extremely uneven length, are headed by verses from the first three chapters of *Genesis*, and indeed the book, as its title shows, is intended to be a commentary on *Genesis*, the general purpose of which is not easily seized by the reader as he makes his way through what seems like a collection of treatises on a highly miscellaneous variety of subjects. Lenoble has, however, well seen what may be the principle of unity in the work. He regards it as mainly directed against all magical and divinatory arts, against Cabalists and occultists of all kinds, against naturalist and animistic philosophers whom Mersenne suspects in general of being either atheists or deists. In other words, the Bible text is being used as a canvas for Mersenne's *summa* against Renaissance magic, its whole way of thinking, and all its off-shoots in the vast contemporary dissemination of magical practices. It is also, suggests Lenoble, a *summa* of Mersenne's own scientific interests, his studies in music, mathematics, physics, astronomy and the like.[2] Thus, within the framework of the Mosaic account of creation, Mersenne is both driving out the old magical way of approaching nature, and also bringing in the new way, the coming way of science and genuine mathematics.

From the vast mass of material in this most important book, which lies between the Renaissance and the modern world, only a few points can be selected. Mersenne is extremely well-informed about the Renaissance magic which he so much detests; probably he made a good deal of use of Del Rio's book against magic which he several times mentions. On Ficino he is very clear-sighted. Ficino does not speak as a Catholic when, in the book *De vita coelitus comparanda*, he affirms that images and characters have

---

[1] M. Mersenne, *Quaestiones celeberrimae in Genesim.* . . . Paris, 1623.
[2] Lenoble, *op. cit.*, pp. 25 ff.

power on all inferior things, which Catholics deny.[1] In another part of the book, where he gives a long and extremely knowledgeable account of the properties of stones and of magic images, he sees the connection which has been made in Renaissance Platonism between magic images of the stars and Platonic ideas:

> Sunt qui ad Platonis ideas recurrant, quae praesint lapidibus, adeout quilibet suam habet ideam, a qua vim & energiam suam accipiat; vel cum Hermete, & Astronomis ad stellas, & imagines coeli (recurrant).[2]

Here he uncovers the magical core of Ficinian Platonism, its confusion of the ideas with magic images and with Hermetism. To attribute such powers to such images seems to him merely insane.

> Verum nemo sanae mentis dixerit illas imagines vim habere, ut constellationes magis influant.[3]

Mersenne is a modern; he has crossed the watershed and is on the same side of it as we are; belief in the power of magic images of the stars seems to him quite mad. A drawing by Mantegna, he thinks, is of more value than all the images of the necromancers.[4] He does not condemn such images because he is afraid of their power but because they are meaningless. Mersenne, who completely discards astrology,[5] naturally also discards astral magic, the miraculous virtue of plants, stones,[6] images, and the whole apparatus upon which *magia naturalis* rested.

---

[1] "Respondeo Ficinum quidem catholicum non esse, ubi nugas illas magicas & astrologicas affert, & probat, ut patet ex lib. 3 de vita coelitus comparanda, in quo characteres & imagines vim in omnia inferiora habere docet, quod singuli vere Cristiani negant." Mersenne, *Quaestiones in Genesim*, col. 1704.

[2] *Ibid.*, col. 1164.

[3] *Ibid.*, col. 1165.

[4] *Ibid.*, *loc. cit.* This reference to Mantegna occurs when Mersenne is condemning the lapidary of Camillus (Leonardus Camillus, *Speculum lapidum*, Venice, 1502) in which Mantegna, Bellini, and Leonardo da Vinci are mentioned; cf. Garin, *Cultura*, p. 397.

[5] Lenoble, *op. cit.*, pp. 128 ff.

[6] In his condemnation of images, however, Mersenne (*op. cit.*, col. 1164) still cites "Catholic philosophers" (i.e. Thomas Aquinas) who have said that the materials or stones of which a talisman is made have power (see above, p. 73).

He condemns the doctrine of the *anima mundi*,[1] or at least the extravagant extension of this indulged in by the Renaissance naturalists who affirm that the world lives, breathes, even thinks. Once again he has detected here the magical core in Renaissance Platonism, for this universal animism in nature was the basis for the operations of the Magus, and the *spiritus mundi* was the vehicle which he used.

Concerning the Cabala, Mersenne would admit an orthodox Cabala, concerned with mystical interpretation of Scripture.[2] But Cabalist magic he, naturally, whole-heartedly condemns, and the whole system of Cabalist angelology and its connections with cosmology.

In the course of this energetic clearance, which demolishes the Hermetist-Cabalist basis of Renaissance magic, Mersenne mentions and condemns all the chief propagators of these views, Ficino, Pico della Mirandola and their successors; he is naturally most severe against arch-magicians, such as Cornelius Agrippa or Trithemius. Against Francesco Giorgi, one of the most celebrated of Hermetic-Cabalists and author of the influential *Harmonia Mundi* he has many passages, and he also devoted another book specifically to refuting him.[3] Patrizi's theory of light comes under review and is condemned.[4] Bruno and Campanella are attacked, the former briefly (Mersenne's main attacks on Bruno come in other books), the latter in long passages.[5] In short Mersenne's vast *Genesis* commentary contains within its covers penetrating critical analyses of almost every aspect of the way of thinking which we have been studying in this book. The life-blood of the Renaissance Magus drains away under this onslaught; his most cherished theories, illusions, and delusions are turning into so much useless lumber in the cold clear light of the new age.

But we have not yet mentioned the chief game which Mersenne is hunting. The dead and gone Hermetist-Cabalists were not so

[1] Lenoble, *op. cit.*, pp. 153 ff.

[2] *Ibid.*, p. 103.

[3] M. Mersenne, *Observationes et emendationes ad Francisci Giorgi problemata*, Paris, 1623.

[4] Mersenne, *Quaest. in Gen.*, cols. 739–40.

[5] Bruno and Campanella are named in the preface to the work as among the chief villains. (Atheos, magos, Deistas, & id genus . . . Campanella, Bruno, Telesio . . .) Campanella's *De sensu rerum* is attacked in detail, col. 1164 ff. For Mersenne on Bruno, see further below, pp. 444–5.

dangerous and abhorrent to him as the living one, Robert Fludd.[1] There can be little doubt that Fludd in whom Mersenne saw, and rightly, a contemporary who was deliberately reviving and re-enforcing with all his power the world view of the Renaissance Magus which Mersenne was bent on destroying, was really the latter's main target. Fludd's works, and particularly his *Utriusque cosmi . . . historia*, were the immediate irritant which precipitated the whole vast counter-flood (if this bad pun may be permitted) of the *Quaestiones in Genesim*. And if we think of how Fludd constantly and for ever quotes Ficino's *Pimander*, equating this with the Mosaic account of creation, we begin to see how Mersenne has planned his book as a reply to that; and we perceive another unifying, guiding principle in his *Genesis* commentary, besides those to which Lenoble has pointed. For Mersenne's own commentary, on its theological side, uses only the Fathers and accredited doctors of the Church. It is not as a Hermetist-Cabalist like Fludd that Mersenne approaches *Genesis*, but as an orthodox Catholic. He is using orthodox *Genesis* commentary as the framework for his attack on Fludd's Hermetist-Cabalist commentary, and on all that had been built on to the Hermes-Moses equation from Pico della Mirandola onwards. Thus, it may be suggested, the true unifying principle of Mersenne's work is Moses, an orthodox Moses, who, turning his face against magic, ushers in the new science.

Mersenne does not often mention Hermes Trismegistus; and when he quotes from the *Hermetica* it is always in Greek, never in Ficino's Latin translation.[2] But he fully realised how basic was Hermes for Fludd and for the whole tradition from whence Fludd derived. The macrocosm-microcosm theory of Fludd's "two worlds" cannot be proved, says Mersenne, because the "Egyptians" teach that man contains the world and because "Mercurius" (also meant by "the Egyptians") calls man a great miracle and like to God.[3]

I have not found in the *Quaestiones in Genesim* any evidence that Mersenne knew when he wrote it of Casaubon's discoveries about

---

[1] On Fludd and the Rosicrucians as Mersenne's chief target, see Lenoble, *op. cit.*, pp. 27 ff.

[2] See for example, Mersenne, *Quaest. in Gen.*, cols. 731, 1750.

[3] *Ibid.*, cols. 1746, 1749.

the *Hermetica*. But soon afterwards he discovered Casaubon and realised what a tool had been provided for his work of demolition of the edifice in which dwelt the Renaissance Magus and his descendant, Robert Fludd. For, if the "Egyptian Moses" was a fake, the corner-stone of the edifice was removed and the whole building must fall into ruin.

Fludd was incensed by Mersenne's attack on him, to which he published angry replies. In his *Sophiae cum moria certamen* (of which the preface is dated Oxford, 1626) he uses most abusive language against the monk, and quotes the passages against himself in the *Quaestiones in Genesim* with detailed rejoinders. In this "Strife of Wisdom with Folly", Fludd presents himself as the representative of deep wisdom, whilst Mersenne is the superficial fool. In his earlier works, Fludd had identified himself with the Rosicrucians and Mersenne had included this mysterious brotherhood in his censures on Fludd, so that the Rosicrucian cause became involved in the Fludd-Mersenne controversy. Hence in another publication, probably partly by Fludd, against Mersenne entitled *Summum bonum* (1629),[1] the highest good is defined on the title-page as "the Magia, Cabala and Alchymia of the Brothers of the Rosy Cross". In this work, when replying to a passage against Ficino in Mersenne's *Quaestiones in Genesim*,[2] the writer quotes at length from Ficino's *Apologia* for his magic which he endorses as representing his own point of view.[3] This in itself is sufficient evidence that Fludd and the Rosicrucians stood for Renaissance Magia, stemming from Ficino, with all its various Cabalist and other accretions, against Mersenne, the rationalist. In another publication of the same year in which there is a passage inveighing against the malice and falsehood of the monk Mersenne, Fludd quotes triumphantly from *Pimander* and the *Asclepius*, thus advancing under the banner of Hermes Trismegistus to defend wisdom against falsehood and malice.[4]

The controversy was watched with interest and excitement by all Europe, as the many references to it in Mersenne's correspondence

---

[1] See above, p. 412.
[2] Mersenne, *Quaest. in Gen.*, cols. 1704–5.
[3] *Summum bonum*, p. 8.
[4] Fludd, *Medicina Catholica*, Frankfort, 1629, p. 36.

testify.[1] I can make no attempt even to mention, much less discuss in detail, all the publications concerned with it. Mersenne's and Fludd's numerous contributions to the dispute were swelled by those of others. For example, Jacques Gaffarel, the Cabalist, joined in on the side of Fludd, whilst Pierre Gassendi, the scientist, came to the assistance and defence of Mersenne.

Mersenne had asked Gassendi to help, since he was tired of replying to Fludd himself, and Gassendi performed this friendly office in 1630 in a publication attractively entitled *Petri Gassendi theologi epistolica exercitatio, in qua Principia Philosophiae Robert Fluddi Medici reteguntur; et ad recentes illius Libros, adversus R. P. F. Marinum Mersennum Ordinis Minimorum Sancti Francisci de Paula scriptos respondetur*. Gassendi appears to take a more moderate tone against Fludd than Mersenne had done, but, as Lenoble has said, "l'impartialité de Gassendi est parfois plus terrible pour Fludd que les emportements de Mersenne",[2] and he is, at bottom, in entire agreement with Mersenne. He prefers, he says, the old Aristotelianism to the misty science of these people (like Fludd) who are completely ignorant of mathematics, who confuse everything with their doctrine of the world soul, who put angels and demons everywhere.

Gassendi's weighty contribution to the controversy was preceded by a letter by Mersenne. It contains a significant passage which shows that Mersenne has found, and is using, the weapon provided by Casaubon. Mersenne accuses Fludd (and the accusation is just) of giving to the writings of "pseudo-Trismegistus"—note the "pseudo"—an authority equal to that of the Scriptures; but these writings now have no authority since what Casaubon has written about them.

> Cum autem Fluddus plures alios authores enumeret, illos solum affero, quorum authoritate in suis libris nititur. Quos inter primum ordinem obtinet pseudo-Trismegistus, cujus *Pymandrum* et alios tractatus Scripturae sacrae authoritati atque veritati pares efficere videtur, et de quorum aestimatione nonnihil, credo, remittet, si legat Casaubonum, prima *ad apparatum Annalium* Exercitatione.[3]

---

[1] See M. Mersenne, *Correspondance*, ed. C. de Waard and R. Pintard, Paris, 1932, indices *sub nomine*; Lenoble, *op. cit.*, pp. 27 ff., etc.

[2] Lenoble, *op. cit.*, p. 29.

[3] The letter is printed in Mersenne's *Correspondance, ed. cit.*, II, pp. 444–5.

E. Garin has quoted this passage as an illustration of how "la grande polemica accesasi intorno al Fludd e ai Rosacroce . . . chiude . . . un periodo della fortuna dell'ermetismo rinascimentale . . .".[1]

Once Casaubon was in the hands of his opponents, Fludd's position was immeasurably weakened, and, as E. Garin says, the whole tradition of Renaissance Hermetism reached a term. No longer will Hermetism maintain the dominating position at the core of main movements, which it had held since Ficino, but will sink underground into esoteric channels, such as the "sogni ermetici dei Rosacroce".[2]

Of the controversies aroused by Robert Fludd the most famous and important is that between Fludd and Kepler.[3] In an appendix to his great work, the *Harmonice Mundi Libri V* (1619) Kepler attacked Fludd; the latter replied in a treatise inserted into the second volume (1621) of his *Utriusque cosmi . . . historia*. Kepler answered with an *Apologia* (1622) to which Fludd again retorted with his *Monochordum Mundi* (1622).

The mighty mathematician who discovered the elliptical orbits of the planets had, in his general outlook, by no means emerged from Renaissance influences. His heliocentricity had a mystical background; his great discovery about the planetary orbits was ecstatically welcomed by him as a confirmation of the music of the spheres; and there are survivals of animism in his theories.[4] Nevertheless, Kepler had an absolutely clear perception of the basic difference between genuine mathematics, based on quantitative measurement, and the "Pythagorean" or "Hermetic" mystical approach to number. He saw with the utmost distinctness that

[1] E. Garin, "Nota sull'ermetismo", *Cultura*, p. 144.

[2] *Ibid.*, p. 146. To the Rosicrucian dreams should be added the pseudo-Egyptian Hermetic dreams of the Jesuit, Kircher.

[3] The importance of the Fludd-Kepler controversy is touched on by E. Cassirer in his *Das Erkenntnisproblem in der Philosophie und Wissenschaft der neueren Zeit*. There is a valuable essay on it by W. Pauli, "The Influence of Archetypal Ideas on the Scientific Theories of Kepler" in C. G. Jung and W. Pauli, *The Interpretation of Nature and the Psyche*, English trans., London, 1955, pp. 147 ff. Lenoble is much concerned with it in *Mersenne ou la naissance du mécanisme*; and see Garin's illuminating remarks in *Cultura*, pp. 143 ff.

[4] See Pauli's essay, cited in the preceding note.

the root of the difference between himself and Fludd lay in their differing attitude to number, his own being mathematical and quantative whilst that of Fludd was Pythagorean and Hermetic. Kepler's masterly analyses of this difference in his replies to Fludd brought this matter out into the clear light of day for the first time and performed a great service in finally releasing genuine mathematics from the agelong accretions of numerology.

In his *Harmonice Mundi*, Kepler has a long passage on Hermes Trismegistus; he has evidently studied the *Corpus Hermeticum* very carefully, particularly the treatise on the "ultores". He identifies the Hermetic teachings with those of Pythagoras; "either Pythagoras is Hermetising, or Hermes is Pythagorising". The passage is so important that it must be quoted in full. (The mention of Camerarius with which it opens refers to the résumé of Camerarius' commentary on the Pythagorean sayings[1] which Kepler has been giving on preceding pages.)

Hactenus Camerarius ex veteribus: quibus pleraque consentientia inculcat Hermes Trismegistus (quisquis ille fuit) filio suo Tatio: cujus haec verba, *Unitas secundum rationem Denarium complectitur, rursumque Denarius unitatem.* Deinde concupiscibilem Animae facultatem componit ex 12. ultoribus, seu vitiis Ethicis, ad numerum signorum Zodiaci, cui Corpus et hanc ad corpus vergentem Animae potentiam subjicit: Rationalem vero facultatem Animae ex Denario et ipse componit Virtutum Ethicarum. Sic quod Pythagoraei celebrant Tetractyn fontem Animarum, et Camerarius plures ait fuisse Tetractyas, non illam solum, quae a quaternarij basi surgit ad summam 10. sed etiam aliam praecipuam, quae ab Ogdoadis basi ad verticem usque colligit summam 36: idem et Tatius hic ex doctrina patris Hermetis innuit, dum tempus ait fuisse, cum ipse ad huc esset in Ogdoade, Octonario: Filium vero Pater ad Pimandrum remittit, de Octonario canentem; in quo sane occurit Octonarius habituum Animae Ethicorum, septem quidem respondentium planetis septem, ut apparet, initio a Luna facto; octavi vero divinioris et quietioris, ad sphaerae puto fixarum ideam. Omnia etiam geruntur per Harmonias; plurima inculcatio *Silentij*, plurima *Mentis*, *Veritatisque* mentio; proponitur et Antrum, Fundus, Penetrale, Crater Animarum, et caetera multa: ut dubium nullum esse possit, quin aut Pythagoras Hermetiset, aut Hermes Pythagoriset. Accedit enim et hoc, quod Hermes Theologiam quandam tradit, cultumque divini numinis; saepe Mosis, saepe Evangelistae Joannis in suo sensu paraphrastes, praesertim de Regeneratione, caeremoniasque discipulo certas inculcat; cum idem

[1] J. Camerarius, *Libellus Scolasticus*, Bâle, 1551.

de Pythagoraeis affirment authores, partem eorum Theologiae varijsque caeremonijs et superstitionibus deditam fuisse; et Proclus Pythagoricus Theologiam in Numerorum contemplatione collocet.[1]

What, in general, I understand from this is that Kepler, being well acquainted with the *Corpus Hermeticum*, regards its basic teachings as in conformity with Pythagorean harmony, the eighth sphere to which the soul ascends (in *C.H.* XIII), with its 36 divisions, being related to the Pythagorean four as the number of the soul. He also knows (and this opens up an entirely new world of sources for Kepler) the Christian Hermetist tradition, by which the *Hermetica* were connected with *Genesis* and with St. John's Gospel. Kepler would thus have been fully able to recognise in Fludd the basis of the latter's *Genesis-Pimander* equation, and of his constant association of Hermes Trismegistus with St. John.

Does Kepler know that the paraphrases of Moses and of St. John by Hermes Trismegistus "whoever he may have been" are of post-Christian date? That is to say, has Kepler read Casaubon? This does not seem clearly indicated in the above passage which I am therefore inclined to think is still reflecting pre-Casaubon religious Hermetism. The remark "aut Pythagoras Hermetiset, aut Hermes Pythagoriset" seems to leave it as an open question as to whether Hermes is the source of Pythagoras (and therefore very early as in the old tradition).

It was at any rate not in ignorance of the Mosaic and Christian or Trinitarian associations of Fludd's Hermetism that Kepler advanced his strong objection to Fludd's inability to distinguish, in his work on harmony, between genuine mathematics and number treated "more Hermetico". These objections are made many times.

[1] J. Kepler, *Harmonice mundi*, in Kepler's *Gesammelte Werke*, ed. M. Caspar, Munich, 1940, Band VI, pp. 98–9. The note to the passage in this edition (p. 534) suggests that Kepler was using the Latin translation of the *Hermetica* by Foix de Candale (Bordeaux, 1574) and Patrizi's *Nova de universis philosophia* (Ferrara, 1591). But the phrase which Kepler quotes literally from *Corpus Hermeticum*, XIII, corresponds exactly to Ficino's translation. According to Kepler, Trismegistus says to his son Tat, "Unitas secundum rationem Denarium complectitur, rursumque Denarius unitatem." Compare Ficino, "unitas secundum rationem denarium complectitur, rursusque denarius unitatem" (Ficino, pp. 1855–6).

For Fludd on *Corpus Hermeticum* XIII and the "ultores", with many quotations in Ficino's Latin, see his *Utriusque cosmi . . . historia*, II, pp. 129–31.

He, Kepler, is using "mathematical demonstrations" in his own work on harmony, whereas for Fludd "Chemists (i.e. Alchemists), Hermetists, Paracelsists" are the true mathematicians.[1] He points out that Fludd's numerical and geometrical arguments rest on the macrocosm-microcosm analogy, whereas he (Kepler) is studying the heavens in themselves and quite apart from such analogies.[2] Hence the illustrations to Fludd's books are "hieroglyphs"[3] or "pictures", whereas Kepler's illustrations are mathematical diagrams and he is arguing as a mathematician:

> Tuis picturis mea comparavi diagrammata; fassus librum meum non aeque atque tuum ornatum esse, nec futurum ad gustum lectoris cuiuslibet: excusavi hunc defectum a professione, cum ego *mathematicum agam*.[4]

Fludd's mathematics are really "mathesis" and "vana geometria" which he utterly confuses with "Chymia" and with "Hermes".[5] Kepler is concerned not with "Pythagorean intentions" but with reality (*res ipsa*).[6] He uses mathematics as a mathematician; whilst Fludd uses them "more Hermetico".[7] If a comparison is to be made between his and Fludd's works on harmony, he will show any reader that "rem mathematicam ego tradam Mathematice, tu Hermetice".[8]

The root of the matter is that "mathesis" or mathematics "more Hermetico" as used by Fludd on harmony means those numerological relationships, ultimately based on astrology, running through the three worlds, the empyrean, the celestial world, and the elemental world, and which bound together the macrocosm and the microcosm. Mathematics in Kepler's sense is quantitative measurement, and in his book he is applying it empirically and only in the celestial world, and there only to the movement of the planets.

> Jam ut propius accedamus ad fundamenta, quibus Robertus de Fluctibus superstruit suam musicam Mundanam; primum ille totum mundum, omnesque tres ejus partes, Empyream, Coelestem, Elementarem, occupat: ego solam coelestem; nec eam totam, sed solos

[1] Kepler, *Harmonice mundi*, Appendix, in *Gesammelte Werke, ed. cit.*, VI, p. 374.

[2] Kepler, *Apologia, Gesammelte Werke, ed. cit.*, VI, p. 386.

[3] "tu (addressing Fludd) rei *figuram vel Hieroglyphicum* effinxeris", *ibid., loc. cit.*

[4] *Ibid.*, p. 396.   [5] *Ibid.*, p. 399.   [6] *Ibid.*, p. 428.

[7] *Ibid.*, p. 432.   [8] *Ibid., loc. cit.*

planetarum motus quasi sub Zodiaco. Ille fisus veteribus, qui vim Harmoniarum ex numeris abstractis esse credebant, sat habet, si quas inter partes concordantiam esse demonstrabit, eas numeris quomodocunque comprehendat, nulla cura, cujusmodi unitates illo numero accumulentur: ego nuspiam doceo quaerere Harmonias, ubi res, inter quas sunt Harmoniae, non possunt mensurari eadem quantitatis mensura . . .[1]

Kepler's firm grasp of the distinction, and lucid exposition of it, is all the more interesting in view of the fact that (as our first quotation shows) he had carefully studied Pythagorean-Hermetic theory of world and soul harmony in the *Hermetica* and knew the tradition of religious Hermetism.

Think of what the position of Giordano Bruno would have been amidst all these controversies! Of Giordano Bruno, one of whose four "guides" of the soul was "mathesis"; who read Hermetic meanings into the Copernican diagram; for whom a compass was not a compass but a hieroglyph; who wrote a book "against mathematicians" illustrated with wildly mystical diagrams. Surely, he would have written violent dialogues against Kepler, the "pedant". Surely he would have been on the side of the Hermetists, of Fludd (though he would not have been sufficiently "Egyptian" for Bruno), and of the Rosicrucians.

And how would Bruno have reacted to Mersenne's *Quaestiones in Genesim*, with its attack on the magical core of Ficinian Platonism, which was Bruno's life-blood; its condemnation of the soul of the world and of the universal animism in living nature, which was Bruno's eternal theme; its deliberate undermining of the position of the Renaissance Magus, which was what Bruno was? Surely he would have rushed to the attack, shouting "Pedant! Pedant!" even more fiercely.

The shade of Giordano Bruno was, in fact, present to the mind of Marin Mersenne. In the prologomena to the *Quaestiones in Genesim* he mentioned him in a list of authors of new philosophies and of "atheists, magicians, deists and such people",[2] but his chief attacks on Bruno are in *L'Impiété des Déistes* where he describes him as "un des plus méchans hommes que la terre porta

---

[1] Kepler, *Harmonice mundi*, Appendix, *Werke, ed. cit.*, VI, p. 375.

[2] Giulio Cesare Vanini (1585–1619) was, with Bruno, one of the chief objects of Mersenne's detestation. Vanini, a Carmelite friar, travelled in Germany, Bohemia, Holland, Switzerland. He tried to establish himself

jamais" and accuses him of "n'avoir inventé une nouvelle façon de philosopher qu'afin de combattre sourdement la religion chrétienne".[1] Mersenne had been reading the "contractions" and was appalled.[2] Though the whole foundation of Bruno's philosophy was utterly bad, yet Mersenne sometimes found truths advanced on the bad foundation. "Quant a Jordan, encore qu'il se serve de mauvais fondemens, neantmoins il est assés probable que le monde est infini, s'il le peut estre. Car pourquoy voulés-vous qu'une cause infinie ait pas un effet infini ?"[3]

Mersenne had realised the "mission" behind Bruno's philosophy, which he describes as "combattre sourdement la religion chrétienne" and regards it with utter abhorrence, and its author as one of the most wicked men who ever lived. This magician, animist, Hermetist had, in fact, been particularly dangerous because he had had a religious mission. Mersenne is right that it was anti-Christian, in the sense that Bruno's universal reform aimed at returning to a supposedly pre-Christian Hermetic Egyptianism. Bruno himself, however, would not have regarded this as necessarily anti-Christian since, as we have seen, he entertained the strange hope that the reform would come within an existing religious framework. If Mersenne knew this he would certainly not have been mollified but confirmed in his view of the danger to orthodox Christianity of Renaissance magic. His clear view of this danger was, indeed, the chief motive behind his determined efforts to stamp it out.[4]

[1] M. Mersenne, *L'Impiété des Déistes*, Paris, 1624, I, pp. 229–30. On Mersenne on Bruno, see the notes to Mersenne's *Correspondance, ed. cit.*, I, pp. 137–8, 147.

[2] *L'Impiété des Déistes*, I, p. 233.

[3] Mersenne, *Correspondance*, III, p. 275; cf. also, *ibid.*, p. 187.

[4] See Lenoble, *Mersenne etc.*, pp. 119 ff., 157 ff.

in France but failed and went to England, where he was, it is said, well received by members of the Anglican church, and apostatised from the Catholic faith in the Italian Protestant church in London. He, however, lost his favour among Anglicans, was imprisoned in the Tower for a month, and returned to Switzerland, which he soon afterwards left for Paris and then Toulouse, where in 1619 he was burned. He has sometimes been compared to Bruno, whose career his own certainly resembles since he travelled in the same countries, though not in the same order, and ended at the stake. Vanini's notions, however, do not seem to me at all like those of Bruno.

Behind the whole controversy which we have been discussing hover those mysterious Rosicrucians. Fludd's works were in defence of the Rosicrucians and attacks on Fludd were also attacks on them. Mersenne was always talking of them.[1] Everyone who took part in the Fludd controversy mentions them; they even appear in Kepler's stately and abstract mathematical pages.[2] And in 1623 a detachment of them actually visited Paris where they put up placards describing themselves as "Invisible Ones" and announcing that they were in possession of many deep secrets of wisdom which those who wished might learn from them.[3] Their visit clashed with the appearance at the same time in Paris of an equally strange and mysterious sect from Spain, calling themselves "Illuminati".[4] That the Invisible Ones came to Paris at the height of the great intellectual battle against all that they represented which Mersenne and his friends were waging adds to the drama of the situation, and if, as has been hinted in this book, there may have been an influence of Bruno on their formation, it becomes even more clear to which side of the controversy Bruno belongs. It might have been as an Invisible One that Bruno would have returned to Paris had he been alive in the seventeenth century.

Richelieu did not receive the Rosicrucians,[5] but when eleven years later Campanella came to Paris he had the powerful cardinal's support[6]—an indication of Campanella's success in switching his ideas (which in their earlier stages had influenced the German movement)[7] into channels acceptable to the powers that be. As we saw, Mersenne was far from enthusiastic about him,[8] and indeed Campanella's astral magic and natural theology would be as archaic and undesirable from Mersenne's point of view as the Magia and Cabala of the detested Rosicrucians.

Thus in these momentous years when the Renaissance world is cracking and the modern world is rising from its ruins, currents and counter-currents still running strongly out of the past swirl

---

[1] See "Rose-Croix" in the indices to Mersenne's *Correspondance*, ed. cit.

[2] J. Kepler, *Apologia* in *Gesammelte Werke, ed. cit.*, VI, p. 445.

[3] P. Arnold, *Histoire des Rose-Croix*, pp. 7 ff.: Mersenne, *Correspondance, ed. cit.*, I, pp. 154–5, note; Lenoble, *op. cit.*, pp. 30–1.

[4] Lenoble, *op. cit.*, p. 31, citing Baillet, *La Vie de Monsieur Descartes*, Paris, 1691, I, p. 107.

[5] Arnold, *op. cit.*, p. 15.

[6] See above, p. 396.   [7] See above, pp. 413–4.   [8] See above, p. 396.

round the protagonists in the epic struggle, the outlines of which are not as yet clear to the spectators. Mersenne[1] and Descartes were suspected of being Rosicrucians because of their recondite interests. And at the same time and place in which Hermetism is in retreat before the onslaughts of Mersenne, aided by Casaubon's discovery, Campanella is prophesying at court that the infant Louis XIV will build the Egyptian City of the Sun.

The seventeenth century is the creative period of modern science, and the Fludd controversies come at the crucial moment when the new turn begins to be made, when the mechanical philosophy of nature provided the hypothesis and the development of mathematics provided the tool for the first decisive victory of man over nature. For "the whole magnificent movement of modern science is essentially of a piece; the later biological and sociological branches took over their basic postulates from the earlier victorious mechanics."[2]

With the history of genuine science leading up to Galileo's mechanics this book has had nothing whatever to do. That story belongs to the history of science proper, to Duhem's researches which demonstrated the advances made during the Middle Ages, and which were gathered up and continued in the Aristotelian school of Padua, to the Renaissance revival of Greek mathematics, to the intensive development of mathematical studies generally on which an influence of Neoplatonism is acknowledged. The phenomenon of Galileo derives from the continuous development in Middle Ages and Renaissance of the rational tradition of Greek science, and it is for this that Mersenne stands as he beats off the terrible magicians.

The history of science can explain and follow the various stages leading to the emergence of modern science in the seventeenth century, but it does not explain *why* this happened at this time, why there was this intense new interest in the world of nature and its workings. Historians of science are aware of a gap here. "For if one thing has at least now grown clear it is that the emergence of modern science was a very complicated affair, and involved a

---

[1] Lenoble, *op. cit.*, p. 31. On Descartes and the Rosicrucians, see below, pp. 452–3.

[2] E. A. Burtt, *The Metaphysical Foundations of Modern Science*, London, 1932, pp. 16–17.

great variety of factors."[1] "In its initial stages, the Scientific Revolution came about rather by a systematic change in intellectual outlook, than by an increase in technical equipment. Why such a revolution in methods of thought should have taken place is obscure."[2] One writer has suggested that what is needed is "historical studies aiming to ferret out the fundamental motives and other human factors involved" behind the scientific movement.[3]

It is here, as a historical study, and particularly as a historical study of motives, that the present book may have a contribution to make towards elucidating these problems. It is a movement of the will which really originates an intellectual movement. A new centre of interest arises, surrounded by an emotional excitement; the mind turns whither the will has directed it, and new attitudes, new discoveries follow. Behind the emergence of modern science there was a new direction of the will towards the world, its marvels, and mysterious workings, a new longing and determination to understand those workings and to operate with them.

Whence and how had this new direction arisen? One answer to that question suggested by this book is "Hermes Trismegistus". And under that name I include the Hermetic core of Ficinian Neoplatonism; Pico's momentous association of Hermetism with Cabalism; the direction of attention towards the sun as the source of mystico-magical power; the magical animation throughout nature which the Magus seeks to tap and to operate with; the concentration on number as a road into nature's secrets; the philosophy, present in both a magical text-book like *Picatrix* and in the philosophical Hermetic writings, that the All is One, and that the operator can rely on the universal validity of the procedures which he uses; finally, and this is in some ways the most important point, those curious historical errors by which "Hermes Trismegistus" was Christianised, so that it was lawful for a religious Hermetist to speculate on the world in his company, to study the mysteries of creation with his assistance, and even

---

[1] J. H. Randall, *The School of Padua and the Emergence of Modern Science*, Padua, 1961, p. 118.

[2] A. C. Crombie, *Augustine to Galileo*, London, 1961 (second edition), II, p. 122.

[3] Burtt, *op. cit.*, p. 305.

(though not all were willing to stretch the point thus far) to operate with the world forces in magic.

The reign of "Hermes Trismegistus" can be exactly dated. It begins in the late fifteenth century when Ficino translates the newly discovered *Corpus Hermeticum*. It ends in the early seventeenth century when Casaubon exposes him. Within the period of his reign the new world views, the new attitudes, the new motives which were to lead to the emergence of modern science made their appearance.

The procedures with which the Magus attempted to operate have nothing to do with genuine science. The question is, did they stimulate the will towards genuine science and its operations? In an earlier chapter in this book I suggested that they did, giving as an example John Dee, who on one level of his mind is a genuine mathematician, in the line leading to the scientific advances, and on another level is attempting to summon angels with practical Cabala. Much more detailed "ferreting out" of the motives behind the work of Renaissance scientists is needed before more positive statements can be made as to the influence upon them of the dominant Hermetic-Cabalist tradition. In his re-examination of the sources of Leonardo da Vinci, E. Garin has drawn attention to Leonardo's mention of "Ermete Filosofo" and to the resemblance of some of Leonardo's doctrines to Ficinian Hermetism.[1] Might it not have been within the outlook of a Magus that a personality like Leonardo was able to co-ordinate his mathematical and mechanical studies with his work as an artist?

Taking a very long view down the avenues of time a beautiful and coherent line of development suggests itself—perhaps too beautiful and coherent to be quite true. The late antique world, unable to carry Greek science forward any further, turned to the religious cult of the world and its accompanying occultisms and magics of which the writings of "Hermes Trismegistus" are an expression. The appearance of the Magus as an ideal at this time was, as Festugière has said, a retreat from reason into the occult.[2] The same writer compares the appearance of the Magus ideal in the Renaissance as similarly a retreat from the intense rationalism of mediaeval scholasticism.[3] In the long mediaeval centuries, both

[1] Garin, *Cultura*, pp. 397 ff.
[2] Festugière, I, p. 63. [3] *Ibid.*, p. 64.

in the West and in the Arabic world, the traditions of rational Greek science had made progress. Hence, it is now suggested, when "Hermes Trismegistus" and all that he stood for is rediscovered in the Renaissance, the return to the occult this time stimulates the genuine science.

The emerging modern science is still clothed in what might be described as a Hermetic atmosphere. Francis Bacon's *New Atlantis* is perhaps not a very good example to take since Bacon's former position as Father of Experimental Science is now weakened. Nevertheless, the *New Atlantis* is a scientist's Paradise where every kind of discovery and invention is put to the service of the happy people. It is ruled by an Order or Society called "Salomon's House" dedicated to the study of the Works and Creatures of God. The Father of Salomon's House rides in the great procession on a chariot on which there is "a sun of gold, radiant upon the top, in the midst".[1] Whether or not there is any real connection between the *New Atlantis* and the *City of the Sun*, those two Utopias come out of the same stream, and the stream is Hermetic, or Hermetic-Cabalist.

The Hermetic impulse as a motive force behind imaginative formulation of a new cosmology is exemplified by Giordano Bruno. From the new approach to him put forward in this book, Bruno once more swings into place as an important landmark in the history of thought, not for the old wrong reasons but for the new right ones.

Ever since Domenico Berti[2] revived him as the hero who died rather than renounce his scientific conviction of the truth of the Copernican theory, the martyr for modern science, the philosopher who broke with medieval Aristotelianism and ushered in the modern world, Bruno has been in a false position. The popular view of Bruno is still roughly as just stated. If I have not finally proved its falsity, I have written this book in vain.

For what is the truth? Bruno was an out-and-out magician, an "Egyptian" and Hermetist of the deepest dye, for whom the

[1] F. Bacon, *Works*, ed. Spedding, Ellis, and Heath, London, 1857, III, p. 155. On the magical background to Bacon's thought, see P. Rossi, *Francesco Bacone: dalla Magia alla Scienza*, Bari, 1957.

[2] Domenico Berti, *La Vita di Giordano Bruno da Nola*, first edition, Florence, 1867.

Copernican heliocentricity heralded the return of magical religion, who in his dispute with the Oxford doctors associated Copernicanism with the magic of Ficino's *De vita coelitus comparanda*, for whom the Copernican diagram was a hieroglyph of the divine, who defended earth-movement with Hermetic arguments concerning the magical life in all nature, whose aim was to achieve Hermetic gnosis, to reflect the world in the *mens* by magical means, including the stamping of magic images of the stars on memory, and so to become a great Magus and miracle-working religious leader. Sweeping away the theological superstructure which the Christian Hermetists had evolved, using Cabala only as subsidiary to Magia, Bruno is a pure naturalist whose religion is the natural religion of the pseudo-Egyptian Hermetic *Asclepius*. Bruno's world view shows what could be evolved out of an extension and intensification of the Hermetic impulse towards the world. Through a Hermetic interpretation of Copernicus and Lucretius, Bruno arrives at his astonishing vision of an infinite extension of the divine as reflected in nature. The earth moves because it is alive around a sun of Egyptian magic; the planets as living stars perform their courses with her; innumerable other worlds, moving and alive like great animals, people an infinite universe.

Drained of its animism, with the laws of inertia and gravity substituted for the psychic life of nature as the principle of movement, understood objectively instead of subjectively, Bruno's universe would turn into something like the mechanical universe of Isaac Newton, marvellously moving forever under its own laws placed in it by a God who is not a magician but a mechanic and a mathematician. The very fact that Bruno's Hermetic and magical world has been mistaken for so long as the world of an advanced thinker, heralding the new cosmology which was to be the outcome of the scientific revolution, is in itself proof of the contention that "Hermes Trismegistus" played some part in preparing for that revolution. The philosophy of Giordano Bruno, instead of being studied as has been done in the past in isolation from its true historical context,[1] can now be examined by historians of thought as a remarkably complete example of a Hermetic world view in the immediately pre-scientific age.

---

[1] The history of attitudes to Bruno would make a fascinating study, the material for which is ready to hand in the monumental *Bibliografia*.

"Hermes Trismegistus" had to be cast off to free the seventeenth century for its advance, and his dating by Casaubon came at the right moment when his work was done. Nevertheless, the history of the emergence of modern science is incomplete without the history of that from which it emerged; Mersenne's reaction cannot be understood without understanding of what he was reacting from; the swing of the pendulum back towards rationalism needs to be seen in the context of the Renaissance revival of the occult.

Moreover, the mechanistic world view established by the seventeenth-century revolution has been in its turn superseded by the amazing latest developments of scientific knowledge. It may be illuminating to view the scientific revolution as in two phases, the first phase consisting of an animistic universe operated by magic, the second phase of a mathematical universe operated by mechanics. An enquiry into both phases, and their interactions, may be a more fruitful line of historical approach to the problems raised by the science of to-day[1] than the line which concentrates only on the seventeenth-century triumph. Is not all science a gnosis, an insight into the nature of the All, which proceeds by successive revelations?

In that interesting human document, Baillet's life of Descartes, we read how the young philosopher, ardently seeking for truth, fell into a kind of enthusiasm "qui disposa de telle manière son esprit . . . qu'il le mit en état de reçevoir les impressions des songes et des visions". It was November 10th, 1619, and he lay down to rest "tout rempli de son enthousiasme, & tout occupé de la pensée d'avoir trouvé ce jour-la les fondemens de la science admirable".[2] In the night he had three consecutive dreams which seemed to him to have come down from on high. We are completely in the atmosphere of the Hermetic trance, of that sleep of the senses in which truth is revealed. The atmosphere is maintained on the following pages which tell of how Descartes heard of the "Frères de

[1] For a discussion of Bruno's atomic theory, that matter is composed of internally animated atoms, see P.-H. Michel, *La cosmologie de Giordano Bruno*, Paris, 1962, p. 66 ff. Bruno probably arrived at this through the introduction of magical animism into the Lucretian cosmology (see above, pp. 246, 248, 265, note 1).

[2] Baillet, *Vie de Descartes*, I, p. 81.

la Rose Croix" who were said to be in possession of a "véritable science".[1] He tried to learn more of them and their secret, but could find out nothing about them, though, on his return to Paris from Germany in 1623 he was suspected of having joined the Rosicrucian brotherhood.[2] This was not true, but it became clear that such a brotherhood was not entirely imaginary because "several Germans and also the Englishman, Robert Fludd, have written in their favour."[3] The atmosphere in which Descartes is casting about for truth is the atmosphere of the great controversy about Fludd and the Rosicrucians.

At about this time, says Baillet, Descartes had almost given up his favourite study of mathematics and geometry which seemed to him to have no certainty.

> Il ne trouvoit rien effectivement qui lui parût moins solide que de s'occuper de nombres tout simples, & de figures imaginaires . . . sans porter sa vuë au delà. Il y voioit même quelque chose de plus qu'inutile; & il croyoit qu'il étoit dangereux de s'appliquer trop sérieusement à ces démonstrations superficielles, que l'industrie & l'expérience fournissent moins souvent que le hazard: & qui sont plutôt du ressort des yeux & de l'imagination que de celui de l'entendement.[4]

This might well be a description of the Fludd type of Hermetic diagram. It will not do for Descartes, who was looking for a "Science générale" which might be called "Mathesis, ou Mathématique universelle".[5] His vision confirmed him in the conviction that mathematics was the sole key to the secrets of nature, and shortly afterwards he invented "a new and most fruitful tool, analytical geometry".[6]

The Cartesian mathesis was a vision of genuine mathematics as the clue to the universe and led to the discovery of a genuinely scientific tool for investigations. A transition has been made to an epoch in which what is still a Hermetic, almost a "Rosicrucian", impulse towards the world results in valid scientific intuitions. But may not the intensive Hermetic training of the imagination towards the world have prepared the way for Descartes to cross that inner frontier?

---

[1] *Ibid.*, p. 87. [2] *Ibid.*, pp. 90–1.
[3] *Ibid.*, p. 108. [4] *Ibid.*, p. 112.
[5] *Ibid.*, pp. 114–15. [6] Burtt, *op. cit.*, p. 97.

In his eagerness to establish a purely objective view of nature as a mechanism, in his enthusiasm for pure mathematics as the only safe tool for objective enquiry, Descartes was left with the problem of mind somewhat embarrassingly on his hands. He provisionally solved the problem in a very crude way, by his so-called dualism, "one world consisting of a huge mathematical machine, extended in space; and another world consisting of unextended thinking spirits. And whatever is not mathematical or depends at all on the activity of thinking substance . . . belongs with the latter."[1] Descartes even assigns an actual place in the body, the conarion or part of the brain, to this "thinking substance" which has to deal with everything which is not part of the vast external machine.[2] This strangely inadequate way of dealing with mind did not long remain unquestioned and since Descartes' day many philosophers and thinkers have struggled with the problem of knowledge, of epistemology, of the relation between mind and matter. Nevertheless, this bad start of the problem of knowledge has never been quite made up. About the external world, man has discovered ever more and more. About his own mind, why he can reflect nature in it and deal with nature in it in this amazing way, he has made much less progress.

Why was Descartes so contemptuous, even one might think, so afraid of the *mens* that he wanted to park it carefully by itself, out of the way of the mechanical universe and mathematics? Might not this be because of the struggle of his world to emerge from "Hermes Trismegistus" (I am again using the name as general coverage) and all that he stood for? The basic difference between the attitude of the magician to the world and the attitude of the scientist to the world is that the former wants to draw the world into himself, whilst the scientist does just the opposite, he externalises and impersonalises the world by a movement of will in an entirely opposite direction to that described in the Hermetic writings, the whole emphasis of which is precisely on the reflection of the world in the *mens*. Whether as religious experience or as magic, the Hermetic attitude to the world has this internal quality.

[1] *Ibid.*, p. 113.
[2] *Ibid.*, pp. 114–15. He, however, qualifies this by saying that we cannot actually give a place in the body to mind, but that it exercises its functions more particularly in the conarion whence it radiates through the rest of the body.

Hence, may it not be supposed, when mechanics and mathematics took over from animism and magic, it was this internalisation, this intimate connection of the *mens* with the world, which had to be avoided at all costs. And hence, it may be suggested, through the necessity for this strong reaction, the mistake arose of allowing the problem of mind to fall so completely out of step and so far behind the problem of matter in the external world and how it works. Thus, from the point of view of the history of the problem of mind and of why it has become such a problem through the neglect of it at the beginning of the modern period, "Hermes Trismegistus" and his history is important. The Fludd controversy cannot be lightly dismissed by the easy assumption that the moderns of those times made no mistakes. They may have discarded notions on mind and matter which, however strangely formulated, may be in essence less remote than their own conceptions from some of the thought of to-day. In any case we ought to know the history of what they discarded, if only to understand the motives which lay behind the triumph of mechanism. And that history uncovers the roots of the change which came over man when his mind was no longer integrated into the divine life of the universe. In the company of "Hermes Trismegistus" one treads the borderlands between magic and religion, magic and science, magic and art or poetry or music. It was in those elusive realms that the man of the Renaissance dwelt, and the seventeenth century lost some clue to the personality of that *magnum miraculum*.

It is as a historical study that I would leave this book with the reader. I have tried to keep in view the main historical outlines of the period and within them to trace the circulation of forces, religious and cultural, ultimately stemming from the impact of "Hermes Trismegistus" (again I use the name to cover the whole movement studied in this book) upon the Italian Renaissance. This influence was in part a hidden influence, and by bringing it to the surface and subjecting it to historical enquiry, new perspectives in which to view familiar phenomena are opened up. My chief aim has been to place Giordano Bruno within such a perspective, and it is my hope that this may of itself clear a road along which others will travel towards new solutions of old problems.

INDEX

458

462

Frances Yates was born in Portsmouth, England. Her father was a naval architect. Constant reading went on in the family and much stimulating conversation; her interests seem to have grown of themselves in this atmosphere. She met the French Renaissance through reading all the books which had belonged to a relative killed in the First World War; this led her to take French in the London B.A. Honours course. Her postgraduate studies expanded into the English and Italian Renaissance and she has remained in those areas ever since. The intense interest in Giordano Bruno began very early; it was through it that she encountered the Warburg Institute. Someone told her that there were a lot of books on Bruno in that library. She joined the staff of the Warburg Institute in 1944 and has been closely associated with its teaching and publishing work ever since. Among her books are *The French Academies of the Sixteenth Century* (1947); *The Valois Tapestries* (1959), and *The Art of Memory* (1966), which contains chapters on Bruno's mnemonics and is complementary to *Giordano Bruno and the Hermetic Tradition*. She has also published many articles, particularly in the *Journal of the Warburg and Courtauld Institutes*, of which she has been one of the editors since soon after its foundation. She has the D. Lit. degree of London University; in 1967 she was elected a Fellow of the British Academy. She has traveled a good deal, particularly in France and Italy, and is well known to a wide circle of scholars and students in many countries. In 1966 she visited the U.S.A., where she has many friends.

VINTAGE HISTORY—AMERICAN

A free catalogue of VINTAGE BOOKS *will be sent at your request. Write to* Vintage Books, 457 Madison Avenue, New York, New York 10022.

VINTAGE HISTORY AND CRITICISM OF
LITERATURE, MUSIC, AND ART

A free catalogue of VINTAGE BOOKS *will be sent at your request. Write to* Vintage Books, 457 Madison Avenue, New York, New York 10022.

VINTAGE POLITICAL SCIENCE
AND SOCIAL CRITICISM

A free catalogue of VINTAGE BOOKS *will be sent at your request.* Write *to* Vintage Books, 457 Madison Avenue, New York, New York 10022.

VINTAGE POLITICAL SCIENCE
AND SOCIAL CRITICISM

A free catalogue of VINTAGE BOOKS *will be sent at your request. Write to* Vintage Books, 457 Madison Avenue, New York, New York 10022.

VINTAGE HISTORY—WORLD

A free catalogue of VINTAGE BOOKS *will be sent at your request. Write to* Vintage Books, 457 Madison Avenue, New York, New York 10022.